ROUTLEDGE LIBRARY EDITIONS: COMEDY

Volume 9

GREEK COMEDY

GREEK COMEDY

GILBERT NORWOOD

Routledge
Taylor & Francis Group
LONDON AND NEW YORK

First published in 1931 by Methuen & Co. Ltd

This edition first published in 2022
by Routledge
4 Park Square, Milton Park, Abingdon, Oxon OX14 4RN

and by Routledge
605 Third Avenue, New York, NY 10158

Routledge is an imprint of the Taylor & Francis Group, an informa business

© Gilbert Norwood 1931

All rights reserved. No part of this book may be reprinted or reproduced or utilised in any form or by any electronic, mechanical, or other means, now known or hereafter invented, including photocopying and recording, or in any information storage or retrieval system, without permission in writing from the publishers.

Trademark notice: Product or corporate names may be trademarks or registered trademarks, and are used only for identification and explanation without intent to infringe.

British Library Cataloguing in Publication Data
A catalogue record for this book is available from the British Library

ISBN: 978-1-032-20971-5 (Set)
ISBN: 978-1-032-21804-5 (Volume 9) (hbk)
ISBN: 978-1-032-21807-6 (Volume 9) (pbk)
ISBN: 978-1-003-27009-6 (Volume 9) (ebk)

DOI: 10.4324/9781003270096

Publisher's Note
The publisher has gone to great lengths to ensure the quality of this reprint but points out that some imperfections in the original copies may be apparent.

Disclaimer
The publisher has made every effort to trace copyright holders and would welcome correspondence from those they have been unable to trace.

GREEK COMEDY

BY

GILBERT NORWOOD, M.A.

FORMERLY FELLOW OF ST. JOHN'S COLLEGE, CAMBRIDGE
PROFESSOR OF CLASSICS AND DIRECTOR OF CLASSICAL STUDIES,
UNIVERSITY COLLEGE, TORONTO

METHUEN & CO. LTD.
36 ESSEX STREET W.C.
LONDON

First Published in 1931

PRINTED IN GREAT BRITAIN

PREFACE

ALL the greatest poets of Greece committed the same unintended offence: their overwhelming excellence thrust into partial or complete oblivion the merits of their less august fellow-writers. Aristophanes was so unquestionably the finest comic playwright of the fifth century that not a single work even of Cratinus has survived. This eclipsing power is still felt in our histories of literature, few readers of which are likely to divine that several of the now fragmentary plays were superior to some written by the master himself and still entirely extant. In this book I have naturally discussed Aristophanes and Menander at length and with deep pleasure; but my chief reason for undertaking it was an ambition to offer, so far as should prove possible, an adequate and illuminating account of numerous minor yet most engaging playwrights. Some of our fragments have been discovered too recently for discussion in earlier books: about the *Demes* papyrus, for example, nothing is to be found save in German periodicals. These considerations have determined the amount of space that I have allotted to the various parts of my subject.

In treating of metre and rhythm I have followed the principles and method used in the corresponding chapter of my *Greek Tragedy*. That chapter was adversely judged by certain admirable scholars, but I confess to being wholly unrepentant: partly because other readers have reported that for the first time they understood something of the subject, partly because the critics I have mentioned gave me little help. They asserted, for instance, that I was mistaken in saying that ictus is stress-accent; but when invited to explain what, then, ictus is, they proved unanimously coy. Prolonged and respectful study of recent books on lyric metre and rhythm has convinced me that they become at crucial moments unintelligible except to the unusually gifted: I at least have learned little from any save the writings of J. H. H. Schmidt, and even from him I have found it necessary to diverge. It is useless for me, or for anyone, to write explanations that do not in fact explain. Those who would have me regard as fundamental Headlam's superb article in the *Journal of Hellenic Studies*, or the work of his skilful and brilliant disciples, cherish a misconception that would make of Greek prosody a morass resembling that wherein students of English prosody are at present floundering. It is possible to scan the verse of Shakespeare, Milton, Wordsworth by simple rules. When the basic principles are grasped, we may proceed to study the subtle and lovely variations executed, within the scheme, by individual masters; and a most vital, most fascinating, study that is. But it must come second, not first. Recent investigators of English verse-technique would teach the student to run before he can walk. That error I have sought to avoid. What I have written here and elsewhere will not, perhaps, reveal to my reader the beauty of Euripidean and Aristophanic poetry; but it will, I hope, give him the indispensable means to such appreciation.

GILBERT NORWOOD

August, 1931

CONTENTS

CHAP.		PAGE
I.	THE HISTORY OF GREEK COMEDY	1
II.	EPICHARMUS	83
III.	CRATINUS	114
IV.	THE SCHOOL OF CRATES	145
V.	EUPOLIS	178
VI.	ARISTOPHANES	202
VII.	MENANDER	313
VIII.	METRE AND RHYTHM IN GREEK COMEDY	365
INDEX		391

GREEK COMEDY

CHAPTER I

THE HISTORY OF GREEK COMEDY

§ 1. INTRODUCTION

DRAMA is the portrayal of a difficulty or problem as presented and solved by the interaction of beings (whether human or not) whose words and deeds are displayed to an audience by performers impersonating them. Comedy is that type of drama which employs action tolerably close to real life and an expression light, charming, often laughable. Allied to comedy, and often confused with it, is farce, which may be defined as exaggerated comedy: its problem is unlikely and absurd, its action ludicrous and one-sided, its manner entirely laughable. Some of the finest work included under the convenient title of "Greek Comedy" should in strictness be called farce.

From our definitions it follows that, although psychology may tell the origin of comedy, history cannot. A comedy is a plot engendered by our sense of the amusing wedded to our instinct for impersonation. But we cannot hope to discover the first occasion on which this kind of performance appeared. "I am pretending to be a cobbler. This man is pretending to be the cobbler's wife. We will now show you how funny married life can be by quarrelling about her shoes and then being reconciled by a customer." One day, of course, a genuine comedy was for the first time acted; but since it was the first, it must have been so rudimentary that no one observed, and therefore remembered and recorded, the change from yesterday's event, whether that was an impersonation without plot, or a plot without impersonation. For plot is vital to drama, however simple: question, complication, and solution must all be present, or there is no drama.

What was the origin of Greek Comedy? To this question the same considerations will or will not be applicable according as comedy was native to Greece or came from elsewhere. This second thesis has never been stated or even hinted by any ancient authority or by any modern student. This question, then, can be no more adequately answered than its predecessor: we must content ourselves with stating the time, place, and circumstances of the first comic drama reported by our authorities. A third question, as to the origin of Athenian Comedy, will resolve itself into an inquiry whether this grew up independently in Attica or was derived from other parts of the Greek world, whether Sicily or elsewhere. That question solved, we shall trace the development of comedy in Athens and its slighter manifestations in other Greek centres; an investigation for which we possess materials tolerably adequate.

Vase-paintings have been fruitfully studied in recent years by students of dramatic origins; but our main source is still the reports [1] of ancient scholars. These latter contributions vary in authority. At one end of the scale stands Aristotle, whose learning, sagacity, and early date constitute an immense claim on our attention. At the other extreme are the stupidities penned by fifth-rate Byzantine pedants while the Crusades trampled past their windows. These deserve practically no respect: the most noted of them, John Tzetzes, owns that he wrote and taught about early

---

[1] These are conveniently presented in Kaibel's *Comicorum Græcorum Fragmenta*, I, i. (all published) which contains also the non-Attic fragments.

drama on the authority of 'that muddle-headed scoundrel Heliodorus,'[1] and only later bethought himself to read the plays he had thus artlessly described. Between Aristotle and the late Byzantines lie a number of writers whose knowledge and ability are of various grades. The best is probably the Anonymus de Comoedia, as he is generally called; with him may be named Platonius and the Scholiast on Dionysius Thrax. These, and others in varying measure, drew upon the Alexandrian scholars, now otherwise lost, whose industry and first-hand knowledge of the texts made them authorities of the first weight. Athenæus, too, should be mentioned, though less valuable for origins. To him we owe an immense number of fragments from lost plays. A man of vast reading, and inordinately proud of it, he conceived the idea of writing the *Deipnosophistæ* or *Experts in Dining*, where certain friends meet at table and illustrate every conceivable aspect of dining with an overwhelming opulence of quotation.

The earliest of Greek, and therefore of European, playwrights was EPICHARMUS, whose achievements shall receive detailed examination later. He was active in Sicily, first at Megara Hyblæa, later in Syracuse, at the close of the sixth and the beginning of the fifth centuries. The Anonymus reports that Epicharmus was " the first to concentrate the scattered elements of comedy by many feats of technique ": that is, when he began to write no comedy existed, only scattered ingredients that awaited a genius for their combination. No doubt his first essays were hardly distinguishable from the mimes[2] that were being composed by others: *Hope* may well have been nothing but the exhibition of a parasite—a mere portrait in quasi-dramatic form; though even here he showed originality, for his parasite was the first in literature. Again, there is no evidence that *Odysseus*

---

[1] Ὁ πεφυρμένος καὶ βδελυρὸς Ἡλιόδωρος (Kaibel, p. 32).
[2] See below, pp. 76-82.

Shipwrecked was more than a " sketch " showing the notoriously versatile hero expounding anachronistic philosophy to his stupefied henchman. But, at some time after his removal from Megara to Syracuse and the court of Hiero, Epicharmus met amid that brilliant assembly the greatest genius between Homer and Plato, the Athenian Æschylus. It is certain that he was familiar with the tragedies, for he made game of an Æschylean peculiarity, and it is hardly possible to doubt that the architectonic qualities therein revealed exercised a strong effect upon his work. In *Busiris*, for example, there must have been genuine plot-structure : problem, what will the strange captive do ?—complication, the meeting of Busiris and his intended victim—catastrophe, the sudden revelation that the victim is Heracles —denouement, the victory and feasting of the demigod. Such work, though the culmination of Epicharmus' career, would (we may assume) strike a reader of the *Acharnians*, not to mention the *Birds*, still less the *Agamemnon*, as narrow in scope, loose in texture, simple in construction : it was nevertheless a splendid achievement—the first comic dramaturgy. To attain this, formidable obstacles were surmounted, chief among them that confronting all pioneers : the very notion of such work had to be evolved. Epicharmus had grown up among writers of mime which contained no action, only descriptions thereof and talk about it. And so his *Hebe's Wedding*, though its theme contained, as we can see now, excellent opportunity for comic action, was written in narrative only. Not the least delightful element in the study of dramatic art is to observe original-minded practitioners at various epochs striving to weave into their fabric threads originally non-dramatic. Peele's *Sir Clyomon and Sir Chlamydes* is narrative stumbling across the boards ; Menander's prologue slowly melts into genuinely dramatic exposition ; in our own day Mr. Eugene O'Neill invents audacious methods of dialogue to secure the self-revelation of discredited soliloquy. So in the dawn

THE HISTORY OF GREEK COMEDY

of comic art Epicharmus transformed narrative into action.

Of other Sicilian playwrights we hear very little. PHORMIS of Syracuse is named by Aristotle[1] with Epicharmus as the inventor of plot; perhaps he helped the master to produce his work. Suidas[2] mentions certain changes he made in the mounting of plays; but he gives six titles of dramas by Phormis. DEINOLOCHUS, of Syracuse or Acragas, a successor of Epicharmus, composed eleven plays; of the five titles that we know, four (*Medea*, etc.) suggest burlesque of legend, and the fifth, *Tragicomedy* (Κωμῳδοτραγῳδία), points the same way. But after this period native comedy seems to have died in the West.

Turning now to Attic Comedy, we find that even Aristotle[3] knows nothing of its earliest phases: official recognition came to it later than to tragedy, before which time the performers were "volunteers"; but it had already received "certain forms" when its known poets appeared in history. Nevertheless, the Byzantines are prepared to tell us a good deal. For example, they relate with delicious particularity that comedy was discovered in the evening; but the day, month and year they fail to divulge. This notion comes from their derivation of the word κωμῳδία, namely from κῶμα, "sleep." But they accept at the same time a derivation from κώμη, "village." From these two etymologies (which cannot both be correct, and indeed neither is) comes their oft-repeated story that country-people, being wronged by influential citizens, came by night into the town and cried aloud their grievances in the streets; the authorities, feeling that such accusations were good for public morals, insisted that the rustics should come forward in the day-time and perform more elaborately; this they

---

[1] *Poetic*, 1449b, 17.   [2] *s.v.* Φόρμος.
[3] *Poetic*, 1449a-b: Αἱ μὲν οὖν τῆς τραγῳδίας μεταβάσεις καὶ δι᾽ ὧν ἐγένοντο οὐ λελήθασιν, ἡ δὲ κωμῳδία διὰ τὸ μὴ σπουδάζεσθαι ἐξ ἀρχῆς ἔλαθεν· καὶ γὰρ χορὸν κωμῳδῶν ὀψέ ποτε ὁ ἄρχων ἔδωκεν, ἀλλ᾽ ἐθελονταὶ ἦσαν. ἤδη δὲ σχήματά τινα αὐτῆς ἐχούσης οἱ λεγόμενοι αὐτῆς ποιηταὶ μνημονεύονται.

did, but fearing their oppressors they disguised themselves by smearing their faces with lees of wine; later, the government put the affair on a sound footing by commissioning poets like Susarion to write the accusations. There is no evidence whatever that this story is true: these writers are in fact thinking of their own time; what they allege of primitive Athens was true of mediæval Constantinople.[1]

Despite the obscurity of this subject, we possess certain important pieces of evidence as to the origin of Athenian Comedy supplied by early vase-paintings, by Aristotle and later writers, and by the structure[2] of the surviving plays. These evidences are eight in number:

(i) Beast-mummeries.
(ii) The lampoon.
(iii) Aristotle's remark about phallic songs.
(iv) Corinthian vase-paintings.

---

[1] In the reign of Theophilus (A.D. 829-42), Nicephorus, the city-prefect, was assailed in a mime for oppressing a widow and was sent to the stake. See Tunison, *Dramatic Traditions of the Dark Ages*, p. 115.

[2] This enumeration ignores two elements in existing comedies that have received much attention in authoritative works, Zieliński's *Gliederung der altattische Komödie*, Mazon's *Essai sur la Composition des Comédies d'Aristophane*, Körte's article *Komödie* in Pauly-Wissowa's *Real-Encyclopädie*, and Pickard-Cambridge's *Dithyramb Tragedy and Comedy*. These are the ἀγών and the epirrhematic syzygy, which both owe their present vogue to Zieliński. Prolonged study of his book leaves the present writer with the impression that it is vastly overrated: not to dwell upon minor points, the two important matters now in question are palmary instances of bad criticism. His long discussion of the epirrhematic syzygy comes simply to this, that whereas in Tragedy the correspondent strophes of any lyric are collected in a consecutive mass, in Comedy they are separated by parts of a scene. But this is not only perfectly obvious: it leads nowhere. As for the ἀγών, the absurdities here are still more glaring. Zieliński, when he finds a play without one, insists that the ἀγών is so vital that we must regard our version as later, and excogitates an ἀγών which existed in the earlier, never asking himself why, if it is vital, Aristophanes actually deleted it. But the whole of his discussion here rests upon an astounding insensibility to the very nature of drama. An ἀγών is a set elaborate conflict between two leading characters. It follows that any play ever written may well have an ἀγών, but well may not—precisely as we find in Aristophanes. There are ἀγῶνες in Greek tragedy, *e.g. Eumenides, Ajax, Hippolytus*. There are ἀγῶνες in non-Greek drama, both tragic and comic, *e.g. Adelphoe, The Merchant of Venice, Julius Cæsar, A Doll's House, Man and Superman*.

THE HISTORY OF GREEK COMEDY

(v) Aristotle's implication as to the comos.
(vi) The Megarian claim.
(vii) The nature and position of the parabasis.
(viii) Features of the post-parabasic scenes.

(i) Primitive mummeries have been familiar in all ages and every quarter of the globe. A group of people disguise themselves as persons or animals and for the pleasure of an audience perform mimic action, which may be dramatic or (more commonly) non-dramatic, like the pageant of Ceres and Juno in *The Tempest* or the lovers' scene in Xenophon's *Symposium*. In Attica the primitive folk-play seems to have specially favoured animal impersonations. Vases painted in a period anterior to the earliest official presentations of comedy show such mummeries of animals or men and animals, and show [1] them as Dionysiac performances —that is, as in some sort precursors of drama properly so-called. For example, a famous vase in the British Museum depicts men dressed as birds and dancing to the music of a flutist; this vase is dated in the neighbourhood of 500 B.C., and almost certainly refers to a theatrical chorus. Another of the same period has a procession of horsemen, whose horses show men's faces below the animal; before these also a flutist is playing. This spirit survived into the literary drama: Magnes, as we shall see, composed beast-plays, and Aristophanes, if he has no *Horses*, has yet *Knights*, mounted on hobby-horses or masquerading men; his wasps are men indeed, but they bear stings; his birds are "genuine." There are many other known instances.[2]

(ii) The lampoon (ἴαμβοι), or short scurrilous address, was very frequent in Attica when crowds gathered for any celebration; such abusive remarks addressed by celebrants to individual bystanders formed one ingredient of Attic Comedy. Our evidence lacks

---
[1] By ivy-tendrils, etc.
[2] See Poppelreuter, *De Comœdiæ Atticæ primordiis*, and Pickard-Cambridge, pp. 245-7.

details, but it is clear so far as it goes. Semos of Delos, in his book [1] on pæans, described the performance of certain φαλλοφόροι (" bearers of the phallus ") who, decked out with garlands of foliage and flowers, advanced into the orchestra and, after a short salutation to Dionysus, ' ran up and jeered at anyone they chose '.[2] There is, however, no indication that their performance was at any point dramatic; still, they appeared in the theatre (though not necessarily in Athens), they followed the phallic-emblem (see the next paragraph), and they uttered lampoons. Next, Aristotle writes concerning Crates that ' he was the first man in Athens to relinquish the lampoon form and compose stories and plots of general application '.[3] Finally, as we have seen, the Byzantines make great play with accusations and reproaches, levelled by rustics against townsmen, as the original stuff of comedy. There was evidently a persistent tradition as to the importance of this element, but Aristotle speaks as if it had to be dropped before comedy could progress. The explanation probably is that Aristotle, having his own day specially in mind, is disposed to regard Crates and his school as the most significant historically among Old Comedy playwrights, because the Middle dramatists derive from them rather than from the satirical school of Aristophanes and others.

(iii) Aristotle asserts that comedy ' originated with those who led the phallic songs '.[4] A procession in honour of Phales, the companion of Dionysus, carried aloft the phallus (a pole symbolizing human fertility) with songs; one man led the singing. We find a specimen of this in the *Acharnians*. Dicæopolis arranges a " skeleton " celebration; his daughter goes

---

[1] Quoted by Athenæus, xiv. 621 f., 622. Cp. the Fescennine verses of Italy.
[2] Εἶτα προστρέχοντες ἐτώθαζον οὓς προέλοιντο.
[3] *Poetic*, 1449b : τῶν δὲ Ἀθήνησιν Κράτης πρῶτος ἦρξεν ἀφέμενος τῆς ἰαμβικῆς ἰδέας καθόλου ποιεῖν λόγους καὶ μύθους.
[4] *Ibid*. 1449a : ἡ μὲν ἀπὸ τῶν ἐξαρχόντων τὸν διθύραμβον, ἡ δὲ ἀπὸ τῶν τὰ φαλλικά, ἃ ἔτι καὶ νῦν ἐν πολλαῖς τῶν πόλεων διαμένει νομιζόμενα.

first with a basket of fruit and other offerings, two slaves bear the phallus, his wife on the roof represents the crowd, and he himself the procession of singers. His ditty proclaims the licentious exploits of Phales, his own glee over his newly-made peace, and contains a scrap of lampoon. This is the kind of celebration to which Aristotle refers; but it is utterly undramatic. Nevertheless, he believes that " leaders " like Dicæopolis originated comedy. Why? He tells us in the same sentence that tragedy was evolved by those who led the dithyramb, and from this analogy we infer that he means: the leader separated himself more and more from his followers (the chorus), making speeches of his own and being in the course of time joined by an additional actor with whom he performed genuinely dramatic scenes that slowly increased in length, interest, and importance.

In the next section we shall find reason to doubt all this. But can we venture to defy so impressive an authority? Here we may, if the opposed evidence is strong. For there can be little doubt that in this part of the *Poetic* Aristotle is perfunctory. Consider the manner in which he writes of Epicharmus: he joins him on to the account of Athenian Comedy without any note as to the vast difference separating non-choric from choric drama; he is thinking of comedy as it is in his own day, when the chorus was unimportant. This casualness may well suggest that he affiliated the phallus-wearing actor of literary Old Comedy to the leader of the pre-literary phallus-bearers, without verifying the alleged connexion.

(iv) In fifth-century Athens the comic actor's costume included the phallus and huge padding of the stomach and posterior: the first item is attested by passages of Aristophanes, and all three by numerous vase-paintings. Comedy being Dionysiac, we are to understand this costume as that attributed to the attendants of Dionysus. But we know that the Athenian idea of the Dionysiac costume was not that just described: on Attic vases the god's male followers are always silenus-satyrs with the tails and ears of horses. On the other hand, Dorian Greeks regularly portrayed these attendants as human, with the phallus and padding. Firstly, such attire (as South Italian vases show) was used by the *phlyakes*—the actors in Italian farce [1]—who often appear as companions of the god. Secondly, dancers thus padded are seen on Chalcidian and Spartano-Cyrenaic vases. Thirdly, they are found above all on the vases of Corinth: it is certain that the Dionysiac thiasos was imagined during the seventh and sixth centuries in Corinth as entirely human, with padding and the phallus. The upshot is that the actors of Athenian Old Comedy regularly wore a costume displaying the physical peculiarities of Peloponnesian attendants on Dionysus, peculiarities entirely foreign to the Attic conception of the thiasos. They are a Peloponnesian element added to, but never completely coalescing with, the genuinely Attic chorus that normally appeared in animal masquerade.

This is a summary of Körte's arguments,[2] which constitute an impressive rebuttal of Aristotle's statement, reported in the preceding section.

(v) Aristotle implies further that comedy—that is, in particular, the comic chorus—arose from the *comos* (κῶμος), the revel-rout of Dionysiac worshippers. He says that the Megarians derive the word " comedy " from *come* (κώμη, " village ")—' denying that comedians were named from participation in the *comos* '.[3] We must believe that he approves this repudiated etymology, not only because of his language here, but in view of what he says concerning the leaders of the phallic songs. These were sung by the revelling procession: Dicæopolis' celebration is a rudimentary *comos*. His suggestion plainly is that the leader developed into the actors, the revellers into the chorus.

---
[1] See below, pp. 73-6.
[2] Pauly-Wissowa's *Real-Encyclopädie*, XI, 1219-21.
[3] *Poetic*, 1448a: ὡς κωμῳδοὺς οὐκ ἀπὸ τοῦ κωμάζειν λεχθέντας.

(vi) The Megarians claimed [1] for two reasons to be the inventors of comedy: it appeared in Nisæan Megara 'under the democracy' and in Sicily was written by Epicharmus 'long before Chionides and Magnes'. As regards Epicharmus, we have seen that this claim was justified. Concerning the alleged drama of Nisæan Megara we have no dates and very doubtful details as to early work; but Aristotle and Aristophanes, with their Scholiasts, tell us something of its quality in the fifth century. These reports [2] depict bad taste in the mounting of plays, and performances that were nothing but crude buffoonery. This implies nothing as to the origin of Attic drama—nor indeed does it in the least disprove an historical affiliation. Aristophanes gives, as instances of 'laughter stolen from Megara,' a couple of slaves scattering nuts among the audience, and 'Heracles robbed of his dinner'.[3] By this accusation of theft he plainly accuses his less gifted colleagues of frequently borrowing from the clownery of Megara. There are several other passages, not confined to Aristophanes, that point the same way; it seems plain that Athenian playwrights had an uneasy sense of obligation. It is to be observed, further, that Aristotle does not reject the Megarian claim. Finally, it is significant that Susarion, despite the Attic dialect of his alleged fragment, is made to call himself a Megarian.[4]

(vii) The parabasis was a part of every Old Comedy and continued into the Middle period, disappearing finally as the chorus dwindled to complete insignificance. It was an elaborate performance at about the middle of the play by the chorus solely, was

---

[1] *Poetic*, 1448a: Διὸ καὶ ἀντιποιοῦνται τῆς τε τραγῳδίας καὶ τῆς κωμῳδίας οἱ Δωριεῖς (τῆς μὲν γὰρ κωμῳδίας οἱ Μεγαρεῖς οἵ τε ἐνταῦθα ὡς ἐπὶ τῆς παρ' αὑτοῖς δημοκρατίας γενομένης καὶ οἱ ἐκ Σικελίας, ἐκεῖθεν γὰρ ἦν Ἐπίχαρμος ὁ ποιητὴς πολλῷ πρότερος ὢν Χιωνίδου καὶ Μάγνητος· καὶ τῆς τραγῳδίας ἔνιοι τῶν ἐν Πελοποννήσῳ) ποιούμενοι τὰ ὀνόματα σημεῖον κτέ.

[2] Conveniently summarized and admirably discussed by Pickard-Cambridge, pp. 274-80.

[3] *Wasps*, 58-60.   [4] See below, pp. 14 sq.

entirely non-dramatic,[1] and its kernel was an address to the audience on behalf of the poet, discussing his art, political crises, and so forth. Such a passage—or rather such a conglomerate of songs and non-dramatic recitative—is *prima facie* inconceivable in the centre of a drama, utterly suspending the action. We may be quite sure, even in the absence of information from our authorities, that it stood originally either before the opening, or after the close, of the action. The second view is the more likely, because it was more natural for the poet to close with an attempt to ingratiate himself with the audience.

(viii) The part of a comedy that followed the parabasis tended to form merely a string of scenes with little structure. It should, however, be confessed that we are here on somewhat dangerous ground. The only complete plays that we possess were written by the same poet, and he gradually developes structure in this part. It might therefore be suggested that such looseness is but an accident of Aristophanes' immaturity, especially when it is remembered that what first-hand knowledge we possess of Cratinus indicates a complete freedom from this weakness: the *Odysses* and the *Dionysalexandros* developed steadily from beginning to end. Nevertheless, Platonius emphatically denies firm structure to Cratinus. Accordingly, when we consider (*a*) what has just been said about the position of the parabasis; (*b*) the fact that these later scenes (except of course the lyrics) are invariably written in iambic trimeters, whereas the earlier part of the play (all that comes between the prologue and the parabasis) is often composed in longer metres; (*c*) that these scenes are often mere buffoonery, showing little or no play of ideas—it is difficult to resist the conviction that this part was at first a mere addendum to please the coarser members of the audience, and was in fact an importation from Nisæan Megara loosely tacked on after the real

---

[1] That is, it contains no action. Nevertheless, the chorus often speaks in character.

finale—the parabasis—just as for many years an English pantomime was followed by the farce of clown, harlequin, columbine, pantaloon and policeman.

From these eight evidences we conceive this strange and elaborate type of comedy to have arisen as follows. In Attica the universal folk-mummery took the form of an animal masquerade attached as *comos* to the worship of Dionysus as god of the vinous revel. Their phallic procession sang lampoons against chance bystanders, sometimes more elaborately against public characters. At first their performance, or at any rate their remarks, were impromptu; later a poet wrote lines for them. When the poet's work attained some elaboration, he wrote an address for the chorus to sing before they withdrew. Next an actor was introduced, partly in imitation of tragedy, partly because the Megarian farce was becoming popular. He was attired in the Peloponnesian manner, and his part was at first mere clowning with the chorus after the parabasis. Later he invaded the earlier part of the performance and was in time provided with a colleague, so that genuine dramatic action became possible. As comedy advanced in the hands of successive artists this scheme was developed: the lyrics increased in beauty and elaboration; plot was developed; topics of deep political or social interest were handled; explanatory scenes,[1] whether by the chief actor (*e.g. Acharnians*) or by gossiping slaves (*e.g. Knights*), came into being; and after the Megarian scenes (so to call them), the *comos* came back into its own, rounding off the play with a finale of triumphant riotousness.

§ 2. Athenian Old Comedy

The earliest poets are, as might be expected, shadowy. Susarion is the first of all: concerning him Tzetzes,[2]

[1] Named πρόλογοι, afterwards to become "prologues" in the modern sense, as written by Menander and his contemporaries.
[2] Kaibel, p. 77.

who gives the fullest account, writes : ' of the so-called first comedy the first and the inventor was the Megarian Susarion, the Tripodiscian, son of Philinus : he, being married to a bad wife who left him, came into the theatre during the Dionysiac festival and pronounced the four following iambic lines, which alone of his writings have been discovered, all the rest being lost : " O yes ! O yes ! Susarion, Philinus' son, a Tripodiscian from Megara, says this : Women are an evil ; nevertheless it is impossible, neighbours, to live in one's house without evil ".' Stobæus adds a fifth line : ' for both to marry and not to marry are evil '. The complete text of this *cri du cœur* runs, then, as follows :

ἀκούετε λεῴ· Σουσαρίων λέγει τάδε,
υἱὸς Φιλίνου Μεγαρόθεν Τριποδίσκιος·
κακὸν γυναῖκες, ἀλλ' ὅμως, ὦ δημόται,
οὐκ ἔστιν οἰκεῖν οἰκίαν ἄνευ κακοῦ·
καὶ γὰρ τὸ γῆμαι καὶ τὸ μὴ γῆμαι κακόν.

Others omit the second line, added, no doubt, by some one who believed in the claim of the Megarians to have originated comedy. But in any case the passage is spurious, for the satire shows a jaded sophistication incredible at the only date possible for Susarion. Others assign him not to the Megarian town, Tripodiscus, but to the Attic deme Icaria. Despite all these doubts, there was certainly a comic poet Susarion of early date, though we have no trustworthy details about his work. The Parian Marble, which belongs to the middle of the third century before Christ, mentions him " under a year which may fall anywhere between 581 and 560 B.C." [1] in a passage that is thus to be restored : " At Athens a chorus of comedians was invented, being established by the Icarians ; the inventor was Susarion ; a prize was first offered consisting of a basket of figs and a barrel of wine ". Such early evidence is not to be rejected. Susarion, in fact, must have been the only

[1] Pickard-Cambridge, p. 280.

THE HISTORY OF GREEK COMEDY 15

notable poet of those who wrote the words for the lampoons of the *comos* when these passed beyond the phase of impromptu abuse. Evidently he was not a comic dramatist in the full sense : but that he was a literary forerunner of comedy is manifest. Hence the statement that he was a Megarian ; his work was a composition, not an improvisation, so that he became an author of scenes, which would at once suggest the Megarian farce, though his performers may not have been actors in the official sense, but members of the chorus. It is significant that one authority, while assigning comedy to Epicharmus, assigns the lampoon to Susarion.[1] Of the other poets who are named as belonging to this pre-natal period of comedy—Euetes, Euxenides and Myllus—we know nothing.

CHIONIDES is named by Aristotle as being, with Magnes, the earliest to compose comedy at Athens : he nowhere mentions Susarion. But Magnes is rather later ; probably Chionides gained the prize at the first official competition in 486 B.C., for Suidas,[2] who calls him ' the originator of Old Comedy,' places him eight years before the Persian War ; that is, in 487-6, by Greek chronology eight years before Salamis. The few fragments are of no interest. Whether Chionides may be regarded as a playwright in the full sense of the word is highly doubtful, since plot-construction, as we shall see, dates in Athens from Cratinus and Crates. The best view is that he gave more form and power to the quasi-drama of chorus and isolated scenes that Susarion had initiated.

MAGNES, according to the Anonymus,[3] was ' an Athenian who competed at Athens, winning eleven

[1] Schol. Dion. Thrax (Kaibel, p. 77): εὑρέθη ἡ μὲν τραγῳδία ὑπὸ Θεσπιδός τινος Ἀθηναίου, ἡ δὲ κωμῳδία ὑπὸ Ἐπιχάρμου ἐν Σικελίᾳ καὶ ὁ ἴαμβος ὑπὸ Σουσαρίωνος. The same writer (*ibid.*) says that he wrote in verse, but there he calls his work comedy (τῆς ἐμμέτρου κωμῳδίας ἀρχηγός).

[2] *s.v.* Χιωνίδης, Ἀθηναῖος, κωμικὸς τῆς ἀρχαίας κωμῳδίας, ὃν καὶ λέγουσι πρωταγωνιστὴν γενέσθαι τῆς ἀρχαίας κωμῳδίας, διδάσκειν δὲ ἔτεσιν ὀκτὼ πρὸ τῶν Περσικῶν.

[3] Kaibel, p. 7. This is confirmed by an inscription (Wilhelm, *Urkunden dramatischer Aufführungen in Athen*, p. 107).

victories. None of his plays survive; those attributed
to him number nine.' Suidas [1] gives him nine plays
and two victories; this divergence shows that in the
days of scholarship little was known of him. The
Scholiasts of Aristophanes, though they have the work
of the learned Didymus before them, can indeed give
the names of the comedies, but seem to possess no
further knowledge. Aristotle himself (in our text of
the *Poetic* [2]) gives nothing save an implication that he
was a contemporary of Chionides. It seems plain that
Magnes' plays had vanished before the Alexandrian
age, and that Didymus could draw on nothing for
information save the *Knights* (see below). As for his
dates, we have four indications: (i) Aristotle puts
Epicharmus 'much earlier' than Magnes; (ii) Suidas [3]
says that Magnes' youth coincided with Epicharmus'
old age; (iii) he was plainly dead when the *Knights*
appeared in 424; (iv) an inscription [4] found in Athens
shows that he was victorious at the City Dionysia of
472. All this points to 500 and 430 as the approximate
dates of his birth and of his death.

He is among those mentioned by Aristophanes as
proofs that the Athenian audience was fickle and cruel
to his predecessors. ' I was slow to come forward
openly as a poet both because of the unique difficulty
of writing comedy, and also because I have long understood *you*, that you are naturally fickle and betrayed
earlier poets when they grew old. First, I knew what
Magnes endured when his hair grew white, he who
had raised many trophies of victory over the choruses
of his rivals; but though he uttered every kind of
sound to please you—played the harp, flapped wings,
showed you Lydians and gall-flies and dyed himself
frog-green—all would not serve. In the end, when
old (how different from his youth!) he was hunted off
the stage despite his years, because his jokes ran dry.' [5]

[1] *s.v.* Μάγνης.   [2] *Poetic*, 1488a, 33.
[3] *s.v.* Μάγνης: ἐπιβάλλει δ' Ἐπιχάρμῳ νέος πρεσβύτῃ.
[4] Wilhelm, *Urkunden*, 18.   [5] *Knights*, 518-25.

Nevertheless, his victories, we have seen, were numerous; this fact, coupled with two others, the titles of his plays and the disregard of the next generation, may give us some notion of his merits. The participles in the fifth and sixth lines of Aristophanes refer to the names of his comedies, the *Harpers* (Βαρβιτισταί), *Birds*, *Lydians*, *Gall-Flies* (Ψῆνες) and *Frogs*. Magnes composed popular beast-fables and his lyrics were probably the most considerable part of his work: he dominated the stage when there was little competition, but the appearance of a genius in Cratinus swept him away. Another reason for the disappearance of Magnes' works is that they were revised to suit later taste. Athenæus [1] speaks of 'the man who composed the writings attributed to Magnes'; Photius [2] says that 'the *Lydians* of Magnes was revised'; and Hesychius [3] most definitely of all: '*Lydizing*, that is, dancing, on account of the *Lydians*, which is preserved, but in a revised form'. Even of these *rechauffés* we possess scarcely anything.

ECPHANTIDES is the only other name of interest belonging to this period. Though undoubtedly later than Magnes, he is called by a Scholiast [4] 'the most ancient poet of the old school,' which shows that he was the earliest comic playwright of whom later antiquity possessed any drama: [5] Magnes, as we have said, disappeared early. He proclaims himself as 'ashamed to write in Megarian' fashion, but despite this claim to artistry he is nicknamed Καπνίας (that is, " flat wine ") by Cratinus, who also parodies his lyric manner. Aristotle [6] mentions a tablet set up by Thrasippus, who had been choregus for Ecphantides.

This early school of " playwrights " was literary, as contrasted with the improvisers who had preceded it; but we have no evidence that they composed genuine

---

[1] ix. 367f., xiv. 646e.
[2] P. 233. 20, under Λυδιάζων.   [3] *s.v.* Λυδίζων.
[4] On Aristotle, *Eth. Nic.*, IV, vi: παλαιότατος ποιητὴς τῶν ἀρχαίων.
[5] Körte, Pauly-Wissowa, XI, 1228.   [6] *Pol.*, 1341a, 36.

plots. They are to be imagined as composing a series of scenes and as more excellent and elaborate on the lyrical side. Development of plot begins, according to Aristotle,[1] with Crates, the pupil of Cratinus; yet the latter is the greatest dramatist before Aristophanes. The explanation is that Crates composed that Comedy of Manners which Aristotle saw ruling the theatre in his own day, whereas Cratinus developed the old lampoon form into a type excellent indeed but obsolete in the fourth century. Crates followed Epicharmus, particularly in his social comedies; Cratinus did not. By the time Magnes was an old man his dramaturgy had become obsolete: Cratinus was writing thoroughly adult comedy. Between the début of Cratinus and the fall of Athens—a period of some fifty years—Greek Comedy saw its Golden Age, which shall be treated here succinctly because detailed treatment of its greatest writers is more conveniently effected in separate chapters. Perfected comedy, despite its unity of technical form, takes on a fourfold aspect derived from its main topics: contemporary manners, burlesque of legend, politics, and fantasy. The last two are familiar because they inspired surviving dramas of Aristophanes: the other two themes are less considered because the works that treat of them have almost vanished. But the *Corianno* of Pherecrates was evidently a notable comedy of manners, and Cratinus composed several burlesques the excellence of which is even now unmistakable. No poet [2] confined himself to one of these types: for example, social comedy appears in the *Wasps* and still more in the *Plutus* of Aristophanes; burlesque of legend—or at least burlesque of its treatment in tragedy—is marked in several of his works, especially the *Thesmophoriazusæ*.

CRATES, under the influence of Epicharmus' social comedy, founded a school of drama that, although

---

[1] *Poetic*, 1449*b*.
[2] Except perhaps very minor poets (such as Alcæus) of whom we know little.

THE HISTORY OF GREEK COMEDY 19

overshadowed by political comedy in the fifth century, was destined to an immensely longer and more fertile, if not more brilliant, career than its rival. His most distinguished followers were PHRYNICHUS, PHERECRATES, and PLATO, who was (next to the three great masters) the most important playwright of the age. To this school a separate chapter is allotted. We shall next discuss the other three leading subjects, fantasy, burlesque of legend, and politics.

Fantasy by its nature imports a vague category, but it excludes at least such plays as the *Knights* and even *Lysistrata*, for it implies not merely imagination, but its unfettered play, imagination bound to no real event of contemporary life. In this period we observe two fanciful motifs invented and repeatedly employed. One is the Cockaigne theme, the picture of a glutton's Eldorado, an edible landscape traversed by rivers of wine and soup. This was originated by Cratinus in his *Riches* (Πλοῦτοι), and we possess several copies of this idea. The *Miners* of Pherecrates portrayed such a region, beneath the earth; Nicophon described a river of soup; so did Crates and Metagenes. But the best of such accounts, according to Athenæus,[1] was written by TELECLEIDES, of whom a complete account may at once be offered; it will be observed that he is interested in politics also.

Of Telecleides' career we can assert only that he belonged to the Periclean age,[2] and that he was a popular but probably commonplace dramatist. He won at least eight [3] victories—three at the City Dionysia, five at the Lenæa—but the Anonymus [4] knows of only six plays. To *Amphictyons* (Ἀμφικτύονες), *The Truth-Tellers* (Ἀψευδεῖς), *Hesiods* (Ἡσίοδοι), *The Chairmen*

[1] VI, 268b.
[2] His first victory was won soon after 446 (Geissler, *Chronologie der altattischen Komödie*, p. 11).
[3] Wilhelm, *Urkunden*, p. 176.
[4] Kaibel, p. 7. Suidas knows him only through Athenæus: Τηλεκλείδης, Ἀθηναῖος, κωμικός. τῶν δραμάτων αὐτοῦ εἰσὶν Ἀμφικτύονες καὶ Πρυτάνεις καὶ Στερροί, ὥς Ἀθήναιος λέγει ἐν τοῖς Δειπνοσοφισταῖς.

(Πρυτάνεις), *The Stiffs* (Στερροί), inscriptions add two, perhaps to be read as *The Furies* (Εὐμενίδες) and *The Soldiers* (Στρατιῶται). *The Stiffs* was produced twice.[1] The AMPHICTYONS seems to have urged concord among the Greek states : such is the suggestion of the title itself, the Amphictyonic Council being a rudimentary League of Nations. One fragment :[2]
' But, oh ye that are best of all citizens at blackmail and litigation, cease your cannibalistic law-suits '—

ἀλλ', ὦ πάντων ἀστῶν λῷστοι σεῖσαι καὶ προσκαλέσασθαι,
παύσασθε δικῶν ἀλληλοφάγων—

refers to concord among the Athenians themselves. In any case, the play contained a picture[3] of " ancient life " :

λέξω τοίνυν βίον ἐξ ἀρχῆς ὃν ἐγὼ θνητοῖσι παρεῖχον.
εἰρήνη μὲν πρῶτον ἁπάντων ἦν ὥσπερ ὕδωρ κατὰ χειρός.
ἡ γῆ δ' ἔφερ' οὐ δέος οὐδὲ νόσους, ἀλλ' αὐτόματ' ἦν τὰ δέοντα·
οἴνῳ γὰρ ἅπασ' ἔρρει χαράδρα, μᾶζαι δ' ἄρτοις ἐμάχοντο
περὶ τοῖς στόμασιν τῶν ἀνθρώπων ἱκετεύουσαι καταπίνειν,
εἴ τι φιλοῖεν τὰς λευκοτάτας. οἱ δ' ἰχθύες οἴκαδ' ἰόντες
ἐξοπτῶντες σφᾶς αὐτοὺς ἂν παρέκειντ' ἐπὶ ταῖσι τραπέζαις.
ζωμοῦ δ' ἔρρει παρὰ τὰς κλίνας ποταμὸς κρέα θερμὰ κυλίνδων,
ὑποτριμματίων δ' ὀχετοὶ τούτων τοῖς βουλομένοισι παρῆσαν,
ὥστ' ἀφθονία τὴν ἔνθεσιν ἦν ἄρδονθ' ἁπαλὴν καταπίνειν,
λεκανίσκαισιν δ' ἀνάπαιστα παρῆν ἡδυσματίοις κατάπαστα.
ὀπταὶ δὲ κίχλαι μετ' ἀμητίσκων εἰς τὸν φάρυγ' εἰσεπέτοντο·
τῶν δὲ πλακούντων ὠστιζομένων περὶ τὴν γνάθον ἦν ἀλαλητός.
μήτρας δὲ τόμοις καὶ χναυματίοις οἱ παῖδες ἂν ἠστραγάλιζον.
οἱ δ' ἄνθρωποι πίονες ἦσαν τότε καὶ μέγα χρῆμα γιγάντων.

' Come, I will describe in full the life that I bestowed upon mankind. Peace, first of all, was regularly on tap. The earth bore no terror or diseases, but necessaries came spontaneously. Wine flowed down all the gullies ; cakes fought with loaves at people's mouths, crying " Please swallow us, if you like the best quality ". Fish came into the house, frying themselves and lying down ready on the tables. A river of soup flowed beside the dining-couches in eddies of stewed meat, and runlets of sauce were at the disposal of those so

[1] Wilhelm, *Urkunden*, p. 204.
[2] Fr. 2. Except where it is otherwise stated, all fragments are quoted from Kock's *Comicorum Atticorum Fragmenta*.
[3] Fr. 1.

inclined: there was plenty of choice where to soak your morsel before swallowing it. On plates were cakes sprinkled with seasoning. Roast thrushes with their pastry flew into your mouth, and the buns made an uproar as they jostled round your teeth. The boys played knuckle-bones with slices of haggis and tit-bits. Men were fat in those days and stalwart giants.' It has been plausibly suggested [1] that the ancient benefactor who recited these blessings was Amphictyon, the eponymous founder of the Council after which this play is named.

From unnamed plays come a few interesting extracts. One concerns blackmailers: [2]

Χαρικλέης μὲν οὖν ἔδωκε μνᾶν, ἵν' αὐτὸν μὴ λέγῃ
ὡς ἔφυ τῇ μητρὶ παίδων πρῶτος ἐκ βαλλαντίου.
τέτταρας δὲ μνᾶς ἔδωκε Νικίας Νικηράτου·
ὧν δ' ἕκατι τοῦτ' ἔδωκε καίπερ εὖ εἰδὼς ἐγὼ
οὐκ ἐρῶ· φίλος γὰρ ἀνήρ, σωφρονεῖν δέ μοι δοκεῖ.

'Charicles gave him a *mina* not to tell that he became his mother's first child by purchase. Nicias, son of Niceratus, gave twelve *minæ*, but the reason I shall not declare though I know it well, for I like the man and think him righteous.' Plutarch [3] tells us he complained that the Athenians had surrendered everything to Pericles—

πόλεών τε φόρους αὐτάς τε πόλεις τὰς μὲν δεῖν τὰς δ' ἀναλύειν,
λάϊνα τείχη τὰ μὲν οἰκοδομεῖν τὰ δὲ τἄμπαλιν αὖ καταβάλλειν,
σπονδὰς δύναμιν κράτος εἰρήνην πλοῦτόν τ' εὐδαιμονίαν τε.

'The tribute of cities and the cities themselves, to bind or unloose; the walls of stone, to build or to cast down; treaties, power, dominion, peace, wealth, and happiness.' Of another passage [4] the Greek is uncertain but the intention plain, that Euripides had collaborating friends:

Μνησίλοχός ἐστ' ἐκεῖνος, ὃς φρύγει τι δρᾶμα καινὸν
Εὐριπίδῃ καὶ Σωκράτης τὰ φρύγαν' ὑποτίθησιν.

[1] By Kock, I, p. 210.
[2] Fr. 41. Charicles was one of the commission of inquiry into the Hermes outrage, and later one of the Thirty Tyrants.
[3] *Pericles*, XVI. Fr. 42.
[4] Frr. 39, 40.

There is no doubt a pun on Φρύγες, the name of a tragedy,[1] and φρύγανα, "brushwood". 'That is Mnesilochus, concocting some new play for Euripides while Socrates puts the fuel underneath.' Perhaps this was a tableau in the *Hesiods*, displayed on the *eccyclema*.

The other favourite fantasy was the story of some divine birth. Such accounts were well known in earlier poetry, for instance the Homeric *Hymn to Hermes* and Pindar's Seventh *Olympian*, but its dramatic handling was originated—so far as comedy [2] is concerned—by HERMIPPUS, who composed *The Birth of Athena* ('Ἀθηνᾶς Γοναί). He seems to have been unimportant as a playwright,[3] but the surviving remnants of his work, both dramatic and non-dramatic, shimmer with a sensuous and delicate charm rarely to be discerned in Attic literature. One example [4] must suffice:

καιροσπάθητον ἄνθεων ὕφασμα καινὸν Ὡρῶν.

'Fresh raiment of flowers close-broidered by fairy-fingers'. So magical is the phrasing that we scarcely recognize the metre as the usual rub-a-dub-dub of Aristophanes. In the writing of nativity-plays Hermippus was followed by NICOPHON with *The Birth of Aphrodite;* POLYZELUS composed a whole series of such dramas—on Dionysus, the Muses, Aphrodite and perhaps Ares; the idea was a favourite in Middle Comedy also. But the drama of fantasy was naturally not confined to these themes. NICOCHARES wrote *Heracles the Play-Producer* (Ἡρακλῆς Χορηγός) and Aristonymus the even quaintlier-named *Frozen Sun* (Ἥλιος Ῥιγῶν), of which also we know nothing; possibly the title means *The Sun-God with a Cold*. The most illustrious instance of fantasy is,

---

[1] But we have no other evidence of a *Phrygians* by Euripides.
[2] Sophocles dramatized the birth of Hermes in his *Ichneutæ*.
[3] His most interesting political fragment (46) is an attack on Pericles, whom he calls βασιλεὺς σατύρων, probably an allusion to Cratinus' *Dionysalexandros:* see below, p. 123.
[4] Fr. 5. The Hours are Nature considered as working subtle and lovely change.

of course, the *Birds*, which seems to have suggested to ARCHIPPUS the idea of his *Fishes*. This poet, who gained one first prize and was ridiculed as the most abandoned punster of his day,[1] is notable for the fact that some ancient critics attributed to him the four doubtful plays of Aristophanes, *Poetry* (Ποίησις), *Islands* (Νῆσοι), *Niobos*, and *Dionysus Shipwrecked* (Διόνυσος Ναυαγός).

Concerning the third topic, burlesque of legend, little need be said in this outline : excellent examples of it will be found in the *Dionysalexandros* and *Odysses* of Cratinus, in the latter part of the *Thesmophoriazusæ*, and in various other works of Aristophanes. No dramatic type has a longer history : it begins with the earliest comic playwright, Epicharmus, continues throughout Old Comedy, and was a favourite pursuit of the Middle writers ; Rhinthon, the *phlyax*, appears to have written nothing else. In most ages it has been a fairly easy and successful dramatic type.

Political themes are the most important and frequent of all. Here the lampoon flourishes, whether as brief incidental gibes at individuals great and small, or as providing the plan of a whole work like the *Knights :* human nature being what it is, an uproarious Old Comedy writer could scarcely conceive a political play without attaching it to personalities. Of this type, the chief exponents were EUPOLIS and ARISTOPHANES, who (together with CRATINUS) were regarded throughout antiquity as beyond compare the great " old " masters. (To each of these a later discussion is devoted.) We may here mention incidentally an attractive poet who did not indeed write on politics, but who distinguished himself in competition with the great playwrights whom we have just named.

AMEIPSIAS is chiefly noteworthy because he twice defeated Aristophanes : in 423 the *Clouds* was placed third and Ameipsias' *Connos* second, Cratinus being first with the *Wine-Flask ;*[2] in 414 the *Birds* came

[1] Schol., *Wasps*, 500.   [2] *Clouds*, Argument IV.

second to Ameipsias' *Revellers*, the third prize falling to Phrynichus' *Hermit*.[1] A notion[2] that ill-feeling existed between Aristophanes and Ameipsias rests on weak evidence. Aristophanes jeers[3] at Ameipsias (together with Phrynichus and Lycis) for hackneyed clowning; this need mean little. On the other side, we hear[4] that Ameipsias derided Aristophanes, saying he must have been born on the fourth of the month: according to a proverb, such persons were fated to toil for others, and Aristophanes produced some of his work under the names of Callistratus and Philonides. Ameipsias composed at least nine plays—we have their titles—and (as has been said) gained at least one first prize, though some have thought that the *Revellers* and the *Connos* were really the work of Phrynichus.[5] CONNOS is named after a famous musician, said to have taught Socrates: it depicted an assembly of sophists. Athenæus writes:[6] 'Ameipsias in *Connos* ... does not number Protagoras in the chorus of thinkers'. This not only gives some idea of the subject: it is important as showing that the chorus consisted of individualized members. In tragedy always, in comedy almost always, the chorus is a company (of maidens or farmers and so forth) all exactly alike. But, as in the *Cities* of Eupolis and the *Birds* of Aristophanes, so here it seems that the separate choristers represented individuals who entered one by one and were announced by name. It is then possible that Socrates was a member of the chorus. He certainly took a part in the play:[7]

Σώκρατες ἀνδρῶν βέλτιστ' ὀλίγων, πολλῶν δὲ ματαιόταθ', ἥκεις
καὶ σὺ πρὸς ἡμᾶς; καρτερικός γ' εἶ.   πόθεν ἄν σοι χλαῖνα γένοιτο;

τουτὶ τὸ κακὸν τῶν σκυτοτόμων κατ' ἐπήρειαν γεγένηται.
οὗτος μέντοι πεινῶν οὕτως οὐπώποτ' ἔτλη κολακεῦσαι.

[1] *Birds*, Argument I.
[2] Meineke, *Fragmenta Comicorum Græcorum*, I, p. 199.
[3] *Frogs*, 1-18.
[4] *Vita* (Dindorf's ed., IV, i. p. 34): τὰ μὲν πρῶτα διὰ Καλλιστράτου καὶ Φιλωνίδου καθίει δράματα· διὸ καὶ ἔσκωπτον αὐτὸν Ἀριστώνυμός τε καὶ Ἀμειψίας τετράδι αὐτὸν λέγοντες γεγονέναι, κατὰ τὴν παροιμίαν, ὡς ἄλλοις πονοῦντα.
[5] Bergk (*Rell. Com. Att.*, 369).   [6] V, 218c.   [7] Fr. 9.

'Socrates, among a few the best, among many the most stupid, hast thou also come to us? This is true fortitude! Whence canst thou get a mantle?... This discomfort is intended as an insult to the shoemakers.[1] Now this man, hungry as he is, never had the hardihood to play the sycophant.' The tone of the passage is much more respectful to Socrates than the *Clouds*, which was performed at the same festival. From SPHENDONE (Σφενδόνη, either "sling" or "bezel") comes one attractive remnant:[2]

τὸ μὲν δόρυ
μετὰ τῆς ἐπιχάλκου πρὸς Πλαταιαῖς ἀπέβαλεν,

'he lost his spear and shield at Platæa'. This most probably refers to the escape from Platæa immortalized by Thucydides; a number of Athenians took part therein. From an unnamed play comes a *scolium* or drinking-catch:[3]

οὐ χρὴ πόλλ' ἔχειν θνητὸν ἄνθρωπον,
ἀλλ' ἐρᾶν καὶ κατεσθίειν· σὺ δὲ κάρτα φείδῃ.

Life is short: a fig for pelf!
Kiss the girls and stuff yourself:
  You'd be wiser,
  Silly miser.

Returning to the description of political comedy, we need to make only two remarks. Firstly, no special importance resides in the fact that some poets attack Pericles, others Cleon, others Hyperbolus, and in the difference between those statesmen. They are attacking "the government," that is all. To suggest, as some have done, that Eupolis and Aristophanes were in the pay of the oligarchic malcontents, is woefully to misapprehend Athenian political life.[4] Granted freedom of speech, it was far easier, far more exciting, far better fun, to assail the favourite of Demos than to assail the opposition. Secondly, these plays are notable for their outspokenness, not merely the freedom

---

[1] Because Socrates always went barefoot. Almost certainly there was in the preceding lines some such remark as 'but where are your shoes?'
[2] Fr. 17. Cp. Thucydides, III, 20-24. [3] Fr. 22.
[4] The *Knights* (see p. 210) is a possible exception to this generalization.

of speech just mentioned. Fifth-century παρρησία meant more than that in the comic drama : not only freedom but licence; the absence not only of fear but of all scruple. Cratinus, we learn, satirized Pericles by innuendo in the *Dionysalexandros*, but that was unusual procedure. Normally, whether in the " elegant " Eupolis, the " bull-eating " Cratinus,[1] or Aristophanes, " the shrine of the Graces," there erupted a volcano of blasting vituperation, imputations of every public and private vileness, couched in language that makes Swift seem half-hearted. Observing this spirit and method, together with the fact that none of the statesmen thus assailed lost a jot of power or reputation, we realize the feeling of Athenians about both politics and art. They perceived clearly the bearing and value of each : they did not pull down Cleon because they saw that Aristophanes was a great poet ; nor did they belittle Aristophanes because they were for Cleon.

These considerations, however, lead us to the one important feature in the external history of Greek drama, the attempt at censorship. There were attacks on individuals and repressive legislation concerning comedy in general. But the first seem to have been outbreaks of Cleon only, who indicted Euripides for impiety and Aristophanes for political improprieties. As for repression in general, we find a good number of allusions to legislation against undisguised personal attack.[2] In all, four repressive laws are alleged.

(i) The " psephism of Morychides," or rather a decree passed in his archonship (440-39) and in force till 438-7. There can be no doubt concerning this : the Scholiast [3] who reports it uses unfaltering language that shows he had a good authority on his desk. 'This (Euthymenes) is the archon in whose year was rescinded the decree forbidding " comedy," [4] proposed in the archonship of Morychides ; it prevailed during that

---

[1] Not much virulence, though a good deal of satire, is to be observed in his fragments ; but see Platonius (quoted on p. 141).
[2] Μὴ κωμῳδεῖν ὀνομαστί. [3] On *Ach.*, 67.
[4] Κωμῳδεῖν being used, as often, of personal satire or lampoon.

year and the two succeeding—those of Glaucinus and Theodorus—after which it was rescinded under Euthymenes.' In this connexion a passage is often quoted from the pseudo-Xenophontean *Constitution of Athens*, written in the first two or three years of the Peloponnesian War, but this is a complete misunderstanding: the writer mentions repression only of attack upon the Commons as such (plays like the *Knights*, that is) and asserts that the Commons actually encourage comedy directed against individuals.[1]

(ii) The "*Lex Antimacheia*," a decree attributed to Antimachus by Scholiasts and others on the strength of the curse invoked on him by Aristophanes: [2] 'May Zeus destroy him evilly for sending wretched me away dinnerless when he was choregus at the Lenæa'. The absurd inference drawn is that Antimachus, by abolishing comedy, deprived the chorus-men of their livelihood; but there were no professional performers at this time; in any case, comedy went merrily on after the *Acharnians*. Aristophanes, of course, means only that Antimachus had failed in his well-known duty, as choregus, of giving a dinner to the performers.

(iii) A Scholiast[3] reports that Syracosius secured the passage of a decree against undisguised satire on the stage; this would be about 415 B.C. He quotes from the *Hermit* of Phrynichus an unfortunately corrupt passage, the general sense of which seems, however, unmistakable: 'Curse Syracosius! He has prevented me from ridiculing those whom I wished.' Whatever this means,[4] it cannot refer to a decree; or

---

[1] *Resp. Ath.*, II, 18.   [2] *Ach.*, 1150 ff.
[3] On *Birds*, 1297: Δοκεῖ δὲ καὶ ψήφισμα τεθεικέναι μὴ κωμῳδεῖσθαι ὀνομαστί τινα, ὡς Φρύνιχος ἐν Μονοτρόπῳ φησί· ψῶρ' ἔχε Συρακόσιον ἐπιφανὴς γὰρ αὐτῷ καὶ μέγα τύχοι. ἀφείλετο γὰρ κωμῳδεῖν οὓς ἐπεθύμουν, διὸ πικρότερον αὐτῷ προσφέρονται.

[4] Syracosius may have baffled Phrynichus by non-legal, perhaps even accidental means: ἀφείλετο suggests not so much direct prohibition as some quite different action that incidentally resulted in Phrynichus' inability. Suppose Syracosius, who was a politician, had made a violent attack on the poet's prospective butts. "I really cannot ridicule men who have been placed beyond censure by the abuse of (the disgusting) Syracosius." Note also the Scholiast's δοκεῖ: he found in his authorities nothing definite about such a law.

—to be quite accurate—it cannot refer to a decree that had any effect. There was an abundance of personal satire in plays immediately following the alleged decree: Syracosius himself, for instance,[1] was laughed at by name in the *Birds*.

(iv) Certain vaguer remarks attribute to a repressive law the change from Old to Middle Comedy:

(*a*) A Scholiast on the *Frogs*[2] writes: 'Not long afterwards Cinesias destroyed the productions (χορηγίας) once for all: wherefore Strattis in the play about him says: "Yonder is the tent of the chorus-slaying Cinesias"'. This seems a mere blunder. Strattis meant that Cinesias (no politician, but a dithyrambic poet) half-killed the singers who had to perform his terrible works. The Scholiast has combined this with the irrelevant fact that after the *Frogs* the importance of comic choruses rapidly dwindled.

(*b*) Tzetzes alleges[3] that Alcibiades not only punished Eupolis for the *Baptæ* but also introduced a decree that comedy should no longer be outspoken, but indirect, whereupon Eupolis himself, with Cratinus, Pherecrates, Plato, and Aristophanes, passed over to "the Second Comedy". This is completely refuted by the known contents of plays subsequent to the *Baptæ*.

(*c*) Horace, in his account of comedy, writes:[4]

> sed in vitium libertas excidit et vim
> dignam lege regi: lex est accepta chorusque
> turpiter obticuit sublato iure nocendi.

'But liberty degenerated into licence and a violence that deserved legal restraint: a law was imposed, and the chorus, deprived of its right to wound, fell into ignominious silence.' This again is chronological confusion.

The upshot is that we know certainly of but one law restraining comedy, that named after Morychides,

---

[1] Denis (*La Comédie grecque*, II, p. 284) gives this and numerous others.
[2] V, 404.   [3] Kaibel, pp. 20 *sq.*, 28.   [4] *Ars Poetica*, 282 *sqq.*

which endured from 440-39 till 438-7, less than three years. Into this period falls the war between Athens and Samos, which might be held to excuse or demand suppression of anything that could embarrass the government. During that period comedies were performed, as we know from inscriptions; but there is no evidence as to the effect of this decree upon their tone. On the other hand, there exists no real proof that any such repression (save of individuals) was even attempted during the long and finally disastrous war against the Peloponnesian Confederacy; and we can point to many extremely bitter and outspoken attacks upon leading statesmen. The natural conclusion is that " Morychides' decree " was an experiment that was felt to have failed.

Old Comedy ended with the fall of Athens at the close of the Peloponnesian War in 404 B.C. A comparison of the *Frogs* (and all that we know of the comic drama just then) with the *Ecclesiazusæ* (and whatever else we gather concerning comedy in general at that date) reveals an enormous change, no less obvious than the gulf between English drama before the Civil War and the drama of the Restoration. Dryden rightly called that interval " the Flood ": his description applies to the change in drama no less than to the political change. Athens went through an experience even more shattering, and Old Comedy was destroyed by the political downfall. Thalia's heart was broken, and though she recovered her poise she never regained her spirits: cleverness, wit and alert interest were not dead, but the old uproarious verve was gone for ever. With this loss of energy and imagination came a weakening on the material side of theatrical art. Men able and willing to pay with the former lavishness for mounting tragedies and comedies could no longer be found. The chief expense had been the chorus of twenty-four men, often elaborately attired; therefore the old chorus was replaced by a commonplace group, whose training too was less exacting. Thus, loss of imaginative energy and loss of riches conspired to change the method of comedy, which became not only more decent in language,[1] but also more pedestrian and plain, with far less song and dance, far more plot: the Comedy of Manners was rapidly becoming the only form.

But, as we have seen, that *genre* was already in some degree at home in the orchestra. It followed that poets who had been practising it before the collapse were able to pass over into the new conditions with comparatively little change of subject or method. Aristophanes as an artist was half-slain by Ægospotami; Plato developed notably, and some ancient scholars assigned him altogether to Middle Comedy. Other men of less moment went straight forward. Whereas, then, Old Comedy in its most magnificent aspects died at the end of the fifth century, there was a period of mere transition for that social comedy which had formed a minor element therein. That transition may be studied not only in Plato but in Aristophanes himself, whose *Ecclesiazusæ* and *Plutus* provide the only examples of Middle Comedy that we possess. But three minor transition-writers shall be considered at once.

THEOPOMPUS, according to Suidas,[2] 'belongs to the Old Comedy and the time of Aristophanes. There are plays and many other writings of his.' (The last words are no doubt due to confusion between the poet and his namesake the historian.) He produced comedies long before Aristophanes' death; for instance, in *The Boys* (Παῖδες) he mentioned Læspodias, who was conspicuous in the last decade of the Peloponnesian War. But he was no less a Middle than an Old Comedian, as even his meagre fragments reveal. The number of his plays is uncertain: we know twenty

---

[1] Cp. Aristotle, *Nic. Eth.*, IV, 1128a, 22: ἴδοι δ' ἄν τις καὶ ἐκ τῶν κωμῳδιῶν τῶν παλαιῶν καὶ τῶν καινῶν· τοῖς μὲν γὰρ ἦν γελοῖον ἡ αἰσχρολογία, τοῖς δὲ μᾶλλον ἡ ὑπόνοια. Crates at least was an exception among the old writers. See p. 147.

[2] s.v. Θεόπομπος.

titles; the Anonymus puts the figure at seventeen, Suidas at twenty-four. We do not know that he ever won the first prize. His longest fragment, from NEMEA,[1] is vastly more like Plautus than Aristophanes. There is a faint whiff of Falstaff and Doll Tearsheet about it, too:

> A. χώρει σὺ δεῦρο, Θηρικλέους πιστὸν τέκνον·
> γενναῖον εἶδος, ὄνομά σοι τί θώμεθα;
> ἆρ' εἰ κάτοπτρον φύσεος ἦν πλῆρες δοθῇς;
> οὐδέν ποτ' ἄλλο. δεῦρο δὴ γεμίσω σ' ἐγώ.
> γραῦ Θεολύτη, γραῦ.
> B.   τί με καλεῖς;
> A.   σέ, φιλτάτη,
> ἵν' ἀσπάσωμαι· δεῦρο παρ' ἐμέ, Θεολύτη,
> παρὰ τὸν νέον σύνδουλον· οὑτωσὶ καλῶς.
> B. Σπινθὴρ τάλας, πειρᾷς με;
> A.   ναί, τοιοῦτό τι.
> φιλοτησίαν δὲ τήνδε σοι προπίομαι·
> δέξαι, πιοῦσα δ' ὁπόσον ἄν σοι θυμὸς ᾖ,
> παράδος τὸ πρῶτον.[2]

'Come hither thou, trusty child of Thericles [*i.e.* a goblet]. Noble shape, how are we to name thee? Verily thou art human nature's mirror, when full in the hand—that's a true word. Come, let me fill thee. Theolyte, old lady! What, Theolyte!' 'Why do you call?' 'To greet you, my dear. Come beside me, Theolyte; come and sit with your new fellow-slave. That's nice.' 'Spinther, you wretch, are you flirting with me?' 'I am, more or less. A pledge to you in this loving-cup! Take it, drink your fill, and pass (it back?).'

Several of his dramas were literary, and in a more dilettante manner than was customary in Old Comedy. ODYSSEUS contained at any rate two quotations:

> χιτῶνά μοι
> φέρων δέδωκας δαιδάλοεν, ὃν ἤκασεν
> ἄρισθ' Ὅμηρος κρομμύου λεπυχάνῳ.[3]

'You brought and gave me a broidered tunic, which Homer admirably compared to the skin of an onion.'

---
[1] The name of a courtesan, which Geissler (*Chronologie*, p. 79) would spell Νεμεάς.
[2] Fr. 32. The last two words cannot be right. Meineke suggests τὸ λοιπόν, which is apt, though not too courteous.
[3] Fr. 33. Cp. *Od.*, XIX, 232 *sq.*

Odysseus, we find, has read what Homer has to say of him! Still more notable, he (or a contemporary) has studied Euripides : [1]

Εὐρίπιδου γάρ' ἔστιν οὐ κακῶς ἔχον,
τἀλλότρια δειπνεῖν τὸν καλῶς εὐδαίμονα.

'There is a sensible remark of Euripides, that the really happy man is he who dines at another's expense.' In the LUXURIOUS MAN ('Ηδυχάρης) occurred the earliest reference in comedy to Plato by name : [2]

ἓν γάρ ἐστιν οὐδὲ ἕν,
τὰ δὲ δύο μόλις ἕν ἐστιν, ὥς φησιν Πλάτων.

'for one is zero, and two are scarcely one, as Plato says'. The PERSIAN [3] (Μῆδος) alluded to fourth-century politics :

ὥς ποτ' ἐκήλησεν Καλλίστρατος υἷας Ἀχαιῶν,
κέρμα φίλον διαδούς, ὅτε συμμαχίαν ἐρέεινεν·
οἷον δ' οὐ κήλησε δέμας λεπτὸν Ῥαδάμανθυν
Λύσανδρον, κώθωνα πρὶν αὐτῷ δῶκε λεπαστήν.

'How once Callistratus enchanted the sons of the Achæans by distributing delightful cash when he requested (?) the alliance. Rhadamanthys-Lysander alone, that slender shape, he did not enchant till he gave him a goblet.' Plutarch [4] tells us that Theopompus compared the Spartans to tavern-keepers, because, after giving the Greeks a taste of the sweet draught of freedom, they poured vinegar for them.

STRATTIS was a weak but pleasing poet whose career began late in the fifth century and continued till at least 375 B.C., as may be gathered from a passage [5] of his *Atalanta*. This alludes to Lagisca, a concubine of Isocrates, the political pamphleteer. Isocrates (born in 436 B.C.) was elderly when he took Lagisca into his house,[6] so that the date of *Atalanta* is 375 B.C. or somewhat later. The Anonymus and Suidas both attribute sixteen plays to Strattis, but we have the

---

[1] Fr. 34.
[2] Fr. 15. Cp. *Phædo*, 96e. The *Phædo* is to be dated about 380 B.C.
[3] Fr. 30.   [4] *Lysander*, XIII.   [5] Fr. 3.
[6] Athenæus, XIII, 592d, προβαίνων τῇ ἡλικίᾳ. Cp. Geissler, *Chronologie*, p. 78.

THE HISTORY OF GREEK COMEDY 33

names of nineteen. His repute was not high: Hesychius, it appears,[1] refers one quotation to 'the vulgar little play of Strattis'. He wrote a good deal of parody, and the PHŒNISSÆ (a burlesque of Euripides) was perhaps his best-known work. In the tragedy Jocasta offers advice to her fratricidal sons, Eteocles and Polynices. We possess two scraps of Strattis' parody. The first [2] runs:

παραινέσαι δὲ σφῶν τι βούλομαι σοφόν·
ὅταν φακῆν ἕψητε, μὴ 'πιχεῖν μύρον.

'A wise admonition I offer to you twain: when boiling porridge, do not mix in perfume.' It is a phrase for wasting costly embellishment upon commonplace things. The second [3] is:

εἴθ' ἥλιος μὲν πείθεται τοῖς παιδίοις
ὅταν λέγωσιν 'ἔξεχ', ὦ φίλ' ἥλιε' . . .

'Then shall the sun obey the children when they cry "Peep out, Mr. Sun" . . . ?' TROILUS, a burlesque of the lost Sophoclean play, catches the eye because the bitter coarseness of one fragment [4] calls to mind Shakespeare's tortured tragedy:

ἦ μήποτ', ὦ παῖ Ζηνός, ἐς ταὐτὸν μόλῃς,
ἀλλὰ παραδοὺς τοῖς Λεσβίοις χαίρειν ἔα.

'Keep thyself from her arms, O son of Zeus, and deliver her to the Lesbians for good and all.' Another passage [5] awakes memories of the *Iliad*:

ἐρινὸν οὖν τιν' αὐτῆς πλησίον
νενόηκας ὄντα;

'Hast thou observed a certain fig-tree close thereby?' This may be part of an assignation between Troilus and Cressida. The SCOURGE OF MANKIND ('Ανθρωπορ-

---

[1] That is, if our MS. is correct. Under κολεκάνοι Hesychius notes: Στράττις ἐν τῷ φορτικῷ δραματίῳ, κτέ. This may be a corruption of ἐν τῷ Φορτικῷ δράματι—'the play entitled *The Vulgar Man*'.
[2] Fr. 45. Cp. Eur., *Phœn.*, 460 sq.
[3] Fr. 46. Cp. Eur., *Phœn.*, 546.   [4] Fr. 41.
[5] Fr. 42. It is the tree mentioned by Andromache to Hector (VI, 433).

3

ραιστής)[1] contained a reminiscence of the most famous [2] *contretemps* that ever delighted the Athenian theatre. An actor named Hegelochus ruined the fine sick-bed scene in Euripides' *Orestes* by a slip in pronouncing v. 279:

ἐκ κυμάτων γὰρ αὖθις αὖ γαλήν' ὁρῶ,

'after the billows once more I see a calm'. The unlucky protagonist gave γαλῆν instead of γαλήν'—'once more do I see a weasel coming out of the waves'. The Scourge seems to have been an archon, whose duty it was to assign protagonists to the competing authors: to no other can the following words [3] be appropriate:

καὶ τῶν μὲν ἄλλων οὐκ ἐμέλησέ μοι μελῶν,
Εὐριπίδου δὲ δρᾶμα δεξιώτατον
διέκναισ' Ὀρέστην, Ἡγέλοχον τὸν Κιννάρου
μισθωσάμενος τὰ πρῶτα τῶν ἐπῶν λέγειν.

'About the dithyrambs I didn't care, but he ruined a masterly play of Euripides, the *Orestes*, by hiring Hegelochus, son of Cinnarus, to play the leading rôle.' The MACEDONIANS (or PAUSANIAS) contained a description [4] of the manner in which the great mantle of Athena was exhibited:

τὸν πέπλον δὲ τοῦτον
ἕλκουσ' ὀνεύοντες τοπείοις ἄνδρες ἀναρίθμητοι
εἰς ἄκρον ὥσπερ ἱστίον τὸν ἱστόν.

'And this robe innumerable men haul like a sail to the top of the mast by ropes on a crane.' The SHADE-SEEKERS (Ψυχασταί) contained a rather effective little lament: [5]

αἱ δ' ἀλεκτρυόνες ἅπασαι
καὶ τὰ χοιρίδια τέθνηκε
καὶ τὰ μίκρ' ὀρνίθια.

---

[1] Some scholars read Ἀνθρωπορέστης (whatever that may mean).

[2] It is mentioned also in Frag. Incert. 60 and in *Frogs*, 303 *sq*. The effect can be estimated in English by reading Edgar's description of the imaginary goblin (*Lear*, IV, vi.) with equal emphasis on "some" and "fiend".

[3] Fr. 1. τῶν ἄλλων μελῶν must mean lyrics as contrasted with plays, by the familiar idiom of ἄλλος. This archon, then, made some blunder about the dithyrambic contest of the same year.

[4] Fr. 30. Strattis said also that giants formed part of the design (Schol. Eur., *Hecuba*, 468).

[5] Fr. 58.

'All the hens and the little pigs are dead, and the little chickens.' The following lyric,[1] from an unnamed play, reads daintily:

πρασοκουρίδες, αἱ καταφύλλους
ἀνὰ κήπους πεντήκοντα ποδῶν
ἴχνεσι βαίνετ', ἐφαπτόμεναι
ποδοῖν σατυριδίων μακροκέρκων
χοροὺς ἑλίσσουσαι παρ' ὠκίμων
πέταλα καὶ θριδακινίδων
εὐόσμων τε σελίνων.

'Ye caterpillars, that amid the garden-foliage pace forward on your fifty feet and cling to the long-tailed elves: ye that move in the country dance beside the leaves of basil and lettuce and fragrant parsley.'

LYSIPPUS belonged, at any rate during part of his career, to the Old Comedy,[2] for we possess one fragment from a parabasis. On the other hand, his most remarkable passage is utterly unlike Old Comedy —lines praising Athens as a show-place, an ancient Venice or other " Mecca of Tourists ". It is astounding to find a contemporary of Aristophanes writing thus:[3]

εἰ μὴ τεθέασαι τὰς 'Αθήνας, στέλεχος εἶ·
εἰ δὲ τεθέασαι μὴ τεθήρευσαι δ', ὄνος·
εἰ δ' εὐαρεστῶν ἀποτρέχεις, κανθήλιος.

'If you have not seen Athens, you are a blockhead; if you have seen her and not been captivated, you are a donkey; if you have felt her charm and scamper off, you are a pack-ass.' Subjoined to this glib little advertisement of *la ville lumière* is a curious passage [4] describing some city of Rhodes as a pleasant spot rather spoiled by the insistence of the inhabitants upon

---

[1] Fr. 66.
[2] In fr. 6 Lampon, the friend of Pericles, is ridiculed.
[3] Fr. 7. Meineke calls this 'encomium elegantissimum' (I, p. 216). It is striking, no doubt, but as poster-rhetoric: τεθήρευσαι is practically a translation of the "lure" that is now a regular garnishment of any town more seductive than Manchester. The passage of pseudo-Dicæarchus (*Descr. Græciæ*, 22) which leads up to our fragment is well worth attention: τὸ καθόλου δ' ὅσον αἱ λοιπαὶ πόλεις πρός τε ἡδονὴν καὶ βίου διόρθωσιν τῶν ἀγρῶν διαφέρουσι, τοσοῦτον τῶν λοιπῶν πόλεων ἡ τῶν 'Αθηναίων παραλλάττει. φυλακτέον δ' ὡς ἐνὶ μάλιστα τὰς ἑταίρας, μὴ λάθῃ τις ἡδέως ἀπολόμενος. οἱ στίχοι Λυσίππου κτέ. Cp. the Introduction to Baedeker's *Paris*, p. xxvii.
[4] Meineke, II, p. 746.

the Sun-God who is their patron: even a certain kind of garland was called "sun-wreath". Here again we feel the tourist atmosphere. However these two passages were used, whether in separate plays or (as is more likely) in the same, Lysippus is writing a rather novel type of comedy. One imagines that he has taken over the idea so brilliantly employed by Eupolis in the *Cities* (and apparently in the *Demes*), but instead of developing a definitely Athenian topic he has composed a living guide-book—twenty-four *choreutæ*, each representing a famous city. Lysippus himself claims originality in the parabasis-fragment [1] already mentioned, which probably comes from his BACCHÆ :

οὐδ' ἀνακνάψας καὶ θειώσας τὰς ἀλλοτρίας ἐπινοίας.

'not furbishing up and treating with sulphur other men's ideas'. Athenæus' desire to prove that 'they cooled wine in order to drink it cooler' provides us with a tantalizing scrap,[2] also from the *Bacchæ* :

A. Ἕρμων.
B.   τί ἔστι;
A.   πῶς ἄγομεν;
B.   τί γ' ἄλλο γ' ἢ
ὁ πατὴρ ἄνωθεν ἐς τὸ φρέαρ, ἐμοὶ δοκεῖν,
ὥσπερ τὸν οἶνον τοῦ θέρους καθεῖκε νώ.

'Hermon!' 'Yes?' 'What has happened to us?' 'Why, of course, father has let us down into the well, I suppose, like wine in summer.' This *Bacchæ* is apparently the only play of Lysippus that survived into the times of Alexandrian scholarship; at any rate it is the only title we possess.

Of the numerous less celebrated authors only ALCÆUS need be mentioned here. On the evidence of Suidas we may believe that he began work in the Old period, but if so he is a strong instance of transition, for his fragments, scanty as they are, contain several non-Attic forms. In the year of the second *Plutus*

---

[1] Fr. 4.   [2] Fr. 1.

THE HISTORY OF GREEK COMEDY

(388 B.C.) he was one of Aristophanes' four rivals. To judge by the titles of his plays, he specialized in erotic drama: in 388 he offered a *Pasiphae*. One of his works was named *Tragicomedy* (Κωμῳδοτραγῳδία), a title used by the Sicilian Deinolochus before him and by Anaxandrides after him.

§ 3. MIDDLE COMEDY

This portion of Greek literature begins with the capture of Athens and the destruction of her empire by Lysander in 404 B.C., so that to this period some works already discussed, including the last two extant plays of Aristophanes, plainly belong. The end [1] of it was marked by the battle of Chæronea in 338 B.C., which brought Greece under Macedonian power and extinguished her political independence. The writing of comedies was industriously pursued: Athenæus [2] tells us that he has himself read more than eight hundred. Nevertheless, this area of literature, in its

---

[1] Since the appearance in 1866 of W. Fielitz' pamphlet, *De Atticorum Comœdia bipartita*, there has been considerable discussion whether Middle Comedy, as such, exists at all; that is, whether we ought not to speak only of Old and Later (or New) Comedy. Fielitz points out that μέση κωμῳδία is mentioned by no author before Apuleius, who calls Philemon *mediæ comœdiæ scriptor* (*Florida*, III, 16): he insists that the tripartition of comedy was the invention of scholars belonging to the age of Hadrian. An admirable brief summary of the subject is given by Körte (Pauly-Wissowa, 1256-8) and a longer discussion by Legrand (*Daos*, pp. 4-10), both of whom decide for the three-fold division. But the whole question is trivial. If our opinion or understanding of any writer who belongs to one or the other alleged periods depended upon the correctness of the bipartition or of the tripartition, that would be another matter. But of course it does not: our view of (let us say) Menander's indebtedness to Crates is not affected in the least by our deciding that there are two lines of demarcation, or one, between them. The whole dispute is about labels and nothing but labels. The really important point is, how do works of various periods differ? not the names of the periods. Now first, there is no doubt that Cratinus, Antiphanes and Menander represent different phases; second, that the type of Antiphanes and his contemporaries develops with no violent break into the type of Menander and his contemporaries. In the present state of our knowledge genuine criticism will allow us to speak of Old, Middle and New Comedy, or of Old and Later Comedy, precisely as we please. In the present book the traditional three-fold division has been followed, mostly because readers prefer shorter sections to longer.

[2] VIII, 336d.

present state, is extremely dull and its authors differ little from one another; for these two reasons we shall not attempt to consider them separately. The only really notable differences are in bulk. Alexis, who, according to Suidas, wrote two hundred and forty-five plays, and Antiphanes, who was even more fertile, account together for one-half of what survives from Middle Comedy, though we possess something at least of no less than thirty-four poets. This vast preponderance of Antiphanes and Alexis shows how beloved they were in antiquity, but the huge number of their plays suggests slightness and triviality. Middle Comedy is a backwater; the fourth century is a century of prose: many single pages of Plato and Demosthenes are worth all these remnants. Between the excitingly varied landscape of Old Comedy and the city of Menander stretches a desert: therein the sedulous topographer may remark two respectable eminences, and perhaps a low ridge in the middle distance, or a few nullahs, and the wayfarer will greet with delight one or two oases with a singing-bird or so; but the ever-present foreground of his journey is sand, tiresome, barren and trickling.

The difference of literary manner between Old and Middle Comedy will best be learned from a study of the later Aristophanes, and the fragments of Antiphanes, Alexis and their colleagues; other differences may be summarized at once. The very shape of comedy begins to waver: the chorus sinks in importance and interest;[1] the parabasis may be omitted. Though the framework is directly inherited from Old Comedy, Middle writers are more indebted for their subjects to Euripides than to any comic dramatist. Love-interest in general, the violation-motif, the recognition by amulets, so frequent in the more melodramatic works of Euripides (for example, in the *Ion*) become frequent. Aristophanes himself used such themes in the *Cocalus*; Anaxandrides built so much on them

[1] Cp. the vigorous fragment of Plato quoted on p. 176.

that he is by one writer credited with the invention of love-affairs and seductions as dramatic material. The *Persa* of Plautus, which is based on a Greek comedy of this period, shows by its manner that such topics were already familiar in that age.[1] In its spirit, again, Middle Comedy stands unmistakably between the Old and the New. It shows some touch of the earlier audacity, combined with a strong leaning towards social comedy, if we may regard as typical the *Plutus*, which contains open defiance of Zeus and the scene of the rich woman with her *gigolo*. There are traces, too, of the old fantasy, or rather of the old indifference to verisimilitude. And to judge by the titles—unfortunately there is little else to rely upon—these playwrights developed that Comedy of Character, whereof Phrynichus' *Hermit* is perhaps the only Old example, which was an indispensable prelude to the perfected Comedy of Manners.

A detailed account of subjects and the like shall be added later; but we may here give conveniently the little that our authorities tell us as to the differences between Old and Middle Comedy. Platonius[2] notes three novelties. First, the topics were changed: whereas Old Comedy censured the wrongdoing of influential men—'generals and judges'—Middle Comedy turned to 'ridicule of stories told by poets'. That is misleading: important as burlesque was, Middle Comedy knew several other themes no less popular; moreover, burlesque was frequent in the earlier period. Second, choric songs fell into disuse. This is untrue; but it is a fact that they became far less important, and that the parabasis disappeared. Third, the masks were wildly distorted. But this clearly refers (or should refer) to New Comedy: for he says that the purpose was to avoid even 'an accidental facial resemblance to some Macedonian official'; and these sensitive Northerners arrived later. The

---

[1] Körte, Pauly-Wissowa, XI, 1264 *sq.* [2] Kaibel, p. 5.

Anonymus,[1] as usual, seems more trustworthy. ' The poets of Middle Comedy did not essay poetic style: they employed the familiar language, and so their merits are rhetorical, poetical qualities being rare in them. They all expend study upon their plots. To the Middle Comedy belong fifty-seven poets; eight hundred and seventeen plays are in existence.'

ANTIPHANES (*circa* 406-332 B.C.) produced his first play about 387 and won thirteen victories. Since the number of his works is variously stated at two hundred and eighty and at three hundred and sixty-five, it is natural to assume that he (and others) wrote for readers also and for production in other places besides Athens.[2] He was of foreign birth, and the Anonymus says that he was given Athenian citizenship by Demosthenes. EUBULUS is described by Suidas as standing on the boundary between Old and Middle Comedy, but he also assigns him to the hundred-and-first Olympiad (376-2); he composed one hundred and four plays. ALEXIS was a naturalized Athenian from Thurii, and an uncle of Menander. He seems to have lived for more than a hundred years (about 390 till at least 287) and so belongs to New Comedy also. Concerning ANAXANDRIDES we possess more interesting accounts. A foreigner from Rhodes or Colophon, he produced his first play in 376 B.C., as we learn from the Parian Marble; according to Suidas, he wrote sixty-five comedies and gained ten victories. Anaxandrides is the only Middle poet mentioned by Aristotle, who tells us that Philemon (the famous New dramatist) acted in his plays.[3] Suidas [4] says that he

---

[1] Kaibel, pp. 8 sq.: τῆς δὲ μέσης κωμῳδίας οἱ ποιηταὶ πλάσματος μὲν οὐχ ἥψαντο ποιητικοῦ, διὰ δὲ τῆς συνήθους ἰόντες λαλιᾶς λογικὰς ἔχουσι τὰς ἀρετάς, ὥστε σπάνιον ποιητικὸν εἶναι χαρακτῆρα παρ' αὐτοῖς. κατασχολοῦνται δὲ πάντες περὶ τὰς ὑποθέσεις. τῆς μὲν οὖν μέσης κωμῳδίας εἰσὶ ποιηταὶ νζ', καὶ τούτων δράματα φέρεται χζ'. This numeral = 607; Meineke alters it to ωιζ' (817) to square with Athenæus (see above).

[2] Machon is known to have written entirely for the Alexandrian theatre (Athen., XIV, 644a).

[3] *Rhetoric*, III, 12. Aristotle quotes him in three other places.

[4] *s.v.*: πρῶτος οὗτος ἔρωτας καὶ παρθένων φθορὰς εἰσήγαγεν. Aristophanes had done this before him in the *Cocalus*.

was the first to introduce love-affairs and seductions into drama: this is untrue, but suggests that such topics were important in his dramas. A lively description of him is preserved by Athenæus.[1] 'Chamæleon of Heraclea in the sixth book of his *Comedy* writes thus: "On one occasion Anaxandrides, when producing a dithyramb at Athens, entered the theatre on horseback and recited part of the libretto. He was handsome and tall, with long hair, and wore a purple cloak with a gold border. But his temper was short, and he showed it about his plays: whenever he missed the prize he took his manuscript into the incense-market and gave it away for wrapping instead of revising it like other people. He thus destroyed many brilliant plays, old age making him peevish with his audience."'

The main topics of Middle Comedy are eating, sex, riddles, philosophy, literature, and life. But these are handled in a special manner, so that even the last becomes far less vague than it seems when summed in one word. That manner is an urbane reflective manipulation, disillusioned and jaded, superficial but dextrous, suggesting a vast club every member of which is a button-holer.

Eating is not what it was in the days of Telecleides, when rivers of soup roared past banks of pastry: not the snorting, teeth-grinding and ear-wagging of Heracles in Epicharmus, but the art of dining. There is not a single fragment that mentions the mere chewing, but a great array dealing with the sponger or parasite, with cooking and with the purchase of food. Alexis was said [2] to have invented the stage-parasite—possibly the most long-lived of all dramatic figures; this of course is wrong,[3] but he was apparently the first to write a play so named. Eubulus tells of one who, invited (as we should put it) to dine at eight, arrived

---

[1] IX, 374*a*, *b*.   [2] By Carystius of Pergamum (Athen., VI, 235*e*).
[3] See the address of the parasite in Epicharmus (p. 103) and the fragment of Eupolis (p. 191).

at breakfast-time, eight a.m.[1] But the dominant figure is the cook. Aristophanes himself ended his career with ÆOLOSICON, about the renowned chef Sicon; and Middle Comedy as a whole sets the cook up as an artist, the genial tyrant and instructor of society. In the THESMOPHOROS of DIONYSIUS a positively professorial outburst [2] expounds the difference between a cook and a mere kitchen-mechanic. 'A cook should always know for whom he is to prepare dinner long before he takes the preparations in hand. The man who considers only the correct method of making a dish and gives no preliminary thought or study to the manner of serving, the time and the place of the repast, is no cook at all but a frying-machine. The difference between the two is immense. Inaccurate speakers will give the name "general" to anyone entrusted with an army, but it belongs rightly to the man who is master of a situation and can take decisions; all others are merely foremen. So with us: any Tom, Dick, or Harry can dress or cut up meat, boil sauces, and use the bellows; but the cook is in a different class' . . . and so forth, with lofty strictures on the inadequate textbook of Archestratus. The idea is otherwise developed in a passage [3] of Alexis, which rises at the end into queer poetry:

> A. οὐκ ἴστε ταῖς πλείσταισι τῶν τεχνῶν ὅτι
> οὐχ ἀρχιτέκτων κύριος τῆς ἡδονῆς
> μόνος καθέστηκ', ἀλλὰ καὶ τῶν χρωμένων
> συμβάλλεταί τις, ἂν καλῶς χρῶνται, μερίς;
> B. ποῖόν τι; δεῖ γὰρ κἀμὲ τὸν ξένον μαθεῖν.
> A. τὸν ὀψοποιὸν σκευάσαι χρηστῶς μόνον
> δεῖ τοὔψον, ἄλλο δ' οὐδέν. ἂν μὲν οὖν τύχῃ
> ὁ ταῦτα μέλλων ἐσθίειν τε καὶ κρινεῖν
> εἰς καιρὸν ἐλθών, ὠφέλησε τὴν τέχνην·
> ἂν δ' ὑστερίζῃ τῆς τεταγμένης ἀκμῆς,
> ὥστ' ἢ προοπτήσαντα χλιαίνειν πάλιν,
> ἢ μὴ προοπτήσαντα συντελεῖν ταχύ,
> ἀπεστέρησε τῆς τέχνης τὴν ἡδονήν.
> B. εἰς τοὺς σοφιστὰς τὸν μάγειρον ἐγγράφω.

[1] Eubulus, fr. 119.
[2] Dionysius, fr. 2, reading ποῦ in v. 7, after Kock. Alexis, fr. 124, gives an elaborate and attractive recipe for restoring the succulence to burnt pork.
[3] Alexis, fr. 149.

Α. ἑστήκαθ' ὑμεῖς, καίεται δέ μοι τὸ πῦρ,
ἤδη πυκνοὶ δ' ᾄττουσιν Ἡφαίστου κύνες
κούφως πρὸς αἴθραν, οἷς τὸ γίγνεσθαί θ' ἅμα
καὶ τὴν τελευτὴν τοῦ βίου συνῆψέ τις
νόμοις ἀνάγκης θεσμὸς οὐχ ὁρώμενος.

'Do you not know that the pleasure given by most of the arts does not depend upon the executant alone, but a part is contributed by his public, if they have taste?' 'In what way? Let a stranger into the secret.' 'The one business of the cook is to prepare the dish competently. Now, if the person who is to eat and appraise it arrives punctually, he assists the artist; but if he comes behind time, either the food must be re-heated because it has been cooked already, or it must be hurried if it has not. In either case æsthetic pleasure is ruined.' 'I see that cooks must be enrolled among the professors.' 'There you stand. My fire burns, and already the hounds of Hephæstus fly in a nimble shower into the air: for them birth and death are enfolded in the same instant by the inexorable law of a mysterious unseen ordinance.' An immense number of these extracts refer to fish, none of them interesting except the description [1] of the manner in which whole nations cook a fish bigger than Crete. This passion engenders hatred of the fishmongers. 'When I see military officers raise their eyebrows haughtily, I certainly feel annoyance but no particular surprise that men honoured by their country should be more pompous than other people. But when I see these damned fishmongers, with eyes bent down and eyebrows reaching the top of their foreheads, I choke with rage.' [2] Another poet is disgusted by their vulgar pronunciation,[3] and a third describes an amusing trick.[4] A law had been passed forbidding fishmongers to water their fish, so that, being unable to keep them so long, they might charge reasonable prices. To evade this, two of them got

[1] Ephippus, fr. 5. [2] Alexis, fr. 16.
[3] Amphis, fr. 30: κτὼ βολῶν for ὀκτὼ ὀβολῶν, etc.
[4] Xenarchus, fr. 7.

up a fight. One fell swooning—close to his fish. 'Somebody shouts "Water! Water!"' Immediately one of his colleagues seized a jug and flung—not a drop over the patient, but the whole lot over the fish. You would have said they had just been caught.'

The relations of men and women as here portrayed are what might have been expected in a society whose intelligence is brilliantly, nay morbidly, active, which longs for a genuine social life, yet has not the courage to emancipate women. Take first the proclamation:

οὐκ ἐτὸς ἑταίρας ἱερόν ἐστι πανταχοῦ,
ἀλλ' οὐχὶ γαμετῆς οὐδαμοῦ τῆς Ἑλλάδος.

'Nowhere in Greece stands a shrine sacred to a wife, but shrines of a courtesan are seen on every hand. No wonder!' The few direct comments on marriage are excellent. 'Magistrates come up for examination once a year, husbands once a day.'[1] 'What is this you tell me? He is married? Why, the last time I saw him he was alive and active.'[2] 'Every bridegroom except Adam has been a fool.'[3] Both Alexis and AMPHIS wrote a WOMAN'S GOVERNMENT (Γυναικοκρατία), of which we know scarcely anything; one fragment suggests a conspiracy of women: 'You must sit in that part of the theatre, over in the outside block of seats, as if you were foreigners'.[4] Allusions to courtesans and their importance are numerous, emphatic and elaborate. XENARCHUS composed a *Priapus* and Eubulus *The Brothel-Keeper;* among the burlesques of legend were a *Calypso* and a *Circe* by ANAXILAS. Verbal obscenity is rare: Aristotle's remark[5] is well known, that Old Comedy wrote indecency, the later comedy innuendo; still, plain statements of the excellence of sensuality are not lacking:

---

[1] Alexis, fr. 162.
[2] Antiphanes, fr. 221. Eustathius (1552) industriously explains: ὡς δῆθεν σήμερον τεθνεώς.
[3] Eubulus, fr. 116.   [4] Alexis, fr. 41.
[5] *Eth. Nic.*, IV, 1128a, 22.

τὰς ἡδονὰς δεῖ συλλέγειν τὸν σώφρονα.
τρεῖς δ' εἰσὶν αἵδε τὴν δύναμιν κεκτημέναι
τὴν ὡς ἀληθῶς συντελοῦσαν τῷ βίῳ,
τὸ πιεῖν, τὸ φαγεῖν, τὸ τῆς Ἀφροδίτης τυγχάνειν.
τὰ δ' ἄλλα προσθήκας ἅπαντα χρὴ καλεῖν.

'The sensible man should collect pleasures. These are three, the genuine factors in life : drinking, eating, sexual indulgence. All the rest must be called appendages.'[1] The social importance of courtesans is shown by the large number of comedies named after them, such as *Antilais*, written by EPICRATES against the most celebrated of all. The descriptions follow familiar lines. 'What a paradox! Harlots always prefer the oldest wine but the newest customer.'[2] Anaxilas has a positive lecture[3] on the bird-of-prey idea, comparing the courtesan to legendary monsters such as Scylla and the Chimæra. One long and picturesque extract[4] details the fraudulent devices whereby they emphasize or create their attractions: cork-soles to increase the height, padding, soot for the eyebrows, white lead, rouge and a drastic scheme to ensure a permanent smile. The doctrine was not unknown, that to consort with them is a form of morality because in this way respectable women are safeguarded : Xenarchus[5] expounds the facile delights of such visits contrasted with the plots and perils of (as we might say) Falstaff at Windsor—stealthily planting a ladder, entering the house by the chimney, or being smuggled in under a consignment of bran. A few passages take a higher tone : mere carnality is replaced by affection. Alexis[6] wrote of some one who fell in love with a picture ; perhaps it " came to life " like Hermione's statue in *The Winter's Tale*. A few tantalizing scraps from the PAMPHILUS of Eubulus tell us that ' there was a big new tavern just opposite the girl's home, and there I lay in wait for her nurse,'

[1] Alexis, fr. 271.
[2] Eubulus, fr. 125 ; cp. Amphis, fr. 23, Epicrates, fr. 9.
[3] Fr. 22.   [4] Alexis, fr. 98.
[5] Fr. 4¹; cp. Eubulus, fr. 67.   [6] Alexis, fr. 40.

to whom he administered sundry jugs of wine.¹ One passage ² shows a tinge of nobility :

> ὡς ὅστις αὐτῆς τῆς ἀκμῆς τῶν σωμάτων
> ἐρᾷ, τὸν ἄλλον δ' οὐδὲ γινώσκει λόγον,
> τῆς ἡδονῆς ἐστ' οὐχὶ τῶν φίλων φίλος,
> ἀδικεῖ δὲ τὸν Ἔρωτ' ἐμφανῶς θνητὸς θεόν,
> ἄπιστον αὐτὸν πᾶσι τοῖς ἄλλοις ποιῶν.

'Passion that adores only the body's surface, ignorant of all other thoughts, is a love of pleasure, not of the beloved : therein a mortal sins openly against the God of Love, destroying human belief in his divinity.'

Riddles had been known in Old Comedy : the *Cleobulinæ* of Cratinus apparently consisted of them ; but this middle period loved them excessively. We may quote one example ³ that possesses some elegance :

> οὐ θνητὸς οὐδ' ἀθάνατος, ἀλλ' ἔχων τινὰ
> σύγκρασιν, ὥστε μήτ' ἐν ἀνθρώπου μέρει
> μήτ' ἐν θεοῦ ζῆν, ἀλλὰ φύεσθαί τ' ἀεὶ
> καινῶς φθίνειν τε τὴν παρουσίαν πάλιν,
> ἀόρατος ὄψιν, γνώριμος δ' ἅπασιν ὤν.

'Not mortal nor immortal, but showing a certain blend and thus living neither in human nor in celestial kind ; ever newly its presence is born and dies ; no one sees its face, yet all know it.'

Philosophy and philosophers are a frequent theme, but mention of them is nearly always casual ; we hear nothing ⁴ of thinkers who lived before this century, and are not astonished to find Alexis ⁵ greeting with joy certain legislation against the philosophers : 'Is this the Academy ? Is this Xenocrates ? God bless Demetrius and the law-givers for telling those who claim to teach the young skill in rhetoric to go to Hell out of Attica.' ⁶ Of fourth-century teachers, outside

---

¹ Eubulus, frr. 80, 81, 82.   ² Alexis, fr. 70.
³ *Id.*, fr. 240. The answer is "Sleep".
⁴ Save that Alexis mentioned the Νῆστις of Empedocles (Kaibel, p. 216).
⁵ Fr. 94. Cp. Diog. Laert., V, 38, and Pollux, IX, 42.
⁶ Under the governorship (317-307) of Demetrius of Phalerum, Sophocles of Sunium secured the adoption of a law that no philosopher, under pain of death, should keep open school without the permission of Senate and People. This passage, then, is later than the date at which we marked the end of Middle Comedy. A good deal of Alexis' very long life falls into the New period.

the Academy and the Pythagorean sect, none is mentioned by name [1] save Aristippus, who was regarded as a teacher of self-indulgence. 'My master in his teens became a student, and applied himself to philosophy. There was a man from Cyrene in town, Aristippus they say, a brilliant sophist—in fact the most distinguished of them all at the time, and outshining his predecessors in debauchery. To him my master paid a talent and so became his pupil. He made little headway at the science, but he did become an expert in dining.'[2] Pythagoreans are mentioned often and generally with a gibe at their squalor: a fragment [3] of the SHE-PYTHAGOREAN (Πυθαγορίζουσα) by Alexis describes this with matchless conciseness: 'no dinner, no soap, no fire, no conversation, no fun and no bath'. For Plato we stand in much better case. Most of our extracts, it is true, are trivial, such as references to his fondness for olives,[4] his pomposity,[5] his loquacity,[6] and mere allusions to his name as the leading "highbrow"; for instance 'Master, what good you are to get out of this I understand less than the Good of Plato'.[7] Nevertheless, a few other passages hold some genuine interest. 'What! You expect to persuade me that there is any lover who worships a beautiful character and ignores physical beauty? What a fool!'[8] This plainly recalls magnificent passages in the *Phædrus* and the *Symposium*. EPHIPPUS [9] gives an elaborate pen-picture of the Platonic fop—well-barbered, exquisitely shod and dressed, with a pose of studied elegance as he begins a political speech. A disquisition [10] on Love as neither male nor female,

---

[1] We learn from Athenæus (IX, 366*b, c*) that the Cynics were mentioned in Antiphanes' *Wallet* (fr. 134), but we have not the poet's words. There was a good parody of Eleatic metaphysical disquisition in his *Cleophanes* (fr. 122), but it is attributed to the sophists in the Lyceum.
[2] Alexis, fr. 36.   [3] *Id.*, fr. 197.   [4] Anaxandrides, fr. 19.
[5] Amphis, fr. 13.   [6] Alexis, fr. 180.
[7] Amphis, fr. 6; cp. Alexis, fr. 152.
[8] Amphis, fr. 15.   [9] Fr. 14.
[10] Alexis (*Phædrus*), fr. 245; cp. Wilamowitz-Moellendorff, *Platon*, ed. 2, I, p. 363, n. 2.

god nor man, etc., probably draws its inspiration from Diotima in the *Symposium*. One long fragment [1] shows real knowledge and insight—a description of scientific research as practised under Plato — not metaphysics, but botany. A " flock of lads " in the hall of the Academy were making classifications of animals, trees, and vegetables. Their chief problem was a pumpkin. " For the first time they fell silent and stood stock-still pondering for a long while with bowed heads. Then suddenly, as they were still bent in contemplation, one of the lads said it was a circular vegetable, a second that it was a grass, and a third suggested a tree.' A physician from Sicily coarsely derides them as idiots, but they are undismayed; Plato, equally serene, encourages them to begin again. It is to be noted that correct division into species is mentioned several times : Epicrates has some real notion of Platonic methods.

Precisely the same temper is to be observed in the discussion and treatment of literature. These are literary poets : they discuss their own profession ; they quote not only earlier writers but themselves, and plagiarize one another ; they parody the tragedians ; above all they are fond of writing burlesques of legend. The first of these items brings up perhaps the most famous fragment [2] of Middle Comedy :

μακάριόν ἐστιν ἡ τραγῳδία
ποίημα κατὰ πάντ', εἴ γε πρῶτον οἱ λόγοι
ὑπὸ τῶν θεατῶν εἰσὶν ἐγνωρισμένοι,
πρὶν καί τιν' εἰπεῖν· ὥσθ' ὑπομνῆσαι μόνον
δεῖ τὸν ποιητήν· Οἰδίπουν γὰρ ἂν μόνον
φῶ, τἆλλα πάντ' ἴσασιν· ὁ πατὴρ Λάϊος
μήτηρ Ἰοκάστη, θυγατέρες, παῖδες τίνες,
τί πείσεθ' οὗτος, τί πεποίηκεν. ἂν πάλιν
εἴπῃ τις Ἀλκμέωνα, καὶ τὰ παιδία
πάντ' εὐθὺς εἴρηχ', ὅτι μανεὶς ἀπέκτονεν
τὴν μητέρ', ἀγανακτῶν δ' Ἄδραστος εὐθέως
ἥξει πάλιν τ' ἄπεισι . . .
ἔπειθ' ὅταν μηδὲν δύνωντ' εἰπεῖν ἔτι,
κομιδῇ δ' ἀπειρήκωσιν ἐν τοῖς δράμασιν,
αἴρουσιν ὥσπερ δάκτυλον τὴν μηχανήν,
καὶ τοῖς θεωμένοισιν ἀποχρώντως ἔχει.

[1] Epicrates, fr. 11.   [2] Antiphanes, Ποίησις, fr. 191.

ἡμῖν δὲ ταῦτ' οὐκ ἔστιν, ἀλλὰ πάντα δεῖ
εὑρεῖν, ὀνόματα καινά, τὰ διῳκημένα
πρότερον, τὰ νῦν παρόντα, τὴν καταστροφήν,
τὴν εἰσβολήν. ἂν ἕν τι τούτων παραλίπῃ
Χρέμης τις ἢ Φείδων τις, ἐκσυρίττεται·
Πηλεῖ δὲ ταῦτ' ἔξεστι καὶ Τεύκρῳ ποιεῖν.

'Your tragedian is altogether the most fortunate of poets. First, his plot is familiar to the audience before a line is uttered—he need only give a reminder. If I just say "Œdipus," they know all the rest: his father was Laius, his mother Jocasta, the names of his sons and daughters, what he has done and what will happen to him. Or let anyone say "Alcmæon," and the very children repeat it all on the spot: "He went mad and killed his mother, and Adrastus in a rage will come on in a minute and go off again." Later, when he can say nothing more and has got his play into a hopeless tangle, he waves his hand, out swings the god on the machine, and the audience is content. We comic playwrights have no such resources: we must invent everything—fresh names, past and present events, the initial idea, the crisis. If our Chremes or Pheidon omits one of these, he is hissed off; but Peleus and Teucer are allowed to do it.' A different thought is gracefully expounded by TIMOCLES:[1] tragedy relieves our sorrows by portraying legendary misfortunes that equal or surpass them. Alexis wrote a *Lover of Tragedy* (Φιλοτραγῳδός); Anaxandrides composed *Comedotragedia*, which may have been a tragi-comedy. A library is described by Alexis:[2]

> *Linus:* Why, go up and take whatever book you please, and you shall read it. Make your choice from the labels. Don't be flurried; take your time. Orpheus is there, Hesiod, the tragedians, Chœrilus, Homer, Epicharmus, literature of every kind. Your choice will show the instinctive bent of your nature.
> *Heracles:* I'll take this.
> *Linus:* Show me what it is first.
> *Heracles:* According to the label, it's a cookery-book.
> *Linus:* You're something of a philosopher, clearly, if you have pitched on Simus' handbook amid such an array of literature.

[1] Fr. 6, *e.g.* τέθνηκέ τῳ παῖς, ἡ Νιόβη κεκούφικεν. [2] Fr. 135.

Heracles: And who is Simus?
Linus: A genius. He has now devoted himself to tragedy; connoisseurs say that of all the actors he is the best cook, and of all cooks he is the best actor.

It is interesting to find Theognis quoted [1]—or rather turned into iambics from elegiacs—at this date. One line of Sophocles [2] is cited, and Euripides several times; [3] his " sigmatism," too, is ridiculed.[4] Eubulus began his comedy about his tragic colleague, the tyrant Dionysius of Syracuse, with an adaptation (or quotation) of Aristophanes' gibes at the incongruity of Agathon's attire.[5] Further, these Middle poets often repeat themselves or plagiarize one another, but the details are interesting only to specialists. Parody is frequent. Timocles in *Orestautocleides* burlesqued the *Eumenides* of Æschylus, and represented [6] his " hero " surrounded by a sleeping assembly of aged courtesans (?) in imitation of Orestes at Delphi amid the Furies. Parody of Euripides is of course more common. AXIONICUS wrote a *Lover of Euripides* (Φιλευριπίδης), but nothing survives therefrom about that poet. All this, however, merges into the elaborate burlesque of legendary plays. The method of these burlesques was of course to accept the heroic framework and by considering it in a modern humdrum manner to extract fun from this incongruity, as Disraeli did in *Ixion in Heaven* and Mark Twain in *A Yankee at the Court of King Arthur*. Thus Orestes and Ægisthus left the stage arm-in-arm, so to speak.[7] The story of Busiris, already burlesqued by Epicharmus and Cratinus, was handled by Ephippus. Heracles asks his terrible host: ' By Heaven, do you not know that I am a Tirynthian of the Argives, who fight all their battles drunk ? ' ' Yes,' replies the negro prince,

---

[1] Theophilus, fr. 6. Cp. Theognis, vv. 457, *sqq*.
[2] Antiphanes, fr. 231; cp. *Antigone*, 712.
[3] *Or.*, 255 in Alexis, fr. 3; *Hipp.*, 415, in Xenarchus, fr. 4; a fragment in Nicostratus, fr. 28.
[4] Eubulus, fr. 26, 27—*Medea*, 476, etc.
[5] *Thesm.*, 136 *sqq*.   [6] Timocles, fr. 25.
[7] Ar., *Poetic*, 1453a: φίλοι γενόμενοι ἐπὶ τελευτῆς ἐξέρχονται.

THE HISTORY OF GREEK COMEDY 51

'that is why they always run away.'[1] Ephippus contrived to introduce in his *Artemis* a satire on Athenian "cupboard-love" of the Thessalian prince Alexander.[2] One special kind of legendary comedy should be noted —the divine-birth play, perhaps the only topic peculiar to Middle Comedy as contrasted with the New; its origin is found in Old Comedy, *The Birth of Athena* by Hermippus. The Middle playwrights composed a large number of such dramas. One passage[3] may be noted, from the BIRTH OF PAN by ARAROS, Aristophanes' son:

ἁρπάσας μόναυλον εὐθὺς πῶς δοκεῖς
κούφως ἀνήλλετο.

'Straightway he snatched the flute and bounded ever so nimbly.' It seems to describe the playing and dancing of the newly-born god and (if so) resembles passages in the *Hymn to Hermes* and the *Ichneutæ* of Sophocles.

The last of our six subjects was life itself. These poets moralized, but their dramas were not studies in morality. 'Nothing is your certain possession except the food on your table. Yet stay! Some one may come up and rob you even of that. Think nothing yours except the mouthful on which you have closed your teeth.'[4] 'Everything can be hidden, with two exceptions: drunkenness and love.'[5] Another fragment[6] is a pallid premonition of the Duke's famous speech in *As You Like It*:

εἶτ' οὐχὶ χρυσοῦν ἐστὶ πρᾶγμ' ἐρημία;
ὁ πατήρ γε τοῦ ζῆν ἐστὶν ἀνθρώποις ἀγρός,
πενίαν τε συγκρύπτειν ἐπίσταται μόνος,
ἄστυ δὲ θέατρον ἀτυχίας σαφοῦς γέμον.

'Then is not solitude a jewel? Does not a man find true life in the country-side, which alone conceals poverty, while the town is a stage where ten thousand eyes view his wretchedness?' The toper is preferred to the philosopher because curious analysis of life

---
[1] Ephippus, fr. 2.   [2] See Kock, II, p. 251.   [3] Araros, fr. 17.
[4] Antiphanes, fr. 204.   [5] *Id.*, fr. 235.   [6] Amphis, fr. 17

hamstrings energy, whereas the unreflective man throws himself freely upon strenuous action.[1] But Alexis [2] extols study with some vigour:

> ἅπαντα τὰ ζητούμεν' ἐξευρίσκεται,
> ἂν μὴ προαποστῇς μηδὲ τὸν πόνον φύγῃς·
> ὅπου γὰρ εὑρήκασιν ἄνθρωποί τινες
> μέρος τι τῶν θείων τοσοῦτο τῷ τόπῳ
> ἀπέχοντες, ἄστρων ἐπιτολάς, δύσεις, τροπάς,
> ἔκλειψιν ἡλίου, τί τῶν κοινῶν κάτω
> καὶ συγγενικῶν δύναιτ' ἂν ἄνθρωπον φυγεῖν;

'All problems are solved by unremitting effort. When you consider that human beings have explained some astronomical facts, despite the distance—the rising, setting and revolution of stars, and the solar eclipses—what commonplace secret of our life here below can escape human intelligence?' One line,[3] trite as it would seem in many periods of literature, shines in this like a gem:

> ἤδη γὰρ ὁ βίος οὑμὸς ἑσπέραν ἄγει.

'My life has now passed into its evening.' But our last example,[4] though it proclaims a despairing hedonism, reaches actual nobility:

> ἆρ' οὐκ οἶσθ' ὅτι
> τὸ καλούμενον ζῆν τοῦτο διατριβῆς χάριν
> ὄνομ' ἐστίν, ὑποκόρισμα τῆς ἀνθρωπίνης
> μοίρας; ἐγὼ γάρ, εἰ μὲν εὖ τις ἢ κακῶς
> φήσει με κρίνειν, οὐκ ἔχοιμ' ἄν σοι φράσαι·
> ἔγνωκα δ' οὖν οὕτως ἐπισκοπούμενος,
> εἶναι μανιώδη πάντα τἀνθρώπων ὅλως,
> ἀποδημίας δὲ τυγχάνειν ἡμᾶς ἀεὶ
> τοὺς ζῶντας, ὥσπερ εἰς πανήγυρίν τινα
> ἀφειμένους ἐκ τοῦ θανάτου καὶ τοῦ σκότους
> εἰς τὴν διατριβὴν εἰς τὸ φῶς τε τοῦθ' ὃ δὴ
> ὁρῶμεν. ὃς δ' ἂν πλεῖστα γελάσῃ καὶ πίῃ
> καὶ τῆς Ἀφροδίτης ἀντιλάβηται τὸν χρόνον
> τοῦτον ὃν ἀφεῖται, καὶ τύχῃ γ' ἐράνου τινός,
> πανηγυρίσας ἥδιστ' ἀπῆλθεν οἴκαδε.

'Do you not know that Life (as we amusingly call it) is but a word, an euphemism for the lot of humanity?

---

[1] Amphis, fr. 33. [2] Fr. 30.
[3] Alexis, fr. 223. [4] *Id.*, Ταραντῖνοι, fr. 219.

My own studied opinion—what verdict will be passed on it I cannot tell—is this. All human affairs are utter insanity, and we who as our turn comes enter upon life are being given a holiday, released from death and the dark to join a carnival, to amuse ourselves in this sunlight whereon we look. The man who laughs most, drinks most, loves most during his hour of holiday, and finds a circle of friends—he has most enjoyed the carnival before he goes back home.'

The literary character of these poets has been satisfactorily, but not perfectly, revealed by the quotations already offered. Its most obvious feature is an almost complete lack of the qualities usually implied by the word " poetry," as indeed the Anonymus has already stated for us. A few of our citations must be excepted; on the other hand, hundreds of fragments that we have not considered here would deepen the main impression. Careful search will produce but the merest handful of passages to contradict it. MNESIMACHUS [1] has an imaginative line : ' Sleep is the first communion of Death '—ὕπνος τὰ μικρὰ τοῦ θανάτου μυστήρια. HENIOCHUS shows a flash of Aristophanic vigour when he makes a man, impatient for his dinner, exclaim ' he could have boiled the brazen bull of Phalaris ten times over by now '.[2] Another quaint idea is used eloquently in Plutarch.[3] ' According to a joke of Antiphanes it was so cold in a certain town that words were frozen the instant they were uttered ; and later, when they thawed, men heard in summer-time the conversations they had held in winter. Thus the words of Plato are delivered to us in youth, but late and hardly do most of us understand them when we have grown old.' Above all must be welcomed this snatch [4] of lyrical loveliness from the FLOWER-GIRLS (Στεφανοπώλιδες) of Eubulus :

---

[1] Fr. 11.   [2] Fr. 2.
[3] *In virtute profectus*, 79 A.
[4] Eubulus, fr. 104. Kock's reading has been altered.

ὦ μάκαρ ἥτις ἔχουσ' ἐνὶ δωματί-
ῳ τι στρούθιον αὐροφόρητον
λεπτότατον περὶ σῶμα συνίλλεται
ἡδυπότην περὶ νυμφίον εὔτριχα
κισσὸς ὅπως πλατάνῳ περιφύεται
αὐξομένας ὥρας ὀλολυγόνος
ἔρωτι κατατετηκώς.

'Ah, happy girl in her cottage, wreathing about her slender form a garland that flutters in the breeze, as round her new-made husband, fragrant of wine, with beautiful hair, she winds her arms like ivy that clasps the plane-tree, pining for love of the nightingale as summer moves to its height.' This dactylic passage is one of the very few lyric fragments: the Middle poets almost exclusively employed the iambic measure. We have indeed a few long anapæstic passages, the most remarkable being that description of scientific research already cited. The chorus was by no means unknown [1] at this date, but its performances were nearly always mere *intermezzi* that have not survived and were probably never copied into the published editions. We have one passage in pæonics.[2] As for the language, it is looser and more casual than in the fifth century: one astonishing example of this is the lateness of the position occasionally given to γάρ and δέ, e.g.,[3]

τὸν μάγειρον εἰδέναι
πολὺ δεῖ γὰρ ἀεὶ . . .
ὃς ἂν εἰς ἑτέραν ληφθῇ δ' ἀποστέλλων πόλιν . . .

Moreover, the elegance of these writers is often a neatness of idea rather than of language—the ἐρημία passage given above is a notable instance. Here we may cite three jokes, one magnificent, one good, and one tolerable. 'He has brought in a perfect gem of a new law, that fishmongers must do their business standing: next year they are to do it hanging.'[4] 'You are far more distrustful than a snail that carries

---

[1] Antiphanes wrote a Χορηγός, Epicrates a Χορός (though Kock doubts this), and the Τροφώνιος of Alexis had a chorus of Bœotians (fr. 237).
[2] Eubulus, fr. 112.   [3] Dionysius, fr. 2; Alexis, fr. 276.
[4] *Id.*, fr. 126.

his house round with him.'¹ 'Footmen are the worst people on earth—except nurses, to be sure; and *they* beat all—except quack-doctors, naturally; for that crew again are the most villainous on earth—unless one wishes to mention fishmongers, of course, who really *are* the worst—after the bankers.' ²

Allusions to contemporary political history are few and trivial. Demosthenes is mentioned for his quibbling ³ or theatrical ⁴ diction, for the affair of Harpalus ⁵ —Δημοσθένης τάλαντα πεντήκοντ' ἔχει—and ironically as a fire-eater who loathes rhetoric.⁶ We find one obscure allusion to the Celts—that is, the Gauls—in the long passage ⁷ (already mentioned) concerning the fish bigger than Crete: the "Macedonian prince" is apparently Alexander the Great, who is perhaps warned to destroy the Gaulish peril instead of attacking Persia : ⁸

παύου φυσῶν, Μακεδὼν ἄρχων·
σβέννυ Κέλτους, μὴ προσκαυθῇς.

'Cease blowing, Macedonian prince! Quench the Gauls, lest you get burnt.' A few passages allude sycophantically to the Diadochi—to the wealth of Seleucus,⁹ to Antigonus and his family,¹⁰ to Ptolemy and his sister.¹¹ Anaxandrides ¹² describes the boisterously ostentatious wedding of the famous Athenian soldier Iphicrates to the daughter of the Thracian King Cotys. The best of these historical scraps is a jesting mention ¹³ of the victory over Adæus, nicknamed " the Fighting-Cock ". An attractive notion (borrowed from the *Cities* of Eupolis) appeared in a play by Heniochus,¹⁴ who laid his scene at Olympia and said so in words resembling those of the Chorus of *Henry the Fifth* : ' All

---

[1] Anaxilas, fr. 34. [2] Antiphanes, fr. 159.
[3] *Id.*, fr. 169; Alexis, fr. 209 *sq.*
[4] Antiphanes, fr. 296; Anaxandrides, fr. 209; Timocles, fr. 38.
[5] *Id.*, fr. 4. [6] *Id.*, fr. 12. [7] Ephippus, fr. 5 *sq.*
[8] So Kock, p. 253. I have altered his προσκαύσῃς.
[9] Antiphanes, fr. 187. Seleucus' pet tiger (apparently an apathetic beast) is mentioned by Alexis, fr. 204.
[10] Alexis, fr. 111. [11] *Id.*, fr. 244. [12] Fr. 41 *sqq.*
[13] Heraclides (Kock, II, p. 435). [14] Fr. 5.

this place that lies around '—the *orchestra*, namely—' is Olympia, and in that booth yonder you must think you see the tent of the state-envoys '. Hither the cities of Greece have come seeking relief from the persecutions of " two women," Democracy and Aristocracy. The whole passage (of eighteen lines) is precisely in the manner of the " New " explanatory prologues.

Hitherto we have said nothing as to plots, because the writers whose quotations give us our fragments are interested in anything rather than the drama as a drama. But we have recently gained part [1] of a papyrus copy of a comedy that may well be Alexis' work, written down in the third century B.C., perhaps before the poet's death, and at last used as mummy-cartonnage. It runs thus: [2]

 Α. τὸ δαιμόνιον τὰ τοιαῦτα τοῖς θνητοῖς σαφῆ
  παραδείγματ' ἐκτίθησιν, ἀλλοτρίαν ὅτι
  ζωὴν ἔχομεν ἅπαντες, ἥν, ὅταν δοκῇ,
  πάλιν παρ' ἑκάστου ῥᾳδίως ἀφείλετο.
  ἀλλ' εἰσιὼν μετὰ τῆς ἱερείας βούλομαι
  τὴν ἐπιμέλειαν τῶν προσηκόντων λαβεῖν.
 ΧΟ. τί ποτ' εὐλαβεῖ, βέλτιστε;
 Β.   πρὸς θεῶν πάρες ·
  διώκομαι γάρ, κατὰ κράτος διώκομαι
  ὑπὸ τοῦ καταράτου κληρονόμου, ληφθήσομαι.
 ΚΛ. ἰοῦ, δίωκε Σωσία, συνάρπασον
  τὸν ἀνδραποδιστήν, λαβὲ λάβ' αὐτόν. οὐ μενεῖς;
 Β. ὦ φιλτάτη Δήμητερ, ἀνατίθημί σοι
  ἐμαυτὸν ἀξιῶ τε σῴζειν.
 ΚΛ.   ποῖ σύ, ποῖ;
 Β. ἤρου με; πρὸς τὴν ἀσφάλειαν ἐνθαδὶ
  ἔδωκ' ἐμαυτὸν ἀντεταξάμην τέ σοι.
 ΚΛ. οὐκ ἔστιν ἀσφάλεια τῷ πεποιηκότι
  τοιαῦτ' · ἀκολούθει θᾶττον.
 Β.   ἄ, ἄ μαρτύρομαι,
  μαρτύρομ' ὑμᾶς, ἄνδρες. ἂν τὴν χεῖρά μοι
  ἱκετηρίῳ τις προσφέρῃ, πεπλήξεται
  παραχρῆμά τ' εὐθὺς τἀπίχειρα λήψεται.
 ΚΛ. τί φής; ὑπὸ σοῦ, μαστιγία;

---

[1] Published by Wilamowitz-Moellendorff in *Sitz-Ber. d. Preuss. Ak. d. Wiss.*, 1918², pp. 743-6. It is discussed also by Fränkel, *Sokrates*, VI, 366, and by Körte, *Sachs. Gesell. d. Wiss. Philol.-Hist. Klasse, Berichte*, 1919, pp. 36-40. It is too recent to appear even in Demiańczuk's *Supplementum Comicum* (1912) and of course is not in Meineke or Kock.

[2] The readings of Körte have been followed, and the spelling conformed to normal English usage: *e.g.* δοκῇ for δοκηι.

B.   νὴ τὸν Δία
        τὸν Ὀλύμπιον καὶ τὴν Ἀθηνᾶν, εὖ γε καὶ
        παλαιστρικῶς, πεῖραν δ' ἐὰν βούλῃ λαβέ.
XO.   ὁρῶντες ἡμεῖς γ' οἱ παρόντες ἐνθάδε
        ἐάσομέν σε παρανομεῖν εἰς τὴν θεὸν;
B.   μὴ τοῦτό γ' ἄνδρες· εὖ γε προσπαίζειν δοκεῖ.

(*The Scene is before a temple of Demeter. A has been addressing the Chorus-leader at some length and now continues.*)

A : ... Such clear proofs does Heaven set before mankind that we all hold our lives as a mere loan, which Heaven, when it thinks well, casually withdraws again from each man.[1] Well, I mean to go inside and make provision with the priestess for the proper course.[2]

(*He enters the temple. A slave rushes in, glancing in terror over his shoulder.*)

Chorus-leader: My friend, what are you afraid of?
Slave: In God's name, let me pass! I am pursued, hotly pursued by the accursed Heir. I shall be caught!

(*Enter the Heir with his slave Sosias.*)

Heir: Halloo! chase him, Sosias! Seize the kidnapper! Catch him, catch him! (*To the Fugitive*) Halt, you!
Slave (*taking refuge at the altar*): Ah, dear Demeter, I make myself thine and implore thee to save me!
Heir: Where are you going, you?
Slave: You ask me? I am taking asylum here and defying you.
Heir: There is no right of asylum for one who has behaved like you. Come with me instantly. (*He advances threateningly.*)
Slave (*To the Chorus, in terror*): No, no! I call you to witness, gentlemen, to witness! (*To his enemies, plucking up courage.*) If anyone lays hands on me, a suppliant, he will get hard knocks and receive his wages without a second's delay.
Heir: What! From you, you whipping-post?
Slave: Yes, by Olympian Zeus and Athena, in good professional boxing form. Try me, if you feel inclined.
Chorus-leader (*to Heir*): Do you think that we bystanders will look on and allow you to commit sacrilege?
Slave: Don't say 'sacrilege,' gentlemen. It's a joke of his, and a good one, I think.

What preceded and followed this lively scene we can only guess; we cannot be sure that the slave's plight is in the first instance connected with the anxieties of the first speaker, though it is easy to suppose that he comes out of the temple and intervenes in the dispute, whereupon some *éclaircissement* ensues—for example, recognition that the slave has been in the right and

[1] Cp. Lucretius, III, 971 : *vitaque mancipio nulli datur, omnibus usu*.
[2] Wilamowitz takes τῶν προσηκόντων as masculine—"my kin," perhaps including a girl.

bringing about what ought to have been the Heir's dearest wish. As a document for the history of drama this passage is important: we cannot do better than quote the masterly comments of Wilamowitz-Moellendorff.

" We find a chorus which participates in the action. . . . It follows that the comedy is older than Menander, because in his work the chorus has no function except dancing between the scenes—he assigns it no words, and if other poets ever diverged from this method there is, however, no trace of such participation as we find here. On the other hand, the note ΧΟΡΟΥ in the second fragment [1] shows that the chorus was employed only as in the *Ecclesiazusæ*. This was therefore a play of the Middle Comedy. That it was no Egyptian imitation like most of the comedies of which remains have been found in the cartonnage, is guaranteed by the excellent diction. Now the oath μὰ τὸν Δία τὸν Ὀλύμπιον καὶ τὴν Ἀθηνᾶν recurs twice in Menander, in the *Plocion* (Gellius, II, 23) and in Priscian, XVIII, 97 (fr. inc. 46 Mein.), but also in the Τοκιστής of Alexis (Athen., VI, 258e). In this connexion we must remember that Alexis was Menander's uncle and teacher. Such a formula could certainly be used by another, but it gives us pause, and παλαιστρικός is attested [2] for Alexis. We have before us a drama of the Middle Comedy, which must be by a celebrated poet, since it is read in Egypt. This justifies the conclusion that it is by Alexis."

§ 4. NEW COMEDY

Between Middle and New Comedy there exists, as we have remarked earlier,[3] no such definite break as lies between the Middle and the Old. Nevertheless, that Macedonian domination which utterly changed

---

[1] A little scrap containing portions of seven lines, above which stand the letters POY.
[2] By Phrynichus, the grammarian; the normal spelling was παλαιστικός.
[3] P. 37.

THE HISTORY OF GREEK COMEDY 59

Greek political life brought changes to the comic drama also. Athens having lost her independence, and public affairs being largely managed by alien administrators, playwrights of necessity turned more than ever from the citizen to the human being. Moreover, the world being opened up to Greeks far more widely by the conquests of Alexander, and the ambitious wars or policies of the Diadochi filling that world with bustle and excitement, life became more adventurous and precarious:[1] those separations and reunions of families, whereof dramatists so often told, are natural results of such widespread alarums. Furthermore, those internal developments that we noticed as distinguishing Middle from Old Comedy advanced definitely and rapidly enough to differentiate of themselves the aspect of the New from that of the Middle. The chorus, as a participant in the action, vanished. There is indeed evidence[2] that it survived till at least the middle of the second century before Christ. But it has no function save to break up the action by its intercalated song and dance; this is the origin of act-divisions. It was regarded as an interruption of the genuine performance, and more than once it is actually so described: 'But look! Here comes a band of revelling youths: let us continue our talk indoors.'[3] Thus the necessity to account for this intrusion brings back the chorus by a quaint accident to its original function as a *comos* or revel-rout. During the Middle period the parabasis had been discontinued; part of its duties was taken over by the prologue, the genesis of which may be clearly perceived in tragedy and in Aristophanes. The moralizing and character-study of the Middle period changes into a fully developed Comedy of Manners: plot reveals character and

---

[1] Cp. Murray, *History of Greek Literature*, p. 378.
[2] Cp. Legrand, *Daos*, p. 422.
[3] Menander, Περικειρομένη, 71 *sq.*, and the Petersburg frag. of Ἐπιτρέποντες (Capps, pp. 89 *sq.*). Precisely the same thing occurs in Gay's *Beggar's Opera*, III, xii.

character creates plot, in an atmosphere of contemporary social conditions. Increasingly subtle psychology produced that curious convention, the " aside," which enjoyed an immensely long vogue, being discarded only in the nineteenth century.

Turning now to a detailed examination of what survives from New Comedy, we shall find it convenient to reserve MENANDER for separate discussion, dealing first with those contemporary playwrights whom he outshone. We may treat of them on the same lines as those followed for their immediate predecessors. The Anonymus puts the number of " New " dramatists at sixty-four; as for the individual poets, we need give special mention to three only: Diphilus, Philemon, and Philippides.

DIPHILUS, a contemporary of Menander—we have no precise knowledge as to dates—was born at Sinope and died in Smyrna, both Asiatic cities, and composed one hundred plays.[1] He stood nearer to Middle Comedy than his colleagues:[2] mythological comedy —that is, burlesque—was more frequent in him. We hear of a *Heracles*, a *Theseus*, and a *Sappho* wherein Archilochus and Hipponax (contemporaries neither of Sappho nor of one another) were introduced as her lovers. It appears that he acted in his own plays: once he did so badly that he was forcibly carried out of the theatre. He repaired to the house of his mistress, Gnathæna, but when he bade her wash his feet she replied: ' Why, I thought they did not allow you to walk.'[3]

PHILEMON, according to the Anonymus,[4] was a Syracusan who obtained Athenian citizenship; ' he produced before the 113th Olympiad '—328-4 B.C.— ' and ninety-seven of his plays are preserved '. Suidas

---

[1] Anon. de Com. (Kaibel, p. 10).
[2] So Meineke, I, p. 447; Kock, II, p. 541.
[3] Told by Lynceus of Samos, *ap*. Athen., XIII, 583 F.
[4] Kaibel, p. 9. According to Strabo (XIV, 671) he was from Solœ in Cilicia.

reports that he flourished in the time of Alexander the Great, shortly before Menander, that he lived to the age of ninety-six or even a hundred and one, and that his death was caused by a fit of immoderate laughter.[1] Philemon was recognized as second only to Menander and frequently defeated him in the competition.[2] The story[3] goes that one day Menander met him and said: 'Pray tell me, Philemon: when you gain the prize from me, do you not blush?' Plutarch relates[4] that Magas, the Macedonian general, who was ridiculed by Philemon, sent the poet a gift of dice and a ball 'as if he were a silly child'; once he was shipwrecked and fell into the hands of Magas, who ordered a soldier to touch his neck with a naked sword and then dismissed him. Philemon expresses an ardent admiration of Euripides:

εἰ ταῖς ἀληθείαισιν οἱ τεθνηκότες
αἴσθησιν εἶχον, ἄνδρες, ὥς φασίν τινες,
ἀπηγξάμην ἂν ὥστ' ἰδεῖν Εὐριπίδην.

'Gentlemen, if the dead really had consciousness, as some say, I would hang myself so as to see Euripides.'[5] Apuleius[6] relates that he died reading in bed.

PHILIPPIDES seems to have possessed a more vigorous personality than any other comic playwright except Anaxandrides. Suidas says his works numbered forty-five, and assigns him to the 111th Olympiad (336-2 B.C.). This seems too early: Plutarch[7] reports that the poet was a friend of Lysimachus, King of Thrace, who received that title in 306 B.C. Aulus Gellius[8] relates that his death was caused by a paroxysm of joy at a victory in the dramatic contest. Plutarch in the passage already mentioned paints an attractive picture. 'Philippides was a friend of Lysimachus, and through

[1] Suidas, *s.v.* Φιλήμων.
[2] He was preferred to him by readers as distinguished from theatre-goers: Demetrius, *De Eloc.*, 193: διὰ τοῦτο δὲ καὶ Μένανδρον ὑποκρίνονται λελυμένον ἐν τοῖς πλείστοις, Φιλήμονα δὲ ἀναγιγνώσκουσιν.
[3] Aulus Gellius, XVII, 4.   [4] *Moral.*, 458a (*De Cohib. Ira*).
[5] Fr. 130.   [6] *Florida*, III, xvi.
[7] *Demetrius*, 894c.   [8] III, 15.

him the people received many benefits at the king's hands. Lysimachus thought it good luck to meet and see him when engaged on any business or campaign. His reputation rested chiefly on a character untainted by the pettiness of courts. Lysimachus once said to him, in a mood of friendly expansiveness: " Tell me, Philippides, what thing of mine shall I share with you?" He replied: "Anything, sir, except state-secrets."' His outburst against the sacrilege of Demetrius, which we shall quote below, is unique in post-Aristophanic comedy for its combination of vigour and courage.

Between Middle and minor New Comedy no profound difference is to be discerned in the fragments themselves: everything said above as to spiritual, moral, social, political and intellectual temper could be repeated here. Burlesque is disappearing, and riddles have lost favour; all the other topics persist, though the emphasis is somewhat different. First, then, as for eating, Athens would seem to have grown a little tired of hearing about fish: we find only two allusions, both in Diphilus,[1] who, as we saw, stands nearest in date to the Middle writers. The parasite [2] of course is not dead, and in *Telesias* Diphilus ' has engraved a consummate picture '[3] of him: NICOLAUS, in one of our longest passages [4] (forty-five lines), describes his legendary origin—the first parasite was Tantalus—and the behaviour that he should follow. There is an imposing array of fragments devoted to the doctrine that a cook must be an artist: he must understand all branches of knowledge—music, medicine, philosophy, war, literature, and so forth. It was he that converted men from cannibalism;[5] he can raise them from the dead by the seductive odours of his masterpieces.[6] One genius does not even enter his kitchen, but listens outside to the notes emitted by the saucepans and

[1] Frr. 33, 66 (Kock, II, pp. 551, 562).   [2] Diphilus, fr. 61.
[3] Athen., 258*e*.   [4] Kock, III, pp. 383 *sq.*
[5] Athenio (III, 369 *sq.*).   [6] Bato, fr. 4.

orchestrates them into a harmony by orders to his scullions.¹

But "love" has become the dramatist's main subject; it has indeed been asserted ² that only two "New" plays were without it, the originals of Plautus' *Captivi* and *Trinummus*. At least one hearty and simple expression ³ of love is to be found :

> τὰς σὰς θεραπεύω μᾶλλον ἀγκάλας ἐγὼ
> ἢ τὰς ἁπάντων τῶν σατραπῶν καὶ βασιλέων
> αὐλάς.

'The courts of all the kings and potentates on earth are less to me than your embrace'—'I'd crowns resign to call thee mine.' Here is a word of shrewdness about those who claim to be enamoured of the character, not the body : 'Why do they not fall in love with the elderly and gross ?'⁴ As before, references to married women are few. APOLLODORUS of Gela wrote a play called Ἀπολείπουσα, probably the FUGITIVE WIFE : 'in my misery I unfastened the well-bucket and made ready the well-ropes'⁵— apparently to slide down and conceal herself. A jealous husband commands⁶ his slaves to 'shut and bar the door; but no carpenter ever made a door so tight that a cat and a lover could not enter'. Courtesans are more conspicuous. In the Middle Comedy they are "historical" persons : they have now become types. A woman brilliantly proves that harlotry is one branch of the teaching profession :⁷ 'Do you think a sophist any better than a courtesan ? ... We educate young men just as well. Compare Aspasia and Socrates, my friend : you will find that her pupil was Pericles, and his Critias.' Simple as this witticism is, it shows more brains than are usual in comedy at this date : there is a power of comparison, of close

---

¹ Damoxenus, fr. 2. ² Körte, Pauly-Wissowa, XI, 1271.
³ *Adesp.*, 145 (III, p. 437).
⁴ Bato, fr. 7. For an extremely unmodern description of athletic grace see Damoxenus, fr. 3.
⁵ Apoll. Gel., fr. 1. ⁶ Apoll. Caryst., fr. 6.
⁷ *Adesp.*, frr. 121, 122 (III, p. 431).

thinking. Usually the New dramatist falls back upon the mere elaboration of one plain idea, such as the cook-artist—he pretends to be thinking, but is only talking.

PHŒNICIDES gives us a notable " slice of life " : [1]

μὰ τὴν Ἀφροδίτην οὐκ ἂν ὑπομείναιμ' ἔτι,
Πυθιάς, ἑταιρεῖν. χαιρέτω· μή μοι λέγε·
ἀπέτυχον· οὐδὲν πρὸς ἐμέ. καταλῦσαι θέλω.
εὐθὺς ἐπιχειρήσασα φίλον ἔσχον τινὰ
στρατιωτικόν· διὰ παντὸς οὗτος τὰς μάχας
ἔλεγεν, ἐδείκνυ' ἅμα λέγων τὰ τραύματα,
εἰσέφερε δ' οὐδέν. δωρεὰν ἔφη τινὰ
παρὰ τοῦ βασιλέως λαμβάνειν, καὶ ταῦτ' ἀεὶ
ἔλεγεν· διὰ ταύτην ἣν λέγω τὴν δωρεὰν
ἐνιαυτὸν ἔσχε μ' ὁ κακοδαίμων δωρεάν.
ἀφῆκα τοῦτον, λαμβάνω δ' ἄλλον τινά,
ἰατρόν. οὗτος εἰσάγων πολλούς τινας
ἔτεμν', ἔκαε, πτωχὸς ἦν καὶ δήμιος.
δεινότερος οὗτος θατέρου μοι κατεφάνη.
ὁ μὲν διήγημ' ἔλεγεν, ὁ δ' ἐποίει νεκρούς.
τρίτῳ συνέζευξ' ἡ τύχη με φιλοσόφῳ
πώγων' ἔχοντι καὶ τρίβωνα καὶ λόγον.
εἰς προῦπτον ἦλθον ἐμπεσοῦσα δὴ κακόν·
οὐδὲν ἐδίδου γάρ· εἴ τι δ' αἰτοίην, ἔφη
οὐκ ἀγαθὸν εἶναι τἀργύριον. ἔστω κακόν,
διὰ τοῦτο δός μοι, ῥῖψον· οὐκ ἐπείθετο.

' By Venus, I can bear the gay life no longer, Pythias. Goodbye. Not a word! I am a failure. It's not my line. I mean to shut down. When I started, I had a military man for my first friend. He talked all the time about his battles, exhibiting his wounds as he did so ; but he never paid anything in. The king was allowing him some pension or other, according to him : he was always talking about it; and because of this same pension the scoundrel was a pensioner of mine for a year. I left him, and took another, a doctor. He used to bring in troops of patients, whom he cut and cauterized—a beggarly parish-doctor. He struck me as more dangerous than the other : the soldier only talked about killing, but the doctor produced his corpses. The third man luck gave me was a philosopher, all beard, gown, and speechifying : there I fell

[1] Fr. 4 (III, p. 334).

into trouble that I ought to have foreseen. He gave me nothing, and if I asked for anything, he said that money was a curse. "All right," said I, "if it is, throw it away, in my direction." He never did.'

The less conspicuous schools of philosophy are rarely mentioned: the "vulgar rhodomontade" (ῥωποπερπερήθρα) of Demosthenes is attributed to 'the eristic Eubulides who asks about Horned Arguments'.[1] That is, he was a member of the Megarian School founded by the Socratic Eucleides. Their puzzles were famous; the Horn (Κερατίνης) appears to have been Eubulides' contribution. More attention is given to those great rivals, Stoicism and Epicureanism. About the former we find mere commonplaces: 'In ten days (he will?) show himself more temperate than Zeno';[2] in Philemon's PHILOSOPHER Zeno was described as 'practising a novel philosophy: he teaches, and takes disciples, in hunger—one loaf, garnished with a dried fig, water to wash it down'.[3] Epicureanism has always possessed this amusing feature, that most of its detractors "show themselves up" artlessly and irredeemably. When Epicurus teaches that pleasure is the greatest good, and when people abuse him for depravity, they reveal with delightful clearness their own private longings. New Comedy is on his side and hostile to the Porch: he is the sensible fellow, the enemy of cranks, (ἄτοποι),[4] the revered teacher of cook-artists,[5] and has indeed revealed the true "way of life" to man. Only by a violent wrench of the mind do we realize that he is the same Epicurus to whom Lucretius gives precisely the same praise.

> A. I entrusted you with the lad and you have ruined him, you scoundrel, persuading him to lead an unnatural life, and now it is all owing to you that he has acquired the habit of drinking before lunch.
> B. What, master? Do you object to his learning about life?
> A. Is *that* what you call life?

[1] *Adesp.*, 294 (III, p. 461). The κερατίνης (sc. λόγος) is given by Diog. Laert., VII, 187: 'If you have not lost a thing, you have it. You have not lost horns, therefore you have horns.'
[2] Poseidippus, fr. 15.   [3] Philemon, fr. 85.
[4] Bato, fr. 3.   [5] Damoxenus, fr. 2.

B. Yes, according to cultivated people. At any rate Epicurus identifies the Good with Pleasure, you know; and pleasure cannot be gained from any other source. . . .
A. Come! Have you ever seen a philosopher drunk or setting his heart on the things you mention?
B. All of them! Certainly these supercilious gentry who hunt for the Wise Man in their schools and colleges as if he was a fugitive slave, as soon as a fish is set before them strike awe into everyone by their skill in laying bare the bones of the subject.[1]

The literary affiliations of these authors continue the family tree from Epicharmus, Crates, Euripides, and Middle Comedy. Their quotations show Euripides the prime favourite:[2] Philippides wrote a play called *The Lover of Euripides* and Philemon's outburst is the most famous passage of post-Aristophanic comedy.[3] The *Sappho* of Diphilus has been mentioned already. Contemporaries appear now and again. There is a remarkable likeness between a brilliant passage of the tragedian Carcinus[4] and this of Philemon:[5]

$$\text{ὁ φθόνος ἐν αὑτῷ τοῦθ' ἐν ἐπιεικῶς ποιεῖ·}$$
$$\text{τὸν αἱρετιστὴν ὄντα τῶν αὑτοῦ τρόπων}$$
$$\text{λυμαίνεται μάλιστα διὰ παντὸς συνών.}$$

'Malice has one excellent quality: the man who harbours it suffers more than anyone, for him it never leaves.' EPINICUS wrote a MNESIPTOLEMUS upon a historian whom he ridicules for his bombast in a pleasant passage,[6] spoken by Mnesiptolemus himself. 'One summer day I saw King Seleucus enjoying a drink of mead. I wrote a description of this to show the world that my art can invest with majesty even casual or trivial themes: "Thasian of elder vintage, and the sweet contribution of the irascible bee from Attic land, he turmoiled in a goblet of molten stone, and bridging the whole liquor with Demeter's grindings he consummated a heat-dispelling drink."'

The "morality" is expressed in that tone of depressed elegance which we noted in Middle Comedy.

---

[1] Bato, fr. 5.
[2] Diphilus, fr. 60; Philippides, fr. 18; *Adesp.*, 115 (III, p. 429).
[3] See above, p. 61.   [4] Fr. 8 (Nauck², p. 800).
[5] Fr. 131.   [6] Fr. 1.

'Love of money is the root of all evil.'¹ 'Time is the universal healer.'² 'Do not rebuke an old man's errors : it is hard to transplant an aged tree.'³ Longer disquisitions expound the difference between the moderate and the excessive use of wine,⁴ the resemblance of life to a voyage,⁵ and the hierarchy of the Universe—men are ruled by tyrants, tyrants by fear ; slaves are under kings, kings under gods, gods under necessity.⁶ A mournful comparison of man with the lower animals is a favourite thought of Philemon's.⁷ Apollodorus (whether of Carystus or of Gela) bitterly exclaims that some men actually are animals :

ἀπραγμόνως ζῆν ἡδύ · μακάριος βίος
καὶ σεμνός, ἂν ᾖ μεθ' ἑτέρων ἀπραγμόνων.
ἐν θηρίοις δὲ καὶ πιθήκοις ὄντα δεῖ
εἶναι πίθηκον · ὦ ταλαιπώρου βίου.

'A quiet existence is sweet: if passed with quiet companions, life is full of happiness and dignity. But amid savage beasts and apes one needs must play the ape—oh, misery !' The Carystian has a long passage ⁸ curiously emphasizing an idea, the vogue ⁹ of which began in the fourth century, that Chance is a definite and positive force in human affairs, not merely the negation of certainty : Chance is convicted not only of stupidity but of being " entirely uneducated " (οὐδὲ παιδείαν ὅλως εἰδυῖα). More commonplace and more modern is the plain man's retort ¹⁰ to an abstemious philosopher. 'You defraud the State by drinking water, for you injure the vinegrower and the merchant ; whereas I assist the revenue by getting drunk.' Here is perhaps the one place ¹¹ in Greek, outside Menander, where we feel the pathetic grace of Terence himself :

---

¹ Apoll. Gel., fr. 4. ² Philippides, fr. 32. ³ Philemon, fr. 147.
⁴ *Adesp.*, 106, 107 (III, p. 423). ⁵ Philemon, fr. 28.
⁶ *Id.*, fr. 31. ⁷ *Id.*, 3, 88, 89, 93. ⁸ Fr. 2.
⁹ It is found here and there earlier : cp. especially Soph., *O.T.*, 1080 *sqq.*; Eur., *Tro.*, 1204 *sqq.*
¹⁰ Bato, fr. 2. ¹¹ Philemon, fr. 71.

οἱ φιλόσοφοι ζητοῦσιν, ὡς ἀκήκοα,
περὶ τοῦτό τ᾿ αὐτοῖς πολὺς ἀναλοῦται χρόνος,
τί ἐστιν ἀγαθόν, οὐδὲ εἷς εὕρηκέ πω
τί ἐστιν. ἀρετὴν καὶ φρόνησίν φασι, καὶ
λέγουσι πάντα μᾶλλον ἢ τί τἀγαθόν.
ἐν ἀγρῷ διατρίβων τὴν τε γῆν σκάπτων ἐγὼ
νῦν εὗρον · εἰρήνη 'στίν · ὦ Ζεῦ φίλτατε,
τῆς ἐπαφροδίτου καὶ φιλανθρώπου θεοῦ.

'The philosophers, so I hear, with vast expenditure of time, try to find what is the Good, yet not one of them has found what it is. They tell us it is Virtue, or Wisdom, or anything rather than the fact. But I, passing my days in the field and digging the earth, have found it now. It is Peace. Ah, kind Heaven! How charming a goddess is she, how loving to mankind!'

Historical allusions are few, and the relations between Philemon and Magas, the Macedonian general, have already been mentioned. The bad influence of demagogues upon politics is described in bitter trochaics by Diphilus,[1] and Apollodorus[2] insists that an evil private life makes an unscrupulous statesman. Far more striking is the fearless outburst[3] of PHILIPPIDES against Stratocles, the sycophant who forwarded the blasphemous and depraved arrogance of Demetrius:

ὁ τὸν ἐνιαυτὸν συντεμὼν εἰς μῆν᾿ ἕνα,
ὁ τὴν ἀκρόπολιν πανδοκεῖον ὑπολαβὼν
καὶ τὰς ἑταίρας εἰσαγαγὼν τῇ παρθένῳ,
δι᾿ ὃν ἀπέκαυσεν ἡ πάχνη τὰς ἀμπέλους,
δι᾿ ὃν ἀσεβοῦνθ᾿ ὁ πέπλος διερράγη μέσος,
τὰς τῶν θεῶν τιμὰς ποιοῦντ᾿ ἀνθρωπίνας.
ταῦτα καταλύει δῆμον, οὐ κωμῳδία.

'He who cut down the year to one month, who took the Acropolis for a hotel and brought courtesans into the presence of the Virgin-Goddess, through whom the frost blighted the vines, through whose impiety the holy robe was torn asunder, when he turned the

---

[1] Fr. 24. [2] Fr. 13.
[3] Philippides, fr. 25. Cp. Plut., *Demetrius*, XII, 24, 26. The last line shows that reproaches or attacks had recently been directed against the frankness, or viciousness, of Comedy.

THE HISTORY OF GREEK COMEDY

honours of the gods into mortal pride. It is these things, not Comedy, that destroy the State.'

The literary manner has undergone no change, save that the sponginess of the diction is more noticeable. A few jokes are quoted. " He is either dead or a schoolmaster ": ἤτοι τέθνηκεν ἢ διδάσκει γράμματα.[1] " For one shilling he plays a tune, and for four shillings he stops playing." [2] The iambic metre is as undistinguished as ever, still showing a love of resolution in the fifth foot, which makes the line close with a silly little scamper, e.g. : [3]

> ἐμαυτὸν ἀδικῶ κοὐκέτ' εἰμὶ θεοσεβής.
> ἐδεῖτο χρῆσαι τὴν σεαυτῆς θυγατέρα.

Poetry, in any but the rhetorical sense, is becoming rarer. " Having passed a rose by, do not look for it again " [4]—ῥόδον παρελθὼν μηκέτι ζήτει πάλιν. Another kind of loveliness is seen in this little picture : [5]

> λεπτὴ δὲ κυρτοῖς ἐγγελῶσα κύμασιν
> αὔρα, κόρη Σκείρωνος, ἡσύχῳ ποδὶ
> προσῆγε πρᾴως καὶ καλῶς τὸν κάνθαρον.

'A faint breeze, born on the cliffs across the sea, broke the swelling waves in laughter and carried the skiff with tranquil pace gently and sweetly to land.' A few words or phrases are so " modern " as to cry aloud for quotation. " Have you bought the street ? " [6]

> τὴν πλατεῖαν σοὶ μόνῳ
> ταύτην πεποίηκεν ὁ βασιλεύς;

" I am wedded to my art " [7]—ἐμοὶ γάρ ἐστιν ἀντὶ γυναικὸς ἡ τέχνη; " a gold-digger " [8]—χρυσοχοεῖν ἐμάνθανε; " the shop-keeping mind " attributed to Mr. Shaw's Bluntschli is exactly translated by κάπηλον φρόνημα; [9] a " night-shirt " is χιτὼν εὐνητήρ; [10] and

---

[1] Kock (III, p. 401): cp. an excellent modern form: "I have three sisters, two living and one in . . ." (Chicago, etc., according to taste).
[2] Adesp., 268 (III, p. 456). [3] Diphilus, fr. 93; Menander, fr. 254.
[4] Adesp., 557 (III, p. 509). [5] Sosicrates, fr. 2.
[6] Philemon, fr. 58. [7] Adesp., 498 (III, p. 500).
[8] Id., 708 (p. 534). [9] Id., 867 (p. 559).
[10] Id., 920 (p. 568).

a portable time-piece is mentioned—περιφέρειν ὡρολόγιον.[1]

Till a few years ago we possessed practically no fragments revealing any of the dramatic qualities possessed by the minor writers of New Comedy.[2] We knew that certain personifications delivered prologues: Fear —" for I am Fear, most uncomely of aspect "[3]—and Air, who, being everywhere—" in Athens, Patræ, Sicily "—knows and can repeat everything.[4] These scraps should perhaps be supplemented by what looks like the complete account [5] of a New Comedy plot bequeathed to us by the quaint co-operation of a neo-Platonist philosopher and a Father of the Church. In condensed form it would run thus. ' Lacydes was so thrifty that when he went out he locked his pantry and placed the key in a desk which he sealed up, thereupon dropping the seal into the pantry through the keyhole. His slaves raided the pantry by breaking the seal, using the key and, when they had eaten and drunk enough, leaving key and seal as before. Lacydes, unable to understand how the victuals had gone, became a pupil of the philosopher Arcesilaus, since he specialized in non-apprehensibility.[6] One day he brought a friend home, and, to prove the correctness of sceptical philosophy, told him about the ring and the seal, to the amusement of the friend, who explained the mystery. Lacydes altered his methods, but the slaves imitated his seal after their thefts, or did not

[1] Bato, fr. 2.
[2] It is customary to regard Plautus and (still more) Terence as evidence for the plots of their Greek "originals". But Plautus is never pressed, because his personality has clearly counted heavily. Terence is much used, but this seems to the present writer unwarranted: see pp. 317, 319.
[3] *Adesp.*, 154 (III, p. 439). [4] Philemon, fr. 91.
[5] Numenius *ap.* Eusebius, *Præp. Ev.*, XIV, 7; Kock, III, pp. 418 *sqq.* That this narrative both in ideas and in language suggests comedy was pointed out by R. Hirzel in *Hermes*, XVIII, pp. 1 *sqq.* This is attractive but not entirely certain. Was the comedy extant or not in Numenius' time? If it was, why did he give it as a novel story (βούλομαί τι διηγήσασθαι ἡδύ)? If not, how could he quote it? Moreover, the description of the slaves as "resembling the slaves of comedy" is very strange if they really were such.
[6] Ἀκαταληψία, a joke on ideas that cannot be grasped and property that is not forthcoming.

even trouble to affix any; and when he reviled them, they took lessons in Stoicism and carried on philosophical disputes with him. Before long his property was utterly despoiled, and at length Lacydes confessed that " the schools have no relation to life ".'[1]

The discoveries [2] made in Egypt during our own time have not only enormously increased our knowledge of Menander, but have also made additions to the non-Menandrian fragments. First, there is a large portion [3] of a prologue, delivered by a god who, after discussing prologue-method, gives the facts that lead up to the play. Two [4] others are rather silly freaks. In one, the first, third, etc., lines are repeated backwards by the second, fourth, etc.:

> Ἔρως, Ἀφροδίτης υἱὸς ἐπιεικής, νέος,
> νέος, ἐπιεικὴς υἱὸς Ἀφροδίτης Ἔρως,
> ἐλήλυθ' ἀγγελῶν τοιοῦτο πρᾶγμά τι,
> πρᾶγμά τι τοιοῦτον ἀγγελῶν ἐλήλυθα. . . .

The other is spoken by Aphrodite, who explains that ' lest you should think me unexercised in poetry ' she will give her information in lines that begin with the letters of the alphabet in order. We have a word or two of the A-line, but the papyrus trails off into unregretted silence. Besides these prologues, we possess a good number of scraps that give glimpses of plot—talk between the young hero and his slave about a girl, misunderstandings between friends or father and son; in short, the kind of conversation familiar to us in the new Menander and in Terence—the dramatic manner, but no strong indications of dramatic structure.

---

[1] A. P. Oppé (*Greek New Comedy*, p. 50) acutely suggests that the slaves may have robbed Lacydes of money also, to aid a love-affair of the young master, as so often elsewhere, and that "it is only natural that the holy father would ignore the worldly side of the play".

[2] Demiańczuk (*Supplementum Comicum*, 1912) and Schroeder (*Novæ Comœdiæ Fragmenta*, etc., 1915) give everything discovered since Kock, except the Menandrea, *Charition* (see below), and the new Alexis fragment (pp. 56 *sqq.*, above).

[3] Demiańczuk, pp. 96 *sq.*; Schroeder, pp. 45 *sqq.*

[4] Dem., pp. 108 *sq.*; Schroeder, pp. 63 *sqq.* Wilamowitz remarks (*Menander*, p. 144): "diese ägyptischen Spielereien beweisen nichts für Athen".

§ 5. Minor Forms of Comedy

The popular rudimentary drama of Greece has been touched on earlier. Epicharmus' work was a splendidly developed instance of such mummeries, and Old Athenian Comedy might be called nothing but an offshoot that grew to gigantic strength, beauty, and variety not only through the genius of its exponents but equally through the blending of nascent drama with the *comos*. We have every excuse for believing that, apart from the best productions of Epicharmus, the non-Attic drama possessed small artistic excellence and that although it had, in whatever modifications, an immensely long existence, individual works enjoyed but short popularity. Nevertheless, it will be interesting to include in our survey a succinct description of the more striking among these rudimentary types: Spartan farce, Italian farce, and the mime. The first two seem more highly wrought local forms of the last.

Athenæus reports thus. 'Among the Spartans there was, according to Sosibius, a certain ancient form of comic amusement; it was unpretentious, since here, too, Sparta aimed at frugality. An imitation, in commonplace language, was given of people stealing fruit or of a foreign physician who talked in a style of which we may gain an idea from the following passage of *The Woman Gathering Mandrakes*, by Alexis [then follow some six lines satirizing the fashion of using Doric Greek in medical discussions]. The name given among the Spartans to those who pursued this kind of sport was *deicelistæ*, as one might say " costumiers " and " mimics ".'[1] He goes on to say that this type of

---

[1] Ath., XIV, 621*d-f*: Παρὰ δὲ Λακεδαιμονίοις κωμικῆς παιδιᾶς ἦν τις τρόπος παλαιός, ὥς φησι Σωσίβιος, οὐκ ἄγαν σπουδαῖος, ἅτε δὴ κἀν τούτοις τὸ λιτὸν τῆς Σπάρτης μεταδιωκούσης. ἐμιμεῖτο γάρ τις ἐν εὐτελεῖ τῇ λέξει κλέπτοντάς τινας ὀπώραν ἢ ξενικὸν ἰατρὸν τοιαυτὶ λέγοντα, ὡς Ἄλεξις ἐν Μανδραγοριζομένῃ διὰ τούτων παρίστησιν . . . (fr. 142, Kock, II, p. 348). ἐκαλοῦντο δ' οἱ μετιόντες τὴν τοιαύτην παιδιὰν παρὰ τοῖς Λάκωσι δεικηλισταί, ὡς ἄν τις σκευοποιοὺς εἴπῃ καὶ μιμητάς. τοῦ δὲ εἴδους τῶν δεικηλιστῶν πολλαὶ κατὰ τόπους εἰσὶ προσηγορίαι. Σικυώνιοι μὲν γὰρ φαλλοφόρους αὐτοὺς καλοῦσιν, ἄλλοι δ' αὐτοκαβδάλους, οἱ δὲ φλύακας, ὡς Ἰταλοί, σοφιστὰς δὲ οἱ πολλοί, Θηβαῖοι δὲ τὰ πολλὰ ἰδίως ὀνομάζειν εἰωθότες ἐθελοντάς.

THE HISTORY OF GREEK COMEDY

player had many names varying from district to district, and disconcerts us by mentioning performers whose show was certainly non-dramatic.[1] But as regards the Spartan plays, all is easy and attractive. These were of the simplest kind: the thief and either the victim whom he outwitted or the detective who outwitted him—perhaps (on sumptuous occasions) all three; the queer outlandish physician, ancestor of Dr. Caius in *The Merry Wives*, impressing the bystanders with his language.[2] No real artist took up the Spartan play: there exists no mention, however vague, of such a writer; and Athenæus, for all his learning, cannot quote from any " book of words," but is reduced to giving a parallel from Athenian Comedy.

The farces of southern Italy were more widely spread both in area and in time; moreover, at least one man of talent engaged in their composition. The performers and the farces alike were named *phlyakes* (φλύακες), and our knowledge of them is derived chiefly from vase-paintings: they acted upon a rough stage, were grotesquely padded in both front and rear, and wore the phallus. Their plays were ludicrous scenes from everyday life or burlesque of legend.

Much the most celebrated author of phlyax-plays was RHINTHON. Suidas writes: ' He was a phlyax of Tarentum, who recast tragic themes in an absurd form; thirty-eight plays of his are in circulation '.[3] In another place [4] he reports: ' Rhinthon was a comic writer of Tarentum, leader of the so-called merry tragedy; that is, the composition of phlyakes. He was the son of [*lacuna*], a potter, and flourished under Ptolemy the First (304-285 B.C.). There are thirty-

---

[1] See what he himself quotes from Semus concerning the φαλλοφόροι and others (622b-d). Cp. p. 8.

[2] Though he spoke a Doric dialect, as the reference to Alexis shows, it must have been a non-Laconian dialect, since Athenæus calls him ξένος.

[3] *s.v.* Τάρας· Ταραντῖνος φλύαξ, τὰ τραγικὰ μεταρρυθμίζων ἐς τὸ γελοῖον. φέρονται δ᾽ αὐτοῦ δράματα λή.

[4] *s.v.* 'Ρίνθων· Ταραντῖνος κωμικός, ἀρχηγὸς τῆς καλουμένης ἱλαροτραγῳδίας, ὅ ἐστι φλυακογραφία. υἱὸς δ᾽ ἦν . . . κεραμέως καὶ γέγονεν ἐπὶ τοῦ πρώτου Πτολεμαίου. δράματα δ᾽ αὐτοῦ κωμικὰ τραγικὰ λή.

eight tragicomedies by him.' John Laurentius Lydus [1] offers a more sensational account, that Rhinthon was the first to write a comedy in hexameters, that Lucilius, the Roman satirist, derived from him the idea of satire in hexameter verse, and that Lucilius' successors "strengthened satirical comedy" by a blend of Rhinthonian metre with the lampoon-style of Cratinus and Eupolis. This cannot be accepted as it stands: Rhinthon did not use the hexameter so far as we can see from his fragments, and Quintilian [2] witnesses that Rome is in no sense indebted to Greece for satire. Finally, the poetess Nossis in her epitaph upon him makes him say:

'Ρίνθων εἴμ' ὁ Συρακόσιος,
Μουσάων ὀλίγη τις ἀηδονίς· ἀλλὰ φλυάκων
ἐκ τραγικῶν ἴδιον κισσὸν ἐδρεψάμεθα.

'I am Rhinthon the Syracusan, a little insignificant nightingale of the Muses, yet from tragic farce I plucked an ivy-garland all my own.' The difference between the statements as to his birthplace probably mean that he was born at Syracuse but passed his career at Tarentum. The claim is unequivocally made for him that he originated a new dramatic type: the name *Rhinthonica* is often used for a special kind of farce. Certainly he differed from Epicharmus in that his works were burlesques not merely of legend but of legend as treated by tragic poets. Yet Cratinus and others wrote such comedy; Rhinthon's originality no doubt consisted in grafting literary burlesque upon the hitherto gross and crude phlyax-drama. Among the titles are *Heracles*, *Iphigenia at Aulis*, *Orestas* (the Doric form), and *Medea*. Our fragments [3] (mostly from lexicographers) are wretchedly meagre—" not a single dog" (οὐδὲ ἧς κύων) and the like. Only one has literary interest, from *Orestas*:

A. ὁ σὲ Διόνυσος αὐτὸς ἐξώλη θείη.
B. Ἱππώνακός γα τὸ μέτρον.
A.   οὐδέν μοι μέλει.

[1] *De Magist.*, I, 41 (Kaibel, pp. 183 sq.).
[2] X, i, 93: *Satura quidem tota nostra est.* But it must not be forgotten that Horace (*Sat.*, I, iv, 6) writes: *Hinc* (the Old Comedy) *omnis pendet Lucilius.*
[3] Kaibel, pp. 185-9.

'May Dionysus himself destroy thee utterly!'
'That is the metre of Hipponax.' 'I don't care.'
A "tragic" character curses another, who, utterly
flinging off stage-illusion, points out that the curse
will not scan [1] as tragic iambics (the otherwise invariable metre of all our fragments). A better conception of Rhinthon is to be gained from South Italian vases.[2]

SOPATER of Paphos was a younger contemporary of
Rhinthon. Our knowledge of him is derived entirely
from Athenæus, who tells us that Sopater was born
in the days of Alexander and survived till the reign
of Ptolemy the Second (285-47 B.C.). Sopater's fragments are a little more copious than Rhinthon's.
Three plays seem to have formed a sequence: *Bacchis*,
The Suitors of Bacchis, *The Wedding of Bacchis*; the
absence of qualification in the first title suggests that
it was the success of *Bacchis* that impelled Sopater to
write a sequel, and then yet another—that is, he did
not plan a triad in the first place. But the only interesting scrap from these three is an allusion to the
Colossus of Rhodes. The titles do not suggest burlesque, like Rhinthon's; nor do the names *Porridge*
(Φακῆ), *The Scientist* (Φυσιολόγος) and others. On
the other hand, we find the titles *Hippolytus*, *Orestes*,
and *A Visit to the Dead* (Νέκυια), evidently a burlesque
of Odysseus' adventure, as this remnant [3] shows:

Ἴθακος Ὀδυσσεύς, τοὐπὶ τῇ φακῇ μύρον,
πάρεστι· θάρσει, θυμέ.

'Odysseus of Ithaca is here, the gilt on the gingerbread; be of good cheer, my heart.' From the
GAULS (Γαλάται) survives a passage [4] devoted entirely
to brisk comment on present-day life. It is by far
the longest phlyax-fragment that has survived:

---

[1] Θείη being a spondee, thus making the line a scazon like those of Hipponax the satirist.
[2] See Heydemann, *Arch. Jahrb.*, I, 260 *sqq.*, and Bieber, *Theaterwesen in Alterthum*, plates 76-86.
[3] Kaibel, p. 195.   [4] *Id.*, p. 193.

παρ' οἷς ἔθος ἐστίν, ἡνίκ' ἂν προτέρημά τι
ἐν τοῖς πολέμοις λάβωσι, θύειν τοῖς θεοῖς
τοὺς αἰχμαλώτους· τοὺς Γαλάτας μιμούμενος
κἀγὼ κατακαύσειν ηὐξάμην τοῖς δαίμοσι
διαλεκτικοὺς τρεῖς τῶν παρεγγεγραμμένων.
καὶ μὴν φιλοσοφεῖν φιλολογεῖν τ' ἀκηκοὼς
ὑμᾶς ἐπιμελῶς καρτερεῖν θ' αἱρουμένους
τὴν πεῖραν ὑμῖν λήψομαι τῶν δογμάτων,
πρῶτον καπνίζων· εἶτ ἐὰν ὀπτωμένων
ἴδω τιν' ὑμῶν συσπάσαντα τὸ σκέλος,
Ζηνωνικῷ πραθήσεθ' οὗτος κυρίῳ
ἐπ' ἐξαγωγῇ, τὴν φρόνησιν ἀγνοῶν.

'[... the Gauls] who have a custom of sacrificing their prisoners to the gods whenever they gain any success in their wars. I, too, in imitation of the Gauls, swore to offer as burnt sacrifice to Heaven three dialecticians belonging to spurious schools. Now, hearing that you men are devoted to philosophy and disquisition, and that your chief tenet is fortitude, I shall test your principles—first of all, by smoking you; next, if during the roasting process I see any of you drawing up his leg, he shall be sold to a Stoic master for exportation as ignorant of philosophy.' This is anything but the coarse clownery that the *phlyakes* are reported to have shown; it is closely similar to late Athenian Comedy, an effect reinforced by the language, rhythm and dialect. Other fragments reveal that Sopater used more variety of metre than Rhinthon, who, indeed, seems to have confined himself to iambic trimeters. Among Sophron's remains are iambic trimeters, a priapean, and a few anapæsts. Rhinthon lived in the West, Sopater in Alexandria, as a few slight allusions show; and it was natural that the phlyax-play should develop differently in those far-sundered regions.

The mime possessed not only inextinguishable vitality—for it flourishes still, and the widest geographical extension—for it has been found in every quarter of the globe, but also great variety of content. We cannot describe it more precisely than this: a mime was a non-choric theatrical sketch of contemporary life, making a popular appeal and depending

THE HISTORY OF GREEK COMEDY 77

in large measure upon facial expression and gesture. Such work varied immensely from place to place, age to age, author to author. Often it was entirely ludicrous; occasionally it was elegantly amusing. One mime would be nothing but an exhibition of crude indecency; another would contain edifying popular philosophy. Scenery was needed for some; others could be given in a dining-room to amuse guests at table. No mime, as far as is known, possessed a true plot.[1] This kind of work showed, as compared with the genuine drama, a declension of art and taste combined with an advance in realism. The mime, as we have seen, was familiar and acceptable in the age of Epicharmus: it continued in favour throughout the days of true comedy and under the Empire first eclipsed, then ousted, the artistic drama in the Roman and the Græco-Roman world alike. Throughout the Middle Ages it flourished, especially in Byzantium, despite the opposition of the Church, which at last took over its methods for the presentation of sacred stories and doctrine. It was thus interwoven with the beginnings of the modern drama. But despite its enormous social, moral, and literary influence, the mime itself was but rarely a piece of literary or dramatic art, and we must here mention only those few writers who invested this rudimentary type of quasi-comedy with artistic form.

The most illustrious composer of mimes was SOPHRON of Syracuse, who flourished in the latter part of the fifth century: we have no precise dates.[2] His mimes, written in Doric prose—according to one

---

[1] Cp. Johannes Laurentius Lydus, *De Magist.*, I, 40: μιμική, τεχνικὸν μὲν ἔχουσα οὐδέν.
[2] Suidas: Σώφρων Συρακόσιος, Ἀγαθοκλέους καὶ Δαμνασυλλίδος· τοῖς δὲ χρόνοις ἦν κατὰ Ξέρξην καὶ Εὐριπίδην, καὶ ἔγραψε μίμους ἀνδρείους καὶ μίμους γυναικείους· εἰσὶ δὲ καταλογάδην, διαλέκτῳ Δωρίδι. καί φασι Πλάτωνα τὸν φιλόσοφον ἀεὶ αὐτοῖς ἐντυγχάνειν, ὡς καὶ καθεύδειν ἐπ᾽ αὐτῶν ἔσθ᾽ ὅτε. On the reference to Xerxes Kaibel writes (p. 152): "Confundi videtur, ut saepius factum, Sophron cum Epicharmo; Sophronis filius Xenarchus Dionysii tyranni aequalis fuit, cp. Phot. *s.v.* Ῥηγίνους."

account,[1] markedly rhythmical prose—were classified as " masculine " and " feminine " ; this division was not made by the Alexandrians, but apparently by Sophron himself, for it is mentioned very early.[2] His works seem to have made no strong impression at first, but they attracted Plato when he sojourned at Syracuse : he introduced them into Athens, and admired them so warmly that he studied them with a view to the character-drawing of his own Dialogues and sometimes slept with them under his pillow.[3] These facts suggest that although Sophron's use of prose implies realism he was yet far more decent than most mime-writers. The division into " male " and " female " shows that if they contained impropriety it was at least not accentuated by any confrontation of the sexes ; and the impressive compliment paid by the greatest writer of antiquity implies that Sophron relied far less on buffoonery than on character-drawing.

For many centuries Sophron's reputation stood high. Apollodorus wrote a commentary in at least three books ;[4] Statius reports[5] that his father taught the works of Sophron in his school at Naples ; a book-label,[6] belonging to the first or second century after Christ, has been found at Oxyrhynchus bearing the inscription : *The Female Mimes of Sophron* ; he was read by Choricius of Gaza in the sixth century.[7]

His fragments, meagre as they are, easily outnumber those of Rhinthon and Sopater. Among the titles we find some of great interest. *The Women Who Say they Will Drive Out the Goddess* (Ταὶ γυναῖκες αἳ τὰν θεὸν φαντὶ ἐξελᾶν) is known to have supplied the

[1] The scholiast on Gregory Nazianzenus (Kaibel, p. 153): Οὗτος (sc. Σώφρων) γὰρ μόνος ποιητῶν ῥυθμοῖς τισι καὶ κώλοις ἐχρήσατο ποιητικῆς ἀναλογίας καταφρονήσας.
[2] Plato, *Rep.*, 451c. Plato nowhere mentions Sophron by name.
[3] Diog. Laert., III 18 : Δοκεῖ δὲ Πλάτων καὶ τὰ Σώφρονος τοῦ μιμογράφου βιβλία ἠμελημένα πρῶτος εἰς Ἀθήνας διακομίσαι καὶ ἠθοποιῆσαι πρὸς αὐτά· ἃ καὶ εὑρεθῆναι ὑπὸ τῇ κεφαλῇ αὐτοῦ.
[4] Athen., VII, 281e-f: Ἐν τῷ γ΄ περὶ Σώφρονος τῷ εἰς τοὺς ἀνδρείους.
[5] *Silvæ*, V, iii, 158.
[6] *Ox. Pap.*, II, 301 : Σώφρονος μῖμοι γυναικεῖοι.
[7] See his *Defence of Mimes*, 3 (Graux, *Textes grecs inédits*, pp. 42 sq.).

model for a part of Theocritus' Second Idyll, and the most celebrated of Theocritus' works, *The Women at the Festival of Adonis* ('Αδωνιάζουσαι) was indebted to Sophron's *Women Watching the Isthmian Games* (Ταὶ θάμεναι τὰ Ἴσθμια); a third mime, *The Fisherman and the Rustic*,[1] probably inspired the Fifth Idyll of Moschus. Little in the fragments will attract any but linguistic specialists, for they are quoted because of such peculiarities. The topics that happen to emerge are mostly eating, drinking, and scratching. One reveals vigorous action: " Pelting the room they filled it with dung "—βαλλίζοντες τὸν θάλαμον σκάτους ἐνέπλησαν.[2] The most striking, and one of the longest, probably comes from the Isthmian mime: Θᾶσαι ὅσσα φύλλα καὶ κάρφεα τοὶ παῖδες τοὺς ἄνδρας βαλλίζοντι· οἷονπερ φαντί, φίλα, τοὺς Τρῶας τὸν Αἴαντα τῷ πάλῳ— " Look at all the leaves and chips the boys are pelting the men with! My dear, it's just like the Trojans in the story pelting Ajax with mud."[3] One of Sophron's characters is known to us by name, a certain Bulias who gave a display of absurdly disjointed rhetoric.[4]

On the literary, not the theatrical, side Sophron found two distinguished successors. THEOCRITUS borrows subjects, as we have seen, and not only throws his *Idylls* (or " little pictures ") into dialogue form as a rule: occasionally he causes the characters to indicate a *mise-en-scène* by their talk. The most elaborate example of this method is the *Adoniazusæ*, containing three separate scenes: the ladies gossiping at home, the crowded streets, and the interior of Ptolemy's palace. But masterly as this poem is, neither here nor elsewhere does Theocritus contemplate stage-production: his exclusive employment of hexameters proves that. HERODAS stands, as regards technique, half-way between Sophron and Theocritus: he writes in metre, but it is the most prosaic of all—the scazon or limping iambic trimeter. His mimes, discovered

---
[1] Ὠλιεὺς τὸν Ἀγροιώταν, i.e.: ὁ ἁλιεὺς τὸν ἀγροιώτην προσαγορεύει.
[2] Kaibel, p. 156.   [3] *Id.*, p. 159.   [4] *Id.*, p. 171.

in 1890, show indeed no more realism than Theocritus' idylls, but far less elegance. They are brief, pungent scenes cast in the simplest theatrical form: a mother describes to a schoolmaster her son's bad behaviour, and begs that he be caned; a party of women visit the leather-worker's shop; and so forth. These are seven excellent little sketches, eminently actable.

Striking examples of crude drama were discovered at Oxyrhynchus[1] in 1897. The MS. contains substantial portions of two dramatic works, which deserve attention as the only extant specimens of genuinely "popular" plays. One is a rudimentary melodrama, and so lies outside our present scope.

The other is a rough blend of romance and low farce which reads like a burlesque of the *Iphigenia in Tauris*. Its title is unknown, and we may provisionally name it CHARITION (*Gracie*), after the heroine. It is mostly in prose, but with a brief lyric passage and a few trochaics. A party of Greeks—including Charition, her brother, a sea-captain, and a buffoon—find themselves among savages upon the coast of the Indian Ocean and escape by making the barbarian king and his subjects drunk. It seems likely that Charition has been a captive among the savages, becoming a priestess (perhaps of Isis) in that far country; and that her brother has led a rescue-expedition. In any case our papyrus gives the last part of the play: near the close of it we find the word καταστολή, which seems to mean "finale". Amusement is provided by the outlandish speech of the savages and their king, though the latter occasionally talks Greek, as when he addresses the Moon-Goddess in lyrics, with a mention of "Indian chiefs" and (perhaps) a "Chinese religious dance". But the chief fun-maker is the buffoon: a frequent stage-direction refers to his obscene crepitations, which come as the climax to a roll of drums;[2] so proud is he of this noise that he addresses it as his patroness

---
[1] *Oxyrhynchus Papyri*, III, pp. 41-57.
[2] So Grenfell and Hunt explain the letter τ.

(κυρία Πορδή) and promises to make a silver statue of her (if they escape, no doubt). The action begins with some one's reporting to Charition his own extrication from some trouble, after which he goes off to bring the boat up. Next, certain savage women return from a hunt with huge bows and nearly shoot the buffoon. The messenger returns and announces: 'Lady Charition, I see the wind is rising, so that we can cross the Indian Ocean and escape. Go inside, then, and fetch your property; if you can carry any of the goddess' offerings, do so.' She replies: 'Fellow, be decent! Those who need rescue should not commit sacrilege while they ask it of the gods. How will they listen to those who sin while seeking pity? . . . Nor do I need those things, but only to see my father's face.' Then comes mention of "neat wine" wherewith the savages are to be incapacitated, 'and here they come!' Later there is a bacchanalian scene consisting, so far as words go, mostly of the gibberish uttered by the bibulous barbarians but containing the king's Greek address to the Moon. He is bound with the sacred girdles. The ship is brought inshore, and after a brief squabble between the captain and the buffoon all the Greeks go aboard. The play ends with Charition's prayer: 'Mistress, be gracious and save thy handmaid!'

Returning to the artistic mime, we find only one distinguished name in post-classical times, that of PHILISTION.[1] He came from Prusa or Sardis,[2] and flourished in Rome at the very beginning of the Christian era.[3] Besides mimes, he wrote a jest-book, *The Laughter-Lover* (Φιλογέλως). Of his work we possess no certain remains, though there are probably traces of him in a third-century jest-book attributed to the grammarians Hierocles and Philagrius. But

---

[1] A full discussion, with sources, will be found in Reich, *Der Mimus*, pp. 423 *sqq.*
[2] Suidas, *s.v.* Φιλιστίων.
[3] Jerome ad Eusebium Chron. Ol., CXCVIa, 2 (A.D. 6) writes: *Philistio mimographus, natione Magnesianus, Romæ clarus habetur.*

his fame was immense : the austere Marcus Aurelius [1] names him among his instances of great men who, like all the rest, met death ; and this implication is but one amongst many. For instance Africanus [2] takes Origen to task for accepting the story of Susannah as canonical, though it smacks of Philistion. There was an opinion [3] abroad that the mime was a further development of genuine comedy, succeeding the New, and apparently Philistion was put forward as the rival of Menander. There exists a collection of couplets called *Maxims of Menander and Philistion;* and though " Philistion " has been altered to " Philemon," the change cannot be regarded as certain.

Nevertheless, there is no evidence that he was genuinely a dramatist, or any other man of his age. Classical comedies were revived in Athens for centuries after him, but the drama as a living art had disappeared.

[1] Εἰς Ἑαυτόν, VI, 47. [2] Migne, *Patrol*, XI, pp. 47 *sqq*.
[3] Cp. Marcus Aurelius, Εἰς Ἑαυτόν, XI, 6.

CHAPTER II

EPICHARMUS

LITTLE is known about Epicharmus' life.[1] That he lived and wrote in Syracuse under the tyrants Gelo (485-78 B.C.) and Hiero (478-67 B.C.) is certain.[2] It is practically certain that he was working for a long time [3] before this, at Megara Hyblæa,[4] in Sicily. It is probable that the poet removed to Syracuse in 483, when Megara was destroyed by Gelo. His birthplace is quite uncertain: Syracuse,[5] Megara Hyblæa,[6] Crastos in Sicily,[7] Samos,[8] Cos,[9] are all mentioned. His birth may be put tentatively at 530 B.C.,[10] his death at 440 B.C.[11]

[1] The best accounts, both of his life and work, are in Lorenz (*Leben und Schriften des Koers Epicharmos*, Berlin, 1864, which contains a collection of the fragments) and A. W. Pickard-Cambridge (*Dithyramb Tragedy and Comedy*, Oxford, 1927, pp. 353-415). The best edition of the fragments is in Kaibel, *Comicorum Græcorum Fragmenta*, I, i, Berlin, 1899.

[2] The Marmor Parium, 71, says under Hiero; Anon. de Com. (Kaibel, p. 17) says Ol. 72 (488-5 B.C.); Timæus (*ap*. Clem. Al., *Strom*., I, 64), under Hiero; Suidas (*s.v.* Ἐπίχαρμος), six years before the Persian Wars (*i.e.* before the invasion of Xerxes).

[3] Aristotle (*Poet*., 1448a, 33 *sq*.) says: Ἐπίχαρμος ὁ ποιητής, πολλῷ πρότερος ὢν Χιωνίδου καὶ Μάγνητος. Now Chionides (Suidas, *s.v.*) appeared first ἔτεσιν ὀκτὼ πρὸ τῶν Περσικῶν. If Epicharmus was "much earlier" than Chionides, he must have been writing by 500 B.C.

[4] That he lived there is proved by the claim (Ar., *Poet*., 1448a, 33) of the Western Megarians that comedy began with them: "for thence came Epicharmus".

[5] Theocritus, *Ep*., XVIII, 6; epigram in Diogenes Laertius, VIII, 78; Suidas, *s.v.*

[6] Suidas, *loc. cit.*   [7] *Ibid.*   [8] *Ibid.*

[9] Diog. Laert., *loc. cit.*, and Suidas, *loc. cit.*

[10] It is probable that he became acquainted with Pythagoreanism before 510 B.C., because about that date the persecution of the sect began.

[11] Diog. Laert., *loc. cit.*, says that he died at the age of ninety, pseudo-Lucian (Μακρόβιοι, 25) at ninety-seven.

He was the earliest comic playwright. The Anonymus tells us:[1] ' He was the first to concentrate the scattered elements of comedy by many feats of technique; his date[2] falls in the seventy-third Olympiad (488-5 B.C.); his composition is sententious, original, and consummate; there survive forty of his plays, but four of these are regarded as spurious '. Aristotle reports that he was " much earlier " than the Athenian comic dramatists Chionides and Magnes.[3] What Epicharmus did, we may be certain, was to elevate the crude buffoonery of the mime into an art-form (however simple), making a written " book ". Nothing is known about any exponent of the embryonic drama which he thus developed; possibly we are to see a literary source or precursor in the lampoonist (not playwright) Aristoxenus of Selinus in Sicily, to whom Epicharmus refers.[4] The degree of elaboration, the amount of structure or plot, thus introduced, we cannot fully determine.[5]

Antiquity admired Epicharmus the philosopher hardly less than Epicharmus the playwright. Hippobotus[6] placed him on a list of philosophers which included Thales and Pythagoras. Diogenes Laertius[7] writes that he was a pupil of Pythagoras, and that ' he left treatises containing physical, ethical, and medical

---

[1] III, 5 (Kaibel, p. 7): οὗτος πρῶτος διερριμμένην τὴν κωμῳδίαν ἀνεκτήσατο πολλὰ προσφιλοτεχνήσας, χρόνοις δὲ γέγονε κατὰ τὴν ογ´ Ὀλυμπιάδα, τῇ δὲ ποιήσει γνωμικὸς καὶ εὑρετικὸς καὶ φιλότεχνος· σῴζεται δὲ αὐτοῦ δράματα μ´, ὧν ἀντιλέγονται δ´. The word γέγονε refers to his *floruit* (cp Rohde, *Rhein. Mus.*, xxxiii, p. 165).

[2] That is, his *floruit*.   [3] Cp. p. 83.
[4] Λόγος καὶ Λόγινα fr. 3 (Lorenz, p. 245 ; Kaibel, p. 107).

οἱ τοὺς ἰάμβους καὶ τὸν ἄριστον τρόπον,
ὃν πρᾶτος εἰσαγήσαθ᾽ Ὡριστόξενος.

The text of the first line is corrupt, ἄριστον being unmetrical. Porson's κὰτ τὸν ἀρχαῖον restores the metre.

[5] See below, pp. 110 *sqq*.

[6] *Ap*. Diog. Laert., I, 42. He wrote a history of philosophy towards the end of the third century B.C.

[7] VIII, 78. The appeal to acrostics surely condemns what it is meant to endorse: such devices are the mark of a completely sophisticated age, and are not certainly known to have existed before the Alexandrian period (Lorenz, p. 67, and Pascal, *Rivista di Filologia*, 1919, p. 58).

EPICHARMUS

disquisitions; in most of the treatises he placed acrostics, wherein he proclaims that the writings are his'. Plutarch surprisingly relates :[1] 'The Romans conferred citizenship upon Pythagoras, so Epicharmus, the comic dramatist (an ancient who acquired the Pythagorean doctrine), tells in a certain work written to Antenor'. A work attributed to Iamblichus says that 'those who wish to utter maxims on any aspect of life propound the ideas of Epicharmus, and practically all the philosophers borrow them';[2] further, that 'among Pythagoras' exoteric hearers was numbered Epicharmus; but he did not join the sect, and on coming to Syracuse he relinquished the open pursuit of philosophy because of Hiero's despotism, and threw their opinions into metre, publishing the doctrines of Pythagoras under the disguise of jest'.[3] Some of this evidence is spurious, but there can be no doubt that Epicharmus studied the doctrines of contemporary philosophers: even if we chose to regard all his extant philosophic fragments as forgeries, the mere fact that forged books on such topics were attributed to him would prove the point. But it is probably a mistake to suppose that he composed an actual philosophic poem *On Nature* (περὶ φύσεως).[4] The fragments were no doubt taken from his plays, the proof being: first, that the longer passages are in dialogue;[5] second, that their metre is iambic, whereas for didactic poetry hexameters were invariably used.[6]

Four great thinkers are (in one way or another)

---

[1] *Life of Numa*, VIII. The λόγος πρὸς 'Αντήνορα was another forgery.
[2] *Life of Pythagoras*, 166. [3] *Ibid.*, 226.
[4] This was held by Lorenz and is accepted by Kaibel. It is supported by a good deal of unsound and random talk about Ennius and Euripides which has been disposed of by Pickard-Cambridge, pp. 365-369.
[5] Plato's method must not cause us to suppose that this argument should face the other way. Dialogue is not an obvious vehicle for philosophical disquisition; and in fact Plato borrowed his dialogue-form from the mimes of Sophron (Diog. Laert., III, 18).
[6] There is, however, some force in Kaibel's argument (*Frag. Com. Græc.* p. 134): 'Attamen quo casu factum esse putabimus ut in eis quae ex fabulis petita esse certo scimus nihil simile reperiamus, quo casu factum ut e sententiis naturalibus ne una quidem cum fabulae nomine tradita sit?'

associated with Epicharmus : Pythagoras, Heraclitus, Xenophanes, Plato. We have just seen how antiquity associated him with Pythagoras ; but there is no clear trace [1] of connexion in the extant fragments. Heraclitus' celebrated doctrine, that all things are in flux (πάντα χωρεῖ καὶ οὐδὲν μένει), that 'we both are and are not' and 'you cannot step twice into the same river' is plainly set forth in this passage : [2]

'*A.* If one chooses to add a unit to an odd number or (if you like) an even one, or to take away a unit from the original number, do you think the number is still the same ? *B.* Not I. *A.* Again, if to a cubit-measure one chooses to add another length, or to cut some off from the former, the original length would surely not remain ? *B.* No. *A.* In the same way now consider mankind : one grows, another dwindles, and we are all subject to change every moment. But what changes by nature, never remaining in the same state, must therefore be different from that which has suffered alteration. Thus both you and I are not the men now that we were yesterday ; later we are others again and never the same according to the same argument.'

With Xenophanes, founder of the Eleatic school, Epicharmus had disagreement, and even a quarrel. Alexander Aphrodisiensis [3] reports that he 'made certain censorious and insulting remarks against Xenophanes, abusing him as stupid and ignorant of reality'. His most famous line :

οὖλος ὁρᾷ, οὖλος δὲ νοεῖ, οὖλος δέ τ' ἀκούει

('All eye is He, all thought, all ear') describing the

[1] Unless we regard as Pythagorean the words τρὶς ἀπεδόθη ζόος, 'thrice he was restored to life' (Lorenz, p. 290, Kaibel, 189), the evidence on examination reduces itself to the pleasant fact that Epicharmus uses the oath 'by the Cabbage' (ναὶ μὰ τὰν κράμβην) and even this he may have borrowed from Ananius, who according to Athenæus (IX, 370*b*) also used it.
[2] Diog. Laert., III. xi (Lorenz, pp. 267 *sq*., Kaibel, 170).
[3] On Aristotle, *Met.*, 1010*a* 5 (οὕτω γὰρ ἁρμόττει μᾶλλον εἰπεῖν ἢ ὥσπερ Ἐπίχαρμος εἰς Ξενοφάνην).

One God, was answered by Epicharmus in the most celebrated words [1] he ever wrote:

νόος ὁρῇ καὶ νόος ἀκούει· τἆλλα κωφὰ καὶ τυφλά

('It is mind that sees, mind that hears: the rest [the senses] are deaf and blind'). Another well-known fragment of Xenophanes vigorously ridicules popular anthropomorphic religion. Epicharmus composed a passage [2] which reads like a parody:

> It is no marvel that we should talk thus and be self-satisfied, convinced that we are fine creatures. For the dog appears to a dog most beautiful, ox to ox, ass to ass, pig to pig.

This assuredly is not bitter opposition, but an imitation with a strong tinge of burlesque; and the most likely view is that Epicharmus here as elsewhere is quoting "one of the leading thinkers of our age" for the purpose of farcical action thus introduced or excused.[3]

His relations with Plato are more perplexing. We read in Diogenes Laertius extracts from a work in four books by Alcimus, perhaps the Sicilian teacher of rhetoric, who lived about 300 B.C. This work was addressed to one Amyntas (probably a Platonist) and contained a supposed proof that Plato borrowed important doctrines from Epicharmus. Diogenes introduces the topic with these uncompromising words:[4] 'Much assistance he (Plato) got from Epicharmus too, the comic poet, for the most part paraphrasing him'. Before proceeding to the evidence adduced by Alcimus, let us note that Plato not merely knew and immensely admired Epicharmus as a comic writer:[5] he also gives, or affects to give, him high rank as a

---

[1] Lorenz, p. 255; Kaibel, 249. Probably Epicharmus supposed Xenophanes to mean that God is perfect in mind and perfect in body, and wished to insist that mind alone is valid, remembering the dictum of Heraclitus that 'eyes and ears are bad witnesses'.
[2] Lorenz, p. 270; Kaibel, 173.   [3] See below, p. 93.
[4] III, 9: πολλὰ δὲ καὶ παρ' Ἐπιχάρμου τοῦ κωμῳδιοποιοῦ προσωφέληται, τὰ πλεῖστα μεταγράψας, καθά φησιν Ἄλκιμος ἐν τοῖς πρὸς Ἀμύνταν, ἅ ἐστι τέτταρα.
[5] *Theætetus*, 152e: τῶν ποιητῶν οἱ ἄκροι τῆς ποιήσεως ἑκατέρας, κωμῳδίας μὲν Ἐπίχαρμος, τραγῳδίας δὲ Ὅμηρος.

philosopher.¹   Now, Alcimus, as reported by Diogenes, adduces four passages of Epicharmus :

(i) Plato's distinction between νοητά and αἰσθητά has been anticipated in Epicharmus' clear discussion of the objects of intellect and the objects of sense. The passage then quoted is that in part translated above (p. 86), which is in fact not Platonic, but Heraclitean.

(ii) Plato's Theory of Ideas, that the ideas are eternal changeless patterns (παραδείγματα) whereof sensible particulars are copies (ὁμοιώματα) may be found in Epicharmus, who speaks thus concerning God and the ideas :

'*A*. Is there such an action as flute-playing? *B*. Certainly. *A*. Now, is a man the same as flute-playing? *B*. No. *A*. Very well : what of a flute-player? What do you think him? A man, no doubt? *B*. Certainly. *A*. Now, do you not think this applies to the Good ?—that the Good is a separate thing, and that whoever by learning knows it, becomes good thereby? Just as one by learning to play the flute becomes a flute-player ; by learning to dance becomes a dancer ; by learning to weave, a weaver ; or similarly, in regard to anything else you like of the kind, he cannot himself become the art, but only an artist.' ²

This seems beyond misconception : everything in a popular Platonic dialogue is present, the Good and the individual participator therein, the examples from handicraft, the acquiescent listener. Are we then to believe that the early Platonic manner flourished before Socrates himself was born? This seems hard to accept for one reason at least—Plato's own silence on this amazing anticipation. For he is not in the habit of concealing such debts : not to mention his attribution of his own theories to Socrates, he expresses the

¹ *Theætetus*, 152*e*.
² Lorenz, p. 269 ; Kaibel, 171. "Action" in the first line translates πρᾶγμα. Croiset (*Hist. de la litt. grecque*, III, p. 453) remarks that we are to suppose this passage introduced by some such premise as : " Is not action proper to man? Yes."

deepest reverence for Parmenides and frequently quotes others. Moreover, even if he had wished to hide this indebtedness, he would scarcely have ventured on the attempt, since the work of Epicharmus was well known in Athens: Antisthenes and Diogenes would have been delighted to inform him in public of so strange a coincidence. The *argumentum ex silentio* is here very strong and lends great support to the contention of Diels[1] that its subject-matter and dialogue-form suggest a fourth-century forger. The composition of bogus Epicharmean works was frequent, as we shall see.

(iii) Alcimus' next proof is an extremely uncouth and obscure remark about the egg and the soul:

> 'Eumæus, wisdom dwells not in one place alone, but whatever lives possesses intelligence also. For the female race of fowls too, if you care to notice, never brings forth living young, but hatches them and causes them to have a soul. Now the quality of this wisdom Nature alone knows, for she has been schooled by herself.'[2]

What Alcimus imagined this to mean is as uncertain as what it actually does mean; for he claims that it anticipates a remark[3] of Plato: 'In what way could animals survive if they did not lay hold of the idea and for this purpose receive intellect by nature?' The two extracts are not parallel: there is nothing but a verbal resemblance. The interest of the passage lies elsewhere—in the fact that it is addressed to Eumæus, which shall be discussed later.[4]

---

[1] *Vorsokratiker*⁴, I, p. 116. Diels thinks the lines may have been an interpolation by the younger Dionysius in the plays of Epicharmus which he caused to be performed at Syracuse for the entertainment of Plato. Suidas (*s.v.* Διονύσιος) tells us that Dionysius wrote a book on *The Poems of Epicharmus*.

[2] Lorenz, p. 270; Kaibel, 172:

Εὔμαιε, τὸ σοφόν ἐστιν οὐ καθ' ἓν μόνον,
ἀλλ' ὅσσα περ ζῇ, πάντα καὶ γνώμαν ἔχει.
καὶ γὰρ τὸ θῆλυ τῶν ἀλεκτορίδων γένος,
αἰ λῇς καταμαθεῖν, ἀτενὲς οὐ τίκτει τέκνα
ζῶντ', ἀλλ' ἐπῳζει καὶ ποιεῖ ψυχὰν ἔχειν.
τὸ δὲ σοφὸν ἁ φύσις τόδ' οἶδεν ὡς ἔχει
μόνα· πεπαίδευται γὰρ αὐταυτᾶς ὕπο.

[3] This is supposed to be *Parmenides*, 129.   [4] P. 101.

(iv) The last passage adduced by Alcimus is that (already mentioned) which describes how each animal thinks its own species the most beautiful. This is an unmistakable reference, not to Plato but to Xenophanes.

After quoting Alcimus' treatise, Diogenes Laertius goes on in his own person: 'That Epicharmus was well aware of his own wisdom may be learnt from the following lines also, in which he prophesies of his future imitator:

> "And as I think—for I do think it—this I know certainly, that in some later time these words of mine will be remembered. Some one will strip them of the metre which now they wear, will give them a garment, a purple robe embroidered with fair language, and, invincible himself, will prove the others but sorry wrestlers."'[1]

> ὡς δ' ἐγὼ δοκέω—δοκέω γάρ—σάφα ἴσαμι τοῦθ', ὅτι
> τῶν ἐμῶν μνάμα ποτ' ἐσσεῖται λόγων τούτων ἔτι.
> καὶ λαβών τις αὐτὰ περιδύσας τὸ μέτρον, ὃ νῦν ἔχει,
> εἶμα δοὺς καὶ πορφύραν λόγοισι ποικίλας καλοῖς,
> δυσπάλαιστος ὢν τὸς ἄλλους εὐπαλαίστους ἀποφανεῖ.

This is a patent forgery. It prophesies far too plainly of Plato, or rather of Plato's plagiarism as Alcimus would have us believe it. One can perhaps imagine Epicharmus saying that his ideas would be stolen. But that he should gratuitously risk time's refutation by adding that the plagiarist would turn his verse into prose, and sumptuous prose too—that is out of the question. Moreover, if these lines had occurred in Epicharmus' genuine or spurious poems, Alcimus could not conceivably have omitted to quote so magnificent an endorsement of his own thesis; and that he did not quote it is shown by the fact that Diogenes quotes them himself immediately on finishing his excerpts from Alcimus.[2] Therefore these lines were forged, and forged later than Alcimus.

The history of the Ψευδεπιχάρμεια, the Epicharmean Forgeries, appears to be briefly as follows:

---

[1] Lorenz, p. 255; Kaibel, 254. (Text as in Lorenz; τός = Attic τούς).
[2] Pickard-Cambridge, pp. 369 sq., thinks that the "prophetic" passage perhaps concluded the introduction to Axiopistus' forged book of Γνῶμαι. Kaibel (p. 138) conjectures that the prophetic passage closed the whole book; Crönert would put it at the beginning.

EPICHARMUS

Alcimus got up his case against Plato by using, not spurious books but the plays themselves as the text stood in his time, that is, not yet sifted by the editor, Apollodorus (first century B.C.). The plays contained additions made by Dionysius the Younger. Alcimus, very stupid or very ignorant of philosophy or very disingenuous, or all three, extracted from Epicharmus passages philosophical indeed, but mostly not Platonic: the single Platonic passage was one of those inserted facetiously by Dionysius. Except at this last point, Alcimus has no connexion at all with spurious Epicharmean work.

Six forgeries are known to us by name. (i) The *Republic*[1] (Πολιτεία), forged by Chrysogonus the Flute-Player remarkably early—not later than 400 B.C. The fragments which we possess are very poor, concerning the importance of reason to man: human reason is derived from the divine. (ii) The *Maxims*[2] (Γνῶμαι), forged by Axiopistus. This was a collection containing some genuine matter and much that was spurious. To this belongs[3] a passage in some fifteen lines—a kind of prospectus proclaiming the value of the book for those dealing with various types of people, and explaining also that the writer, Epicharmus (named), having been twitted with inability, despite his wisdom, to write tersely, has here shown that he can. To this collection belongs the prophetic passage about a prose plagiarist. (iii) The *Canon*[4] (Κανών), also forged by

[1] Athenæus, XIV, 648d: τὴν μὲν ἡμίναν οἱ τὰ εἰς Ἐπίχαρμον ἀναφερόμενα ποιήματα πεποιηκότες οἴδασι, κἂν τῷ Χείρωνι ἐπιγραφομένῳ οὕτως λέγεται· καὶ πιεῖν ὕδωρ διπλάσιον χλιαρόν, ἡμίνας δύο. τὰ δὲ ψευδεπιχάρμεια ταῦτα πεποιήκασιν ἄνδρες ἔνδοξοι Χρυσόγονός τε ὁ αὐλητής, ὥς φησιν Ἀριστόξενος ἐν ὀγδόῳ Πολιτικῶν Νόμων, τὴν Πολιτείαν ἐπιγραφομένην. Φιλόχορος δ' ἐν τοῖς Περὶ Μαντικῆς Ἀξιόπιστον τὸν εἴτε Λοκρὸν γένος εἴτε Σικυώνιον τὸν Κανόνα καὶ τὰς Γνώμας πεποιηκέναι φησίν. Chrysogonus flourished late in the fifth century B.C. (Athen., XII, 535d), Aristoxenus about a century after him.
[2] See last note. The "prospectus" passage is in neither Lorenz nor Kaibel, having been discovered later at El-Hibeh in Egypt. The text was given first by Grenfell and Hunt (*Hibeh Papyri*, I, i), later by Diels (*Vorsokratiker*⁴, I, p. 116), and by Pickard-Cambridge, pp. 369 sq.
[3] According to Crönert (*Hermes*, XLVII, pp. 402 sqq.).
[4] See Athen., XIV, 648d (quoted above).

Axiopistus. Nothing is known about it. (iv) *Chiron* [1] (Χείρων), a book of unknown date and authorship, probably about medicine, the instruction being delivered by that famous teacher, the Centaur Chiron. (v) *Cookery* ('Οψοποιία), also of unknown date and authorship. This is thought to have formed part of the *Chiron*, or even to be identical with it.[2] (vi) *Antenor* (Πρὸς Ἀντήνορα) which contained the statement that the Romans conferred citizenship upon Pythagoras. Nothing is known about the book save this fact, quoted by Plutarch.[3]

Epicharmus must have been (for whatever reasons and in whatever tone) a notable exponent of philosophy —of contemporary thought, however, not by supernatural means an exponent of Platonism. But there is no reason to postulate a directly didactic poem analogous to that of his brilliant neighbour Empedocles. Far more likely is the theory that his philosophical disquisitions were worked into the fabric of his comedies. This finds support in a statement quoted above, that in fear of Hiero the poet published Pythagorean doctrines under the disguise of jest. The supposed reason was no doubt non-existent: Hiero's "tyranny" was scarcely so pervasive and alert as to persecute a man who remarked that eggs need hatching and that $x + 1$ does not equal x. Pindar, we know, did not fear to give that prince admonitions as to personal ambition and domestic policy; Epicharmus himself, though he offended Hiero by an objectionable remark uttered in the presence of Hiero's wife,[4] nevertheless used marked candour [5] towards him at other times without any recorded

---

[1] See Athen., XIV, 648*d* (quoted above). We have one line from it: 'drink twice as much warm water—two quarts'.

[2] Susemihl, *Philologus*, LIII, p. 565. Kaibel (p. 144) points out that ἡμίνα, quoted by the Antiatticista from the 'Οψοποιία, is quoted by Athenæus from the *Chiron*.

[3] *Life of Numa*, VIII. [4] Pseudo-Plutarch, *Apophth. Reg.*, 175c.

[5] Plutarch, *Quomodo quis adulatorem*, 68a: τοῦ Ἱέρωνος ἀνελόντος ἐνίους τῶν συνήθων, καὶ μεθ' ἡμέρας ὀλίγας καλέσαντος ἐπὶ δεῖπνον αὐτόν, Ἀλλὰ πρώην, ἔφη, θύων τοὺς φίλους οὐκ ἐκάλεσας.

punishment. Epicharmus discussed philosophy in his comedies playfully because he chose to do so.

But why did he choose? Are we to believe that in order to popularize philosophy he decided against a didactic poem and put doctrine into his comedies so as to render it palatable? The fatal objection is that Epicharmus has no philosophy at all in the sense now intended. Empedocles' system is clear enough: but Epicharmus offers statements now of Heracliteanism, now of Eleaticism, now of Pythagoreanism. Such eclecticism it would have been absurd to promulgate seriously, when people could read Heraclitus and Xenophanes, hear Pythagorean lectures, for themselves. There remains another, far more probable, view [1]— that Epicharmus, instead of using comedy as a vehicle for doctrine, used doctrine as a vehicle for comedy, just as did Molière in (for instance) *Le Mariage Forcé*. Plutarch [2] writes: ' But such cases in general rather resemble those passages of Epicharmus from which the sophists derived their " increasing argument ": [3] the man who formerly got the loan owes nothing to-day, having become another; the man invited yesterday to dinner arrives to-day unbidden, for he is some one else.' This points unmistakably to the doctrine of Heraclitus that all things are in a state of flux, so that we are to-day not what we were yesterday.[4] Lorenz suggests a laughable scene: ' You have come to dinner? I never invited you!' 'Oh yes, you asked me yesterday.' ' But you are a different man to-day. Don't you know your philosophy? *You* have no invitation: please go home.' This conception could plainly be elaborated into excellent comedy similar to the scene where Molière's Pyrrhonian philosopher Marphurius finds his own doctrine of doubt and suspended judgment turned against him.

[1] Lorenz, pp. 180-5.
[2] *De Sera Numinum Vindicta*, xv, 559b: this passage points almost certainly to a scene of comedy.
[3] For the αὐξανόμενος λόγος, see p. 94.
[4] See the fragment discussed on p. 88.

Another element in Epicharmus is the study of rhetorical method. Sicily during his lifetime [1] produced the first teacher of rhetoric, Corax, whose pupil, the brilliant sophist Gorgias, exercised so marked an influence upon Athenian prose. Epicharmus made two contributions to the nascent art that was to grow into the giant force that corrupted Greek politics and half slew Roman literature. He invented two rhetorical figures, both derived from his wayward interest in philosophy.

The first is the Growth Proposition [2] (ὁ αὐξανόμενος λόγος), exemplified admirably by the fragment that culminates in the assertion 'You and I are not the same men to-day that we were yesterday'. Chrysippus the Stoic, who wrote a treatise on this figure of rhetoric, attributed its invention to Epicharmus. Plutarch [3] adroitly applies the idea to certain political theorists who would release the state from responsibility for earlier misdeeds. And in his *Life of Theseus* [4] he writes:

'The ship of thirty oars, wherein he sailed and returned safe with the young people, was preserved by the Athenians till the days of Demetrius of Phalerum. They used to remove the old timbers and put new strong planks into the fabric, so that the ship became for the philosophers a disputed example, raising the Growth Proposition, some saying that the ship remained the same ship, others insisting that it was different.'

The other rhetorical figure was the famous *climax* or "ladder" (κλῖμαξ), often called by our authorities

---

[1] According to doubtful authority Corax was influential under Hiero (476-67 B.C.). See Blass, *Attische Beredsamkeit*, I, p. 18.
[2] Bernays (*Rhein. Mus.*, VIII, p. 283 n) rightly maintains that the phrase is analogous to ὁ ἐγκεκαλυμμένος λόγος—that it means "the Increasing-Man Proposition". This rhetorical figure must not be confused with the *Sorites*. Mr. Pickard-Cambridge, however (p. 376), identifies the two. But whereas in the Growth Proposition a man instantly becomes another man, in the *Sorites* the point is that you cannot tell how long he remains the same.
[3] *De Sera Num. Vindicta*, 559a sqq. See p. 93 above.
[4] Chap. XXIII.

"building up" (ἐποικοδόμησις).[1] Its form is a series of statements, the second member in each being identical with the first member of the following statement. Thus Epicharmus writes : 'From the sacrifice came the feast, and from the feast came drinking, and from drinking revelry, and from revelry misbehaviour, and from misbehaviour a lawsuit, and from the lawsuit the condemnation, and from the condemnation came fetters, the stocks and a fine'.[2] All terms save the first and last being repeated, we observe a "building-up" or "staircase" (*climax*) :

καταδίκα—πέδαι, σφαλός, ζαμία.
δίκα—καταδίκα
ὑανία—δίκα
κῶμος—ὑανία
πόσις—κῶμος
θοίνα—πόσις
θυσία—θοίνα

Epicharmus no doubt used the figure for quaint purposes, showing (as here) that a good thing can insensibly change into a bad by slight alterations,[3] as in the modern

[1] See the passages collected by Cope on Arist., *Rhet.*, I, 1365a, 10 (VIII, 31). Aristotle (*loc. cit.* and *De Gen. Anim.*, I, 724a) plainly regards Epicharmus as the inventor of this figure, though Eustathius in his commentary on *Iliad*, II, 102-8 (Hephæstus gave the sceptre to Zeus, he to Hermes, etc.) and on *Iliad*, XX, 214 *sqq.* (genealogy of Hector from Zeus) regards these lines as already exemplifying the κλῖμαξ or σχῆμα κλιμακωτόν. But Homer gives only an impressive enumeration ; there is no whimsical change from good to bad, as in Epicharmus, or crescendo as in Demosthenes. Quintilian (IX, iii, 54-57), who regards *gradatio, quæ dicitur* κλῖμαξ, as going downstairs, not upstairs, quotes from Calvus : *Non ergo magis pecuniarum repetundarum quam maiestatis, neque maiestatis magis quam Plautiæ legis, neque Plautiæ legis magis quam ambitus, neque ambitus magis quam omnium legum est.*

[2] Lorenz, p. 271 ; Kaibel, 148 :

A. ἐκ μὲν θυσίας θοῖνα,
ἐκ δὲ θοίνας πόσις ἐγένετο. B. χαρίεν, ὥς γ' ἐμοὶ[δοκεῖ]
A. ἐκ δὲ πόσιος κῶμος, ἐκ κώμου δ' ἐγένεθ' ὑανία,
ἐκ δ' ὑανίας δίκα [τάχ', ἐκ δίκας δὲ κατα]δίκα,
ἐκ δὲ καταδίκας πέδαι τε καὶ σφαλὸς καὶ ζαμία.

[3] This figure may perhaps be the origin of the *Sorites*. In any case it seems to have come into Epicharmus' mind as an exemplification of the Heraclitean flux : that philosopher had gone so far as to say not only that 'we are and are not' but also that 'good and bad are the same'. So here : the holy and elevating θυσία is shown to produce, by the most trivial changes, the bad and degrading fetters and stocks.

game of changing a word into its opposite by altering only one letter at a time. Plainly this device is capable of serious rhetorical force, as in the sentence of Demosthenes: οὐκ εἶπον μὲν ταῦτα, οὐκ ἔγραψα δέ· οὐδ' ἔγραψα μέν, οὐκ ἐπρέσβευσα δέ· οὐδ' ἐπρέσβευσα μέν, οὐκ ἔπεισα δὲ τοὺς Θηβαίους.¹ It is worth noting too that in both Epicharmus and Demosthenes the last member is longer than the rest: we have now reached the new level—the 'landing,' as it were.

We cannot say whether Epicharmus or Corax began the systematic study of rhetoric: the latter, however, composed a Manual (τέχνη) and not even Diogenes Laertius ascribes any such book to the poet. But not only did he invent the two figures just described: he is also interested in antitheses, puns, and accurate distinctions of similar words. Among the first are two clever epigrams:

οὐ λέγειν τύγ' ἐσσὶ δεινός, ἀλλὰ σιγῆν ἀδύνατος.²
'You are not clever at speaking, but bad at silence.'
οὐ φιλάνθρωπος τύγ' ἐσσ'· ἔχεις νόσον· χαίρεις διδούς.³
'You are not generous: you enjoy giving things away.'

From *The Male and Female Argument* (or Proposition, or whatever it may have been—Λόγος καὶ Λογίνα—and the name suggests that the whole play was concerned with rhetoric ⁴) comes an excellent pun: ⁵

A. ὁ Ζεύς μ' ἐκάλεσε Πέλοπί γ' ἔρανον ἱστιῶν.
B. ἦ παμπόνηρον ὄψον, ὦ τᾶν, ὁ γέρανος.
A. ἀλλ' οὔτι γέρανον, ἀλλ' ἔρανόν γά τοι λέγω.

A feebler instance is the joke about the four-legged tripod which would need an Œdipus to expound it (τετράπους, τρίπους, Οἰδίπους).⁶ Discrimination be-

---
¹ *De Corona*, 179, quoted as a κλῖμαξ by Demetrius, περὶ ἑρμηνείας (*De Elocutione*), 270.
² Lorenz, p. 263; Kaibel, 272.   ³ Lorenz, p. 263; Kaibel, 274.
⁴ See below, p. 106.   ⁵ Lorenz, p. 245; Kaibel, 87.
⁶ Lorenz, p. 262; Kaibel, 149.

tween words of similar sound occurs.[1] As a false antithesis Aristotle [2] notes :

τόκα μὲν ἐν τήνοις ἐγὼν ἦν, τόκα δὲ παρὰ τήνοις ἐγών,

'Sometimes I was with them, sometimes among them.' A more surprising feat of literary scholarship is his alleged addition of certain letters to the Greek alphabet.[3]

Hitherto we have dealt only with certain important but not dramatic features in Epicharmus' work. Turning to his comedies as such, we find a tantalizing heap of brief fragments from the thirty-six pieces which he wrote: of none can we feel sure that we know its scope and structure, but we do know something of the contents of a few. His works apparently fell into three classes, though we must beware of assuming that these did not merge into one another. It seems likely nevertheless that these different types of comedy were addressed to different kinds of audience.

The first category contained mythological travesties, burlesque versions of stories about gods or heroes—Dionysus, Odysseus, and especially Heracles, whose adventures and gluttony provided such copious material for later comic playwrights; so far as we know this use of Heracles began with Epicharmus. The play of which we are least ignorant is HEBE'S WEDDING (Ἥβας Γάμος), though even here our fragments are mostly lists of fish and other eatables. The play must have dealt with a scene in Heaven, where the marriage-feast of Hebe and Heracles (officially deified but still

---

[1] συνεκρίθη and διεκρίθη, ἀπῆνθεν and ἦνθεν (Lorenz, p. 258; Kaibel, 245).

[2] Lorenz, p. 273; Kaibel, 147; Aristotle, *Rhet.*, III, 9 (1410*b*, 3). (The text of Aristotle reads ἐν τήνων, the quotation in Demetrius, *De Elocutione*, 24, reads ἐν τήνοις). Blass, however (*Attische Beredsamkeit*[2], I, p. 16*n*), denies this on the ground that τῆνος . . . τῆνος mean the same as the Attic ὁ μέν . . . ὁ δέ. . . . Norden, however, takes it as a false antithesis (*Ant. Kunstprosa*, I, 25), as does Demetrius (*loc. cit.*): ἴσως γελωτοποιῶν οὕτως ἀντέθηκεν, καὶ ἅμα σκώπτων τοὺς ῥήτορας.

[3] See Lorenz, p. 73. According to tradition (Pliny, *Nat. Hist.*, VII, 57) Epicharmus' contemporary (and perhaps his associate) Simonides introduced ζ, ψ, η, and ω, Epicharmus himself θ and χ.

mortally hungry) was celebrated. Later the poet produced a second and probably longer version called the MUSES.[1] Of these two plays all we possess [2] in addition to the menu is:

(i) 'But we gods call them whitings (λεύκας).'

(ii) 'And *sciphias* and *chromis*, which according to Ananius is in spring the finest of all fish, as is *anthias* in winter.'[3]

(iii) 'Poseidon came in person, bringing in Phœnician luggers . . .' (further fish).

(iv) Athena played on a flute the war-dance for the Dioscuri (Castor and Pollux), whence it is that the Spartans go into battle with flute-music.[4]

(v) 'And the costly *elops* (fish) . . . a single specimen, and that Zeus took and ordered that it be set aside for himself and . . . for his wife.'[5]

(vi) There was a company — not a "chorus" — of seven Muses, named after famous rivers and lakes, who apparently brought and recommended each her own selection of fish. These water-muses were daughters of Pieros and Pimpleis.[6]

A few points are clear. The scene was in Heaven and the subject was the marriage-feast of Hebe and Heracles. There were long and absurdly erudite lists of eatables.[7] Quite a number of gods took part in the action. Athena has retained the flute which in

---

[1] Athenæus, III, 110*b*; Ἐπίχαρμος δ' ἐν Ἥβης Γάμῳ καὶ Μούσαις—τοῦτο δὲ τὸ δρᾶμα διασκευή ἐστι τοῦ προκειμένου—ἄρτων ἐκτίθεται γένη.

[2] Lorenz, pp. 230-40; Kaibel, pp. 98-104.

[3] The Greek words are names of fish, whose identification with known species is doubtful and unimportant. Ananius was a writer of lampoons.

[4] First statement in Athenæus, IV, 184 *sq.*, first and second in a scholium on Pindar, *Pyth.*, II, 127. Epicharmus' own words are not given, but he plainly made both statements.

[5] A corrupt passage: the dots mark the corruptions. Hera may have been given some pathetically cheap fish.

[6] Pieros and Pimpleis are parents invented by Epicharmus from the poetical names of the Muses, Pierides and Pimpleides. They are facetious, translated by Pickard-Cambridge (p. 384) as "Fat" and "Fill".

[7] Some lines are rather attractive, *e.g.* Lorenz, p. 231; Kaibel, 53:

καρκίνοι θ' ἵκοντ' ἐχῖνοί θ', οἳ καθ' ἁλμυρὰν ἅλα
νεῖν μὲν οὐκ ἴσαντι, πεζᾷ δ' ἐμπορεύονται μόνον.

other versions she threw away after the first trial on observing how her features were distorted by playing it. Epicharmus' contemporary Ananius is, by a jesting anachronism, mentioned as already flourishing in the days of Heracles. Finally—a highly important fact—many of the events (possibly all) were not shown but narrated, some (probably all) of these by a god.[1] Other features may be safely guessed, at any rate a superhuman display of gluttony by Heracles. Attempts have been made to find, or rather to postulate, plot-development here: the play would have the form of a rudimentary trilogy—Hera's intrigue against the marriage, her failure, her reconciliation and the feast. For this absolutely no evidence is forthcoming, though (as we shall see) there is a strong likelihood that Epicharmus sooner or later adopted the germ of the trilogy-form.[2]

This mythological class included BUSIRIS. Busiris was a king of Egypt who by the advice of an oracle sacrificed one foreigner each year on the altar of Zeus as a means to avert famine. Heracles on his way to the Far West of Africa (the Quest of the Hesperidean Apples) came to Egypt and was seized for sacrifice, but turned the tables on his captors and slew Busiris. Such is the story told by Apollodorus. All we know concerning Epicharmus' treatment is that after[3] his triumph Heracles celebrated an orgy, described in language whose frenzied vigour resembles that of Athenian Old Comedy:

> πρᾶτον μὲν αἴ κ' ἔσθοντ' ἴδοις νιν, ἀποθάνοις.
> βρέμει μὲν ὁ φάρυγξ ἔνδοθ', ἀραβεῖ δ' ἁ γνάθος,
> ψοφεῖ δ' ὁ γόμφιος, τέτριγε δ' ὁ κυνόδων,
> σίζει δὲ ταῖς ῥίνεσσι, κινεῖ δ' οὔατα.

'Why, first, you would die if you saw him eating. Rumbles issue from the gullet, the jaw clatters, the grinders bang, the dog-tooth shrieks, he whistles

---

[1] Kaibel (p. 98) suggests Hermes.   [2] See below, pp. 112 sq.
[3] So it is usually understood (e.g. by Pickard-Cambridge, p. 384). But the passage may rather have been part of a speech in which this year's just-captured and amazing victim is described to the waiting Busiris.

through his nostrils and works his ears.'[1] There is something Æschylean here, and something of Rabelais' Gargantua. We note again that the wonderful sight is reported as happening off-stage.

ODYSSEUS THE DESERTER (Ὀδυσσεὺς Αὐτόμολος) probably treated the story found in Homer,[2] that Odysseus penetrated into Troy disguised as a beggar, to spy upon the Trojans. Three fragments are of interest. One is in anapæsts:[3]

ἁ δ' Ἀσυχία χαρίεσσα, γυνά,
καὶ Σωφροσύνης πλατίον οἰκεῖ.

'Peace is charming, lady, and she dwells next door to Moderation.' This may well be part of Odysseus' talk with Helen inside Troy (if he ever got there—see below). Another passage[4] is a good example of burlesque by anachronism.[5] The text is corrupt, but the sense fairly plain: 'I was keeping a sucking-pig of my neighbours for sacrifice at the Eleusinian mysteries, but I lost it, Heaven knows how: it was no fault of mine. And he said I was intriguing with the Greeks and had betrayed the pig.' Thirdly, in a papyrus fragment[6] we read what may be a soliloquy of Odysseus in this play: he determines not to risk entering Troy, but merely to invent a narrative of his expedition and relate it to the admiring Greeks on his return. If this is correct, we have here a brilliant stroke of technique. Epicharmus, being induced by contemporary conditions of dramatic art to give his most laughable "scenes" in narrative, here like an

[1] Lorenz, p. 223; Kaibel, 21. Pollux (IX, 45) mentions also a word ῥογός used by Epicharmus in *Busiris* for "granary"; no doubt there was a scene of superhuman pantry-storming.
[2] *Od.*, IV, 242-60; also in the lost *Little Iliad*. A similar idea occurs in the Sinon passage of Vergil (*Aen.*, II, 57-198).
[3] Lorenz, p. 247; Kaibel, 101. Γυνά is probably vocative.
[4] Lorenz, p. 247; Kaibel, 100.
[5] Compare the reference to Ananius in *Hebe's Wedding*.
[6] Kaibel, fr. 99 (not in Lorenz, having been discovered later). There are scholia to the papyrus fragment, in which occur the words πόρρω καθεδοῦμαι καὶ προσποιήσομαι πάντα διαπεπρᾶχθαι; 'I shall sit at a distance and pretend to have accomplished everything'. Unfortunately there is no clear proof that the fragment comes from this play. Its text is defective.

artist uses his limitations and turns the necessity for mere narrative into a feature of his plot.

HERACLES AND THE GIRDLE (Ἡρακλῆς ὁ ἐπὶ τὸν ζωστῆρα) seems to have given a battle between him and an army of Pygmies who rode upon "huge Ætnæan beetles". From this detail Aristophanes may have taken his idea for Trygæus' steed in the *Peace*. From PHILOCTETAS we have one notable line : 'No dithyramb can be written by a teetotaller' (οὐκ ἔστι διθύραμβος ὅκχ᾽ ὕδωρ πίῃς), which was copied by the jovial Cratinus.¹ Among the plays that centre in Odysseus perhaps the most interesting is ODYSSEUS SHIPWRECKED (Ὀδυσσεὺς Ναυαγός), if we are to take it that the fragment ² on the hatching of chickens is therefrom derived. That passage is addressed to Eumæus, famous from the *Odyssey* as the swine-herd of Odysseus. We should then have to assume that the hero landed after his shipwreck, not upon Phæacia as Homer says, but upon his own island. In any case the mention of Eumæus in the fragment is very important as showing that Epicharmus did introduce philosophical disquisition into his "heroic" plays. All that we know for certain about *Odysseus Shipwrecked* is that it mentioned a word for " the bottom of the mast "³ and Diomos, a Sicilian herdsman, who invented bucolic poetry.⁴ The CYCLOPS no doubt treated the Homeric story : 'pour it into the cup and bring it' (φέρ᾽ ἐγχέας εἰς τὸ σκύφος). In the SIRENS was a description of feasting which suggests that the appeal to Odysseus' love of knowledge, represented in Homer, was changed by Epicharmus into an appeal to his " inner man ". It is punctuated by the envious moans of some second person. The REVELLERS (Κωμασταί) or HEPHÆSTUS dealt with a subject that must have been after Epicharmus' heart. Hera, displeased with her son Hephæstus because of his

---

¹ Fr. 199, ὕδωρ δὲ πίνων χρηστὸν οὐδὲν ἂν τέκοις, interpreted by Horace (*Ep*., I, xix, I, *sq*.) as referring to poetry. See below, p. 116.
² See p. 89. ³ Ὀρθίαξ (Pollux, X, 134).
⁴ Βουκολιασμός (Athen., XIV, 619a, b).

lameness, ejected him from Heaven; in revenge he sent his mother a cunningly wrought throne: it imprisoned her and none could extricate her. Hephæstus refused to return and open his mechanism, till Dionysus was sent, made him drunk, and brought him back triumphantly amid a revel-rout of Satyrs. Unfortunately our fragments do not help.[1] In AMYCUS was found the boxing-match between Polydeuces (Pollux), and Amycus, king of the Bebryces. This play is important for Epicharmus' stage-craft. Not only is it likely that the audience were delighted by a really good [2] (or delightfully absurd) boxing contest on the stage and by a " boxing tune ": [3] no less than three characters seem to have taken part in one place:

Ἄμυκε, μὴ κύδαζέ μοι τὸν πρεσβύτερον ἀδελφεόν,[4]

'Amycus, do not revile my elder brother': at the end the barbarian was " packed up " like Nicarchus in the *Acharnians*. The TROJANS (Τρῶες) contained the splendid line:

Ζεὺς ἄναξ, ἀν' ἄκρα ναίων Γαργάρων ἀγάννιφα,[5]

'Sovran Zeus, mid snowy splendour throned on topmost Gargarus'; and perhaps the diminutive Πριαμιλλύδριον belongs to this play.

The second type of comedy composed by Epicharmus is the social—the portraiture of contemporary life and character. In HOPE or WEALTH (Ἐλπὶς ἢ Πλοῦτος) appeared the first, and a masterly, depiction of what became a stock-character in Athenian

---

[1] Photius tells that the story of the trick-chair comes in this play; he does not mention the return of Hephæstus. If the outline given above is that followed by Epicharmus, we undoubtedly have the rudimentary trilogistic form discussed on p. 111. Possibly the words οὐδὲ ποτθιγεῖν ἐγὼν τεῦς ἀξιῶ (Lorenz, p. 244, Kaibel, 85) may have been words of Hephæstus refusing to release Hera.

[2] See the vigorous narrative in Theocritus (XXII, 76-134). Obvious as is the notion that Epicharmus really presented this, it may nevertheless have been merely reported; and the Theocritean passage slightly supports this latter view, as Theocritus was familiar with Epicharmus' work.

[3] See Pollux, IV, 56, where ποιητικόν should no doubt be πυκτικόν.

[4] Lorenz, p. 220; Kaibel, 6.

[5] So Kaibel, 130; Lorenz (p. 253) has a different reading.

Comedy—the parasite. One fragment [1] is almost the longest of Epicharmus and by far the most important:

συνδειπνέω τῷ λῶντι, καλέσαι δεῖ μόνον,
καὶ τῷ γα μηδὲ λῶντι κωὐδὲν δεῖ καλεῖν.
τηνεῖ δὲ χαρίεις τ' εἰμὶ καὶ ποιέω πολὺν
γέλωτα καὶ τὸν ἱστιῶντ' ἐπαινέω.
καί κά τις ἀντίον τι λῇ τήνῳ λέγειν,
τήνῳ κυδάζομαί τε κἀπ' ὧν ἠχθόμαν.
κἤπειτα πολλὰ καταφαγών, πόλλ' ἐμπιών,
ἄπειμι. λύχνον δ' οὐχ ὁ παῖς μοι συμφέρει,
ἕρπω δ' ὀλισθράζων τε καὶ κατὰ σκότος
ἐρῆμος. ὅκκα δ' ἐντύχω τοῖς περιπόλοις,
τοῦθ' οἷον ἀγαθὸν ἐπιλέγω τοῖς θεοῖς, ὅτι
οὐ λῶντι πλεῖον ἀλλὰ μαστιγοῦντί με.
ἐπεὶ δέ χ' εἴκω οἰκάδις καταφθαρείς,
ἄστρωτος εὕδω καὶ τὰ μὲν πρᾶτ' οὐ κοῶ,
ᾆς κά μ' ἄκρατος οἶνος ἀμφέπῃ φρένας.

'I dine with whoever wishes—he needs only to invite me; yes, and with the man who doesn't wish—no need of invitation. At table, I am witty and cause much laughter. I praise our host, and if anyone wishes to contradict him, I insult the man and take the quarrel on myself. Then, full of meat and drink, I depart. No servant accompanies me with a lantern, but I trudge along all by myself, stumbling in the dark. Whenever I meet the watch I thank my stars that they are satisfied with thrashing me. And when I reach home all to pieces I lie without bedclothes, not noticing their absence so long as the potent wine enfolds my brain.'

From Athenæus, to whom we owe this admirable extract, we learn that this parasite is the earliest in dramatic literature. We can only guess at the action of the piece: the fragments do not help us, though there is another passage of four lines describing the parasite: its text is doubtful, but the last line seems plain—' he empties a tankard at one draught as if it were a noggin '.[2] Nevertheless, it is an attractive

[1] Athenæus, VI, 235f-236b. Printed here practically as in Lorenz, pp. 226-8. Kaibel gives much the same.

[2] ἄμυστιν ὥσπερ κύλικα πίνει κύμβιον—a little cup and a big. The MSS. give τὸν βίον for κύμβιον, but 'draining the cup of life' is much more like Menander than Epicharmus. Kaibel (34), however, retains it.

suggestion¹ that 'Hope was represented by the parasite always on the look-out for an invitation, and Πλοῦτος by one of his patrons (or victims) very unwilling to invite him,' and that the piece ' consisted of a series of farcical encounters between the parasite and the rich men who tried to shake him off'.

Despite the achievements of Aristophanes, the Comedy of Manners had a longer career in the ancient world than what is known as Old Comedy; and one would have been glad to study its first manifestation in Sicily. But this second class of Epicharmean drama has left even more scanty relics than the first. Except the parasite-passage we have scarcely anything. PLUNDER (Ἁρπαγαί) may² have dealt with knaves (various types, perhaps, as the title is plural) who prey on the weakness of human nature: some four lines give a description of 'villainous soothsayers who worm their way into the confidence of silly women' at varying fees. There was also a reference to public life: ἁ δὲ Σικελία πέποσχε ('and Sicily has suffered' or 'experienced'). A more striking bit of comment on contemporary events is quoted³ from another play: 'That Anaxilaus wished to annihilate Locri and was thwarted by Hiero, Epicharmus also relates in ISLANDS.' The PILGRIMS (Θεαροί, Attic Θεωροί, 'envoys to a religious festival') described how the members of a sacred embassy to Delphi examined the temple treasures, a topic which frequently recurs in Greek poetry.⁴

The MEGARIAN WOMAN (Μεγαρίς) was perhaps an

---

¹ Pickard-Cambridge, p, 399.
² Unfortunately for the supposition in this sentence the fragment is a simile: ὡσπεραὶ πονηραὶ μάντιες, κτέ (Lorenz, p. 221; Kaibel, 9).
³ By the Scholiast on Pindar, *Pyth.* I, 98. The event took place in, or just before, 476 B.C. From an unnamed work is quoted another sentence about politics: ἀγρὸν τὰν πόλιν ποιεῖς (Lorenz, p. 278; Kaibel, 169): 'You make the city a field,' *i.e.* turn it into a wilderness (cp. Tennyson, *Aylmer's Field*).
⁴ In Æschylus' lost play Θεωροὶ ἢ Ἰσθμιασταί, Sophron's mime ταὶ θάμεναι (= θεώμεναι)ⁱ τὰ Ἴσθμια, Euripides' *Ion*, Herodas IV, and Theocritus' *Adoniazusæ*.

early example of the type so common in Attic New Comedy (*The Girl of Andros, of Perinthus*, etc.). It contained two descriptive passages, the longer corrupt, but apparently a vigorous caricature of some one with ' a bony head like a stag's '.[1] The other is a charming line : [2]

εὔυμνος καὶ μουσικὰν ἔχουσα πᾶσαν φιλόλυρος,

' Graced with song, mistress of melody, in love with the harp.' This may, then, have been a character-play, as was perhaps the RUSTIC ('Αγρωστῖνος). From this latter comes the remark : ' How swiftly the formidable Fisticuff walks about ! ' [3] He was a boxing-trainer, called after his habits like persons in Ben Jonson and others. Epicharmus was the first comic poet to represent drunken men : he was followed in this by Crates in the *Neighbours*. It has been ingeniously suggested [4] that Epicharmus invented also the Swaggering Soldier, so familiar in later comedy: there are no fragments to this effect, but though we find Lamachus in the *Acharnians*, the type in general could hardly have been evolved in fifth-century Athens, where the professional soldier was unknown ; on the other hand, he was a notable figure in the Syracuse of Gelo and Hiero.

The third class of Epicharmean comedy presented a conflict, not of opposite characters or even of types, but of non-human entities or abstractions—a duel of claims between personifications, like the contention between Water and Wine in Walter Map, and the thirteenth-century French *débats*. To this category belonged EARTH AND SEA (Γᾶ καὶ Θάλασσα): the fragment ' nor does (she ?) bear vines ' suggests antiphonal proclamation of fruits on the one hand, fishes on the other ; and Ælian [5] gives the familiar news that

---

[1] Lorenz, p. 245 ; Kaibel, 90.   [2] Lorenz, p. 246 ; Kaibel, 91.
[3] Lorenz, p. 219 ; Kaibel, 1.
[4] By H. Wysk (see Körte, Pauly-Wissowa, XI, 1225).
[5] *Nat. Hist. An.*, XIII, 4.

in this play many fish were mentioned. We have also the attractive phrase 'to cook the breakfast porridge'.[1] By far the most striking example is the curiously named ΔΟΓΟΣ ΚΑΙ ΛΟΓΙΝΑ. This means a male and female, but of what species is rendered obscure by the notorious difficulty of the word λόγος, which even Faust in Goethe found baffling. The title has been taken to mean "Male and Female Argument" (Plea ? Reason ? Theory ?) and an obvious analogue to this occurs in the duel between the Just and Unjust Λόγοι in Aristophanes' *Clouds*; or it may signify a male and female personification of rhetoric.[2] Conceivably we have here the original, or an earlier instance, of the male and female mimes in which Sophron excelled.

Passing now to the remains that, while genuine,[3] cannot be at present referred to any particular comedy, we find some of the most famous lines in Greek literature. One has been discussed already:

νόος ὁρῇ καὶ νόος ἀκούει· τἆλλα κωφὰ καὶ τυφλά,

''Tis mind that sees, mind that hears: the rest are deaf and blind.' Even more celebrated is the surly shrewdness of

νᾶφε καὶ μέμνασ' ἀπιστεῖν· ἄρθρα ταῦτα τᾶν φρενῶν,

'The sinews of wisdom are sobriety and ceaseless

---

[1] Πῶλτον ἕψειν ὄρθριον (Lorenz, p. 225; Kaibel, 23).
[2] It contains the joke about γέρανος (see above, p. 96), which suggests that the whole drama was a riot of rhetorical jokes and puzzles. This is only a guess, but if it is right it meets the difficulty presented by the mention of Zeus and Pelops in the γέρανος passage: "the characters were mythological; and it is not quite clear how the Masculine and Feminine Reason fitted in with these" (Pickard-Cambridge, p. 398). The whole thing may have been a dialogue between (as we might say) Mr. and Mrs. Wordsworth, or between Major Premise and Miss Barbara Celarent—an elaborate set-to of cross-questions and crooked answers, in which Zeus and Pelops were introduced to lend "verisimilitude" like the Muses, etc., in the arithmetical problems of the *Anthology*.
[3] The authenticity of some or all has been questioned. They appeared no doubt in Axiopistus' book of γνῶμαι: but though the book as such was a forgery, that is no reason for supposing that no single γνώμη was Epicharmean.

distrust.'[1] This peasant-like, Hesiodic, vigour is heard again in

αὗτα φύσις ἀνθρώπων, ἀσκοὶ πεφυσαμένοι,[2]

'Men are nothing but inflated wineskins.' Again:

συνεκρίθη καὶ διεκρίθη κἀπῆνθεν, ὅθεν ἦνθεν, πάλιν,
γᾶ μὲν εἰς γᾶν, πνεῦμα δ' ἄνω· τί τῶνδε χαλεπόν; οὐδὲ ἕν.

'They came together and were separated once more, returning whence they came: earth to earth, spirit aloft. What is hard in this? Nothing.'[3] The conversational crispness of another recalls Menander:

εὐσεβὴς βίος μέγιστον ἐφόδιον θνατοῖς ἔπι,

'The best provision for the journey of life is piety.'[4] Finally the celebrated maxim χαλεπὰ τὰ καλά ('beautiful things are hard') was "mentioned" by Epicharmus.[5] Here is a maxim which one would have insisted was disguised Menander were it not quoted by Xenophon:[6]

τῶν πόνων πωλοῦντι πάντα τἀγάθ' ἁμῖν τοὶ θεοί,

'All our blessings are sold us by the gods at the price of toil'. A good deal subtler is the adage: γνῶθι πῶς ἄλλῳ κέχρηται, 'know how he has used another' (if you think of making a man your friend).[7] Epicharmus has left us a flat contradiction of a theory very precious to Pindar, whom he must have met and known:

ἁ δὲ μελέτα φύσιος ἀγαθᾶς πλέονα δωρεῖται, φίλοι.

'Training, my friends, confers more benefit than nature.'[8] Zenobius[9] quotes from Epicharmus a statement that 'five judges judged the comedians'. Apparently the poet wrote ἐν πέντε κριτῶν γούνασι κεῖται

---

[1] Lorenz, p. 160; Kaibel, 250.
[2] Lorenz, p. 257; Kaibel, 246. The words are no doubt genuine, but they will not scan. Diels (*Vorsok.*⁴, I, p. 122) reads: ἅ γα φύσις ἀνδρῶν τί ὂν; ἀσκοὶ πεφυσιαμένοι. This can be scanned by main strength; but, rough as Epicharmus is, he never wrote such a line.
[3] Lorenz, p. 258; Kaibel, 245.   [4] Lorenz, p. 258; Kaibel, 261.
[5] Schol. Plato, *Cratylus*, 384a.
[6] *Memorabilia*, II, i, 20 (Lorenz, p. 259; Kaibel, 287).
[7] Lorenz, p. 260; Kaibel, 264.
[8] Lorenz, p. 261; Kaibel, 284 (reading δωρεῖται φίλοις).
[9] III, 64 (Lorenz, p. 278; Kaibel, 229).

as a proverbial phrase meaning 'the decision is not in our hands'. We cannot infer, however, that Sicily had competitions in comedy as had Athens.

His language [1] is Doric Greek, of the mild Sicilian kind (much nearer to Attic than the Doric of Sparta), using the digamma fitfully; it contains a few words borrowed from Latin—e.g. ὀγκία or οὐγκία (*uncia*) and κύβιτος (*cubitus*). The metre which he most often employs is the trochaic tetrameter,[2] which an ancient grammarian [3] actually named " Epicharmus' measure," although it had been used before him by Archilochus and Solon. Iambics too are common. Of anapæsts we possess but three fragments (that quoted above from *Odysseus the Deserter*, a passage from the Περίαλλος about Semele dancing to music, and ἐν πέντε κριτῶν γούνασι κεῖται) though he wrote two whole plays in that metre.[4] There is no evidence that he ever used lyrical metres. His versification is somewhat rough.[5] The plays contained some dancing and some indecency, how much of each we cannot say.[6] Parody was uncommon.[7] The length of the plays is uncertain, but there is fairly good reason to estimate it at an average of some four hundred lines.[8] Epicharmus' fame was

---

[1] Details in Lorenz, pp. 148-56.
[2] For this and other metrical terms see Chapter VIII.
[3] C. Marius Victorinus (Keil, *Gramm. Lat.*, VI, p. 84): *tetrametrum catalecticum, quod Archilochium et Epicharmium vocatur.*
[4] *The Dancers* (Χορεύοντες) and the *Victorious Athlete* ('Επινίκιος).
[5] Not because he is writing comedy. For example, he often neglects the diæresis in the trochaic tetrameter, which Aristophanes regularly observes.
[6] Whether the phallus was worn is unknown, but must be regarded as likely. It was regular both in Athenian old comedy and in the performances of the φλύακες in S. Italy. Vase-paintings frequently show this. (The reproductions are expurgated in English books.)
[7] Athenæus (XV, 698c), after remarking that parody was invented by Hipponax, adds: κέχρηται δὲ καὶ ὁ Ἐπίχαρμος ὁ Συρακόσιος ἔν τισι τῶν δραμάτων ἐπ' ὀλίγον. A parody of Homer (λαοὶ τοξοχίτωνες, ἀκούετε Σειρηνάων) is quoted by the Schol. on *Iliad*, XIX, 1.
[8] Birt, *Antike Buchwesen* (pp. 496 sq.), combining the facts (i) that in the Alexandrian edition each play of Aristophanes filled one volume, (ii) that the plays of Epicharmus filled ten volumes (Porphyrius, *Life of Plotinus*, xxiv), makes the average length of the latter between three and four hundred lines. This arithmetic is in itself dubious (see Pickard-Cambridge, p. 406), but it is attractive: the apparent simplicity of Epicharmus' plots suggests a length far less than the Aristophanic.

widespread. Apollodorus, a pupil of Aristarchus, made the Alexandrian text in ten books, and separated off the spurious works. Plato knew his work well and puts him at the " summit " of comedy.[1] Theocritus writes of him with affectionate respect.[2] Plautus was influenced by him, according to Horace, in some manner not easily determined;[3] Ennius named his Pythagorean poem *Epicharmus*;[4] centuries later Statius couples him with Hesiod as an authority on farming,[5] and Columella[6] associates him with Hiero as an enthusiast for that pursuit.

The most important facts about Epicharmus are three qualities that give a potent fascination to this half-seen figure.

First, he possessed the Sicilian manner, an attractive blend of the Italian (not Roman) and the Athenian. All that we know of the ancient Sicilian temperament reveals a certain richness, gusto, colour, showing plain kinship with that early Italian spirit which illumines even the fog of Plautus with a rare yet jovial beam. Most Greeks had no sense of humour: many of them had wit, but that rich zest which is one necessary element in humour was denied them; the Sicilian possessed humour, a touch of the racy, the crude, of

[1] *Theætetus*, 152e. [2] *Epigram* XVIII.
[3] Horace, *Ep.*, II, i, 58: *Plautus* (dicitur) *ad exemplum Siculi properare Epicharmi*. It is very hard to find any "haste" in either poet. Christ (*Gesch. der Griech. Litt.*, § 179) refers *properare* to the rapidity of resolved feet, Bernhardy (II, ii, p. 526) to "the lively tone of the conversation"; Mahaffy (*Hist. of Gk. Lit.*, I, p. 403) says it "seems only to apply to the easy flow of the dialogue"; Pickard-Cambridge (p. 408) thinks it perhaps refers to the rapidity of Epicharmus' "patter" or to the interchange of question and answer; similarly Denis (*La Comédie grecque*, I, p. 75) explains by "la verve, le mouvement, l'entrain"; Baiter-Orelli (on Horace) think the reference is to tense speed of plot; Lorenz (pp. 211-216) seems to agree with Mahaffy. None of these explanations is likely, and the third is apparently untrue of Epicharmus, fantastically untrue of Plautus. Christ's view is the least improbable.

[4] Very few fragments of this are left. The metre is the trochaic tetrameter. Ennius relates that he dreamed he was dead; in the lower world (it appears) Epicharmus expounded Pythagorean doctrines. As L. Müller (*Quintus Ennius*, p. 112) says, this need not mean that he quoted Epicharmus or translated any book περὶ φύσεως. Vahlen too (*Enn. poes. rel.*, p. xciii) thinks the relationship merely formal.

[5] *Silvæ*, IV, iii, 150. [6] I, i.

sympathy with what is seen to be absurd. On the other side, he was still a Greek, sometimes a good deal of an Athenian:[1] quick-witted, undisdainful of intellect, eager to rationalize the chaotic and then to irrationalize the systematic. At the court of Syracuse Pindar and Æschylus the pre-Periclean were welcome guests, but Plato was ejected with contumely. In such a circle Epicharmus was naturally at home, and his comedies too, with their quaint combination of Heraclitean flux and the staircase leading from church to gaol. Plautus could have written of the parasite cudgelled by the watch; Aristotle could have expounded the Heraclitean Flux in iambic verse. Epicharmus did both.

Second, his work was admirable but primitive drama. Here are three statements, all of which need careful exposition and understanding.

It was certainly drama—the working out of a situation by the collision of contrasted personalities. Not only do our authorities regularly call Epicharmus a "comic poet" ($\kappa\omega\mu\omega\delta o\pi o\iota\acute{o}\varsigma$) and his work "plays" ($\delta\rho\acute{a}\mu\alpha\tau a$): even in our meagre fragments we find that the *Amycus* showed three persons interacting. It is in virtue of this confrontation, this interaction, that Epicharmus is to be called the earliest comic playwright: that is what Aristotle[2] means by attributing to him the introduction of "plots" or "plays with a story" ($\mu\hat{\upsilon}\theta o\iota$). His predecessors bequeathed to him, not drama but the raw material thereof: Aristoxenus of Selinus was a lampoonist, Ananius wrote satires, the anonymous theatrical entertainers of Megara and Syracuse concocted mimes. That is, Aristoxenus gave him lessons in language, Ananius in observation, the mime-composers in farcical scenes. Epicharmus welded these elements (and others, for example his

---

[1] Thucydides (VIII, 96, 5) calls the Syracusans μάλιστα ὁμοιότροποι (sc. τοῖς 'Αθηναίοις).

[2] *Poetic*, 1449b, 5 sqq. : τὸ δὲ μύθους ποιεῖν Ἐπίχαρμος καὶ Φόρμις τὸ μὲν ἐξ ἀρχῆς ἐκ Σικελίας ἦλθε, where Ἐπίχαρμος καὶ Φόρμις is excised by Susemihl. Cp. also 1448a, 33 sq.

own humour and his knowledge of contemporary thought) into a connected story told by action—into a *play*, one part of the definition of which is that there is a pre-ordained point at which it must stop. Next, this authentic drama was primitive.[1] Grysar's theory, that Epicharmus wrote in a trilogistic or quasi-trilogistic form, is not so much erroneous as misleading. From what has just been said it will be clear that some Epicharmean plays must have exhibited development, phases of action, and it is impossible to deny that had we a complete example Grysar could identify Aristotle's beginning, middle, and end. It is certain,[2] too, that Epicharmus knew Æschylus' work, and Æschylus wrote trilogies. But to argue for these reasons that the Sicilian dramas were analogous to the *Oresteia* is to play with words. Apart from the silence of all ancient authorities about trilogistic form, and the rudimentary development necessary in a pioneer, the great argument against Grysar is the striking fact that a great deal of Epicharmus is not dramatic strictly at all, but narrative. Many an incident which (one would suppose) might have been shown to the spectators and

[1] The extremes of opinion are represented by Grysar and Kaibel. The former (*De Doriensium Comœdia*, Köln, 1828) asserts a trilogistic development: *e.g.* in Hebe's Wedding the opposition of Hera, her placation, the marriage-feast. Kaibel (Pauly-Wissowa, VI, 36) insists that Epicharmus did not write comedies (κωμῳδίαι) in the full sense at all. His work, says Kaibel, belongs to the sphere of comedy, Epicharmus is called a κωμικός, but his pieces are called κωμῳδίαι by no authority, only δράματα—a distinction probably due to the insight of the first editor, Apollodorus; the works were "eben Possen," which certainly showed (like Attic comedy) a comic element in the treatment, but which dispensed with the κῶμος, the peculiar Attic garnishing. This is accepted by Wilamowitz (*Einleitung in d. gr. Tragödie*, pp. 54 *sq.*). It is refuted by the fact that on this theory Epicharmus (despite Aristotle and the Anonymus) made no change at all in the shape of Sicilian "drama". Croiset (*Hist. de la litt. grecque*, III, 433 *sq.*) suspects that Epicharmus wrote prologues, because of the narrative passages.

[2] Æschylus at Hiero's request produced in Syracuse a new play (Αἰτναῖαι) and a revival of the *Persæ*. Epicharmus joked at Æschylus' fondness for the word τιμαλφεῖν (Schol. on *Eum.*, 626) and some plays of Epicharmus bore the same titles as some of Æschylus (*e.g. Promatheus, Philoctetas*—the Doric spelling). An attempt has been made to relate him to satyric drama: Croiset (p. 443) thinks the latter influenced him; Mahaffy (*Hist. of Gk. Lit.*, II, 406) reverses the relationship; K. O. Müller (*Gesch. der griech. Literatur*, II, 246) points to notable differences between the two types.

brought the house down, was apparently treated like the preliminary dispute for the tragic throne in the *Frogs*[1] or the healing of Plutus. Greek " drama," of course, had to be developed from pure narrative to fully dramatic presentation—and never quite reached it, as the Messengers' speeches in tragedy show, and the prologues of Menander. It is important nevertheless to remember that the technique of Epicharmus must have developed to some degree, and probably developed to a marked degree because of his removal to Syracuse[2] and a more cosmopolitan society. No doubt he began with the current mime-form. No doubt his first dramatic essays were half mime, half comedy. Finally, we can hardly deny that in his latest years the narrative element was less prominent. But the nearest he came to the alleged trilogistic form was a comedy with, to be sure, three distinguishable phases (as in all playwrights), a beginning, a middle, and an end. His most completely articulated piece would be analogous, not to the *Oresteia* but to a one-act comedy of our own time. Of this type *Busiris* was no doubt an example. As for Epicharmus' work being not only rudimentary but admirable, it is worth while to remark that his excellence does not reside in brilliance of style, as some writers assert. A glance at the more important fragments that we have quoted will show that his composition, though vigorous, is clumsy—his composition, strictly so called. Individual lines such as νᾶφε καὶ μέμνασ' ἀπιστεῖν κτέ., are admirable in their phrasing. But continuous composition shows him gawky and fumbling in diction. On the other hand, his shrewdness, his observation of character, are first-rate. Epicharmus, in fact, resembles Ennius. His originality in conceiving and developing

---

[1] Vv. 771-83. Later, of course, the claimants proceed to a very elaborate conflict *coram populo*.
[2] Körte (Pauly-Wissowa, XI, 1223) asserts that "for us and for the ancients the only discernible period of his activity falls in his last years, in the Syracuse of the Deinomenidae" (Gelo and Hiero). This is quite unfounded.

EPICHARMUS

dramatic situations has been already exhibited so far as our meagre materials allow.

Thirdly, Epicharmus shed his energies over both the Greek and the Roman world. Constant trade and the travels of such men as Æschylus [1] and Plato brought his work home to the audiences and playwrights [2] of Athens, and so of all Greece proper and the Asiatic cities and islands which regarded Athens as their intellectual metropolis. The political relations of Hiero and Syracusan commerce spread Sicilian culture over South Italy, so that aboriginal clownery and nascent drama were moulded and invigorated by Epicharmus, whose influence upon the *phlyakes* cannot be exactly assessed but cannot be doubted. So it is that the modern world owes to this earliest master, through Aristophanes and Menander, through Plautus [3] and the *commedia del' arte*, a great deal more than it dreams. In him lie the germs both of Alceste and of Falstaff. From the obscurity of time and distorted story his voice comes in snatches like a friendly shout that reaches us fitfully at the mercy of casual winds and rock-contours, a cheery but tantalizing utterance from a rich vivid personality.

[1] Cp. Capps, *Columbia Univ. Lectures on Gk. Lit.*, p. 130.
[2] Alexis names Epicharmus as part of a poetical library (see above, p. 49). Archippus wrote a play 'Ἡρακλῆς Γαμῶν (*Heracles the Bridegroom*), which perhaps (Soph., *Trach.*, 460) dealt with the same subject as Ἥβας Γάμος. The Schol. on *Peace*, 185, says that Aristophanes is borrowing from Epicharmus' *Sciron* (see Lorenz, pp. 251 *sq.*). The famous psephisma, μὴ κωμῳδεῖν ὀνομαστί (see pp. 26 *sqq.*), may have caused the Athenian dramatists to look back for inspiration to Epicharmus (see Lorenz, pp. 207 *sq.*). Zieliński (*Gliederung*, p. 243) points out that Epicharmus' name is not mentioned earlier than Plato, and finds no trace in Aristophanes of any knowledge of Epicharmus. The "Megarian farce," however, so often described in Aristophanes and others, may well refer to Sicily as well as to the Peloponnese. But it must be confessed that the "parallels" between Aristophanes and our fragments of Epicharmus, which von Salis (*De Doriensium Ludorum in Comœdia Attica Vestigiis*, Basel, 1905), adduces, are unconvincing.
[3] K. O. Müller (*Gesch. d. gr. Lit.*, II, p. 244) points to the Doric, not Athenian, spelling of Miccotrogus' name in the *Stichus*. The obscure passage of Horace (*Ep.*, II, i, 58: see p. 109) proves at any rate that some Roman scholars saw a literary affiliation.

CHAPTER III

CRATINUS

CRATINUS,[1] the son of Callimedes, is said to have belonged to the Athenian tribe Œneis.[2] His life may be dated roughly at 490-20 B.C.[3] Twenty-eight titles are known to us, but our authorities [4] put the figure at twenty-one. Cratinus gained nine [5] first prizes, one of them in 423 B.C., when his *Wine-*

[1] Suidas, *s.v.*: Κρατῖνος, Καλλιμήδους, Ἀθηναῖος, κωμικός, λαμπρὸς τὸν χαρακτῆρα· φιλοπότης δὲ καὶ παιδικῶν ἡττημένος. ἦν δὲ τῆς ἀρχαίας κωμῳδίας. ἔγραψε δὲ δράματα κά. ἐνίκησε δὲ θ′.
[2] Zenobius, III, 81, Suidas, *s.v.* Ἐπειοῦ δειλότερος. Körte (Pauly-Wissowa, XXII, 1647) rejects this statement as derived from some joke that assigned the vinous poet to the tribe of Vintagers. This is the rage of scepticism which cold-heartedly denies joyous coincidences. It is absurd to say that the story is untrue merely because it would be delightful if it were true. There is nowhere a hint of any other tribe for Cratinus.
[3] The Πυτίνη was produced in 423; as we hear of no later play we can assume that he died not many years later. The apparent evidence of the *Peace* must, however, be used with caution. That comedy appeared in 421 and reports Cratinus' death thus (vv. 700 *sqq.*):

    EP. τί δαί; Κρατῖνος ὁ σοφὸς ἔστιν;
    TP.   ἀπέθανεν
        ὅθ' οἱ Λάκωνες ἐνέβαλον.
    EP.   τί παθών;
    TP.   ὅ τι;
        ὡρακιάσας· οὐ γὰρ ἐξηνέσχετο
        ἰδὼν πίθον καταγνύμενον οἴνου πλέων.

This would put Cratinus' death in or before 421. But it may be only a joke, and there had been no invasion of Attica since 425, two years before the *Wine-Flask*. Next, his first victory was won about 453 B.C. In view of Cratinus' merits one naturally assumes that he was then still under forty. This gives *circa* 490 as the date of his birth, which agrees well enough with the description of him as an old man in Aristophanes' *Knights* (v. 533), produced in 424.
[4] Suidas, *s.v.* Κρατῖνος and Anon. de Com. (Kaibel, p. 7).
[5] Suidas, *ibid.* The lists in the inscriptions given by Wilhelm (*Urk.*, 107 and 123) give six City and three Lenæan victories. The Schol. on *Knights*, 528, says that Cratinus beat his rivals παμψηφεί, 'by all the votes'.

114

Flask (Πυτίνη) defeated the *Connos* of Ameipsias and the *Clouds* of Aristophanes.[1] In 425 his play [2] came second to the *Acharnians* and in 424 to the *Knights*.[3] These are the only dates in his career that are quite certain, though we shall see that other plays can be dated with confidence.

In 424 B.C., when Cratinus was perhaps within sight of seventy, a brisk and brilliant young poet produced a comedy called the *Knights* in which he took upon himself to rebuke Athens for neglect of old poets who had served her well. In the course of these remarks the impish Muse of Comedy inspired him to patronize Cratinus in language of delightful impertinence and pathetic admiration (vv. 526-36):

εἶτα Κρατίνου μεμνημένος, ὃς πολλῷ ῥεύσας ποτ' ἐπαίνῳ
διὰ τῶν ἀφελῶν πεδίων ἔρρει, καὶ τῆς στάσεως παρασύρων
ἐφόρει τὰς δρῦς καὶ τὰς πλατάνους καὶ τοὺς ἐχθροὺς προθελύμνους·
ᾆσαι δ' οὐκ ἦν ἐν συμποσίῳ πλὴν ' Δωροῖ συκοπέδιλε '
καὶ ' τέκτονες εὐπαλάμων ὕμνων '· οὕτως ἤνθησεν ἐκεῖνος.
νυνὶ δ' ὑμεῖς αὐτὸν ὁρῶντες παραληροῦντ' οὐκ ἐλεεῖτε,
ἐκπιπτουσῶν τῶν ἠλέκτρων καὶ τοῦ τόνου οὐκέτ' ἐνόντος
τῶν θ' ἁρμονιῶν διαχασκουσῶν· ἀλλὰ γέρων ὢν περιέρρει,
ὥσπερ Κοννᾶς, στέφανον μὲν ἔχων αὖον δίψῃ δ' ἀπολωλώς,
ὃν χρῆν διὰ τὰς προτέρας νίκας πίνειν ἐν τῷ πρυτανείῳ,
καὶ μὴ ληρεῖν ἀλλὰ θεᾶσθαι λιπαρὸν παρὰ τῷ Διονύσῳ.

'Next Cratinus comes to mind, who once in full torrent of glory flowed over the level countryside, sweeping along uprooted oaks, plane-trees and rivals. So mightily did he flourish that nothing could be sung at wine-parties except " Rule Britammany ! " and " Minstrels, deftly build the song ". But now ! Look at him, drivelling out of tune—pegs dropping out, strings loose, joints starting ! And you—you !— feel no pity for this senile loafer with the faded garland and the destroying thirst, though you ought to reward his past triumphs with free drinks for the rest of his life, make him drop his hopeless plays and sit as a dapper spectator in the front row.'

---

[1] *Clouds*, Argument V.
[2] The Χειμαζόμενοι (*Acharnians*, Argument *ad. fin.*).
[3] The Σάτυροι (*Knights*, Argument II).

Aristophanes spoke too soon. This stinging mixture of praise and pity brought the elderly genius to his feet. 'Nearly seventy and ruined by drink, am I? Ho!' Next year at the City Dionysia he produced the WINE-FLASK (Πυτίνη) and defeated [1] his ambiguous eulogist with a play that boldly took up the imputations of Aristophanes. From the fragments and a scholium on the *Knights* [2] we gain a fair conception of the plot. Cratinus' wife, Comedy herself, complains to his friends that Cratinus is neglecting her and consorting with Drunkenness (Μέθη)—'formerly I was his wife, but now no more' (γυνὴ δ' ἐκείνου πρότερον ἦ, νῦν δ' οὐκέτι) [3] —and wishes to bring an action against him for ill-treatment. Cratinus used to be a good husband, but now he runs after every pretty wine-skin that he sees.[4] It appears that these friends, who form the chorus, have come forward in order to keep the case out of court by making Cratinus see reason. In a speech that was probably the culmination of the drama, Cratinus explained, or defended, or gloried in, his new way of life: it contained the famous line [5] ὕδωρ δὲ πίνων οὐδὲν ἂν τέκοι σοφόν: 'but if he drinks water he can create nothing wise'. We possess practically nothing else about it, only the dazed comment: [6]

> ἄναξ Ἄπολλον, τῶν ἐπῶν τῶν ῥευμάτων.
> καναχοῦσι πηγαί, δωδεκάκρουνον τὸ στόμα,
> Ἰλισσὸς ἐν τῇ φάρυγι· τί ἂν εἴποιμ' ἔτι;
> εἰ μὴ γὰρ ἐπιβύσει τις αὐτοῦ τὸ στόμα,
> ἅπαντα ταῦτα κατακλύσει ποιήμασιν.

'Holy Apollo! What a torrent of verse! A bubbling well! His mouth is a twelve-spouted fountain, his throat a river, his . . . comparisons fail me! Unless some one plugs his mouth, he will flood the whole district with poetry.' We may conjecture that he entered embracing the Wine-Flask which gives its

---

[1] Aristophanes took his failure very badly. In his second version (*Clouds*, 518-62) of the defeated play he reads the Athenians a vigorous and bitter lecture on their bad taste in putting the *Clouds* below the work of Cratinus and Ameipsias.
[2] V. 400, ἐν Κρατίνου κῳδίον.   [3] Fr. 182.
[4] Fr. 183.   [5] Fr. 199.   [6] Fr. 186.

name to the play and which (needless to say) symbolized his new love, Methe.¹ His recalcitrance is proved by the passage ² where a friend cudgels his brains for some device to cure the infatuation:

> πῶς τις αὐτόν, πῶς τις ἂν
> ἀπὸ τοῦ πότου παύσειε, τοῦ λίαν πότου;
> ἐγᾦδα. συντρίψω γὰρ αὐτοῦ τοὺς χόας,
> καὶ τοὺς καδίσκους συγκεραυνώσω σποδῶν,
> καὶ τἄλλα πάντ' ἀγγεῖα τὰ περὶ τὸν πότον,
> κοὐδ' ὀξύβαφον οἰνηρὸν ἔτι κεκτήσεται.

'How, oh how, can one check his drinking, his excessive drinking? I have it! I'll smash his jugs, I'll shatter his jars like a thunderbolt, and every other drinking-vessel: he shan't have so much as a winesaucer to his name.' But somehow Cratinus is later reconciled to Comedy and expresses his repentance:

> ἀτὰρ ἐννοοῦμαι δὴ τὰ τῆς μοχθηρίας
> τῆς ἠλιθιότητός τε τῆς ἐμῆς.³

'Well, well: I realize how wicked my stupidity has been.' How this change of heart is induced we can only guess: perhaps Comedy steals the Wine-Flask and thus brings the poet to his knees.⁴

Of the other fragments some are interesting although we cannot tell what connexion they had with the story just outlined. There would seem to have been a racy discussion of young politicians: each was relegated to some spot better suited to his habits than the Pnyx: e.g.: ⁵

> Ὑπέρβολον δ' ἀποσβέσας ἐν τοῖς λύχνοισι γράψον.

¹ One is reminded of that uproarious reprobate Merrythought in *The Knight of the Burning Pestle*. For the idea that the πυτίνη was embraced and apostrophized compare the coal-basket scene in *Acharnians*, 331-5.
² Fr. 187. ³ Fr. 188.
⁴ Two fragments have suggested this. Fr. 189 runs:

> ὄψει γὰρ αὐτὴν ἐντὸς οὐ πολλοῦ χρόνου
> παρὰ τοῖσι δεσμώταισι καταπιττουμένην.

'You shall see her before long receiving a coat of pitch from the gaolers'—that is, 'don't worry: I've only sent her to the repairers.' Comedy would then be consoling Cratinus, who despite his reformation grieves for his discarded love, now thrown on the world. To such a sad reverie fr. 190 may belong:

> ἆρ' ἀραχνίων μεστὴν ἔχεις τὴν γαστέρα;

'Can it be that you have nothing to fill your belly but spiders' webs?'
⁵ Fr. 196.

'Put Hyperbolus out and write him up in the Lamp-Market,' Hyperbolus being a lamp-merchant. Some of the proposed destinations would (we are to hope) be funnier than this,[1] and the whole oration would resemble Koko's topical song: "I've got him on the list". Finally, we are told [2] that 'Cratinus, hearing this (the passage from the *Knights* quoted above) wrote the *Wine-Flask*, in which he reviles [3] Aristophanes for plagiarizing Eupolis'.

But by far the most attractive and important of Cratinus' comedies, in the present state of our knowledge, is the DIONYSALEXANDROS.[4] Till 1904 our meagre collection of citations told nothing of the plot, but in that year Grenfell and Hunt published a papyrus, discovered at Oxyrhynchus, containing a good deal of the Argument.[5]

'... These [6] address the audience concerning the poets,[7] and when Dionysus appears they mock and jeer at him. Dionysus, being offered by Hera unshaken sovereignty, by Athena success in war, and by Aphrodite the possession of charm and surpassing beauty, adjudges the victory to Aphrodite. Next he sails to Sparta, abducts Helen, and returns to Mt. Ida. But soon, hearing that the Greeks are ravaging the land, he flees to Alexander,[8] hides Helen in a basket as [a goose?], disguises himself as a ram, and awaits the upshot. Alexander arrives, detects them both, and orders them to be taken to the ships, intending to

---

[1] An apparently vigorous one lurks in the distorted Greek of fr. 195.

[2] Scholiast on *Knights*, 531. Eupolis' connexion with the *Knights* is discussed below (pp. 210 sq.).

[3] We have no quotation of his words.

[4] In discussing this play I am much indebted, of course to Grenfell and Hunt, but also to the admirable article of M. Croiset in the *Revue des Études grecques*, XVII (1904), pp. 297-310, and the very full and masterly treatment by Körte in *Hermes*, XXXIX (1904), pp. 481-98.

[5] *Oxyrhynchus Papyri*, IV, 69-72. The text here given (from Grenfell and Hunt) opens where the Greek begins to be consecutive.

[6] The chorus of satyrs.

[7] The Greek is defective. Grenfell and Hunt make out "on behalf of the poet".

[8] Paris, son of Priam.

hand them over to the Greeks. But Helen objects; he takes pity on her and withholds her, to make her his wife, but Dionysus he despatches to be handed over. The satyrs escort Dionysus with encouragement and assurances that they will never desert him. In the play Pericles is most convincingly satirized by innuendo as having involved the Athenians in the war.'[1]

This document puts us for the first time in possession of a correct notion as to Athenian mythological comedy. Cratinus took the familiar story of Helen, Paris, and Agamemnon's expedition. Into this he thrust Dionysus and an attendant rout of satyrs, giving to the god, for most of the play, the part assigned by the legend to Paris, but of course making it ridiculous. (One detail of the fun is preserved: whereas Paris was promised the most beautiful woman on earth, here the no doubt less attractive Dionysus is offered a prospect of becoming irresistible himself.) Then, at the close, orthodox legend is reinstated: Dionysus disappears, and Paris stands forth as responsible to the Greeks for the retention of Helen.

[1] ... καὶ παραφανέντα τὸν Διόνυσον ἐπισκώπτουσι καὶ χλευάζουσιν. ὁ δὲ παραγενομένων [παραγγελλομένων, Körte] αὐτῷ παρὰ μὲν Ἥρας τυραννίδος ἀκινήτου παρὰ δ' Ἀθηνᾶς εὐτυχίας κατὰ πόλεμον τῆς δ' Ἀφροδίτης κάλλιστόν τε καὶ ἐπέραστον αὐτὸν ὑπάρχειν κρίνει ταύτην νικᾶν. μετὰ δὲ ταῦτα πλεύσας εἰς Λακεδαίμονα καὶ τὴν Ἑλένην ἐξαγαγὼν ἐπανέρχεται εἰς τὴν Ἴδην. ἀκούσας δὲ μετ' ὀλίγον τοὺς Ἀχαιοὺς πυρπολεῖν τὴν χώραν φεύγει πρὸς τὸν Ἀλέξανδρον καὶ τὴν μὲν Ἑλένην εἰς τάλαρον ὥσπερ [τυρὸν G. and H., χῆνα Körte] κρύψας, ἑαυτὸν δ' εἰς κριὸν μετασκευάσας, ὑπομένει τὸ μέλλον· παραγενόμενος δ' Ἀλέξανδρος καὶ φωράσας ἑκάτερον ἄγειν ἐπὶ τὰς ναῦς προστάττει ὡς παραδώσων τοῖς Ἀχαιοῖς. ὀκνούσης δὲ τῆς Ἑλένης ταύτην μὲν οἰκτείρας ὡς γυναῖχ' ἕξειν ἐπικατέχει, τὸν δὲ Διόνυσον ὡς παραδοθησόμενον ἀποστέλλει. συνακολουθοῦσι δ' οἱ σάτυροι παρακαλοῦντές τε καὶ οὐκ ἂν προδώσειν αὐτὸν φάσκοντες. κωμῳδεῖται δ' ἐν τῷ δράματι Περικλῆς μάλα πιθανῶς δι' ἐμφάσεως ὡς ἐπαγειοχὼς τοῖς Ἀθηναίοις τὸν πόλεμον.

The fragmentary Greek that precedes what is here printed contains a reference to Hermes. The second column is headed

Διονυσ
— η
Κρατ

where η means "eighth," which according to Körte (*Hermes*, XXXIX, 484 *sq.*) refers to an alphabetical arrangement of Cratinus' works in the Alexandrian library. Flickinger (*Classical Philology*, 1910, 7 *sqq.*) takes it as chronological, and dates the *Dionysalexandros* at 445 B.C., referring to the Spartan invasion of 446.

As to the details of the *Dionysalexandros*, it is necessary to observe that our information practically begins with the parabasis. We are told that 'they address the spectators,' whether on behalf of the poet or 'concerning the poets'.[1] Either reading points to a parabasis of a kind familiar in Aristophanes. What preceded the parabasis? Our tattered Greek mentions "seeking," and Hermes, who assuredly acted as conductor of the three goddesses to be judged by the mortal. After the parabasis, Dionysus "appears". The word is notable—not ἐπιφανέντα, appropriate to a glorious apparition, but παραφανέντα, which suggests some one "popping in" rather jauntily and unexpectedly. This, together with the derision of the satyrs, probably gives a clue to the early action. It may be that Hermes, having brought the three goddesses to Mt. Ida for judgment by Paris, cannot find him [2] and is at his wits' end, since such important ladies cannot be kept waiting, especially on a mountain-side and prepared for a beauty-contest; and that his difficulty is solved by a sudden proposal that Dionysus (providentially near at hand) shall act as judge. Who makes this proposal? Probably not the god himself, but his satyr-followers in his momentary absence, for it seems that they have to describe their candidate to the doubtful Hermes:

A. στολὴν δὲ δὴ τίν' εἶχε; τοῦτό μοι φράσον.
B. θύρσον, κροκωτόν, ποικίλον, καρχήσιον.[3]

'Tell me, what was his attire?' 'A Bacchic wand, a saffron shawl, an embroidered robe, a goblet.'

Dionysus "pops in" and the plan is discussed.

---

[1] Rutherford (*Classical Review*, XVIII, p. 440) would read περὶ υῶν ποιήσεως. "When the *Dionysalexander* was produced the project for the legitimizing of the younger Pericles was either debating or accomplished." He would date the play at 430, a year practically certain on other grounds (see below).

[2] Hence the "seeking" (ζητ—?).

[3] Fr. 38. The tense of εἶχε may mean that Hermes is about to set forth in quest of Dionysus: 'when last seen, was wearing....'

Perhaps he is attracted by the task of impersonating a prince and wearing royal gear, but is disillusioned:

οὔκ, ἀλλὰ βόλιτα χλωρὰ κᾡσπώτην πατεῖν.[1]

'Nothing of the kind: (you will have to) walk on fresh dung and filthy wool.' But he accepts the proposition and adds theatrically rustic attire to his effeminate Bacchic garb. The chorus greet with jeers his boast that he is several kinds of herdsman in one:

ποιμὴν καθέστηκ' αἰπόλος καὶ βουκόλος.[2]

The next thing we know of is the Judgment of Paris-Dionysus and its result, though with no details. It is quite in accord with the intoxicated Time-Spirit of Old Comedy that Dionysus sails to Sparta, woos Helen, and returns with her while the chorus (we are to suppose) sings an ode. The Greek expedition, too, makes the journey to Troy at a miraculous speed. The terrified Dionysus conceals Helen and himself. Her he puts into a basket disguised as something thereto appropriate—what, we do not know, because the papyrus is defective here. The best proposal is that of Körte, a goose,[3] because of the Leda story. Dionysus disguises himself as a ram: the famous line [4]

ὁ δ' ἠλίθιος ὥσπερ πρόβατον βῆ βῆ λέγων βαδίζει,

'and the simpleton walks along saying "Ba! Ba!" like a sheep,' refers no doubt to the industrious but amateurish efforts of Dionysus to sustain the character. The true Paris arrives, urged probably by the Greek invasion to discover the culprits and release his country by their surrender. Some detective [5] work is necessary

---

[1] Fr. 39. Flickinger (*loc. cit.*, p. 9) aptly suggests that fr. 42, παραστάδας καὶ πρόθυρα βούλει ποικίλα, points at the ambitious building schemes of Pericles.

[2] This is, however, not certainly to be referred to this play (fr. 281).

[3] A faint support for this from outside is fr. 46, which contains the rare word χηνοβοσκοί. We are to take the goose as a parody of the swan, as indeed it is.

[4] Fr. 43. This line is often quoted as an argument for the "reformed" pronunciation of Greek: "a sheep does not say *bee, bee; bay, bay* is much more like the sound".

[5] Cp. φωράσας in the Argument.

before the disguise is penetrated: the scene of the Megarian pigs in the *Acharnians* may suggest how the detection of Helen was conducted. Finally Dionysus is merely ejected from the story, but the charms of Helen overthrow the purpose of Paris, and matters are in train for the ten years' war. The play perhaps ended with a marriage-feast of Alexander and Helen.[1]

It is difficult to interpret precisely the final sentence of the Argument that " Pericles is most convincingly satirized by innuendo as having involved the Athenians in the war ". It is plain enough from these words that Dionysus represents Pericles ; that the ravaging of the Troad—which must have been emphasized in the play, or it would never have got into this brief summary [2] —is meant to recall the first invasion and the exasperating sight of fire rising from Acharnæ ;[3] that the amorous adventure of Dionysus corresponds to the scandalous stories about Aspasia's[4] part in the outbreak of war. It is possible, too, that the surrender of Dionysus to the Greeks hinted at the Spartan demand that Athens should expel the " accursed " Alcmæonidæ, that is, Pericles.[5] But whereas, judging by the practice of contemporary playwrights, we should have expected a perfectly explicit comparison, the Argument plainly indicates another treatment, satire by insinuation. In the present state of our knowledge it is best to accept this view, and to believe that Cratinus is primarily concerned with a riotous travesty of the legend, and works contemporary satire into the fabric purely as an undertone.

[1] Cp. frr. 40, 44, 45.
[2] The Argument says πυρπολεῖν τὴν χώραν. Now the invaders did of course ravage the country, but the phrase is not *prima facie* likely in a concise description. One would have expected εἰσβαλεῖν ὡς πολιορκήσοντας. The inference is that Cratinus dwells on the devastation in a manner inappropriate to one alluding to the *Iliad*, but very appropriate to one with the Peloponnesian invasion in his mind.
[3] Cp. Thucydides, II, 19-23.
[4] Just as Pericles = Dionysus = Paris, the cause of war, so was Aspasia named Helen by Eupolis in the *Prospaltii*.
So Wilamowitz-Moellendorff, *Gott. gel. Anzeigen*, 1904, p. 665.

Two other points should be made : (i) It is possible that Hermippus refers to this play in the fragment [1] that begins βασιλεῦ σατύρων. If so, the allegory must have been more transparent for Cratinus' contemporaries than for the writer of the Argument. (ii) Is Tzetzes, who contradicts Aristotle about the number of actors in early comedy, himself contradicted by this Argument ? Aristotle had written [2] that 'no one knows who fixed the number of comic actors'. Tzetzes reports [3] that 'Cratinus was the first to fix the number of actors at three'. Is it a fact that the *Dionysalexandros* needs four actors ? In the scene where Dionysus judges the three goddesses, we apparently need four, not to mention Hermes. But it may well have been that Hera, Athena, and Aphrodite are all silent. We moderns should, of course, expect a striking address from each, but the practice of Aristophanes [4] shows that he at any rate—and if so, why not Cratinus ?— would have been content to make each " whisper " to Hermes, who would then report [5] her offer. That scene would demand only two actors, with three mutes.

The date is not quite certain. One would naturally place it early in the war because of the political allusions, but not later than Pericles' death. This gives 430 or 429. Clear evidence for the former year is obtained if we assume that the satyr-fragment of Hermippus could not have been written had not Cratinus already made Dionysus-Pericles a leader of satyrs.[6] Now the passage of Hermippus belongs to a play (whether the *Fates* or

---

[1] Fr. 46, from the Μοῖραι. See above, p. 22.
[2] *Poetic*, 1449b, 3.
[3] Kaibel, p. 18 : ἐπιγενόμενος δὲ ὁ Κρατῖνος κατέστησε μὲν πρῶτον τὰ ἐν τῇ κωμῳδίᾳ πρόσωπα μέχρι τριῶν στήσας τὴν ἀταξίαν. By πρόσωπα Tzetzes must mean "actors" : "characters" (the usual meaning of πρόσωπα) would make nonsense.
[4] *E.g. Peace*, 957 *sqq*.
[5] Cp. the Argument: παραγγελλομένων παρὰ μὲν Ἥρας κτέ, where the verb is however Körte's emendation for παραγενομένων.
[6] See Croiset, *loc. cit.*, pp. 309 *sq.*, and Wilamowitz-Moellendorff, *loc. cit.*, pp. 665 *sqq*.

not) produced in 430. The conclusion would then be that Hermippus' comedy appeared at the City Dionysia, and the *Dionysalexandros* at the Lenæa, of 430.

Another blend of whimsical legend-distortion and satire on contemporaries was to be found in NEMESIS, a deliberately bungling travesty of the birth of Helen compounded by some queer alchemy with the fortunes of that great but unromantic Athenian, Pericles. Later writers give the story thus:[1] " Zeus fell in love with Nemesis, a maiden of Rhamnus in Attica, who changed herself into all shapes so as to elude his embraces. Finally she became a swan, and Zeus, turning himself into a swan also, bade Aphrodite, in the shape of an eagle, pursue him. The fugitive bird found a refuge with Nemesis, who thus, in due course, laid an egg. This was taken by Hermes to Leda in Sparta; she hatched it and produced Helen." That Nemesis, not Leda, was Helen's mother had been affirmed by Stasinus, the epic poet who composed the *Cypria*. The laughably stupid notion of two mothers is, of course, an attempt to harmonize the Nemesis story with the Leda story; whether it is an invention of Cratinus' own one does not know, but would like to believe.[2]

In the fragments we find some one, whether Aphrodite or Hermes, giving Zeus the great idea: 'Well, you must become a large bird'—ὄρνιθα τοίνυν δεῖ σε γίγνεσθαι μέγαν.[3] After his metamorphosis the god (an amazing figure of fun, no doubt, like the comic fowls on the famous British Museum vase) is heard explaining that his appetite has changed with his shape: 'So that when at meals I enjoy the food, and everything in the garden is lovely to eat'.[4] In four lines [5] of pseudo-tragic diction Leda is commanded to complete the birth of Helen:

---

[1] What follows is a combination of Eratosthenes, *Catast.*, 25, and Hyginus, *Astron.*, VIII, p. 374.
[2] There is no hint anywhere that the combined version is earlier than Cratinus; and Eratosthenes ends his own version with the words ὥς φησι Κράτης (Κρατῖνος, Valckenär) ὁ ποιητής.
[3] Fr. 107.   [4] Fr. 109.   [5] Fr. 108.

Λήδα, σὸν ἔργον · δεῖ σ' ὅπως εὐσχήμονος
ἀλεκτρυόνος μηδὲν διοίσεις τοὺς τρόπους,
ἐπὶ τῷδ' ἐπῳζουσ', ὡς ἂν ἐκλέψῃς καλὸν
ἡμῖν τι καὶ θαυμαστὸν ἐκ τοῦδ' ὄρνεον.

'Leda, 'tis thy task to assume all the habits of a graceful hen, brooding on this egg, so that from it thou mayst hatch for us a fowl most wondrous fair.' Two allusions are found to Sparta, Leda's home, one [1] of them a pun on *spartinos*, which means "made of rope". With all this Pericles was in some way connected. Plutarch [2] writes that the comic poets ridiculed Pericles because of his abnormally long head, and that Cratinus in *Nemesis* wrote: μόλ', ὦ Ζεῦ ξένιε καὶ καραιέ. ('Come, O Zeus alien and headlong.') What, and how vital, was the connexion between Pericles and the legend is uncertain. But the comic playwrights were fond of joking about his relations with Aspasia, who is sometimes represented as a Hera to his Zeus. It is an excellent conjecture,[3] based partly on the word ξένιος ("alien") just quoted, partly on the complicated birth of Helen, Zeus' child, that the whole play was a skit on the family affairs of Pericles, who (having lost his legitimate sons) had proposed the abrogation of the bastardy law so that he might adopt the son born to him by Aspasia. If so, the play can be dated with certainty at 429 B.C.

The CHIRONS (Χείρωνες) seems to have been regarded by Cratinus himself as his finest play. At the close he wrote: [4]

ταῦτα δυοῖν ἐτέοιν ἡμῖν μόλις ἐξεπονήθη,

[1] Fr. 110. Cp. *Birds*, 814-16.
[2] *Pericles*, III. The MSS. give μακάριε or κάριε as the last word. These are variously emended into καραιέ and καράνιε (*quasi* κεραύνιε), in order to justify Plutarch's statement about the head. Jokes on this peculiarity of Pericles are frequent. Cp. in particular the notable fragment from Cratinus' *Thracian Women* (fr. 71) discussed below (pp. 134 *sq.*).
[3] See Kock (I, p. 49). Körte, however (*Jahresb. über Klass. Altertumsw.*, 152 (1911), 257, 8), points out that not Zeus and Helen, but Zeus and Heracles, are the appropriate subjects of such reference, and concludes that we cannot say what the connexion was between the *Nemesis* and Pericles.
[4] Fr. 237; Aristides, XLIX, 387. Cobet thought that the two years were those during which satire of contemporary persons was forbidden by Athenian law (μὴ ὀνομαστὶ κωμῳδεῖν. Cp. pp. 26 *sqq.*).

'this I hardly completed in two years,' adding a challenge to all other poets to do as well in the whole of their lives. Its theme was that favourite topic, the baseness of to-day contrasted with the noble past. In *Chirons*, however, the difference appears to have been political only.[1] These Chirons, who formed the chorus, were a multiplication of a single figure, the Centaur Chiron, famous for his immense knowledge and wisdom, which made him to Greek imagination a great instructor of youth. Early enough to be attributed to Hesiod, there existed a body of writing known as *Chiron's Maxims*, and it was as such mentors that the chorus appear:

σκῆψιν μὲν Χείρωνες ἐλήλυμεν, ὡς ὑποθήκας[2] . . .

The passage breaks off because Hephæstion, who quotes it, is not interested in the speech or the play, but only in the fact that Cratinus used ἐλήλυμεν for ἐληλύθαμεν. 'Ostensibly we Chirons have come so as to . . . maxims.' They have been summoned to give sage advice, but their real purpose is . . . it may have been horse-play, or a comic song, or almost anything else. The reason for invoking their aid was disgust with the Periclean *régime*. Somewhere occurred a lyrical parody of legend:[3]

Στάσις δὲ καὶ πρεσβυγενὴς Κρόνος ἀλλήλοισι μιγέντε
μέγιστον τίκτετον τύραννον,
ὃν δὴ κεφαληγερέταν θεοὶ καλέουσιν.

'Strife and primeval Cronos mingling together brought to birth a mighty monarch, him whom gods name the high-brow Jove.' For this Athenian Zeus a consort was provided:[4]

Ἥραν τέ οἱ Ἀσπασίαν τίκτει Καταπυγοσύνη
παλλακὴν κυνώπιδα,

---

[1] Not this play, but *Riches*, was the first of the comedies depicting the Athenian Golden Age of fantastic comfort. See below, p. 139.
[2] Fr. 235.
[3] Fr. 240: κεφεληγερέταν is a joke for νεφεληγερέταν, "cloud-gathering," the Homeric epithet of Zeus.
[4] Fr. 241. Κυνῶπις, 'with eyes like a dog's' (proverbial of shamelessness) is a parody of βοῶπις, the Homeric epithet of Hera.

'and to him (Cronos) Lewdness bare Hera-Aspasia, the concubine with the eyes of bitchery'. From the complaints against the rule of these deities comes apparently the phrase δωροδοκούντων αἲξ οὐρανία, 'the Horn of Plenty for bribe-takers':[1] this may be a general charge of corruption in politics, or may allude to Pericles' institution of payment for public services. That Strife is said to be his mother points to the bitter struggles—with Cimon, Thucydides, and others—by which he rose to primacy in Athens.

On the chance of remedying this corruption the malcontent (we are to suppose) summons Chiron, and finds his prayer lavishly answered by a whole squadron of cantering Centaurs, each bringing a battery of maxims. Later the malcontent (probably by their advice) determined to call up from the dead the one Athenian statesman who had been both wise and incorruptible—Solon himself. There followed a ceremony of incantation, containing the words:[2]

ἄγε δὴ πρὸς ἕω πρῶτον ἁπάντων ἴστω καὶ λάμβανε χερσὶν
σχῖνον μεγάλην.

'Come now, first of all turn towards the East and take in your hands a great squill.' This no doubt formed part of the ceremony whereby the ghost of Solon was raised from Hades.[3] He duly appeared, and we possess two lines from his opening speech:[4]

οἰκῶ δὲ νῆσον, ὡς μὲν ἀνθρώπων λόγος,
ἐσπαρμένος κατὰ πᾶσαν Αἴαντος πόλιν.

'And I dwell on an island, strewn (so at least men say) throughout the country of Ajax.' It was Solon's dying command that his ashes should be scattered over the island of Salamis. What part was taken by the great law-giver and patriot is not plain. Nor do we find what we should expect—quotations, exact or parodied, from Solon's work, at any rate among the remains of it that we possess, nor does any ancient

[1] Fr. 244.   [2] Fr. 232.
[3] It has, however, been thought part of an incantation against Pericles ὁ σχινοκέφαλος (*Thracian Women*, fr. 71).
[4] Fr. 228.

writer mention such passages; there is perhaps one scrap.[1] But it was almost certainly he who delivered a description of the innocence and happiness that marked an earlier generation of Athenians. Of their primitive ways we are told:[2]

> οἷς ἦν μέγιστος ὅρκος
> ἅπαντι λόγῳ κύων, ἔπειτα χήν, θεοὺς δ' ἐσίγων.

'Whose most solemn oath in any speech was the dog, then the goose: they named no god.' To this large-hearted simplicity the words ἐξ ἀσαμίνθου κύλικος λείβων[3] may apply: they appear to mean (as is appropriate to the wine-loving Cratinus) 'pouring libations from a goblet as big as a bath-tub'. This description of early bliss is reflected in a lyric of the chorus:[4]

> μακάριος ἦν ὁ πρὸ τοῦ βίος
> βροτοῖσι πρὸς τὰ νῦν, ὃν εἶχον ἄνδρες
> ἀγανόφρονες ἡδυλόγῳ σοφίᾳ βροτῶν περισσοκαλλεῖς.

'Blessed, compared with to-day, was the life of earlier mortals, which was lived by radiant-hearted men made wondrous fair by the charming voice of mortal wisdom.' A couple of lines[5] recall the gleaming loveliness wherewith Pindar[6] pictures the blessed who live at ease:

> ἁπαλὸν δὲ σισύμβριον ἢ ῥόδον ἢ κρίνον παρ' οὓς ἐθάκει·
> μετὰ χερσὶ δὲ μῆλον ἕκαστος ἔχων σκίπωνά τ' ἠγόραζον.

'The soft mint or rose or lily nestled beside their ear: with an apple and a staff in hand they haunted the piazza.' But, as was said, the outcome of Solon's reappearance on the scene of his reforms is unknown:

---

[1] Hesychius quotes the word αὐτόφορτοι as being used here: ὁ δὲ Κρατῖνος ἐν Χείρωνι (sic) τοὺς τὰ κοινὰ φορτιζομένους ἔφη (fr. 248). It ought not to mean that, as Kock points out. Possibly it is a reminiscence of the famous αὐτὸς κῆρυξ (Solon, fr. 1 Bergk), which means both 'auctioning off my own cargo' and 'myself the herald' (of our disgrace in Salamis).

[2] Fr. 231. Socrates' favourite oath, then, was extremely old-fashioned.

[3] Fr. 234.

[4] Fr. 238. It is hard to believe that Cratinus wrote βροτοῖσι, ἄνδρες, βροτῶν, all three; but no satisfactory emendation has been proposed.

[5] Fr. 239. I have printed what seems to give the best sense and scansion.

[6] Ol., II, 75 sqq.; fr. 95 (Boeckh).

there is one line[1] that seems to depict him doing justice upon wicked citizens:

καὶ πρῶτον μὲν παρὰ ναυτοδικῶν ἀπάγω τρία κνώδαλ' ἀναιδῆ,

'first I drag three shameless brutes from before the Naval Board'. The date of the *Chirons* lies in the last few years before the outbreak of the Peloponnesian War.[2]

ODYSSES ('Οδυσσῆς) is the plural of "Odysseus" with the meaning "Odysseus and his comrades". It was a merry burlesque of the Cyclops-episode in Homer; and, being concerned entirely with legend, is assigned to the period (439-7 B.C.) during which the licence of comedy was restricted by law. Platonius reports that this play had neither lyrics nor parabasis,[3] and that it contained censure of no one, only ridicule of the *Odyssey*.[4]

[1] Fr. 233. The ναυτοδίκαι acted as a grand jury in cases of alleged assumption of citizenship by aliens. If they found a "true bill," the case came before the Heliæa.

[2] Geissler (*Chronologie*, pp. 20 *sq*.) puts it later than 440 in view of Aspasia's notoriety, but earlier than 431 because there was apparently no mention of the war. Again, in view of "Morychides' decree," which stopped personal satire in 439-7, he puts it at 436-2.

[3] Kaibel, p. 4: τοιοῦτος οὖν ἐστὶν ὁ τῆς μέσης κωμῳδίας τύπος, οἷός ἐστιν ὁ Αἰολοσίκων Ἀριστοφάνους καὶ οἱ Ὀδυσσεῖς Κρατίνου, καὶ πλεῖστα τῶν παλαιῶν δραμάτων οὔτε χορικὰ οὔτε παραβάσεις ἔχοντα. Körte (Pauly-Wissowa, XXII, 1652) contradicts Platonius "because fragments 144 and 145 certainly come from choric songs, and frag. 146 probably from the parabasis". But there is nothing whatever to show that anapæsts were always sung: many of them were delivered in recitative; and fr. 144 being entirely in parœmiacs, an apparently unique arrangement (Hephæstion, 8, 8), we cannot assume either method of rendering. Fr. 145 may belong to the long anapæstic measure, or to the system of parœmiacs just mentioned, or the heroic hexameter (used elsewhere in 'Οδυσσῆς), which was certainly not sung, but chanted in recitative. Fr. 146 is so corrupt textually that it cannot be scanned at all. Kaibel (*Hermes*, XXX, 1895, p. 75) explains the text of Platonius quite differently. "The lack of a chorus (*i.e.* of choric songs) refers to the *Aiolosikon*, and the Middle Comedy; the 'Οδυσσῆς of Cratinus is quoted as an instance of non-political comedy, which had this in common with the *Aiolosikon*, that in both a literary travesty or parody took the place of political satire." The truth appears to be that there was of course a chorus, but not "lyrics" (χορικά) as Platonius says; nevertheless they chanted anapæsts. As to a parabasis, the only "proof" is the obscure and corrupt single line (?)

οὐκ ἰδίᾳ τάδ' οὐκ ἐτὸν θοι τἀπὶ Χαριξένης

(fr. 146) which to be sure, Kaibel (p. 81) writes thus:

οὐκ ἴδι' ἄττ', ἀλλ' οὐκέτ' ὄνθ' οἷα τἀπὶ Χαριξένης.

[4] Kaibel, p. 5: οἱ γοῦν Ὀδυσσεῖς Κρατίνου οὐδενὸς ἐπιτίμησιν ἔχουσι, διασυρμὸν δὲ τῆς Ὀδυσσείας τοῦ Ὁμήρου.

Though there were no choric songs, there was a chorus, the companions of Odysseus. These apparently opened the drama with the words :

σιγάν νυν ἅπας ἔχε σιγάν,
καὶ πάντα λόγον τάχα πεύσει·
ἡμῖν δ' Ἰθάκη πατρίς ἐστιν,
πλέομεν δ' ἅμ' Ὀδυσσέι θείῳ.

'Silence, now! Every one keep silence, and you shall learn the whole story. Our country is Ithaca, and we are at sea with glorious Odysseus.'[1] These brisk lines in unusual rhythm[2] are plainly the opening chant of the sailors, who may be supposed to enter the orchestra in a boat on rollers, like Charon in the *Frogs*. To this craft we may find an allusion in the phrase νεοχμόν τι παρῆχθαι ἄθυρμα: 'that a new-fangled toy has been brought along'.[3] These words are, however, usually explained[4] as "a new type of

[1] Fr. 144. It is held by Bergk (*Rel. Com. Att.*, p. 160), followed by Meineke (II, p. 100), Kock (*ad loc.*), Körte (Pauly-Wissowa, XXII, 1652) and Kaibel (*Hermes*, XXX, 1895, p. 81) that this passage belongs to the end. Kock's argument is amazing : " ad extremam fabulam haec chori verba pertinere docet Eurip. Cycl., 708-9". The real arguments are (i) that in Homer Odysseus' name is revealed only at the end ; (ii) that the singular πεύσει suggests an address to Polyphemus. But, as for (i) the revelation may have been to the audience ; and, for (ii), the singular πεύσει is explained by the singular ἔχε with ἅπας. Strong arguments for placing the passage at the opening are, that the whole tone of the first two lines suggests a prologue, and that πλέομεν, while quite unnatural to a sentence the only purpose of which is to reveal Noman's true name, does on the other hand fit a general preliminary announcement perfectly.
[2] They are all paroemiac anapaests (see pp. 373 *sq.*). [3] Fr. 145.
[4] So Meineke and Kock, who suggests as the final verse of the play :

ἡγεῖσθ' ἔξω · μετρίως δὲ δοκεῖ νεοχμόν τι παρῆχθαι ἄθυρμα,

which involves the gratuitous miracle that Aristophanes, in the last line of the *Clouds*, imitated the last line of Cratinus' *Odysses* without detection by his Scholiasts, Athenæus, or the lexicographers. As for the metre, Meineke says that Elmsley (on *Medea*, p. 268) was wrong in thinking these words part of an anapæstic tetrameter. He cannot possibly know this (see above, p. 129), but is misled by his desire to associate the passage with the σιγάν νυν fragment. Kaibel (*loc. cit.*, p. 81) also puts these words at the close, as part of the parabasis in which he believes, despite Platonius ; he agrees too that they mean a new kind of play. Of course ἄθυρμα could quite well be used of a literary or musical composition ; but it need not. The only argument (not very strong) in favour of the boat is the word παρῆχθαι—"brought along" (or even "alongside"). On the other hand, ἄθυρμα does not suit the boat, unless it were a "toy" or "delight," as indeed it may well have been, careering round the orchestra on rollers while Odysseus gazed at the Great Bear, no doubt in the wrong direction.

comedy," the poet being for a time debarred by law from the normal contemporary satire. But whether ἄθυρμα means the ship or not, there are plain allusions to the progress of the voyage—not only the direction : [1]

ἐπ' ἀριστέρ' ἀεὶ τὴν ἄρκτον ἔχων λάμπουσαν, ἕως ἂν ἐφεύρῃς . . .

'ever keeping on your left the radiant Bear, until you find . . .,' but also words [2] almost certainly uttered in presence of the audience by a man on the freak-ship :

τίνες αὖ πόντον κατέχουσ' αὖραι; νέφος οὐράνιον τόδ' ὁρῶμαι.

'What new breezes sweep the sea? Yonder I espy a cloud in the heavens.' This line, we know,[3] occurred very early in the play. The same scene no doubt contained the unusual rhythm of

ὡς ἂν μᾶλλον τοῖς πηδαλίοις ἡ ναῦς ἡμῖν πειθαρχῇ,

'so that our ship may more readily obey the steering-oars'.[4] All these lines clearly belong to the opening, where the Greeks approach Sicily and the home of Polyphemus.

In due course Odysseus offers wine to the Cyclops, with a delicious joke. Homer's story is that Polyphemus, after drinking, is so delighted that he asks the stranger his name and is told "Noman" (Οὖτις). So familiar is this to Cratinus and his hearers that Odysseus is ludicrously supposed equally familiar with it. 'Come now, take this wine; drink it at once, and straightway ask me my name' :

τῇ νῦν τόδε πῖθι λαβὼν ἤδη, καὶ τοὔνομά μ' εὐθὺς ἐρώτα.[5]

---

[1] Fr. 149. The words are a reminiscence of Calypso's instruction, *Od.*, V, 276 *sq.* In Cratinus they may well have been uttered by Odysseus on shipboard to his steersman.

[2] Fr. 138.

[3] Hephæstion (VIII, 5) says that Cratinus wrote it εἰς τοὺς Ὀδυσσέας εἰσβάλλων.

[4] Fr. 139. Hephæstion (*loc. cit.*) quotes it to show that in anapæstic tetrameters the penultimate foot may be a spondee.

[5] Fr. 141. Kock sees the joke, but others have laboured to make the passage "sensible," *e.g.* Herwerden: . . . λαβών. ἤσθη καὶ τοὔνομά μ' εὐθὺς ἐρωτᾷ. But Meineke (*ap.* Kock), in his startled recoil from Cratinus' absurdity, becomes funny over again by himself:

τῇ νῦν τόδε πῖθι λαβὼν ἤδη · μὴ τοὔνομά μ' εὐθὺς ἐρώτα.

The artless cannibal drinks and exclaims zestfully

οὔπω "πιον τοιοῦτον οὐδὲ πίομαι
Μάρωνα.¹

'Never did I, and never shall I, drink such—Maro.' Later, Polyphemus and his benefactor discuss Odysseus, doubtless because the Cyclops, knowing the prophecy that Odysseus shall blind him, is curious as to his enemy's whereabouts:

ΚΥΚ. πώποτ' εἶδες, εἰπέ μοι,
τὸν ἄνδρα;
ΟΔ. Λαέρτα φίλον παῖδ'; ἐν Πάρῳ,
σικυὸν μέγιστον σπερματιὰν ὠνούμενον.²

'*Cyc.* Tell me, have you ever seen the man? *Od.* Laertes' dear son? I saw him in Paros, buying a huge ripe pumpkin.' The casual tone of Odysseus is admirable. Welcker[3] suggests that Cratinus represents his hero as traversing the world in quest of delicious edibles.

When Polyphemus turns upon the Greeks it is perhaps only after he has given them (contrary to Homer) intentional hospitality:

ἧσθε πανημέριοι χορταζόμενοι γάλα λευκόν,
πυὸν δαινύμενοι, κἀμπιπλάμενοι πυριάτῃ.⁴

'Ye sat all day battening upon fresh milk, feasting on whey, gorging yourselves with beestings.' Certainly they appear to have offended him in some definite manner, to judge by the first words of his inevitable outbreak:[5]

ἀνθ' ὧν πάντας ἑλὼν ὑμᾶς ἐρίηρας ἑταίρους,
φρύξας, ἑψήσας, κἀπ' ἀνθρακιᾶς ὀπτήσας,
εἰς ἅλμην τε καὶ ὀξάλμην, κᾆτ' ἐς σκοροδάλμην
χλιαρὸν ἐμβάπτων, ὃς ἂν ὀπτότατός μοι ἁπάντων
ὑμῶν φαίνηται, κατατρώξομαι, ὦ στρατιῶται.

---

[1] Fr. 135. Maro is the man from whom Odysseus got the wine (*Od.*, IX, 196).

[2] Fr. 136.

[3] *Kleine Schriften*, I, 322. There is little beyond the present passage to support this charming theory. Still fr. 147 does mention 'a warm fillet of fish' (τέμαχος ὀρφὼ χλιαρόν) and fr. 148 'large sucking-pigs' (δέλφακας μεγάλους). Cp. the *Cyclopes* of Callias (fr. 5), τί γὰρ ἡ τρυφερὰ καὶ καλλιτράπεζος Ἰωνία εἴφ' ὅ τι πράσσει.

[4] Fr. 142.

[5] Fr. 143. Kock points out that ἐρίηρας ἑταίρους and στρατιῶται are no doubt ironical quotations from Odysseus.

'Wherefore, seizing all you trusty comrades, I shall roast you, boil you, bake you on coals, plunge you into brine and vinegar-brine and warm garlic-brine; and whichever of you strikes me as best cooked I shall devour, O soldiers.' One line depicts the panic of these unhappy guests—'Others are skulking under the beds':

ἄλλοι δ' ἀλυσκάζουσιν ὑπὸ ταῖς κλινίσιν.[1]

Perhaps a verse [2] of unknown authorship belongs to this comedy:

τίς δέ σ' ἐτύφλωσεν; τίς ἀφείλετο λαμπάδος αὐγάς;

'But who has blinded you? Who has taken away the beams of the lamp (*i.e.* your single eye)?' It would of course be the inquiry of the other Cyclopes,[3] and if so, we may believe in the theory [4] that this comedy had a double chorus, of twelve Greek sailors and twelve Cyclopes.

Much less is known about the THRACIAN WOMEN (Θρᾶσσαι), which contained allusions to contemporary politics, but was mostly concerned with the Athenian worship of that Thracian goddess, Bendis, whose all-night festival caused Socrates to visit Cephalus and engage in the most celebrated of his conversations.[5] Little is now to be read, however, concerning the religious or ceremonial element. We know from Hesychius [6] that Cratinus mentioned Bendis, giving her the epithet δίλογχος, that is " having two functions " —the heavenly and the infernal—" for they think the moon is Bendis and Artemis ". To Artemis as huntress the word ἀρκύωρος [7] may point, as it means " warden of the nets ". And Photius,[8] the lexicographer, quotes from this play the word κύβηβος, which he defines as 'possessed, dominated by, the mother of the gods'.

[1] Fr. 137.   [2] Fr. 150.   [3] Cp. *Od.*, IX, 403 *sqq.*
[4] Kaibel (*loc. cit.*). This able article contains some highly doubtful imaginings, as for example (p. 81) that Odysseus brought the hostile semi-chorus over to his side by a speech on the advantages of democracy.
[5] Plato, *Republic*, 354A.   [6] *s.v.* δίλογχον (fr. 80).   [7] Fr. 79.
[8] *s.v.* κύβηβος (fr. 82). Virgil (*Aen.*, X, 220) calls Cybele herself Cybebe.

The Bendidean element must have been large, since the play is named from the foreign worshippers who brought the cult to Athens and who may have provided even more noise than religion. Indeed a grave probability exists that these outlandish priestesses provided something between a revival-service and a jazz-band. For the word συρβηνεύς is quoted as from the *Thracian Women*, and a chorus of these was one 'in which each performer must sing whatever he is inclined to sing, paying no attention to the conductor'; it is also defined as 'persons who play the flute with uproar'. There is an anonymous line,

τυρβηνέων τι καινὸν ἐργαστήριον,

'a novel studio of jazz-singers,' which it is tempting to assign to our play.[1]

As for public affairs, we light upon a sparkling and important passage [2] about the usual victim:

ὁ σχινοκέφαλος Ζεὺς ὁδὶ προσέρχεται
Περικλέης, τᾠδεῖον ἐπὶ τοῦ κρανίου
ἔχων, ἐπειδὴ τοὔστρακον παροίχεται.

'Yonder comes our squill-headed Zeus, Pericles, wearing the Concert-Hall on his skull because the tiling has disappeared.' This is full of excellent matter which must have sent storms of laughter bellowing along the benches. Pericles is Zeus because virtual sovereign of Athens and the Empire, and squill-headed as afflicted with an elongated head. Sensitive about this deformity, he habitually wore a great helmet, for which the Concert-Hall is here substituted. It commemorated the overthrow of the Persian invaders, and, being built in imitation of Xerxes' state-marquee, had a dome which the lively Cratinus imagines as a hat suitable to the long-headed Attic Zeus. Of course, he must have some covering, because all the tiles have been blown away—or have blown over. It is a brilliant *double entente*. When the tiling is blown off a house, some new protection is needed, even if we have to

---

[1] For the whole wild business see Kock on fr. 84 (συρβηνεύς).
[2] Fr. 71.

steal a public building. And when the threat of ostracism, the tile-vote of censure, has blown over, can we wonder if the threatened statesman in his relief struts about town with our latest architecture instead of a hat?

Pericles escaped ostracism in 444, so that this comedy may be confidently dated at 443 or very soon after. Little else survives of which we can make anything. In the previous year Psammetichus, king of Egypt, had bestowed on the Athenians a great gift of corn and (apparently) of gold. Cratinus refers to attempted embezzlement of this:

ὅτι τοὺς κόρακας τἀξ Αἰγύπτου χρυσία κλέπτοντας ἔπαυσαν,[1]

'because they thwarted the crows that would steal the Egyptian gold plate'.

The ARCHILOCHI ('Ἀρχίλοχοι) seems to have been a highly important play: for instance it might have made more definite for us the relation between Cratinus and the only earlier poet known to have influenced him. The title apparently means "Archilochus and his friends". The date is fixed closely by the pathetic praise bestowed on Cimon, who must have died a little before: [2]

κἀγὼ γὰρ ηὔχουν Μητρόβιος ὁ γραμματεὺς
σὺν ἀνδρὶ θείῳ καὶ φιλοξενωτάτῳ
καὶ πάντ' ἀρίστῳ τῷ Πανελλήνων πρόμῳ
Κίμωνι λιπαρὸν γῆρας εὐωχούμενος
αἰῶνα πάντα συνδιατρίψειν. ὁ δὲ λιπὼν
βέβηκε πρότερος.

'For I, too, Metrobius the clerk, rejoiced in the prospect of spending all my life with Cimon, that glorious and most hospitable man, far the best chieftain of all Greece, passing a mellow old age amid good cheer. But he has left us and gone before.' Cimon died in camp before Citium in 449 B.C., so that this comedy probably belongs to 448. As for its subject, we know that a "swarm" of poets appeared: it

[1] Fr. 73. Meineke reads ἔπαυσεν, making an allusion in the parabasis to the poet's own services. The incident is mentioned by Pherecrates also in the Δουλοδιδάσκαλος (fr. 47).
[2] Fr. 1.

is probable that they were all epic (or at least hexameter) poets [1] and possible that they were hauled up out of Hades on a fisherman's hook like the philosophers in Lucian.[2] The title shows that mordant criticism abounded, Archilochus being proverbial for that : one fragment [3] mentions it :

εἶδες τὴν Θασίαν ἅλμην οἷ' ἄττα βαΰζει;
ὡς εὖ καὶ ταχέως ἀπετίσατο καὶ παραχρῆμα.
οὐ μέντοι παρὰ κωφὸν ὁ τυφλὸς ἔοικε λαλῆσαι.

'Did you notice how the Thasian brine-sauce cries aloud ? How well and rapidly and promptly he made reprisals ! But there is no likelihood of this being a blind man talking to the deaf.' Meineke [4] thinks that certain distinguished poets held a carnival of mutual detraction, thus all being named Archilochi.

In the LAWS (Νόμοι) it is almost certain that Solon, the lawgiver, appeared : the line [5]

ὑμῶν εἷς μὲν ἕκαστος ἀλώπηξ δωροδοκεῖται,

'each of you is a bribe-taking fox,' irresistibly recalls the famous warning against Peisistratus uttered by Solon to his countrymen :

ὑμέων δ' εἷς μὲν ἕκαστος ἀλώπεκος ἴχνεσι βαίνει.

It has been thought [6] that this play was a protest against the recent curtailment of the powers held by the Areopagus. However that may be, Meineke's [7] charming idea deserves applause, that in the line [8]

ἢ πρεσβῦται πάνυ γηράλεοι σκήπτροισιν ἄκασκα βιβῶντες,

'Verily as old men sorely stricken with years, moving gently forward with their staves ' . . . is meant a procession of decrepit Laws which forms the chorus.

---

[1] Diog. Laert., *Proem.*, XII : καὶ οἱ ποιηταὶ σοφισταί, καθὰ καὶ Κρατῖνος ἐν Ἀρχιλόχῳ (sic) τοὺς περὶ Ὅμηρον καὶ Ἡσίοδον ἐπαινῶν οὕτως καλεῖ.

[2] Fr. 2. οἷον σοφιστῶν σμῆνος ἀνεδιφήσατε. There is no proof that (as we might have expected) these ancients were pitted against contemporaries of Cratinus.

[3] Fr. 6. Thasos was Archilochus' home ; it was famous for its *sauce piquante*.

[4] II, p. 25.   [5] Fr. 128. Cp. Solon, fr. X, 6 (Bergk).
[6] Bergk (*Rell. Com. Att.*, p. 132).   [7] II, p. 89.   [8] Fr. 126.

We may imagine that Solon, their father, acted as their champion and comforter.

The EUNEIDÆ (Εὐνεῖδαι—a guild of cithara-players who performed the music at religious services) is said [1] to have been found beneath the pillow of Alexander the Great after his death. It was full of parodies,[2] among them that " Rule Britammany " of which Aristophanes [3] speaks. It contained one of the very few pathetic passages [4] that we know from Cratinus:

στένομεν μεμνημένοι
ἥβης ἐκείνης νοῦ τε τοῦδε καὶ φρενῶν,
ὅτι οὐ φιλοῦσί πως μετ' ἀλλήλων μένειν.

'We sigh to think of our distant youth and of our present shrewdness, that they refuse to dwell together.' Further, one of Cratinus' audacious compounds occurred in this work—ἀμφιανακτίζειν, ' to sing hymns that begin *Praise ye the Lord* '.[5] Nothing is known of the plot, but the title, the frequency of parody, and the phrase τέκτονες εὐπαλάμων ὕμνων [6] suggest that the *Euneidæ* treated of song-writers and their various styles, as the *Archilochi* of epic poets.

Of no other play written by Cratinus can we draw an outline, however faint. Let us then examine certain fragments grouped according to their subjects.

A good number throw light on theatrical history or the profession of a playwright. Some archon distinguished himself by refusing choruses both to Sophocles and to Cratinus. The later fact is attested by Hesychius; [7] as for the former, Cratinus writes of this archon in the HERDSMEN: [8]

ὃς οὐκ ἔδωκ' αἰτοῦντι Σοφοκλέει χορόν,
τῷ Κλεομάχου δ', ὃν οὐκ ἂν ἠξίουν ἐγὼ
ἐμοὶ διδάσκειν οὐδ' ἂν εἰς Ἀδώνια.

[1] Ptolemæus Hephæstio *ap.* Photius, *Bibl.*, 192, p. 151.
[2] Athenæus, XV, 689c.   [3] *Knights*, 529. See above, p. 115.
[4] Fr. 65. Kock suggests the above full version; but the last line is almost entirely his composition.
[5] The 'nomes' of Terpander regularly began with the words ἀμφί μοι αὖτις ἄνακτα or the like. Aristophanes, too, parodies this opening (*Clouds*, 598).
[6] Fr. 70. See *Knights*, 530, and p. 115 above.
[7] *s.v.* πυρπερέγχει.   [8] Fr. 15.

'Who refused Sophocles' request for a chorus, but gave one to Cleomachus' son,[1] whom I should think unfit to produce a play for me even at the feast of Adonis.' In another place [2] the ingenious poet contrives to combine, and no doubt infuriate, two of his most distinguished contemporaries in a single deadly word:

ὑπολεπτολόγος, γνωμοδιώκτης, εὐριπιδαριστοφανίζων.

'A subtle logic-chopping, epigram-chasing Euripidaristophanizer!' It is as if W. S. Gilbert had called some one an Ibsene-Pinero. Other passages deal vivaciously with the audience. They are apparently credited with good taste because they attend dramatic performances with the regularity of seasonal winds:

ἐτήσιοι γὰρ πρόσιτ᾽ ἀεὶ πρὸς τὴν τέχνην.[3]

But elsewhere he feels it necessary to bid them have all their wits about them and appreciate original work: [4]

ἀφυπνίζεσθαι χρὴ πάντα θεατὴν
ἀπὸ μὲν βλεφάρων αὐθημερινῶν ποιητῶν λῆρον ἀφέντα.

'Wake up, all you spectators, and shake from your eyelids the rubbish of ephemeral poets.' Cratinus, as we have had opportunity to observe, cherished no mean opinion of his own powers: another fragment about the audience justifies him—poetry, dignity, playfulness, all charmingly blent: [5]

χαῖρ᾽ ὦ μέγ᾽ ἀχρειογέλως ὅμιλε ταῖς ἐπίβδαις,
τῆς ἡμετέρας σοφίας κριτὴς ἄριστε πάντων·
εὐδαίμον᾽ ἔτικτέ σε μήτηρ ἰκρίων ψόφησις.

'Hail, ye throngs that laugh on the other side of your faces next morning, the world's best judges of my art: your mother, the thunder of the benches, bore you to happiness.' On another occasion, when defeated,

---

[1] Gnesippus, ridiculed in Cratinus' Ὧραι (fr. 256) as a tragic poet who used an effeminate chorus.
[2] Fr. 307. These notable words are reported by the Scholiast on Plato, *Apology*, 19c: Ἀριστοφάνης ... ἐκωμῳδεῖτο ἐπὶ τῷ σκώπτειν μὲν Εὐριπίδην, μιμεῖσθαι δ᾽ αὐτόν, κτέ.
[3] Fr. 23. [4] Fr. 306.
[5] Fr. 323. It is charming despite its obscurity, and only of genuine poetry can this ever be said. For the metre see p. 390.

he appears to have called the auditorium 'a sink of spectators'.[1] It was some such reverse that provoked an eloquently indignant address to his Muse :[2]

ὅτε σὺ τοὺς καλοὺς θριάμβους ἀναρύτουσ' ἀπηχθάνου.

'When thou didst meet disfavour though drawing from thy wells those fair dithyrambs.'

Next, it is convenient to assemble here certain examples of Cratinus' fertility of invention. CLEOBULINÆ, named after a famous composer of puzzles, seems to have depicted a number of women (Cleobulina and her friends) who propounded riddles. RICHES (Πλοῦτοι[3]) was important as the first example of a very favourite[4] type of comedy, which portrayed an imaginary Golden Age :

οἷς δὴ βασιλεὺς Κρόνος ἦν τὸ παλαιόν
ὅτε τοῖς ἄρτοις ἠστραγάλιζον, μᾶζαι δ' ἐν ταῖσι παλαίστραις
Αἰγιναῖαι κατεβέβληντο δρυπετεῖς βώλοις τε κομῶσαι.[5]

'Among whom Cronos was king of yore, when they used loaves for dice and the wrestling-schools were strewn with Æginetan cakes that fell from the trees and blossomed out of the sods.' Not only did Heaven send them up blessings (crops, etc.) without their labour—αὐτόματα τοῖσι θεὸς ἀνίει τἀγαθά[6]—but the most exquisite fish swam (or walked ?) up, introducing themselves by name to the pampered lieges of Cronos.[7] The MEN OF SERIPHOS (Σερίφιοι) dealt with an exploit of Perseus, who, by means of the Gorgon's head, turned into stone the whole island and

---

[1] Fr. 347. Photius says that Cratinus used the phrase Λέρνη θεατῶν in the sense κακὸν θέατρον. Hesychius says of Λέρνη θεατῶν : παροιμία τίς ἐστιν Ἀργολικὴ Λέρνη κακῶν . . . τὰ γὰρ ἀποκαθάρματα εἰς τοῦτο τὸ χωρίον ἐνέβαλλον.

[2] Fr. 36. This line comes from a play with the curious name Διδασκαλίαι —*Dramatic Productions*. Probably the play dealt entirely with recent dramatic history and contained comment on the poet's contemporaries and on his own career. Hesychius (*s.v.* πυρπερέγχει) tells us that the Βουκόλοι opened with a dithyramb.

[3] The point of the plural is uncertain.   [4] Athenæus, VI, 267e *sqq.*
[5] Fr. 165.   [6] Fr. 160.
[7] Fr. 161. The above seems the only way of explaining ἐγὼ γάρ εἰμι θυννὶς κτέ.

its inhabitants. The words αἶρε δεῦρο τοὺς βρικέλους,[1] 'raise hither the tragic masks,' suggest a ludicrously terrific scene in which Perseus directed the property-man to haul into view some dreadful mask already familiar to his audience from tragedy. The tale of Andromeda was introduced, for we learn that Cratinus called her " bait "[2] for the monster. Perseus in his journey through the air saw the City of Slaves, inhabited by villainous *nouveaux riches*.

A few delightful passages may be cited that have come down to us merely as metrical instances. The verse named after Cratinus himself is exemplified in an amusing blend of another man's line with words of Cratinus' own :

εὔιε κισσοχαῖτ' ἄναξ χαῖρ', ἔφασκ' Ἐκφαντίδης.[3]

'O Dionysus ivy-crowned, hail!—to quote Ecphantides.' The simple frolicking rhythm[4] has been developed into a rather befuddled but happily drunken roll, the effect of which is perhaps even more evident in another specimen—' this chorus can bear all, endure all ' :

πάντα φορητὰ πάντα τολμητὰ τῷδε τῷ χορῷ.[5]

One can almost see Cratinus' feet treading on one another. The Phalæcean is beautifully presented in this couplet :[6]

χαῖρ' ὦ χρυσόκερως βάβακτα κήλων
Πάν, Πελασγικὸν Ἄργος ἐμβατεύων.

'Hail, thou of the golden horns, revelling and lustful, Pan that hauntest Pelasgian Argos.'

As a last quotation let us take two lines,[7] from an unnamed comedy, which exhibit Cratinus' whimsical fancy, love of good cheer, and vigorous diction :

γαυριῶσαι δ' ἀναμένουσιν ὧδ' ἐπηγλαϊσμέναι
μείρακες φαιδραὶ τράπεζαι τρισκελεῖς σφενδάμνινοι.

---

[1] Fr. 205.   [2] Fr. 216 (δελέαστρα).
[3] Fr. 324. This is τὸ καλούμενον Κρατίνειον (Hephæstion, XV, 24). See below, p. 388.
[4] That is, the measure found in the first three words (εὔιε . . . ἄναξ) and used by Aristophanes in a lovely little song (*Knights*, 551 *sqq.*). See below, pp. 209, 388.
[5] Fr. 324.   [6] Fr. 321. See below, p. 389.   [7] Fr. 301.

'Here in wanton splendour await us radiant damsels —three-legged tables of maple-wood.'

A definite conception of Cratinus' spirit and work, save in one highly important particular, may be gained from the fragments that we have discussed. His only model appears to have been Archilochus, the great satirist, and his attacks were no less unsparing. Platonius writes : [1] 'Cratinus, the poet of the Old Comedy, is bitter in abuse, as being an imitator of Archilochus. Unlike Aristophanes, who avoids the vulgarity of invective by infusing charm into his gibes, he simply sets down his invective against offenders bald-headed, as the phrase goes.' That Cratinus is ruthless no one doubts ; but that he wrote with charm, even in full attack, is equally plain from our fragments. But for many generations the only feature of Old Comedy that struck readers was its frank invective. This was the effect of the Roman imperial *régime*. Nevertheless, Cratinus was regarded by all ancient scholars and critics as the first great comic playwright, Epicharmus being important in their eyes rather as a social satirist, " philosopher," and moralist. An interesting comment [2] describes him as 'very poetical, composing in the Æschylean manner,' a verdict probably founded on the satyric plays of Æschylus and justified even by their fragments—indeed, in a sense, by the tragedies also.

The exception referred to above is the dramaturgy of Cratinus, his power to construct plots, " drama " in the most exact sense. We possess in fact only one [3]

---

[1] Kaibel, p. 6 : Κρατῖνος, ὁ τῆς παλαιᾶς κωμῳδίας ποιητής, ἅτε δὴ κατὰ τὰς Ἀρχιλόχου ζηλώσεις, αὐστηρὸς μὲν ταῖς λοιδορίαις ἐστίν· οὐ γὰρ ὥσπερ Ἀριστοφάνης ἐπιτρέχειν τὴν χάριν τοῖς σκώμμασι ποιεῖ, τὸ φορτικὸν τῆς ἐπιτιμήσεως διὰ ταύτης ἀναιρῶν, ἀλλ' ἁπλῶς κατὰ τὴν παροιμίαν γυμνῇ τῇ κεφαλῇ τίθησι τὰς βλασφημίας κατὰ τῶν ἁμαρτανόντων. Later he is called πικρὸς λίαν and his vehemence (τὸ σφοδρὸν τοῦ Κρατίνου) is mentioned casually in a discussion of Eupolis, which shows that it was a familiar element in him.

[2] Anon. de Com. (Kaibel, p. 7) : γέγονε δὲ ποιητικώτατος, κατασκευάζων εἰς τὸν Αἰσχύλου χαρακτῆρα.

[3] The splendid passage (*Knights*, 526-36) already discussed has no bearing on this topic. Aristophanes in *Clouds*, 739-47, does indeed describe the contents of plays written by his predecessors, but it is impossible to apply the

ancient observation on his plot-technique. Platonius [1] writes: 'Though admirably inventive in the opening and scheme of his plays, he rends his plots to pieces as he goes on, and fills up his plays with inconsequent matter'. On general grounds this is precisely what we should have expected. We know that comedy arose in Sicily from scattered scenes which Epicharmus welded together.[2] We know also that most of Aristophanes' plays show strictly dramatic development only in the first half, the second being composed of little rudimentary scenes demonstrating the point and value of the comic achievement performed by the protagonist.[3] Cratinus, who lies chronologically between Epicharmus and Aristophanes, was practically certain not to have constructed comedies analogous in technique to the *Œdipus Tyrannus* or even the *Prometheus*. But this neat and satisfying theory is sorely menaced, if not destroyed, by the epoch-making discovery of the Argument to the *Dionysalexandros*. Our information reveals a play surpassing in structural excellence every known work of Aristophanes except the *Thesmophoriazusæ* and thus flatly contradicting Platonius. Further, it is fairly clear that the *Odysses* was of the same type; but there was little proof in it of Cratinus' constructive skill, as he followed the main lines of the Homeric story. Concerning the *Wine Flask* we cannot say much under this head,[4] and nothing at all of the

description to Cratinus' work, whether Aristophanes wishes us to do so or not. The passage is true only of "Megarian" comedy (whether written by Megarians or by Athenians): it is absurdly untrue of the man who composed *Nemesis*, *Dionysalexandros*, and the *Wine-Flask*. The Scholiast on *Peace*, 740, reports that 'some say he is hinting at Cratinus as author of such plays' (τινὲς δέ φασιν εἰς Κρατῖνον αἰνίττεσθαι, ὡς τοιαῦτα ποιοῦντα δράματα). We cannot, of course, in the present state of our knowledge, deny that Cratinus may have written such "slapstick" farce in his early days.

[1] Kaibel, p. 6: εὔστοχος δὲ ὢν ἐν ταῖς ἐπιβολαῖς τῶν δραμάτων καὶ διασκευαῖς, εἶτα προϊὼν καὶ διασπῶν τὰς ὑποθέσεις οὐκ ἀκολούθως πληροῖ τὰ δράματα.
[2] See above, pp. 84, 110.   [3] See below, pp. 299, 302 sq.
[4] What we are told of the plot suggests (when we remember Aristophanes) that the conversion of Cratinus occurred about the middle of the action, to be followed by scenes depicting his success as a reformed character. This is only a guess: it has no other support than the fact that the reported details do not seem enough to fill a play.

CRATINUS

other plays. But the *Dionysalexandros* is an unmistakable and impressive proof that Platonius has given a report erroneous or (at least) too sweeping. Yet he no doubt derives his brief summary from the work of real critics like Didymus, who had Cratinus' whole work before him.

The facts are probably as follows. Epicharmus did influence Attic comedy, but Cratinus was not among those influenced. The first playwright so affected was Crates, who composed social comedy on the model afforded by Epicharmus' *Hope or Wealth*, *Plunder*, *The Pilgrims*, *The Woman of Megara*. Cratinus seems to have been independent of all this. His only literary precursor was Archilochus, a very great but entirely non-dramatic poet. As for drama, all that Cratinus found available for his instruction was tragedy, and the crude genuinely Attic comedy practised by Chionides and Magnes. In these circumstances his early work naturally would be precisely what Platonius describes it as being. Gradually by his own genius and (it is surely impossible to doubt) by the example of the tragedians, among whom Æschylus was of most profit to him, he worked his way to a complete structural technique: the *Dionysalexandros*, written when Cratinus was at least fifty-five, proves this beyond question.

As regards three factors in dramatic composition, literary style, theme, and plot-construction, the achievement of Cratinus was remarkable. Late in his life (as we have just seen) he became the first man who ever wrote a fully constructed comedy. As for theme, he originated political comedy, though his work in this respect was perhaps rudimentary. The "bald-headed" onslaughts of which Platonius speaks were invectives against private individuals: this seems certain from the indirectness of political satire which marked his latest work.[1] A more specific theme which

---

[1] Even the notable gibe at Pericles in the *Thracian Women* may have been only incidental; and that play belongs to Cratinus' middle period.

he introduced (in his Πλοῦτοι) was the Golden Age of fantastic material prosperity. Again, so far as we can see, the Old Comedy owes its literary manner to Cratinus: the rich vigour, the poetical power, the zestful fun, the command of idiom, are all exemplified even in our fragments. Horace's remark,[1] that Lucilius is "entirely derived" from Athenian Old Comedy, becomes less surprising as we ponder the earliest of its great exponents. Cratinus is the Falstaff of Greek literature: a rich jovial personality [2] glows from every isolated line that the metrician or the dictionary-maker has flung to us. He offers a superb blend of great intellect and uproarious good-humour; and after the *Knights* appeared he could say with Sir John: "I am not only witty in myself, but the cause that wit is in other men".

[1] *Sat.*, I, iv, 6: *hinc omnis pendet Lucilius.*
[2] Cp. *Frogs*, 357: Κρατίνου τοῦ ταυροφάγου γλώττης βακχεῖ' ἐτελέσθη, and Tucker's admirable remarks.

CHAPTER IV

THE SCHOOL OF CRATES

§ 1. Crates

THE eminence of Crates receives impressive testimony from two illustrious writers and critics. Aristophanes, in that famous parabasis where he describes the cruelty of the Athenian public to his predecessors, writes thus [1] concerning Crates:

οἴας δὲ Κράτης ὀργὰς ὑμῶν ἠνέσχετο καὶ στυφελιγμούς,
ὃς ἀπὸ σμικρᾶς δαπάνης ὑμᾶς ἀριστίζων ἀπέπεμπεν,
ἀπὸ κραμβοτάτου στόματος μάττων ἀστειοτάτας ἐπινοίας·
χοῦτος μέντοι μόνος ἀντήρκει, τοτὲ μὲν πίπτων τοτὲ δ' οὐχί.

'What bad tempers, what outrages, Crates endured from you!—he who with small expense gave you lunch before he sent you home, kneading up the wittiest ideas by aid of a fastidious style. Nevertheless, he, too, pursued a career of mingled failure and success, the only man of them to hold out.' Aristotle, after mentioning the plot-work of Epicharmus and Phormis, goes on: [2] 'At Athens, Crates was the first to relinquish the lampoon-form and compose stories or plots of general application'. In a later age the Anonymus writes: [3] 'Crates of Athens. This man, they say, began as an actor. He succeeded Cratinus, was extremely funny and gay, and was the first to

---
[1] *Knights*, 537-40.
[2] *Poetic*, 1449b, 7: τῶν δὲ Ἀθήνησι Κράτης πρῶτος ἦρξεν ἀφέμενος τῆς ἰαμβικῆς ἰδέας καθόλου ποιεῖν λόγους καὶ μύθους.
[3] Kaibel, p. 7: Κράτης Ἀθηναῖος, τοῦτον ὑποκριτὴν φασι γεγονέναι τὸ πρῶτον, ὃς ἐπεβέβληκε Κρατίνῳ, πάνυ γελοῖος καὶ ἱλαρὸς γενόμενος, καὶ πρῶτος μεθύοντας ἐν κωμῳδίᾳ προήγαγε. τούτου δράματά ἐστιν ἑπτά.

introduce drunken persons into comedy. There are seven plays by him.' The Scholiast on the Aristophanic passage says: ' He was a poet of comedy, who first acted Cratinus' plays, and later became a poet himself'. Suidas reports: ' Crates of Athens, a comic playwright whose brother was Epilycus, an epic poet. There are seven[1] plays of his: Γείτονες (*Neighbours*), Ἥρωες (*Heroes*), Θηρία (*Wild Beasts*), Λάμια (*Goblin*), Πεδῆται (no doubt a mistake for Παιδιαί, *Games*), Σάμιοι (*Samians*). He wrote also certain prose works.' ' Crates of Athens, another[2] comic playwright, also belonging to the Old Comedy. Three plays of his are in circulation: Θησαυρός (*Treasure*), Ὄρνιθες (*Birds*), Φιλάργυρος (*Miser*).'

Aristotle's statement might seem to imply that Crates was earlier than Cratinus, since the latter, too, composed plots. But the later tradition clearly holds Crates for a successor of Cratinus, and Aristophanes, by mentioning him later, must surely mean that he was Cratinus' junior. The probable explanation is that, although the Sicilians and Cratinus and Crates all constructed plots, Crates innovated by diverging from Cratinus' method (which was to write comedies against specific persons)[3] and composing plays of general application: he is influenced by Epicharmus and prepares the way for the Comedy of Manners.

The description given in the *Knights* refers mostly to style. Aristophanes' word ἐπινοίας (" ideas ") may point to his plots, but could mean incidental dexterities of character-drawing or literary " conceptions " such as epigrams. In any case the passage shows that there existed between Cratinus and Crates as great a

---

[1] One title is lost from the list that follows, probably Τόλμαι.
[2] The two Cratetes are a mistake of Suidas. But we must not necessarily attribute the three last plays to our Crates. Θησαυρός and Φιλάργυρος look like Middle or New titles; the Ὄρνιθες (of which no fragments survive) is thought by Meineke (I, p. 64) to have been a recension of Magnes' play. The prose works are probably those of Crates, the philosopher and tragic poet.
[3] This is the meaning of ἰαμβικὴ ἰδέα: there is no direct reference to the iambic metre, but to the lampoons for which that metre was at first exclusively employed.

THE SCHOOL OF CRATES

difference in style as Aristotle shows there was in plot. The word ἀστειοτάτας means the height of wit, a perfect urbanity; and the phrase κραμβότατον στόμα is an excellent Attic rendering of what we call "the classical manner in literature". Crates is in this respect the forerunner of Middle and New Comedy, and also in his avoidance of verbal indecency.[1]

Tradition assigns him to Cratinus as an actor of his plays, but study of Epicharmean social comedy led him into revolt against his great instructor. Crates' adherence to the restrained and elegant manner had the natural but, for us, melancholy result that he was not quotable, and so was rarely quoted. The dates of his career, if not of his life, can be determined with fair accuracy. From Eusebius[2] we learn that he 'came into notice' in 450 B.C., no doubt the date of his first production. He was clearly dead by the time (424 B.C.) Aristophanes wrote of him in the *Knights*. The number of his plays is put at eight by Meineke.[3] He won at least three victories.[4] Nothing else is really known about him.[5]

The only play of Crates concerning which we possess substantial information is the BEASTS (Θηρία). Athenæus[6] mentions it as second in time to the *Riches* of Cratinus in his list of extracts from Old Comedy dealing with "the ancient life," and shows that the play contained two disputants, each putting forward his view or claim:

---

[1] In a recently-discovered fragment (Demiańczuk, p. 29) there is a modest little cough: ἡδὺ γὰρ κἀκεῖνο τὸ δρᾶν, λέγεσθαι δ'οὐ καλόν. Cp. Philemon, fr. 126: ἀλλ' αἰσχύνομαι λέγειν, κτέ.

[2] In Jerome's version (II, 105, Schoene).

[3] I, p. 64. Fifteen titles are to be found in Kock, some being of very doubtful authenticity.

[4] At the Lenæa (cp. Wilhelm, *Urkunden*, 123). We do not know how he fared at the City Dionysia.

[5] The Scholiast on Aristophanes (*loc. cit.*) says: ἐξεωνεῖτο τοὺς θεατὰς καὶ τὴν τούτων εὔνοιαν, which is no doubt derived from the gibe of some rival, that he threw nuts and the like among the spectators, a practice of which we read several times in Aristophanes.

[6] VI, 267e.

A. ἔπειτα δοῦλον οὐδὲ εἷς κεκτήσετ' οὐδὲ δούλην,
   ἀλλ' αὑτὸς αὑτῷ δῆτ' ἀνὴρ γέρων διακονήσει;
B. οὐ δῆθ'· ὁδοιποροῦντα γὰρ τὰ πάντ' ἐγὼ ποιήσω,
A. τί δῆτα τοῦτ' αὐτοῖς πλέον;
B.   πρόσεισιν αὖθ' ἕκαστον
   τῶν σκευαρίων ὅταν καλῇ τι. παρατίθου τράπεζα.
   αὕτη παρασκεύαζε σαυτήν. μάττε, θυλάκισκε.
   ἔγχει, κύαθε. ποῦσθ' ἡ κύλιξ; διάνιζ' ἰοῦσα σαυτήν.
   ἀνάβαινε, μᾶζα. τὴν χύτραν χρῆν ἐξερᾶν τὰ τεῦτλα.
   ἰχθύ, βάδιζ'. ἀλλ' οὐδέπω 'πὶ θάτερ' ὀπτός εἰμι.
   οὔκουν μεταστρέψας σεαυτὸν ἁλὶ πάσεις ἀλείφων.[1]

'What, shall no one possess a male or female slave? Shall an aged man have to wait on himself?' 'Certainly not; I will cause everything to walk.' 'And what good will that do them?' 'Each of the utensils will come up of itself when he calls it. "Get into position, Table. Come now, lay yourself. Trough, begin kneading. Pour in, Ladle." Where is the Cup? "Be off and rinse yourself. Cake, climb on the table." The Jug ought to have poured out the beetroot. "Fish, come along. 'But I'm not fried on the other side yet.' Well, turn yourself over and sprinkle yourself with salt and oil."'

Next, the speaker's rival is heard:[2]

ἀλλ' ἀντίθες τοι· ἐγὼ γὰρ αὐτὰ πάμπαλιν
τὰ θερμὰ λουτρὰ πρῶτον ἄξω τοῖς ἐμοῖς
ἐπὶ κιόνων ὥσπερ διὰ τοῦ παιωνίου
ἐπὶ τῆς θαλάττης, ὥσθ' ἑκάστῳ ῥεύσεται
εἰς τὴν πύελον, ἐρεῖ δὲ θὔδωρ 'ἀνέχετε'.
ἔπειτ' ἀλάβαστος εὐθέως ἥξει μύρου
αὐτόματος, ὁ σπόγγος τε καὶ τὰ σάνδαλα.

---

[1] Fr. 14.

[2] Fr. 15. An interesting but difficult passage. Note first the perhaps unparalleled crasis of two words separated by a pause—τοι ἐγώ pronounced as τοὐγώ. τόδ'· ἐγώ has been suggested, and may serve. ἐπὶ κιόνων means an aqueduct, as rare among Greeks as common among Romans. τὸ παιώνιον ("healing-place") was no doubt a hospital, but this is the only extant mention of one at this time in Athens. ἐπὶ τῆς θαλάττης is not understood by Meineke or Kock, who appear to take it as indicating that the hospital was in the Piræus. A pretty piece of topography! What Londoner, if he meant "I am going to Greenwich Hospital" would say "I am making for the sea"? Θάλαττα probably means a "tank". The evidence is not strong, but the remarks of Verrall (*Agamemnon*, ed. 2, pp. 217 *sq.*) may be reinforced by Herodotus, VIII, 55, where we learn that the pool of salt-water on the Acropolis was called Θάλασσα. The fifth line is well explained by Kock "ipsa aqua alveo repleto dicet *inhibete aquam*".

THE SCHOOL OF CRATES

'Now mark the contrast. I for my part will first bring my friends the hot bath-water itself into the tank on pillars as at the hospital, so that it shall flow into the bath-tub for each person; and the water shall say "when!" Next, a jar of ointment shall instantly arrive of itself, accompanied by the sponge and slippers.'

The two disputants are perhaps allegorical. What is the point of their dispute? It is easy to reply that " one of them recommends a life of luxury and ease, the other a simple life in accordance with natural laws";[1] but quite wrong, for two reasons. For, strangely enough, the " disputants " agree (so far as our fragments extend): both alike depict a condition of life in which comforts will be automatically provided. In fact, had we not Athenæus' clear testimony, we could imagine most of the second passage as being (save for the metre) a continuation of the first. The other objection is that neither describes a life of archaic simplicity, but a world in which all contemporary comforts find a place, being, however, provided with miraculous promptness and efficiency. No one would believe in a debate comparable to that of the Just and Unjust Arguments in the *Clouds*, were it not that Athenæus introduces the second passage thus:[2] ' Immediately thereupon the person who espouses the contrary argument says . . .' The opposition must lie between two competing methods of securing a condition which both agree is desirable: a miraculous *confort moderne*.

This play is called *Beasts* because talking animals took an important share in it. Apparently they formed the chorus, and we possess a passage[3] in which their champion urges men to abstain from a meat diet:

A. καὶ τῶν ῥαφάνων ἕψειν χρὴ . . .
ἰχθῦς τ' ὀπτᾶν τούς τε ταρίχους, ἡμῶν δ' ἀπὸ χεῖρας ἔχεσθαι.
B. οὐκ ἄρ' ἔτ' οὐδὲν κρέας, ὡς ὑμεῖς λέγετ', οὐδ' ὁτιοῦν ἐδόμεσθα,
οὐδ' ἔτι χορδὰς οὐδέ τάκωνας ποιησόμεθ' οὐδ' ἀλλᾶντας;

[1] Meineke, II, p. 237.   [2] VI, 268a.   [3] Fr. 17.

'And you ought to boil radishes . . . fry fish and kippers, and keep your hands off us.' ' So we shall eat, according to your programme, not a scrap of meat any more, and not even get ourselves tripe or rissoles or sausages ? '

Outside the *Beasts* there is little of interest. In the Neighbours (Γείτονες) Crates introduced drunken men to the comic stage of Athens. A passage [1] from the Samians may be quoted for its wildly mysterious matter and the attractive though still cryptic vigour of its close :

σκυτίνη ποτ' ἐν χύτρᾳ τάριχος ἐλεφάντινον
ἧψε ποντιὰς χελώνη πευκίνοισι κύμασιν,
κάρκινοι ποδάνεμοί τε καὶ τανύπτεροι λύκοι
ὑσοριμαχεῖν ἄνδρες οὐρανοῦ καττύματα.
παῖ' ἐκεῖνον, ἄγχ' ἐκεῖνον. ἐν Κέῳ τίς ἡμέρα;

' Once upon a time the sea-tortoise fired an ivory kipper with pine-waves in a leather jug. Crabs, fleet as the wind, and long-feathered wolves . . . the soles of Heaven. Hit him! Choke him! What day is it in Ceos ? ' It is comforting to find that Aristophanes understood this : in the second version of the *Thesmophoriazusæ* [2] he alluded to the ivory kipper with envious delight. The Games (Παιδιαί) has been thought [3] to have had a chorus, each member of which represented a different sport ; we have a fragment which refers to a kissing-game. Among the untitled extracts occurs the line : [4]

ἀλλὰ σικύαν ποτιβαλῶ τοι, κἄν τὺ λῇς, ἀποσχάσω.

' But I will put a cupping-iron on you, and if you wish I will cut a vein.' It is Doric Greek. Our physicians use Latin, the Roman physicians used Greek, Athenian physicians used a non-Attic dialect.

§ 2. Phrynichus

This playwright, though an Athenian, was alleged by his rivals to be of foreign birth.[5] Phrynichus'

---

[1] Fr. 29. In the fourth line ὑσοριμαχεῖν (if nothing else) is corrupt. The τάριχος ἐλεφάντινον is possibly an oyster.
[2] Fr. 333.   [3] Bergk, *Rell. Com. Att.*, 131.
[4] Fr. 41.   [5] Schol., *Frogs*, 14.

THE SCHOOL OF CRATES

début was in 429 B.C.;[1] the latest date in his career that we can be sure of is 405 B.C., when he presented the *Muses*. He wrote ten plays, all the titles of which are known; but whether he ever won the first prize we cannot say, unless it is true that he was the real author of the *Revellers* produced by Ameipsias.

The longest fragment[2] comes from EPHIALTES (Ἐφιάλτης, " nightmare " or " incubus ") :

ἔστιν δ' αὐτούς γε φυλάττεσθαι τῶν νῦν χαλεπώτατον ἔργον.
ἔχουσι γάρ τι κέντρον ἐν τοῖς δακτύλοις,
   μισάνθρωπον ἄνθος ἥβης·
εἶθ' ἡδυλογοῦσιν ἅπασιν ἀεὶ κατὰ τὴν ἀγορὰν περιόντες.
ἐπὶ τοῖς δὲ βάθροις ὅταν ὦσιν, ἐκεῖ τούτοις, οἷς ἡδυλογοῦσιν,
μεγάλας ἀμυχὰς καταμύξαντες καὶ συγκύψαντες ἅπαντες
   γελῶσιν.

'To protect oneself from them is the most difficult task of the present day, for they have a sting in their fingers, the heartless charm of youthful beauty. Then they flirt with every one incessantly as they walk up and down the market-place; but when they get on the benches, after inflicting great scratches, they all put their heads together and laugh at those whom they beguile.' It is a terribly vivid bit of observation. Apparently the Ephialtes of this play is the inhuman lovely young person—the " vampire " of our more melodramatic literature—who tears at men's hearts and derides their agony.[3] This is a needed footnote to Plato's *Symposium* and *Charmides*.

Concerning the HERMIT (Μονότροπος) we possess some scraps of fact. From its title one gathers that it was a character play : no other " Old " example is

---

[1] Suidas, *s.v.* Φρύνιχος, writes : κωμικὸς τῶν ἐπιδευτέρων τῆς ἀρχαίας κωμῳδίας. ἐδίδαξε γοῦν ἐπὶ τῆς πϛ' Ὀλυμπιάδος. That is, his career began in 435-2 B.C. (ἐπιδευτέρων refers to date : cp. γοῦν). But this is probably wrong. From the Anonymus (Kaibel, p. 8) we learn that Eupolis' first play appeared in 429 B.C., and that Phrynichus began in the same year as Eupolis.

[2] Fr. 3. περιόντες is a variant form of περιιόντες. The triple - αντες at the end is ugly.

[3] Kaibel, however (*Hermes*, XXIV, 1889, 35 *sqq.*), identifies these people with Phrynichus' own rivals in comic drama. There is no evidence whatever for this, unless we are (with Kaibel) to take βάθρα as "the stage". The word is never so used elsewhere, but means "benches"—whether in the theatre or not.

known. It obtained the third prize in 414 B.C., when Ameipsias[1] was first with the *Revellers* and Aristophanes second with the *Birds*. Meton, the celebrated mathematician, who, in the *Birds*, offers to " town-plan " the cloud-city, is mentioned[2] as a hydraulic engineer:

> A. τίς δ' ἐστὶν ὁ μετὰ ταῦτα φροντίζων;
> B.   Μέτων
>   ὁ Λευκονοιεύς.
> A.   οἶδ'· ὁ τὰς κρήνας ἄγων.

'Who is the next thinker?'[3] 'Meton of Leuconea.' 'I know: the man who guides the well-water.' Nicias, too, is mentioned, in language[4] that implies he is the first engineer of the day:

> ἀλλ' ὑπερβέβληκε πολὺ τὸν Νικίαν
> στρατηγίας πλήθει τε κἀξευρήμασιν.

'Why, he surpasses Nicias in the number of commands he has held, and in his inventions.' Syracosius, too, came in for comment.[5]

The MUSES contained what is now the most familiar fragment[6] of Phrynichus:

> μάκαρ Σοφοκλέης, ὃς πολὺν χρόνον βιοὺς
> ἀπέθανεν, εὐδαίμων ἀνὴρ καὶ δεξιός,
> πολλὰς ποιήσας καὶ καλὰς τραγῳδίας
> καλῶς δ' ἐτελεύτησ'· οὐδὲν ὑπομείνας κακόν.

'Blessed is Sophocles, who passed so many years before his death, a happy man and brilliant, who wrote many beautiful tragedies and made a beautiful end of a life that knew no misfortune.' Meineke[7] held that this comedy portrayed a contest (perhaps between Sophocles and Euripides) for the primacy in poetry, with the

---

[1] As Phrynichus also wrote a Κωμασταί, it has been thought that there was but one such play, written by Phrynichus but produced under the name of Ameipsias, because of a law forbidding any comic dramatist to compete with more than one piece. The *Connos* of Ameipsias has also been attributed to him.
[2] Fr. 21.   [3] The Greek is probably corrupt.
[4] Meineke, p. 589; Kock, fr. 22. Cp. *Birds*, 363.
[5] Schol., *Birds*, 1297. See above, pp. 27 sq.
[6] Fr. 31.   [7] I, p. 157.

Muses as judges. The only support for this lies in the allusion [1] to a trial :

> ἰδού, δέχου τὴν ψῆφον· ὁ κάδισκος δέ σοι
> ὁ μὲν καταλύων οὗτος, ὁ δ' ἀπολλὺς ὁδί.

'See, take your voting-pebble. This is the urn for acquittal, this for destruction.' It is likely enough that another eulogy [2] of Sophocles belongs to this drama :

> οὐ γλύξις οὐδ' ὑπόχυτος, ἀλλὰ Πράμνιος.

This play obtained the second prize in 405 B.C., when Aristophanes was first with the *Frogs* and Plato third with the *Cleophon*.

Among the citations from unnamed dramas we find an amusing reference to the Mutilation of the Hermæ :

> A. ὦ φίλταθ' Ἑρμῆ, καὶ φυλάττου, μὴ πεσὼν
> σαυτὸν παρακρούσῃ καὶ παράσχῃς διαβολὴν
> ἑτέρῳ Διοκλείδᾳ βουλομένῳ κακόν τι δρᾶν.
> ΕΡΜ. φυλάξομαι, Τεύκρῳ γὰρ οὐχὶ βούλομαι
> μήνυτρα δοῦναι τῷ παλαμναίῳ ξένῳ.

'(Farewell?) beloved Hermes: mind you don't fall and injure yourself, thus providing slander for some new Diocleidas bent on harm.' 'Yes, I'll be careful: I don't wish to give blood-money to that accursed foreigner, Teucrus.' [3]

Finally, we learn from the *Clouds* that Phrynichus composed a comedy (the title is unknown) in which a drunken old woman travestied Andromeda and was eaten by the sea-monster. The crispness of Aristophanes' language [4] awakens lively regret that we have not so much as a word left from Phrynichus' own rendering of this spirited concept :

> Εὔπολις μὲν τὸν Μαρικᾶν πρώτιστον παρείλκυσεν,
> ἐκστρέψας τοὺς ἡμετέρους Ἱππέας κακὸς κακῶς,
> προσθεὶς αὐτῷ γραῦν μεθύσην τοῦ κόρδακος εἴνεχ', ἣν
> Φρύνιχος πάλαι πεποίηχ', ἣν τὸ κῆτος ἤσθιεν.

Eupolis 'dragged in for the sake of the *cordax*[5] a drunken hag whom Phrynichus used ages ago, her whom the

[1] Fr. 32. [2] Fr. 65. It alludes to various brands of wine.
[3] Fr. 58. [4] *Clouds*, 549 *sqq*. [5] An indecent dance.

monster ate'. The imperfect tense ἤσθιεν may mean "was for eating," which suggests repeated rushes of the reptile and correspondent shrieking recoils of the woman (perhaps a *cordax à deux*), continued so long as the audience cheered; or it may mean "was eating," which implies slow and difficult deglutition while the victim performed the *cordax* with her disengaged portion.

It is plain that we possess at present materials insufficient for a full judgment on Phrynichus. Ancient opinion was diverse. The Anonymus calls him 'one of the most notable' among the old comic playwrights.[1] Aristophanes derides him, together with Lycis and Ameipsias, as a composer of trite vulgarities;[2] but the Scholiast notes that 'nothing of this kind is to be found in the extant comedies, though it is likely that examples occurred in the lost plays'. The same writer reports that Phrynichus 'is ridiculed for the mediocrity of his poems, for plagiarism, and for an imperfect ear'. These charges are probably quoted from the comedies of Phrynichus' rivals. Didymus of Alexandria thought it worth while to write a commentary on his work, at least on the *Cronos*. One surmises that Phrynichus was a sound humdrum comic poet of Ben Jonson's calibre.

§ 3. PHERECRATES

Of this poet the Anonymus writes a notice unfortunately corrupt. 'Pherecrates of Athens was victorious in the archonship of Theodorus (?) and emulated Crates, whose actor he was. Further, he refrained from abuse, and gained a reputation for introducing new topics, showing himself fertile in plots.'[3] The number of plays is given by Suidas as

[1] Anon., *de Com.* (Kaibel, p. 7). The ἀξιολογώτατοι are Epicharmus, Magnes, Cratinus, Crates, Pherecrates, Phrynichus, Eupolis, Aristophanes.
[2] *Frogs*, 1-18.
[3] Anon., *de Com.* (Kaibel, p. 8): Φερεκράτης Ἀθηναῖος· νικᾷ ἐπὶ Θεάτρου. γενόμενος δὲ ὑποκριτὴς ἐζήλωκε Κράτητα καὶ αὖ τοῦ μὲν λοιδορεῖν ἀπέστη, πράγματα δὲ εἰσηγούμενος καινὰ ηὐδοκίμει γενόμενος εὑρετικὸς μύθων. The first sentence has been emended by Dobree: νικᾷ ἐπὶ Θεοδώρου—that is, 437 B.C. Capps (*American Journal of Philology*, 28, pp. 197 *sq.*) would read ἐπὶ Πυθοδώρου, giving 431 B.C.

seventeen. Of these, four[1] were by some ascribed to other playwrights. It is probable that these non-authentic plays were later revisions.

In the SAVAGES ("Ἄγριοι), which was produced in 420 B.C.,[2] the poet pours charming ridicule upon that favourite topic, the Golden Age. Plato, the philosopher, intimating in a remarkable passage[3] that the "noble savage" is a myth and that the vilest Athenians are superior to any wild man, mentions 'a sort of savages, like those whom the poet Pherecrates produced last year at the Lenæan festival. Believe me, if you fell in with such people as the misanthropists met in that chorus, you would be delighted to encounter Eurybatus and Phrynondas.' Apparently certain Athenians, like Pisthetærus and Euelpides in the *Birds*, grown disgusted with their own country, set out to find the alleged noble race of savages, among whom existed that primitive simplicity of life described in one of the fragments:[4]

> οὐ γὰρ ἦν τότ' οὔτε Μανῆς οὔτε Σηκὶς οὐδενὶ
> δοῦλος, ἀλλ' αὐτὰς ἔδει μοχθεῖν ἅπαντ' ἐν οἰκίᾳ·
> εἶτα πρὸς τούτοισιν ἤλουν ὄρθριαι τὰ σιτία,
> ὥστε τὴν κώμην ὑπηχεῖν θιγγανουσῶν τὰς μύλας.

'For in those days no one had any Old Joe or Mary Ann: the women had to do all the housework themselves. Yes, and they used to grind the flour early in the morning, till the village resounded with the millstones.' We may suppose this to be part of an enthusiastic address by the leader of the expedition, to which the chorus perhaps offered a dubious welcome, depicting the real plight of the savages:[5]

---

[1] Ἀγαθοί (Strattis), Μεταλλῆς (Nicomachus), Πέρσαι (an unknown), Χείρων (Plato or Nicomachus). Unfortunately the last three dramas contained some of the most striking among the Pherecratean fragments.
[2] Athenæus, 218*d*: ἐδιδάχθησαν δὲ οἱ Ἄγριοι ἐπ' Ἀριστίωνος ἄρχοντος.
[3] *Protagoras*, 327*d*.
[4] Fr. 10. Manes and Secis are well-known slave-names. Kock rightly objects to the last three words: θιγγανουσῶν is absurd, and needs the genitive. He would read περιαγουσῶν.
[5] Fr. 13. The precise meaning of ἔνθρυσκος and of βράκανος is unknown.

ἐν θρύσκοισι καὶ βρακάνοις
καὶ στραβήλοις ζῆν · ὁπόταν δ'
ἤδη πεινῶσι σφόδρα,
ὡσπέρει τοὺς πουλύποδας
* * * νύκτωρ περιτρώγ—
ειν αὑτῶν τοὺς δακτύλους.

'... to live on pig-nuts, berries, and wild olives; but, when downright hungry, to gnaw their own fingers at night as cuttle-fish do.' It is possible that the savages received these inverted missionaries with hostile dread and retreated into their wigwams: γέρροις ἀποσταυροῦνται, ' they fence themselves off with hurdles '. A comic siege of their wattled stronghold is suggested by the vigorous lines : [1]

ὅδε δὴ δελφίς ἐστι μολιβδοῦς δελφινοφόρος τε κεροῦχος,
ὃς διακόψει τοὔδαφος αὐτῶν ἐμπίπτων καὶ καταδύων.

' Look, here is a leaden dolphin and the spar to carry it. This will smash their floor by falling in and plunging through.' The result of this onslaught is debated: [2]

A. ἦ μὴν σὺ σαυτὸν μακαριεῖς, ὦ τᾶν, ὅταν
οὑτοί σε κατορύττωσιν.
B.   οὐ δῆτ', ἀλλ' ἐγὼ
τούτους πρότερον. οὗτοι δὲ μακαριοῦσ' ἐμέ,
καίτοι πόθεν λήνους τοσαύτας λήψομεν;

' My word, you'll congratulate yourself, my dear sir, when these fellows are burying you.' ' Not a bit of it! I'll bury them first, and they'll congratulate me. But where shall we get enough coffins?' Bloodshed is no doubt averted, and we find traces of discussion between the Athenians and the savages : [3]

οὐδ' ἀποπροσωπίζεσθε κυάμοις; πώμαλα.

' Don't you even clean your faces with beans?' ' O dear no!' This suggests that the aborigines rub

---

[1] Fr. 12. The language suggests a passage of Thucydides (VII, 41), the scholium on which borrows the words of Pherecrates. In Thucydides the reference is to sinking ships by dropping leaden weights from a height. And in Pherecrates καταδύων suggests as much. But it is hard to imagine a naval scene in the play (like the massed attack by canoes in *Robinson Crusoe*); therefore we should regard καταδύων as intransitive, and the whole idea transferred from sea- to land-fighting.
[2] Fr. 5.   [3] Fr. 9.

THE SCHOOL OF CRATES

themselves with the inside of bean-pods, as the Zulus use banana-skins for cleaning their teeth.

CORIANNO (Κοριαννώ) is the most interesting of all his works. Here Pherecrates gives a glimpse of a domestic interior and one or two hints of the love-intrigue so frequent in later comedy. The piece bears a courtesan's name, and it appears to have depicted a father and son both entangled, or wishing to be entangled, with Corianno or her like. We have fragments [1] of their quarrel:

> ἀπαρτὶ μὲν οὖν ἐμοὶ μὲν εἰκός ἐστ' ἐρᾶν,
> σοὶ δ' οὐκεθ' ὥρα.

'On the contrary, for me this is just the right time to have an affair : for you the season is past.'

> ὑοσκυαμᾷς ἀνὴρ γέρων ὤν.

'You have a bee in your aged bonnet.'

> ὦ Ζεῦ πολυτίμητ', ἆρ' ἀκούεις ἅ με λέγει
> ὁ πανοῦργος υἱός;

'O worshipful Zeus, hearest thou what my villainous son says of me?'

Other extracts offer a notable presentation of ordinary home-life in a manner quite unlike Aristophanes but reminding us of Herodas. First we see a mother (probably Corianno herself) and her daughter (named Glyce).

> A. φέρε δὴ κατακλινῶ, σὺ δὲ τράπεζαν εἴσφερε
> καὶ κύλικα κἀντραγεῖν, ἵν' ἥδιον πίω.
> B. ἰδοὺ κύλιξ σοι καὶ τράπεζα καὶ φακοί.
> A. μή μοι φακούς, μὰ τὸν Δί', οὐ γὰρ ἥδομαι.
> ἢν γὰρ τράγῃ τις, τοῦ στόματος ὄζει κακόν.[2]

'Ah, now for the settee! Bring in a table and cup and a bit of something to improve the wine.' 'Here is a cup, a table, and some lentils.' 'No lentils for me, good Heavens! I don't like them : they make your breath smell.'

These two are visited by a lady friend, and the

---

[1] Frr. 71, 72, 73.   [2] Fr. 67.

conversation, though on an inferior [1] plane, recalls the celebrated chat in Theocritus' *Fifteenth Idyll* :

> A. ἐκ τοῦ βαλανείου γὰρ διέφθος ἔρχομαι,
> ξηρὰν ἔχουσα τὴν φάρυγα.
> B.   δώσω πιεῖν.
> A. γλίσχρον γε μοῦστὶ τὸ σίαλον νὴ τὼ θεώ.
> Γ. τί λάβω κεράσαι σοι; τὴν κοτυλίσκην;
> A.   μηδαμῶς
> μικράν γε. κινεῖται γὰρ εὐθύς μοι χολή,
> ἐξ οὗπερ ἔπιον ἐκ τοιαύτης φάρμακον.
> εἰς τὴν ἐμήν νυν ἔγχεον τὴν μείζονα.
>
> *   *   *   *   *   *
>
>   ἄποτ' ἐστ', ὦ Γλύκη.
> B. ὑδαρῆ 'νέχεέν σοι;
> A.   παντάπασι μὲν οὖν ὕδωρ.
> B. τί εἰργάσω; πῶς ὦ κατάρατε δ' ἐνέχεας;
> Γ. δύ' ὕδατος, ὦ μάμμη.
> B.   τί δ' οἴνου;
> Γ.   τέτταρας.
> B. ἔρρ' ἐς κόρακας. βατράχοισιν οἰνοχοεῖν σε δεῖ.[2]

Visitor : I've come from the baths all boiled, and my throat is parched.
Hostess : You shall have a drink.
Visitor : Well, my spittle is sticky, by the Holy Twain.
Glyce : You'll have the noggin?
Visitor : No, no, if it's a little one. My stomach turns at one in a moment, ever since I drank medicine out of such a cup. (*Produces a formidable goblet from her gown.*) Just pour it into mine—it's bigger. (*Glyce mixes wine and pours some into this receptacle. After one sip the visitor recoils.*) It's undrinkable, Glyce !
Hostess : Did she give you too much water?
Visitor : Too much? She gave me nothing else !
Hostess (*to Glyce*): What have you done? You little wretch, how did you mix it?
Glyce : Two measures of water, mammy.
Hostess : And how many of wine?
Glyce : Four.
Hostess : To Hell with you! You would make a good barmaid for a crowd of frogs.[3]

The metrician Hephæstion quotes three remarkable lines from *Corianno* :

> ἄνδρες, πρόσχετε τὸν νοῦν
> ἐξευρήματι καινῷ
> συμπτύκτοις ἀναπαίστοις.

---

[1] The two older women are coarse : for instance ἔρρ' ἐς κόρακας is equivalent to swearing.
[2] Frr. 69, 70. The fourth line is corrupt : I have given Kock's emendation.
[3] Four of wine to two of water would be regarded by most Greeks as a very strong mixture.

'Sirs, give heed to a new invention, the collapsed anapæst.' These are " Pherecrateans."[1]

To this same category of amorous plays the OLD WOMEN (Γρᾶες) perhaps belonged. The fragments are trivial, but there is a reference [2] to old women recovering their youth, the phrase Ἀθηναίαις αὐταῖς τε καὶ ταῖς ξυμμάχοις [3] (which suggests a revolt of Athenian women such as occurs in Aristophanes), and an allusion to carrier-pigeons: ἀπόπεμψον ἀγγέλλοντα τὸν περιστερόν,[4] 'Send off the dove with a message'. It may have been carrying a love-letter: the same notion appears more plainly in PETALE: [5]

ἀλλ' ὦ περιστέριον ὅμοιον Κλεισθένει,
πέτου, κόμισον δέ μ' εἰς Κύθηρα καὶ Κύπρον.

'But, O thou tiny dove Falstaffian, take wing and bear me to Cythera and Cyprus.'

CRAPATALI (Κραπάταλοι—meaning unknown, except that it is something trivial or valueless) seems to have been a queer extravaganza about Hades. Pollux [6] says that Pherecrates expounded the coinage of the Lower World: eight *ciccabi* make one *psothia*, two *psothiæ* make one *crapatalus*, which is the equivalent of the Attic drachma. Apparently some one asks the way to Hades and is thus directed: [7]

ὦ δαιμόνιε, πύρεττε μηδὲν φροντίσας,
καὶ τῶν φιβάλεων τρῶγε σύκων τοῦ θέρους
κἀμπιμπλάμενος κάθευδε τῆς μεσημβρίας,
κᾆτα σφακέλιζε καὶ πέπρησο καὶ βόα.

'My dear fellow, catch a fever carelessly, eat early figs in summer, and after a hearty meal sleep at midday; then fall into convulsions, get a temperature, and shout.' Two famous dead persons (if not more) appeared, so that we must imagine the action as taking place in Hades. The speaker of ὡς ἄτοπόν ἐστι μητέρ'

---

[1] Fr. 79. See below, pp. 389 *sq*.   [2] Fr. 35.
[3] Fr. 34. The word Ἀθηναίαις caused much head-shaking among the lexicographers, the true feminine of Ἀθηναῖοι being Ἀττικαί. But the whole phrase is a parody of legal language in the masculine.
[4] Fr. 33.   [5] Fr. 135.   [6] IX, 83.   [7] Fr. 80.

εἶναι καὶ γυνήν,[1] is surely Jocasta, and we know [2] it was Æschylus who said

> ὅστις γ' αὐτοῖς παρέδωκα τέχνην μεγάλην ἐξοικοδομήσας.

'Seeing that I handed down to them an art that I had built up to majesty.' It may be that to this place belongs the description [3] of early choruses :

> ὁ χορὸς δ' αὐτοῖς εἶχεν δάπιδας ῥυπαρὰς καὶ στρωματόδεσμα.

'Their chorus wore dirty rugs and bedding-ropes.' These two passages suggest that the *Crapatali* contained a discussion of early drama, like the *Frogs*. A passage [4] from the parabasis mentions the poet by name :

> τοῖς δὲ κριταῖς
> τοῖς νῦν κρίνουσι λέγω
> μὴ 'πιορκεῖν μηδ' ἀδίκως
> κρίνειν, ἢ νὴ τὸν φίλιον
> μῦθον εἰς ὑμᾶς ἕτερον
> Φερεκράτης λέξει πολὺ τούτ—
> ου κακηγορίστερον.

'And the judges (of plays) now in session I bid not to break their oath or judge unrighteously; else, by Friendly Zeus, Pherecrates will deliver against you another play far more slanderous than this.'

The DESERTERS (Αὐτόμολοι) has been thought a political play because of one passage : [5]

> οὗτοι γὰρ ἡμῖν οἱ κακῶς ἀπολούμενοι
> ἐπαμφοτερίζουσ' ἐμποδὼν καθήμενοι.

'For these wretches squat in our path and shilly-shally.' This is known [6] to be an allusion to the wavering policy of Argos in the Peloponnesian War. But one extract proves nothing about the whole plot: the political allusion may be quite incidental, and none of the other fragments (so far as we know) points in the same direction. Indeed the only striking one looks quite different. Clement of Alexandria writes : [7]

---

[1] Fr. 91.　　　　[2] Schol., *Peace*, 748; fr. 94.
[3] Quoted by Eustathius, *Od.*, 1369, 43, as from Pherecrates, without any play-title (fr. 185).
[4] Fr. 96.　　[5] Fr. 19.　　[6] Schol., *Peace*, 477.
[7] *Strom.*, VII, p. 846; fr. 23.

'That comic poet Pherecrates in his *Deserters* makes the gods themselves grumble at mankind about their sacrifices.' Then follow six lines the text of which is imperfect but which complain that men eat almost all the offering and give useless remnants to the gods. This, together with the title of the play, might suggest that (as in Aristophanes' *Peace*) the *gods* have deserted mankind.

Of the ANT-MEN (Μυρμηκάνθρωποι) more can be made. Kock [1] has ingeniously suggested that "Pherecrates combined the legend of Deucalion's flood, which included Attica, with that of the ants whom Zeus transformed into men as a favour to Æacus". An allusion to the flood may be found in the line [2] ἀλλ' ὡς τάχιστα τὸν γέρονθ' ἱστὸν ποίει—'Quick! Turn the spindle into a mast.' Deucalion rigs up an impromptu ark (out of a meal-tub, it may be) and takes his wife's spindle to carry the sail (possibly an old tunic). It appears, too, that since of course these survivors have nothing to eat but fish they grow utterly tired of what was in ordinary Greek life an esteemed dainty:

μηδέποτ' ἰχθύν, ὦ Δευκαλίων, μηδ' ἢν αἰτῶ παραθῇς μοι.[3]

'Never set fish before me, Deucalion, not even if I ask for it.' They seem, indeed, to have been so bored by their voyage that one of them began to talk to the fish that approached their vessel.[4] Bad weather added to their troubles: οἴμοι κακοδαίμων, αἰγὶς αἰγὶς ἔρχεται—'Alas! Bad luck! A storm! a storm!'[5] Their landing (perhaps on Ægina, the island of Æacus) seems to be described: ξένη γυνὴ γραῦς ἀρτίως ἀφιγμένη [6] —'a foreign old woman, just arrived'. As for the ant-men, Kock sees a reference to them in the words [7]

[1] I, p. 178.
[2] Fr. 114. A spindle was called γέρων because it was surmounted by an image of the bearded Hermes.
[3] Fr. 180. Cp. Kingsley, *Water-Babies*, Chap. III: "Winchester apprentices shall covenant, as they did three hundred years ago, not to be made to eat salmon more than three days a week".
[4] Fr. 113.   [5] Fr. 117.   [6] Fr. 119.   [7] Fr. 118.

ὕστερον ἀρᾶται κἀπιθεάζει τῷ πατρί ('later he prays and beseeches his father')—" this is to be understood of Æacus who, when he has lost his citizens, prays his father Zeus to give him others, however created". Another passage [1] depicts the swarming arrival of the ants. This must have been an original and amusing comedy.

We pass now to the doubtful plays. According to Harpocration [2] and Photius,[3] the MINERS (Μεταλλῆς) was attributed by the critic Eratosthenes to one Nicomachus. Apparently his verdict was based upon diction, and our fragments certainly contain things not to be expected in the "extremely Attic"[4] Pherecrates. This play is notable for several reasons. First we possess a fragment running to the sensational length of thirty-four lines; it need scarcely be said that it deals with edibles. Next, the subject was a version of Paradise—an extremely earthly Paradise. We are to understand that certain miners, working in the silver-mines at Laureion in Attica, fell through into the Lower World and discovered this Arabian Nights Restaurant. The long fragment need not be printed: it is like a poor copy of the passage in Telecleides—rivers of soup, dainties asking to be eaten, etc. The catalogue is interrupted thus:

οἴμ' ὡς ἀπολεῖς μ' ἐνταῦθα διατρίβουσ' ἔτι,
παρὸν κολυμβᾶν ὡς ἔχετ' εἰς τὸν Τάρταρον.

'Confound you! I'm disgusted that you waste your time here, when you could all of you dive just as you are into Hell.' This is, "if the Lower World is so delightful, go back there". The wording shows that the narrator of the catalogue is a woman and that she has brought companions, a chorus of the miners who have so wonderfully "struck oil".

The PERSIANS (Πέρσαι) is also of dubious authorship.[5] It appears to have been yet another Arabian

---

[1] Fr. 121.   [2] s.v. Μεταλλεῖς.   [3] s.v. εὐθὺς Λυκείου.
[4] Ἀττικώτατος (Athenæus, 268e).
[5] Our authorities several times (Athenæus, 78d, 502a, 684f, 685a, and Schol., *Frogs*, 365) write Φερεκράτης ἢ ὁ πεποιηκὼς τοὺς Πέρσας, etc.

THE SCHOOL OF CRATES

Nights' Entertainment, and, curiously enough, to have been inspired by precisely the same idea as those famous tales. The *Arabian Nights* was coloured by the gorgeous stories that had spread over Arabia concerning Persian wealth; so was this Athenian *Persæ*, the notion of which seems to have been that Persian gold would abolish poverty in Greece. One fragment [1] closely resembles a passage in Aristophanes' *Plutus* :

τίς δ' ἔσθ' ἡμῖν τῶν σῶν ἀροτῶν ἢ ζυγοποιῶν ἔτι χρεία,
ἢ δρεπανουργῶν ἢ χαλκοτύπων ἢ σπέρματος ἢ χαρακισμοῦ;
αὐτόματοι γὰρ διὰ τῶν τριόδων ποταμοὶ λιπαροῖς ἐπιπάστοις
ζωμοῦ μέλανος καὶ Ἀχιλλείοις μάζαις κοχοδοῦντες ἐπιβλὺξ
ἀπὸ τῶν πηγῶν τῶν τοῦ πλούτου ῥεύσονται, σφῶν ἀρύτεσθαι.
ὁ Ζεὺς δ' ὕων οἴνῳ καπνίᾳ κατὰ τοῦ κεράμου βαλανεύσει.
ἀπὸ τῶν δὲ τεγῶν ὀχετοὶ βοτρύων μετὰ ναστίσκων πολυτύρων
ὀχετεύσονται θερμῷ σὺν ἔτνει καὶ λειριοπολφανεμώναις.
τὰ δὲ δὴ δένδρη τἀν τοῖς ὄρεσιν χορδαῖς ὀπταῖς ἐριφείοις
φυλλοροήσει, καὶ τευθιδίοις ἁπαλοῖς κίχλαις τ' ἀναβράστοις.

'But what further need have we of your ploughmen or harness-makers, your sickle-manufacturers or bronze-founders, or sowing or fencing? For spontaneously there will flow through the cross-roads rivers of dark soup in a spate of rich dumplings and Achilles-buns, gurgling forth from the fountains of wealth for men to draw thereof. Zeus shall bathe the tiles with a rain of mellow wine, and from the roof jets of grapes and cheese-cakes shall spout together with hot soup and salad. The trees on the mountains shall shed boiled chitterlings, tender cuttlefish-steaks, and roast thrushes.' Some one (perhaps Poverty herself, as in Aristophanes) has been pointing out that universal wealth will destroy civilization, since no one will practise the useful trades for a livelihood. The reply is 'we shall not need the useful trades'.

The only other fragment [2] of interest belongs to a type affected by others besides this author—a romantic "conceit" which compares to charming natural objects, not parts of the body (as in so many lyrists) but functions of the body:

[1] Cp. Ar., *Plutus*, 507 *sqq*.   [2] Fr. 131. The metre is Priapean.

ὦ μαλάχας μὲν ἐξορῶν, ἀναπνέων δ' ὑάκινθον,
καὶ μελίλωτινον λαλῶν καὶ ῥόδα προσσεσηρώς
ὦ φιλῶν μὲν ἀμάρακον, προσκινῶν δὲ σέλινα,
γελῶν δ' ἱπποσέλινα καὶ κοσμοσάνδαλα βαίνων.

It is like a quiet echo of the overwhelming raptures in the *Song of Solomon*. 'The light of thy eyes is as mallows, thy breath the hyacinth; in thy speech dwells the honey-lotus and roses upon the movement of thy lips. Yea, thy kisses are marjoram, the touch of thy body is parsley, thy laughter the horse-parsley, and thy footfall is shod in the petals of flowers.'

CHIRON, attributed by some to Nicomachus,[1] by others to Plato,[2] has left mysteriously diverse fragments: parodies of Hesiod, a reference to, or parody of, the ninth *Iliad*, and a long fragment on the degradation of music. The first class refer with queer elaboration to the duty of politeness to unwelcome guests. Next we have

A. δώσει δέ σοι γυναῖκας ἑπτὰ Λεσβίδας.
B. καλόν γε δῶρον, ἕπτ' ἔχειν λαικαστρίας.[3]

'He will give you seven Lesbian women.' It is the offer of Agamemnon to Achilles as reported by Odysseus. But Lesbos had lost its reputation since Homeric days, and the answer comes: 'A glorious gift indeed—seven courtesans!' Plutarch[4] tells us that 'Pherecrates, the comic poet, brought on Music dressed as a woman, mangled in every limb: he depicts Justice inquiring the cause of this outrage and Music saying...' Then follow twenty-five lines[5] describing the successive corruptions of the art by the musicians Melanippides, Cinesias, Phrynis, and Timotheus.

Even though not authentic, the fragments of these three plays help to complete our notion of Pherecrates; for had they not been in his manner they would never have been attributed to him. On the whole we form a tolerably definite picture of this playwright. He

[1] Athenæus, 364a. [2] Meineke, I, p. 76.
[3] Fr. 149. Cp. *Iliad*, IX, 270-2.
[4] *De Musica*, 1141, 2. That he refers to the *Chiron* is proved by Nicomachus Gerasenus, p. 274 (ed. Janus, Teubner).
[5] Fr. 145.

belongs, as the Anonymus reports, to the school of Crates, exhibiting an elegant originality without much trace either of political preoccupations or personal invective.[1] He seems to have been a peculiarly sensitive man: besides several proofs of his passion for good taste in music, among them the exclamation [2] that listening to a bad singer is like wearing a wreath of thorns, we are to remember those beautiful, if somewhat richly perfumed lines, ὦ μαλάχας μὲν ἐξορῶν and the rest: though they come from the *Persæ*, they may well be his. He is in fact for us more notable than Crates himself as an exponent of the urbane side of Old Comedy. To that period, indeed, he belongs only in part. Not only the features already indicated, but also the remarkable *Corianno*, suggest that in spirit at least—we do not know when he died [3]—he belongs even more than Plato or Phrynichus to the Middle Comedy. This impression is strengthened by the "non-authentic" dramas: a later generation relished him enough to touch his work up for revival.

§ 4. PLATO

Next to the three Masters, Plato is the most important Old Comedian. Athenæus called him "brilliant in style";[4] we possess a large number of fragments and can gain glimpses of whole plays; like Aristophanes, Plato illustrates the transition from Old to Middle Comedy—indeed, he was by some allotted to the second period.[5]

---

[1] There is only one such, an attack on Alcibiades' morals (fr. 155).
[2] Fr. 24.
[3] Geissler (*Chronologie*, p. 42) says he was certainly dead by 400 B.C. There is no evidence for this.
[4] Suidas, s.v. Πλάτων: ἔστι δὲ λαμπρὸς τὸν χαρακτῆρα, ὥς φησιν Ἀθήναιος ἐν τοῖς Δειπνοσοφισταῖς. This remark is not to be found in our text of Athenæus.
[5] Anon., de Com. (Kaibel, pp. 13 sq.): γέγονε δὲ τῆς μὲν πρώτης κωμῳδίας ἄριστος τεχνίτης οὗτος ὁ Ἀριστοφάνης καὶ Εὔπολις, τῆς δὲ δευτέρας Πλάτων, τῆς δὲ τρίτης Μένανδρος. The Scholiast on Dionysius Thrax (Kaibel, p. 15) writes: τῆς δὲ μέσης καὶ αὐτῆς μὲν πολλοὶ γεγόνασιν, ἐπίσημος δὲ Πλάτων τις, οὐχ ὁ φιλόσοφος, ἀλλ' ἕτερός τις. ὁμοίως κἀκείνου τὰ δράματα οὐ φαίνεται. Suidas, however, says (s.v.) that Plato was a contemporary of Aristophanes, Phrynichus, Eupolis and Pherecrates.

The number of his works is given as twenty-eight by both the Anonymus and Suidas, though the latter's enumeration includes thirty titles; how many victories he gained is unknown. His first production fell in the eighty-eighth Olympiad (427-4),[1] and as Athenian dramatists generally began their careers young, we may tentatively date his birth at 450 B.C. His activity lasted till at least 385;[2] and the fact that some authorities assign him to the Middle Comedy suggests that he survived that date by a considerable time. The only personal fact about Plato known to us is given thus by our fullest authority:[3] '*Imitating Arcadians*. This phrase is used by Plato in *Peisander*, about those who endure distress for others: though very warlike, they never gained any victory for themselves, but helped many others thereto. Thus Plato said he imitated the Arcadians, because, owing to poverty, he supplied others with the comedies that he had himself composed.' This may be an exaggerated rendering of the fact that (like Aristophanes) Plato induced others to father his dramas.[4] Had he been really a hack composing plays for well-to-do ambitious amateurs, one would have expected either that a larger number of plays would be attributed to him by tradition, or else that his authorship would leak out in the ages of scholarship.[5]

Plato is perhaps the most important instance of transition: part of his work was unmistakably Old, part unmistakably Middle. His transitional quality is

---

[1] Cyril, *Contra Iulianum*, I, p. 1313 (Migne, p. 522): ὀγδοηκοστῇ ὀγδόῃ τὸν κωμῳδὸν Ἀριστοφάνην Εὔπολίν τε καὶ Πλάτωνα γενέσθαι. This is of course not the birth year, but the *floruit*.

[2] Cp. Geissler, *Chronologie*, p. 74.

[3] Arsenius (*Violetum*, ed. Walz, p. 76). The gist of this occurs in Suidas also under the same lemma.

[4] Διὰ πενίαν would have then to be explained away. Naeke (*ap.* Meineke, I, p. 163) believed that, Plato having referred to the Arcadians, the grammarians irrelevantly recalled the hire paid to Arcadian soldiers, and so imported the financial element into their account.

[5] Only one instance of this is known. *Alliance* was attributed to Cantharus as well as to Plato (Priscian, *Inst. Gram.*, XVIII, p. 182, Krehl).

marked by his linguistic novelties [1] and by a change of outlook : in his early time we find him writing political [2] comedy; later he turns to romantic and erotic drama, a nascent comedy of manners.

ALLIANCE (Συμμαχία) contained a description [3] of a game played by street-boys :

εἴξασιν γὰρ τοῖς παιδαρίοις τούτοις, οἳ ἑκάστοτε γραμμὴν
ἐν ταῖσιν ὁδοῖς διαγράψαντες διανειμάμενοι δίχ' ἑαυτοὺς
ἑστᾶσ', αὐτῶν οἱ μὲν ἐκεῖθεν τῆς γραμμῆς, οἱ δ' αὖ ἐκεῖθεν ·
εἷς δ' ἀμφοτέρων ὄστρακον αὐτοῖς εἰς μέσον ἑστὼς ἀνίησιν,
κἂν μὲν πίπτῃσι τὰ λεύκ' ἐπάνω, φεύγειν ταχὺ τοὺς ἑτέρους δεῖ,
τοὺς δὲ διώκειν.

' They resemble those children whom you may see in the street any day : they draw a line across the road and divide themselves into two companies, standing one on each side of the line. One, standing between these, tosses a tile into the air. If it falls white side up, one company must run away and the other must pursue.' Bergk [4] thought this a reference to ostracism, and the Alliance that famous coalition between Nicias and Alcibiades against Hyperbolus.[5] Meineke [6] was content to refer it to the quarrels of the Greek States. Kock [7] took a similar view, believing that the play (like *Lysistrata*) urged friendship and concord upon the Greeks. As a fact, there is no clear evidence that this passage, or the whole play, had any political colour at all. Our extract may allude to private persons who are at a deadlock in some dispute and who do not know which side is to (or can) take the initiative—like the people in Sheridan's *Critic*. The only other interesting point is that the first sentence of the play contained γάρ (" for ")—ἐγὼ γὰρ ὑμῖν ἦν φράσω [8]—which shows that Plato's style was sometimes deliberately casual.

But politics were certainly the theme of GREECE

---

[1] See the details in Meineke, I, pp. 164 *sq.*—*e.g.* μανάκις for ὀλιγάκις, ἐλεῖτον the future of ἐλαύνω, ἀράχνιον with second syllable long.
[2] He claims (fr. 107) to have been the first to attack Cleon.
[3] Fr. 153. The game was called ὀστρακίνδα. At the end of the third line αὖ scans as short by "weak hiatus". See p. 367.
[4] *Rell. Com. Att.*, pp. 261, 312.   [5] See below, pp. 169 *sq.*
[6] I, p. 185.   [7] I, p. 641.   [8] Fr. 152.

or the ISLANDS; from it we catch a faint echo of those dreadful days when Athens was facing her new life after the collapse of 404 B.C. and the complete loss of her empire. So much seems to follow from the lines : [1]

εἰ μὲν οὖν ταύτην σὺ τὴν θάλατταν ἀποδώσεις ἑκών·
εἰ δὲ μή γε, ταῦτα πάντα συντριαινῶν ἀπολέσω.

'If thou wilt restore this sea willingly, well and good ; otherwise I will destroy all this with my shattering trident.' The allusion must be to the sea-power wrested by Sparta from Athens, which is championed by Poseidon, not only the sea-god but also the patron of the Athenian knights. Whom Poseidon threatens we can but guess ; the most natural person is Zeus himself.[2] Whether Plato was supporting or denouncing dreams of *revanche* cannot be determined. Another vigorous fragment [3] points to the public demoralization of Athens :

εἴξασιν ἡμῖν οἱ νόμοι τούτοισι τοῖσι λεπτοῖς
ἀραχνίοις, ἃν τοῖσι τοίχοις ἡ φάλαγξ ὑφαίνει.

'Our laws resemble those filmy webs that the spider weaves upon the walls.' The fact that Photius' lexicon quotes from this play τάξαι in the sense of τιμῆσαι ("assess"), joined to the alternative title *Islands*, may suggest that in this comedy was a scheme for reconstituting the empire. The importance of Poseidon may have been great. A word [4] said to mean "a breaking wave" is quoted: possibly the god was described as stepping upon Attic soil from the sea. Finally, a brilliant scrap of description, not quoted, unfortunately, but only paraphrased [5] from Plato,

---

[1] Fr. 23. For the last word, which is bad Attic for ἀπολῶ, Kock would read ἀποκλύσω. But Meineke is no doubt justified in retaining ἀπολέσω as one of Plato's "late" features.

[2] The god seems to be threatening that he will wreck the world : his menace resembles that of the Sun-God in *Od.*, XII, 383 : δύσομαι εἰς Ἀΐδαο καὶ ἐν νεκύεσσι φαείνω.

[3] Fr. 22. The scansion of ἀραχνίοις has already been noted. Kock, following Porson, prints the passage as iambics but with a change of his own which retains the early scansion of ἀραχνίοις.

[4] σκώληκα. Cp. Photius, *s.v.*

[5] Sextus Empiricus, *Adv. Rhet.*, II, p. 296.

may well belong to this play. 'But among those who give a home to rhetoric the laws are remodelled every day, for example in Athens, as is remarked by Plato, the poet of Old Comedy: for if one is absent for only three months (says he) one no longer recognizes the city, but like those who roam about at night one finds lodging next to the fortifications as if one were a pony-postman—so far as the laws are concerned it is a different town'.

HYPERBOLUS (Ὑπέρβολος) was an attack upon the famous demagogue who, after Cleon's death, rose to power despite lack of education, despicable character, and alleged foreign origin—he could not even speak good Attic:[1]

> ὁ δ' οὐ γὰρ ἠττίκιζεν, ὦ Μοῖραι φίλαι,
> ἀλλ' ὁπότε μὲν χρείη διῃτώμην λέγειν
> ἔφασκε δὴ τω μην, ὁπότε δ' εἰπεῖν δέοι
> ὀλίγον, ὀλίον ἔλεγεν.

What Hyperbolus said for διῃτώμην was naturally doomed to corruption by copyists: perhaps we should read ἔφασκ' ἐδιῃτώμην.[2] This play treated the famous ostracism of the demagogue, who, having sought to induce the Athenians to ostracize either Nicias or Alcibiades so that he might deal more easily with the other, was hoist with his own petard: Alcibiades persuaded Nicias to join hands with him, and their combined parties secured the ostracism of Hyperbolus.[3] Plato's comedy must have dealt fully with this overthrow,[4] for we have fragments that precede and that follow it. First:

---
[1] Fr. 168.
[2] So Meineke, I, p. 192, but in II, p. 669, he prefers ἐδιαιτώμην.
[3] In 417 B.C. See Plutarch, *Alcibiades*, XIII, *Nicias*, XI, *Aristides*, VII.
[4] Geissler, however (*Chronologie*, pp. 49 sq.), dates the *Hyperbolus* at 419 or 418, before the ostracism, because "it is not appropriate to the art of the comedians to make a person no longer dangerous the chief character of a play". It follows that the comment καίτοι πέπραγε κτέ. cannot belong to the *Hyperbolus* (Kock had already placed it among the ἄδηλα). This is very unconvincing. πέπραγε is primary, not historic, and so fits better a final comment on what has just happened than a reference to something definitely in the past. Moreover, the "no longer dangerous" argument would (in its essentials) have prevented Aristophanes from writing the *Frogs*.

> A. εὐτυχεῖς, ὦ δεσπότα.
> B. τί δ' ἔστι;
> A. βουλεύειν ὀλίγου ἔλαχες πάνυ.
> ἀτὰρ οὐ λαχὼν ὅμως ἔλαχες, ἢν νοῦν ἔχῃς.
> B. πῶς ἦν ἔχω νοῦν;
> A. ὅτι πονηρῷ καὶ ξένῳ
> ἐπέλαχες ἀνδρί, μηδέπω γὰρ ἐλευθέρῳ ...
> B. ἄπερρ'· ἐγὼ δ' ὑμῖν τὸ πρᾶγμα δὴ φράσω·
> Ὑπερβόλῳ βουλῆς γάρ, ἄνδρες, ἐπέλαχον.

'Congratulations, master!' 'On what?' 'You came within an ace of a seat on the senate. But though you missed it, you got it, if you understand.' 'How do you mean?' 'Because you were appointed as second string to a low foreigner, not to a free man, thank Heaven'... 'Be off! (*To the audience*) I will explain the affair to you myself. The fact is, gentlemen, I was appointed second string to Hyperbolus on the Senate...'[1] The last two lines show that this passage came early in the play. Later we find the well-known comment[2] on this ostracism:

> καίτοι πέπραγε τῶν τρόπων μὲν ἄξια,
> αὑτοῦ δὲ καὶ τῶν στιγμάτων ἀνάξια·
> οὐ γὰρ τοιούτων οὕνεκ' ὄστραχ' εὑρέθη.

'Yet his fate, though appropriate to his conduct, is not appropriate to himself and his servile birth: it was not for his type that ostracism was devised.' The Athenians, Plutarch[3] reports, felt that ostracism, which had been inflicted upon men like Aristides, was degraded by its application to Hyperbolus, and they never used that device again.

From the FESTIVALS ('Ἑορταί), the plot of which is entirely unknown, comes a handful of miscellaneous scraps, two of which may be quoted. Some one who used the double *tau* instead of *sigma* was thus greeted:

> εὖ γέ σοι γένοιθ', ἡμᾶς ὅτι
> ἔσωσας ἐκ τῶν σῖγμα τῶν Εὐριπίδου.

---

[1] Frr. 166, 167. (The third line is an Euripidean quibble.) For every man appointed to the senate a second man was selected in case the first proved ineligible on scrutiny. Hyperbolus is certain to be "unseated on appeal".

[2] Meineke, II, p. 669; Kock, fr. 187, among the ἄδηλα (see above).

[3] *Nicias*, XI.

THE SCHOOL OF CRATES

'Bless you for saving us from the esses of Euripides.' It is quoted by the Scholiast on the famous line (*Medea*, 476), ἔσωσά σ', ὡς ἴσασιν Ἑλλήνων ὅσοι.... Another fragment [1] recalls the Chicago merchant's remark about pigs: "We use everything but the squeal":

> τῶν γὰρ τετραπόδων οὐδὲν ἀποκτείνειν ἔδει
> ἡμᾶς τὸ λοιπόν, πλὴν ὑῶν· τὰ γὰρ κρέα
> ἥδιστ' ἔχουσι, κοὐδὲν ἀφ' ὑὸς γίγνεται
> πλὴν ὑστριχὶς καὶ πηλὸς ἡμῖν καὶ βοή.

'We ought in future to kill no animal except the pig: its meat is delicious, and nothing in a pig is lost except the bristles, the mud and the squeal.'

The SPARTANS or the POETS (Λάκωνες ἢ Ποιηταί) represented a banquet at which there was discussion about rival poets or poetical schools. We possess a fragment [2] that is clearly "Middle"—a picture of "manners".

> A. ἄνδρες δεδειπνήκασιν ἤδη σχεδὸν ἅπαντες.
> B.   εὖ γε.
> τί οὐ τρέχων σὺ τὰς τραπέζας εἰσφέρεις; ἐγὼ δὲ
> λίτρον παραχέων ἔρχομαι.
> A.   κἀγὼ δὲ παρακορήσων.
> σπονδὰς δ' ἔπειτα παραχέας τὸν κότταβον παροίσω.
> τῇ παιδὶ τοὺς αὐλοὺς ἐχρῆν ἤδη πρὸ χειρὸς εἶναι,
> καὶ προσαναφυσᾶν.
> B.   τὸ μύρον ἤδη παράχεον βαδίζων
> Αἰγύπτιον, κᾆτ' ἴρινον· στέφανον δ' ἔπειθ' ἑκάστῳ
> δώσω φέρων τῶν ξυμποτῶν. νεοκρᾶτά τις ποιείτω.
> A. καὶ δὴ κέκραται.
> B.   τὸν λιβανωτὸν † ἐπιτιθεὶς εἶπε † ...
> σπονδὴ μὲν ἤδη γέγονε, καὶ πίνοντές εἰσι πόρρω.
> καὶ σκόλιον ᾖσται, κότταβος δ'ἐξοίχεται θύραζε.
> αὐλοὺς δ' ἔχουσά τις κορίσκη Καρικὸν μέλος τι
> μελίζεται τοῖς συμπόταις, κἄλλην τρίγωνον εἶδον
> ἔχουσαν, εἶτ' ᾖδεν πρὸς αὐτὸ μέλος Ἰωνικόν τι.[3]

---

[1] Fr. 28. The last clause is queerly expressed. Normally the Greek would mean 'we get nothing but...' This makes no sense, and ἀφ'... γίγνεται must be regarded as *tmesis*.

[2] Fr. 69.

[3] The division between speakers is conjectural. Meineke (II, p. 638) declines such division, thinking that the whole is delivered by one person, who imitates the after-dinner bustle. This is rather attractive: a skilful pantomimist would make a great success, whereas a mere description of such well-known things would be absurd. In the third line Casaubon read νίπτρον ("washing-water") for λίτρον ("powdered soap"). The ninth line will not scan: read perhaps ἀνεῖπε, "announce". After that line Cobet saw a lacuna, for some time must have passed. The compounds with παρά refer to the waiters' progress along the tables. Μύρον, with στέφανος, corresponds to our cigars.

'The gentlemen have nearly all finished dinner by now.' 'Good! Hurry, you, and bring out the tables. I'll go and supply the soap.' 'I'll sweep up the crumbs, pour the libations and fetch out the *cottabos*. That girl ought by now to have her pipes ready and tune up.' 'Now move along serving the perfume—first Egyptian, then orris-root; next I'll bring a garland for each of the guests. Some one mix a fresh bowl of wine.' 'That's done.' 'Throw incense on the fire. .... Now the libation has been poured, drinking is well under way, the catch has been sung and they are removing the *cottabos*. A damsel with pipes is playing a Carian tune to the guests, and I saw another with a little harp to which she was singing an Ionian tune.'

Two other passages from the *Spartans* should be noted. As so often, some one rose from the dead:

> Α. καὶ μὴν ὄμοσόν μοι μὴ τεθνάναι.
> Β.   τὸ σῶμ' ἐγώ,
>   ψυχὴν δ'ἀνήκειν ὥσπερ Αἰσώπου ποτέ.[1]

'See here! Swear to me that you are not dead.' 'I affirm that my body is dead, but that my spirit has risen like Æsop's once on a time.' Who rises, we do not know; and the fact that none of our three [2] authorities names him suggests that he is not in himself a remarkable figure, though he was perhaps important to the plot. But the passage may be a purely incidental joke. Finally, the proof that poetry was discussed is afforded (in addition to the title) by these lines: [3]

> ὅταν δέωμαι γωνιαίου ῥήματος,
> τούτῳ παριστῶ καὶ μοχλεύω τὰς πέτρας.

'When I need a corner-stone phrase, I (borrow from this man?) and lever the rocks.' It is evidently meant that a feeble poet uses the work of some vigorous

---

[1] Fr. 68.
[2] Schol., *Birds*, 471; Schol., *Wasps*, 125; Suidas, *s.v.* ἀναβιῶναι.
[3] Fr. 67. τούτῳ παριστῶ is corrupt. Meineke would make the first line a question and the second a reply, reading παρίστω ("Stand beside this man") and μόχλευε: he thinks Æschylus appeared in the play.

predecessor[1] as a quarry. The feeble poet is the tragedian Sthenelus, for we are told by Harpocration[2] that he is derided in this drama as a plagiarist.

The difficulty mentioned earlier, that Aristophanes attributes Cratinus' death to a Spartan invasion of Attica,[3] but that no invasion occurred at the relevant time, has possibly been solved by an ingenious conjecture[4] that the " Laconian inroad " was the invasion of the theatre by Plato's Λάκωνες. These scenic Spartans not only dined but are to be supposed to break the wine-cask whose loss killed Cratinus with grief.

Possibly the most important fact about Plato is that in several of his plays sexual passion is a main theme. At least three instances are to be found in his work. Concerning EUROPA we know little; but our chief fragment[5] is plainly the introduction to a salacious, or at least luscious, passage. Zeus has been contemplating the slumber of Europa as his opportunity, but some one begins to point out to him the superior attractions of a woman awake. Zeus (it seems) asks for details, and our fragment ceases. The LONG NIGHT (Νὺξ Μακρά) probably treated the same story as Plautus' *Amphitruo*. One fragment,[6]

ἐνταῦθ' ἐπ' ἄκρων τῶν κροτάφων ἕξει λύχνον
δίμυξον,

' there he will have upon his head a lamp with two wicks,' suggests a means whereby (as in Plautus) the audience may distinguish the god from the man whom he impersonates. We command better knowledge of ZEUS REVILED (Ζεὺς Κακούμενος). How Zeus himself was concerned does not appear, but his son Heracles

---

[1] Æschylus is an obvious suggestion. He is addressed in *Clouds*, 1399, as καινῶν ἐπῶν κινητὰ καὶ μοχλευτά.
[2] P. 166, 3: καὶ ἐν ταῖς διδασκαλίαις εὑρίσκεται ὁ Σθένελος τραγῳδίας ποιητής. ἐκωμῴδει δὲ αὐτὸν ὁ τοὺς Πλάτωνος Λάκωνας γράψας ὡς ἀλλότρια ἔπη σφετεριζόμενον. This is the only doubt expressed anywhere as to the authenticity of the Λάκωνες. Because of this Zieliński (*Rhein. Mus.*, XXXIX, pp. 303 sqq.) regards the play as a "literature-comedy" of the fourth century.
[3] *Peace*, 701 : ὅθ' οἱ Λάκωνες ἐνέβαλον.
[4] Cobet, *Obs. crit. in Platonem*, p. 87 ; Bergk, *Rell. Com. Att.*, p. 187.
[5] Fr. 43.
[6] Fr. 84.

is deeply involved. The first fragment [1] shows him in the house of a courtesan, amusing himself with the *cottabos* under the business-like eye of the girl's master :

> A. πρὸς κότταβον παίζειν, ἕως ἂν σφῷν ἐγὼ
> τὸ δεῖπνον ἔνδον σκευάσω.
> HP. πάνυ βούλομαι.
> ἀλλ' ἄγγος ἔστ' ;
> A. ἀλλ' εἰς θυείαν παιστέον.
> HP. φέρε τὴν θυείαν, αἶρ' ὕδωρ, τὰ ποτήρια
> παράθετε. παίζωμεν δὲ περὶ φιλημάτων.
> A. * * * * ἀγεννῶς οὐκ ἐῶ
> παίζειν. τίθημι κοττάβεια σφῷν ἐγὼ
> τασδί τε τὰς κρηπῖδας ἃς αὕτη φορεῖ,
> καὶ τὸν κότυλον τὸν σόν.
> HP. βαβαιάξ, οὑτοσὶ
> μείζων ἀγὼν τῆς Ἰσθμιάδος ἐπέρχεται.

Master: ... to play at *cottabos* while I prepare dinner for the two of you within.
Heracles: Excellent ! But have you a vessel ?
Master: Oh, you can use a mortar.
Heracles: Fetch it, bring water, set out the cups. Let us play for kisses.
Master: ... more sportsmanship, please ! *I* will fix your stakes—the shoes she is wearing, and your goblet.
Heracles: Gosh ! This match is going to be a bigger event than the Isthmian Games.

The hero's goblet, we are to suppose, is a possession not only capacious but valuable, vastly surpassing the shoes. The girl is an expert player, as is shown by a fragment [2] where she good-naturedly tries to improve his game. In fact, here is the ancient analogue of a modern *motif* : the big-hearted guileless officer on leave, the beautiful decoy, and the quiet little game of cards in the luxurious flat. Later, it seems that she wins the goblet (τὸν κότυλον φέρει [3]) and that, as the sport proceeds, Heracles is deprived gradually of all, even his most trivial possessions.

PHAON was equally amorous. The story taken by Plato as groundwork was no doubt that reported by Servius : ' Phaon was a ferryman who used to convey his neighbours from Lesbos to the mainland for hire.

---

[1] Fr. 46.   [2] Fr. 47.
[3] Fr. 48. Athenæus, XI, 478e. For this meaning φέρεται was to be expected, and the passage may mean 'he is bringing the goblet' (as who should bring the Rajah's ruby with him to the flat).

THE SCHOOL OF CRATES

But Venus, who had transformed herself into an old woman, he carried across for nothing. She bestowed on him as reward an alabaster vase of ointment. With this he began to anoint himself every day, and caused women to fall in love with him.'[1] We possess a long fragment [2] depicting the result. Aphrodite [3] addresses a throng of women who passionately desire to meet Phaon. He is in seclusion [4] and she acts as the doorkeeper, prescribing the elaborate sacrificial presents that must be offered to her and other powers (with erotic names) before admission is granted. Another passage,[5] of eighteen lines, shows us a man studying " a new cookery-book of Philoxenus," and reading out a list of aphrodisiac foods. This may be brought into connexion with the fact that one character in *Phaon* was an old man in love with a music-girl whom he rapturously addresses thus : [6]

ὦ χρυσοῦν ἀνάθημα,
ὦ τοῖσιν ἐμοῖς τρυφεροῖσι τρόποις . . . ὦ γλυκὺς ἀγκών.

' O golden crown of mine, O thou . . . to my wanton temper, O sweet embrace ! ' That *Phaon* was a product of Plato's later period is shown, not only by the cookery-book (a " Middle " and " New " *motif*) and by the use of παρουσία for " affluence,"[7] but particularly by the statement [8] of a Scholiast that this comedy was produced in the archonship of Diocles, that is, in 391.

[1] Servius on Virgil, *Æn.*, III, 279.
[2] Fr. 174. Farnell (*Classical Quarterly*, XIV, pp. 139 *sqq.*) explains the whole speech as a parody of ritual enactment of sacrifices. In particular, κυσί τε καὶ κυνηγέταις (v. 16) is a skit on directions given for visiting the temple of Asclepius in the Piræus.
[3] That she is the speaker is shown by her calling herself κουροτρόφος and demanding not merely presents but sacrifices (προθύεται).
[4] This may be a reminiscence of Cratinus, who had said (Athenæus, II, 69d) of Phaon that Aphrodite herself fell in love with him and hid him 'amid fair lettuces' (ἐν καλαῖς θριδακίναις).
[5] Fr. 173. Plato gives here a burlesque of the Δεῖπνον written by Philoxenus of Cythera.
[6] Fr. 178. The phrase γλυκὺς ἀγκών may mean 'sour grapes'; see Thompson on Plato, *Phædrus*, 257d.
[7] Fr. 177.   [8] On *Plutus*, 179.

The COSTUMES (Σκευαί) was a play about the theatre, and probably about the decline of tragedy. Two poets are in one passage [1] pitted against each other, poets ridiculed by Aristophanes also:

> ἄψαι μόνον σὺ κἂν ἄκρῳ τοῦ Μορσίμου,
> ἵνα σου πατήσω τὸν Σθένελον μάλ' αὐτίκα.

'You just lay a finger on Morsimus, and I'll instantly stamp on your Sthenelus.' The ruin of choric dancing is vigorously described: [2]

> ὥστ' εἴ τις ὀρχοῖτ' εὖ, θέαμ' ἦν · νῦν δὲ δρῶσιν οὐδέν,
> ἀλλ' ὥσπερ ἀπόπληκτοι στάδην ἑστῶτες ὠρύονται.

'So if anyone danced well, there was something to watch; but nowadays they do nothing: like paralysed men they stand stock-still and howl.' *Cleophon* (an attack on the demagogue) was defeated at the Lenæan festival of 405 by the *Frogs* and by the *Muses* of Phrynichus. In the *Resident Aliens* (Μέτοικοι) the nominative ἐμαυτός occurred. *Victories* (Νῖκαι) ridiculed Aristophanes for the colossal image of Peace. *Peisander* satirized the famous oligarch of that name and the distinguished orator Antiphon; it contained also the phrase "imitating the Arcadians" which we have discussed earlier.

Conspicuous among the extracts from unnamed plays stands a rather noble address [3] to the tomb of Themistocles, who died in exile but whose remains were secretly brought back by his friends and buried in Attica on Cape Sunium:

> ὁ σὸς δὲ τύμβος ἐν καλῷ κεχωσμένος
> τοῖς ἐμπόροις πρόσρησις ἔσται πανταχοῦ,
> τούς τ' ἐκπλέοντας τ' εἰσπλέοντάς τ' ὄψεται,
> χὠπόταν ἅμιλλ' ᾖ τῶν νεῶν θεάσεται.

'And thy tomb, heaped in a fair spot, shall be hailed by merchantmen from every quarter; it shall watch the vessels homeward and outward bound, and be a

---
[1] Fr. 128. [2] Fr. 130.
[3] Fr. 183. The whole idea is based on that magnificent boast of Hector in *Iliad*, VII, 81-91. The regattas off Sunium are mentioned in *Knights*, 555; cp. Thuc., VI, xxxii, 2.

THE SCHOOL OF CRATES

spectator when the ships are racing.' It is a beautiful farewell to the founder of a naval empire. Here is an excellent attack [1] on talk-politicians :

> ἢν γὰρ ἀποθάνῃ
> εἷς τις πονηρός, δύ' ἀνέφυσαν ῥήτορες·
> οὐδεὶς γὰρ ἡμῖν Ἰόλεως ἐν τῇ πόλει,
> ὅστις ἐπικαύσει τὰς κεφαλὰς τῶν ῥητόρων.

'For if one scoundrel dies, there spring up two other politicians : we have no Iolaus in Athens to cauterize the heads of politicians.' Another delightful fragment [2] introduces a man who says he is a statue :

> A. οὗτος, τίς εἶ; λέγε ταχύ· τί σιγᾷς; οὐκ ἐρεῖς;
> B. Ἑρμῆς ἔγωγε Δαιδάλου φωνὴν ἔχων
> ξύλινος βαδίζων αὐτομάτως ἐλήλυθα.

'Hi! who are you? Tell me at once! Why silent? Come, speak!' 'Hermes am I, the work of Dædalus, endowed with speech; here self-propelled I come on wooden feet.'

---

[1] Fr. 186. The joke in the first sentence is perhaps unparalleled in ancient literature, but has a well-deserved vogue to-day in various forms, *e.g.* "one of them was a professor and the other was stupid too!".

[2] Fr. 188. The broken scansion in the first line is in notable contrast with the tragic rhythm that follows.

CHAPTER V

EUPOLIS

EUPOLIS, son of Sosipolis, was born at Athens in 445 B.C. and produced his first play in the course of his seventeenth year; that is, in 429 B.C.[1] Suidas[2] attributes to him seven victories but only seventeen plays in all; the Anonymus puts the number at fourteen. That his life was short cannot be doubted. Various stories of his death, however untrue in detail, agree in placing it before the close of the Peloponnesian War (404 B.C.); we may take it, then, that he died in early middle age. As to the manner of his death, three accounts were offered. The most widely reported was that Alcibiades, enraged by Eupolis' attack on him in the *Baptæ*, caused the poet to be drowned during the famous voyage to Sicily in 415 B.C.[3] Suidas[4] relates that 'he died in the Hellespontine region during the war against Sparta: as a result, poets were forbidden to serve in war'. This refers, no doubt, to the battles of Cynossema (411) or of Ægospotami (404). Finally Ælian[5] reports that Eupolis died in Ægina, and that his dog crouched on the tomb till he died of grief, wherefore the spot was named Κυνὸς Θρῆνος, or Dog's Dirge.

[1] Anon., *de Com.* (Kaibel, p. 8): Εὔπολις Ἀθηναῖος ἐδίδαξεν ἐπὶ ἄρχοντος Ἀπολλοδώρου, ἐφ' οὗ καὶ Φρύνιχος· γεγονὼς δυνατὸς τῇ λέξει καὶ ζηλῶν Κρατῖνον πολύ γε λοίδορον καὶ σκαιὸν ἐπιφαίνει. γέγραπται δὲ αὐτῷ δράματα ιδ'. We know fourteen titles, including the probably spurious *Helots*.

[2] Εὔπολις· καὶ οὗτος ιζ' ἐτῶν γεγονὼς ἤρξατο ἐπιδείκνυσθαι καὶ ἐδίδαξε δράματα ιζ'. ἐνίκησε δὲ ζ'. καὶ ἀπέθανε ναυαγήσας κατὰ τὸν Ἑλλήσποντον ἐν τῷ πρὸς Λακεδαιμονίους πολέμῳ. καὶ ἐκ τούτου ἐκωλύθη στρατεύεσθαι ποιητήν. τὰ δὲ δράματα αὐτοῦ Αἶγες, Ἀστράτευτοι ἢ Ἀνδρόγονοι, καὶ ἄλλα.

[3] Cp. Platonius (Kaibel, p. 4): ἴσμεν γοῦν τὸν Εὔπολιν ἐπὶ τῷ διδάξαι τοὺς Βάπτας ἀποπνιγέντα εἰς τὴν θάλασσαν ὑπ' ἐκείνου εἰς ὃν καθῆκε τοὺς Βάπτας. The story is certainly untrue: see below, p. 189.

[4] See above.   [5] *Nat. Hist. An.*, X, 41.

This faithful friend (says Ælian) had already shown his devotion by killing Eupolis' slave, Ephialtes, who had stolen some of the poet's manuscripts.

Eupolis was invariably placed beside Cratinus and Aristophanes as one of the three Masters of Old Comedy;[1] he collaborated in the *Knights;* he won seven first prizes in his brief career; with the *Flatterers* he defeated Aristophanes' *Peace* in 421 B.C. Platonius[2] writes: 'Eupolis shows magnificent imagination in his plots. His opening scenes are great, and he excites in the play itself that imagination which other poets stir in the parabasis, being powerful enough to bring up figures of legislators from the dead, and through their mouths to advocate the passing or repeal of laws. This loftiness is matched by his charm and the aptness of his jests.' All this reveals a very great comic dramatist, who corresponded to Sophocles as Cratinus to Æschylus and Aristophanes to Euripides. Unfortunately our fragments are too meagre for anything but a hint of this excellence: even Cratinus is in far better case.

The DEMES (Δῆμοι, the wards or parishes of Attica) was apparently one of his finest works; it has been called "the most important political comedy of all time";[3] of late it has gained even more attractiveness for us by Lefèbvre's discovery in Egypt of three papyrus-leaves, which were published in 1911.[4] These

---

[1] *E.g.* Horace, *Sat.*, I, iv, 1:
    Eupolis atque Cratinus Aristophanesque poetæ
    atque alii, quorum comœdia prisca virorum est. . . .
Quintilian, X, i, 65: *Plures eius auctores: Aristophanes tamen et Eupolis Cratinusque præcipui.*

[2] Kaibel, p. 6: Εὔπολις δὲ εὐφάνταστος μὲν εἰς ὑπερβολήν ἐστι κατὰ τὰς ὑποθέσεις· τὰς γὰρ εἰσηγήσεις μεγάλας τῶν δραμάτων ποιεῖται, καὶ ἥνπερ ἐν τῇ παραβάσει φαντασίαν κινοῦσιν οἱ λοιποί, ταύτην ἐκεῖνος ἐν αὐτοῖς τοῖς δράμασιν, ἀναγαγεῖν ἱκανὸς ὢν ἐξ Ἅιδου νομοθετῶν πρόσωπα καὶ δι' αὐτῶν εἰσηγούμενος ἢ περὶ θέσεως νόμων ἢ καταλύσεως. ὥσπερ δέ ἐστιν ὑψηλὸς οὕτω καὶ ἐπίχαρις καὶ περὶ τὰ σκώμματα λίαν εὔστοχος.

[3] Körte (Pauly-Wissowa, XI, 1238).

[4] *Catalogue général des antiquités égyptiennes du musée de Caire*, no. 43227, *Papyrus de Ménandre*, par M. Gustave Lefèbvre, Cairo, 1911. The papyri belong to the fourth or fifth century after Christ. The chief discussions

remains extend over one hundred and seventeen lines, but the papyrus is in such bad condition that by no means all of this mass can be read ; we have, however, a few substantial pieces, including a portion of the parabasis. We must keep three aspects clearly separate : the main outline of the plot, which no one disputes ; the details that we learn from trustworthy ancient authorities ; the undoubted facts to be gained from the papyri. Only then can we consider the probable or possible things that emerge from the papyri by assistance of likely or dubious conjecture.

First, then, it is agreed by all that some one,[1] distressed by the plight of Athens, brought from the dead certain Athenian Worthies to help the State.

Secondly, three ancient writers amplify the above. Plutarch [2] tells us that (i) the Worthies were statesmen, (ii) Pericles was among them, (iii) Pericles was named last, (iv) Myronides (or Pyronides) [3] answered Pericles' question about his surviving son. The Scholiast on

---

of reading and interpretation are those of Körte (*Hermes*, 47, pp. 276 *sqq.*), Keil (*Göttingische Nachrichten*, 1912, pp. 237 *sqq.*), Jensen (*Hermes*, 51, pp. 321 *sqq.*), Robert (*Göttingische Gelehrte Anzeiger*, 1918, pp. 321 *sqq.*), and Körte (*Verhandlungen der Sächs. Akad. d. Wiss. zu Leipzig*, phil.-hist. Klasse, 71, 1919).

[1] One naturally supposes a living Athenian or Athenians, and we shall see below that it was certainly Nicias, whether assisted or not by Myronides (or Pyronides); but Hermann (*Opusc.*, V, p. 292) thought it was Hermes, the divine ψυχοπομπός.

[2] *Pericles*, III : Ὁ δ' Εὔπολις ἐν τοῖς Δήμοις πυνθανόμενος περὶ ἑκάστου τῶν ἀναβεβηκότων ἐξ Ἅιδου δημαγωγῶν, ὡς ὁ Περικλῆς ὠνόμαστο τελευταῖος, ὅ τι περ κεφάλαιον τῶν κάτωθεν ἤγαγες (Kock, fr. 93). *Ibid.*, XXIV : δοκεῖ δὲ καὶ τὸν νόθον ἐκ ταύτης (sc. Ἀσπασίας) τεκνῶσαι, περὶ οὗ πεποίηκεν Εὔπολις ἐν Δήμοις αὐτὸν μὲν οὕτως ἐρωτῶντα· ὁ νόθος δέ μοι ζῇ; τὸν δὲ Μυρωνίδην ἀποκρινόμενον·

καὶ πάλαι γ' ἂν ἦν ἀνήρ,
εἰ μὴ τὸ τῆς πόρνης ὑπωρρώδει κακόν.

[3] In *Pericles*, XXIV (see above) Μυρωνίδην is merely a "Byzantine conjecture" for Πυρωνίδην (Wilamowitz-Moellendorff in *Hermes*, 54, p. 69). Who Pyronides may have been we do not know. Myronides is of course the celebrated victor of Œnophyta (456 B.C.): he has in two places been read into the papyrus. But by quaint ill-luck his first letter is in both places illegible—the name may be that of his shadowy rival Pyronides. Körte supposes that the character is "Pyronides" indeed, but that this is a nickname for Myronides (cp. "Labes" for "Laches" in the *Wasps*).

Aristides,[1] the rhetorician, names the Worthies as Miltiades, Aristides, Gelon and Pericles; Gelon is undoubtedly a mistake for Solon.[2] This writer mentions Eupolis, but does not name the play that is in his mind; still one cannot seriously doubt that it is the *Demes*. Finally, Galen[3] says that Nicias was one of the characters.

Thirdly, the papyri reveal the following facts:
(a) *As regards authorship*:
(i) The first two leaves at least belong to the *Demes* of Eupolis. For we read in one place πέττειν and, underneath it, γγενωμ, with three undecipherable letters following. Unless we postulate an amazing coincidence, these words must belong to a fragment already known to us:[4]

τὸ χαλκίον
θέρμαινέ θ' ἡμῖν καὶ θύη πέττειν τινὰ
κέλευ', ἵνα σπλάγχνοισι συγγενώμεθα.

(ii) Nevertheless, a few lines below we read ... ου τ' ἐκείνου καὶ φρενῶν, which, clearly suggesting Cratinus' line ἥβης ἐκείνης νοῦ τ' ἐκείνου καὶ φρενῶν,[5] seems to imply that Cratinus wrote the papyrus-play. The words should, however, be regarded as a quotation by Eupolis from Cratinus.[6]

---

[1] III, p. 672 (Dindorf): Εὔπολις ἐποίησεν ἀναστάντα τὸν Μιλτιάδην καὶ Ἀριστείδην καὶ Γέλωνα καὶ Περικλέα. This and other passages show what we are to make of the statement by the Scholiast on *Acharnians*, 64: Εὔπολις ἐν Δήμοις εἰσάγει τὸν Πεισιστράτον βασιλέα. He means merely that Eupolis called P. a king.

[2] Gelon was a Sicilian tyrant and never had any close connexion with Athens.

[3] See below, p. 183.

[4] Fr. 108. This proof was pointed out by Körte (*Berl. Philol. Wochenschrift*, Dec. 9th, 1911).

[5] Εὐνεῖδαι, fr. 1 (Meineke); cp. fr. 65 (Kock).

[6] Our papyrus cannot belong to the *Euneidæ*, for the *Euneidæ*, being anterior to the *Knights* (v. 529 of which quotes from it), cannot have mentioned the expedition to Mantinea. The language, too, shows that this is a quotation:

ἤρχετον σὺ καὶ Σόλων
ἤβης τ' ἐκείνης νοῦ τ' ἐκείνου καὶ φρενῶν.

ἤρχετον suits ἤβης, but goes awkwardly with the other genitives.

(b) *As regards date:*

(i) The expedition to Mantinea, which occurred in 418, is mentioned in lines tolerably perfect:

εἰς δὲ Μαντίνειαν ὑμᾶς οὗτος οὐ μέμνησθ' ὅτι
τοῦ θεοῦ βροντῶντος ὑμῖν οὐδ' ἐῶντος ἐμβαλεῖν
εἶπε δήσειν τοὺς στρατηγοὺς πρὸς βίαν ἐν τῷ ξύλῳ ; [1]

'Do you not remember that, when Heaven thundered upon you and forbade you to invade Mantinea, this man said he would pillory the generals by force?'

(ii) 'The people in the Long Walls' (τοὺς ἐν μακροῖν τειχοῖν) are spoken of in a passage to be discussed later. The words are possibly an indication of date:[2] country-dwellers have been forced by the Spartan invasion of Attica to dwell in the fortified area. Unfortunately, this happened in two periods, that preceding Sphacteria in 425,[3] and that following the occupation of Decelea in 413.[4]

(c) *As regards plot:*

(i) Certain people came back from the dead. The most unmistakable proof is the phrase ἤρχετον σὺ καὶ Σόλων—'when you and Solon governed'. Some one is addressed who was a ruler (or statesman) in an earlier generation: he is not necessarily a contemporary of Solon's, but he must be ancient or he would not be coupled with him. Strong confirmation is given by the protest quoted from Euripides:[5] τί τοὺς θανόντας οὐκ ἐᾷς τεθνηκέναι; 'Why do you not suffer the dead to remain dead?'

---

[1] The generals were Nicias, Nicostratus, and Laches—all members of the peace-party; and in any case Nicias could be depended on to accept unfavourable omens. The expedition was led by Nicostratus and Laches (Thuc., V, 61).

[2] So Körte takes them (*Hermes*, 47, pp. 295 *sq.*). He insists that the Worthies must have been summoned because of a great misfortune. None had happened in the former Long Walls period, but the Sicilian disaster just preceded the second. Now, as for the second, the year 413 will not serve, for Agis invaded Attica later than the dramatic festivals of that year (ἦρος εὐθὺς ἀρχομένου, Thuc., VII, xix, 1). We are therefore left with one year only for the production of the *Demes*, 412, since Eupolis fell in 411. (But why should his play not have been produced at one of the festivals of 411? They occurred before the fighting season began.) We shall later see reason to reject all this.

[3] Thucydides, II, xvii.   [4] *Id.*, VII, xxvii, 5.   [5] Fr. 507, Nauck.

(ii) The third leaf shows a whole scene with fair completeness. Some blackmailer " proves " that he is a just man by relating how he dealt with a foreigner (from Epidaurus, it seems) whom he saw coming into the Agora with barley in his beard. Pretending to believe this a proof of villainy—that he has been drinking κυκεών [1]—he extorted a hundred gold staters from him. ' If a man pays he may do what he likes ' appears to be the blackmailer's boasted justice. The person to whom he gives this lecture may be Aristides. Whoever it is, he has the blackmailer arrested and punished despite his protests, after which he issues to Athens some proclamation about justice.

The date of the play can be fixed very closely. It was produced after Mantinea (418) and before Nicias left Athens for ever in 415. This means that the apparently valuable evidence about the Long Walls must be disregarded, and we may do so with little misgiving.[2]

We may now proceed to deal with the play in detail so far as is possible. The Worthies were summoned by Nicias,[3] who stated to them the grievous plight of Athens and begged their help. Some fragments describe the evil conditions that have prompted this necromancy :

καὶ λέγουσί γε
τὰ μειράκια προιστάμενα τοῖς ἀνδράσιν.

' Yes, and the lads get up and speak before the men.' [4]

---

[1] Körte (*Hermes*, 47, p. 308) points out that the κυκεών was the Eleusinian mystery-drink. He then refers the scene to the famous travesty committed by Alcibiades, just before the Sicilian expedition, and so gains further support for his dating of the play.

[2] After all the discussions, we simply do not know the point of the reference to οἱ ἐν μακροῖν τειχοῖν. Therefore we have no right to say that the mere mention of them must supply a date by reference to the dates of the Spartan inroads. There may be half-a-dozen reasons why people lived there between the invasions. Some of the first refugees may have "stayed on"; and so forth.

[3] See fr. 91, Meineke, II, 455. According to Galen (V, p. 38, ed. Kühn) the person who conversed with Pericles was Nicias.

[4] Fr. 310.

Some especially objectionable politician is apparently referred to in the lines :[1]

> ὃν χρῆν ἔν τε ταῖς τριόδοις καὶ τοῖς ὀξυθυμίοις
> προστρόπαιον τῆς πόλεως κάεσθαι τετριγότα.

'Who ought to burn, sputtering at the cross-roads, among the rubbish as the city's scapegoat.' The speaker's hope in the Worthies is that they will cause 'our country to bloom and flourish again'—ἀμβλυστονῆσαι καὶ χλοῆσαι τὴν πόλιν.[2] One passage[3] may point to the ceremony of evocation :

> τὸ χαλκίον
> θέρμαινέ θ' ἡμῖν καὶ θύη πέττειν τινά
> κέλευ', ἵνα σπλάγχοισι συγγενώμεθα.

'Heat the cauldron for us and bid some one knead incense, that we may deal with the offerings.'

The new papyrus apparently makes the Four Worthies arrive in a body and sit in a row ; compare the words of Plutarch :[4] 'Eupolis in the *Demes*, inquiring about each of the statesmen that have ascended from Hades, remarks (since Pericles had been named last) :

> ὅ τι περ κεφάλαιον τῶν κάτωθεν ἤγαγες.

"You have brought the crown of the lower world ".' Seven lines describing the unique eloquence of Pericles form perhaps the best-known passage of Greek Comedy outside the work of Aristophanes :[5]

> A. κράτιστος οὗτος ἐγένετ' ἀνθρώπων λέγειν·
> ὁπότε παρέλθοι δ', ὥσπερ ἀγαθοὶ δρομῆς
> ἐκ δέκα ποδῶν ᾕρει λέγων τοὺς ῥήτορας.

---

[1] Fr. 120. The metre is Eupolidean ; the passage no doubt belongs to the parabasis. For the sentiment compare *Frogs*, 732 *sq.*
[2] Fr. 105. [3] Fr. 108.
[4] *Pericles*, III (quoted above). The papyrus reads, according to Jensen's restoration (*loc. cit.*, p. 329) :

> ἐπεὶ δοκῶ τοὺς ἄνδρας ἤδη τούσδ' ὁρᾶν
> καθημένους, οὕς φασιν ἥκειν παρὰ νεκρῶν, κτέ.

(of παρὰ νεκρῶν the MS. gives only the first α.)
[5] Fr. 94. Curiously enough it is precisely this power that Alcibiades in a celebrated passage of Plato (*Symp.*, 215E) denies to Pericles and assigns to Socrates. It is commonly thought that Pericles left his κέντρον in Thucydides—that the Funeral Speech (II, 35-46) contains real Periclean phrases.

B. ταχὺν λέγεις μέν, πρὸς δέ γ' αὐτοῦ τῷ τάχει
πειθώ τις ἐπεκάθιζεν ἐπὶ τοῖς χείλεσιν,
οὕτως ἐκήλει, καὶ μόνος τῶν ῥητόρων
τὸ κέντρον ἐγκατέλειπε τοῖς ἀκροωμένοις.

'This was the most consummate speaker in the world. Whenever he came forward, like a good runner he overtook the orators though they had ten feet start.' 'A rapid speaker, indeed; but besides his speed, a strange charm sat upon his lips, such a wizard was he; and alone of orators he left his sting in the hearer.' At some point in the action Pericles asks of his illegitimate son, and is told by Myronides :[1] ' he would long ago have been a man had he not quailed before the disgrace of his birth '.[2] Further dispraise of the younger Pericles must have followed, for his father laments :[3]

οὐ δεινὸν οὖν κριοὺς ἐμ' ἐκγεννᾶν τέκνα,
ὄρνεις δ' ὁμοίους τοὺς νεοττοὺς τῷ πατρί;

'Is it not shocking that while birds beget chicks resembling their fathers, my children should be rams?'

Of the other three, Solon has scarcely anything, perhaps nothing, to say in our fragments, though one may think that his style is to be recognized in

ἀνὴρ πολίτης πουλύπους ἐς τοὺς τρόπους.[4]

'A citizen who behaves like a cuttle-fish.' From Miltiades there comes the outburst [5] that suggested a famous phrase to Demosthenes :

οὐ γὰρ μὰ τὴν Μαραθῶνι τὴν ἐμὴν μάχην
χαίρων τις αὐτῶν τοὐμὸν ἀλγυνεῖ κέαρ.

'By Marathon, mine own battle, none of them shall grieve my soul unchastised.' This is probably the same victory which is said, in an obscure fragment,[6]

[1] Or perhaps Pyronides: see above. [2] Fr. 98.
[3] Fr. 99. Κριούς refers to a proverb about ungrateful children, ἐπεὶ τὰς φάτνας πλήττουσιν οἱ κριοί (Zenobius, IV, 63).
[4] Fr. 101. We should say "a chameleon". Meier (quoted, but with disapproval, by Kock) thought that Theramenes was meant.
[5] Fr. 90. Cp. Dem., *De Corona*, 208 : μὰ τοὺς Μαραθῶνι προκινδυνεύσαντας τῶν προγόνων. Eupolis in his second line is himself borrowing from Euripides (*Medea*, 304, 307).
[6] Fr. 116, where see Kock's discussion.

to eclipse the triumph of all succeeding generals. Aristides bulks more largely to our view. Nicias asks him (how like Nicias !) ' By what means did you become just ? ' The answer is

> ἡ μὲν φύσις τὸ μέγιστόν ἐστ', ἔπειτα δὲ
> κἀγὼ προθύμως τῇ φύσει συνελάμβανον.[1]

' Nature's is the largest share : then I eagerly assisted her.' Not a thrilling rejoinder ; but it recalls the old opposition of " nature " and " instruction " that so continuously exercised the mind of Pindar. In the papyrus there is a good deal more concerning Aristides (probably) and justice : see the passage about the blackmailer mentioned above. After committing the blackmailer to the stocks he delivers an oration concerning justice which begins :

> ἐγὼ δὲ πάσῃ προσαγορεύω τῇ πόλει
> εἶναι δικαίους, ὡς ὃς ἂν δίκαιος ᾖ. . . .

' I issue proclamation to all Athens, that men shall be just. For whosoever is just . . .'

So much for the part played by the Four Worthies. Returning to the evocation, we find that one of them asks the reason for this summons :

> λέγ' ὅτου 'πιθυμεῖς, κοὐδὲν ἀτυχήσεις ἐμοῦ.[2]

' Tell your wish, and you shall have all from me.' No doubt Nicias and Myronides explained at length, giving details of the evil conditions in Athens. A number of uninteresting fragments would fit in here, and perhaps some of those tentatively assigned above to the opening of the play. Certainly here must have occurred the vigorous appeal : [3]

> καὶ μηκέτ', ὦναξ Μιλτιάδη καὶ Περίκλεες,
> ἐάσατ' ἄρχειν μειράκια κινούμενα,
> ἐν τοῖν σφυροῖν ἕλκοντα τὴν στρατηγίαν.

' And henceforth, lord Miltiades and Pericles, debar from office the depraved lads who trail their com-

---

[1] Fr. 91.   [2] Fr. 114.
[3] Fr. 100. The text is not quite certain, nor the meaning of the last line —' who haul their generalship in their ankles,' literally.

missions in the gutter.' This explanatory scene closed apparently with the lines : [1]

καὶ τοῦ μὲν ἐν κύκλῳ γε παύσομαι λόγου,
φράσω δέ σοι τὸ πρᾶγμα διὰ τῶν χωρίων.

This is obscure, because it depends partly upon word-play.[2] The gist of it is : ' I will cease talking at large and let the Athenian parishes speak for themselves.' Aristides (or Miltiades) has already been told ' You Worthies shall learn how much worse off all the demes are now than of yore, when you and Solon ruled '. At this point, then, the complaints and entreaties of the spokesmen are taken up and given particularity (comic or pathetic or both) by members of the chorus who present [3] the Attic demes. It is a device resembling the splendid conception of our poet's *Cities*. None of the fragments can be referred with certainty to these detailed complaints.

Near the end came this passage : [4]

A. ἀναθῶμεν νῦν χἠμεῖς τούτοις τασδὶ τὰς εἰρεσιώνας
καὶ προσαγήλωμεν ἀπελθόντες.
B. χαίρετε πάντες.
A. δεχόμεσθα.

' Let us, too, adorn them with these harvest wreaths, depart and do worship.' ' Fare ye all well ! ' ' We accept.' It is a reverent farewell offered to the Four.

The longest fragment [5] of all would fit in at various points :

καὶ μὴν ἐγὼ πολλῶν παρόντων οὐκ ἔχω τί λέξω,
οὕτω σφόδρ' ἀλγῶ τὴν πολιτείαν ὁρῶν παρ' ἡμῖν.
ἡμεῖς γὰρ οὐχ οὕτω τέως ᾠκοῦμεν οἱ γέροντες,
ἀλλ' ἦσαν ἡμῖν τῇ πόλει πρῶτον μὲν οἱ στρατηγοὶ
ἐκ τῶν μεγίστων οἰκιῶν, πλούτῳ γένει τε πρῶτοι,
οἷς ὡσπέρει θεοῖσιν ηὐχόμεσθα· καὶ γὰρ ἦσαν·
ὥστ' ἀσφαλῶς ἐπράττομεν· νυνὶ δ', ὅταν τύχωμεν,
στρατευόμεσθ' αἱρούμενοι καθάρματα στρατηγούς.

---

[1] Fr. 106.
[2] Probably Eupolis here calls the parishes χωρία instead of δῆμοι because χωρίον means "place" not only geographically but also scientifically—"locus" or "area" as in a diagram : each man of the chorus has his special post or χωρίον from which he steps forward to speak his short contribution.
[3] How, is not plain. There were over a hundred demes, only twenty-four choristers. Probably twenty-four named demes were presented, chosen for their importance or comic utility (queer names, interesting members, etc.).
[4] Fr. 119. The division between speakers is uncertain.
[5] Fr. 117.

'Indeed, despite the abundance of matter I know not what to say, so deeply pained am I by the spectacle of our present public life. This was not the way we aged men lived formerly. First of all, the generals that our city employed came from the greatest houses, men prominent in wealth and birth, to whom we prayed as if they were gods, as indeed they were; so that our affairs were safe. But to-day, when the fit takes us, we go to war electing scoundrels as our generals.' Probably it is the opening of an elaborate speech made by Nicias or Myronides to the chorus, and leading up to the suggestion that, in default of decent contemporary leaders, the Four should be summoned. Nothing further can be gleaned as to the plot: we do not even know what definite result accrued from this experiment in political necromancy.

Concerning the BAPTÆ (Βάπται)[1] our chief source is the Scholiast on Juvenal, II, 91 *sq.*:

> talia secreta coluerunt orgia tæda
> Cecropidam soliti Baptæ lassare Cotytto.

'Such orgies were celebrated with secret torches by the Baptæ, who were wont to tire Athenian Cotytto.' On this passage the Scholiast remarks: '*Baptæ* is the name of a book wherein shameless persons are described by Eupolis, who represents Athenian men dancing in female guise until the music-girl is tired. So the *Baptæ* were effeminate men, under which title Eupolis wrote a comedy, wherefore he was killed by Alcibiades, whom he had especially attacked.' Of all this but little is found in our fragments. There remain a reference[2] to the magic wheel employed for weaving spells; the cry of ecstatic invocation, εὐαὶ σαβαῖ; three or four lines of lyric trochees describing the lewd motions of a musician;[3] and an obscure

---

[1] The meaning is doubtful. Literally it means "dippers," but baptismal rites were by no means peculiar to the Cotyttia. Meineke (I, p. 123) suggests "those who dye their hair"—that is, as a part of their effeminacy. Lobeck (*Aglaophamus*, II, p. 1019) takes the name as a reference to ritual washing.
[2] Fr. 72.   [3] Fr. 77.

scholium [1] on Æschines reporting that the Baptæ had an obscene vocabulary of their own. Further light on the plot is perhaps given by Hesychius, who writes, under the entry *Cotytto :* ' Eupolis, in his hatred of the Corinthians, introduces a certain vulgar divinity '.[2] If we assume [3] that our poet spoke of Cotytto in only one drama, we may with Meineke interpret Hesychius as showing that Eupolis' purpose was ' to assail the criminal lust of the Corinthians (among whom the worship of Cotytto was highly revered) and so bring the rites of Cotytto into contempt, thus preventing their reception into Athens.'

But the chief interest of the *Baptæ* lies in its connexion with Alcibiades, a possible reference to whom is found in the line ὅτι οὐκ ἀτρύφερος οὐδ' ἄωρός ἐστ' ἀνήρ [4]—' because he is a man of fashion in the prime of life '. The story was well known [5] that, when the Athenian Armada was on its way to Sicily in 415 B.C., Alcibiades caused Eupolis to be drowned because of the attack on himself in the play. An epigram makes him exclaim :

βάπτεις μ' ἐν θυμέλῃσιν, ἐγὼ δέ σε κύμασι πόντου
βαπτίζων ὀλέσω, νάμασι πικροτάτοις.

' You " dip " me in the theatre, but I will dip you in the sea-waves' bitter flood and slay you.' But the story, as Cicero [6] tells us, was rejected by Eratosthenes, who pointed out that there were later plays by Eupolis. What connexion existed between this comedy and the famous burlesque of religious mysteries that contributed to Alcibiades' recall from his Sicilian command ? That outrage was a travesty of Demeter's

[1] Fr. 82. See Meineke, I, p. 335, and II, p. 451.
[2] Ὁ μὲν Εὔπολις κατ' ἔχθος τὸ πρὸς τοὺς Κορινθίους φορτικόν τινα δαίμονα διατίθεται. Meineke, followed by Kock, takes διατίθεται as 'in scena exhibet'. It is possible, as Meineke (II, p. 121) says, that the disreputable *psaltria* was Cotytto herself.
[3] This assumption is fairly safe : Cotytto was not well known in Athens, though her worship was received into that city (Kaibel, Pauly-Wissowa, VI, 1233). Lucian writes (*adv. indoct.*, 27) : ἀνέγνως καὶ τοὺς Βάπτας, τὸ δρᾶμα ὅλον ; εἶτ' οὐδέν σου τἀκεῖ καθίκετο οὐδ' ἠρυθρίασας γνωρίσας αὐτά ;
[4] Fr. 69.   [5] See above, p. 178.   [6] *Ad Atticum*, VI, 1.

worship, and she was incomparably better known and more revered in Athens than Cotytto. The likeliest view is that Eupolis produced his play in 415 B.C., a few months before the Sicilian expedition set sail, and that it conveyed, not a direct censure of Alcibiades' misconduct, but a burlesque of it, no doubt with hostile intent. Cotytto was substituted for Demeter because the former goddess was vastly more suitable to the comic stage than the latter. One deeply interesting fragment has nothing to do with all this, but concerns the quarrel between Eupolis and Aristophanes. It is a scrap [1] from the parabasis:

κἀκείνους τοὺς Ἱππέας
συνεποίησα τῷ φαλακρῷ τούτῳ κἀδωρησάμην.

'And that play, the *Knights*, I generously helped our Baldhead to write.' But this it will be more convenient to discuss elsewhere.[2]

The FLATTERERS (Κόλακες), which in 421 B.C. won the first prize over the *Peace* of Aristophanes, was a social satire, depicting the reckless self-indulgence and ostentatious hospitality of Callias, the son of Hipponicus, and the rapacity of the parasites who fleeced him; among these latter was Protagoras, the most renowned of all sophists. This comedy, then, was apparently the analogue of Plato's *Protagoras*, in which that sophist and some of his rivals, together with Socrates, meet in Callias' house. There may well have been a burlesque lecture delivered by the distinguished guest, but there are only two hints of this:

ἔνδοθι μέν ἐστι Πρωταγόρας ὁ Τήϊος,
ὃς ἀλαζονεύεται μέν, ἀλιτήριος,
περὶ τῶν μετεώρων, τὰ δὲ χαμᾶθεν ἐσθίει.[3]

'Indoors is Protagoras of Teos, who orates pretentiously, the scoundrel, about the celestial, but eats the terrestrial.' This is the stock accusation, so familiar in the *Clouds*, that the typical teacher of scientific

[1] Fr. 78. [2] See below, pp. 210 *sq*. [3] Fr. 146.

thought is a philosophic Stiggins. A scrap of bogus science is given : [1]

πίνειν γὰρ αὐτὸν Πρωταγόρας ἐκέλευ', ἵνα
πρὸ τοῦ κυνὸς τὸν πνεύμον' ἔκκλυστον φορῇ.

'For Protagoras bade him drink to irrigate his lungs before the dog-days.' But the fragments are mostly sentences about the ways of parasites. One of them deserves careful study. It treats exactly the same topic as the admirable passage in Epicharmus' *Hope*: immensely less vigorous, it reveals nevertheless greater skill in composition, and the authentic Athenian limpidity.[2] It is the longest complete portion of Eupolis that we possess, delivered by the chorus (composed of flatterers) in their parabasis:

ἀλλὰ δίαιταν ἣν ἔχουσ' οἱ κόλακες πρὸς ὑμᾶς
λέξομεν· ἀλλ' ἀκούσαθ' ὡς ἐσμὲν ἅπαντα κομψοὶ
ἄνδρες· ὅτοισι πρῶτα μὲν παῖς ἀκόλουθός ἐστιν
ἀλλότριος τὰ πολλά, μικρὸν δέ τι κἀμὸν αὐτοῦ.
ἱματίω δέ μοι δύ' ἐστὸν χαρίεντε τούτω,
οἷν μεταλαμβάνων ἀεὶ θάτερον ἐξελαύνω
εἰς ἀγοράν, ἐκεῖ δ' ἐπειδὰν κατίδω τιν' ἄνδρα
ἠλίθιον, πλουτοῦντα δ', εὐθὺς περὶ τοῦτόν εἰμι.
κἄν τι τύχῃ λέγων ὁ πλούταξ, πάνυ τοῦτ' ἐπαινῶ,
καὶ καταπλήττομαι δοκῶν τοῖσι λόγοισι χαίρειν.
εἶτ' ἐπὶ δεῖπνον ἐρχόμεσθ' ἄλλυδις ἄλλος ἡμῶν
μᾶζαν ἐπ' ἀλλόφυλον, οὗ δεῖ χαρίεντα πολλὰ
τὸν κόλακ' εὐθέως λέγειν, ἢ 'κφέρεται θύραζε.
οἶδα δ' Ἀκέστορ' αὐτὸ τὸν στιγματίαν παθόντα·
σκῶμμα γὰρ εἶπ' ἀσελγές, εὖτ' αὐτὸν ὁ παῖς θύραζε
ἐξαγαγὼν ἔχοντα κλοιὸν καρέδωκεν Οἰνεῖ.

'But we will describe to you the life of flatterers: just hear what complete exquisites we are. First, we have a page at our heels: he is mostly another man's —I have little share in him myself. For clothes, I possess these two delightful garments, in one or the other of which I march forth every day into the market-place. Once there, whenever I espy some one with no brains but plenty of money, I am at him instantly. If my plutocrat lets fall a remark, I praise it vehemently,

[1] Fr. 147.
[2] Fr. 159. The metre is the "first Priapean". Œneus at the end is 'the eponymous hero of the tribe Œneis, in the deme of which, called Κειρίαδαι, was the βάραθρον' (Kock).

filled with pretended rapture. Next we make off dispersedly to dine at the table of others, where the flatterer must straightway discharge a flood of wit or be flung out into the street. I remember that happening to Acestor, who began life as a slave: he made an indecent joke, and the servant haled him out of doors in a wooden collar and had him thrown into the pit.'

MARICAS (Μαρικᾶς—' a barbarian boy's nickname,' says Hesychius) was produced in 421 B.C. It was a satire directed against the demagogue Hyperbolus, attacked under a barbarian name, just as Cleon is called the " Paphlagonian " in the *Knights*. One of our fragments is a parody of a familiar Æschylean passage.[1] As opponent to Hyperbolus, Eupolis puts forward Nicias, concerning whom the longest fragment [2] says :

>   MAP. πόσου χρόνου γὰρ ξυγγεγένησαι Νικίᾳ;
>   B. οὐδ' εἶδον, εἰ μὴ 'ναγχος ἑστῶτ' ἐν ἀγορᾷ.
>   MAP. ἀνὴρ ὁμολογεῖ Νικίαν ἑορακέναι.
>   καίτοι τί παθὼν ἂν εἶδεν, εἰ μὴ προυδίδου;
>   Γ. ἠκούσατ', ὦ ξυνήλικες,
>   ἐπ' αὐτοφώρῳ Νικίαν εἰλημμένον;
>   B. ὑμεῖς γάρ, ὦ φρενοβλαβεῖς,
>   λάβοιτ' ἂν ἄνδρ' ἄριστον ἐν κακῷ τινί;

Maricas : How long is it since you met Nicias ?
Citizen : I haven't even seen him, except when he was standing in the market-place the other day.
Mar. : The man owns to having seen Nicias ! and how could he have seen him unless treason were afoot ?
Others : You hear, gossips, that Nicias has been caught red-handed ?
Cit. : What, you lunatics ? Could you possibly catch that excellent man in any misdeed ?

Eupolis is deriding the wild and unscrupulous accusations of disloyalty to the State that demagogues loved to bring against distinguished conservatives. We learn further about Maricas from Quintilian [3] that ' he

---

[1] Fr. 192. Cp. Æsch., *Persæ*, 65.
[2] Fr. 181. The passage is given by Plutarch (*Nicias*, IV) who says: ὁ δ' ὑπ' Εὐπόλιδος κωμῳδούμενος ἐν Μαρίκᾳ προάγων τινὰ τῶν ἀπραγμόνων καὶ πενήτων λέγει· πόσου κτέ.
[3] I, x, 18: *Maricas, qui est Hyperbolus, nihil se ex musicis scire nisi litteras confitetur.* Cp. *Knights*, 188 *sq.*

owns to knowing naught of culture except the alphabet'. But he picked up experience by "knocking about" Athens:

> καὶ πόλλ' ἔμαθον ἐν τοῖσι κουρείοις ἐγὼ
> ἀτόπως καθίζων κοὐδὲ γιγνώσκειν δοκῶν,

'learned much in the barber-shops, sitting unsuspected and pretending not to understand'.[1] Even from the surviving scraps it is plain that there must have been some likeness between *Maricas* and Aristophanes' *Knights*, produced four years earlier. And a charge of bungling parody was made by Aristophanes in the *Clouds*[2]—a diatribe composed, for greater pungency, in Eupolis' own favourite metre.

The CITIES (Πόλεις) was probably one of the most charming and vigorous comedies ever produced in Athens. The Cities were the subject-states of the Athenian Empire: each member of the chorus represented some famous town and entered separately (like the birds in Aristophanes), being described in a few "topical" lines by one of the main persons, his companion adding to the description a facetious footnote of his own. The greatest of the allies was presented in lines that must have aroused a tempest of proud applause:[3]

> αὕτη Χίος, καλὴ πόλις . . .
> πέμπει γὰρ ἡμῖν ναῦς μακρὰς ἄνδρας θ' ὅταν δεήσῃ
> καὶ τἄλλα πειθαρχεῖ καλῶς, ἄπληκτος ὥσπερ ἵππος.

'Here comes Chios, a beautiful city . . . for she sends us cruisers and men at need, in all ways nobly loyal, like a horse that needs no goad.' Probably the Chian chorister was decked with naval gear, as the next two fragments suggest:

> Τῆνος αὕτη
> πολλοὺς ἔχουσα σκορπίους ἔχεις τε συκοφάντας.[4]

'Tenos comes next, holding scorpions in plenty and snake-like sycophants.' The last figure in the pro-

[1] Fr. 180.   [2] vv. 553-6. See pp. 210 *sq.*, 388.
[3] Fr. 232.   [4] Fr. 231.

cession was a brilliant apparition in spangles. Her description[1] is very brief, and therefore, no doubt, we are to suppose the loss of at least one line; but we possess here the contribution of the facetious confidant or clown:

> A. ἡ δ' ὑστάτη ποῦ 'σθ';
> B. ἥδε Κύζικος πλέα στατήρων.
> A. ἐν τῇδε τοίνυν τῇ πόλει φρουρῶν ἐγώ ποτ' αὐτὸς
> γυναῖκ' ἐκίνουν κολλύβου καὶ παῖδα καὶ γέροντα,
> κἀξῆν ὅλην τὴν ἡμέραν τὸν κύσθον ἐκκορίζειν.

Little is left concerning the other twenty-one cities: possibly the line πεφυτευμένη δ' αὕτη 'στὶν ἢ ψιλὴ μόνον;—'is this planted with fruit-trees or merely bare?'—alludes to another.[2] The lexicographer Harpocration reports that Eupolis in this comedy mentioned ἀμόργινα, a kind of dress-fabric; so the island of Amorgos may have been presented.

What was the purpose of this exciting pageant? Almost certainly to introduce a plea for better treatment of the subject-allies; in addition to the normal strain of the Peloponnesian War, they had recently seen their tribute to the Athenian exchequer doubled by Cleon. The evidence that Eupolis not only discussed their plight but also championed them is not strong, but must be regarded as fairly adequate. First, a number of Athenians were censured by name:[3] this in itself, of course, is very weak, but it gains a little strength from the Procession of Allies. Second, one or two passages probably imply speeches of complaint by the Allies: it is possibly one of the Cities that laments she does not own a necessary utensil.[4] But another fragment[5] is vastly more important: it perhaps contains a feminine participle and certainly points to slavery and a possible change of masters:

> κακὰ τοιάδε
> πάσχουσα, μηδὲ πρᾶσιν αἰτῶ;

[1] Fr. 233. Ποῦ in the first line is strange.
[2] Fr. 230. [3] Frr. 207, 209, 210, 213, 235.
[4] Fr. 224: ἐμοὶ γὰρ οὐκ ἔστ' οὐδὲ λάσαν' ὅπου χέσω.
[5] Meineke, II, pp. 519 sq.; Kock, fr. 225. Meineke, however, reads κ.τ. πάσχουσιν, οὐδὲ π. αἰτοῦσιν.

EUPOLIS

'When I suffer such miseries, am I not even to beg for a new master?'

Further, we gain glimpses of a contest between those who urge mildness towards the subject-states and the inheritors of Pericles' doctrine, 'Keep the allies in hand'.[1] For instance, possibly:

> ὡς ὑμῖν πάντως ἐγὼ
> ἀποκρινοῦμαι πρὸς τὰ κατηγορούμενα.[2]

'Since I will reply by all means to your base charges.' And the proud question, τί δ' ἔστ' Ἀθηναίοισι πρᾶγμ' ἀπώμοτον;[3]—'What deed will any man swear Athenians cannot perform?'—points to Cleon's reckless imperialism. A corrupt passage[4] from an anonymous grammarian indicates the same spirit, praising the man who is eager for office. The other party seem to have read a lesson from Athenian history. Miltiades is mentioned, 'who bequeathed us our Marathonian heritage'— ὃς τὴν Μαραθῶνι κατέλιφ' ἡμῖν οὐσίαν[5]—and there is a curious passage about Cimon:[6]

> κακὸς μὲν οὐκ ἦν, φιλοπότης δὲ κἀμελής,
> κἀνίοτ' ἂν ἀπεκοιμᾶτ' ἂν ἐν Λακεδαίμονι,
> κἂν Ἐλπινίκην τήνδε καταλιπὼν μόνην.

'Base he was not, but wine-loving and careless. Sometimes he would sleep from home in Lacedæmon, leaving Elpinice alone here.' To the same party may belong the sentence οὐ γὰρ πολυπράγμων ἐστίν, ἀλλ' ἀπλήγιος[7]—'for he is not a busybody, but a simple man'—and a gibe[8] at incompetent generals:

> οὓς δ' οὐκ ἂν εἴλεσθ' οὐδ' ἂν οἰνόπτας πρὸ τοῦ,
> νυνὶ στρατηγοὺς ἔχομεν. ὦ πόλις πόλις,
> ὡς εὐτυχὴς εἶ μᾶλλον ἢ καλῶς φρονεῖς.

---

[1] Thuc., II, xiii, 2.
[2] Fr. 219. But if this is an instance, the first words must be made to scan. Hermann adds κακῶς μου (after τά). This gives the verse Eupolidean metre, in which case no doubt the passage is part of the parabasis. Then it would not have the meaning suggested above, but would refer to the poet himself and his detractors.
[3] Fr. 217.   [4] Fr. 234.   [5] Fr. 216.
[6] Fr. 208.   [7] Fr. 222.   [8] Fr. 205.

'Men whom in earlier times you would have refused appointment as wine-inspectors we find generals to-day. O my country, my country, how richer thou art in good luck than in good sense!' Here is a vivid little picture [1] of a demagogue:

> Συρακόσιος δ' ἔοικεν, ἡνίκ' ἂν λέγῃ,
> τοῖς κυνιδίοισι τοῖσιν ἐπὶ τῶν τειχίων·
> ἀναβὰς γὰρ ἐπὶ τὸ βῆμ' ὑλακτεῖ περιτρέχων.

'Syracosius making a speech is like a pup on a wall: as soon as he mounts the platform he runs about barking.'

No details of the plot are reported. But it is possible that the appeal for clemency—naturally successful in the poet's hands—resulted in a marriage or pairing-off of "cities" and Athenians. That the sexual possibilities of a "female" chorus would not be overlooked is certain; and at one place, even in our scanty fragments, a man is rebuked for attempting to flirt with one of the "cities":

> ὁ Φιλῖνος οὗτος, τί ἄρα πρὸς ταύτην βλέπεις;
> οὐκ ἀπολιβάξεις εἰς ἀποικίαν τινά; [2]

'I say, Philinus! Why are you gazing at her? Take yourself off to a colony.' And some one says ἔχω γὰρ ἐπιτήδειον ἄνδρ' αὐτῇ πάνυ [3]—'I have an entirely suitable husband (or man) for her.' It is conceivable that there was a marriage-procession of these pairs to rites in the *opisthodomos* or rear-chamber of the Acropolis. We know [4] that Eupolis mentioned in this play that the allies were bidden to bring their tribute to Athens at the City Dionysia. This treasure, after being exhibited in the theatre, was stored in the Acropolis; and the striking words ἣν οὐκ ἀνέῳξα πώποτ' ἀνθρώποις ἐγώ [5]—'which I have never yet opened to mankind'—may refer to the inmost sanctuary. One may well imagine a great final procession of "married" allies and Athenians accompanying the treasure to its sacred abiding-place.

[1] Fr. 207. [2] Fr. 206. [3] Fr. 229.
[4] Schol. on *Acharnians*, 504. [5] Fr. 220.

That is all we can now say of what must have been a beautiful, stirring, and brilliant comedy. Its date falls before the Sicilian expedition: Chios had not yet revolted—that happened in 412 B.C.; and Stilbides, the famous seer who accompanied Nicias to Sicily,[1] was still in Athens.[2]

The BRIGADIERS (Ταξίαρχοι) was a lively *pièce d'occasion*. Phormio, the Athenian naval commander who so brilliantly distinguished himself in the early years of the Peloponnesian War, takes the god Dionysus as an apprentice, and nearly all our fragments remind us of that scene in the *Frogs* where the same god irritates Charon by his ineptitude as an oarsman. They are not in themselves attractive, but one may be cited:[3]

ὅστις πύελον ἥκεις ἔχων καὶ χαλκίον
ὥσπερ λεχὼ στρατιῶτις ἐξ Ἰωνίας.

'Since you have turned up with a bath-tub and a kettle, like a soldier's wife in Ionia who has just had a baby.' The god intends to "boil his peas" and scandalizes the hard-living Phormio by his luxurious kit, like the officers of the Guards who infuriated Wellington by putting up umbrellas during a battle. Phormio makes short work of his paraphernalia, and appears to send off a female slave of the god's to the auction-block.[4] The curious occasion of this play is related by the Scholiast on Aristophanes.[5] 'This Phormio was an Athenian by birth, a son of Asopichus. After brilliant service as a general he became poor, and, being unable to pay the hundred *minæ* of his audit,[6] he lost his franchise. He was living in the

[1] Plutarch, *Nicias*, XXIII.
[2] Fr. 211. Geissler (*Chronologie*, p. 39) dates the play confidently at the Great Dionysia of 422, because of the allusion (fr. 209) to Amynias.
[3] Fr. 256. [4] Fr. 258.
[5] *Peace*, 347. One sentence is difficult and corrupt: ὁ δὲ δῆμος βουλόμενος λῦσαι τὴν ἀτιμίαν ἀπεμίσθωσεν αὐτὸν τῶν ρ' μνῶν τοῦ Διονυσίου κτέ. See Boeckh and Meineke in the latter's *Fragmenta Com. Graec.*, II, pp. 527 sq., from which the above explanation is borrowed.
[6] Τῆς εὐθύνης.

country when the Acarnanians begged for him as a commander; this request he refused, saying that a disfranchised man could not accept it. Then the People, wishing to annul his disability (suffered him to pay off the hundred *minæ* by a sacrifice to Dionysus ?). So Androtion writes in the Third Book of his *Attica*.' Since it was difficult to annul a fine owed to the State, a fiction was practised. Phormio was appointed to perform a trivial task, apparently a sacrifice or service to Dionysus, and was given as " wages " the amount of his huge fine. Eupolis represents the " service " to the god as his training in Phormio's camp. The date of this comedy is 428 or 427 B.C., about the time of Phormio's death (428).

In NON-COMBATANTS (Ἀστράτευτοι) occurred an intriguing passage taken partly from Sophocles:

μήποτε θρέψω
παρὰ Περσεφόνῃ τοιόνδε ταῶν, ὃς τοὺς εὕδοντας ἐγείρει [1]

' lest I should rear in Persephone's kingdom a peacock like that which arouses the sleepers'. In HELOTS (Εἵλωτες), if he wrote the play, which is highly doubtful,[2] Eupolis mentioned Stesichorus, Alcman and Simonides with respect; and certainly he somewhere complained that Pindar had become obsolete because most people had grown too vulgar to appreciate him.[3] The GOLDEN AGE [4] (Χρυσοῦν Γένος) appears to have been a sarcastic eulogy of the Cleonian régime:

ὦ καλλίστη πόλι πασῶν, ὅσας Κλέων ἐφορᾷ,
ὡς εὐδαίμων πρότερόν τ' ἦσθα νῦν τε μᾶλλον ἔσει.

' Fairest of all cities under Cleon's eye, how happy wast thou of old, and how much happier shalt thou

---

[1] Fr. 36. Cp. Soph. fr. 890 (Jebb-Pearson):
κερκίδος ὕμνοις
ἢ τοὺς εὕδοντας ἐγείρει.

[2] Our authorities mostly speak of ὁ τοὺς Εἵλωτας ποιήσας or the like.

[3] As to Pindar, we have Athenæus' paraphrase (I, iii a): ὡς τὰ Πινδάρου ὁ κωμῳδοποιὸς Εὔπολίς φησιν, ἤδη κατασεσιγασμένων ὑπὸ τῆς τῶν πολλῶν ἀφιλοκαλίας.

[4] Produced at the Great Dionysia of 424 B.C., according to Geissler, (*Chronologie*, p. 35).

henceforth be!' *Autolycus* was a bitter and coarse attack on a young athlete who, in 421 B.C., won the *pancration* at the Panathenæa and for whom his patron, Callias, prepared the entertainment described in Xenophon's *Symposium*. Eupolis wrote two versions of it, the first being produced under the name of Demostratus [1] in 420 B.C.

Among the fragments whose provenance is unknown are a few attractive passages. Two refer to Socrates:

δεξάμενος δὲ Σωκράτης τὴν ἐπίδειξιν ᾄδων
Στησιχόρου πρὸς τὴν λύραν οἰνοχόην ἔκλεψεν.[2]

'Socrates, consenting to give a display, sang to the lyre a poem of Stesichorus and stole a wine-jug meanwhile.'

μισῶ δὲ καὶ τὸν Σωκράτη, τὸν πτωχὸν ἀδολέσχην,
ὃς τἄλλα μὲν πεφρόντικεν
ὁπόθεν δὲ καταφαγεῖν ἔχοι τούτου κατημέληκεν.[3]

'Socrates, too, I hate, the beggarly chatterbox, who has thought out everything else but neglected to discover a source of food.' Our authority for the former passage asserts that 'Eupolis, brief as is his mention of Socrates, attacks him more vigorously than Aristophanes in the whole of the *Clouds*'.[4] Of Cleon we are told that he was the first to use, in his despatches to the people, the epistolary salutation Χαῖρε.[5] Photius, who tells [6] us that the Lacedæmonians bore the monogram Λ on their shields, quotes from Eupolis the vivid words:

ἐξεπλάγη γὰρ ἰδὼν στίλβοντα τὰ λάμβδα.

'His heart shook when he saw the glittering lambdas.' Is this a reference to Cleon's defeat and death at Amphipolis?[7] Our list may close with an expostula-

---

[1] Cp. Athenæus, V, 216*d*.
[2] Fr. 361. Some would refer this fragment to the Κόλακες. It is in the same metre as the parasite fragment.
[3] Fr. 352. [4] Scholiast on *Clouds*, 96.
[5] Fr. 308. It was after the capture of Sphacteria.
[6] *s.v.* Λάμβδα: fr. 359.
[7] Thuc., V, 10. Cp. especially οἱ ἄνδρες ἡμᾶς οὐ μενοῦσιν κτέ.

tion to the Athenian audience similar to the manifestoes of Terence :

ἀλλ' ἀκούετ', ὦ θεαταί, τἀμὰ καὶ ξυνίετε
ῥήματ'· εὐθὺ γὰρ πρὸς ὑμᾶς πρῶτον ἀπολογήσομαι . . .
ὅτι παθόντες τοὺς ξένους μὲν λέγετε ποιητὰς σοφούς,
ἢν δέ τις τῶν ἐνθάδ' αὐτοῦ μηδὲ ἓν χεῖρον φρονῶν
ἐπιτιθῆται τῇ ποιήσει πάνυ δοκεῖ κακῶς φρονεῖν,
μαίνεταί τε καὶ παραρρεῖ τῶν φρενῶν τῷ σῷ λόγῳ.
ἀλλ' ἐμοὶ πείθεσθε πάντως· μεταβαλόντες τοὺς τρόπους,
μὴ φθονεῖθ' ὅταν τις ἡμῶν μουσικῇ χαίρῃ νέων.[1]

'Nay, spectators, hear and understand my remarks, for to you first will I straightway offer my defence. (I cannot imagine ?) what has put it into your heads to call foreign poets brilliant, whereas if any local man, with quite as good ability, addresses himself to poetry, you think him a perfect fool—he is mad and wandering in his wits by your account, sir. Nay, accept my advice altogether : change your ways and feel no malice when any of us (native Athenians devotes himself ?) to art.' The complaint about foreign rivals must, of course,[2] refer to Athenians suspected of possessing no genuine right to citizenship. Probably the man in view is Aristophanes, frequently called a foreigner[3] by his enemies and at loggerheads with Eupolis since the rupture of their friendship over the composition of the *Knights*.

These lines have been called *elegantissimi*.[4] This criticism well illustrates the perils surrounding students of fragmentary literature : after perusing a thousand scraps about fried fish, the weary researcher hails any passage above that level as a jewel of poetry. This passage is, as a fact, extremely flat and obvious in

---

[1] Fr. 357. Kock with probability supposes a lacuna after the second line. In the fifth, τῷ σῷ λόγῳ implies that the speaker suddenly turns or points to some particular person. Kock would read παρεκρεῖ τῶν φρενῶν ὁ σῶς λόγος ('good sense'), which is very dubious Greek. In the last line he suggests συνών for νέων, which is certainly hard. Richards (*Classical Quarterly*, I, p. 31) would read μουσικὴν (or μουσικῇ) χαίρῃ ποῶν.

[2] No mere ξένος could compete in the Athenian dramatic contests, though citizens of allied States could do so ; notable instances are Achæus of Eretria and Ion of Chios, the tragedians.

[3] Cp. below, p. 202.   [4] Meineke, I, p. 111.

style, a description fitting nearly all the fragments that we have discussed. Eupolis lacked the rich vigour of Cratinus and the sparkle of Aristophanes. Even that charm whereof ancient critics [1] write is seldom apparent in the verbal style of his surviving poetry. His eminence consisted rather in ideas and their dramatic exposition.

[1] *E.g.* Macrobius, VII, v. 8: *notus est omnibus Eupolis, inter elegantes habendus veteris comœdiæ poetas.*

CHAPTER VI

ARISTOPHANES

ARISTOPHANES was born about 445 B.C. and belonged to the deme Cydathenæon, of the tribe Pandionis. His father was named Philippus, his mother Zenodora. His rivals often accused him of foreign birth: Lindus and Camirus in Rhodes, Ægina and Egypt were all mentioned as his birthplace. Apparently the family possessed an estate in Ægina, which may have been the occasion for these stories. Aristophanes' first play, the *Banqueters*, appeared when he was not more than eighteen. Forty-four plays in all were attributed to him, four of these—*Poetry, The Shipwrecked Man, The Islands, Niobos*—being, however, assigned by some to Archippus. The poet was more than once attacked by the statesman Cleon, but he escaped punishment. Early in life he became bald. He had three sons, Philippus, Araros, and Nicostratus or Philetærus. Several of his works were produced under the name of another, sometimes Philonides, sometimes Callistratus, and his last two plays, *Cocalus* and *Æolosicon*, under the name of his son Araros, whom he wished to launch as a comic playwright. The date of his death is unknown, but cannot have occurred before 388 B.C. It is said that Dionysius, tyrant of Syracuse, asked Plato to describe the constitution of Athens, whereupon the philosopher sent him the works of Aristophanes. To Plato also is attributed the epitaph : [1]

Αἱ Χάριτες τέμενός τι λαβεῖν ὅπερ οὐχὶ πεσεῖται
ζητοῦσαι, ψυχὴν εὗρον Ἀριστοφάνους,

[1] Certainly not by Plato, in whose day a τέμενος was not a building, but a sacred enclosure, which could not be imagined as falling.

'The Graces, seeking a shrine that could not fall, discovered the soul of Aristophanes.' This meagre outline gives all the facts of which we can be certain.[1] That the ancient world, which was in a position to make a full comparison of Aristophanes and his rivals, looked on him as by far the greatest Old Comedian, is proved by the fact that of him alone did it preserve entire plays. These number eleven, which shall now be considered in chronological order.

The ACHARNIANS ('Αχαρνῆς, men of Acharnæ, a deme seven miles north of Athens) was performed at the Lenæa of 425 B.C. under the name of Callistratus, and obtained the first prize, defeating the works of Cratinus (Χειμαζόμενοι) and of Eupolis (Νουμηνίαι).

Dicæopolis is discovered waiting in the Pnyx, the meeting-place of the National Assembly. But for him, the scene is deserted, and he complains of the supineness of his fellow-citizens. At length the Pnyx fills, and we have a lively caricature of the Assembly; Dicæopolis sends a messenger to Sparta to make peace for him on his private account. This man returns with " peace-wine," which Dicæopolis accepts rapturously, and retires to his farm to celebrate, after six years' intermission, the Vintage-Festival. But the scent of this wine reached some old charcoal-burners of Acharnæ, the bitterest section of the war-party in Athens; they pursue the messenger, vowing death to the man who has dared to make peace. At the moment when Dicæopolis is preparing his celebration they come upon the scene as the chorus of the play, and he is on the point of being stoned to death when he saves himself by a burlesque of a scene in Euripides: rushing into the house he comes back with a basket of charcoal and a sword, threatening to slay the Acharnians' darling. This deadly peril unmans the chorus, who give Dicæopolis permission to state his

---

[1] The ancient Lives (of which we have five) give other details purely imaginary or based on the poet's own remarks; for example, that the king of Persia inquired on whose side he was (*Ach.*, v. 646).

case. In order to obtain the tattered garments of a suppliant he applies to Euripides, and wheedles out of his victim a ludicrous assortment of beggar's odds and ends; thus equipped, he confronts the chorus to make his speech—an account, jocular in tone but deeply serious in intention, of the causes of the Peloponnesian War, showing that the Athenians have taken up arms for frivolous reasons. Half the chorus are won over, half are obdurate; the two sections come to blows, and the war-at-any-price party calls to Lamachus for help. Lamachus stalks on to the stage, a martial figure in grotesquely terrifying armour. In his brush with Dicæopolis he has no arguments to offer, only threats and abuse: at last he retires beaten. With the departure of this champion all opposition to Dicæopolis disappears: the whole chorus are henceforth on his side, and deliver their parabasis.

The rest of the play depicts the blessings which Dicæopolis has secured. A Megarian enters, compelled by famine to sell his two little daughters, whom he disguises as pigs; then a Bœotian, who brings to market an eel, the Athenian's favourite but long-absent delicacy. The informers who interfere with Dicæopolis' traffic are handled mercilessly. Lamachus sends his servant to buy some of the dainties that Dicæopolis has acquired, but his request is rejected. A herald enters to proclaim the Feast of Pitchers and the usual prize—a skin of wine—for the drinker who empties his jug first. Dicæopolis determines to compete, and begins to cook various dainties for his feast. Two heralds enter; one orders Lamachus to march off, in spite of the snowstorms and the festivities at home, to guard the Bœotian frontier; the other summons Dicæopolis to eat his dinner at the house of the Priest of Dionysus. After a song by the chorus both champions return. First comes Lamachus, preceded by a mock-tragic messenger who describes the dreadful injury which has disabled his master; the warrior is half-carried on to the scene by two soldiers.

On the other side Dicæopolis enters, incapacitated also, but by intoxication, and supported by two flute-girls. He has won the prize for rapid drinking; the chorus hail him as the victor, and he leads them out in procession.

This comedy, written perhaps before the poet was twenty years old, is not only brilliant, not only a masterpiece: it contains all, or nearly all, the excellences that he was ever to exhibit. The elaborate burlesque of the Athenian Assembly, the exquisite parody [1] of Euripides' *Telephus*, the ode translated below, which is perhaps unsurpassed in its kind, the riotous jollity with which the play ends—these are the outstanding charms of the *Acharnians*. The play has its more ephemeral side. It is not only a comedy; it possesses some of the qualities of a political pamphlet: Aristophanes puts forth all his powers to turn his countrymen against the war, and his last scenes bear witness that there is a jingoism of peace as well as a jingoism of war.

As for the main topic, the first reflexion of every reader since Ægospotami must be amazement that the Athenian republic allowed the play to be presented at all. Despite the tolerance and rights of minorities of which so much is heard, no state save fifth-century Athens would have endured, in the midst of a war, any play so definitely criticizing the author's fellow-countrymen, so openly stating a case for the enemy. And there can be no doubt that Aristophanes is to be taken seriously: here, as so often, beneath the surface of laughable or bitter nonsense, can be plainly felt a strong opinion and a passionate appeal. He undoubtedly wishes that the war should end, but the agony of later years has not yet entered his soul: we find only one hint of the future *Lysistrata*, in the line ' she is a woman and not to blame for the war '.[2]

---

[1] Denis, however, points out (*La Comédie grecque*, I, p. 323) that Dicæopolis makes no real use of the beggar's gear thus elaborately secured.
[2] v. 1062.

The superficial absurdity, however, must be held to include Lamachus, the treatment of whom is precisely like that of Socrates in the *Clouds*. Aristophanes wishes to discredit the war-party, and so, selecting its most prominent member, without scruple attaches to him whatever ridicule the ideal " sabre-rattler " may be held to deserve.

In lyrical power this play stands high among the eleven. Its finest passage is the song about peace and war, of which this version may give some idea :

> Dost thou see, thronging city? His cunning so quaint is,
>   The truce he has made crowns him king of the mart.
> All household utensils, all roastable dainties,
>   Yea, blessings in showers have gladdened his heart!
>   Ne'er again shall the War-God have welcome from me,
>   Or join in our feast and our national song,
> The quarrelsome drunkard! All happy were we,
>   Till his tipsy intrusion wrought havoc and wrong.
> He bullied and brawled, while to quiet his ire
>   I said, 'Sit and drink ; pass the loving-cup round.'
> But he rammed our vine-props deeper down in the fire,
>   And spilled, like a brute, all our wine on the ground.
>
> [*Feathers from poultry flutter out of the house.*]
>
> This banquet's exciting our friend : see the traces!
>   All these feathers are proof that he's festive and gay.
> O Peace, foster-sister of Love and the Graces,
>   How blind to thy beauty our eyes till to-day!
>   O might kindly Cupid, with garlanded tresses
>   Like the dream of a painter, bring thee to my arms!
> Dost thou deem me too old for thy fertile caresses?
>   To a threefold exploit I'd be roused by thy charms.
> First the vine-shoots I'd plant, then young figs in a line,
>   And thirdly the vines that I'd tenderly raise ;
> And a ring-fence of olives the farm to confine,
>   And anoint us with oil on the festival days!

The KNIGHTS ('Ἱππῆς, the Athenian cavalry—a class social, political, and financial, as well as military) was produced at the Lenæa of 424 B.C. under the poet's own name—the earliest he so produced—and obtained the first prize.

Two slaves of the stupid and irascible old man Demos (the Athenian People) discuss their evil plight. Recently the master has bought a Paphlagonian slave, who has become his favourite and bullies the other slaves. It soon becomes plain that the Paphlagonian is Cleon, the malcontents Nicias, the conservative statesman, and Demosthenes, the distinguished soldier. 'The other day,' the latter relates, 'I kneaded a Spartan cake at Pylos, but Paphlagon, with utter knavery, dodged me, snatched it up and himself presented it to our master.' Demosthenes persuades Nicias to steal Cleon's collection of oracles: among them is found a prophecy that Cleon shall be supplanted by a Sausage-seller. He duly appears and is persuaded to undertake his high destiny of overthrowing Cleon and becoming the greatest man in Greece: his fears are overborne and his claims shown to be incomparable —scoundrelism, impudence, and ignorance. Then Cleon rushes out, accusing them of treason; the chorus of knights gallops [1] up to their aid, chasing and buffeting Cleon. There follows a violent contest of abuse between the rival statesmen. At length Cleon departs to denounce the Sausage-seller before the Senate, and his antagonist makes off in pursuit. After the parabasis he returns and relates how he discomfited Cleon by outbidding him before the Senate with lies and sycophancy. Cleon returns in fury and calls forth Demos, whom both rivals seek to cajole, first by arguments, then by gifts, and the recitation of bogus oracles. At length Demos renounces Cleon and takes Agoracritus (this we find, is the Sausage-seller's name) as his steward. Next comes a brief second parabasis, at the close of which Agoracritus proclaims that he has rejuvenated Demos, who appears from the Propylæa as the splendid Athenian People as it was in the days of Aristides and Miltiades. He is ashamed of his recent stupidities and determines to live in the fine ancient fashion.

The *Knights* is a bad and stupid play. Certain small passages are excellent, and some important historically; but as a whole this saturnalia of falsetto

---

[1] Riding hobby-horses, perhaps (so van Leeuwen, p. xvii of his edition).

Billingsgate, this anthology of verbs meaning "to kick in the stomach" and the like, is astounding after the *Acharnians*. The fact is, Aristophanes has spoiled his play by losing his temper: his suffocating rage against Cleon has caused him to forget that anger, however justified, cannot of itself project a work of art. Consider this trash,[1] hardly worth reprinting, certainly not translating:

> ΚΛ. ὦ Δῆμ', ἐγὼ μέντοι παρεσκευασμένος
> τρίπαλαι κάθημαι βουλόμενός σ' εὐεργετεῖν.
> ΑΛ. ἐγὼ δὲ δεκάπαλαί γε καὶ δωδεκάπαλαι
> καὶ χιλιόπαλαι καὶ προπαλαιπαλαίπαλαι.
> ΔΗ. ἐγὼ δὲ προσδοκῶν γε τρισμυριόπαλαι
> βδελύττομαί σφω καὶ προπαλαιπαλαίπαλαι.

Perhaps even more juvenile is the Sausage-seller's reply to Cleon's boast that he has a chest full of oracles. 'But I have a garret and two lodging-houses full.'[2] Of that vigorous inventiveness wherein the *Acharnians* is rich, scarcely anything can be seen: his greatest effort is to portray the People and its statesmen as a silly old man with plotting slaves.

The incidental merits are three. First, in the less hysterical passages we enjoy that nervous yet utterly simple Attic style which Aristophanes, when he chooses, can write as well as Plato himself:

> καὶ νὴ Δί' ἄλλα γ' ἐστί μοι κόβαλα παιδὸς ὄντος.
> ἐξηπάτων γὰρ τοὺς μαγείρους ἐπιλέγων τοιαυτί·
> 'σκέψασθε, παῖδες· οὐχ ὁρᾶθ'; ὥρα νέα, χελιδών.'
> οἱ δ' ἔβλεπον, κἀγὼ 'ν τοσούτῳ τῶν κρεῶν ἔκλεπτον...
> καὶ ταῦτα δρῶν ἐλάνθανόν γ'· εἰ δ' οὖν ἴδοι τις αὐτῶν,
> ἀποκρυπτόμενος ἐς τὼ κοχώνα τοὺς θεοὺς ἀπώμνυν·
> ὥστ' εἶπ' ἀνὴρ τῶν ῥητόρων ἰδών με τοῦτο δρῶντα·
> 'οὐκ ἔσθ' ὅπως ὁ παῖς ὅδ' οὐ τὸν δῆμον ἐπιτροπεύσει.'[3]

A commonplace version might run thus:

> And yes, my word! I'd other tricks when quite a little fellow.
> The butchers: how I swindled them! You should have heard me bellow:
> "Look, boys! A swallow! Spring is here! Look! Seeing is believing."
> So up they stared, and while they stared a cutlet I was thieving.
> And nine times out of ten it worked, but at the tenth to save it
> I clapped the meat between my thighs and gave my affidavit.
> A gentleman in public life, who watched this exhibition,
> Exclaimed: "That lad is bound to rise: he'll make a politician."

[1] vv. 1152 *sqq.* [2] v. 1001. [3] vv. 418 *sqq.*

It is a delightful blend of Mr. Charles Chaplin stealing the pies one by one in *A Dog's Life*, and of Jowett proclaiming " that young man will go far ". Secondly, an excellent little scene occurs near the end,[1] a quaint parallel to the climax of *Macbeth*. Cleon, apparently ruined, has yet one resource. ' Surrender the ring of office? Never! I have a Pythian oracle that reveals the one man who shall overthrow me.' Then, as he questions the Sausage-seller on the details of his career, the truth gradually reveals itself that before him stands the Man of Destiny: the younger generation is not knocking, but kicking, at the door. Unlike Macbeth, however, he collapses utterly and disappears with borrowed words of tragedy on his lips:

> Alas! God's oracle is all fulfilled.
> The wheel is come full circle: sit me on't
> And trundle hapless me behind the scenes.
> Garland of mine, this parting breaks my heart.
> Farewell! Another soon shall call thee his—
> Luckier than I, but ah! how less a thief!

Thirdly, the main parabasis must be reckoned among the best things Aristophanes ever wrote. We have discussed elsewhere [2] the memorable account of his predecessors, Magnes, Cratinus, and Crates. It contains also two delicious songs to Poseidon and Athena, thrown for the most part into the dainty rhythm [3] so familiar to our own children: " Here we go round the mulberry-bush ":

> Ἱππι' ἄναξ Πόσειδον, ᾧ
> χαλκοκρότων ἵππων κτύπος
> καὶ χρεμετισμὸς ἁνδάνει
> καὶ κυανέμβολοι θοαὶ
> μισθοφόροι τριήρεις.
>
> Cruisers with iron prows that race
> Bringing the cash from Chios and Thrace,
> Neighing of steeds and thudding hooves:
> These are the joys your heart approves,
>   Cavalry-God Poseidon!

The *antepirrhema* playfully depicts the valour shown by the knights' horses in the expedition to Corinth.

---

[1] vv. 1227-52.   [2] Pp. 16 *sq.*, 115 *sq.*, 145 *sqq.*   [3] See below, p. 376 *sq.*

It is notable that the poet, while so fiercely deriding the sensational feat of a democrat at Pylos, should rhapsodize over this insignificant exploit of the aristocratic knights.[1]

This discrepancy raises a particular question concerning his treatment of Cleon—something more than the general topic of unfairness. Was the poet directly and definitely suborned by the oligarchs to make this attack? Despite the complete absence of any external evidence, no one can avoid at least asking that question who considers, not so much the violence of this play as the absence of light and shade effect. Elsewhere he allows something in favour of his butts: here is unremitting rancour. And when we ask whether the occasion was such as to condone unrelieved virulence, we note at once that it was displayed at the very moment when Cleon had deserved most excellently of his countrymen: his exploit at Pylos and Sphacteria was no less valuable than spectacular. It is a curious reflexion that throughout the performance Cleon must have been seated in the front row of spectators, this distinction having been conferred precisely because of Pylos; it is still more notable that despite this unparalleled torrent of abuse he was soon afterwards elected a general.

A highly interesting piece of literary history concerns the *Knights*: Eupolis collaborated in it. In the *Clouds* Aristophanes writes: ' First of all Eupolis brought on his clumsy *Maricas*, a travesty of my *Knights* as stupid as himself.' On this the Scholiast [2] remarks: ' Eupolis in the *Baptae* says on the contrary that he helped Aristophanes with the *Knights*. He means the final parabasis. His words are " That play the *Knights*, too, I helped the bald-headed to

---

[1] Couat, *Aristophane et l'ancienne comédie attique*, p. 88.
[2] On *Clouds*, 554. Eupolis' words are (with an omission made by the Scholiast):

$$\kappa\dot{\alpha}\kappa\epsilon\dot{\iota}\nu\text{ous } \text{τοὺς } \text{Ἱππέας}$$
$$\text{συνεποίησα τῷ φαλακρῷ } \ldots \text{ κἀδωρησάμην.}$$

write . . . and made him a present thereof ".' Moreover, Cratinus twitted Aristophanes with plagiarizing Eupolis.[1] Finally, on the second parabasis of the *Knights* the Scholiast says : ' From the words ὅστις οὖν τοιοῦτον ἄνδρα some say that Eupolis wrote the parabasis, since he says " I helped the bald-headed to write ".' The natural assumption is : Eupolis wrote that part of the parabasis that deals with Hyperbolus, and, when in his *Maricas* he wrote a whole play against Hyperbolus, took back what was his own and used it, much to Aristophanes' annoyance.

The CLOUDS (Νεφέλαι) was produced [2] at the Great Dionysia of 423 B.C. and obtained the third prize, being defeated by the *Wine-Flask* of Cratinus and the *Connos* of Ameipsias.[3]

Strepsiades, an old rustic, cannot sleep for thinking of the debts in which he is involved by his son Pheidippides, who indulges a passion for horseracing. He begs his son to enter the " thinking-shop " of Socrates as a student : these sophists can make him so clever that he will win all suits brought by the creditors. Pheidippides refuses, and the father determines to undergo the training himself. He is shown round the school and at length sees a figure swinging aloft in a basket—Socrates himself, who has ascended into purer air for the sake of clearer thought. Hearing Strepsiades' errand, the sage descends and summons his patronesses, the Clouds, who inspire all windy and pretentious artists and thinkers ; he then gives a long lecture on meteorology. Strepsiades is taken indoors while the chorus of Clouds deliver the parabasis. Socrates returns, disgusted with Strepsiades' stupidity. They begin discussion in the open air, and in the end Socrates is so exasperated that he expels the senile undergraduate. Strepsiades appeals to the

---

[1] Ὡς τὰ Εὐπόλιδος λέγοντα (Schol. on *Knights*, 528).
[2] Under the name of Philonides ; the author of the Life says that he produced the plays written by Aristophanes against Socrates and Euripides.
[3] Or Phrynichus. See p. 24.

chorus, who suggest that he should send his son for instruction. Pheidippides now consents, and Socrates agrees to teach him the " two pleas " ; there follows the famous contest between the Just Argument and the Unjust, who describe in turn their effects upon the young—the old system of education, inculcating good manners, good morals, and athletics; and the new, which flings aside traditional restraint, bidding the youth indulge all his passions. At length the Just Argument, forced to confess that practically everyone in Athens follows his rival's teaching, throws up his case. Pheidippides is taken indoors for instruction under the fashionable system. Strepsiades returns, distressed by the approach of settling-day: he is delighted to find that his son is now fully prepared to baffle the creditors; they go within to celebrate his " graduation " with a dinner. Two creditors appear, and Strepsiades discomfits them by showing off mysterious scraps of learning obtained from Socrates. But soon he reappears in very different mood. The dinner has been a heart-breaking fiasco: Pheidippides has not only quarrelled with his father about literary criticism, but, in an access of artistic fervour, has almost strangled him. The son comes out offering to justify his conduct by the new learning, and Strepsiades finds that the devices he had meant for his own defence can be used for his undoing. In his rage and despair he leads his slaves to an attack on the thinking-shop, to which he sets fire, the horrified inmates scurrying forth with squeals.

That our text of the *Clouds* is not entirely the same as that performed in 423 B.C. all of course agree: there is a passage in the parabasis concerning the play's reception which must be later, and must have replaced something else. But can we go further? Is it possible to say how much else is new? If so, can we with any precision determine the shape of the original play? Finally, if these alterations were extensive, why were they made? We have three ancient sources of information : two of the Arguments, and quotations from the first version.

The fifth Argument reads : ' The first *Clouds* was produced in the City during Isarchus' archonship, when Cratinus was victorious with the *Wine-Flask*, and Ameipsias with *Connos*. Wherefore Aristophanes, unexpectedly rebuffed, thought he must again produce the second version and rebuke the audience. But he met with far worse failure on the later occasion and did not again bring forward his revision. The second *Clouds* appeared in Ameinias' archonship '—that is, in 422 B.C.[1] The sixth Argument reads : ' This is the same as the earlier, but it is partially revised, as if the poet had decided to present it anew but gave up the plan for whatever reason. Now there was a complete recasting, affecting practically every part. Some elements were removed, some remodelled ; the arrangement was altered and the relation of the characters changed. [The wholesale revisions were such as these.] For instance, the parabasis of the chorus was altered, and where the Just Argument talks to the Unjust, and finally where Socrates' school is set on fire.' This evidently combines two different accounts : one said that only a slight revision (perhaps merely the re-writing of the parabasis passage) took place ; the other, that there were drastic and widespread changes.

Thirdly, we have a few quotations " from the *Clouds* " which are not to be found in our text. One runs :

Εὐριπίδης δ' ὁ τὰς τραγῳδίας ποιῶν
τὰς περιλαλούσας οὗτός ἐστι τὰς σοφάς.

' This is Euripides, who writes the garrulous scientific tragedies.' But Diogenes Laertius, from whom the citation comes, is talking about the rumour that Socrates helped the poet with his tragedies. This

---

[1] Whether our version was ever acted cannot be stated with certainty ; but it was not in 422 B.C., for the references (vv. 551 *sqq.*) to plays about Hyperbolus show that the parabasis cannot have been written till 419 B.C.

sense cannot be extracted from the Greek just given, which must accordingly be emended to Εὐριπίδου or Εὐριπίδῃ. We thus get a passage apparently unimportant—a scrap of a description of Socrates—but one nevertheless not found in our *Clouds*. Another is:

ἐς τὴν Πάρνηθ' ὀργισθεῖσαι φροῦδαι κατὰ τὸν Λυκαβηττόν.

The gender and the subject-matter show that this refers to the chorus: 'Making off in anger to Mt. Parnes along Lycabettus'. This looks at first like a difference in plot, but it is perfectly easy to suppose that the Clouds are speaking about themselves and 'the angry withdrawal' they made in the past, or may make in the future, 'on beholding some foolish act of the Athenian people'.[1] Thirdly, vv. 412-19 are quoted by Diogenes Laertius[2] with numerous slight changes. This has been taken as a passage from the first *Clouds* addressed to Socrates, whereas the similar lines in our version are addressed to Strepsiades. It is more likely[3] that they have been adapted from our text by Diogenes to suit his own discussion of Socrates.

These evidences are to be reinforced by study of any signs of alteration that may be discovered in our text.[4] The facts appear to be as follows:—

Firstly, Strepsiades' course of study was originally successful. As they stand now, the scenes of his tuition, though in themselves excellent, are inept when read in the light of the whole drama. Why not cause Pheidippides to do at once what he does in the end, submit to the sophistic teaching? Why thrust in the Strep-

---

[1] Mr. B. B. Rogers, *Introduction* to his translation, p. xiv.   [2] II, v. 27.
[3] As excellently demonstrated by van Leeuwen, *Proleg.*, xxiv *sq.*
[4] From the voluminous "literature" the following works may be singled out: Zieliński, *Die Gliederung der altattischen Komödie*, pp. 34-52; Kock, *Einleitung* to his edition, pp. 24-47 (an English translation will be found in Humphrey's edition of the *Clouds*, Ginn & Co., 1888); Schwandle, *De Aristophanis Nubibus Prioribus;* van Leeuwen, *Prolegomena* to his edition, pp. ix-xxviii. Zieliński makes penetrating and illuminating remarks on our topic, mixed with utterly wild pronouncements—for instance, the (fortunately irrelevant) account of Socrates' back-garden, the lane, the removable garden-wall.

siades scenes, which (on the other hand) are far too long for a flash in the pan ? Note in particular two points which it seems impossible to evade. (*a*) Despite his preliminary foolishness about metres and the like, Strepsiades does seem to be progressing.[1] (*b*) Since Pheidippides has at length fulfilled his father's wish and so become capable of beating off the creditors for him, it is astonishing that, when the creditors actually arrive, not the young man, but the old, meets and outfaces them. Secondly, it follows from this that Pheidippides' part in the first *Clouds* was vastly less than in the later: perhaps no more than to provide the distresses that drive his father into the sophistic circle. But from this again follows the disappearance of two great scenes: the magnificent contention between the Just and the Unjust Arguments, the brilliantly witty dispute between father and son. So far as the former dispute is concerned, we have the support of the Sixth Argument. Thirdly, Socrates remained throughout as he was depicted early in the drama, an atheistic and pedantic physical philosopher: he was not presented as a corrupter of the young. The main proof of this is the negative witness in Plato's *Apology*. There Socrates summarizes Aristophanes' attack upon him thus:[2] 'Socrates is a wicked busybody who studies subterranean and celestial things and makes the worse plea the better and teaches others the same notions. . . . You saw for yourselves in the comedy of Aristophanes a so-called Socrates swinging about there, saying that he was treading the air, and talking a great deal of other nonsense about which I know nothing at all.' If the poet had gone on to show Socrates as a corrupter of the young—which is precisely what happens in our text—it is inconceivable that Socrates should omit to mention something so profoundly relevant to his purpose. Fourthly, the *finale* exhibited no such paroxysm of resentment in Strepsiades against the sophists nor the burning of the thinking-shop, but presented

[1] vv. 758. [2] *Apology*, 19b, c.

just the reverse. The first statement is proved by the words of the Argument, that one of the new passages was the firing of the school. But the second rests on grounds entirely different; that is, on mere analogy, but analogy difficult to disregard. Aristophanes' method throughout his career (so far as we know it) is the ironical. He takes a fantastic project and not only carries it to success, but crowns it at the end with spectacular triumph. In our *Clouds* absurdity and knavery are exposed, the chorus make a complete *volte-face*, sanity returns and Socrates is discomfited with a mechanical completeness that reminds a modern of Pecksniff's downfall.

We are then to suppose that the original comedy showed Strepsiades as, at first no doubt a stupid, but later an accomplished, pupil of the sophists: he carries out his purpose of baffling the creditors—which, indeed, he does in our play, though that part may have been longer and better. After this we postulate something for which, to be sure, there is practically no evidence in our play—a riotously jovial *kermesse* celebrating the triumph of the modern teaching. Practically no evidence, but perhaps a little. The famous " midwifery " of Socrates is mentioned [1] even in our text, and who can say to what marvellous sophistic Athena our elderly hero gave birth?

The *Clouds* offers the most brilliant, and perhaps the most profound, comparison ever written of traditional and innovating theories of education. Certain modern errors that have been, each in its day, cardinal and dominant are here completely avoided: right education is right not because it produces wealth or social advancement or good character or good citizenship, but because it deepens and enriches the individual soul. The " good citizenship " error, almost unchallenged in our own day, was indeed not difficult to avoid in Aristophanes' time: the Unjust Argument produced Alcibiades, who ruined his country by his

---

[1] vv. 135-9. Cp. the "bedroom" scene, vv. 694 *sqq.*

counsels to Sparta; the Just Argument produced Nicias, who ruined his country because he did not understand eclipses.

It is unfortunate for the poet's reputation in our more conscientious world that he selected for his butt the noblest of all pagan teachers. However much of their own personalities Plato and Xenophon may have imported into their accounts of Socrates, it is unquestionable that the *Clouds* gives a wild caricature. Nevertheless, Socrates cannot have been to any Athenian in 423 B.C. what he is to us after the *Phædo* and twenty-five centuries of reverent tradition and study ; that is to say, though of course Aristophanes " knew better," there was nothing specially wicked in taking Socrates as a butt; and his reasons are easy to detect. He wished to attack " the sophistic movement," he must select some person as representative,[1] and the natural choice was undoubtedly Socrates, who had some real affinity with the sophists, was very well known, and showed peculiarities of face, gait, and manner that made him a godsend to any actor.[2] Whether this attack had any share in the condemnation of Socrates twenty-four years later is a question often debated. Plato in the *Apology* certainly implies that it had, but that he later acquitted Aristophanes seems to be proved by the magnificent scenes of the *Symposium*. The second Argument states that our comedy was a *ballon d'essai* sent up at the instance of Anytus and Meletus (two of the accusers in 399 B.C.), ' for they moved cautiously because Socrates had many devoted friends, especially the coterie of Alcibiades, which, indeed, prevented the poet from gaining the prize with this play.' This of course is nonsense : Meletus at this date was at most a young boy, and in any case what accuser would deliberately wait for a quarter of

---

[1] As a matter of fact, most people would know that the κρείττων λόγος and the ἥττων λόγος were an idea of Protagoras.

[2] He was ridiculed in other comedies also: the Πανόπται of Cratinus, the Παράσιτοι of Eupolis, the Κόννος of Ameipsias or Phrynichus.

a century? But the chief point is that Athenian opinion was not formed by the comic stage: Cleon was incessantly abused, yet he enjoyed unquestioned political primacy from the death of Pericles to his own.

Perhaps nothing in the whole range of comic literature is finer than the scientific discussions. Socrates has summoned the Cloud goddesses, who come and greet him in tones that overwhelm Strepsiades: 'Heavens! That voice! How august, and solemn, and imposing'—

ὦ γῆ τοῦ φθέγματος, ὡς ἱερὸν καὶ σεμνὸν καὶ τερατῶδες.

'Yes,' answers the Sage, 'for they alone are goddesses: all the others are nonsense.' Strepsiades is startled: 'What about Zeus?' 'Zeus! Don't be silly. There's no such person.' The worried pupil offers evidence that Zeus does exist—the rain and the thunder—but is informed that all such things are caused by the Clouds. 'How?' he asks. Socrates gives the "rationalistic" (and correct) explanation, twice referring to "Force" or "Necessity" (ἀνάγκη).[1] 'But who is it that exerts the force? Isn't it Zeus?'—ὁ δ'ἀναγκάζων ἐστὶ τίς αὐτάς, οὐχ ὁ Ζεύς, ὥστε φέρεσθαι; This is a great moment. The bogus scientist's worst habit is to "explain" difficulties by translating them into Latin or Greek: Molière pilloried but did not cure it when his quack-doctor "explained" that opium sends us to sleep because it possesses *virtus dormitiva*.[2] Strepsiades, vastly more alert here than when discussing metre, seizes the point and will not be put off. But Socrates has a reply: at any rate he carries the account one step farther back. 'Zeus? Certainly not! It is the vortex of the Universe (αἰθέριος δῖνος).' Strepsiades, to our disappointment, fails to inquire: 'But what causes the vortex? Isn't it Zeus?' And why does he not? Another fundamental thought for scientists and teachers: he thinks he understands

---

[1] Ἀνάγκη is significantly invoked later, on morals (v. 1075).
[2] *Le Malade Imaginaire, Troisième Intermède*.

though he does not, and so halts contented and mistaken. We observe that he imagines Dinos ("Vortex") to be a proper name, the name of One really ultimate. He nods his head sapiently:

Δῖνος, τουτί μ' ἐλελήθει,
ὁ Ζεὺς οὐκ ὤν, ἀλλ' ἀντ' αὐτοῦ Δῖνος νυνὶ βασιλεύων.

'Vortex! Ah, stupid of me. . . . No Zeus, of course. . . . Vortex is king instead of him nowadays.'[1] But the finest stroke by far is to come: Aristophanes plays on us, the audience, one of the greatest jokes ever made. We, too, have thought we understand, halting therefore contented. But at the very close of the drama we are thunderstruck to find that Strepsiades, being no scientist, instead of taking *dinos* to mean "vortex" as we and Socrates did, has given it the only significance he knows. In his final rage and despair he turns to the big jar that stands beside his door, and savagely addresses it: 'Unhappy that I am, to think *you* a god, when you are nothing but earthenware!'[2] *Dinos*, we suddenly remember, means not only "vortex" but "jar" also. All this time Strepsiades has been hugging this precious discovery that his old jar accounts for the wonders of meteorology. Comedy is rarely sublime, but here it is so, in the most skilfully damaging exposure of pseudo-science and sham education ever penned.

Later, in a beautiful and memorable harangue, the Just Argument describes " the old system of education ". Much of it seems to modern readers a strange medley of the English " public school spirit " and " deportment for young ladies " of the eighteen-sixties: no feature of Athenian life, as portrayed by both Aristophanes and Plato, is so amazing as the treatment of boys at one moment as if they were young soldiers, at the next as if they were lovely and alluring girls. The Just Argument describes how they used to tramp schoolwards all together and in orderly manner— εὐτάκτως ἀθρόους, the "crocodile" in fact; on the

[1] vv. 380 *sq.*   [2] vv. 1472 *sqq.*

other hand they went without overcoats even if it snowed heavily. At their singing-lesson any original rendering was punished with a severe thrashing: this sounds familiar, but—in the gymnasium they were to adopt a modest attitude 'lest the bystanders saw anything improper'. What a comment on the traditional notion of " the grand old Greeks " and their sane respect for the body, etc., etc., by one who was a grand old Greek himself! Even worse follows: on departure from the wrestling-ground they were made to smoothe the sand whereon they had sat, so as to leave no suggestive marks.

Whatever the methods employed to reach it, the object of the " old education " was on the whole that which has been set before Western boyhood for many generations. Its spiritual culmination Aristophanes crystallizes into a noble phrase:[1] τῆς αἰδοῦς μέλλεις τἄγαλμ' ἀναπλάττειν. 'You are to fashion in your heart the image of nobility' is a weak translation; Aristophanes has given the Attic equivalent of 'Your body is the temple of the Holy Ghost'. He concludes with that memorable and lovely picture, a marvellous prophecy of the summer term in our universities;[2] and, by one of those divine accidents that shed a final glory upon the greatest moments of literature, he actually uses the traditional name of all universities:

ἀλλ' εἰς Ἀκαδήμειαν κατιὼν ὑπὸ ταῖς μορίαις ἀποθρέξει
στεφανωσάμενος καλάμῳ λευκῷ μετὰ σώφρονος ἡλικιώτου,
μίλακος ὄζων καὶ ἀπραγμοσύνης καὶ λεύκης φυλλοβολούσης,
ἦρος ἐν ὥρᾳ χαίρων, ὁπόταν πλάτανος πτελέᾳ ψιθυρίζῃ.

' No, you shall repair to the grove of Academus and, garlanded with white reeds, run your laps beneath the olives with a sound-hearted friend of your own year, fragrant of bryony and quiet leisure and the silver poplar as she casts her leaves, rejoicing in the spring season, when the plane-tree whispers to the elm.'

[1] v. 995.
[2] Much of that intoxicatingly beautiful novel, Mr. Compton Mackenzie's *Sinister Street*, might be called a vast commentary on the whole speech of the Δίκαιος Λόγος.

The gospel of the Unjust Argument also exhibits notable qualities: first, that plain gracefulness and trenchancy whereof Aristophanes was so brilliant a master; second, a sparkling proclamation of the doctrine of complete self-expression, that to withstand any temptation is sin. One line [1] may be selected as a perfect example of both qualities:

χρῶ τῇ φύσει, σκίρτα, γέλα, νόμιζε μηδὲν αἰσχρόν.

'Give rein to your nature, prance and laugh, think nothing shameful.' The application of this which follows holds special interest: 'If you are taken in adultery, refer your accuser to Zeus, notoriously weak in such matters: how can a mortal like you be stronger than a god?' It is the argument employed by the young debauchee in Terence [2] to defend not a seduction but a particularly vile rape, and as so employed is vigorously denounced by St. Augustine. Other arguments, whether they clash with this or not, are to be met here: for instance, the cave-man notion—γυνὴ σιναμωρουμένη χαίρει [3]—above all, the clinching question, 'What good did any one ever get from being chaste?' [4] The other Argument, more just than wise, instead of answering (as Plato would have answered) that it is a good in itself, tries to offer examples of (so to put it) virtuous apprentices who have become Lord Mayor, and is of course worsted. This exposition of sophistic immoralism is developed with sparkling verve by Pheidippides later: he begins with a juvenile rapture that stirs and wins the heart:

ὡς ἡδὺ καινοῖς πράγμασιν καὶ δεξιοῖς ὁμιλεῖν
καὶ τῶν καθεστώτων νόμων ὑπερφρονεῖν δύνασθαι.

It is unmistakable, this cry of the converted soul, this ecstasy as of a youth who suddenly realizes Beethoven or Botticelli in the marrow of his soul. So precious is

---
[1] v. 1078.
[2] *Eunuchus*, vv. 584 *sqq*. Cp. St. Augustine, *Confessions*, I, xvi. Mr. Rogers well quotes *Merry Wives*, V, v.
[3] v. 1070.   [4] vv. 1060 *sq*.

that rapturous irradiation of the spirit, that one wonders at times whether it is not the illumination that matters rather than the truth or falsehood of its cause. Yet the words seem so bare and obvious: where does the glamour reside? Translate them as best you may, and your magic gold turns to withered leaves overnight: "How sweet to rise above convention, living amid novelty and brilliance!"

What follows is a real argument, some new ideas and some capital jokes. 'Consider cocks and other creatures. They hit back at their fathers, yet how do they differ from us, except that they don't go in for politics?' 'Well, if you take cocks as your models in everything, why don't you eat dirt and sleep on a perch?'[1] Again, Strepsiades remarks:[2] 'You need not revenge yourself on me for the beating I gave you when a child: you can bestow them on your own son'. Pheidippides is not to be caught. 'And suppose I never have one? All my howls will have gone for nothing, and you will have had the laugh of me, safely dead'—μάτην ἐμοὶ κεκλαύσεται, σὺ δ' ἐγχανὼν τεθνήξεις. His great argument is the famous doctrine of νόμος "convention". 'That a son should not strike his father is only a convention: it was some man that set it up; and I, another man, am at full liberty to establish a new convention.'[3] This antithesis of "nature" and "convention" was the most original, most instructive, and most dangerous contribution of the Sophists to Greek thought; its best expression is the superb outburst of Callias in Plato's *Gorgias*.[4] The peril that it contained is shown comically here and tragically in Athenian history: the Just Argument truly says 'some day Athens will realize what lessons you are giving to her fools'.[5]

The WASPS (Σφῆκες) was produced at the Lenæa of 422 B.C. The text of the First Argument is corrupt,

---

[1] vv. 1427 *sqq.* [2] vv. 1434 *sqq.*
[3] vv. 1421 *sqq.* (paraphrased).
[4] 482c-486d. [5] vv. 918 *sq.*

and no further detail about the contest is quite certain, but the facts appear to be that the first prize fell to the *Rehearsal*, written by Aristophanes [1] and produced by Philonides, the second prize to the *Wasps*, written and produced by Aristophanes, and the third to Leucon's *Ambassadors*.

Two slaves, Sosias and Xanthias, are on guard outside a house. They explain that, together with Bdelycleon (" Cleon-hater "),[2] their old master's son, they are keeping captive their master Philocleon (" Cleon-lover "). He is madly in love with his work as a juryman, and the power he wields over wealthy or noble defendants; he votes invariably for condemnation. Bdelycleon is determined to cure him by forcible detention at home. The frantic old man makes ingenious attempts to escape, but in vain. The chorus of " Wasps " enter, aged jurymen armed with great stings symbolizing their ferocity in condemnation; they are on their way to the law-courts and have called to bring Philocleon. They encourage him to one more attempt: he bites through the netting and begins to let himself down by a rope. His captors awake and there follows a mêlée in which Bdelycleon wins. Then he insists on proving to his father that the supposed power and splendour of a juryman's life are nothing but slavery to the politicians. After vigorous speeches on each side, both Philocleon and the chorus are convinced. But the old man is lost: what is he now to do with his life? Bdelycleon arranges law-business for him in comfort at home. The household is ransacked for

---

[1] It may be objected: "Then he is still ventriloquizing, in the *Rehearsal* contemporaneous with the *Wasps* in which (vv. 1017-22) he repudiates the practice". It is probably enough to answer: "At any rate he does not ventriloquize in the *Wasps* itself, and so much consistency as that is enough for Aristophanes". Anyone who cannot accept this seems driven back on van Leeuwen's idea (*Mnemosyne*, XVI, 251) that the *Wasps* was produced at the Great Dionysia of 422, some weeks after the ventriloquial *Rehearsal*.

[2] To those who search for blunders in Aristophanes the fact may be pointed out that Philocleon would never have given his son such a name; still less could he himself have been named in admiration of a statesman who was himself an infant (if he was born at all) when the rite took place. Again, the captive at v. 169 is toothless, but at v. 368 he bites through the net.

utensils to represent the furnishings of the court; a defendant is found in the dog Labes,[1] accused by another dog of stealing a Sicilian cheese. When the pleadings, with the witnesses (the dish, the grater, etc.) have been heard, Philocleon is tricked into placing his pebble in the wrong urn. Finding that he has voted for acquittal, he swoons. Bdelycleon comforts him and promises to take him into smart society. The parabasis follows, a discussion of the poet's career and merits, and a proclamation of the valiant deeds performed by the Wasps against barbarian invaders. In the next scene Bdelycleon coaches his father in the manners and small talk of fashionable people; then comes a brief second parabasis. Xanthias enters, describing Philocleon's outrageous behaviour at a dinner-party. Soon the old man returns, followed by people whom he has insulted on the way: he cheerfully snubs them with scraps of irrelevant repartee; moreover, to his son's indignation, he has carried off the flute-girl from the party. Bdelycleon forces him into the house, but after awhile he emerges to challenge all the tragic dancers in Athens to a competition. The three sons of Carcinus come forward, and with a display of high kicking the play ends.

The *Wasps* is a delightful, indeed a haunting, play; but it is queer and puzzling too. What is the subject? Most will answer "the poet's object is to cure Athenian passion for legal business"—that is, he has written satire, half friendly, half contemptuous, of a prevailing fad. Others will reply: "the poet's purpose was to make the dicasts appear monsters of caprice and injustice."[2] But at least one able exponent[3] of Aristophanes finds a totally different purpose. "It has for its object the rupture of the alliance which existed between the demagogues on the one hand, and

---

[1] A reference to the attack by Cleon upon Laches, who had led an expedition to Sicily in 425 B.C.
[2] Grote, *History of Greece*, Part II, ch. vi, note (quoted by Mr. Rogers).
[3] Mr. B. B. Rogers, *Introduction*, pp. xvi-xix.

the dicasts, who constituted their main support and stay in the popular assemblies, on the other. . . . The one matter referred to arbitration, the one matter debated, the one matter decided, is this, Are the dicasts, as the demagogues tell them, really lords of all, or are they in reality mere tools and slaves of the demagogues themselves?" But these theories ignore the initiation of Philocleon into smart society and his adventures there, which fill the last four hundred lines; as a whole, then, the play depicts the weaning of a silly old man from his silly old business.

Turning now to a more detailed consideration, we remark three main features of interest. The chief parabasis contains a passage of importance for students of Aristophanes' poetical quality, and indeed of poetry in general. The *Wasps* describe their achievement at Marathon :[1]

> ἔσμεν ἡμεῖς, οἷς πρόσεστι τοῦτο τοὐρροπύγιον,
> Ἀττικοὶ μόνοι δικαίως ἐγγενεῖς αὐτόχθονες,
> ἀνδρικώτατον γένος καὶ πλεῖστα τήνδε τὴν πόλιν
> ὠφελῆσαν ἐν μάχαισιν, ἡνίκ' ἦλθ' ὁ βάρβαρος
> τῷ καπνῷ τύφων ἅπασαν τὴν πόλιν καὶ πυρπολῶν,
> ἐξελεῖν ἡμῶν μενοινῶν πρὸς βίαν τἀνθρήνια.
> εὐθέως γὰρ ἐκδραμόντες ξὺν δορὶ ξὺν ἀσπίδι
> ἐμαχόμεσθ' αὐτοῖσι, θυμὸν ὀξίνην πεπωκότες,
> στὰς ἀνὴρ παρ' ἄνδρ', ὑπ' ὀργῆς τὴν χελύνην ἐσθίων·
> ὑπὸ δὲ τῶν τοξευμάτων οὐκ ἦν ἰδεῖν τὸν οὐρανόν.
> ἀλλ' ὅμως ἐωσάμεσθα ξὺν θεοῖς πρὸς ἑσπέραν.
> γλαῦξ γὰρ ἡμῶν πρὶν μάχεσθαι τὸν στρατὸν διέπτετο·
> εἶτα δ' εἱπόμεσθα θυννάζοντες ἐς τοὺς θυλάκους,
> οἱ δ' ἔφευγον τὰς γνάθους καὶ τὰς ὀφρῦς κεντούμενοι·
> ὥστε παρὰ τοῖς βαρβάροισι πανταχοῦ καὶ νῦν ἔτι
> μηδὲν Ἀττικοῦ καλεῖσθαι σφηκὸς ἀνδρικώτερον.

This is utterly simple—how simple no modern reader can appreciate till he seeks to translate it : human language could not be plainer. Yet it is glorious, too, attaining the sublime with those words πρὸς ἑσπέραν, a fine example of a device too rarely noted : at the height of emotional tension a great author will at times achieve the culminating triumph of making us feel at home amid that splendour, by inserting a trivial fact that is

[1] vv. 1075 *sqq.*

true indeed but at the first incurious glance strangely unneeded. So amid the overwhelming speed and glory of Hector as he bursts through the gates, Homer stays to tell us that ' in his hands he carried two spears ';[1] so in the divine muster-roll of faithful patriarchs, ' Jacob, when he was a dying, blessed both the sons of Joseph, and worshipped, leaning upon the top of his staff ';[2] so here, after the heroic struggle at Marathon under Persian arrows that hid the sun, so many were they, ' nevertheless with God's help we thrust them back as evening drew on '. Mr. Rogers has rendered our passage with no little skill and fire :

> We on whom this stern-appendage, this portentous tail is found,
> Are the genuine old Autochthons, native children of the ground ;
> We the only true-born Attics, of the staunch heroic breed,
> Many a time have fought for Athens, guarding her in hours of need ;
> When with smoke and fire and rapine forth the fierce Barbarian came,
> Eager to destroy our wasps-nests, smothering all the town in flame,
> Out at once we rushed to meet him : on with shield and spear we went,
> Fought the memorable battle, primed with fiery hardiment ;
> Man to man we stood, and, grimly, gnawed for rage our under-lips.
> Hah ! their arrows hail so densely, all the sun is in eclipse !
> Yet we drove their ranks before us, ere the fall of eventide :
> As we closed, an owl flew o'er us, and the GODS were on our side !
> Stung in jaw, and cheek, and eyebrow, fearfully they took to flight,
> We behind them, we harpooning at their slops with all our might :
> So that in barbarian countries even now the people call
> Attic wasps the best, and bravest, yea, the manliest tribe of all !

Secondly, we may admire, side by side, admirable little comic scenes of two utterly different kinds. Philocleon's attempt to acquire the well-read talk of the fashionable supplies us with pretty and amusing vignettes : for instance, the scholarly gentleman's game of capping verses, which between Bdelycleon and his father, of course, degenerates into a familiar absurdity of our own music-halls. Then, in quite another key, the attempts of the elderly captive to escape from his own house are as good as anything even Aristophanes has invented in the way of zestful and ingenious drollery. ' What is this noise in the chimney ? Hullo ! Who are you ? ' ' I'm the smoke coming out.' Philo-

---

[1] *Iliad*, XII, 462 *sqq.*   [2] *Hebrews*, xi, 21.

cleon asks that his donkey may be led forth and sold. It duly appears, staggering like the pet ram of Polyphemus; and (sure enough) a new Odysseus is discovered under its belly. 'My dear sir, who *are* you?' Every child on the benches knows the answer, but what a roar when it comes! 'Noman, of course.'

The third element is more pervasive: an air of what a modern reader is at first inclined to call the Middle or even the New Comedy—elegant wit rather than satire and boisterous fun. Opinions may well differ as to the strength of this quality in the *Wasps*. We may go so far as to allege that while keeping to his "Old" method in the *Rehearsal* he deliberately essayed another kind of work in this drama; the other extreme is to see nothing but a slight and incidental relaxation.

Let us note first certain small points. There is a clear reminiscence[1] of the amusing *climax* in Epicharmus:

κακὸν τὸ πίνειν· ἀπὸ γὰρ οἴνου γίγνεται
καὶ θυροκοπῆσαι καὶ πατάξαι καὶ βαλεῖν,
κἄπειτ' ἀποτίνειν ἀργύριον ἐκ κραιπάλης.

'Drinking is bad: the result of wine is kicking at doors, assault and battery, and later a fine to pay when your headache has gone.' Perhaps a snatch[2] of love-poetry should be cited here: ἕως γάρ, ὦ μελίττιον—'Honey, the dawn has come'. The first fifty-three lines are bad introductory patter, almost so described by the poet, who makes Xanthias proceed: 'Well now, let me expound the idea of our play to the spectators'. Nor is his explanatory speech very good: at one place he sinks to the Plautine level. After inviting the audience to guess what malady afflicts Philocleon and receiving absurd imaginary answers from the butts on the benches, he goes on: 'Silly nonsense! You will never guess it. Well, if you wish to know, keep silence now, for I will at last tell you the master's disease.'

ἄλλως φλυαρεῖτ'· οὐ γὰρ ἐξευρήσετε.
εἰ δὴ 'πιθυμεῖτ' εἰδέναι, σιγᾶτε νῦν.
φράσω γὰρ ἤδη τὴν νόσον τοῦ δεσπότου.

[1] vv. 1253 sqq. Cp. above, pp. 94 sq.   [2] v. 367.

From afar one hears with a shiver those club-footed Roman iambics. The dog-trial provides an amazing contrast with the vigour and variety of the escape-scenes: nothing could well be more languid—for a reader. As a spectacle it was no doubt more attractive, but the walking utensils are another example of precisely the manner in question. Observe, further, two points neither good nor bad, but unmistakably " late," so far as our imperfect evidence goes. The slaves for the first time have rôles of some importance throughout: contrast the *Knights*, where after great initial services to the plot Nicias and Demosthenes drop entirely out of sight. Here for the first time we find a plain hint of the Getæ and Traniones who pervade and often dominate Roman comedy. The abduction of the girl-musician is almost an accidental freak, but it is entirely in the spirit of later work.

Finally, two scenes that are in any case of the first importance may reasonably be placed under this same head.

In the argumentative passages high spirits make way for brain-work. Compare Dicæopolis' stump-speech about the causes of the war—Aspasia's damsels, the Seriphian puppy, the frantic chaos of the shipyards—with Bdelycleon's lecture on Athenian revenue and its manipulation by shifty demagogues. The whole spirit has changed. ' First, calculate roughly—not with a table, but on your fingers, the total revenue that we draw from our subject-states, adding in the separate additional payments and the numerous one-per-cent taxes—court-fees, mining-rents, market-dues, harbour-dues, ground-rents, confiscations. The grand total of all this comes to nearly two thousand talents. Next set aside from this the yearly payment of six thousand jurymen (" and never have more been harboured on our soil "), and we find, of course, that it makes a hundred and fifty talents.'[1] At once the conclusion is drawn: ' Why, that means that the jurymen get

---

[1] vv. 656 *sqq*.

less than a tenth of the whole revenue!' Again, 'To-day there are a thousand cities paying us tribute. If we instructed each to feed twenty men, that would mean delicate fare for twenty thousand good democrats.'[1]

Or compare our chorus with the Acharnians. Even when bitterly antagonistic to Bdelycleon their wrath is utter mildness after the hurricane of fury that shakes the pursuers of Dicæopolis. They are wasps for but a part of the action; otherwise they are charming old rustics. Their *parodos* or entrance-song is completely delightful. The poet has shed upon it, what is not usual for him, a gentle radiance: humdrum life lit up by the observer's sympathy. He loves the picture he has painted, and describes it beforehand in haunting lines:[2]

> λύχνους ἔχοντες καὶ μινυρίζοντες μέλη
> ἀρχαιομελισιδωνοφρυνιχήρατα.

'Carrying lanterns and humming ancient songs, the charming honey of Phrynichus' *Phœnissæ*.'

> Lights in their hands, old music on their lips,
> Wild honey and the East and loveliness.

After a while their lanterns (one almost said "lanthorns") are espied glimmering in the distance and the old fellows come trudging along amid mutual encouragements to bestir their creaky bones. Their very names are pleasant—ὦ Στρυμόδωρε Κονθυλεῦ and the rest—

> William Dewy, Tranter Reuben, Farmer Ledlow late at plough.

But these pleasantly obsolete gaffers look back, like Justice Shallow, on a boisterous hell-raking youth:

> πάρεσθ' ὃ δὴ λοιπόν γ' ἔτ' ἐστίν, ἀππαπαῖ παππαιάξ,
> ἥβης ἐκείνης ἡνίκ' ἐν Βυζαντίῳ ξυνῆμεν
> φρουροῦντ' ἐγώ τε καὶ σύ· κᾆτα περιπατοῦντε νύκτωρ
> τῆς ἀρτοπωλίδος λαθόντ' ἐκλέψαμεν τὸν ὅλμον,
> κᾆθ' ἥψομεν τοῦ κορκόρου κατασχίσαντες αὐτόν.[3]

[1] vv. 707 *sqq*.
[2] vv. 219 *sq*. The exquisite verse-translation is by Professor Gilbert Murray (*Ancient Greek Literature*, p. 214).
[3] vv. 235 *sqq*. Cp. *Henry IV*, Pt. II, III, ii.

This has been to all intents and purposes translated for us by the best of pens. " The same Sir John, the very same. I see him break Skogan's head at the court-gate, when a' was a crack not thus high : and the very same day did I fight with one Sampson Stockfish, a fruiterer, behind Gray's Inn. Jesu, Jesu (ἀππαπαῖ παπαιάξ), the mad days that I have spent ! " This is a world better than examining Cleon's entrails.[1]

The PEACE (Εἰρήνη) was produced at the Great Dionysia of 421 B.C., and won the second prize, being defeated by the *Flatterers* (Κόλακες) of Eupolis and defeating Leucon's *Clansmen* (Φράτορες).

Two slaves of Trygæus, an Athenian husbandman, are discovered feeding a gigantic beetle with dung. Trygæus mounts the beetle and flies aloft in imitation of Bellerophon on Pegasus, intending to expostulate with Zeus for allowing the Peloponnesian War to continue. Arrived in Heaven, he finds Hermes only : the other gods, disgusted by the suicidal folly of the Greeks, have removed to the remotest summit, leaving Polemos (War) to work his will. He has buried the Peace-goddess in a cave, and now enters bearing a mortar in which he intends to make a huge salad, braising leeks (Prasiæ in Laconia), onions (Megara), cheese (Sicily), and honey (Athens). He asks his servant Tumult for a pestle. ' But we have none : we only moved in yesterday.' ' Then run and fetch one from Athens.' In a moment the slave returns with news that the Athenian pestle is lost (Cleon is dead). Polemos sends to Sparta, but learns that she has lent hers to others and it is lost (Brasidas has died in Thrace). He disgustedly withdraws and Trygæus seizes this respite to summon the friends of peace to rescue the goddess. The chorus enter, hysterical with joy, and are about to begin work when Hermes comes back and threatens to reveal their plan to Zeus ; with presents and flattery he is appeased. The stones are removed, ropes are attached to the lay-figure of Peace, and work

---

[1] *Knights*, 375 *sqq.*

begins. But it does not prosper, because some (Argives, etc.) are not trying or are even hindering. At length, the farmers alone undertake the task and amid loud shouts the goddess at length appears with her handmaids Opora ('Οπώρα, " Fruit ") and Theoria (Θεωρία, " Holiday " [1]), presented by real persons. There is great rejoicing, and Hermes describes how Peace disappeared : Pheidias, the sculptor, got into trouble, and his friend Pericles, fearing to share his fate, started the war ; the rest followed from the stupidity of the masses and the corruption of politicians. The parabasis praises the lofty methods of Aristophanes and derides his vulgar rivals ; an ode expounds the true spirit of the Comic Muse. Theoria is presented to the Senate ; Opora is to be the wife of Trygæus. Peace herself is to be consecrated with a ritual which is duly begun but is interrupted by Hierocles, a seer, who delivers bogus oracles to stop the proceedings and tries in vain to get a share of the sacrificial meat. There follows a second parabasis depicting the joys of peace in the countryside. Trygæus, busied with the wedding-preparations, is interrupted by tradesmen to whom the cessation of war has brought prosperity or ruin. Two boys who are to sing at the wedding come out for practice. Lamachus' son knows nothing but warlike passages from Homer, and is snubbed. Cleonymus' son sings a couplet from Archilochus, how that poet (like Cleonymus) threw his shield away. The play ends with a jovial marriage-song.

One Argument says : ' The theatrical chronicle mentions another *Peace*. . . . " It is therefore a question," remarks Eratosthenes, " whether he produced the same play again or offered another which has not survived." Crates, however, knows of two plays, for he writes: " At any rate in the *Acharnians* or

---

[1] Perhaps the least bad single word for θεωρία, which means a jolly expedition to some sacred celebration—exactly what "pilgrimage" meant to Chaucer. But that word has now associations of solitariness and toil which make it useless here.

Babylonians or in the second *Peace* ". Moreover, certain passages are incidentally quoted which are not found in the existing text.' We possess four fragments [1] to which this last sentence applies :

(i) A. τῆς πᾶσιν ἀνθρώποισιν Εἰρήνης φίλης
πιστὴ τρόφος ταμία συνεργὸς ἐπίτροπος
θυγατὴρ ἀδελφή· πάντα ταῦτ' ἐχρῆτό μοι.
B. σοὶ δ'ὄνομα δὴ τί ἐστιν;
A.   ὅ τι; Γεωργία.

A. Peace, dear to all mankind, found in me her faithful nurse, stewardess, helper, guardian, daughter and sister—all these in one.
B. And what is your name?
A.   Husbandry.

(ii)   τὴν δ' ἀσπίδα
ἐπίθημα τῷ φρέατι παράθες εὐθέως.

'Quick! Put the shield on the well for a cover.'

(iii) ἰὼ Λακεδαῖμον, τί ἄρα πείσει τήμερον;

'Ah, Sparta! What shalt thou suffer to-day?'

(iv) πόθεν τὸ φῖτυ; τί τὸ γένος; τίς ἡ σπορά;

'Whence comes this sprig? What is its kind? How was it planted?'

Before considering this evidence for two editions, it will be convenient to indicate certain features [2] in our own text.

(i) The conduct of Zeus is unintelligible. We are told [3] that the gods have washed their hands of Greece, leaving it at the disposal of Polemos; it is he who has imprisoned the goddess. Yet, when Trygæus proposes to free her, Hermes warns [4] him that Zeus has announced the death penalty for anyone who does so; and when Trygæus ignores this, it is Zeus to whom Hermes shouts, not Polemos, though it was Polemos who Trygæus feared might be aroused by the jubilations of the chorus.[5]

(ii) It seems impossible to say who form the chorus. When Trygæus summons them, they are described [6] as 'farmers, merchants, carpenters, crafts-

---

[1] Kock, frr. 294-7.
[2] Among these need not be included the remark of the Ionian in vv. 45 *sqq.*, which has often been taken to imply that Cleon is still alive (despite vv. 255 *sqq.* and 648 *sqq.*). Κεῖνος refers to the beetle, not to Cleon.
[3] vv. 195 *sqq.*   [4] vv. 371 *sqq.*
[5] v. 310.   [6] vv. 296 *sqq.*

men, resident aliens, foreigners, islanders, all folk ';
and he has just before addressed himself to ' Men of
Greece '. Next moment the chorus enter, describing
themselves as ' All-Hellenes '.[1] Nevertheless, in their
first ode they unmistakably speak as Athenians only.[2]
When hauling up the goddess they include Megarians [3]
and other non-Attic people; but in the Second Parabasis they are all Athenians.[4]

As for the chorus, the non-Athenians may form a
παραχορήγημα.[5] With the chorus of Athenians there
enter a company of Argives, Spartans, etc., to whom the
phrase ' O Men of All Greece ' is addressed. These
subsidiary persons join in the first attempts to rescue
Peace, but disappear when the chorus proper—the
band of Attic farmers—take over the task themselves.[6]
But the other point, the intrusive mention of Zeus
and the death-penalty, seems utterly baffling. It is very
small; still, why is it there? Moreover, the Scholiast
tells us of Polemos' first speech : ' Some say that Zeus
speaks these words '.[7] It is impossible to avoid the
conclusion then our text presents a combination of two
versions.

We find then one passage in our text that would
of itself suggest what the Romans called *contaminatio*.
Let us look now at the external testimony. Though
the assumption of two versions is usually to be condemned, we stand here in different case. It is impossible to set aside the Third Argument, for its writer
had before him the work of two weighty and early
critics, Eratosthenes and Crates. His language is
crisp and definite : evidently he knows what he is talking about. We are to conclude that the library of
Alexandria, where Eratosthenes worked, had a copy
of but one edition, whereas the library of Pergamum,
where Crates worked, possessed copies of two editions.[8]

---

[1] v. 302.   [2] vv. 355 *sq.*   [3] v. 500.
[4] Cp. particularly v. 1183.   [5] But see below.
[6] v. 508 : ἄγ' ὦνδρες αὐτοὶ δὴ μόνοι λαβώμεθ' οἱ γεωργοί.
[7] On v. 236.   [8] Kaibel (Pauly-Wissowa 979).

The numerous and complicated discussions [1] that have been spun like a cocoon round this play must not cause us to forget how few the details are that we know concerning its history. They seem to amount to these, and no more. (i) We have *a* version of the *Peace*; (ii) we know there were two versions; (iii) in ours occurs an irrational passage about Zeus; (iv) the goddess Husbandry appeared in one version. In the absence of more information, the simplest view appears to be this. At the Great Dionysia of 421, a *Peace* was presented which, if not almost the same as ours, must have been very like it: that is, it contained the pestle-scene and the rescue of a goddess connected with peace. But it had not our Zeus-passage: Hermes shouted to Polemos, not to Zeus. At some other festival—in what year cannot be determined—another *Peace* [2] was presented. This cannot have contained the Polemos-scene, for it would not be true that Brasidas and Cleon were lately dead. The place of Polemos was taken by Zeus; or, rather, the fear of Zeus replaced the fear of Polemos. Husbandry took the place of the three divinities shown in the other *Peace*. It is possible that the choruses were simpler than in our version: a pan-Hellenic chorus in the Polemos-Peace drama, a chorus of Attic farmers [3] in the Zeus-Husbandry drama. Long afterwards some play-fancier [4] made a " still better " play than either of these versions by putting into one the most attractive portions of the other.

[1] The most startling theory is Zieliński's (*Gliederung*, pp. 63-79). He believes that the earlier version (not ours) was produced in 422 and that ours is a revision thereof, made to serve as framework for the dedication in the theatre (Dionysia, 421) of a statue of Peace begun by Pheidias (cp. v. 605, ἦρξεν αὐτῆς Φειδίας) and finished by one of his pupils.
[2] Some modern scholars identify this other peace-play with the *Farmers* (Γεωργοί).
[3] Cp. the Second Argument: ὁ δὲ χορὸς συνέστηκεν ἔκ τινων 'Αττικῶν γεωργῶν.
[4] That such persons existed we know from *Anecdota Bekkeri*, 39: Ἐπικαττύειν καὶ πτερνίζειν: τὸ παλαιὰ ἐπισκευάζειν, ἡ μεταφορὰ ἀπὸ τῶν τοῖς παλαιοῖς ὑποδήμασιν ἕτερα καττύματα καὶ πτέρνας προσραπτόντων. λέγουσι δὲ ἐπὶ τῶν τὰ παλαιὰ τῶν δραμάτων μεταποιούντων καὶ μεταραπτόντων.

The *Peace*, as we have it, whatever its eccentricities, remains a brilliant and delightful play. Nowhere, even in the *Birds*, does the poet show greater ease: every kind of charm radiates from him without effort. Compare the opening lines with those of the *Wasps* : there we read mere back-chat ; here, the introduction really introduces, for the first sentence takes us into the heart of the plot. High spirits provide two of the best incidental jokes he ever made : ' Eat the Sibyl,' [1] and Trygæus' remark [2] to the audience on descending once more to *terra firma* : ' From the sky you looked ever so stupid ; but now that I see you close you look worse '. But the charm is most evident when literature itself forms the theme. The whole parody of *Bellerophon* is perfect, especially the hero's serio-comic anapæsts addressed, as he gains a wider prospect over earth's surface, to all, even to a man down at the docks, whose untimely necessities may lure his soaring beetle back again. Among the incidental allusions to Sophocles,[3] Euripides,[4] Cratinus,[5] and the quotations from Homer,[6] and Archilochus,[7] shines one of his brightest jewels. When Trygæus returns to earth his servant asks whether it is true that when we die we become stars. ' Certainly,' replies his master ; ' for instance—

Ἴων ὁ Χῖος, ὅσπερ ἐποίησεν πάλαι
ἐνθάδε τὸν ἀοῖόν ποθ' · ὡς δ' ἦλθ', εὐθέως
ἀοῖον αὐτὸν πάντες ἐκάλουν ἀστέρα—

' Ion of Chios, who long ago wrote his *Dawn* here on earth : as soon as he came they all named him " Star of Dawn ".' It may be that from this place Shelley drew inspiration for the glory that irradiates the forty-sixth stanza of *Adonais*. It is an exquisite instance of that device whereby one poet praises another in terms of that other's achievement : Ion had written

ἀωῖον ἀεροφοίταν
ἀστέρα μείναμεν ἀελίου λευκοπτέρυγα πρόδρομον.

---

[1] v. 1116. [2] vv. 82 *sqq*. [3] vv. 531, 695 *sqq*.
[4] vv. 532 and perhaps 1012 *sqq*. [5] vv. 700 *sqq*. Cp. p. 173.
[6] vv. 1273 *sqq*. [7] vv. 1298 *sq*.

'We awaited the star that wanders through the dawn-lit sky, pale-winged courier of the sun.'

Another poet whom Aristophanes is never slow to discuss is himself. In the first parabasis he claims two merits. First, he has banished vulgarity from the comic stage—'jokes about rags and flea-campaigns, the everlasting Heracles In The Bake-House and the slave who gets a thrashing so that his fellow may work off the well-known joke. . . .'[1] Such things may, of course, be found in our poet himself, but they are incidental. His second claim is to have made Comedy a great art form : ἐποίησε τέχνην μεγάλην ὑμῖν κἀπύργωσ' οἰκοδομήσας—precisely the manner in which he elsewhere writes of Æschylus.[2] The means to this loftiness are 'stately language, cultivated ideas and jests '— ἔπεσιν μεγάλοις καὶ διανοίαις καὶ σκώμμασιν οὐκ ἀγοραίοις —and an impressive object of satire : Cleon, arrayed in superhuman (and sub-human) terrors.[3] Thus the poet has shown himself a paladin [4] of the theatre by attacking the dragon, 'not satirizing the trivial men and women of private life '—οὐκ ἰδιώτας ἀνθρωπίσκους κωμῳδῶν οὐδὲ γυναῖκας—like the school of Crates. That " paladin " is not too high praise is suggested by his sudden outburst of downright chivalry towards Cleon, of all people. He attacked him while he lived, but when Hermes seems on the verge of a diatribe against the tanner who kept the war in being, Trygæus interrupts firmly : ' Cease, cease, Lord Hermes, do not say it! . . . He is no longer ours, but yours,' and so forth.[5]

Many will find the greatest charm of this play in its exquisite pictures of country life. It has been admirably observed [6] that the earliest idyllic poetry

---

[1] vv. 739 sqq.   [2] E.g. Frogs, 1004.
[3] vv, 739 sqq. The fantastic word-picture of Cleon's anatomy is borrowed from the Wasps.
[4] 'Ἡρακλέους ὀργήν τιν' ἔχων τοῖσι μεγίστοις ἐπεχείρει. It is an amusing and striking fact that he can mention Heracles as the type both of drama that he derides (v. 741) and of drama that he praises (v. 752), without confusing either his ancient audience or his modern readers.
[5] vv. 648 sqq.
[6] By Professor J. S. Phillimore, in *Pastoral and Allegory* (Oxford, 1925).

ARISTOPHANES

of Greece is found in Aristophanes, at the time when the country population of Attica, confined by war for years behind city-walls, was tempted to idealize rural life.

> ἀλλ' ἀναμνησθέντες ἄνδρες
> τῆς διαίτης τῆς παλαιᾶς,
> ἣν παρεῖχ' αὕτη ποθ' ἡμῖν,
> τῶν τε παλασίων ἐκείνων
> τῶν τε σύκων τῶν τε μύρτων,
> τῆς τρυγός τε τῆς γλυκείας
> τῆς ἰωνιᾶς τε τῆς πρὸς
> τῷ φρέατι τῶν τ' ἐλαῶν
>   ὧν ποθοῦμεν,
> ἀντὶ τούτων τήνδε νυνὶ
> τὴν θεὸν προσείπατε.

' Come, lads, remember the old-time life that She once bestowed on us, those cakes of dried fruit, the figs and myrtle-berries, the sweet new wine, the violet-bed that fringed the well, the olives dear to memory : for all those gifts salute this our goddess to-day.' [1] The second parabasis contains his finest work in this kind : [2]

> Ah, there's nothing half so sweet as when the seed is in the ground.
> God a gracious rain is sending, and a neighbour saunters round.
> O Comarchides ! he hails me : how shall we enjoy the hours?
> Drinking seems to suit my fancy, what with these benignant showers.
> Therefore let three quarts, my mistress, of your kidney-beans be fried,
> Mix them nicely up with barley, and your choicest figs provide ;
> Syra run and shout to Manes, call him in without delay,
> 'Tis no time to stand and dawdle pruning out the vines to-day,
> Nor to break the clods about them now the ground is soaking through.
> Bring me out from home the fieldfare, bring me out the finches two.
> Then there ought to be some beestings, four good plates of hare beside
> (Hah ! unless the cat purloined them yesterday at eventide ;
> Something scuffled in the pantry, something made a noise and fuss) ;
> If you find them, one's for father, bring the other three to us.
> Ask Æschinades to send us myrtle branches green and strong ;
> Bid Charinades attend us, shouting as you pass along.
>   Then we'll sit and drink together,
>   God the while refreshing, blessing,
>   All the labour of our hands.

This passage bears a marked verbal resemblance to Plato's description of the unphilosophic delights enjoyed in ' the city of pigs ' ; [3] it may be more attractively

---

[1] vv. 571 sqq. [2] vv. 1140 sqq. (tr. Rogers).
[3] *Republic*, 372 a-d.

described as a blend of Hesiod, Theocritus and Christmas as portrayed by Dickens.

Fun, both verbal and spectacular, is plentiful: the picture [1] of the unfortunate rustic who finds himself listed by trickery at the last moment to join a military expedition, the monstrous beetle at his repast 'working his feelers round thus, like a man coiling a ship's cable,' [2] the sudden references to theatrical conditions—'sacrifice the sheep behind the scenes and save the pocket of the *choregus*,' [3]—Trygæus' agonized appeal to the stage-carpenter for a safe passage through the air; [4] and of spectacular comic effects there are no less than three, all first-rate—the tragi-comic ascent to Heaven, the salad of Polemos, and the rescue of Peace with all the Hellenic States hauling at the ropes.

The BIRDS (Ὄρνιθες) was produced at the Great Dionysia of 414 B.C. under the name of Callistratus, and obtained the second prize; Ameipsias was first with the *Revellers* (Κωμασταί); Phrynichus third with the *Hermit* (Μονότροπος).

Two elderly Athenians, Pisthetærus and Euelpides, disgusted with the litigious atmosphere of Athens, seek a new city, and for this reason visit the Hoopoe, who, having once been a man, can sympathize with them, and being now a bird has travelled far. Pisthetærus has an inspiration: let the birds found a city in the air and so become masters of the Universe. The Hoopoe calls the tribes of birds and they begin to flock in; but, finding that the visitors are human beings, age-long foes of the birds, they are at point to tear them to pieces. The Hoopoe at length induces them to hear Pisthetærus' proposals. He makes a long speech about the primitive glories of the birds and the loss of their dignities. The chorus wildly proclaim that they will recover their sovereignty of the Universe or die: let Pisthetærus advise them. He urges the foundation of a city in the clouds and dilates

[1] vv. 1179 *sqq*.
[2] vv. 35 *sqq*.
[3] vv. 1020 *sqq*.
[4] v 174.

upon the ease with which the birds will establish themselves as dispensers of all blessings and all punishments. This plan is acclaimed, and the Chorus sing their celebrated parabasis. First [1] a brief song (*commation*) is sung to the nightingale; then come the *anapæsts* or *parabasis* proper, an address to mankind describing the earliest history of the Universe, and the importance of the birds to every function of human life, ending (in the *pnigos*) with promises of complete felicity to men if they will worship the birds; there follows a song (*ode* or *strophe*) to the Woodland Muse; the *epirrhema* recites the advantages a man will find if he joins the birds; the *antode* (or *antistrophe*) describes the swans as divine singers that fill Heaven with amazed delight; the *antepirrhema* dilates on the advantages of wings if a man stays in his earthly surroundings. Pisthetærus and Euelpides return, grotesquely plumed, and the future city is named Nephelococcygia (" Cloudcuckootown "), Euelpides is sent off to superintend the building, while Pisthetærus organizes the sacrificial service to the new gods. But he is interrupted by a poet already furnished with odes to the new city, an oracle-monger, a town-planning expert, an inspector or visiting commissioner, and a dealer in ready-made laws. All these are chased away, and a second parabasis follows. A messenger brings news that the city is finished: another reports that some god has got past the sentries: the intruder proves to be Iris, sent by Zeus to expostulate with mankind for the cessation of sacrifices. Pisthetærus utters the harshest threats against Zeus and packs her off. A herald brings tidings of the enthusiasm for the birds that has sprung up among mankind: multitudes are now on their way to apply for feathers. Three of these arrive, a son who wishes to strangle his father, the poet Cinesias, and a professional informer; each is shrewdly dealt with. A topical song is followed by the arrival of Prometheus,

[1] As this parabasis is not only magnificent but contains all the technical divisions (except the rare *antipnigos*), their names and contents have here been catalogued.

who sneaks in under a large umbrella in case Zeus sees him. The gods (he reports) are starving, and will send an embassy; Pisthetærus must not merely demand the sceptre from Zeus, but insist also that Basileia ("Royalty") be given to him for a wife. After another topical song the envoys come in: Poseidon, Heracles, and an uncouth barbarian deity. They at length accept the conditions, and Pisthetærus departs to bring his bride. After a third song a messenger announces the overwhelming splendour to which the hero has attained. The chorus sing a marriage-ode; the bride and groom enter amid rejoicing, and all move off in triumph.

This comedy is universally acclaimed as the finest masterpiece of Aristophanes. Furthermore, it is entirely unencumbered by the historico-literary questions that are the food of researchers; granted a sound knowledge of Greek, the play holds no more difficulty for a modern reader than does *The Tempest*. The one "difficulty" that can be said to arise has been imposed on the poet wantonly from without. Why did he write the play? or what is he satirizing? Ancient scholars will have it that he ridicules the litigiousness of his countrymen: for this practically no evidence can be found.[1] Modern scholars often assert that he is satirizing the boundless schemes of conquest that now excited Athens, which a few months before had despatched the famous and ill-starred Syracusan Expedition. That Aristophanes meant to ridicule these imperial dreams there is no shred of proof;[2] and when he does intend to ridicule

[1] In vv. 39 *sqq.* we are told by Euelpides that incessant δίκαι are their reason for leaving Athens; but we hear no more of this, and when explaining their wishes to the Hoopoe they say nothing about it. It is a casual excuse of the poet's to set his men off on their search for "a cosy city".

[2] There is not even a reference to the Expedition beyond the allusion (vv. 145 *sq.*) to the *Salaminia* which was sent to fetch Alcibiades back. Süvern's essay, in which Heaven is the Peloponnese, the birds the Athenians who will starve them out, etc., surely need detain no one: the only excuse for seeking allegory, in any work that does not openly proclaim itself as such, is that the work cannot be understood on ordinary lines. So with Mr. E. G. Harman's view that the Athenian democracy is forced to make terms with the exiles.

anybody or anything his intention is hardly doubtful. In the *Birds* his purpose, for anyone not obsessed by research-mongering, is almost too obvious to state: it was the working out of a glorious comic fancy—" let us build a city at ' the Thermopylæ of the Universe ' and dictate terms to gods and men ". We should hardly be justified even in asserting that it satirizes the irresponsible day-dreams of man (whether Greek or barbarian) in his weaker moments. No one at all is derided:[1] this is a fairy-tale gloriously funny and gloriously told. If we still ask: " And why does he leave political comedy for the purely fantastic ? " it might be enough to reply: " Because he chooses. Seven years have elapsed since his last extant play, the *Peace*, and he has conceived other ideas."[2] Or we may believe that his refusal to write politics is but a sign that he is only too conscious of them: that during these years the growing villainy and recklessness induced by continued war or treacherous peace have sickened him of humanity, and he turns deliberately for relief to a castle in the air. If that is so, we have three, not two, works of war-hatred produced by Athenians of genius: the *Birds* should be placed beside the *Trojan Women* and those frightful chapters [3] where Thucydides depicts the degeneration of Greece. There is a grim fascination in collecting so magnificent, so strangely assorted, a trio. But we must remember a fact that damages such an idea. Glorious fantasy as the *Birds* is, it is not an entirely irresponsible lark in the empyrean, but shows a disconcerting touch of practicality. We need not dwell upon the matter-of-fact vigour wherewith Pisthetærus makes his proposal : ' Very well. My first instruction is that there should

---

[1] In the sense here intended. There are of course brief incidental lampoons in the lyrics.

[2] Van Leeuwen (*Prolegomena ad Aves*, pp. xii *sq.*) remarks that "this comedy opens a series of plays aloof from public life and humdrum affairs, their subjects being either borrowed from tragedy or amusing inventions of the poet's own ".

[3] III, 82-84.

be a single bird commonwealth; next, the whole air—all intermediate space—must be surrounded by a circular wall of large bricks, like Babylon.'[1] This is a brisk organizing brain, indeed, with no touch of Aladdin or Ariel; but that may be attributed to the clear-cut mental temper of all Athenians. Far more striking is the morality. When wretches from earth arrive hoping to find delightful scope and facilities for their wickedness in this novel Jerusalem, Pisthetærus reads them stern and edifying lectures.[2]

Has the play any flaws? Perhaps none. The Basileia idea may be thought too overwhelming. No doubt we are meant to take, and do take, the whole story as fun: Pisthetærus himself, on hearing of the miraculously rapid completion of Nephelococcygia says: 'It sounds to me as if it were truly a lie';[3] and Iris penetrates the terrific bastions without so much as noticing them.[4] Nevertheless, to enjoy the wildest story we must entertain a spurious momentary belief in it; and if we do, the Basileia passages might seem more suited to Shelley's *Prometheus Unbound* than to Aristophanic drollery. But we have no business to harbour memories of Shelley and other more orthodox writers on the divine government; this passage is only another proof of the un-Hebraic lightness wherewith Athenians could on occasion take their religion. It is reinforced by other things: Poseidon swears by Poseidon like any Athenian knight;[5] and Pisthetærus goes to the extreme of blasphemy when he harshly tells Iris:[6] 'If Zeus annoys me further, I will burn the house over his head'. This attitude provides some excellent fooling. What is to happen when Zeus dies? Can Heracles inherit? No; but Poseidon, his next legitimate kin. 'Ah! But suppose,' Heracles objects, ' he makes special provision for me at his death.' ' The

---

[1] vv. 550 *sq.*
[2] His treatment of the unnatural son (vv. 1336 *sqq.*) is very noteworthy.
[3] v. 1167.   [4] v. 1210.
[5] v. 1614.   [6] vv. 1246 *sqq.*

law won't allow that,' Pisthetærus answers firmly, and reads him an extract from Solon's code.

Excellent as the fun is, the chief interest of the *Birds* lies elsewhere, in dramatic structure and lyrical beauty. Had this comedy followed the lines of its predecessors, we should have found, between the erection of the new city and the triumphant wedding with Basileia (who would not have been mentioned earlier), nothing except a series of scenes demonstrating, indeed, the birds' power and glory but showing no increase of significance or tension. Now, though the Unnatural Son, Cinesias, and the Informer are analogous to the intruders who come to beg peace-wine from Dicæopolis, there occur in addition two scenes that are not only first-rate fun but also give the second half of the play an organic development. It becomes clear that the action has not really closed with the completion of the cloud-city, as the *Peace* closed with the rescue of the goddess. If Pisthetærus' position is to be secure, he must grasp the sceptre itself; still more, he must contract a divine marriage. These are new ideas—ideas that the Athenian has not himself conceived: and they must be imparted to him by Prometheus, a new-comer to the story. Further, whereas the poet might even so have despatched his hero at once to Heaven armed with this advice, the confrontation is first set before our eyes in the reception of the celestial ambassadors. Throughout the second half of this play we find, then, a genuine dramatic development—a new thing in Aristophanic drama so far as we know it.

But the fame of the *Birds* rests for the most part upon its lyrical magnificence: the Hoopoe's summons to his mate the Nightingale, with its peerless and haunting close:[1]

διὰ δ' ἀθανάτων στομάτων χωρεῖ
ξυμφωνος ὁμοῦ
θεία μακάρων ὀλολυγή,

[1] vv. 220 *sqq.*

'from seraphic lips in pealing unison resounds the celestial Hallelujah'; then, as in a moment he passes from the intense splendours of the empyrean to the lowliest wayside nooks, that fresh spring-time joyousness [1] wherewith he calls together the birds of ploughland, garden, and hillside, of the marsh-channels, the 'lovely meadow of Marathon,' and the sea-wave, in throbbing music that echoes the sweetest singer of the past—

ὧν τ' ἐπὶ πόντιον οἶδμα θαλάσσης
φῦλα μετ' ἀλκυόνεσσι ποτῆται,

'your tribes flit with the halcyon over billows of the open sea'; [2] the little song [3] that depicts the happy life of birds at every season, 'during winter sporting in caverned rocks with mountain-nymphs'; and the superb Messenger's speech [4] concerning Pisthetærus' apotheosis; above all, that august address [5] in the first parabasis where 'mankind, whose dim existence likens them to the leaves in their generation' hear the story of primeval chaos and the birth of Love :

ἐξ οὗ περιτελλομέναις ὥραις ἔβλαστεν Ἔρως ὁ ποθεινός,
στίλβων νῶτον πτερύγοιν χρυσαῖν, εἰκὼς ἀνεμώκεσι δίναις,

'therefrom as the seasons revolved blossomed forth Eros, the world's desire, the sheen of gold upon his pinions, his force like the tornado'.

And the Universe is thus shaken to pieces and irradiated with cataclysmic splendours by the action of two elderly men who left Athens because they wished for a little peace and quiet in their old age!

LYSISTRATA (Λυσιστράτη, 'She who disbands armies') was produced, with what success is not known, at the Lenæan festival of 411 B.C., under the name of Callistratus.

Lysistrata summons the women of Greece to combine in stopping the Peloponnesian War. She pro-

---

[1] Observe the quaint and charming art whereby the poet develops bird-cries into articulate speech, e.g. vv. 228 sq. : ἰὼ ἰὼ ἰτὼ ἰτὼ ἰτώ, ἴτω τις ὧδε . . . .
[2] vv. 250 sq. Cp. Alcman's famous fragment.
[3] vv. 1088 sqq.   [4] vv. 1706 sqq.   [5] vv. 685 sqq.

poses to force the men of all the Greek States to make peace by refusing them sexual intercourse until they do. Her colleagues at length agree. Hardly has their oath been recited when a clamour is heard. Lysistrata's second plan has succeeded: the older Athenian women have seized the Acropolis, including the State treasury. The foreigners depart to spread the sex-strike over Greece, and the Athenian women barricade themselves in the Acropolis. A semi-chorus of old men arrives, bearing timber and fire to smoke the invaders out. They are confronted by a semi-chorus of old women carrying jugs of water; there follows a struggle in which the men are drenched. Enter a Commissioner [1] who has come to draw money for naval expenses from the Treasury, but finds himself locked out. He orders the gates to be burst in, but Lysistrata herself opens them. The Commissioner commands his police to arrest her and her companions, but they are worsted and she is allowed to state her case: the Treasury has been seized by women, who can manage it better than men; women have been snubbed hitherto, but now they mean to take public affairs in hand. The Commissioner departs in dudgeon, and the semi-choruses sing injuriously against one another. Lysistrata comes forth despondent: her followers are wearying of the strike and offering every kind of excuse to slip off home. She exposes and baffles these deserters and makes an appeal for patience; 'remember that the men are feeling the strain too'. After more altercatory songs from the semi-choruses, Cinesias arrives, longing for his wife Myrrhine: she agrees to relent, but after keeping him absurdly on tenterhooks, disappoints him. Next a Spartan herald arrives; meeting the Commissioner, he reports that the Peloponnesian confederates have been reduced to such straits by domestic defection that they are ready to make peace. He and the Commissioner agree to the appointment of plenipotentiaries.

[1] Πρόβουλος, one of the Committee of Public Safety appointed after the Sicilian disaster (Thuc., VIII, i, 3).

The two semi-choruses are reconciled, and form a single chorus. The Spartan and Athenian envoys appear and are made friends by Lysistrata; all go into a banquet, after which there are songs and dances by Spartans and Athenians.

Lysistrata is indecent and grave, brutal and tender, quaint and smart, political and frolicsome, all by turns. If we do perceive one general characteristic amid all this, it is weariness: though *Lysistrata*, if compared with fourth-century comedy, shows a vigour positively volcanic, it nevertheless appears jaded beside the *Birds* and the *Frogs*. The explanation is that frightful overthrow in Sicily, which for the time broke even Aristophanes' spirit. When his semi-choruses at last combine, they begin with these amazing words:[1] 'Gentlemen, we are not preparing to utter a single ill word against any citizen: no, our intent is to say and do all the good we can, for the troubles already on our hands are enough'. Small wonder that the *Lysistrata* is patchy —sometimes (in the indecent parts) riotously funny, sometimes (in the argumentative passages) so anxiously reasonable, so devoid of sparkle, that one might imagine we are listening to anapæsts written by Xenophon:

$$\pi\hat{\omega}\varsigma\ \dot{o}\rho\theta\hat{\omega}\varsigma,\ \ddot{\omega}\ \kappa\alpha\kappa\acute{o}\delta\alpha\iota\mu\text{ον},$$
$$\epsilon\dot{i}\ \mu\eta\delta\dot{\epsilon}\ \kappa\alpha\kappa\hat{\omega}\varsigma\ \beta\text{ου}\lambda\epsilon\text{υο}\mu\acute{\epsilon}\nu\text{οι}\varsigma\ \dot{\epsilon}\xi\hat{\eta}\nu\ \dot{\upsilon}\mu\hat{\iota}\nu\ \dot{\upsilon}\pi\text{ο}\theta\acute{\epsilon}\sigma\theta\alpha\iota;$$
$$\ddot{o}\tau\epsilon\ \delta\dot{\eta}\ \delta'\ \dot{\upsilon}\mu\hat{\omega}\nu\ \dot{\epsilon}\nu\ \tau\alpha\hat{\iota}\sigma\iota\nu\ \dot{o}\delta\text{οι}\hat{\varsigma}\ \phi\alpha\nu\epsilon\rho\hat{\omega}\varsigma\ \dot{\eta}\kappa\text{ού}\text{ο}\mu\epsilon\nu\ \ddot{\eta}\delta\eta,$$
$$'\text{ο}\dot{\upsilon}\kappa\ \ddot{\epsilon}\sigma\tau\iota\nu\ \dot{\alpha}\nu\dot{\eta}\rho\ \dot{\epsilon}\nu\ \tau\hat{\eta}\ \chi\acute{\omega}\rho\alpha\cdot'\ '\mu\grave{\alpha}\ \Delta\acute{\iota}'\ \text{ο}\dot{\upsilon}\ \delta\hat{\eta}\tau\acute{},'\ \epsilon\dot{i}\phi'\ \ddot{\epsilon}\tau\epsilon\rho\acute{o}\varsigma\ \tau\iota\varsigma\cdot$$
$$\mu\epsilon\tau\grave{\alpha}\ \tau\alpha\hat{\upsilon}\theta'\ \dot{\eta}\mu\hat{\iota}\nu\ \epsilon\dot{\upsilon}\theta\grave{\upsilon}\varsigma\ \ddot{\epsilon}\delta\text{ο}\xi\epsilon\nu\ \sigma\hat{\omega}\sigma\alpha\iota\ \tau\grave{\eta}\nu\ \text{‘Ε}\lambda\lambda\acute{\alpha}\delta\alpha\ \kappa\text{οι}\nu\hat{\eta}$$
$$\tau\alpha\hat{\iota}\sigma\iota\ \gamma\upsilon\nu\alpha\iota\xi\grave{\iota}\nu\ \sigma\upsilon\lambda\lambda\epsilon\chi\theta\epsilon\acute{\iota}\sigma\alpha\iota\varsigma.[2]$$

'Wretch! How could it be right if we were not allowed to advise you even when your plans were wrong? So when we began to hear you openly saying in the street, " There is not a man left in the country," and another answering, " No, by Heaven," we women at once decided to combine for the rescue of Greece.' At the opening of her appeal to the women whom she has summoned Lysistrata says, ' I am sure you all miss

---

[1] vv. 1043 *sqq*. [2] vv. 521 *sqq*.

your husbands who are away at the war'; and three of them reply. In any other of his plays, however pathetic the answers might have been, one at least would have been amusing too; here, all three speak mere matter-of-fact.

This depression has suffused other parts of the work with subdued colours such as are not common in our poet. Cross as the old men and old women are, something of the " dear old soul " clings to them that culminates, when they are reconciled, in a Darby and Joan scene. These aged besiegers of the stolen Acropolis, mumbling about their lumbago and getting the smoke of the deadly torches in their poor bleared eyes, so that their stanzas end with the piteous little refrain [1]

> φῦ φῦ (not φεῦ, φεῦ)
> ἰοὺ ἰοὺ τοῦ καπνοῦ,
> "Pff! Pff! Drat the smoke,"

how charming they are, and how they thrill us with their memories of another siege of the same citadel in those great days when the Spartan invader was forced to slink out of it!

> οὕτως ἐπολιόρκησ' ἐγὼ τὸν ἄνδρ' ἐκεῖνον ὠμῶς
> ἐφ' ἑπτακαίδεκ' ἀσπίδων πρὸς ταῖς πύλαις καθεύδων.

'So fiercely did I besiege the Spartan! we bivouacked before the gates sixteen deep, under arms all night.' [2] They are—they must be—the same grumpy old fellows whom we met in the *Wasps*: here is Strymodorus again,[3] at any rate. Their female opponents are less interesting; and both sides grow so angry that there is a good deal of low talk; but all comes right in the end, and when each aged lady helps her *vis-à-vis* on with his coat and takes the gnat out of his eye ('Just look! Mercy! What a monster!'[4]) we half expect her to break out into the Greek equivalent of *John Anderson, my Jo*.

---
[1] vv. 294 sq.   [2] vv. 281 sq.
[3] v. 259, cp. *Wasps*, v. 233. He has been mentioned in *Ach.*, 273, also.
[4] v. 1031.

It is in women that the pathos of this play is mostly concentrated. There is not much of it, but nowhere among the hard-hearted unhumorous Athenians (except, of course, in Euripides) do we find any strong sense of the pathetic,[1] and *Lysistrata* is the tenderest of Aristophanes' works. We can see and hear—how plainly!—the Athenian woman, dreading a snub, but in anguish for her country: ἀλγοῦσαι τἄνδοθεν ὑμᾶς ἐπανηρόμεθ' ἂν γελάσασαι [2]—' grieving within, we used to ask you gaily . . .' Lysistrata has a stinging retort [3] (worthy of, almost borrowed from, Euripides) to the question, ' What concern have *you* in the war ? '—

καὶ μήν, ὦ κατάρατε,
πλεῖν ἤ γε διπλοῦν αὐτὸν φέρομεν, πρώτιστον μέν γε τεκοῦσαι
κἀκπέμψασαι παῖδας ὁπλίτας. . . .

' What, you villain? We endure twice our share of it, nay more : first because we bear sons and send them out as soldiers.[4] . . . Then :

τῆς δὲ γυναικὸς σμικρὸς ὁ καιρός, κἂν τούτου μὴ 'πιλάβηται,
οὐδεὶς ἐθέλει γῆμαι ταύτην, ὀττευομένη δὲ κάθηται.

(A man may easily marry late), ' but a woman's day is brief, and if she lets it slip no one seeks to marry her : she sits telling her fortune '.

Such passages for a moment transform the boisterous farce of fifth-century Athens into something strangely like the *comédie larmoyante* of La Chaussée and his school ; it has been plausibly urged [5] that the extreme grossness of other scenes was intended as a deliberate antidote to excessive seriousness. There is some truth in the suggestion, but it is misleading, for the poet's natural method of putting any idea was the farcical, which, for Athens, included a great deal of indecency. So much we can observe in any of the plays he had already composed. The novelty here is that sex lies at the very root of the play : theoretically, of

---

[1] The increase of compassion is perhaps the only genuine superiority of the modern over the ancient world.
[2] v. 512.
[3] vv. 588 *sqq.*, cp. *Medea*, 248 *sqq.*
[4] Cp. vv. 649 *sqq.*
[5] Rogers, *Introduction*, p. ix.

course, the women's strike could be treated with austere propriety, but not in a fifth-century comedy. He might have composed a play depicting only the women's seizure of the Treasury and Lysistrata's political and social arguments : he would have been indecent more incidentally, as in the *Wasps* or *Peace*. The strike is introduced for its own sake, an undoubtedly rich mine. The passages that depict the distress of the unnamed Spartans and Athenians are (however broad) robustly laughable and unseductive ; but the scene of Cinesias and Myrrhine is deliberately prurient. Connected only in part with this latter is another element. For the first time in extant literature we find here a notion that has been enormously exploited in modern writing—what may be most succinctly described by a few once incessant phrases : " lovely woman," " the fair sex," " the ladies, God bless 'em." Here is one example : [1]

> τί δ' ἂν γυναῖκες φρόνιμον ἐργασαίατο
> ἢ λαμπρόν, αἳ καθήμεθ' ἐξηνθισμέναι,
> κροκωτοφοροῦσαι καὶ κεκαλλωπισμέναι
> καὶ Κιμμερίκ' ὀρθοστάδια καὶ περιβαρίδας ;

' But how can women perform any wise or glorious exploit ? We sit about with our golden curls, dressed in becoming shades, made up to charm, wearing dainty shoes and frocks from abroad that show off the figure.' It is on this that Lysistrata herself chiefly relies.[2]

The weakness of general effect in this play is due not only to basing the action upon two ideas (the sex-strike and the seizure of the Acropolis) but also to looseness of technical structure. The two choruses combine very late ; as a result, there is no parabasis. This primitive construction, and the fact that the dramatist contented himself with tying two plot-notions together, point to a certain hurry and casualness [3] in his own mind. A few weeks after the *Lysistrata* he produced

---

[1] vv. 42 *sqq.* Cf. vv. 149 *sqq.*, 551 *sqq.*   [2] vv. 46 *sqq.*, 551 *sqq.*
[3] Note, as a symptom of this, the contradiction between vv. 107 and 129 *sqq.* Lysistrata's friends might have made a virtue of necessity.

a brilliant masterpiece, and it is natural to suppose that our play was thrown off as a hasty *pièce d'occasion*. This would account not only for the pervasive lack of strength but also for the peculiar close, which contains none of the customary fireworks and is bulked out, pleasantly enough but rather tamely, by those Athenian and Spartan choruses that remind a modern reader of the ballets in *Le Bourgeois Gentilhomme* and *Le Malade Imaginaire*, and are in fact a reversion to the primitive comos-finale.

The THESMOPHORIAZUSÆ (Θεσμοφοριάζουσαι, 'Women celebrating the Thesmophoria'—a festival sacred to the Mother and the Maid) was produced at the Great Dionysia of 411 B.C.[1] There is no Argument and we know nothing of its success.

Euripides enters, bringing his elderly kinsman, Mnesilochus,[2] to the house of Agathon, the elegant tragic poet. Agathon's servant announces in high-flown anapæsts that his master is deep in composition. While waiting, Euripides explains his errand to Mnesilochus: the Athenian women, angered by Euripides' attacks on them in his plays, have determined to use this day of the female festival, the Thesmophoria, for a meeting at which they will decide whether he is to be slain. Euripides intends to despatch Agathon, disguised as a woman, to plead his cause. Agathon now appears, accompanied by a chorus with which he rehearses a composition; Euripides puts his request, which is urbanely but firmly rejected. Mnesilochus steps into the breach, is shaved by Euripides, dressed in female garments supplied by Agathon, and moves forward to the Thesmophorian temple and the assembly. A woman proposes that Euripides be put to death: he has poisoned family life by filling men's minds with suspicion. Another

---

[1] At v. 1060 'Echo' says she 'acted with Euripides in this same place last year': that is, our play came out the year after Euripides' *Andromeda*. This latter belongs to the year 412 (cp. Scholiast on *Frogs*, 53).

[2] Never so named in our text; see below.

complains that he has ruined her florist's business by persuading the men that there are no gods. Next, the disguised Mnesilochus pronounces a racy and scandalous address on the immoral doings of " herself " and others, seeking to show that Euripides has told but a fraction of the truth. The meeting clamours in protest, and a bawling-match follows between the first orator and Mnesilochus, which the chorus-leader stills on the approach of Cleisthenes, who brings news that Euripides has sent a disguised kinsman to spy on the women. Detective work is rapidly begun and Mnesilochus is unmasked. Cleisthenes goes to fetch a magistrate, leaving the women to watch their captive, who attempts escape by a burlesque of Euripides' *Telephus*: he seizes a baby from one of his foes and (finding that it is a wineskin) sheds its blood. He next decides to summon Euripides' aid by a device from *Palamedes*: carving his message on scraps of wood he flings them abroad as Œax threw inscribed oar-blades into the sea. The parabasis follows, concerned mostly with the superiority of women to men. Mnesilochus now tries another play, *Helena*. He acts the forlorn Helen and Euripides enters as Menelaus to rescue " her," but the wardress is not deceived; when the magistrate arrives with a policeman, Euripides perforce withdraws, and Mnesilochus is trussed up to a board. After a dance and song by the chorus, Euripides and the prisoner engage in a parody of the *Andromeda*, but the barbarian constable refuses to allow the release of " Andromeda." The chorus sing again, after which Euripides in his own person approaches them and offers terms: if they will favour the rescue, he will promise never again to revile women. They agree, and he disguises himself as an old woman taking a dancing-girl to a party. The latter so enthrals the policeman that he goes off with her, to find on his return that the crone and the prisoner have vanished. The chorus misdirect his pursuit, and the play ends.

Ancient authorities mention another *Thesmophori-*

azusæ. All we know of it is (i) that Demetrius of Trœzen called it *Thesmophoriasasæ* [1]—' Women who *have celebrated* the Thesmophoria '—which may suggest that the lost play continued the story of ours; (ii) that the prologue was delivered by Calligeneia,[2] a goddess after whom the last day of the Thesmophoria was named; (iii) a few fragments: one forbids the use of wines that will excite masculine passion;[3] there is a long list of women's jewellery, etc.;[4] Agathon's fondness for antitheses is mentioned;[5] Euripides' *Antiope* was perhaps parodied;[6] the *agon* is referred to by name.[7] There are two more striking remnants—the lines[8] about the " ivory kipper " mentioned by Crates " with casual and effortless brilliance "— λαμπρὸν ἐκόμιζεν ἀπόνως παραβεβλημένον—and three verses[9] that are apparently of the first importance:

μήτε Μούσας ἀνακαλεῖν ἑλικοβοστρύχους
μήτε Χάριτας βοᾶν ἐς χορὸν Ὀλυμπίας·
ἐνθάδε γάρ εἰσιν, ὥς φησιν ὁ διδάσκαλος.

' And not to summon " Muses of curling tresses " nor to call " Olympian Graces to the dance "; for they are here, as the poet says.' Finally (iv) we find this in an ancient Life of Euripides : ' They say, too, that women, because of the censures he passed on them in his poems, attacked him at the Thesmophoria with murderous intent; but they spared him, first because of the Muses, and next on his undertaking never to abuse them again '.[10]

Three assumptions seem legitimate. First, there was a strong similarity between the two plays named *Thesmophoriazusæ* : this conclusion rests on the passage in the Life and on the fragment about aphrodisiac wine. Next, Mnesilochus appeared. For in our play Aristophanes calls him a " kinsman " (κηδεστής)

[1] Athenæus, I, 29a.
[2] Schol. on *Thesm.*, 298.
[3] Fr. 317.
[4] Fr. 320.
[5] Fr. 326.
[6] Fr. 327.
[7] Fr. 331 : ἀγὼν πρόφασιν οὐ δέχεται.
[8] Fr. 333. See above, p. 150.
[9] Fr. 334.
[10] Nauck, *Eur.*, I, 7.

only of Euripides, never giving him a name; moreover, v. 1206, 'hurry home to your wife and children,' is quite unsuitable as addressed to the speaker's stepfather. Nevertheless, the name is used by the Scholiast and inserted by copyists before many speeches of the kinsman. The inference is that Aristophanes called him Mnesilochus in the lost play and the name was naturally but wrongly attached later to our anonymous character. Finally, the Muses in person took part in the lost comedy. But they did not form the chorus or any part of it.[1] Their number had already long been fixed at nine, and that would have wrecked the symmetry of the chorus, or two semi-choruses, which invariably totalled twenty-four. Moreover, in the fragment that asserts the presence of Muses and Graces the words are added 'as the poet says': this points to something unusual, or casual, or even doubtful—to anything rather than their presence as members of the normal and official chorus. As for the Graces, the fragment says they were present, like the Muses; but the Life passage does not mention them: we can say nothing of their function. The inference is that a serious defence of Euripides was advanced, and was supported by Muses whom he brought forward. How the scenes went it is hardly worth while to conjecture: the poet may have sent in some or all of the Muses as a secondary chorus to sing either real songs of Euripides or parodies of them. Further, the right person to conduct this defence would seem to be Euripides himself.

For dazzling wit and irresistibly laughable farce combined this play is perhaps the world's finest masterpiece. It is as charming as the *Gondoliers*, as funny as Bottom's interlude in *A Midsummer Night's Dream*, equal in its racy rhetoric to *Man and Superman*. Among Aristophanes' works, only the *Birds* and *Frogs* can rank with it; and those dramas are placed above the

---

[1] As Zieliński (*Gliederung*, p. 90) asserts.

rest by virtues not entirely comic. But this play is a glittering marvel—glorious foolery suffused by a thrice-refined intellectual virtuosity that never misses a point, never overstresses it; the urbanity of Meredith, the *gaminerie* of Villon, the zestfulness of Chaucer. All these strangely assorted qualities are here displayed in bewildering opulence to complete a jewel of light comedy. That it is not oftener so acclaimed must be attributed to but one cause: an indecency too pervasive for the amputation so frequently performed upon the *Acharnians* and the *Wasps*. There is no bowdlerizing the *Thesmophoriazusæ*, yet no honest reader is likely to deny that its indecency succeeds in being richly comic: prominent instances are the detection of Mnesilochus and the artless excitement of the uncouth foreign policeman over the alluring little creature who dances "like-a da flea in da rug" (ὥσπερ ψύλλο κατὰ τὸ κῴδιο).

Aristophanes is ever excellent in parody, but here he surpasses himself. In the first minute of the action he gives us a brief lecture from Euripides on the origin of human organs (by an engaging innovation, nothing more improper than the eye and ear), then goes on to a burlesque of Agathon's diction, rhythm, and music, which means little to us in the absence of Agathon's own work; even so we are cheered by the neatness with which the clown's low and unappreciative comments fit into the rhythm of the very superior verse which it interrupts. For him the only appeal lies in what is now lost, the music—'how flirtatious, how luscious, and lascivious!' Agathon's explanation that a poet must dress to suit his topic, contains a pleasant little passage [1] about earlier poets, some of whom we are surprised to hear mentioned in Athens at this date; indeed Agathon implies that they are *recherché* reading: 'Besides, it is bad taste for a poet to look oafish and shaggy. Remember that Ibycus—you know him,

---

[1] vv. 159 *sqq.*

of course ?—and Anacreon of Teos and Alcæus, those alchemists of rhythm, wore dainty hair-ribbons and lived in exotic delicacy; Phrynichus—him I am sure you have heard—was handsome in costume as in person, which is precisely the reason why his plays were handsome too. *Le style, c'est l'homme.*' This same scene contains also a toothsome little parody [1] of Agathon's iambic manner:

> ὦ πρέσβυ πρέσβυ, τοῦ φθόνου μὲν τὸν ψόγον
> ἤκουσα, τὴν δ' ἄλγησιν οὐ παρεσχόμην,

a wondrously urbane version of " hard words break no bones ":

> O aged one, the censure of thy spite
> I hear, yet suffer no responsive pang.

But parody is not always needed: when Euripides asks Agathon to confront the murderous women on his behalf, the other (always with a good memory of the poets) replies in an apt and damaging quotation from Euripides' own work: ' You value life; why should your father not ? ' [2]

Later in the play, Mnesilochus' captive plight is made the occasion for burlesque of no less than four Euripidean tragedies. *Telephus* has been employed already, in the *Acharnians* : here the situation is even more amusing, and the " murder " is really performed. The *Palamedes* scene is brief but laughable : ' confound this R ! ' [3] mutters the hero, amid his tragic anapæsts, when he comes upon the first curved letter in the message he is carving. The other two are superb. It might almost be alleged that the best merit of Euripides' *Helena* is to have inspired this glorious five minutes of fooling. The Helen presented by a bedraggled elderly Athenian, Euripides as his own shipwrecked Menelaus, are excellent; but the edge

---

[1] vv. 146 *sq.* This is one of the Agathonesque antitheses referred to above.
[2] vv. 133 *sq.* (*Alcesis*, 691).   [3] Τουτὶ τὸ ῥῶ μοχθηρόν (v. 781).

of the whole affair is the comments of the wardress, naturally bewildered yet standing no nonsense.

> MN. κἀγὼ μὲν ἐνθάδ᾽ εἴμ᾽· ὁ δ᾽ ἄθλιος πόσις
> οὑμὸς Μενέλαος οὐδέπω προσέρχεται.
> τί οὖν ἔτι ζῶ;
> ΓΥ.   τῇ κοράκων πονηρίᾳ.
>
> Mn. And here I linger, but my hapless spouse
>   Menelaus comes not nigh. What keeps me then
>   Alive?
> Wardress.   Remissness of the carrion crows.[1]

The pseudo-Menelaus paying no attention to her uncanonical, though shrewd, interruptions, she puts his stupidity down to the horrors of shipwreck: ' still rather sea-sick, aren't you, stranger?'[2] In the recognition scene, "Helen" makes an excellent, if disreputable pun,[3] and to her husband's excited cry ' Lady, what sayst thou? Turn those orbs on mine!' she, remembering those awful moments in which she has been shaved for her part, replies, ' I dare not turn on thee this ruined face'.[4] In the *Andromeda* burlesque Euripides bears two rôles. As Echo, in a heartless parody of the lovely opening scene, he repeats first the laments of his weather-beaten Andromeda, then the policeman's bewildered ejaculations in broken Greek, which the barbarian supposes are uttered by the captive and for which he maltreats him. Later, assuming the character of Perseus ' cleaving the middle heaven on wingèd feet,' he appeals to the constable's good nature, only to find that, though ready enough to connive at the hero's strange passion, he refuses to allow the proposed rescue.

The *eccyclema* is employed, not only to produce and withdraw Agathon with his gear, but also to change the scene. After Mnesilochus has been prepared for his expedition, we are supposed to leave Agathon's house and approach the temple. At this point a manu-

[1] vv. 866 sqq. [2] v. 382.
[3] v. 912: ὦ χρόνιος ἐλθὼν σῆς δάμαρτος ἐσχάρας, where the original (*Helena*, 572) has ἐς χέρας.
[4] vv. 902 sq.

ARISTOPHANES

script gives one of our rare stage-directions : '*A cry of worshippers. The Temple is pushed forth.*'[1] Another point of stage-management is raised by the shaving of Mnesilochus : it shows what could be done with a comic mask. Prose is used in the first part of the she-herald's proclamation. Mnesilochus is present as a captive throughout the parabasis : in all other plays known to us the actors withdrew here. The finale is abnormal, being entirely without the customary fireworks.

The FROGS (Βάτραχοι) was produced, under the name of Philonides, at the Lenæa of 405 B.C., and obtained the first prize, Phrynichus being second with the *Muses*, Plato third with *Cleophon*. The play was so greatly admired for its parabasis (recommending amnesty and union of all citizens in view of the public danger) that it was produced a second time.[2]

The god Dionysus, disguised as Heracles, and followed by his slave Xanthias, knocks at the door of his brother, Heracles. He explains his errand : disheartened by the dearth of tragic poets since Euripides' death, he wishes to descend and fetch him back. Heracles suggests various routes to Hades, and Dionysus selects the ferry-boat of Charon. This soon comes into sight,[3] but Xanthias is refused a passage because he did not fight at Arginusæ : he must run round the lake. Meanwhile Dionysus has to row the boat ; he is heartened, then enraged, by the croaking chorus of the frogs. Disembarking, the god is joined by Xanthias, and after some moments of terror they hear the Iacchus-throng : these, who form the chorus, are a band of initiated men and women whose religion makes Hades for them a place of joy and splendour.

[1] After v. 276 : Ὀλολύζουσι. Τὸ ἱερὸν ὠθεῖται. Cp. "*Bed put forth*" in *Henry VI*, Pt. II, III, ii.
[2] The Third Argument says : Οὕτω δὲ ἐθαυμάσθη διὰ τὴν ἐν αὐτῷ παράβασιν, καθ' ἣν διαλλάττει τοὺς ἐντίμους τοῖς ἀτίμοις καὶ τοὺς πολίτας τοῖς φυγάσιν, ὥστε καὶ ἀνεδιδάχθη, ὥς φησι Δικαίαρχος.
[3] On rollers, no doubt ; and the voyage of Dionysus is a tour of the orchestra. Cp. the *Odysses* of Cratinus (p. 130, above).

The travellers arrive at King Pluto's door, and Dionysus announces himself to the porter Æacus [1] as Heracles. Æacus flies into a rage—'You are the scoundrel who stole our dog Cerberus'—and rushes off to fetch the Gorgons. Dionysus in terror persuades Xanthias to exchange clothes with him and pose as Heracles; whereupon a maidservant comes out of the palace, greets "Heracles" and describes the banquet that Queen Persephone has prepared for him. Xanthias is about to follow when Dionysus insists on becoming Heracles again. Next moment, however, he is assailed by two landladies whom the real Heracles on his former visit to Hades ate out of house and home without payment. With bitter threats they rush off to fetch their champions,[2] Cleon and Hyperbolus; Dionysus wheedles his slave into again assuming the guise of Heracles. Æacus returns with constables, but Xanthias puts on a bold front, offering his "slave" for torture in the Athenian fashion. Dionysus exclaims: 'I am a god — touch me at your peril'. Xanthias remarks: 'All the more reason for scourging him: if he is a god, he will feel nothing'. Dionysus rejoins: 'Then, if *you* are a god, why not be thrashed too?' Xanthias agrees, and Æacus tests them by alternate blows, but their stoicism and cunning baffle him, and he takes them within to be examined by Pluto and Persephone. The chorus deliver their celebrated parabasis. Æacus returns with Xanthias, whose pretensions have now been exposed, and tells him that there is great excitement among the dead. Æschylus used to hold the throne of tragedy, but Euripides, when he came down recently to Hades, claimed it; there is to be a contest, with Dionysus as the judge. After a vigorous ode of expectation, the conflict begins, with Dionysus as the buffoon. With great skill, vigour and mutual abuse the two poets compare their character-drawing, diction, subject-matter, moral effect, their

---

[1] Traditionally so called, but nameless in the text.
[2] Both had died some years before this date.

prologues (with the famous oil-flask joke against Euripides), their lyrics, and finally the weight of their lines, to test which Dionysus uses a huge pair of scales. At last he announces that he cannot choose : ' one of them I think wise, in the other I delight '. But urged by Pluto to make up his mind, he invites the rivals to give Athens advice concerning Alcibiades. When they have done so, Dionysus chooses Æschylus, and the victor is accompanied by the chorus on the first stage of his journey up to earth.

This magnificent comedy won as warm admiration in ancient as in modern days : with the *Clouds* and *Plutus* it formed the Byzantine collection for school-reading. Concerning its political wisdom, and its allusions to the distress of Athens, little need be said here, despite the terrible urgency of those topics ; for the main interest of the *Frogs* lies elsewhere. Arginusæ has just been fought.[1] The politicians Cleophon [2] and Theramenes [3] are briefly satirized. Æschylus and Euripides are invited [4] to give their views on Alcibiades. The parabasis urges [5] with pathetic vigour that the oligarchic machinations of Phrynichus should be overlooked and that all Athenians, whatever their past or their party, should be encouraged to strive in unity for the preservation of the storm-tossed Commonwealth.

For us the *Frogs* possesses small interest as an historical document, compared with the *Hellenica* of a less gifted author. Its merits are three : magnificent farce, magnificent lyrics, magnificent high comedy.

The last, that renowned contest between Æschylus and Euripides, need not here be discussed in detail, for it belongs rather to the history of tragedy ; but a few main points should be observed. First, this is real criticism, and valuable criticism. Its amusing manner should not engender any belief that Aristophanes is " writing with his tongue in his cheek," a thing he never does : consider his prayer to Demeter that he may

[1] vv. 33, 49, 190, 693.   [2] vv. 678, 1532.   [3] vv. 541, 967.
[4] vv. 1422 *sqq.*   [5] vv. 686-705.

blend much that is earnest with much that is absurd.[1] The latter half of this play is not only a masterpiece of wit and poetic gaiety : it is also a treatise into which have gone hard brain-work, common sense, and a deeply serious view of art :

> τίνος οὕνεκα χρὴ θαυμάζειν ἄνδρα ποιητήν ;
> δεξιότητος καὶ νουθεσίας, ὅτι βελτίους τε ποιοῦμεν
> τοὺς ἀνθρώπους ἐν ταῖς πόλεσιν.

'On what grounds should a poet be admired ? The adroit illumination and betterment of his public.'[2] It is nowadays a natural criticism that too much stress is laid on the practical "usefulness" of poetry, none on the deep and permanent pleasure that is an end in itself ; and this bias leads to the absurdity of praising [3] "divine Homer" because he taught military science. But it certainly represents one side of the importance of art, and Aristophanes would apply it to comedy as to tragedy. This he keeps always before his eyes, as we have just seen from his prayer to the august Demeter ; it comes out again in his protest against '*unseasonable vulgarity*'.[4] In the second place, this is no indiscriminate onslaught upon Euripides. Bitterly as our poet feels against him even in the grave, as he has felt for twenty years, he sees faults in his rival also, and permits Euripides to defend himself skilfully, often convincingly. There is little doubt that he actually quotes remarks made by Euripides in conversation : the discussion [5] of the *Choephoræ* is almost certainly an instance, as is the magnificent description [6] of his realism :

> οἰκεῖα πράγματ' εἰσάγων, οἷς χρώμεθ', οἷς ξύνεσμεν,
> ἐξ ὧν γ' ἂν ἐξηλεγχόμην· ξυνειδότες γὰρ οὗτοι
> ἤλεγχον ἄν μου τὴν τέχνην· ἀλλ' οὐκ ἐκομπολάκουν
> ἀπὸ τοῦ φρονεῖν ἀποσπάσας, οὐδ' ἐξέπληττον αὐτοὺς
> Κύκνους ποιῶν καὶ Μέμνονας κωδωνοφαλαροπώλους.

[1] vv. 391 sq.   [2] vv. 1088 sqq.
[3] vv. 1034 sqq. Cp. Professor Gilbert Murray's excellent note on pp. 126 sq. of his translation.
[4] v. 358.   [5] vv. 1119 sqq.   [6] vv. 959 sqq.

'The life we know—that was my subject—the substance of our daily experience, where I could be proved right or wrong: the audience yonder could pronounce on my art. I never drugged them with windy bombast or stampeded them with the jingling accoutrements of legendary swashbucklers.' Thirdly, Aristophanes is right, not about the quality of Euripides' work, but about its effects. A noble and beautiful poet Euripides certainly was; but, whether he should be blamed for it or not, the intellectual and artistic influence whereof he was the most distinguished exponent ruined the Athenian spirit.

The lyrics show a range wide even for Aristophanes. In the simple light-hearted songs of the frog-chorus sunshine becomes audible:[1]

> φθεγξόμεσθ', εἰ δή ποτ' εὐ-
> ηλίοις ἐν ἀμέραισιν
> ἠλάμεσθα διὰ κυπείρου
> καὶ φλέω, χαίροντες ᾠδῆς
> πολυκολύμβοισι μέλεσιν.
> ἢ Διὸς φεύγοντες ὄμβρον
> ἔνυδρον ἐν βυθῷ χορείαν
> αἰόλαν ἐφθεγξάμεσθα
> πομφολογοφλάσμασιν.

> Sing we now, if ever hopping
>   Through the sedge and flowering rushes,
> In and out the sunshine flopping
> We have sported, rising, dropping,
>   With our song that nothing hushes.

> Sing, if e'er in days of storm
>   Safe our native oozes bore us,
> Staved the rain off, kept us warm,
> Till we set our dance in form,
>   Raised our hubble-bubbling chorus.

Contrasted with the commonplace urbanity of a stanza[2] on the politician Theramenes is that combination of diabolical skill and thunderous vigour wherewith the contest of the tragic Masters is heralded:[3] it is as if Homer had a nightmare of a shipyard invaded by lions. The words γομφοπαγῆ πινακηδὸν ἀποσπῶν γηγενεῖ

---
[1] vv. 242 sqq. (Professor Gilbert Murray's translation).
[2] vv. 533 sqq.　　　　　　　　　　　　　[3] vv. 814 sqq.

φυσήματι would be invaluable to anyone who sought the best Greek for " blowing up a battleship ". Contrasted with this divine rowdiness is a later passage [1] that should be cited for its evidence concerning the education, or rather the literary knowledge, of contemporary Athenians : ' If you fear that the audience may be rather stupid and not follow your subtle discussion, forget your dread. It is no longer so : they are trained, and every one notes the clever points with a book in his hand.[2] Their wits are naturally powerful, and now they are whetted indeed. So away with misgivings ! Go to all lengths, confident in the culture of your audience.' The whole second half of the *Frogs* confirms this suggestion : Aristophanes must have known that it was safe to offer a mass of dramatic, literary, and musical criticism which, though deliciously sauced, is nevertheless long, elaborate, and in places subtle.

Other lyrics are masterpieces in yet other kinds. The parody of Euripidean monodies, despite our lack of the music, we can still appreciate :[3] the song about a stolen hen is a delightful burlesque of Euripidean pathos, terror, verbal repetitions, and sudden homely details. The parodos provides a notable instance of virtuosity. One song[4] opens with a lively though religious stanza :

> Ἴακχε πολυτίμητε, μέλος ἑορτῆς
> ἥδιστον εὑρών, δεῦρο συνακολούθει
> πρὸς τὴν θεὸν
> καὶ δεῖξον ὡς ἄνευ πόνου
> πολλὴν ὁδὸν περαίνεις.
> Ἴακχε φιλοχορευτὰ συμπρόπεμπέ με.

There follow two playful stanzas, where the torn garment reveals a girl's breast. This detail so charms Dionysus that he joins in, using the second half only of the same stanza-form ; and Xanthias also jumps

---

[1] vv. 1109 *sqq.*
[2] Like Dionysus who read the *Andromeda* on ship-board (vv. 52 *sq.*).
[3] vv. 1331 *sqq.*
[4] vv. 399-444.

forward, breaking the last line with a result not merely secular but pleasantly oafish : [1]

ΔΙ. ἐγὼ δ' ἀεί πως φιλακολου—
θός εἰμι καὶ μετ' αὐτῆς
παίζων χορεύειν βούλομαι.
ΞΑ. κἄγωγε πρός.

The chorus take over this truncated stanza, alter its metre slightly to a more sing-song manner, and employ it for a series of little lampoons such as were the germ of Attic comedy :

βούλεσθε δῆτα κοινῇ
σκώψωμεν Ἀρχέδημον,
ὃς ἑπτέτης ὢν οὐκ ἔφυσε φράτερας;

After five of these, the stanza becomes still less poetical and is used for ordinary question and reply. 'Can you tell us whereabouts Pluto lives?' 'It is quite close. . . .' And the last stanza is the least hymn-like of all, divided between two persons and concluding with a joke about ' the eternal bug-in-a-rug ' :

ΔΙ. αἴροι' ἂν αὖθις, ὦ παῖ.
ΞΑ. τουτὶ τί ἦν τὸ πρᾶγμα
ἀλλ' ἢ Διὸς Κόρινθος ἐν τοῖς στρώμασιν;

The farcical scenes are not merely among the best he ever wrote : they remind us for once of both Shakespeare and Molière by their combination of splendid gusto and consummate finish. That scene where the two landladies assail their supposed defaulting customer reads like the germ of the verbal affray between Falstaff and " Dame Partlet the hen ".[2] Moreover, like Sir John, Heracles knows intimately the lower social life and the topography of the—capital : for " Hell is a city much like London " as Shelley said ; or, as Aristophanes implies,[3] like Athens. Molière excels perhaps all other dramatists in the deftness wherewith he distils not only much fun from a situation but (if

---

[1] The sudden thump of the monosyllable πρός at the stanza's very end is delicious. A similar effect is found in Meredith's *Phœbus with Admetus*: "Danced in rings with girls, like a sail-flapped mast".
[2] *Henry IV*, Pt. I, III, iii.   [3] vv. 108 *sqq*.

one may dogmatize on such a theme) literally all the fun. In this play the Greek approaches the Frenchman. Consider that scene where Xanthias, once more disguised as Heracles, is invited by Persephone to a banquet. Most playwrights, and Aristophanes himself at the *Acharnians* level, would have made Xanthias gleefully enter the palace, leaving Dionysus to pine through the keyhole. A vastly richer effect is gained by causing Xanthias, amid the stupefaction of all who know Heracles, to reply: 'Many thanks, but I must decline'. A similar touch appears in the brawl with the hostesses: after devouring mountains of provender and avoiding the bill by a pretence of homicidal madness that sent Dame Partlet and her colleague fleeing upstairs, the hero decamped—with the door-mats under his arm (v. 567). Other instances may easily be observed in the trial by scourging.

The ECCLESIAZUSÆ ('Εκκλησιάζουσαι, 'Women attending the Athenian legislative assembly'—" The Ladies in Parliament "[1] as we may phrase it) was produced in 392,[2] with what success is not known.

Praxagora awaits before dawn other women of Athens, who slip out of their houses one by one, disguised in their husbands' clothes. They discuss a plan to attend the Assembly as citizens and vote for a proposal that government should be handed over to the women. Disguising themselves still further with false beards, they rehearse; Praxagora makes a speech [3] amid applause, and the other women as chorus follow [4] her to the Pnyx. Blepyrus, Praxagora's husband, enters grumbling: he has wished to leave his bed and go outside for an urgent purpose, but could not find

---

[1] This is the title of the late Sir G. O. Trevelyan's brilliant *jeu d'esprit*.
[2] The Scholiast on v. 193 mentions an alliance, made in 394, as having happened 'two years earlier'.
[3] It contains one of those strange blunders of Aristophanes which will be discussed below (p. 299): Praxagora gives a most emphatic description of the conservatism shown by women when she is on the point of inaugurating a catastrophic revolution.
[4] Thus the orchestra is vacated by the chorus in the course of the action: this is rare.

his clothes. He therefore comes on dressed in his wife's gown and shoes, and is doing his best in the semi-darkness when a friend arrives, converses with him, and departs to the Assembly. Blepyrus is still busy when one Chremes arrives from the Assembly and tells how a mob of white-faced voters have pushed through a proposal to entrust the State to women. They retire, and the chorus return to shed their disguises, greeting Praxagora, who has been elected Generaless to carry out the Women's Policy. She launches into an account of the new régime : everything is to be held and used in common—wealth, meals, sexual relations. The rest of the play deals with these three subjects in order. First comes a man who collects all his goods and packs them for delivery to the public store amid the jeers of another who prophesies the collapse of the scheme. But when a Heraldess announces that the free public banquet is about to begin, the cynic is filled with public zeal and hurries off to do his share of eating. Then comes the sexual " reform " : a youth consumed by passion for a girl is dragged to and fro and quarrelled over by three hags in virtue of the new law that the ugliest must come first. Finally Blepyrus is summoned to the banquet with the chorus.

This is the work of a broken-hearted man. The ruin of Athens in 404 B.C. was a genuine disaster by which the world lost a unique and invaluable kind of civilization. This is not the place to discuss that calamity at large, but we are to realize that it was reflected in the individual life of our poet. Such realization is only too easy : a comparison of the *Ecclesiazusæ* and the *Frogs* brings it home to the most casual reader with such poignancy that at times his fancy hears Lysander's trumpets blare over the toppling walls of that ' glamorous City violet-crowned, bulwark of Hellas, haunted by divine presences '. To compare this with the *Birds* is like setting *Count Robert of Paris* beside *Old Mortality*. Almost everywhere the work is neat, sensible, and jaded : [1] the old verve, the broad-chested riotous fun, have utterly gone : and when he seeks to recover it we find only a mechanical monstrosity like the famous longest word [2] in Greek, a procession of one hundred and sixty-nine letters (*plus* an iota subscript), indicating a medley of fish, flesh, fowl, and sauces. Any Greek at any street corner could have manufactured this : it is entirely different from his earlier witty fabrications such as the delightful ἀρχαιομελισιδωνοφρυνιχήρατα. The mighty irresponsible genius has dwindled into a mere accomplished writer : he who had known Periclean Athens found himself in later middle life among men very like those whom Demosthenes reproached in vain.[3] That anonymous cynic who so easily sees through the fire-new communism of Praxagora is a first faint intimation of the *Græculus*, the Levantine, who was to be the joke and scorn of later generations.

That it does not lack interest, however, goes without saying. But little of this is purely artistic ; most is either academic or documentary. Let us consider first the artistic side. There are a few good jokes. One is the reason for which Athens accepts the proposal to entrust the State to women : ' It was felt that here was the only device that had never been tried before '.[4] The brief reference to ' the suffragette and the policeman,' [5] as the phrase would have run a few years ago, and the suggestion that the conscientious citizen is arranging his household gear for a procession to the pawnshop [6] may raise a smile. The youth haled to and fro by the lewd and hideous crones who dispute

---

[1] One terrible example will be enough (vv. 489 *sqq.*):

ἀλλ' ἐγκονῶμεν · τοῦ τόπου γὰρ ἐγγύς ἐσμεν ἤδη
ὅθενπερ εἰς ἐκκλησίαν ὡρμώμεθ' ἡνίκ' ἦμεν ·
τὴν δ' οἰκίαν ἔξεσθ' ὁρᾶν, ὅθενπερ ἡ στρατηγὸς
ἔσθ' ἡ τὸ πρᾶγμ' εὑροῦσ' ὃ νῦν ἔδοξε τοῖς πολίταις.

[2] vv. 1169 *sqq.*
[3] Public service is now a trade like bricklaying (vv. 299 *sqq.*), and genuine public spirit is dead (vv. 767, 797 *sq.*).
[4] vv. 456 *sq.* [5] vv. 258 *sq.* [6] vv. 755 *sqq.*

his favours provokes to-day not laughter but nausea; nevertheless his lament ' I am the new Procrustes' [1] is a flash of genuine wit. When Praxagora has coached her friends in the masculine deportment needed for the success of their plot in the Assembly, one lady complacently adds ' Yes, and I've brought my knitting,' or words to that effect.[2]

Though the lyrics of the chorus are negligible and have indeed partly disappeared, some of the solos are attractive in a debased and trivial manner. The amorous scenes contain three duets, over which the poet half audibly yawns before delivering them: [3]

κεἰ γὰρ δι' ὄχλου τοῦτ' ἐστὶ τοῖς θεωμένοις. . . .

' Even though it bores the audience. . . .' Then comes the disgusting antiphony of the Girl and the Hag. When the Youth appears, he and the Hag sing a duet in that scolion-metre the most famous instance of which is the Harmodius-Song. The other two duets have refrains, a very rare thing at this date and frequent in no period of ancient poetry:

ἄνοιξον, ἀσπάζου με.
διά τοι σε πόνους ἔχω.
Open, and welcome me;
Sorely I yearn for thee.

The academic or documentary aspects of this play possess, as we said, greater interest.

First, the *Ecclesiazusæ* is more rational than its predecessors: it insists, for better or for worse, on consistency, common sense. The initial idea, that women should invade and dominate the Assembly, wild as it seemed in the poet's time, is enormously less fantastic than the errands of Trygæus and Dionysus —not to mention the fact that such theories were in the air. The rest of the play is almost startlingly " sensible ". When he composed the *Birds*, Aristophanes did not ask himself how the stones of Cloud-cuckootown hung in the sky. Here the women practise

[1] v. 1021.   [2] vv. 88 *sq.*   [3] v. 888.

carefully beforehand lest they betray themselves at the meeting. In earlier plays no explanation of detail is asked for unless the poet wishes to make a joke in reply.[1] But here we are shown the women getting away after their imposture and removing their disguises: there is even an interrogatory [2] by Praxagora's husband: 'Where *have* you been?' An admirer of her oration asks how she learned to speak so well, and she gives a perfectly normal answer [3] worthy of Xenophon. The discussions of policy are for the most part genuine argumentation. When Praxagora explains that all property must henceforth be held in common, Blepyrus asks: 'What of persons who possess no real estate but only cash, the amount of which cannot be checked (ἀφανῆ πλοῦτον)?'[4] But the best example is that passage [5] where the cynical citizen reminds his credulous friend of previous financial expedients: vigorous and sensible, but quite unamusing, it is as near to a speech by Lysias as to Dicæopolis' stump-oration. Again, one of the first things done by the new female government is to suppress prostitution.

Another inescapable note is the misery of the people. The most boisterous and light-hearted of the earlier plays leave it clear enough that most Athenians were not only poor but knew they were poor; the difference is that in the earlier time they did not break their hearts over it. Since Ægospotami, Athenians were poor without hope or pride, and the whole temperature of the theatre has therefore changed: it is like a transition from the poor of Dickens to the poor of George Gissing. In Old Comedy the poverty-stricken Athenian dined with Pherecrates or Telecleides in a magic world where the very landscape was eatable. Turn to the Eldorado of Euæon [6] in this play: 'I will tell you how to save Athens and her people. If the

---

[1] When Dionysus inquires how the Athenian two obols got to Hades, he is told 'Theseus brought them' (*Frogs*, 141 *sqq.*).
[2] vv. 520 *sqq.*   [3] vv. 243 *sq.*   [4] vv. 597 *sqq.*
[5] vv. 812-29.   [6] vv. 413 *sqq.*

fullers supply woollen capes in mid-winter to all who need then none of us will ever catch pleurisy again. Further, all who have no bed or blankets should go after their baths to the tanners' shops to sleep : if he shuts them out in winter, he is to be fined three fleeces.' This may be called fanciful in the sense that it is ' economically unsound ' ; as art it is only too realistic.

A third point of interest is the relationship between this comedy and Plato's *Republic*. Unmistakable likenesses appear : the community of property and of women, and on this latter the comment [1] that society will be more closely bound together because each person will look on men of a certain age as being each perhaps his father, and on every such woman as perhaps his mother. Plato himself is possibly mentioned by name.[2] On the other hand, it is unlikely that the *Republic*, as we know it, appeared before the *Ecclesiazusæ*, because it seems to contain clear allusions [3] to this play. It may be that the *Republic* was brought out in two parts, between the publication of which our play was produced ; or we may prefer to believe that the dialogue was published as a whole after the comedy, but that Plato's notions had already become well-known in Athens. This latter is the likelier view.

PLUTUS, or WEALTH (Πλοῦτος), was produced in 388 B.C., its four rivals being the *Spartans* of Nicochares, *Admetus* of Aristomenes, *Adonis* of Nicophon, *Pasiphae* of Alcæus.[4] What prize it gained is unknown.

[1] vv. 641 *sqq*.
[2] 'Plato' ('Broad-Shoulders') was of course only a nickname of Aristocles ; and Bergk (*ap*. Meineke, II, 1162) thinks that the diminutive Aristyllus (*Eccl.*, 647, *Plutus*, 314, fr. 538) refers to the philosopher. This has been vigorously rejected (cp. van Leeuwen, *Prolegomena ad Eccl.*, p. xiii, n.), and Stallbaum (*Resp. præf.*, p. lxxii), taking it that Plato is not so much as named or hinted at, regards this silence as proof that Aristophanes is not thinking of the *Republic* at all.
[3] *Rep.*, 450*e*, 456*b*, 452*b*, *c*. The question is fully and judiciously discussed by Adam (*Republic*, Vol. I, App. I), who thinks it probable "that Plato had the *Ecclesiazusæ* and its author in his mind when he wrote that part of the fifth book which deals with the subject of women and children".
[4] At this date the three competing comedies had been replaced by five. Note that nearly all these titles are proper names : only one play is named after its chorus, another of the numerous proofs that the importance of the chorus was rapidly diminishing.

The slave Carion grumbles that he and his master, Chremylus, are following a blind man from the shrine of Apollo. Chremylus explains that, being righteous but unprosperous, he asked the oracle whether his son should follow his example or become a rogue. The god bade him follow the first person he met: it proved to be this blind "man," who reveals himself as the god of Wealth, blinded by Zeus because he determined to consort only with the just, wise, and well-behaved; since then he has always fallen in with the wicked. Chremylus and Carion show him that he is really master of the Universe, and offer to restore his power by taking him to the temple of Asclepius to recover his sight, and help only the good henceforth. He goes into the house, and Carion summons the chorus of poor husbandmen, to whom he tells the news. He and they sing and dance a rustic ditty. Chremylus returns, meeting his friend Blepsidemus, who is convinced that the report of wealth means a huge theft by Chremylus. At last reassured, he prepares to accompany them to the shrine, when the two friends are confronted by a horrible spectre, Poverty, who insists on proving that they contemplate a crime in seeking to expel her from Greece: she is the cause of all that is good in life. After a vigorous debate they drive her away and depart with Plutus. Later [1] Carion returns exultantly, announcing the success of the treatment, which he describes at length to Chremylus' wife. Plutus returns with his patron: henceforth he will favour only the good. This new régime is illustrated by three pairs of people: a just man who has at length found prosperity and a blackmailer who is ruined; a rich and hideous old woman and her *gigolo*; the god Hermes, who is glad to desert from Heaven for a scullion's post in Chremylus' household, and a priest who is appointed to lead the procession that is to instal Plutus in the

---

[1] After an interval marked by the word ΧΟΡΟΥ in our MSS. This indicates a song now lost.

rear-chamber of Athena's temple. The chorus follow, rejoicing.

As so often, the ghost of another version peers at us from the murk of the scholia and other such literature. The evidence falls into three groups. (i) Certain passages imply merely the existence of two versions. Eight words are cited by Pollux and others, as occurring in the *Plutus*, which are not found in our text. This evidence is inconclusive.[1] (ii) Three passages imply or state that our version is the later: the Scholiast on *Frogs*, 1093, gives three lyric lines, which are not in our text, as occurring in " the first Plutus "; two verses of our text are quoted as from " the second Plutus ".[2] (iii) Four passages[3] imply or state that our version is the earlier. For instance, on v. 1147 (about Thrasybulus' occupation of Phyle) the Scholiast remarks that the words must have been interpolated from the second *Plutus*, because the event happened in the fifth year after the play. Without attempting to determine here the reasons for these variations, we may confidently assert three things. First, there were two plays called *Plutus*, separated by twenty years: it is impossible to suppose that the basic assumption of all the passages just adduced is a mere blunder. Second, our play is the later; if there is anything at all in criticism, it is absolutely certain that our feeble Middle Comedy could not have been composed between the *Thesmophoriazusæ* and the *Frogs*. Thirdly, the earlier play, though no doubt called by the same title, must have been very different from ours, for the reason just given.

The *Ecclesiazusæ*, we said, was a poor play. The *Plutus* is not only poor; it is poor but honest. There is a horrible shabby-genteel air about it, suggesting to an English reader that the next queer word attributed

---

[1] See van Leeuwen's examination (*Prolegomena*, pp. v-x).
[2] v. 992 quoted by Schol. Ven. on *Il.*, XXIII, 361; v. 1128 quoted by Athenæus, 368*d*.
[3] Schol. on *Plutus*, 173, 179, 972, 1147.

to it by some newly-discovered lexicographer will mean "a horse-hair sofa" or "an antimacassar". When Carion says to Chremylus' wife, "it happened before you could have swallowed ten cups,"[1] we assure ourselves only with an effort that they are not cups of tea drunk in the company of Blepsidemus' wife.[2] The *Plutus* owed its position in the Byzantine selection of three surely not to its merits but to the same causes that prompt its choice to-day for school-reading: the easiness of its Greek and the comparative absence of indecency. It belongs entirely to the Middle Comedy in virtue of the following features. (i) The chorus is negligible: no part of the plot depends upon it, except indeed that a lapse of time is needed here and there, which was represented by a song and dance; all the lyrics have disappeared (being, no doubt, *intermezzi* of small merit) except the song about the Cyclops and Circe. (ii) The slave Carion is far more independent, both in manner and in function, than his colleagues of earlier plays. Not only does he call his master "you blockhead"[3] and his remarks "nonsense,"[4] but he is also important to the action: he summons the chorus, sings the Cyclops-song with them, and delivers the Messenger's speech;[5] an equally "late" touch is that he steals food like his Plautine descendants.[6] (iii) That pervasive lack of *brio*, that jaded facility noted in the *Ecclesiazusæ*, is obvious here also. Consider this passage:[7]

> μετρίου γὰρ ἀνδρὸς οὐκ ἐπέτυχες πώποτε.
> ἐγὼ δὲ τούτου τοῦ τρόπου πώς εἰμ' ἀεί,
> χαίρω τε γὰρ φειδόμενος ὡς οὐδεὶς ἀνὴρ
> πάλιν τ' ἀναλῶν, ἡνίκ' ἂν τούτων δέῃ.

'Yes—you never met a temperate man, but I am more or less of that kind: I rejoice beyond any man in

---

[1] v. 737.
[2] It is impossible not to observe that v. 972—ἀλλ' οὐ λαχοῦσ' ἔπινες ἐν τῷ γράμματι—supplies the perfect Greek idiom for Mrs. Gamp's stern command, "No, Betsey! Drink fair, wotever you do!"
[3] v. 46 (ὦ σκαιότατε).   [4] v. 23 (λῆρος).   [5] vv. 653 *sqq*.
[6] v. 320.   [7] vv. 245 *sqq*.

frugality and in expenditure too, whenever each is necessary.' Two lines at least are unmistakably Plautine : [1]

> ὡς σεμνὸς οὑπίτριπτος · αἱ κνῆμαι δέ σου βοῶσιν
> 'ἰοὺ ἰού,' τὰς χοίνικας καὶ τὰς πέδας ποθοῦσαι.

'What a supercilious knave ! Your shanks are shouting " Ow ! ow ! " yearning for the shackles and fetters.' (iv) The Attic style grows not merely pallid : [2] it begins to disintegrate : Aristophanes allows himself a word-order unparalleled in his other works : [3]

> ἐσδὺς γάρ ποτε
> οὐκ εἶχεν ἐς τὴν οἰκίαν οὐδὲν λαβεῖν.

> χαίρειν μὲν ὑμᾶς ἐστίν, ὦνδρες δημόται,
> ἀρχαῖον ἤδη προσαγορεύειν καὶ σαπρόν.

> πολλοὶ μὲν γὰρ τῶν ἀνθρώπων ὄντες πλουτοῦσι πονηροί.

Its merits are soon told. Despite what has just been said, we gain a few glimpses of the old Aristophanes. When Plutus, dazed by the suggestion that he may regain his sight, stammers his terror of Zeus, Chremylus answers with a touch of Pisthetærus : 'What, you most craven of all gods ? Do you suppose that the majesty and thunderbolt of Zeus will be worth sixpence if you regain your sight even for an hour ? ' [4] There are a few witty phrases. ' Rich ? Why, you may each become a Midas, if you can get donkey's ears.' [5] ' You could draw me through a finger-ring.' ' Aye, if the ring were the rim of a sieve.' [6] Blepsidemus' obstinacy is laughable : despite all assurances, he is convinced that Chremylus' reputed wealth must be the fruit of robbery. When his friend swears by

[1] vv. 275 sqq.
[2] See van Leeuwen (*Prolegomena ad Plutum*, pp. xix sq.) for an interesting account of the language and a note on the commonplace names of Chremylus and Blepsidemus.
[3] vv. 204 sq., 323 sq., 502.
[4] vv. 123 sq.
[5] v. 287. Unless we give the plural Μίδας a rather awkward translation, we perform the amazing feat of foisting upon Aristophanes a joke that he does not make—"Midasses". Cp. the gorgonzola in *Acharnians*, 1124 sq.
[6] vv. 1036 sq. Cp. *Henry IV*, Pt. I, II, iv : " I could have crept into any alderman's thumb-ring ".

Poseidon, he cautiously asks: 'You mean the Sea-God?'[1] A hint of pathos clings to the playful reminiscence of one among those great figures that Aristophanes knew—a tiny scrap of Sophocles,[2] now these many years in his grave: στιβάδα σχοίνων κόρεων μεστήν, ἣ τοὺς εὕδοντας ἐγείρει, 'a rush mat full of bugs *arousing them that slumber*'.

We have often noted the earnestness of Aristophanes: here it makes its most emphatic entry, and actually repudiates comedy by name. Poverty, stung by a taunt of Chremylus, exclaims: 'You seek to scoff and play the buffoon (κωμῳδεῖν), snapping your fingers at seriousness'.[3] Nothing could show more plainly the change that has come over the "comic" stage: we have, in fact, left farce for comedy—a type of play which counts nothing alien that is human, however serious it may be. So it comes about that we find a brief but illuminating picture of the "sycophant," to give him his traditional but absurd name. As a fact, this type, so frequent in Athens, is really a blackmailer; and in the *Plutus* we get a real hint of the reason for his frequency and indeed for his existence: namely, a grave defect in the administration of the law. Offenders might often go free because there was no official to watch over the operation of a law, so that everything depended on the chance intervention of public-spirited members of the public. Naturally, when the offenders began to bribe these amateur prosecutors, public spirit rapidly grew into a profession.[4]

Poverty's share in the action is for several reasons deeply interesting. First, her position is stated with cogency as well as seriousness: destroy the metre and one might be reading a light Platonic dialogue—

ἀλλ' οὐδ' ἔσται πρῶτον ἁπάντων οὐδεὶς οὐδ' ἀνδραποδιστὴς
κατὰ τὸν λόγον ὃν σὺ λέγεις δήπου.[5]

[1] vv. 394 *sqq*.
[2] v. 541. Cp. Soph., fr. 890 (Jebb-Pearson). There are reminiscences of Solon also (v. 193) and Pindar (vv. 144 *sqq*.).
[3] v. 557.
[4] See the discussion, vv. 906-919, where the point of the whole is ὁ βουλόμενος. [5] vv. 522 *sq*.

'But, first of all, there will not *be* any slavers, according to your own argument.' When Chremylus describes the evils which, he says, Poverty inflicts on mankind, 'in place of a bed a reed mat full of bugs,' the stone for a pillow, and so forth, she answers, with a precision more natural to Prodicus or Hippias than to Trygæus, very clearly and well:[1] 'You have not described my life, but reviled that of beggars. . . . The beggar's life, whereof you speak, is existence without possessions, whereas the poor man's is a life of thrift and industry, with no superfluity but no deficiency either.' Secondly, this *agon* or debate between Chremylus and the goblin testifies to the economic and spiritual result for Athens of her fall from political greatness: here the *Plutus* reinforces the *Ecclesiazusæ*. Thirdly, the dispute fails amazingly to square with the plot. Chremylus' idea is plain enough: to restore Plutus' sight and thus give riches only to the virtuous, leaving the wicked to indigence. It is the notion widely accepted in times both ancient and modern, and by people more highly esteemed than Chremylus, that persons who pay in one currency should be repaid in another, that virtue should be recompensed by prosperity—money, good repute, health, or happiness—an artless theory that is not only refuted by experience but also reveals our genuine opinion of virtue as an unpleasant device for securing something that is pleasant. Such is the idea of Chremylus, perfectly clear, however vulgar and stupid; and this we see fulfilled after the return of Plutus: the Just Man rich, the Blackmailer ruined. But in the dispute with Poverty all is changed.[2] Every one is to be rich, otherwise her very admirable argument would fall to pieces. But Chremylus nowhere points this out. In this part

---

[1] vv. 548 *sqq.*

[2] Aristophanes cannot be acquitted of a complete failure to remember what he is talking about. For instance, in vv. 495 *sqq.*, 630, 826, only the good benefit; in vv. 401 and 1004, etc. (the base gigolo) the bad are to benefit as well as the good; even in the dispute with Poverty, Chremylus at one time (vv. 499 *sqq.*) voices his original purpose.

of the play, then, we intend not to reward virtue, but to cure poverty. Fourthly, the dispute closes with a strange hitch in the plot, or rather a clumsy readjustment. Poverty has no difficulty in proving that the reformers are wrong: her remarks are a translation into Attic thought and language of the Grand Inquisitor's song in the *Gondoliers*: " A king there lived . . ." Chremylus is defeated. But if so, what becomes of our triumphant *finale*? He is therefore made to say: ' Even if you convince me, I shall act as if you had not convinced me ';[1] and the comedy proceeds exactly as if Poverty had never entered the theatre. Aristophanes has tied together two ideas utterly different in their outcome but possessing a superficial likeness since they are both concerned with the incidence of poverty. As a consequence the last words of the goblin, weighty as they are, find no result in the sequel: ' Verily the day will come when you will send for me ';[2] but it may well be that Aristophanes intends these words as a hint that I am a better economist than I pretend to be '.

Besides the eleven extant comedies, we possess fragments approaching one thousand in number, more than half coming from named plays: but there are only six works concerning which we can claim definite knowledge, and but two the main outlines of which can be stated with confidence.

The BANQUETERS (Δαιταλῆς) was the first comedy of Aristophanes, produced in 427 B.C.[3] when he was perhaps only seventeen years old, under the name of one of his acquaintances—either[4] Callistratus or Philonides—and won the second prize.[5] The poet

[1] v. 600: οὐ γὰρ πείσεις, οὐδ᾽ ἢν πείσῃς.   [2] vv. 608 sq.
[3] Anon., *de Com*. (Kaibel, p. 8): ἐδίδαξε δὲ πρῶτον ἐπὶ ἄρχοντος Διοτίμου διὰ Καλλιστράτου.
[4] For Callistratus see last note. For Philonides cp. Schol. on *Clouds*, 531 (ταῖς ἑτέρα).
[5] Schol., *Clouds*, 529.

himself makes striking mention of this initial success.¹
In our version of the *Clouds* he reproaches his audience
for failing to appreciate the earlier version, and
proceeds : ²

> ἐξ ὅτου γὰρ ἐνθάδ᾽ ὑπ᾽ ἀνδρῶν, οἷς ἡδὺ καὶ λέγειν,
> ὁ σώφρων τε χὠ καταπύγων ἄριστ᾽ ἠκουσάτην,
> κἀγώ, παρθένος γὰρ ἔτ᾽ ἦ, κοὐκ ἐξῆν πώ μοι τεκεῖν,
> ἐξέθηκα, παῖς δ᾽ ἑτέρα τις λαβοῦσ᾽ ἀνείλετο,
> ὑμεῖς δ᾽ ἐξεθρέψατε γενναίως κἀπαιδεύσατε·
> ἐκ τούτου μοι πιστὰ παρ᾽ ὑμῖν γνώμης ἔσθ᾽ ὅρκια.

' For ever since the Chaste Man and the Rake won the highest praise in this theatre from men (of high repute ?) and I, being still a maid and not yet allowed to bear a child, exposed my offspring, which another girl took and adopted, and you generously cherished and reared it—since then I have sure testimonies of your opinion.' The second line indicates the main theme of the *Banqueters*. Our youthful poet begins his career with a study of contemporary education : he compares two young men reared by their father in different surroundings, one amid the old fashioned régime of the countryside, the other in the new-fangled city ways. The first becomes a chaste sober youth, the second a debauchee. We catch glimpses of the father's disappointment in the city youth :

> ἀλλ᾽ οὐ γὰρ ἔμαθε ταῦτ᾽ ἐμοῦ πέμποντος, ἀλλὰ μᾶλλον
> πίνειν, ἔπειτ᾽ ᾄδειν κακῶς, Συρακοσίαν τράπεζαν,
> Συβαρίτιδάς τ᾽ εὐωχίας καὶ Χῖον ἐκ Λακαινᾶν.³

' But when I sent him, he did not learn those subjects, but drinking, vile singing, Syracusan dinners, Sybaritic luxury, and Chian wine from Laconian goblets '— liqueurs by the tumblerful, as we might say. The lad's appearance, too, is ultra-fashionable :

> καὶ λεῖος, ὥσπερ ἔγχελυς, χρυσοῦς ἔχων κικίννους.⁴

' Sleek as an eel, wearing golden curls.' At one point

---
[1] That the passage refers to the *Banqueters* is shown by the scholia.
[2] *Clouds*, 528-533.   [3] Fr. 216.
[4] Fr. 218. Compare, for all this, Mr. Kipling's *Mary Gloster*.

the father, precisely as in the *Clouds*,[1] invites his son to ' sing one of the old favourites ' :

ᾆσον δή μοι σκόλιόν τι λαβὼν Ἀλκαίου κἀνακρέοντος.[2]

' Come, take (the myrtle-branch) and sing me a catch of Alcæus or Anacreon.' No doubt the other answers like Pheidippides and renders something that his auditor describes as " blackguardly filth ".[3] Part of the examination is more technical. Galen[4] writes : " The old man from the Banqueters' deme [5] calls upon his depraved son to expound, first, the meaning of the word κόρυμβα, and next, ' what do they call ἀμενηνὰ κάρηνα ? ' The other, however, replies by propounding this kind of thing from the obsolete words on Solon's pillars about various lawsuits : ' Well, let your son, this brother of mine, explain what they mean by ἰδυῖοι ! ' " The old man, proud of his own and his model son's skill in the traditional Homeric learning, is answered by his more modern son with a budget of equally queer words from a less fashionable body of writing, just as a later parent, scandalized by ignorance of Horace and Virgil, might be asked, " Well, what's a dicotyledonous plant ? "

We are probably to suppose that the Rake has really pursued legal studies ; at any rate another piece[6] of dialogue (also preserved by Galen) shows him overwhelming his father with strange words taken from rhetoricians ; and the studies of law and of rhetoric were closely allied.

A. ἀλλ' εἶ σορέλλη καὶ μύρον καὶ ταινίαι.
B. ἰδοὺ σορέλλη · τοῦτο παρὰ Λυσιστράτου.
A. ἦ μὴν ἴσως σὺ καταπλιγήσει τῷ χρόνῳ.
B. τὸ καταπλιγήσει τοῦτο παρὰ τῶν ῥητόρων.

[1] vv. 1355 sqq.   [2] Fr. 223.
[3] Ὦ πορνεία καὶ ἀναιδεία (fr. 226, Kock, who reads ὦ παρανοία κτέ).
[4] *Præf. Lex. Hippocr.* (Kühn, XIX, pp. 66 sq.; fr. 222). Κόρυμβα (*Iliad*, IX, 241) means "prows" ; ἀμενηνὰ κάρηνα is usually translated "strengthless heads" ; ἰδυῖοι the ancient lexicographers explain as μάρτυρες.
[5] This is either a mistake of Galen's or a joke of the poet's. Who the banqueters were is explained below.
[6] Fr. 198.

A. ἀποβύσεταί σοι ταῦτά πη τὰ ῥήματα.
B. παρ' Ἀλκιβιάδου τοῦτο τἀποβύσεται.
A. τί δ' ὑποτεκμαίρει καὶ κακῶς ἄνδρας λέγεις
καλοκἀγαθεῖν ἀσκοῦντας;
B.   οἴμ', ὦ Θρασύμαχε,
τίς τοῦτο τῶν ξυνηγόρων τερθρεύεται;

'Oh, you are a coffineer and incense and funeral-garlands.' 'Coffineer, forsooth! A word borrowed from Lysistratus.' 'Verily you shall be over-straddled in time.' 'Over-straddled! Indeed, a parliamentary remark!' 'This talk of yours shall be estopped somehow.' 'Alcibiades' contribution, this *estopped*.' 'Why this scrutiny? Why abuse men who practise genteelishness?' 'Ugh, Thrasymachus! Which of the barristers uses that bombastic word?' A reference to these imposing legal researches of the Rake is perhaps to be found in the phrase:[1]

εἰ μὴ δικῶν τε γυργαθοὺς ψηφισμάτων τε θωμοὺς
φέροντες,

'... unless bringing baskets of law-suits and heaps of decrees'. The father bids his son 'Come back and make yourself useful on the farm after all this expensive education'. He is rebuffed:[2]

ὅστις αὐλοῖς καὶ λύραισι κατατέτριμμαι χρώμενος,
εἶτά με σκάπτειν κελεύεις;

'After I've worn myself to a shadow with practice on the flute and lyre, do you stand there and tell me to dig?' Some brief passages[3] imply a set-to between the brothers themselves: one corrupt fragment mentions 'playing truant'—ἀπεδίδρασκες ἐκ διδασκάλου.[4]

This ill-feeling at length (it appears) reaches such a height that the Rake, instead of directly assaulting his father like his successor in the *Clouds*, hales him off to court with the intent to prove him an alien:

ἐθέλω βάψας πρὸς ναυτοδίκας ξένον ἐξαίφνης ἀποφῆναι.[5]

[1] Fr. 217.   [2] Fr. 221.
[3] *E.g.* fr. 206: φέρ' ἴδω, τί σοι δῶ τῶν μύρων; ψάγδαν φιλεῖς; 'Videtur filius improbus per ironiam fratri de unguentis suis quidquid velit offerre' (Kock).   [4] Fr. 199.
[5] Fr. 225. The last word is supplied by Kock. On the ναυτοδίκαι Hesychius writes (*s.v.*): οἱ ἐπὶ τοῦ ἐμπορίου δικασταί, ὑφ' ὧν καὶ αἱ τῆς ξενίας ἐκρίνοντο δίκαι.

'I wish to ply the oar to the Navy-Board and show (him? you?) up instantly as a foreigner.' The old man is not afraid: 'If he fails to get his fifth of the votes, let him go hang!'[1] We possess a rather fine scrap of his defence before the Board: 'Call my witnesses—the ancient kings of Attica!'—τὸν Ἐρεχθέα μοι καὶ τὸν Αἰγέα κάλει.[2] Though we can hardly suppose[3] that they answered the summons, no doubt the elderly Athenian won his case. It may be that he used his opportunity to read the whole of Athens a lesson:[4]

εἰς τὰς τριήρεις δεῖν ἀναλοῦν ταῦτα καὶ τὰ τείχη,
εἰς οἷ' ἀνάλουν οἱ πρὸ τοῦ τὰ χρήματα.

'We ought to spend this on the fleet and the fortifications on which the men of old spent their money.' The "reported" form of the Greek here, and another passage,[5] that describes (in the past tense) the assembling of the jury, suggest that the trial-scene is not depicted, but merely related.

This family quarrel provided the main interest of the *Banqueters*: Aristophanes, as we saw, practically calls his play *The Chaste Man and the Rake*. But there were other elements. These Banqueters were an official company: every year the king-archon caused each deme to select twelve men who dined once a month in a temple of Heracles and were named παράσιτοι as guests of that god.[6] In our play we are to suppose that the Chorus of twenty-four represented twelve παράσιτοι proper with a son of each. That is a conjecture of Bergk's,[7] supported not only by the exigencies

---

[1] Fr. 201. [2] Fr. 211.
[3] F. E. Roetter, however (*De Daetalensium fabula*, p. 13) thinks that one or both actually appeared. His "evidence" is Schol. *Wasps*, 823: εἶχον δὲ καὶ οἱ ἥρωες πανοπλίαν, καὶ δῆλον ἐκ τῶν Δαιταλέων.
[4] Fr. 220. Hall and Geldart read δεῖ μ'. [5] Fr. 210.
[6] Athenæus, VI, 235c, Pollux, VI, 12, and others. Cp. especially the long fragment (vv. 21-30) of Diodorus, a playwright of the Middle Comedy (Kock, II, p. 420).
[7] *Ap.* Meineke, II, p. 1024. (The fragments of Aristophanes in Meineke's corpus were edited by Bergk.) For the practice of a man taking his son he quotes Isaeus, IX, 30: Εἰς τοίνυν τὰ ἱερὰ ὁ πατὴρ ὁ ἐμὸς τὸν Ἀστύφιλον

of arithmetic [1] but also by the fact that it would be artistically good to have one half of the chorus supporting the father, the other half his depraved son, though (no doubt), as elsewhere in Aristophanes, the two companies came to enthusiastic agreement in the end.[2] The official banquet formed of course a background to the elaborate dispute between father and sons. But in the course of the celebration occurred a feature [3] of profound interest, to which an important fragment [4] unmistakably points :

ἐπιδείπνιον βασιλεὺς θέαν
τοῖς δαιταλεῦσιν, ὥσπερ ἄξιον λόγου,
χαριζόμενος τὸ δρᾶμα τοῦτ' ἐδείκνυεν.

'The king-archon, to pleasure the banqueters with an after-dinner spectacle, exhibited this play as worth consideration.' There is no reasonable doubt that this comedy contained a subsidiary drama [5] (possibly dramas)—a " play within a play "—an inserted entertainment for guests (the actors of the main piece) precisely like the most famous instance of all, in *A Midsummer Night's Dream*. The dispute between father and son being settled, the parabasis closes the question, and the guests celebrate both the reconciliation and the festival by giving ' a little play of our own,'

παῖδα ἦγε μεθ' ἑαυτοῦ ὥσπερ καὶ ἐμὲ πανταχῇ, καὶ εἰς τοὺς θιάσους τοὺς Ἡρακλέους ἐκεῖνον εἰσήγαγεν, ἵνα μετέχοι τῆς κοινωνίας. But see Wyse (who reads θιασώτας) *ad loc*. Fahraeus (*De argumento atque consilio Daetalensium*, p. 35) rightly points out that the father and sons cannot have been ordinary guests, as the chorus made up the full number.

[1] This obvious principle of equality in the semi-choruses is astonishingly denied by the Scholiast on *Knights*, 589, but on æsthetic grounds it is impossible to accept his statement.

[2] That the chorus consisted (whether in whole or in part) of old men who supported the earlier ways of life, is proved by one word, ἐψυχρολουτήσαμεν (fr. 237)—'we bathed in cold water'. This is no doubt part of a censure upon the θερμὰ λουτρά (cp. *Clouds*, 1043 *sqq*.) favoured by a more luxurious age. But the interesting point is that it must belong to the chorus (not to the father, as Kock supposes) because it is impossible to scan the word except as part of a pæonic system, and these were invariably delivered by the chorus.

[3] The whole subject of "episodes" in Old Comedy has been discussed more fully in *Classical Philology*, XXV (1930), pp. 217 *sqq*.

[4] Bergk, p. 1029. This fragment has disappeared from our collections since Meineke withdrew the attribution in his fifth volume (i, p. 62). But it should be restored to Aristophanes : see the article mentioned in the preceding note.

[5] Ranke, *de Aristophanis vita*, p. cccxi, followed by Bergk, 1024 *sqq*.

under direction of the actor who has throughout impersonated the king-archon. For this " episode " the chorus of the *Banqueters* provides a chorus from its own number, and perhaps more than one " episode " was given.¹

Aristophanes, like Shakespeare, was fond of this method. In the *Thesmophoriazusæ* we have miniature parodies of several Euripidean tragedies, in the *Wasps* a mimic law-suit. But these are closely knit with the main plot. Other instances perhaps occurred in the Δράματα ἢ Κένταυρος. In this first comedy we may safely assume that the " show " was a mere intercalation. The language of the fragment proves this : it is ' an after-dinner spectacle' given by the archon as ' worthy of note '. Such phrasing implies work on a different plane, and perhaps also parody of recent or contemporary drama : the youthful playright may have driven home his contempt for vulgar Megarian farces by a burlesque or series of burlesques.²

Aristophanes' next play, the BABYLONIANS (Βαβυλώνιοι), which was produced in 426 B.C. under the name of Callistratus,³ involved the youthful poet in serious trouble. We know several things about it, but to fit them all into one plot is difficult.⁴

In the *Acharnians* ⁵ (produced in the following year, 425 B.C.) Dicæopolis says, on behalf of the author : ' And for myself, I know what I suffered from Cleon because of last year's comedy. He haled me into the Council Chamber, slandered me with a gabble of lies, and drenched me with a torrent of muddy eloquence till I very nearly perished under his fetid pettifoggery.' On this the Scholiast remarks : ' The *Babylonians*

---

¹Orion (49, 10) writes : καὶ Δαιταλεῖς δρᾶμα 'Αριστοφάνους, ἐπειδὴ ἐν ἱερῷ 'Ηρακλέους δειπνοῦντες καὶ ἀναστάντες χοροὶ ἐγένοντο. The last three words unmistakably suggest the procedure described above ; note the plural χοροί.
²So Bergk, *ap*. Meineke, p. 1025.
³Photius, 499, 1, and Suidas, *s.v.* Σαμίων ὁ δῆμος.
⁴What follows is a summary of an article in *Classical Philology*, XXV, pp. 1 *sqq*.
⁵vv. 377 *sqq*.

is meant, which Aristophanes produced before the *Acharnians* and in which he reviled many: for he ridiculed the magistrates (whether selected by lot or by vote) and Cleon in the presence of the allies. For he exhibited a play, the *Babylonians*, at the Dionysiac festival, which is celebrated in the spring, and at which the allies used to bring their tribute; and therefore Cleon in anger indicted him before the citizens for wrong-doing, as having acted so with intent to insult the People and the Senate. He indicted him for foreign origin also and brought him to trial.' Later in the same speech Dicæopolis remarks:[1] 'For not now will Cleon slander me, that I am reviling Athens in the presence of foreigners; for we are by ourselves and the contest [among comic playwrights] is at the Lenæa, and no foreigners are yet present, for neither tribute nor allies have arrived from the cities.'

There is some obscurity about this trial. We do not know its outcome, though the poet's language and the fact that his career was unchecked make it plain that he was at any rate not severely punished. Further, if Callistratus fathered the play, why was Aristophanes attacked? It is an obvious reply that no doubt every one in Athens knew the real author, yet a Scholiast informs us that it was Callistratus who was brought before the Senate. But the passage in the *Acharnians* about the author's plight surely settles the question, unless, indeed, we are to suppose that Callistratus wrote that passage.[2] It seems certain that Aristophanes himself was indicted, but that Alexandrian scholars (and the Scholiast who followed them) were confused by the presence of Callistratus.

[1] *Acharnians*, 502 *sqq*. Cp. vv. 630 *sqq*. and perhaps *Wasps*, 1285 *sqq*., though this last passage may refer to a later imbroglio (see the Scholiast on *Wasps*, 1285: "Ἄδηλον πότερον τῆς Καλλιστράτου εἰς τὴν βουλὴν εἰσαγωγῆς καὶ νῦν μιμνήσκεται, ὅτι αὐτὸν Κλέων εἰσήγαγεν, ἢ ἑτέρας κατ' αὐτοῦ γενομένης Ἀριστοφάνους, εἰ καὶ μὴ εἰσαγωγῆς, ἀλλὰ ἀπειλῆς τινός, ὅπερ καὶ μᾶλλον ἐμφαίνεται.' Ἐκεῖνά τε γὰρ ἀναπολεῖν ἀρχαιότερα ἔσται, νῦν τε ὡς περὶ αὐτοῦ λέγει).
[2] The surprising suggestion of J. H. Gunning (*De Babyloniis Aristophanis*, p. 75). Kaibel (Pauly-Wissowa, II, 975) held that the γραφὴ ξενίας was never brought forward, and is a mistaken conjecture of the Scholiast on the *Acharnians*.

What was the poet's offence? Very strangely, none of our authorities gives us clear details, but the conclusion usually [1] drawn from our fragments is that the subject-allies of Athens were represented as a chorus of branded slaves working in the mill of their master, Demos. The poet himself in the *Acharnians* gives only one line [2] that can conceivably support this startling theory:

καὶ τοὺς δήμους ἐν ταῖς πόλεσιν δείξας ὡς δημοκρατοῦνται.

'He showed how democratic rule affects the masses in our subject states.' His treatment of this theme was bold: παρεκινδύνευσ' εἰπεῖν ἐν Ἀθηναίοις τὰ δίκαια— 'he dared to speak justice among Athenians'.[3] Bold, indeed, in the midst of a war that Athens was fighting to keep her empire, with one eye upon possible insurgents, when the revolt and chastisement of Mytilene were fresh in all minds; at the very moment, too, when the audience contained envoys from all these subjects! But, though Aristophanes must have gone far (as we may well deduce from Cleon's wrath and from the speech in the *Acharnians*) he did not go so far as that.

Our authorities [4] yield only the following facts as regards the alleged slave-mill in which the allies were imprisoned. There were certain slaves, branded (or perhaps tattooed, and of disconcerting aspect, who worked in a penal mill. They were of some importance [5] in the play. They were (or were named by the poet) Babylonians; [6] they were not Samians.[7] There is no

[1] *E.g.* by Kaibel (Pauly-Wissowa, XI, 975).
[2] *Ach.*, 642.   [3] *Ibid.*, 645.
[4] Plutarch, *Pericles*, XXVI; Hesychius, *s.vv.* Σαμίων ὁ δῆμος and Ἰστριανά; Photius, *s.vv.* Σαμίων κτέ and στιγών; Suidas, *s.v.* Σαμίων; *Et. Magn.*, *s.v.* ζώστειον.
[5] This follows from the number of references just given.
[6] This may mean only "barbarians". Hesychius explains the name as οἱ βάρβαροι παρὰ τοῖς Ἀττικοῖς and Suidas as παῖδες; that is, "slaves".
[7] Gunning (p. 7) well points out, that if they were Samians, Plutarch (see above) could not have called Aristophanes' line a riddle. They belong to some other nation and are more or less subtly called Samians because of their "lettering" (an allusion to the branding that occurred in the war between Samos and Athens).

reason at all to suppose that they were, or in any sense represented, members of the subject-states. But a further point of great importance is certain : these "Babylonians" formed the chorus, or at any rate *a* chorus. Whenever a Greek play has a plural name, that name is the name of the people composing the chorus, save that in the *Frogs* the chorus proper consists of the Initiated, while the frogs form a subsidiary chorus.[1] One fragment undoubtedly refers to the Babylonians as the chorus :

ἦ που κατὰ στοίχους κεκράξονταί τι βαρβαριστί.

'No doubt they will stand in rows and screech some barbarian ditty.'[2]

The god Dionysus was himself brought to trial, almost certainly by Athenian demagogues. 'So in the *Babylonians*, too, of Aristophanes we shall hear that the *oxybaphon* was a cup; when Dionysus says of the demagogues at Athens that when he had come away to the trial they asked him for two *oxybapha*; for we cannot suppose this to mean anything else than that they asked him for goblets.'[3]

A third element was the landing of some person or persons from a ship : the fragments reveal little, but their number suggests that this feature of the play was important. One implies that a character of the play watches the landing (which happens "off") and reports it, as is often done with horse-races in our own theatres :

εὖ γ' ἐξεκολύμβησ' οὑπιβάτης ὡς ἐξοίσων ἐπίγειον.[4]

'Splendid, that dive the marine made to bring the cable ashore!'

The fourth and last feature of importance, was an exposure of the fulsome rhetoric wherewith envoys from the cities [5] hoodwinked the Athenian assembly.

---

[1] Bergk (pp. 969 *sq.*) thought that Persian attendants on an envoy from the Great King formed the chorus or perhaps a παραχορήγημα, and that the envoy's speech was a parody of Gorgias.
[2] Fr. 79.   [3] Athenæus, XI, 494*d*; fr 70.   [4] Fr. 80.
[5] That is, almost certainly, from the subject-states ; cp. vv. 642 *sq.*

Aristophanes' speech [1] of exculpation in the *Acharnians* emphasizes this, and shows that the flattery was not commonplace but sophisticated and literary. It has therefore been conjectured [2] (but wrongly, as we shall see) that the speaker of such deceptive eulogies was Gorgias himself, the distinguished sophist and teacher of eloquence, who had come to Athens in the year before the *Babylonians* as an envoy of his native town, Leontini in Sicily, and had persuaded the Athenians to send a squadron thither; [3] all we know is that Aristophanes said a good deal about flattering and over-eloquent envoys. We possess one clear allusion to such rhetoric from the *Babylonians*, the delicious picture of a spell-bound audience: [4]

ἀνέχασκον εἰς ἕκαστος ἐμφερέστατα
ὀπτωμέναις κόγχαισιν ἐπὶ τῶν ἀνθράκων.

'Every man of them was gaping up precisely like roasting shell-fish on the coals.'

These, then, are our four elements: (*a*) the chorus consisted of branded or tattooed barbarian slaves from a penal mill; (*b*) the god Dionysus was brought to trial and was entangled with demagogues; (*c*) some person or persons landed from a ship; (*d*) the rhetorical flattery of envoys was exposed. Can we build these into a plot? To help us we have two ancient accounts of the play: Aristophanes himself tells us (i) that he was attacked bitterly for reviling Athens in the presence of allies; (ii) that he showed the (methods or effect) of democratic rule upon those allies (and—as above—that he exposed flattering orators); the Scholiast already quoted reports that Aristophanes derided the magistrates, both (iii) those appointed by lot and (iv) those elected, and (v) that he derided Cleon.

We thus obtain a possible outline of the play.

[1] *Ach.*, 634 *sqq.*
[2] Ranke, *Vita Aristophanis*, § 33, followed by Bergk (p. 969) and others.
[3] Diodorus, XII, 53.
[4] Fr. 68. The passage may refer to the reception of the envoys or equally well to the trial of Dionysus.

Dionysus, with his wild Orientals, enters Attica, and his followers are thrown into prison. He somehow obtains their (temporary?) deliverance, stations them in the orchestra as chorus,[1] and puts himself forward as the best representative of Athens because he presides in the theatre, which contains citizens, foreign envoys, and the allies bearing their tribute. To him enter certain allied envoys who deliver absurdly florid eulogies of Athens in order to secure benefits (for instance, a reduction of their tribute-assessments). He derides and exposes them, no doubt in a speech ludicrously damaging to Athens herself, for which he is attacked by Cleon and another, and dragged off to trial. On his return he relates his experiences: how the demagogues sought to blackmail him, how he spell-bound the judges by his eloquence and finally triumphed. The chorus congratulate him and perform the parabasis. Dionysus, now secure (perhaps as king), very likely announces the permanent liberation of his attendants and (more certainly) deals severely with the bureaucracy, members of which come in one by one to curry favour with the new power: first a civilian (perhaps a Prytanis), then a soldier, perhaps others. The comedy may have ended by a proclamation of Dionysus: ' I must now depart to other countries (as usual during my earlier career): to you, citizens of Athens, I leave my blessing and the command that ' etc., etc. There is no evidence whatever that Aristophanes in this play championed the allies.

The FARMERS (Γεωργοί), produced soon after 425 B.C.,[2] is usually supposed[3] to have resembled the *Peace* in urging the country population of Attica to insist on stopping the Peloponnesian War. There is no evidence for this. All we know on this side is that

---

[1] Fr. 66: ἴστασθ' ἐφεξῆς πάντες ἐπὶ τρεῖς ἀσπίδας.
[2] The Nicias-passage shows that it appeared soon after the Pylos affair (425 B.C.). Capps (*American Journal of Philology*, 32, p. 429) assigns it to the Dionysia of 424 B.C.
[3] Cp. for instance Bergk, pp. 984 *sq.* Fritzsche (*De Daetalensibus*, pp. 131, note 71) supposed this comedy a second edition of the *Peace*.

the play appeared early in the war, contained allusions to several fruits, and depicted the chorus of farmers returning to their beloved countryside : [1]

> ἐξ ἄστεως νῦν εἰς ἀγρὸν χωρῶμεν · ὡς πάλαι δεῖ
> ἡμᾶς ἐκεῖ 'ν τῷ χαλκίῳ λελουμένους σχολάζειν.

'Now let us leave town for the country : it is high time we were taking our ease there after a bath in the bronze tub.' But the incidents may very well have been quite different [2] from those of the *Peace*. Indeed, one fragment [3] makes this fairly certain :

> A. ἐθέλω γεωργεῖν.
> B.   εἶτα τίς σε κωλύει;
> A. ὑμεῖς. τί δ'εἰ δίδωμι χιλίας δραχμὰς
> ἐάν με τῶν ἀρχῶν ἀφῆτε;
> B.   δεχόμεθα·
> δισχίλιαι γάρ εἰσι σὺν ταῖς Νικίου.

'I wish to work on my farm.' 'Well, who is preventing it?' 'You! Suppose I offer you a thousand drachmæ to let me escape office?' 'Done! It makes two thousand with those Nicias paid.' The last words point at Nicias' fear of responsibility and at his famous resignation of the generalship to Cleon during the affair of Pylos.[4]

A charming passage,[5] opening with an echo of a lovely Euripidean song, voices the husbandman's yearning :

> Εἰρήνη βαθύπλουτε καὶ ζευγάριον βοεικόν,
> εἰ γὰρ ἐμοὶ παυσαμένῳ τοῦ πολέμου γένοιτο
> σκάψαι κἀποκλάσαι τε καὶ λουσαμένῳ διελκύσαι
> τῆς τρυγὸς ἄρτον λιπαρὸν καὶ ῥάφανον φαγόντι.

> O Peace, thou well of riches, and O my teem of steers,
> If only I might cease from war and delve again my ditches,
> Or prune the long-neglected vine and bathe when toil was over,
> Then eat my lunch in clover and quaff the season's wine!

---

[1] Fr. 107.
[2] The line ἐν ἀγορᾷ δ'αὖ πλάτανον εὖ διαφυτεύσομεν (fr. 111) may mean that in this play the Aristophanic fantasy was the transformation of Athens into a country-paradise : αὖ suggests that the sentence is part of an enumeration (of marvellous "developments"?). Note also the strange words (see below) οὖθαρ ἀγαθῆς χθονός : perhaps the soil is to undergo a miraculous change. [3] Fr. 100.
[4] So Plutarch (*Nicias*, 8) by whom the fragment is quoted.
[5] Fr. 109. The first two words are borrowed from Euripides' *Cresphontes* (fr. 453 Nauck).

Another lyric [1] inspired perhaps the most famous saying in later pagan Greek literature :

ὦ πόλι φίλη Κέκροπος, αὐτοφυὲς Ἀττική,
χαῖρε λιπαρὸν δάπεδον, οὖθαρ ἀγαθῆς χθονός.

'O beloved city of Cecrops, native-born Attica, hail, thou radiant land, good soil of loamy richness !' From this Marcus Aurelius [2] took his great outburst : ' He can say " Dear city of Cecrops " : wilt thou not say " Dear city of God " ? '

GERYTADES (Γηρυτάδης) is a name of unknown meaning. The Athenian poets sent a deputation to Hades seeking assistance from the shades of the old Masters ; for delegates they chose the leanest and lightest of their number, as having already one foot in the grave : [3]

A. καὶ τίς νεκρῶν κευθμῶνα καὶ σκότου πύλας
   ἔτλη κατελθεῖν;
B.   ἕν' ἀφ' ἑκάστης τῆς τέχνης
   εἱλόμεθα κοινῇ γενομένης ἐκκλησίας,
   οὓς ᾖσμεν ὄντας ᾁδοφοίτας καὶ θαμὰ
   ἐκεῖσε φιλοχωροῦντας.
A.   εἴσι γάρ τινες
   ἄνδρες παρ' ὑμῖν ᾁδοφοῖται;
B.   νὴ Δία
   μάλιστά γ'.
A.   ὥσπερ Θρᾳκοφοῖται;
B.   πάντ' ἔχεις.
A. καὶ τίνες ἂν εἶεν;
B.   πρῶτα μὲν Σαννυρίων
   ἀπὸ τῶν τρυγῳδῶν, ἀπὸ δὲ τῶν τραγικῶν χορῶν
   Μέλητος, ἀπὸ δὲ τῶν κυκλίων Κινησίας.

' Nay, who hath dared descend to the hiding-place of the dead and the gates of darkness ? ' ' An assembly was convened and we all chose one from each craft, who we knew were Hades-trippers and had often shown a wish to go there.' ' What ! are there Hades-trippers among you ? ' ' There are indeed, by Zeus.' ' Like

---

[1] Fr. 110. This fine apostrophe is strange in our poet. He makes fun in the *Acharnians* (639 *sq.*) of λιπαρός as applied to Athens, and the last three words are untrue (cp. Thucydides, I, ii, 5, τὸ λεπτογέων).

[2] IV, 23 : Ἐκεῖνος μέν φησι Πόλι φίλη Κέκροπος, σὺ δὲ οὐκ ἐρεῖς·Ὦ πόλι φίλη Διός;

[3] Athenæus, XII, 551a (fr. 149). The first line is borrowed from Euripides (*Hecuba*, 1).

Thrace-trippers?' 'Certainly.' 'And who may they be?' 'First, Sannyrion from the comic poets, then Meletus from the tragic choruses, and from the lyric poets Cinesias.' The explanation is almost certainly not given by one of the delegates: some one else introduces them or leads them down to Hades. This is proved by the words with which the door-keeper, or other inhabitant of Hades, receives the explanation:[1]

ὡς σφόδρ' ἐπὶ λεπτῶν ἐλπίδων ὠχεῖσθ' ἄρα.
τούτους γὰρ ἦν πολλῷ ξυνέλθῃ ξυλλαβὼν
ὁ τῆς διαρροίας ποταμὸς οἰχήσεται.

'On what frail hopes, then, have you been building! Those men (not "you") . . . the River Stynx will whirl away out of sight.'

What is the object of this deputation? It has usually been supposed that help and instruction in literature were sought from the great departed. Bergk[2] accordingly assumed that the play was somewhat like the *Frogs* and later in time, because both Sophocles and Euripides must have been dead if we are to imagine a dearth of poetic genius in Athens. Körte[3] believed that the delegates brought back from Hades Ancient Poetry, a female lay-figure like the goddess in the *Peace*. But there is no evidence whatever that the living poets descended for inspiration or instruction in their art. So far as our fragments go, another theory is more attractive—'In these days poetry has fallen

[1] Fr. 150. The second line is corrupt.
[2] Pp. 1004 *sq.* Sophocles died while the *Frogs* was actually being written, and Bergk puts the *Gerytades* "several years" later—naturally, since he imagines that the two plays had similar plots. Even if his reason is wrong, his dating appears to be correct. Sannyrion is prominent at the date of the *Gerytades* and his career seems to have begun in 404 B.C., the year after the *Frogs*. (Meineke, I, p. 263; Geissler, however, *Chronologie*, p. 64, dates his Δανάη at 407-404).
[3] *Jahresb.*, 152 (1911), p. 271. We have a new fragment (*Papiri Greco-Egizii*, II, i, Col. II, 9):

φέρε νῦν ἐγὼ τὴν δαίμον' ἣν ἀνήγαγον
ἐς τὴν ἀγορὰν ἄγων ἱδρύσωμαι βοῖ.

Körte first assumes that this passage belongs to the *Gerytades* because it refers to a descent into Hades and then suggests that Sannyrion and his colleagues have brought ἀρχαία ποίησις back with them.

into such disesteem that we cannot make a living: let us ask the great poets of the past if they can give us a meal in Hades.' There are two arguments for this view. First, that the new indifference to culture, not the badness of poets, is the source of trouble, seems clear from the extract :[1]

> τότε μὲν . . . σοῦ κατεκοττάβιζον ἄν,
> νυνὶ δὲ καὶ κατεμοῦσι, τάχα δ' εὖ οἶδ' ὅτι
> καὶ καταχέσονται.

'In those days . . . they would invoke your name at the *cottabos*, but now they vomit over you and I am certain that matters will not stop there.' This surely means that some great figure, whether Dionysus, or a Muse, or Poetry, is insulted by former partisans: it can scarcely refer to discredit brought about by the bungling work of poets or musicians.[2] The second argument is that many of our fragments allude to eating and none contains any advice about improvements in literature, though naturally there are parodies.[3] Nor was the meal any 'banquet in honour of our distinguished colleagues from Earth'. The visitors were so famished that they ate the wax off their notebooks—

> τὴν μάλθαν ἐκ τῶν γραμματείων ἤσθιον.[4]

Still clearer are these lines :[5]

> A. ἆρ' ἔνδον ἀνδρῶν κεστρέων ἀποικία;
> B. ὡς μὲν γάρ εἰσι νήστιδες, γιγνώσκετε.

'Have we got a colony of cormorants in the house?' 'Well, you know they are ravenous.' Perhaps it was

---

[1] Fr. 152. The person addressed is supposed by Bergk to be Dionysus, by Kock Poetry.
[2] *Frogs*, 95 and 366 (quoted by Kock) are not relevant.
[3] Cp. the first line quoted above (p. 289). And the Scholiast on Sophocles' *Electra*, 289, says: "this too Aristophanes has parodied in *Gerytades*".
[4] Fr. 157. Ἤσθιον might of course be "I ate". The line is, however, more likely to be a report to the Committee of Reception on the appetite of their visitors. Bergk charmingly suggests that Sannyrion and his friends grew so hungry on the road that they consumed the edible part of their letters of introduction.
[5] Fr. 156.

the dinner-hour of which the speaker of another line was thinking :

πόλος τόδ' ἐστίν ; εἶτα πόστην ἥλιος τέτραπται ; [1]

'Is this a dial-finger? Well, what hour does the sun mark?' Some items in the menu were "topical" but unappetizing. Each envoy was offered the type of literature appropriate to him. Of Cinesias (no doubt) it is said, ' look after him and feed him on solos'—θεράπευε καὶ χόρταζε τῶν μονῳδιῶν.[2] And we are to suppose it was Meletus who, as a tragic poet, was confronted by a dish of tragedy : [3]

A. καὶ πῶς ἐγὼ Σθενέλου φάγοιμ' ἂν ῥήματα ;
B. εἰς ὄξος ἐμβαπτόμενος ἢ ξηροὺς ἅλας.

'Why, how can I eat passages of Sthenelus?' 'Dip them in vinegar or dry salt.'

The ISLANDS (Νῆσοι) was one of the four quasi-Aristophanic plays attributed by ancient scholars to Archippus. The chief fragment [4] is an effective proclamation of an old topic that has made the fortune of many poets since Aristophanes, who seems, indeed, to have been the very first demonstrator of the difference between grassy nooks and hot, noisy streets :

ὦ μῶρε, μῶρε, ταῦτα πάντ' ἐν τῇδ' ἔνι·
οἰκεῖν μὲν ἀργὸν αὐτὸν ἐν τῷ γῃδίῳ
ἀπαλλαγέντα τῶν κατ' ἀγορὰν πραγμάτων,
κεκτημένον ζευγάριον οἰκεῖον βοοῖν,
ἔπειτ' ἀκούειν προβατίων βληχωμένων
τρυγός τε φωνὴν εἰς λεκάνην ὠθουμένης,
ὄψῳ τε χρῆσθαι σπινιδίοις τε καὶ κίχλαις,
καὶ μὴ περιμένειν ἐξ ἀγορᾶς ἰχθύδια
τριταῖα, πολυτίμητα, βεβασανισμένα
ἐπ' ἰχθυοπώλου χειρὶ παρανομωτάτῃ.

'Ah, foolish one ! All this is summed up here—to dwell on your little farm yourself at ease, freed from the worries of town-life, possessing your own trim team of oxen ; and then to hear the bleating sheep and the new wine's voice as it is forced out into the bowl ; to dine on fieldfares and thrushes, not waiting for tiny

[1] Fr. 163. Apparently the visitors are being shown the sights of Hades, including the South Pole. [2] Fr. 154. [3] Fr. 151. [4] Fr. 387.

fish from the market, three days old, very dear, and pawed over by the appraising fingers of a cheating fishmonger.' It is very easy to say that this comedy, therefore, was meant to remind the agricultural citizens of the blessings they miss by a continuance of the war. But as a matter of fact this passage would fit either peace or war at almost any date. Nevertheless, the chorus no doubt represented the islands allied to Athens: but the alliance may have been the Second Confederacy, of the fourth century, not the fifth century Empire. They entered singly, and a brief fragment [1] about this resembles a passage in the *Clouds* :

A. τί σὺ λέγεις; εἰσὶν δὲ ποῦ;
B. αἰδὶ κατ' αὐτὴν ἣν βλέπεις τὴν εἴσοδον.

'What's that? Where are they?' 'Yonder in the very entrance that you are watching.' One at least of them has been ill-treated, whether by gods or men : [2]

ὡς ἐς τὴν γῆν κύψασα κάτω καὶ ξυννενοφυῖα βαδίζει.

'Look how she comes with drooping head and clouded countenance!' Perhaps it is this beclouded look that makes some one exclaim, in the child's phrase, 'Peep out, Mr. Sun!'[3]

The SEASONS (Ὧραι) had a plot apparently unique—a contention between the established deities of Attica and the foreign gods who were beginning to gain a foothold. Cicero [4] writes : 'New gods and night-long vigils held in their honour are attacked by Aristophanes, that witty poet of the Old Comedy, with such vigour that in his play Sabazius and certain other gods are condemned as foreigners and expelled from the State.' This refers to the *Seasons*, as our fragments reveal. Sabazius is mentioned, 'the Phrygian flute-player '— τὸν Φρύγα, τὸν αὐλητῆρα, τὸν Σαβάζιον.[5]

[1] Fr. 388. Cp. *Clouds*, 325 sq.
[2] Fr. 395.   [3] Fr. 389.
[4] *De Legibus*, II, 15: *Novos vero deos et in his colendis nocturnas pervigilationes sic Aristophanes facetissimus poeta veteris comediæ vexat, ut apud eum Sabazius et quidam alii di peregrini iudicati e civitate eiiciantur.*
[5] Fr. 566.

A. ὄψει δὲ χειμῶνος μέσου σικυούς, βότρυς, ὀπώραν,
στεφάνους ἴων ῥόδων κρίνων κονιορτὸν ἐκτυφλοῦντα.
αὐτὸς δ' ἀνὴρ πωλεῖ κίχλας, ἀπίους, σχαδόνας, ἐλάας,
πυόν, χόρια, χελιδόνια, τέττιγας ἐμβρυείους.
ὑρίχους δ' ἴδοις ἂν νειφομένους σύκων ὁμοῦ τε μύρτων·
ἔπειτα κολοκύντας ὁμοῦ ταῖς γογγυλίσιν ἀμῶσιν.
ὥστ' οὐκέτ' οὐδεὶς οἶδ' ὁπηνίκ' ἐστὶ τοὐνιαυτοῦ.
καίτοι μέγιστον ἀγαθόν, εἴπερ ἔστι δι' ἐνιαυτοῦ
ὅτου τις ἐπιθυμεῖ λαβεῖν.
B.   κακὸν μὲν οὖν μέγιστον.
εἰ μὴ γὰρ ἦν, οὐκ ἂν ἐπεθύμουν οὐδ' ἂν ἐδαπανῶντο.
ἐγὼ δὲ ταῦτ' ὀλίγον χρόνον χρήσας ἀφειλόμην ἄν.
A. κἄγωγε ταῖς ἄλλαις πόλεσι δρῶ ταῦτα πλὴν Ἀθηνῶν·
τούτοις δ' ὑπάρχει ταῦτ' ἐπειδὴ τοὺς θεοὺς σέβουσιν.
B. ἀπέλαυσαν ἄρα σέβοντες ὑμᾶς, ὡς σὺ φῄς;
A.   τιὴ δή;
B. Αἴγυπτον αὐτῶν τὴν πόλιν πεποίηκας ἀντ' Ἀθηνῶν.[1]

This belongs, of course, to the dispute between the established gods and the intruders, whose respective spokesmen are perhaps Athena and Sabazius. 'In mid-winter you may see pumpkins, grapes, fruit, and garlands of violets, roses, and lilies in blinding, whirling medley. The same man sells thrushes, plums, honey-comb, olives, beestings, tripe, swallow-blossom, and eggs of the cicala. You can see baskets buried in drifts of figs and myrtle-berries at once; they harvest melons at the same time as turnips. No one any longer knows what season of the year it is. That is surely an immense boon, to get whatever one wishes throughout the year.'

'No! An immense evil. If they had not these things, they would not desire them or spend money on them. I should have lent them these for a brief time and then withdrawn them.'

'So do I, to every city except Athens. They possess these things securely, because they revere the gods.'

'They are rewarded then, according to you, for revering you gods?'

'What do you mean?'

'You have made their city Egypt instead of Athens.'

The proclamation of benefits must be made by the

[1] Fr. 569.

spokesman of the old gods, as Athenians did in fact pride themselves on this abundance. Comparison of this passage with the title of the play suggests that the chorus was a pageant of various fruits.

Of the other comedies we know too little for even a tentative description: one can do no more than pick out isolated fragments. In DAUGHTERS OF DANAUS (Δαναΐδες) was a discussion [1] of earlier comedy:

ὁ χορὸς δ' ὠρχεῖτ' ἂν ἐναψάμενος δάπιδας καὶ στρωματόδεσμα,
διαμασχαλίσας αὑτὸν σκελίσιν καὶ φύσκαις καὶ ῥαφανῖσιν.[2]

'The chorus would dance in rugs and bedding-cords, their beef and sausages and carrots tucked under their arms.' The first line recalls our domestic charades; the second seems to mean that they were paid in kind by the choregus and carried their wages with them into the performance to ensure their safety. 'So uncomplicated a task was poetry for them'—οὕτως αὐτοῖς ἀταλαιπώρως ἡ ποίησις διέκειτο.[3]

WOMEN UNDER CANVAS is probably [4] the meaning of Σκηνὰς Καταλαμβάνουσαι. The Athenian women have come forth and set up their tents in order to watch some spectacle or procession. One of them describes her wine-goblet as her "fellow-spectator" (συνθεατρία).[5] In this play Aristophanes put forward a defence of himself as a part of the action, not merely in the parabasis, as so often.[6] Possibly there was an elaborate examination or trial of the poet, if we may judge from this fragment: [7]

καὶ μὴν ἄκουσον, ὦ γύναι, θυμοῦ δίχα
καὶ κρῖνον αὐτὴ μὴ μετ' ὀξυρεγμίας.

---

[1] Fr. 253.   [2] Fr. 253.   [3] Fr. 254.
[4] It has been thought to mean *Women Rushing the Theatre*, i.e. seizing the men's seats before the latter arrive. But though σκηνή is used for the stage-buildings, there is no evidence that σκηναί ever meant "the theatre," including the auditorium. Casaubon (*ad* Athen., IV, 20, p. 301) thought the women set up booths in the market-place and streets like merchants: this, however, would be σκηνὰς ποιοῦσαι, says Kock, who offers the explanation followed above.
[5] Fr. 472.
[6] The metre is the iambic senarius, never used in the parabasis.
[7] Fr. 473.

'Come now, lady : listen dispassionately and judge for yourself without bile.' We have two striking lines [1] from his defence :

χρῶμαι γὰρ αὐτοῦ τοῦ στόματος τῷ στρογγύλῳ,
τοὺς νοῦς δ' ἀγοραίους ἧττον ἢ 'κεῖνος ποιῶ.

The Scholiast on Plato [2] tells us that 'Aristophanes was derided for imitating Euripides though scoffing at him'; he then quotes the gibe [3] of Cratinus, and adds Aristophanes' own explanation, as above : 'for I use his elegance of style, but my ideas are less vulgar than his.' [4]

Among the *Incertarum Fabularum Fragmenta* only a few need mention here.

Slang is rare in Aristophanes, but he nicknames the head a basin : ἵνα μὴ καταγῇς τὸ σκάφιον πληγεὶς ξύλῳ [5] 'lest you get a blow from a log and break your basin'. Somewhat similar is Ἀφροδίτης γάλα [6] (" milk of Venus ") as a fancy name for a certain wine. Mascots are mentioned as being favoured by blacksmiths :

πλὴν εἴ τις πρίαιτο δεόμενος
βασκάνιον ἐπὶ κάμινον ἀνδρὸς χαλκέως.[7]

'Unless one in his need bought the mascot that a smith hung over his furnace.' They seem to have been clay images of Hephæstus.[8] Striking proof of the Athenian ear for difference in pronunciation is found :

διάλεκτον ἔχοντα μέσην πόλεως
οὔτ' ἀστείαν ὑποθηλυτέραν
οὔτ' ἀνελεύθερον ὑπαγροικοτέραν.[9]

'Using the intermediate Athenian accent—neither the city-speech with its tinge of effeminacy nor the coarse tone with its tinge of rusticity.' Two shreds should be recorded because, brief as they are, they show kinship with New Comedy : μεσέγγυον τὴν μείρακα

---

[1] Fr. 471. [2] *Apology*, 19c. [3] See above, p. 138.
[4] From this comedy, it may be added, Pollux (unwilling that his royal pupil Commodus should be ignorant even of life's seamy side) has culled the Greek word for a burglar's "jemmy": μόχλισκος.
[5] Fr. 604. [6] Fr. 596. [7] Fr. 592.
[8] Schol., *Birds*, 436. [9] Fr. 685.

καταθέσθαι ¹—' to hand the girl over to a third party' (till some dispute is settled); and ἀνήσω κροκύδα μαστιγουμένη ²—' I shall be flogged till I lose my wool,' the interest of which is that a female slave speaks.

Finally we note certain interesting remarks on dramatic history. Æschylus is made to say: ' myself devised the dances for my choruses '—τοῖσι χοροῖς αὐτὸς τὰ σχήματ' ἐποίουν.³ It is apparently in reply to this that some one says: ⁴

τοὺς Φρύγας οἶδα θεωρῶν,
ὅτε τῷ Πριάμῳ συλλυσόμενοι τὸν παῖδ' ἦλθον τεθνεῶτα,
πολλὰ τοιαυτὶ καὶ τοιαυτὶ καὶ δεῦρο σχηματίσαντας.

' I remember watching the Phrygians, when they came with Priam to ransom his dead son, performing many figures—this way and that way and hither.' A famous piece of gossip about Euripides is voiced in the lines: ⁵

Κηφισοφῶν ἄριστε καὶ μελάντατε·
σὺ δὴ ξυνέζης εἰς τὰ πόλλ' Εὐριπίδῃ
καὶ ξυνεποίεις, ὥς φασι, τὴν τραγῳδίαν.

' Cephisophon, best and blackest of men, you shared Euripides' life in most things, and (so they say) helped to beget his works.' A splendid though reluctant eulogy of the poet whom Aristophanes so often derided is found in a fragment ⁶ of uncertain authorship:

ὁ δ' Ἀναξαγόρου τρόφιμος χαιοῦ στρυφνὸς μὲν ἔμοιγε προσειπεῖν
καὶ μισογέλως καὶ τωθάζειν οὐδὲ παρ' οἶνον μεμαθηκώς·
ἀλλ' ὅ τι γράψαι τοῦτ' ἂν μέλιτος καὶ Σειρήνων ἐτετεύχει.

' The foster-son of worthy Anaxagoras I found austere and morose in conversation: he had not learned to joke even over his wine. But whatever he wrote was filled with honey and magical voices.' One would like to believe that Aristophanes wrote that.

---

¹ Fr. 650.   ² Fr. 651.   ³ Fr. 677.
⁴ Fr. 678. The allusion is to *The Phrygians or Hector's Ransom*.
⁵ Fr. 580.
⁶ Quoted by Aulus Gellius, XV, xx, 8, who attributes it to Alexander Ætolus. Nauck claims it for Aristophanes, comparing the *Vita Euripidis*, ii, 92, 116 (Dindorf).

Aristophanes was endowed with superb wit, splendid poetical genius, immense vitality. In virtue of these three gifts he may truly be called great, but they are the only elements of greatness that he possesses. He is neither a great humorist nor a great playwright.

He is not a great humorist, for he is without pity or reverence. That is not to say that he is a monster, only that in character he is a normal Athenian. The achievements of Athens blind us at times to the limitations of the Attic spirit, which accentuated the defects as well as the virtues of Hellenism. That mental clarity, that instinctive perception of outline, which projected the heroic figures of Homer, the science of Hippocrates, Sophoclean tragedy, and the logic of Aristotle, made it inevitable that humour should be rare in the art and daily life of that brilliant people: among the Athenians it was even less common than elsewhere. Humour observes and rejoices in the penumbra of character and events; its method is a rich blurring of outline. Wit insists upon the exact shape of thought and gains its effects by remorseless rendering of outline. Humour is emotional, wit intellectual. The humorist sympathizes with those at whom he laughs; the wit may be all compact of malice. Falstaff is a disreputable old man, but we are all exceedingly fond of him; Don Quixote is an impossible old simpleton, but we adore him. For what character in Aristophanes do we feel more than a tepid liking? The truth is that he has created no character at all. No author can create people unless he loves human beings, and there is no evidence that Aristophanes loved anyone in particular; at most, he shows an occasional sympathy for types, as in *Lysistrata*, nor can anyone forget those charming old persons of the *Wasps* and *Peace*, perhaps a memory of childhood. He is almost everywhere metallic, like W. S. Gilbert, who reveals no tenderness save when he sets himself deliberately to write a love-song, whose pathos is turned on mechanically at the double rap of the conductor's baton, and whose incessant derision of elderly women betrays a complete absence of humour amid an opulence of wit. On this side certainly Aristophanes is the Athenian Gilbert.[1]

Nor is he a great playwright. He could indeed conceive and carry through gloriously clever and amusing situations; but, in addition to what has just been said concerning his persons, we must recognize that the structure of his dramas is on the whole loose and faltering. The method of Aristophanic composition is to write the first part magnificently in construction as in wit, and after the parabasis to throw on the stage a jumble of little scenes each of which may be splendid or mediocre, but which merely illustrate the main idea of the play, and could be cut down or multiplied with ease.[2] If we refuse to be blinded by his reputation, we may easily see how these plays were composed, for a clue lies plainly before us in the mistakes which the attentive reader may so frequently detect. These are both great and small: they vary in importance from the fact that Philocleon is at one moment toothless and at the next bites through his cords, to the hopeless muddle of the *Plutus*. Except when we are certain that two versions existed and were (long after) ineptly combined, we should accept the natural explanation. Aristophanes conceived a splendid comic idea and then wrote ahead, dashing off lyrics and scenes just as they occurred to him; when the play was "finished," finished it was. He never went back and removed even those trivial inconsistencies that might have disappeared under a stroke of the pen. Why did he not? He simply did not care, and for two reasons. First, he is writing for an audience who will see the play once, not for a reader who moves backwards and forwards over his text with a watch-maker's goggle in his eye, and in his mind an awestruck belief in the

---
[1] *Plutus*, 1041 *sqq.*, for instance, reads like the germ of certain Katisha passages.
[2] The historical reasons for this do not alter the fact.

crystalline perfection of everything Greek. In the second place, he is more often writing farce than comedy, in the sense attached to the word " comedy " since Menander; and one of the peculiarities of farce is that the author can play the fool as heartily as his characters. As everyone knows, Aristophanes does this in great things: he is irresponsible—' the naughty darling of the Graces' as Goethe named him—and would have laughed loudly had he been informed that no one can fly to Heaven on a beetle. This irresponsibility extends to inconsistency and lack of logic as well as to his famous " unfairness ".

His one dramatic excellence is fertility in comic ideas, the invention of a magnificent initial concept, and an immense merit this is. He shows a vast sense of fun, of imagination envisaging the incongruous. No writer in the world can be compared with him in this titanic power to make a whole play one huge acted joke. Other comic playwrights merely take a situation of interest and tension, to portray therein persons who act and hold forth amusingly. This situation is often commonplace, even if the treatment is glorious; thus the Gadshill robbery and its sequel, merely as events, have small value, though the treatment surpasses everything else of its kind. Here Aristophanes is the opposite of Shakespeare. The situation for him is everything, the personages little; for the figure of Falstaff he substitutes the religion of Dinos. A play by him would still be a comedy even if no one uttered a verbal joke. For the whole thing is a joke. The most penetrating, as the most brilliant, modern passage ever written about him indicates this in language that recalls his own. Heine[1] sees " a deep

---

[1] *Reisebilder*, III, ii, 11: " Zeigt sich in des Grafen Werk keine Spur von einer tiefen Weltvernichtungsidee, die jedem aristophanischen Lustspiele zum Grunde liegt, und die darin, wie ein phantastisch ironischer Zauberbaum, emporschiesst mit blühendem Gedankenschmuck, singenden Nachtigallnestern und kletternden Affen. Eine solche Idee, mit dem Todesjubel und dem Zerstörungsfeuerwerk, das dazu gehört, durften wir freilich von dem armen Grafen nicht erwarten."

idea of world-annihilation lying at the base of each Aristophanic comedy, which, like a fantastically ironic fairy-tree, shoots upwards therein bearing gorgeous blossoms of thought, melodious nightingale-nests and climbing monkeys"; in another sentence he extols "the jubilee of death and the fireworks of destruction". The world-annihilation, the jubilee of death, the fireworks of destruction, are all names for that one explosive idea which is in each play Aristophanes' greatest feat, the essence of his dramaturgy. The universe and our life therein are unintelligible to the ordinary man; the artist's function is to make it by a stroke of imaginative genius intelligible and then by a stroke of interpretative genius to make the ordinary man understand it when by imagination so manipulated. And those three phrases of Heine point to Aristophanes' own method of manipulation—not indeed reducing the universe to nothing, but blowing it to pieces and building with the shards a new fantastic universe that lasts for a rainbow moment like the soap-bubble blown by a child. Such is his work in the *Birds* above all, and in others too; even where the fantasy is less titanic, the instinct yet remains to project some ludicrous notion that sets the world upside-down and then to work it out with gay defiance of reason and morality. Needless to remark, he is not the slave of his own imagination: he is too much the Athenian for that. So it is that we have had occasion to call his method ironic: his phantasmagorias are the offspring of intellect wedded to fancy. This joyous topsy-turvydom is the special glory of Aristophanes: no one has rivalled him here, but a few moderns show some touch of his bizarre imagination. Cervantes depicts a noble soul that insists on living the age of chivalry in a prosaic world; but Don Quixote is romantic and pathetic, not comic at all: Sancho follows him precisely to give comic relief. W. S. Gilbert portrays the fairy world entangled with British peers and policemen, a youth apprenticed to piracy as if to a humdrum law-abiding trade; but the idea tails off into a series of harshly intellectual jokes and a splendid efflorescence of emotional or jesting lyrics. Swift begins, indeed, his accounts of Lilliput and Brobdingnag with an admirably fantastic idea; but the two kingdoms are perfectly rational, and the hero's stature is nothing but a device for giving us a novel perception of their rationality and of the author's satire; the Houhymnmns are so far from fantastic that their very reason for existence is to satirize our fantastic folly and wickedness. There is no complete parallel to these imaginative flights of Aristophanes, except in a noble imitation of the man himself written by a genius even greater than he. In the *Symposium* [1] Plato has attributed to him a speech concerning love which is a superb reflexion, not of his verbal style (though what do we know of Aristophanes' conversation? [2]) but of something far more difficult to render, his imaginative process. Once we human beings were rotund creatures with two faces and two sets of limbs. But God in his wrath slit each down the middle, and thus formed new people with but one face, two legs, and so forth; so that now each of us runs to and fro about the world looking for his other half. This glorious blend of fun, grotesquerie, poetical force and loveliness is absolute Aristophanes.

We have observed repeatedly that the construction of these plays is loose; but a development, an improvement of structure, must not be overlooked. In his early [3] work, the exposition and triumph of the " annihilating " idea may in strictness be said to constitute the play proper. Then comes the parabasis, of course no part of the drama at all, in the normal

---

[1] 189c-193c.
[2] The reader who has been expecting quotation from Browning's *Aristophanes' Apology* should ask himself whether that great poet has here given us anything whatever of value, whether in poetry or in criticism. As for the immediate question, if Aristophanes was in private life as verbose as Browning makes him, we should have had news of the astounding fact from Cratinus.
[3] Whether what follows is entirely true of the *Banqueters* and the *Babylonians*, as well as of the *Acharnians*, we cannot say.

sense of that word. There follows a section rudimentary in structure, however excellent otherwise; the action does not develop. All that we find is a demonstration of the effects wrought by the hero's success. Then the play closes with some spectacular climax that crowns his success with complete recognition and glory.[1]

Of this method our earliest extant play is a good instance, though the final triumph of Dicæopolis and the discomfiture of the war-party represented by Lamachus is less striking than the exploit of the Sausage-Seller, not to mention Trygæus and Pisthetærus. But a slow and faltering advance on this method at once begins. The *Acharnians* shows no development between the parabasis and the finale: but in the *Knights* Demos grows more and more impressed by the Sausage-Seller's merit. Of the *Clouds* in this connexion little is to be made: throughout, even in the early part, it is utterly ramshackle. The *Wasps* reveals more firmness, but the minor scenes, instead of leading up to the finale, lead really to nothing at all, and the " end " is merely tied on by the poet. One might suppose him to have realized his weakness in this part of dramatic work and to be floundering in quest of a better form. In the *Birds* he makes a genuine improvement. It contains a brilliant series of intruders,[2] but also two organic scenes: Iris, showing the first effect of the blockade of Olympus, and the celestial embassy which leads up with ease and vigour to the finale. Next, *Lysistrata* develops throughout, more steadily but less powerfully than the *Birds*. In place of " intruders " we find the interview between Cinesias and Myrrhine, showing (just as intruder-scenes would have shown) the effect of the sex-strike, but doing so with more elaboration and finish. More-

---

[1] Among our eleven comedies three lack this: the *Clouds* has lost its original finale; the *Wasps* has only drunken excitement; the *Thesmophoriazusæ* closes admirably but with no fire-works at all.

[2] Even to this element a slight structure is here given: the intruders come back and interrupt one another (vv. 1052, etc.).

over, the embassies not only exhibit the same effect on whole nations, but lead up to the close precisely as do Poseidon and his colleagues in the *Birds*. In the *Thesmophoriazusæ*, construction reaches the greatest perfection that Aristophanes, so far as we know, achieved. Its later half is filled with the attempts of Euripides to rescue his kinsman; these are not comments on what has preceded, but a thoroughly dramatic continuation of the kinsman's exploit. Nevertheless, the attempt falls into a series of scenes, even here: splendid as these are, they have less structural excellence than a single, more complicated, rescue would have possessed. Now follows a decline. The *Frogs* shows a peculiar formation. In the latter half we find indeed a series of scenes that certainly lead up to a finale, but by a merely arithmetical accumulation, as in the *Knights*. Nevertheless, such a serial arrangement is necessary to the idea of this particular play. And to the second part the earlier is (*prima facie*) auxiliary, containing as it does Dionysus' expedition for the purpose of fetching Euripides. But this homogeneity, admirable when briefly stated, is damaged by the incidental passages of the early part, especially the thrashing-scene, which is so fine that we forget for a while the main purpose of the comedy. The *Ecclesiazusæ* possesses a good scheme, but *Plutus* shows, in this respect as in others, a woeful falling-off: it reverts to the early feebleness of construction.

But the strictest scrutiny leaves him with those three splendid merits: wit, poetry, vitality. Let us consider them in turn.

Wit, fun, and humour are each the amusing self-expression of one who envisages the incongruous. When the intellect is the function employed, wit results; when it is the imagination, fun results; when it is the emotions, humour results. These definitions help to explain why a child always appreciates fun, humour rarely, wit never. Aristophanes, we have already observed, has no humour because (in the normal Athenian way) his emotions are repressed, if not atrophied. But wit, the intellectual rendering of incongruity, lights up every page of his work, ranging from puns, such as the ἐσχάρας of " Helen " to the Dinos jest that in a sense runs through many hundred lines of the *Clouds*. For though neatness is essential to wit, brevity is not : Shakespeare makes Polonius say so only to render his verbosity still more ridiculous ; the essence is not so much brevity as a short-circuiting of ideas. That masterpiece—" Advice to those about to marry : Don't "—is perfect not only because the point lies in a single word, but because the ideas are telescoped together. Literature can be terse and dull like Parmenides' hexameters on Nature or Longfellow's *Psalm of Life*, long-winded and witty, like Millamant's famous lecture on matrimony in *The Way of the World*, or a hundred passages of Plato. It is the telescoping of ideas that counts ; that is to say, while the nature of wit is the intellectual rendering of incongruity, its method is to leave something for the hearer to supply and to appreciate all the more zestfully for that very reason. When Donne writes " If you can think these flatteries, they are," he achieves wit, or would achieve it did he not ruin the effect by adding the idea that he has overleaped : " For then your judgment is below my praise ". So in the story of the man who drew his revolver upon another, explaining that he had determined to shoot anyone whom he found uglier than himself. One version continues : " The other answered, ' Shoot ! ' " ; the alternative version gives : " Well, if I'm really uglier than you, I don't want to live, so shoot ! " The first version is wit ; the second has no merciful name. Balzac, in *Le Curé de Tours*, has written with brilliance, yet none of the Polonian " brevity," a passage in which the reader is left to decide " which is which ". " Cet endroit est un désert de pierres, une solitude pleine de physionomie, et qui ne peut-être habitée que par des êtres arrivés à une nullité complète ou doués d'une force d'âme prodigieuse. La maison dont il s'agit avait toujours été occupée par des abbés, et appartenait à une vieille fille nommée mademoiselle Gamard." Two instances only shall be offered from Aristophanes himself. When the donkey staggers forth from Bdelycleon's house, his son does not remark: 'Bless me! Where have I met something like this before? Homer? Homer? Let me see . . .' No: 'Why dost grunt, if not carrying some Odysseus?' That is wit. "Helen" in the *Thesmophoriazusæ* is begged by "her husband" to look him in the face. Suppose she had replied, 'Oh, my dear, surely you remember that you shaved me for this part in the First Act. You made a dreadful job of it: I'm too much of a fright to look at anyone.' That would have been fun, but not wit. What she actually says is: 'I dare not turn on thee my ruined face'.

Indecency falls sometimes under the category of fun, sometimes of wit. For there are two kinds of indecency: the crude and the subtle. The former has been regarded by vast numbers of people in all ages as funny only because of that incongruity to which we have referred: since a thing is normally unmentionable, mention of it is an incongruity and therefore (to uncomplicated souls) instantly amusing though embroidered with no charm of phrase or neatness of idea. The subtle kind of obscenity, that which shows some art in its expression, has caused an immense amount of cogitation, heart-searching, consumption of ink and paper. Theoretically, it should be ranged with decent wit or decent fun, precisely as jokes about bald men arrogate to themselves no special category. That we decline so to regard it is due to a notion that something wicked or morbid invests the excretory and genital functions: just as we are intellectual above the neck, so are we sinful below the waistline. The vast modern preoccupation with sex has for one result an incessant, nervous, and largely disingenuous discussion of great writers whose work contains indecency; and among

ARISTOPHANES

these, side by side with Rabelais, Aristophanes is the most prominent.

It is a commonplace of criticism that Aristophanes' indecency is broad, uproarious, virile ; that it contains nothing insidious or seductive ; that here he resembles Fielding, not Sterne ; that, like the cleanly-built Englishman of popular novelists, though he may be " no saint," he nevertheless loathes the insinuating, the quasi-artistic, the subtly luscious phases of sexual attraction. This is a complete mistake. There is no kind or aspect of impropriety that cannot be found in his surviving work : his head is in the stars ; his feet are planted firmly in the mud. Not only are bodily functions, normal and abnormal, mentioned with frequency, gusto and detail; not only does the arrival of a female (whether human or divine) involve a prompt suggestion that she be put to sexual activity, as when Pisthetærus threatens to punish Iris' trespass with rape and when Trygæus hands over Opora to the Athenian Senate with elaborate instructions : now and again we may remark a subtler, more essentially lewd, prurience, that brings to mind no longer Rabelais or Shakespeare, but the more insidiously seductive deftness exhibited by certain later practitioners of graphic and theatrical art.

Whether he should be blamed for this it is too late to ask : he is dead, with all the carnal loveliness that excited him. Our only question is : should we read him ? By reading him, we surely mean the study of his work as he wrote it, unexpurgated ; for to leave the improprieties out of Aristophanes is like omitting from Dickens all reference to drink. " But why not leave out such passages, confess freely that the poet is thereby mutilated, and nevertheless derive instruction or amusement from the residue ? " That suggestion raises into the light our whole feeling about literature—not merely Greek, but all literature. Are we to treat a great author as a tradesman from whose wares we select the oddments marked on our shopping-list (in other words, demanded by our preconceived idea of what the young should learn), or as an original interpreter of life, to whom if we listen we must listen unreservedly, since it is precisely for the original, and therefore novel, and therefore shocking, elements in his work that we began to listen at all? The former plan will presumably engender good citizens, the latter educated men and women; and we shall choose according as we put the individual or the community first.

Of the three qualities wherefor, we said, Aristophanes may truly be called great, the second was poetical splendour. But he rivals Plato himself in versatility. It is, indeed, impossible to describe " the Aristophanic style ": he so often parodies some obscure dithyrambist or august tragedian, or writes dialect, or, speaking for himself, changes from exquisite descriptive lyric to coarse hard-hitting topical songs, from crazy discussion to flamboyant mob-oratory. But when he is not performing these varied and exciting feats, we find ourselves face to face with a great master of urbanity, a *grand seigneur* of literature, an accomplished and splendid Atticist. Despite the magnificence of much Athenian literature, perhaps the highest achievement of the Attic writers, certainly the achievement that has least often been paralleled, was that they said exactly what they meant with crispness and grace. Almost every other writer says as much as he means only at the cost of saying or implying in addition a great deal that he does not mean. An apt precision of statement is in English so rare that any considerable passage thus composed is regarded as fine literature: hence the reputation of Goldsmith. But to achieve this precision, and beauty therewith, is (outside Greek) the rarest of all excellences: Lincoln's Gettysburg speech is a miracle, and a brief miracle. In this regard Aristophanes is perhaps the most notable even among Athenians: the other poets naturally do not rival him here, because they are more remote from everyday speech; Lysias is more commonplace, Isocrates more self-conscious ; Plato's nearest manner is more casual. Here is the " ordinary " Attic superlatively well written : [1]

> ὦ ποθεινὴ τοῖς δικαίοις καὶ γεωργοῖς ἡμέρα,
> ἄσμενός σ' ἰδὼν προσειπεῖν βούλομαι τὰς ἀμπέλους,
> τάς τε συκᾶς, ἃς ἐγὼ 'φύτευον ὢν νεώτερος,
> ἀσπάσασθαι θυμὸς ἡμῖν ἐστὶ πολλοστῷ χρόνῳ.
>
> ὡς καλὸν ἔχουσα τὸ πρόσωπον ἆρ' ἐλάνθανες.
>
> ὡς ἡδὺ καινοῖς πράγμασιν καὶ δεξιοῖς ὁμιλεῖν,
> καὶ τῶν καθεστώτων νόμων ὑπερφρονεῖν δύνασθαι.
>
> μάτην ἐμοὶ κεκλαύσεται, σὺ δ' ἐγχανὼν τεθνήξεις.

Above and below this plain athletic elegance lie two other kinds of writing. The lyrics bring to mind the exhilaration of champagne, the flashing of spray in sunlight, the glad efflorescence of whatever in humanity or the world around us is spontaneously glad and vivid. On the other side lies his ordinary iambic dialogue, and it is curious that here, though he was charged with imitating Euripides and confessed that he used that poet's elegance of diction, no beauty at all can be discovered by the modern reader, except the borrowed charms of parody, as in the glorious Messenger's speech from Heaven in the *Birds*. The reason is that all this part of his work is practically prose. Both he and others wrote a few short scraps of prose, in proclamations and the like, but otherwise Greek drama never [2] evolved prose dialogue, despite the example of Plato. As a result, Menander, writing realist drama and needing a realist medium, uses a deliquescent verse that foreshadows the too rhythmical " prose " of Vanbrugh and the fashion which thereafter ruled the English stage till the days of Pinero. Before Menander the decline began (in this as in so much else) with Euripides, who, though he can when he chooses write iambics of an almost Sophoclean splendour, usually elects for a more commonplace manner. Aristophanes stands between Euripides and

---

[1] *Peace*, 556 *sqq.*; *Ach.*, 990; *Clouds*, 1399 *sq.*; *ib.* 1436.
[2] Except in mimes (see for example p. 79).

Menander. Instances may be found in abundance: the following passage [1] may be quoted because it is amusing also:

αἴσχιστα γάρ τοί μ' ἠργάσατο Λυσίστρατος
ὁ σκωπτόλης. δραχμὴν μετ' ἐμοῦ πρώην λαβὼν
ἐλθὼν διεκερμάτιζετ' ἐν τοῖς ἰχθύσιν,
κᾆπειτ' ἐνέθηκε τρεῖς λοιπίδας μοι κεστρέων·
κἀγὼ 'νέκαψ'. ὀβολοὺς γὰρ ᾠόμην λαβεῖν·
κᾆτα βδελυχθεὶς ὀσφρόμενος ἐξέπτυσα·
κᾆθ' εἷλκον αὐτόν.

All that remains to be remarked about Aristophanes' style is a strange inability to use the word γέρων without saying γέρων ὤν.[2]

As for the vitality of Aristophanes, a deep sense of it is the first experience of every one who approaches him and the final impression as we look up at length from these extraordinary pages. If we ignore the two last works, written after the glory had faded that made him possible, we find a vibrant tingling personality, a profound gusto for every side of life and human activity, for every artistic means to their expression. Aristophanes, no less finished a townsman than Charles Lamb, loved the country as passionately as Thoreau; he rivals Pindar in poetic imagination, Dickens in his zest for fun, even buffoonery; at one moment he rejoices in style with all Pater's thrilled delicacy, at another he is as philistine as a cart-horse. His only lack was compassion, and so it was that when he and his City fell on evil days he found nothing to sustain him, no interest in life save to rake over embers from which the fire had departed. But while the Empire yet stood

---

[1] *Wasps*, 787 *sqq*. But the most prosaic line in Aristophanes is not iambic at all (*Plutus*, 509): εἰ τοῦτο γένοιθ' ὁ ποθεῖθ' ὑμεῖς, οὔ φημ' ἂν λυσιτελεῖν σφῷν.

[2] Wherever γέρων can grammatically take the participle it receives it (except in *Plutus*, 258, and even there Meineke would read γέροντας ὄντας for γ. ἄνδρας): *Ach.*, 222; *Knights*, 533; *Clouds*, 129; *Wasps*, 278, 1192, 1384; *Peace*, 698; *Birds*, 1256; *Ecclesiazusæ*, 323; *Plutus*, 1066. Euripides is surely laughing at this habit when he makes Tiresias (*Bacchæ*, 188 *sq*.) utter the hideous sentence:

ἐπιλελήσμεθ' ἡδέως
γέροντες ὄντες.

he rejoiced in life and art, fun and politics, pleasure and wisdom, during that radiant age when all these were still interwoven, pouring forth the treasures of his poetry with prodigal splendour. That is the secret of his charm and of his immortality : he is not only magnificent, he is prodigal—not indeed thoughtless, but living in the glorious present, with no premonition of scholiasts and essayists, researchers and editors. Here is no shame, no misgiving : it does not occur to him that a time may arrive when people will ask themselves whether he is suitable for the Young Person. You may discover in Aristophanes every kind of impropriety save one : cant. Thus in spite of all he is still admired and read, though perhaps not a single person now living could bear the presence of his robust sagacity, his merciless candour. When we extol freedom of speech, we mean licence to utter our own blasphemies, not those of others : the most enlightened connoisseur of " advanced " literature, painting and sculpture is quite as deeply wounded, shocked, antagonized by eulogies of Longfellow, Landseer, and the Albert Memorial as any Philistine by Joyce, Gauguin, or Epstein. But this unaccountable Athenian was both the Wycherley and the Tennyson of his age : he adores what he burned and burns what he adored with lightning vicissitude. In short, he employs that celebrated *parrhesia*—not mere " free speech," but the right to say whatever enters his head. In our day he would be expelled from every Y.M.C.A. in Boston and from every *boîte* in Montmartre. We are hagridden by logic, a good servant but a bad master : he flings logic to the winds, rioting in beauty and bestiality, wisdom and folly, with no care for the chilling morrow. We praise him because he is safely dead ; but, as Heine remarked on hearing that the King of Prussia enjoyed the *Birds*, if the genuine Aristophanes were alive, we should very soon see him accompanied by a chorus of policemen. Yet, though we could not endure his scorching and dazzling genius in full power among us, we cannot refrain from turning our eyes to that distant beacon of wit, satire, rollicking gusto, exhilarating poetry. One of us loves Aristophanes' songs, another chuckles over his indecency, a third counts his prepositions for a doctor's degree, a fourth compares him as a dramatic artist with Molière, as an historical document with Theognis. He would have been vastly surprised, and would have given us some nickname in forty-seven letters; for such divided interest is a sign of our failure to recover the spirit of fifth-century Athens.

CHAPTER VII

MENANDER

MENANDER, who was born in 342-1 B.C. and died in his fifty-second year, 291-0,[1] was an Athenian citizen, son of Diopeithes and Hegesistrata, and nephew of Alexis, who is said to have taught him dramatic composition. Another of his teachers was Theophrastus,[2] Aristotle's successor, who wrote not only the celebrated *Characters*, but also a treatise *On Comedy*. Among the companions of his youth were Epicurus, the philosopher, and Demetrius of Phalerum, who later became Macedonian governor of Athens and gave the dramatist his protection during that troubled period; when Demetrius fell into disrepute, Menander narrowly escaped impeachment as his friend.[3] The poet was a man of wealth and family,[4] and (save for a cast in his eye) notable good looks.[5] Suidas reports that he was "utterly crazy about women": the name of his mistress, Glycera, became celebrated, and he is said to have put her into one of his plays.[6] Menander's first comedy appeared when he was twenty. He wrote one hundred and five (or eight) plays in thirty years, but obtained the prize only eight times,[7] his first victory being won by *Anger*

---

[1] The precise dates of his life and career are doubtful. Those given above are stated by Christ, *Griech. Literaturgeschichte*, ed. 4, p. 322.
[2] Diog. Laert., V, 2.   [3] *Id.*, V, 79.
[4] Λαμπρὸς καὶ βίῳ καὶ γένει (Anon., *de Com.* Kaibel, p. 9).
[5] Suidas, *s.v.*
[6] Athen., 594*d*. Körte, *Hermes*, 54, pp. 87 *sqq.*, does not believe that this Glycera ever existed.
[7] Aulus Gellius, XVIII, 4.

('Οργή) in 315 B.C.;[1] Philemon, it is said, often defeated him.[2] He lived all his life in Athens, refusing the invitation of King Ptolemy Soter, who wished him to settle in Alexandria.[3] He died, according to one account,[4] while bathing in the harbour of the Piræus, and was buried beside the road from Athens to the port;[5] his statue was placed in the theatre. Practically at the moment of his *début* as a dramatist his three greatest contemporaries died—Alexander, Demosthenes and Aristotle; while he was still a young man the two most important post-Platonic philosophies, Epicureanism and Stoicism, were inaugurated in his native city.

Throughout later antiquity Menander's fame was immense, surpassed by that of no other poet save Homer and Virgil: the vast array of quotations in ancient writers and the constant allusions to his name show that he was regarded as the finest comic playwright of Greece. In this opinion readers of every grade and nation concurred. That eminent Greek critic, Aristophanes of Byzantium, affected to doubt which of the two, Life and Menander, had copied the other;[6] and the best of all Roman critics, when advising students of oratory in their reading, names Menander as almost sufficient in himself.[7] At the other end of the scale, an ignorant and befuddled Byzantine can still say, after so many centuries, that Menander is "the star of the New Comedy, as we have learned ".[8] The intervening distance both of time and of scholarship is filled by ardent praise from poets and critics, essayists, orators, and scientists. Lucian's *Dialogues of Courtesans*

---

[1] Capps, *American J. of Phil.*, XXI, p. 61. Others think that 'Οργή was his first play, produced (then) in 321.

[2] For a story about this see above, p. 61.

[3] Pliny, *Nat. Hist.*, VII, 30; Alciphron, *Ep.*, II, iii.

[4] Scholiast on Ovid, *Ibis.*, 589. But Ovid may be referring to Eupolis.

[5] Pausanias, I, ii, 2.

[6] Schol. Hermogenes (Walz, *Rhetores Græci*, IV, p. 101): 'Ω Μένανδρε και βίε, πότερος ἄρ' ὑμῶν πότερον ἀπεμιμήσατο;

[7] Quintilian, X, 1, 69.

[8] Ὅς ἄστρον ἐστὶ τῆς νέας κωμῳδίας—an iambic line of unknown authorship (Bekker, *Anecd.*, 749).

are said to be derived entirely from Menander.¹ In Southern Gaul, seven centuries after the poet's death, Sidonius Apollinaris ² gave his son a lesson in comparative literature by setting work of Terence and of Menander side by side on his desk. Propertius,³ Ovid,⁴ and Ausonius ⁵ refer to him as the poet *par excellence* of love or wantonness; even the austere Persius ⁶ translates from him a scrap of revealing dialogue. That amiable pedant Aulus Gellius preserves anecdotes and dates concerning him. Phædrus,⁷ the fabulist, paints a picture of him in his habit as he lived:

> unguento delibutus, vestitu adfluens,
> veniebat gressu delicato et languido.

'Bathed in scent, his gown worn negligently, he moved with affected languid gait.' Alciphron has left two imaginary letters exchanged by Menander and Glycera, full of charm and tender pride: 'Don't I mend your masks and try on the costumes, and stand about in the wings squeezing my fingers together as I wait for the house to applaud?'⁸

But the most notable witness to his vast renown is Plutarch,⁹ that nobler Boswell of a whole civilization. "The style of Menander shows so uniform a polish, such a harmonious blend of manner, that while it traverses a wide range of emotion and character, adapting itself to all shades of personality, its unity is apparent, its individuality unimpaired amid diction normal, customary and inevitable. Yet if the subject happens to demand noisy bombast, all the stops are pulled out; after a moment, he pushes them back without jarring, and restores the normal pitch of his utterance. There have been many renowned craftsmen, but no workmen ever made a shoe, no theatrical artist a mask, no costumier a garment, that fitted equally

---

[1] Schol. in Luc., p. 275 (Rabe). [2] IV, 12. [3] IV, v, 43.
[4] *Amores*, I, xv, 18; *Tristia*, II, 369 sq. [5] *Parech. Cent. Nupt.*
[6] V, 161 sqq. [7] VI, i, 11 sq.
[8] Alc., *Ep.*, II, iv, 19. [9] *Moralia*, 853-4.

well man and woman, child, elder and slave; yet Menander has so blent his diction that it suits every character, every rank, every age; and that though he was still a youth when he laid hand to the work and died at the zenith of his poetical and theatrical skill, the very moment when (as Aristotle says) a writer's style makes its most notable and far-reaching progress. A comparison, therefore, of Menander's earliest plays with those belonging to his middle and final periods will reveal what new achievements he could have added even to the latter . . . Menander's charm makes him utterly satisfying, for in these works that present with universal appeal the splendours of Greece, society finds its culture, the schools their study, the theatre its triumph. The nature and possibilities of literary elegance were by him revealed for the first time: he has invaded every quarter of the world with his invincible glamour, bringing all ears, all hearts, under the sway of the Greek language. What sound reason for entering a theatre does the cultivated man ever find, except Menander?"

One might go on indefinitely culling quotations and praise from pagans and Christians, from Seneca [1] and Horace [2] and Manilius.[3] Scholarly editions and essays were not wanting, by Lynceus of Samos,[4] by Soteridas [5] of Epidaurus, by Sellius,[6] by Aristophanes of Byzantium.[7] He strongly influenced Roman drama, and thereby mediæval writers (including Hroswitha, the learned nun of Gandersheim) and the majority of modern comic dramatists, including Molière himself,

---

[1] *Nat. Quæst.*, IVa, Præf., 19.
[2] *Ep.*, II, 57; *Sat.*, II, iii, 11.
[3] V, 47 *sqq.*: *Qui vitae ostendit vitam*, etc.
[4] Athen., 242b.   [5] Suidas, *s.v.*
[6] Suidas, *s.v.* Ὅμηρος: Sellius wrote περιοχαὶ τῶν Μενάνδου δραμάτων.
[7] Certain linguistic purists (see below, p. 351) censured Menander's vocabulary, and some critics accused him of "theft". Cæcilius of Calacte said that in his Δεισιδαίμων he copied out the Οἰωνιστής of Antiphanes from beginning to end. One Latinus wrote περὶ τῶν οὐκ ἰδίων Μενάνδρου. The book of the critic Aristophanes mentioned above was of this kind, though he admired Menander greatly: παράλληλοι Μενάνδρου τε καί ἀφ' ὧν ἔκλεψεν ἐκλογαί. (For all these see Eusebius, *Præp. Ev.*, X.)

through whom his spirit has passed into the social drama of our own day, in England by means of the Restoration playwrights and Sheridan.

Till recently our knowledge of Menander rested on three insufficient bases: a collection of fragments laboriously scraped together by modern scholars from the ancient authors who quoted him; the *One-Line Maxims* (Γνῶμαι Μονόστιχοι); the comedies of Terence and Plautus. The Latin plays no doubt give us a general idea of the topics and methods of New Comedy; but that Terence (not to mention Plautus) merely translated Menander in the modern sense of that word, is demonstrably untenable.[1] The *Maxims* are an ancient collection the mere existence of which attests the poet's reputation as an epigrammatist. Among them are some famous lines:

> φθείρουσιν ἤθη χρήσθ' ὁμιλίαι κακαί.[2]
> 'Bad associates spoil a good character.'
>
> Ὡς χάριέν ἐστ' ἄνθρωπος, ὅταν ἄνθρωπος ᾖ.[3]
> 'How delightful is a human being, when he is human!'

Others are more commonplace, but still good:

> Γύμναζε παῖδας, ἄνδρας οὐ γὰρ γυμνάσεις.[4]
> 'Train children, for men you will not train.'
>
> Ζῶμεν γὰρ οὐχ ὡς θέλομεν, ἀλλ' ὡς δυνάμεθα.[5]
> 'We live, not as we would, but as we can.'

Mixed with these are " epigrams " merely ludicrous:

> Οὐδεὶς τὸ μέλλον ἀσφαλῶς ἐπίσταται.[6]
> 'No one has accurate knowledge of the future.'
>
> Εἰ θνητὸς εἶ, βέλτιστε, θνητὰ καὶ φρόνει.[7]
> 'Friend, if you are a mortal, think mortal thoughts.'

A great deal of the collection is not Menandrian: for instance, we know that Θεοῦ θέλοντος κἂν ἐπὶ ῥιπὸς

---

[1] This topic has been discussed at length in *The Art of Terence*. Briefly: Terence learned his craft, and borrowed scenes, from Menander; but the available (highly various) evidences overwhelmingly imply that he was original in the structure and the spirit of his plays.

[2] v. 738 (Meineke)—the famous quotation (1 *Cor.* xv, 33) of St. Paul: "Evil communications corrupt good manners". The line has been attributed to Euripides.

[3] v. 562 (Meineke).   [4] v. 104 (M.).   [5] v. 190 (M.).
[6] v. 412 (M.).   [7] v. 173 (M.).

πλέοις [1]—'If God wills, you may go to sea on a hurdle'—was written by Simonides of Amorgos. The fragments proper do not place Menander utterly beyond Antiphanes and Alexis in the Middle Comedy, or Philemon and Diphilus in the New.

But the position has been completely altered by the famous discoveries [2] of papyri in Egypt. The dry sand has preserved whatever happened to be committed to it, but the documents were often even then defective: the celebrated finds at Oxyrhynchus were made in the village rubbish-heaps, and so even to-day we possess no complete comedy of Menander. But of three plays we have so considerable a bulk that we can form a satisfactory notion of each; and concerning some half-dozen others we have attractive though scrappy information; other passages again belong to unidentified plays. Far the most important MS. is the so-called Cairo papyrus, found in 1905 at Aphroditopolis by Gustave Lefèbvre: " the poet of Venus rose from the dead in the town of Venus," as Körte phrases it. This priceless MS. contains parts of five works, the *Hero*, *Arbitration*, the *Samia*, *The Shorn Lady*, and a nameless play. Over this and its lesser companions, together with small pieces and mere shreds containing but some half-dozen letters, the united scholarship of the world has for a quarter of a century toiled with microscope and photographic camera, with limitless patience, immense ingenuity and learning, to build up a trustworthy text of these lightly-written comedies, as the Chinese Emperor lavished all his jewels on the effort to complete one casement of Aladdin's palace.

---

[1] v. 671 (M.).
[2] The "literature" about these is already extensive. The most useful writings are: (i) texts: Körte, *Menandrea* (editio maior), ed. 2, Leipzig, 1912; Sudhaus, *Menandri reliquiae nuper repertae*, ed. 2, Bonn, 1914; (ii) annotated editions: Capps, *Four Plays of Menander*, Boston, 1910; van Leeuwen, *Menandri Fabularum Reliquiae*, ed. 3, Leyden, 1919; Allinson, Loeb Text and Translation, London, 1921; Waddell, *Selections from Menander*, Oxford, 1927; (iii) discussions: Wilamowitz-Moellendorff, *Menander: Das Schiedsgericht* (pp. 11-172), Berlin, 1925; Murray, *Menander* (pp. 9-34 of Powell and Barber's *New Chapters in Greek Literature*), Oxford, 1929.

It has been a delightful and unparalleled experience thus to observe a great writer rising slowly from the dead and speaking in ever less muffled tones. Our steadily mounting excitement as we gradually compose a coherent scheme of *The Shorn Lady* must differ much from the interest of those others who sat back comfortably, supplied by a prologuizing deity with whatever information they needed. But this triumph of discovering literature unknown to the greatest scholars of the past, this half-illegitimate thrill in the perusal, have now and again influenced criticism untowardly. One result is that we proudly insist on knowing more than we can know. Our good fortune goes to our heads like strong wine, and we talk as if we possessed the whole hundred odd comedies that Menander wrote. We insist that Terence is a mere translator, so that we may illustrate the work we do possess by quoting what " Menander has said " in the *Andria* or the *Adelphoe*.[1] At times the passion to pretend that we know everything passes into downright hysteria. Even before the discoveries, it caused one enthusiast [2] to write : " The remarks of Donatus on the Latin play [*Andria*] succeed in proving this fidelity of imitation. But even where I cannot establish its exactitude, I feel it, I divine it." This ardour induced him actually to translate the most famous line of Terence—*homo sum : humani nihil a me alienum puto*[3]—into Greek and to print his version upon his title-page. This has been far outdone since the discoveries were made. But as we grow more

[1] Wilamowitz-Moellendorff, *Menander*, pp. 121 : " Im Heautontimorumenos lässt es Menander Abend werden und wahrend eines Zwischenaktes die Nacht verstreichen". But this is rare : in other places Wilamowitz expresses doubt of the Terentian evidence (*e.g.* pp. 139 : " von der genialen Wildheit des Plautus ganz abzusehen, kann ich nach wiederholter Prüfung mich nicht getrauen, selbst die Übersetzungen des Terenz als Ganzes für Menander zu verwenden "). Prof. L. A. Post, though in *The Dramatic Art of Menander* (*Harvard Studies in Classical Philology*, XXIV, pp. 111-45) he uses the Latin plays freely as evidence for Menander's practice, takes a very different view in his excellent and much later *Menander : Three Plays* (1929). Legrand, throughout *Daos*, makes much use of both Plautus and Terence.

[2] Benoit, *La Comédie de Menandre*, pp. 224.   [3] *Heaut.*, v. 25.

familiar with our new possession, we shall be less prone to such unbalanced transports.

Among the "old fragments" there are not many passages of deep interest. Some of the single lines have already been given from the *Maxims*, to which may be added the celebrated 'He whom the gods love dies young' (Ὃν οἱ θεοὶ φιλοῦσιν ἀποθνήσκει νέος [1]) and the superb ἄνθρωπος· ἱκανὴ πρόφασις εἰς τὸ δυστυχεῖν,[2] 'Sorrow? Of course! Isn't he human?' —this may do at a pinch. The same disillusionment is expressed with urbane and devastating elaboration in a passage from the SUPPOSITITIOUS CHILD [3] (Ὑποβολιμαῖος):

> παύσασθε νοῦν ἔχοντες· οὐδὲν γὰρ πλέον
> ἀνθρώπινος νοῦς ἐστὶν ἄλλο τῆς τύχης,
> εἴτ' ἔστι τοῦτο πνεῦμα θεῖον εἴτε νοῦς.
> τοῦτ' ἔστι τὸ κυβερνῶν ἅπαντα καὶ στρέφον
> καὶ σῷζον, ἡ πρόνοια δ' ἡ θνητὴ καπνὸς
> καὶ φλήναφος. πείσθητε κοὐ μέμψεσθέ με·
> πάνθ' ὅσα νοοῦμεν ἢ λέγομεν ἢ πράττομεν
> τύχη 'στίν, ἡμεῖς δ' ἐσμὲν ἐπιγεγραμμένοι.
> τύχη κυβερνᾷ πάντα· ταύτην καὶ φρένας
> δεῖ καὶ πρόνοιαν τὴν θεὸν καλεῖν μόνην,
> εἰ μή τις ἄλλως ὀνόμασιν χαίρει κενοῖς.

'Cease having sense. Mortal sense is nothing more than chance, whether that is divine spirit or sense. It is this that governs, steers, and preserves all things; human forethought is vapour and rubbish. Be convinced, and you will not blame me. All our thoughts, words and acts are Chance, and we are sealed as hers. Chance governs all: unless we delight in empty names, this goddess alone must we call Mind and Providence.' That is not cynicism,[4] but rather quietism, as revealed in a beautiful passage [5] surviving from the same play:

[1] Fr. 125.
[2] Fr. 263. Cp. Philemon fr. inc. 100: ἐμέθυον· ἱκανὴ πρόφασις εἰς θἀμαρτάνειν.
[3] Frr. 482, 483 (Kock): I have, however, given Meineke's reading (IV pp. 212 sq.).
[4] In any case, as need hardly be said, we must beware of taking isolated passages as giving the dramatist's own view.
[5] Fr. 481. The translation is by Professor Gilbert Murray (*op. cit.*), who evidently reads καταλύσεις βελτίονας. For the πανήγυρις idea cp. Alexis (pp. 52 sq.).

τοῦτον εὐτυχέστατον λέγω,
ὅστις θεωρήσας ἀλύπως, Παρμένων,
τὰ σεμνὰ ταῦτ' ἀπῆλθεν, ὅθεν ἦλθεν, ταχύ,
τὸν ἥλιον τὸν κοινόν, ἄστρ', ὕδωρ, νέφη,
πῦρ· ταῦτα, κἂν ἑκατὸν ἔτη βιῷς, ἀεὶ
ὄψει παρόντα, κἂν ἐνιαυτοὺς σφόδρ' ὀλίγους,
σεμνότερα τούτων ἕτερα δ'οὐκ ὄψει ποτέ.
πανήγυριν νόμισόν τιν' εἶναι τὸν χρόνον,
ὃν φημι, τοῦτον ἢ 'πιδημίαν, ἐν ᾧ
ὄχλος, ἀγορά, κλέπται, κυβεῖαι, διατριβαί·
ἂν πρῶτον ἀπίῃς, καταλύσεις βελτίονας
ἐφόδι' ἔχων ἀπῆλθες, ἐχθρὸς οὐδενί.

> I count it happiness
> Ere we go quickly thither whence we came
> To gaze ungrieving on these majesties,
> The world-wide sun, the stars, water and clouds,
> And fire. Live, Parmeno, a hundred years
> Or a few months, these you will always see,
> And never, never, any greater things.
> Think of this life-time as a festival
> Or visit to a strange city, full of noise,
> Buying and selling, thieving, dicing stalls
> And joy-parks. If you leave it early, friend,
> Why, think you have gone to find a better inn ;
> You have paid your fare and leave no enemies.

The Lucretian note is plainly heard. Moralizing is indeed a marked feature in Menander, and an excellent scene of *Arbitration* will show how dextrously he could weave it into his dialogue. Sometimes he is tart : ' All fathers are fools '[1]—a good example of truth-telling by terse exaggeration, like Mr. Shaw's remark that every man over forty is a scoundrel. But usually he is mellower : ' Generosity (as some call it nowadays) has degraded all life to villainy, for no wrongdoer meets punishment.'[2] Poignancy is conveyed by utter plainness : ' Waiting is so wearisome ! '—οὕτω τι πρᾶγμ' ἔστ' ἐπίπονον τὸ προσδοκᾶν.[3] More sophisticated is this reflexion [4] drawn from theatrical affairs : ' In a chorus you will find that not all sing, but two or three stand dumb at the end of the line to fill up the number. So in the world : every one occupies room,

---

[1] *Heaut.*, fr. 144.   [2] Fr. incert. 579.
[3] *Citharistes*, fr. 287.
[4] *Heiress*, fr. 165. This has been held to prove that Menander used a chorus. He did (see pp. 333, 342), but this passage might refer to tragedy or dithyramb.

but only those live who have livelihood.' One passage [1] merits close attention from students of comparative literature :

> ὅταν εἰδέναι θέλῃς σεαυτὸν ὅστις εἶ,
> ἔμβλεψον εἰς τὰ μνήμαθ' ὡς ὁδοιπορεῖς.
> ἐνταῦθ' ἔνεστ' ὀστᾶ τε καὶ κούφη κόνις
> ἀνδρῶν βασιλέων καὶ τυράννων καὶ σοφῶν
> καὶ μέγα φρονούντων ἐπὶ γένει καὶ χρήμασιν
> αὑτῶν τε δόξῃ κἀπὶ κάλλει σωμάτων.
> κᾆτ' οὐδὲν αὐτοῖς τῶνδ' ἐπήρκεσεν χρόνον.
> κοινὸν τὸν Ἅιδην ἔσχον οἱ πάντες βροτοί.
> πρὸς ταῦθ' ὁρῶν γίνωσκε σαυτὸν ὅστις εἶ.

'When thou wishest to know thyself, what thou art, look at the tombs as thou journeyest. Therein are bones and light dust of men that were kings, tyrants, and sages, men proud of birth and wealth, their own glory and comeliness. Yet none of these things defended them against Time : all mortals come alike to death. Looking on these, learn what thou art.' How august an array of passages on this theme—not merely death, but the vanishing of all earthly pomp and brightness in the grave—rises into the mind of a modern student ! How engrossing to compare the varieties of pathos and loveliness in poems of so many generations, from Homer's lamentations to the resigned musings of Hardy, above all the verses of Francis Beaumont, perhaps the closest in thought to Menander, and not the least beautiful !

> Mortality, behold, and fear,
> What a change of flesh is here !
> Think how many royal bones
> Sleep within this heap of stones.
> Here they lie, had realms and lands
> Who now want strength to stir their hands ; . . . .
> Here the bones of birth have cried
> ' Though gods they were, as men they died ' :
> Here are sands, ignoble things,
> Dropt from the ruin'd sides of kings.

Nor could a more perfect example be found of the difference between the " classical " and the " romantic " styles, or rather between the Attic and the Elizabethan :

[1] Fr. incert. 538.

Menander's Greek is the plainest possible expression; Beaumont's last couplet is a triumph of literary Gothic.

These " old " fragments have less to say of love than we should have expected. A lover tries in vain to describe the kiss that was his undoing.[1] ' Or was it like a storm at sea ? No : you have a breathing-space to shout : " God help us ! Haul at the ropes ! " But one touch of her lips, and that instant I was drawn under.' Among the polygamous Thracians anyone who has but four or five wives is called " a wretched bachelor ".[2] From TREASURE (Θησαυρός) comes a quaint passage on Love's usury : ' They who postpone love till old age have to pay additional interest for all those years '.[3] One comedy was named after the renowned courtesan Thais : the famous " evil communications " is by some ascribed to it. Allusions to other social elements are less common. ' A gentleman should distinguish himself in war : agriculture is a slave's business.'[4] On the other hand : ' Not even if God formed him could any soldier be a man of elegance ': κομψὸς στρατιώτης, οὐδ' ἐὰν πλάττῃ θεός, οὐδεὶς γένοιτ' ἄν.[5] A few attractive bits of adventurous narrative occur. ' When they saw us rounding the headland, they quickly went aboard and put out to sea.'[6] ' Many had left the stockade and were plundering the villages.'[7]

Next may be grouped six comedies,[8] concerning each of which as a whole we may claim some meagre knowledge.

The FARMER (Γεωργός) was by several years the earliest of the new discoveries : in 1897, M. Jules Nicole found in Egypt a papyrus, containing eighty-seven lines, now known as the Geneva fragment; a Florentine papyrus, published in 1912, added some

[1] Fr. incert. 536.   [2] *Ib.*, 548.   [3] Θησαυρός, fr. 235.
[4] Fr. incert. 642.   [5] *Ib.*, 732.
[6] 'Ἁλιεῖς, fr. 15.   [7] 'Ἀσπίς, fr. 77.
[8] Quotations from these follow the reading and numbering of Körte's second edition, except as regards "old" fragments of them, the reference for which is (as usual) to Kock.

fragmentary lines. Quintilian alludes to the prologue in words unfortunately obscure ;[1] a passage of the *Anthology* implies that this play was concerned with jealousy.[2] What we now possess reveals something of the story amid touches of pathos, excitement, and fun.

A Youth explains that he has returned home from Corinth to find his Father pushing forward preparations for the Youth's marriage to his half-sister ;[3] this plan the Youth resists, for he wishes to marry some one else —a girl whom he has seduced, the daughter of Myrrhine, who lives next door. This speech of the Youth apparently formed the prologue. Next Myrrhine and the nurse Philinna come out : they have heard of the wedding and resent the treatment of Myrrhine's daughter. To them enter Daos, slave of the Father, bringing from the farm flowers and other decorations for the wedding : 'I suppose no one ever tilled a more pious estate. It produces myrrh, capital ivy, and all these flowers. If you plant anything else, it gives correct and just return—exactly what you put in.' Seeing Myrrhine, he reports " splendid news ". Clæenetus, the old man on whose farm Myrrhine's son (probably named Gorgias) is working, has gashed his leg beautifully ($\chi\rho\eta\sigma\tau\hat{\omega}\varsigma$ $\pi\acute{\alpha}\nu\upsilon$) while digging ; better still, the wound grew inflamed. His slaves neglected the sufferer, but Gorgias tended him. Clæenetus in gratitude questioned him concerning his family, and so heard about his sister and the poverty of the three. Clæenetus felt a touch of nature that makes the whole world kin,[4] and promised to marry the girl. Daos congratulates Myrrhine on their escape from poverty and enters the Father's house, leaving her in anguished perplexity.[5]

[1] XI, iii, 91.
[2] *Anth. Pal.*, XII, 233. The Γεωργός is coupled with the Μισούμενος and the Περικειρομένη.
[3] She is ὁμοπατρία, therefore there was no objection of principle. A ὁμομητρία was out of the question.
[4] Ἔπαθέν τι κοινόν (v. 71).
[5] Since her daughter cannot marry Clæenetus, whether because she is his daughter as well as hers, or because she is with child by the Youth, or for both reasons.

We have nothing more but scraps. It is, however, easy to suppose that Cleænetus proves to be the father of Gorgias and his sister, that he now marries Myrrhine and by giving his daughter a dowry induces the Father to consent to her marriage with the Youth; Gorgias may have paired off with the Father's daughter. The events that set things in motion are illuminating. Cleænetus, in his desire " to make some return " (χάριν ἀποδοῦναι) for Gorgias' tendance,[1] promises to marry the sister. It is assumed that this will be greeted with joyful relief; Cleænetus, probably a " sympathetic " old man, regards his purpose as a reasonable reward for Gorgias' kindness. This proposal, on which primarily the whole action swings—or a considerable part of it—is an excellent evidence of Athenian feeling about marriage, a feeling of which we must ceaselessly remind ourselves if we are not to be repelled or mystified by ancient comedies.

A good part of the Argument of the PRIESTESS (Ἱέρεια) is found in a fragment [2] from a book which seems to have given a complete collection of Menander's plots. All that we formerly possessed of this play was a phrase about " the peeping ass," and seven lines [3] on superstition. ' Madam, no god saves one man by means of another. For if a man by using cymbals draws the god to his wishes, he is greater than the god. No, Rhode : these are the instruments of daring wickedness invented by shameless men and constructed to turn our generation into a laughing-stock.' Our new Argument, so far as it is legible, runs thus.[4] ' The former husband of the priestess . . . having recovered, tried to seek out the son whom he loved. His servant was persuaded to be brought to the priestess under pretence of being possessed, in order that he might be

---

[1] A charming point: they are probably father and son, though neither knows it.
[2] *Ox. Pap.*, X, pp. 83 *sqq*. The account of the *Priestess* is followed by the beginning of the Argument of the *Imbrians* (Ἴμβριοι).
[3] Fr. 245.
[4] The translation is by Grenfell and Hunt. The dots indicate lacunæ in the papyrus.

accorded treatment; and he secretly obtained information and discovered the truth. The true son of the mother of the supposititious child, desiring to marry the daughter of the priestess, sent his brother to speak with the priestess about him. While the women were talking [the old man, who] had become suspicious, and especially in consequence of the information of his servant that there was a difference in personal appearance, addresses the younger of his neighbours' sons as his own. The youth discerning his mistake intimidates his brother in advance, saying that the old man was mad and was declaring every young man to be his son. Accordingly when the old man subsequently learned the truth and addressed the elder as his son, the latter sends him away as being mad. At the same time . . . the old man having recovered his son marries the priestess, and the son receives the daughter of his foster-parents and the younger and true son of the neighbours receives the daughter of the priestess whom he had loved, and the marriages of all three pairs are celebrated. . . . Such are the incidents of the plot. The play is one of the best.' It is clear that there was an element of farce in the attempt of the father to identify his son, and also perhaps in the " symptoms " of the slave-detective who entered what appears to have been the Priestess's private lunatic-asylum. Very likely her elderly bridegroom at the close read her a lesson on quasi-religious psychotherapy, of which the fragment about cymbals would form a part.

The HERO ($"H\rho\omega\varsigma$) stands first [1] in the Cairo papyrus. Into the usual rape-story intrudes the slave Daos, who loves Plangon and to shield her takes the responsibility for her plight. The opening scene shows him agonizing in love and suspense, owing to the absence of his master, who has promised Plangon to him. What happens to

---

[1] One play originally preceded it, for our first play is headed $\kappa\theta$ (29). The missing twenty-eight pages would contain nearly one thousand lines, just the correct length for a Menandrian play.

this noble slave we do not know except that he is disappointed of his beloved, who marries her violator. As we possess the first two pages devoted to the play, we gain certain introductory matter. First comes, or came, the title;[1] next, a metrical argument in twelve lines, from which we learn the "story," including the resolve of Daos. Finally, there is a list of *dramatis personæ*, nine in number, including "the god Hero," who is named third. This Hero was no doubt a deified ancestor, the genius of the family, like the *Lar familiaris* who speaks the prologue of Plautus' *Aulularia*. We are no doubt to understand, not only that he knows all the past events, but also that his benevolent interest brings about a happy solution of all the difficulties. As he is named third, after Geta and Daos, it is clear that his prologue (lost) must have been delivered after the introductory scene in which Daos reveals to Geta his love, anxiety and (now lost) his purpose. This arrangement is not unparalleled and shall be discussed later.

Interest attaches to the FLATTERER (Κόλαξ) mostly because Terence[2] states that he has taken over into his *Eunuch* two of the characters, the parasite and the braggart soldier. The youth Pheidias and the soldier Bias both desire the same girl, the property of a slave-dealer or *leno*. Pheidias converses bitterly with some one: his father has gone away on business, leaving him an insufficient allowance. The conversation condemns the injustice of Heaven in permitting the scoundrel Bias to become rich. 'I suppose he has betrayed a city or a satrap or a camp—that is clear, for no just man ever grew rich quickly': οὐδεὶς ἐπλούτησεν ταχέως δίκαιος ὤν. 'Oh to denounce him in public for demoralizing us by showing that wickedness pays!' Later, an old slave dilates to Pheidias on the danger of flatterers, who bring great men to naught. Another passage shows the slave-dealer's business worries.

---

[1] We have only ΕΝΑΝΔΡΟΥ.   [2] *Eunuchus*, prol. 30 *sqq.*

'He will bring along sixty companions—as many as Odysseus led to Troy!—shouting and threatening: "Scoundrel! Have you sold her to a man with more money?"' One of the old fragments shows a cook offering sacrifice before a dinner of τετραδισταί, or men who dined together on the fourth of the month. It is likely that Pheidias was one of these, and as that day was sacred to Aphrodite Pandemos it is an attractive suggestion[1] that by her favour Pheidias wins the girl and humiliates Bias. Whether the assailants whom the dealer fears are the fellow-clubmen of Pheidias or Bias' comrades-in-arms is not plain, unless we bring in the Terentian play. There the soldier Thraso with his flatterer Gnatho makes an abortive attack on the house where the heroine is living. Some of the old fragments closely resemble passages in Terence: Bias boasts of having surpassed King Alexander in toping, and Struthias laughs at the memory of his leader's witticism upon some Cyprian. Our papyrus contains a scholium about Astyanax of Miletus, a noted Olympian victor, who distinguished himself in 316 B.C.; the *Flatterer* was therefore written not long after, and is a rather early play.

The HATED LOVER (Μισούμενος) was unusual and attractive in that it showed a " sympathetic " soldier.[2] For once ancient allusions, combined with " old " fragments, tell us something of the plot.[3] Thrasonides is a young soldier who has distinguished himself in the service of the Cyprian king.[4] He holds in his house a girl (whether purchased by him or taken prisoner in war) whom he wildly loves, named Crateia:

---

[1] Of van Leeuwen, *op. cit.*, p. 244.
[2] Hence this play is said (by modern scholars, not by any ancient authority) to have resembled the Περικειρομένη. But the central figure of the latter is plainly the girl; in the Μισούμενος it was probably the lover.
[3] There is no evidence for Kock's statement (III, p. 97) that "the girl was at length torn from him by a youthful rival". Kock was plainly generalizing from the usual procedure with regard to the *miles*.
[4] Fr. 340.

'A cheap serving-maid has cowed me, a thing no enemy has ever done'[1]—

παιδισκάριόν με καταδεδούλωκ' εὐτελές,
ὃν οὐδὲ εἶς τῶν πολεμίων οὐπώποτε.

But she repulses him: the title of the play suggests some definite grievance: 'his military uncouthness,' we are told.[2] Thrasonides, however, does not abuse his position and power—that is the notable feature. 'She is in my house: I can act, and wish to act, like one frantically in love, but I do not.'[3] At night he cannot sleep for distress, but leaves the house and paces the street. This created an effective scene, very likely the first, which would expound the situation: at any rate several of our old fragments fit in here. Thrasonides' restlessness has disturbed his batman Geta, who complains with the freedom often found in New Comedy slaves. 'Why don't you sleep? You are destroying me by this tramping up and down.'[4] His master confides in him.[5] 'Have you never been in love, Geta?' 'No: I never had a full stomach.' Thrasonides laments his hard fate[6] and makes the remarks about Crateia that we quoted first. Geta begs him to go indoors:[7] 'I see I shall have to lock you in at nights.'[8] Then or later Thrasonides meditates suicide;[9] he sends gifts and requests to the girl, and there was probably a scene of supplication, for we are not only told[10] that he 'implores and weeps,' which suggests an interview with her in presence of the audience: we have also two lines probably spoken by her: 'Sooner or later drunkenness will strip off this

---

[1] Fr. 338.
[2] Libanius, xxxi, iv, 512 (Reiske): στρατιωτικὴν ... ἀηδίαν νοσοῦντα τὸν ἄνθρωπον εἰς ἀπέχθειαν αὐτῷ κινῆσαι τὴν ἐρωμένην. Evidently he did not act so violently as Polemon in the Περικειρομένη, but apparently repelled her by his boasting and perhaps by exhibiting his wounds (cp. Phœnicides fr. 4, on p. 64). Othello used his experiences more tactfully.
[3] Fr. 336.   [4] Fr. 341.
[5] Fr. 345. (The situation is very like that in Theocritus, X, 7 sqq.) But the fragment does not certainly belong to this play.
[6] Frr. 335, 337.   [7] Fr. 342.   [8] Fr. 343.
[9] Arrian, Diss. Epict., IV, i, 19 sq.   [10] Ibid.

would-be deceptive pretence'.[1] Crateia's father arrives: no doubt he has been searching for her and arrives at a critical moment to ransom her. Father and daughter rapturously embrace: Thrasonides comes upon them and is enraged by the sight.[2] 'He looks a gray-haired old man—sixty, I should say—nevertheless, he shall rue it. You there! Whom do you think you are embracing and kissing?' The explanation is apparently given later to Thrasonides by his own father: he is filled with consternation, and we hear him begging his father to bring about his marriage with Crateia.

The APPARITION (Φάσμα), according to Terence,[3] was badly adapted by his enemy Luscius Lanuvinus, and in a note on Terence Donatus gives the story of Menander's play. A young man's stepmother had before her marriage born a daughter, whom she caused to be brought up secretly next-door. In order to have the girl's company, she made a passage through the wall between the houses. This aperture she masked by a kind of shrine, whither she often retired as if to her devotions. The young man saw the girl and imagined her a goddess; gradually the facts became known, he fell in love with her, and the play ended with their marriage. We possess only two passages. One is part of the prologue, consisting perhaps of a dialogue between two divinities.[4] The other is a brisk conversation-narrative of a freedman and the young Pheidias, who is apparently at the stage where he thinks the lady supernatural but already loves her; for he expresses his trouble more vaguely than most Menandrian (or other) lovers. The freedman rates him amusingly. 'You are too well-off. Your whole life is a sleep. What is wrong with you is that you have

---

[1] Fr. 339.
[2] Another likeness to the Περικειρομένη.
[3] *Eunuchus*, prol., 9.
[4] So Körte, p. lvi. He notes that second-person forms occur and compares the Luxuria and Inopia of Plautus' *Trinummus*. Sudhaus accounts for the second-person forms by supposing that the prologue-speaker quotes some one.

no genuine troubles, so you need an imaginary cure. You had better take up religion.'

There remain three comedies of which we possess really substantial knowledge.

The earliest is known as SAMIA, or the *Woman of Samos* (Σαμία), though we are not certain that this was really its title. The reasons for putting it early in the poet's career are a reference [1] to the parasite Chærephon, which smacks rather of Middle Comedy, and the strongly farcical manner of the interview between Demeas and Niceratus.

We open where Demeas is addressing a long narrative to the audience. '. . . for as soon as I entered I bustled my household along to prepare for the wedding.' He himself was busy in the store-chamber and noticed that amid the confusion the baby had been left crying alone in a room from which the pantry opened. Moschion's old nurse descended from the attic and began to comfort the child: ' Darling baby! Treasure! Where is Mammy?' Then she talked to herself and revealed to the unseen listener that the child is Moschion's. Warned by a fellow-servant that the master was within earshot, she took it away. Demeas came out quietly and after a while saw the Samian girl, Chrysis, suckling the baby. He is filled with horror: the child is hers, but who is the father? Demeas himself, or— ? He will not put the thought into words, for the youth has always been well-conducted and shown reverence for Demeas. But the nurse's words! Here his monologue is interrupted by his slave Parmenon,[2] who enters, chaffing the cook engaged for the wedding dinner. Demeas summons Parmenon and asks him ' Whose is the baby?' Parmenon with some embarrassment replies that it belongs

---

[1] v. 258, Körte: cp. p. xxxiii of his edition.
[2] What is the plot-value of this scene? It makes no difference at all to Demeas' feelings and later action. Why, then, insert it? Mainly to break up Demeas' soliloquy, which would otherwise be too long; secondarily to give a little relief: Demeas' brief questioning has its amusing side, and the cook is the stock comic figure in these plays.

to Chrysis. 'And who is the father?' 'You, master.' Demeas in a rage asserts that Moschion is the father, and threatens Parmenon, who runs away, leaving the other in a fury of pain and anger. But it cannot be Moschion's fault, for if it were he would still be opposed to his father, whereas he has given no explanation and has welcomed the suggested marriage. No; Chrysis must have tempted and overborne him. Moschion cannot have deliberately wronged Demeas, 'not if he were ten times merely an adopted son'. In anguish he strives to tear love from his heart, determined to thrust Chrysis out of the house. But he must not tell her the true reason: there is a good pretext in her adoption of the baby. He rushes into the house, almost knocking over the cook, who has come out looking for Parmenon.[1] In a moment Demeas returns with Chrysis and a nurse carrying the baby. Despite her amazement, grief, and affectionate pleading, he insists that she shall depart: he took her from a life of poverty, and this is her gratitude; let her seek her proper place among the lowly courtesans. He goes within, leaving her at the door, weeping. Their neighbour, Niceratus, enters, bringing a scraggy sheep for sacrifice. Chrysis tells him that she has been cast out for adopting the baby, though Demeas had not been angry at the time. (*At this point occurs a gap of about a hundred and forty lines.*) Demeas and Niceratus have been conversing excitedly, and now Niceratus, exclaiming 'All is lost!' rushes into his house. Demeas soliloquizes in alarm on the other's hot temper. 'I ought to be put to death! . . . Heavens, how he is shouting! There! He is calling for *fire!* He says he will burn the baby!! In a minute I shall see a roast grandson!!!!' Niceratus flounces out again: Chrysis (he says) has persuaded his wife and daughter to confess nothing and refuses to hand over the child. 'Don't be surprised if I kill the woman!' 'Don't do that, Niceratus,' falters Demeas.

[1] This incident has no value beyond avoiding an empty stage: the cook talks for a moment until Demeas returns.

'I just thought I'd tell you,' explains the other, leaping into his house once more. Next moment, the terrified Chrysis, carrying the child, runs out pursued by her host, who brandishes his walking-stick. Demeas throws himself between them and bids Chrysis retreat into his house [1] while he engages in a tussle with Niceratus. After she has disappeared the two seniors calm down a little and take to verbal conflict. In the end Demeas consoles his neighbour by reminding him of the story about Zeus and Danae. 'Doesn't your roof leak anywhere?' 'Everywhere. What of it?' 'In Danae's case Zeus turned himself into gold; this time it is water. Depend upon it: your daughter's child is of divine birth.' Moreover, says Demeas, Moschion will certainly marry her: 'put everything in order for the wedding'. (*Interval, in which the chorus performs.*) Moschion soliloquizes. He is so enraged by his father's accusation, though it has now been met and withdrawn, that he is inclined to go soldiering in Bactria or Caria. But he cannot leave Plangon, whom he loves. Still, he will pretend that he is going, so as to teach his father a lesson. Parmenon is sent by him to fetch a sword and a military cloak, but returns from the house without them, announcing that the marriage is afoot: all is well. Moschion drives him in again with savage blows to fetch the gear, and stands pondering: 'But suppose father doesn't beg me to stay, loses his temper, and agrees to my departure?'

It has been thought better to give an account of the *Samia* first in this form rather than to begin with a reasoned but devitalized " story of the play," that the reader may relish the blend of suspense, amusement, and annoyance at enigmas inevitable for those who approach Menander's text as it now stands.

The story, then, is somewhat as follows. Demeas

---

[1] Exactly reversing his recent treatment of Chrysis. The wild fun of the scene may have been increased by "business" in which he and she interchange their earlier gestures.

has a Samian mistress called Chrysis, and they are heartily fond of one another, but he does not wish to have a child. He and Niceratus have both been from home for a considerable time. During their absence Chrysis bears a child [1] to Demeas, but it is still-born. Moschion seduces Plangon, daughter of Niceratus; apparently they dare not marry because Niceratus is poor [2] and therefore Demeas would not consent. Plangon bears a child which Moschion brings to his father's house, where Chrysis nurses it as if her own. All these facts are familiar to every one in the two houses, except the fathers, who know only that Chrysis has found a child which she persuades Demeas to let her adopt.[3] Then Demeas, imagining an affair between Chrysis and Moschion, turns her out and she is given refuge in Niceratus' house. Demeas [4] taxes Moschion with his fault and learns that Plangon, not Chrysis, is the child's mother; Niceratus sees or hears something in his own house between Chrysis, Plangon, and his wife (all three or any two of these) that makes him wonder about the baby's parentage; he consults Demeas, who ought to be the father of any child of Chrysis; the drift of their conversation forces Demeas to tell Niceratus that the baby is Plangon's, but his desire to shield Moschion makes him profess not to

---

[1] This, with what follows, seems the best account of the baby, or babies.
[2] Cp. the skinny sheep and the leaky roof.
[3] Probably he finds her with it on his return and consents to a *fait accompli*.
[4] The statements in this sentence cover the gap of 140 lines. They do not agree entirely with any of the editors, but none of these has offered an explanation that fits what immediately follows the gap and is completely plausible in itself; for instance, Allinson's idea, that Niceratus has been informed that the baby adopted by Chrysis is a foundling of unknown parentage, does not account for Niceratus' furious pursuit of the baby. In the explanation given above there is one weakness: it fails to show how the conversation between the two elders leads Demeas into the statement about Plangon; but that is not a flaw, only an incompleteness. Whether "taxes" is the right word or not, vv. 271-293 show that Moschion now knows of Demeas' former suspicion, which Demeas had intended to mention to no one (vv. 136 *sq.*). That Niceratus knows of Plangon's baby and does not know who is its father, the Zeus-passage proves incontestably: otherwise it would be as irrelevant as it is absurd.

know the father. This revelation drives Niceratus to frenzy: he chases Chrysis with his own grandson out of his house, but is calmed [1] at last by Demeas' promise that Moschion shall marry his daughter. Later Moschion makes a plan to pretend that he is going abroad as a soldier, in disgust with his father, and in this he persists though Parmenon tells him that the wedding preparations are afoot and all is well.

The rest is in outline obvious. Moschion acknowledges to all that he is the father of Plangon's child and they are married. Chrysis is reconciled to Demeas; it may be that she is discovered to be an Athenian and so is married to him; she may even prove to be Moschion's sister. But at least two difficulties remain. Why does Moschion angrily wave aside Parmenon's news that all is well because the wedding preparations are in progress? There seems to have been trouble from the beginning about some marriage of Moschion's: to whom, and what is its relation with his love for Plangon?[2] The other point is the youth's pretended enlistment. Certainly it is introduced with fair plausibility; but to what can it lead, for he does not intend to leave home?[3] Now, Moschion has expected to be begged to stay; later he has misgivings: 'Suppose father is angry and lets me go! A pretty fool I shall look!' This leads us to suppose that Menander followed neither one line nor the other, but gave the interview a novel turn: Demeas, stung by grief and indignation, cries: 'Ah! If only you were really my son!' Moschion, thunderstruck to find that he is only an adopted son and has meditated so ungrateful

---

[1] The brilliant nonsense about Zeus has nothing to do with this: beyond amusing the audience, it has but one purpose—to give Niceratus time to simmer down.

[2] We may provisionally accept the view (van Leeuwen, p. 98) that Demeas, at first actually or potentially opposed to Moschion's marriage with Plangon, has suddenly seen cause to arrange the marriage. This would account both for the seduction and for the marriage preparations. But even so, one does not understand Moschion's attitude towards Parmenon's news.

[3] The extraordinarily clever and satisfying explanation that follows is van Leeuwen's (p. 100).

a return for nurture on which he has no claim, begs forgiveness and then asks about his true parents. This would bring about a scene of birth-tokens, and so perhaps the recognition of Chrysis as his sister.

Thus, possessing little more than one-third of this play, we can nevertheless work out the plot with tolerable confidence. We can even see how the construction depends on the pyschology: Demeas' refusal to tell Chrysis the genuine reason for her expulsion, Moschion's concealment of his love from Demeas, his false enlistment—all these are levers of the action, and all spring from character. To Demeas' opening speech it is hard to render full justice—a triumph of the "New" manner: elegant without affectation, detailed without elaboration, exciting yet unhurried, it is a masterpiece of urbanity in style, of clearness in narration. Let anyone seek in Homer, Euripides, Plato, or the Orators, such perfect relation of a story containing several characters, household topography, varied emotion, and he will realize what Menander has achieved. Another first-rate passage is the expulsion, a touching scene of pathos on both sides. Chrysis' love, pain, and bewilderment are admirably depicted, but Demeas' plight is magnificent drama; the misery that he is forced to suppress heightens and excuses the cruel rage that he is at liberty to display. At the same instant he is hateful, pitiable, and absurd. Finally, the interview between the fathers is delicious, ranging from touches of the same pathetic comedy to knockabout farce. Niceratus popping in and out of his front-door with instalments of his bloodthirsty plan is quite as good as Ford's attempts to catch Falstaff.

In the SHORN LADY (Περικειρομένη) plot-details were probably complicated even in the first instance by a vivacious coming-and-going, which includes an abortive siege, as in Terence's *Eunuchus*. It will therefore be convenient to give the story first.

The wife of a Corinthian named Patæcus died in

giving birth to twins, a boy and a girl ; at the same time
he lost his fortune in a shipwreck and therefore exposed
the infants. These were discovered by a poor old
woman who kept the girl but handed over the boy to
a rich lady named Myrrhine. When times grew bad,
the old woman gave her foster-child, Glycera, to a
soldier, Polemon, for his concubine. As her end
approached, realizing that Glycera's position was
insecure and that she might need the help of her rich
brother, the old woman told Glycera all that she herself
knew and gave her the birth-tokens found with her.
She died. Polemon bought a house next to that in
which Myrrhine is living with her adopted son
Moschion, who thinks he is her real son (and with her
husband Patæcus ?). Glycera has told no one of her
relationship to Moschion, not wishing to spoil his
brilliant position. But Moschion, while Polemon is
absent, has conceived a passion for Glycera, and one
evening as she stood at her door, he ran up, threw his
arms round her and began to kiss her. Knowing that
he was her brother she did not recoil.[1] At that moment
Polemon returned, saw the encounter, and imagined
that Moschion was a favoured rival. Moschion made
himself scarce ; Polemon in fury cut off Glycera's
hair and retired in dudgeon to a country house ; the
girl took refuge with Myrrhine. Moschion thinks
she has done this so as to be near him, but his self-
complacency is destroyed by Myrrhine's stern refusal
to permit his advances. Polemon soon repents and
sends his slave Sosias to the town-house on trivial
errands—really to see what is going on—and finds that
Glycera has left him. He and his followers prepare
to storm [2] her refuge, but Patæcus makes him see

---

[1] v. 37 : οὐκ ἔφυγε.
[2] I cannot refrain from recording a strange and touching fact. Sudhaus (who was killed in the Great War) writes in the brief preface to his second edition, over the date 12th August, 1914 : " Οἱ παῖδες ἐπὶ τὰ πελτία ['To arms, my lads !'] was the last verse that I annotated on the first of August. Twenty-four hours later I was standing on the frontier." Countrymen of Mr. A. E.

reason. The soldier begs Patæcus to intercede with Glycera and in his artless suffering insists on showing him the attractive belongings that he has given her. Something among her possessions makes Patæcus curious about her origin. Next he has an interview with her, urging a reconciliation. She replies with firmness and dignity. Her self-defence leads her to produce the casket of her birth-tokens, and Patæcus finds that she is his daughter. Still she says nothing of Moschion; but somehow his parentage comes to light. Polemon arrives, knowing at last that the kiss was " innocent " and feverishly urging his slave, Doris, to bring about a reconciliation: he is more afraid than ever that Glycera, having found a wealthy father, will not return to him. But she greets him with loving forgiveness, Patæcus gives her a substantial dowry, and the marriage is arranged. Of this Moschion is a concealed auditor, but when his father tersely continues: 'I have another wedding to arrange: for my son I am taking Philinus' daughter,' the youth suddenly cries ' Good God ! ' and our papyrus ends with amusing abruptness.

The date of the *Shorn Lady* lies in the latest years of the fourth century, when Menander was about forty. Our evidence is a mention of the " Corinthian troubles ";[1] and other passages show that the scene was laid in Corinth. The selection of this city rather than Athens is vital. Glycera is not, indeed, a wife, but the most reputable kind of concubine.[2] Now, in Athens Polemon would have possessed a legal right to force her to return home,[3] and the bottom would have

Housman will note with a thrill that the passage (vv. 202 *sqq.* Sudhaus) goes on to speak of a mercenary army:

Οἱ παῖδες ἐπὶ τὰ πελτί'. οὗτοι πρὶν πτύσαι
διαρπάσονται πάντα, κἂν τετρωβόλους
καλῆς.

[1] Körte (p. xliii) dates the play at 305 or 304, Capps (p. 146) at 302 or 301.
[2] Polemon says (v. 239): ἐγὼ γαμετὴν νενόμικα ταύτην. Cp. *pro uxore* in Terence (*Andria*, 273) and *in uxoris loco* (*Heaut.*, 104).
[3] This was the right of a husband over his wife unless indeed she succeeded in a suit of ἀπόλειψις, and it is a natural assumption that this right included a παλλακή also.

dropped out of our play. As it is, Pataecus tells him bluntly: 'She may have loved you; but now that she is grievously offended you must win her back: she is her own mistress (ἑαυτῆς ἐστ' ἐκείνη κυρία)'.[1] The *locale* of the drama thus makes possible a human and permanently interesting situation. The prologue presents two important features. As in the *Hero* and in *Arbitration*, it occurs after the first act, when the attention of the audience has been gained, and tells the earlier history of 'the girl whom you saw just now'.[2] It is delivered by Ignorance (Ἄγνοια) who states[3] that she intends to bring about the revelation and recognition. What a promise to put into the mouth of personified ignorance! Is there any excuse? We shall see.

Even in its mutilation, this is a fascinating work, full of sparkle and gracious charm. There are many things we do not know: the relation of Pataecus to Myrrhine, what part Habrotonon the courtesan plays[4] —even whether she speaks or not—whether Moschion drives away[5] the besiegers or skulks till they have gone,[6] how his relationships are revealed, and often who is the speaker of a given line. But at least two beautiful qualities are here unmistakable. One, strange though it appears, lies in construction. For, however defective one's knowledge of the details, it is plain that Menander has wrought superbly: he has achieved that most difficult, rarest and most charming feat of a dramatist, to make the plot *solve itself*. Glycera finds her father and secure happiness because of Polemon's outrage; that outrage was caused by Moschion's amorous outbreak *combined with* Glycera's reception of it; and that combination happens only because their origin is a secret. Moschion is discovered to be

---

[1] vv. 241 *sqq.*   [2] v. 7.   [3] vv. 42 *sqq.*
[4] She has no doubt been playing the flute at the party wherewith Polemon sought to drown his sorrows; but why does he bring her into town for the onslaught upon Myrrhine's house? (One of the rare obscenities in the extant Menander is addressed to her.)
[5] So Körte, p. xli.   [6] So Allinson, p. 251.

her brother precisely because no one (save Glycera) knows that he is. Menander was naturally proud of this masterpiece: he causes Glycera to expound part of it in her last words to Polemon, and he indicates the quality of the whole by giving his prologue to Ignorance, of all people, who boasts that she will reveal all.

Further, there is beautiful characterization. Pataecus and the slaves do not count for much here, and Moschion is not striking, though we enjoy his bumptious [1] pride in his imaginary powers as a lady-killer, which makes him clay in the none too skilful fingers of Daos. Polemon is more vivid. His passion for Glycera, his sudden madness of jealousy, his remorse, his artless pleading with Pataecus and simple pride in the delightfulness of his beloved when arrayed in her wonderful clothes, and his half-hysterical talk with the slave-girl who is to plead his cause ('Excellent! Excellent! Go in. I'll make you a free woman this very day, Doris ')—all these skilful touches combine to win our rather amused affection. And each of those qualities is directly dramatic: every one of them causes a development of the action. Glycera herself is the radiant centre of the whole comedy. Loving Polemon deeply, she yet will not return to him at the price of her self-respect: 'After this let him wreak his insolence on others: he has wickedly ill-treated me as though I were a slave.'[2] But in the hour of his suppliant repentance she forgives, with no weak sentimentality or patronizing tartness, but with the sunny wisdom of a fine nature: 'Why yes; for it was your fit of anger that began all our happiness'.[3] Her trouble sprang entirely from the goodness and sagacity wherewith she guarded the comfort of her unconscious and undeserving brother. When Polemon taxed [4] her with infidelity, two words from her would have made all well,

---

[1] He resembles the young country squires of English social comedy, for instance Tony Lumpkin in *She Stoops to Conquer*.
[2] vv. 315 *sqq*.   [3] vv. 443 *sqq*.
[4] We do not possess this scene, but it must have been acted or reported early in the play.

but they were not spoken, and she quietly faced his brutal yet not unnatural anger. All these virtues unite to compose a beautiful scene whereof a mutilated passage survives, the interview [1] in which Patæcus urges her to be reconciled to her lover. So much is plain, that she not only refuses to accept love on such unworthy terms but sees occasion also to defend herself for taking refuge in the house where Moschion lives. ' Can you believe that I fled to his mother so that he should marry me ?—or no : why that ?—in hopes to become his mistress ? If so, should we not both have avoided his parents ? Would he have thus rashly brought me to his father ? Should I without a blush have embraced such folly as to offend Myrrhine and give you a suspicion of my immodesty that nothing would wipe out ? Can it be that you, Patæcus—you too !—have come to me convinced of that, thinking that I was such an one ? ' Patæcus answers with kindness, but urges the " wise " course, that she return to her protector ; she replies firmly : ' I best know my own affairs '.[2] In this strength is no hardness : the long-past sorrow of another draws from her an instant cry of sympathy.[3]

Glycera has been described as " almost Shakespearian," which is meant as high praise but is in fact ruinously bad criticism. There can be little comparison between the two dramatists. Shakespeare's heroines are either vastly greater, more vital, than Glycera, or vastly inferior to her—in character, however, they surpass her in beauty of language. It would be ludicrous to speak of Cleopatra in the same breath as of her. On the other side, Cordelia, Miranda, and Desdemona are mere lovely puppets, dramatically effective only in a negative way—that is, by the force of the opinions and emotions they arouse in others. Imogen and Portia of Belmont may, by their enterprise, remind us a little of Glycera ; but Portia is in no danger, and of Imogen we know that ' her beauty and her brain go

---

[1] vv. 301 *sqq.*   [2] v. 326 : ἐγῴδα τἄμ' ἄριστα.   [3] v. 377.

not together'. As for the Helena of *All's Well*, her dogged bed-hunting may arouse compassionate wonder and even respect, despite the cold-blooded indecency of her stupid talk with the Clown; but she is wooden, utterly below the gallant finely-strung girl whom Menander portrays.

Most notable of all is ARBITRATION ('Επιτρέποντες, ' persons submitting their dispute to an arbitrator ') which was among the most celebrated Menandrian works and of which we possess some three-fifths: one mass gives no less than three hundred and sixty consecutive lines.

The reader comes abruptly upon two quarrelling slaves: Daos, a shepherd, and Syriscus, a charcoal-burner, with whom is his wife, carrying a baby. They submit their cases to an old man who approaches, Smicrines. Daos explains [1] that a month ago he found in the woods a baby, which he at first decided to rear; later he began to count the cost, and when his acquaintance Syriscus begged the child he handed it over. Afterwards, Syriscus heard of certain ornaments exposed with the child and is now demanding them. Skilful argumentation is laid before Smicrines, Daos insisting that Syriscus has enough already and should not demand jewellery as well as child, Syriscus urging that the child is being robbed not only of property but also of a clue to his parentage. Smicrines adjudges the jewellery to the infant and the infant to Syriscus, and departs after making Daos surrender the trinkets. Syriscus is counting them over into his wife's gown when Onesimus, another slave, catches sight of a ring, which he recognizes as belonging to his master Charisius, who lost it when drunk. He takes it for delivery to Charisius. An interval [2] follows, after which Onesimus comes out and tells the audience that he has several

---

[1] Here Menander commits the fault which Terence (*Eun.*, prol., 10 *sqq.*) twits Luscius Lanuvinus with committing in his version of the Θησαυρός—causing the defendant to open the case.
[2] Marked by ΧΟΡΟΥ in the MS.

times been on the point of showing the ring to Charisius but has shirked, for his " revelations " have already got him into trouble. " Again and again he says ' Zeus destroy the evil man that told me this ! ' I fear he may be reconciled with his wife and kill me who told him this and know the secret." While Onesimus stands irresolute, Habrotonon comes out, but neither sees the other for a while. He mutters over his perplexity. Her remarks show that she is a musician whom Charisius has hired for his party ; she has been in his house two days, but he has had no amorous dealings with her. Syriscus enters and talks about the ring to Onesimus, who explains (part of) his hesitation. The ring proves Charisius father of the baby ; he lost it during the Tauropolia, an all-night festival celebrated by women ; clearly there was a rape and the unknown girl has exposed the infant thus begotten. Syriscus goes. Habrotonon, who has overheard, comes forward and discusses the affair with Onesimus. She remembers observing at that very festival a girl belonging to the company for whom she herself was playing : she wandered away by herself and came back with her clothes torn and in great distress. Who this girl was Habrotonon did not know, but she would recognize her if they met. This may well be the child's mother, but Habrotonon feels that she must first discover its father, since, though the child's ring belonged to Charisius, he may have parted with it in some other way, and so need not be the father. Till she finds who wronged the girl she saw, she is unwilling to reveal the rape to the girl's friends, of whom it would be necessary to ask her name and family. Habrotonon therefore decides to pose, with infant and ring, to Charisius as the child's mother. If he lost the ring while committing the rape, he will reveal it ; then, knowing the father, she will seek the true mother. Incidentally she will surely be given her freedom as a reward ; she promises to give Onesimus credit also. He remains to soliloquize on her cunning, till he sees Smicrines approaching in excitement. The text now tails off into scraps, but apparently he withdraws and Smicrines enters talking angrily about the dissolute behaviour of his son-in-law Charisius.

Another fragment shows Habrotonon recognizing some woman (either Pamphile, the wife of Charisius, or Sophrone, the old nurse of Pamphile) and revealing that she is not the mother but has so given it out in order to find the true mother. They enter the house to confer (and no doubt the baby is restored to its mother, Pamphile, who learns that Charisius, her husband, is its father). Onesimus enters and relates that he has watched Charisius over-hearing a conversation between his wife and her father Smicrines, which has filled Charisius with violent remorse. Onesimus dreads punishment for slandering Pamphile, and retreats on hearing his master's approach. Charisius in an agonized soliloquy reproaches himself for punishing his wife because of an involuntary act similar to one that he himself voluntarily committed: she has nobly told her father that she married him for better for worse; with what stupid pride he has requited her!

In a much briefer passage Habrotonon reveals to Charisius that the child, which he knows to be his, is also the child not of Habrotonon but of Pamphile.

Another, evidently close to the end, shows Smicrines again furiously approaching the house, apparently to fetch his daughter away by force. Onesimus reads him a lecture on morals and theology, finally revealing (supported by Sophrone) that Smicrines has a legitimate grandson.

This account ignores a number of passages. Readers who examine *Arbitration* in any of the editions will gain a fuller conception of this comedy; but the idea gained will depend upon the edition used, for many of our papyrus scraps are so tattered that reconstructions diverge disconcertingly. Certain characters—Chærestratus and the Cook [1]—hover fitfully on the

---

[1] We know from Athen., 659b, that he provided the funny element.

verge of our knowledge. The St. Petersburg fragment (parchment, not papyrus), if correctly assigned [1] to this play, shows that Charisius' quarrel with his wife has gone so far that he is actually living in a brothel.[2] We are not certain that Pamphile had a speaking part: her speech of loyalty is only reported by Charisius. Above all, we do not know how important Habrotonon's imposture was: that is, how long did she pose as the mother? Was it long enough to create a new situation for Pamphile? That is a vital question.[3]

But the mere " story " is plain enough. At a midnight festival Charisius violated Pamphile; neither saw the other's face, but the girl snatched a ring from him during the struggle. Four months later she was given with a large dowry by her father Smicrines in marriage to Charisius. Later the husband went away on business, and during his absence Pamphile bore a child, the result of her misfortune. Helped by Sophrone, she exposed it together with certain tokens, including the ring. Charisius' slave, Onesimus, discovered these facts and on his master's return divulged them to him. Charisius, in rage, left his wife and stayed

---

[1] By Capps (pp. 34 *sq.*), followed by van Leeuwen, Wilamowitz and others.

[2] The house next to that of Charisius is supposed to belong to Chærestratus but to have been rented by a *leno*.

[3] In any case her imposture gives her importance. Thus Wilamowitz, (p. 124) regards her fortunes and those of Pamphile as equally engrossing. But was there a substantial part of the play during which she was accepted by all as the mother? If so, as Croiset (*L'Arbitrage*, p. 2) aptly remarks, she both prepares and retards the solution. Capps (p. 39) seeks to prove that when Smicrines and Pamphile engage in the talk overheard by Charisius, they cannot have been told that Charisius is father of Habrotonon's child; but his proof fails because we cannot assume (see his own text) that Smicrines goes in to see Pamphile at the same time that Habrotonon enters to tell Charisius her story. There is an admirable German play, *Das Schiedsgericht*, "translated by Alfred Körte, completed by Friedrich von Oppeln-Bronikowski" (Leipzig, no date), which assumes, and makes striking use of, the assumption that Pamphile does hear Habrotonon's story. It contains an impressive speech (p. 60) to this effect: "My rival overbears me in the eyes of Charisius because she has a child and I have none. I put my baby away so as to keep my husband, and through that very fact I am losing him." This is excellent, precisely that blend of pathos and clever ratiocination so notable in Euripides and bequeathed by him to Menander.

in a neighbouring house, where he lived dissolutely; in particular he hired a girl-musician, Habrotonon, but did not actually co-habit with her owing to his love for Pamphile. Smicrines, hearing of this extravagant behaviour, and trembling for the dowry more than for his daughter,[1] comes to fetch her home. On the way he arbitrates between Daos and Syriscus, thus unconsciously saving his grandson for his true parents. He seeks in vain to persuade Pamphile to leave Charisius. Habrotonon lays the plan already described. Charisius learns almost at the same moment both that he is the father of an illegitimate child and that his wife, whom he has treated brutally for bearing one against her will, regards him with unselfish loyalty. After realizing his own vanity and baseness he learns that his child and his wife's are one and the same; he goes within and the three are united. Smicrines, who has gone back to town, returns to take his daughter away by force, learns the truth from Onesimus and Sophrone, and is reconciled. Habrotonon (surely) is given her freedom; probably she speaks for Onesimus and gains his liberty also; no doubt these two marry.

The two important scenes that survive witness eloquently to Menander's power, each in a different way. Habrotonon's talk with Onesimus exemplifies his skill in plot. First she describes the night-scene at the Tauropolia, briefly but how vividly! 'At that time I did not know what a man was.... Suddenly she ran up—no one with her—crying and tearing her hair; her frock was ruined—such a lovely delicate dress! It was just one rag'—

> εἶτ' ἐξαπίνης κλάουσα προστρέχει μόνη,
> τίλλουσ' ἑαυτῆς τὰς τρίχας, καλὸν πάνυ
> καὶ λεπτόν, ὦ θεοί, ταραντῖνον σφόδρα
> ἀπολωλεκυῖ', ὅλον γὰρ ἐγεγόνει ῥάκος.

[1] Cp. Schol. Ambros. on *Odyssey*, VII, 225: Κομιδῇ γὰρ σμικρολόγος φαίνεται (sc. ὁ Ὀδυσσεὺς) προστάσσων τῶν φιλτάτων τὴν κτῆσιν, ὡς παρὰ Μενάνδρῳ ἐν Ἐπιτρέπουσιν (a good evidence of the fame of this play).

Then she lays her plan: there can be few examples of complication so elegantly constructed—" spun " is the better word. She considers every one, the baby that has won her affection (ὡς κομψόν, τάλαν—' so nice, bless it ! '), the girl at the Tauropolia, and Charisius. When we have appreciated this (not before) Onesimus drily adds: ' And you, no doubt, will get your freedom '. She agrees, with passionate hope, but we are sure that her other motives too are strong. Her plan itself is marked by the same delightful balance. She has to find the father while finding the mother, with no clues save one, the ring; it is a strange dramatic algebra: how to solve one equation containing two unknown quantities.

The arbitration scene is of the opposite kind. All is perfectly easy as a matter of construction, and interest is confined to presentation. Menander succeeds by his skill in forensic eloquence, which drew the warmest praise from Quintilian [1] himself. That he borrows the situation from Euripides' *Alope* matters little: the arguments plainly cannot have been taken from the tragedian. Daos and Syriscus give truly admirable displays: eloquent, convincing and somewhat amusing too, because though they make excellent sense they have a touch of formality that suggests burlesque of the professional barrister. And they are delightfully contrasted. Daos' speech is austerely logical, quite unadorned, appealing to the intelligence alone. His story gives the facts with utter bareness, implying a superhuman honesty. ' He kept on all day. I yielded to his prayers and arguments. I gave the child. He went away, invoking a thousand blessings. When he got the child he kissed my hands '—

> ὅλην τὴν ἡμέραν
> κατέτριψε· λιπαροῦντι καὶ πείθοντί με
> ὑπεσχόμην. ἔδωκ'· ἀπῆλθεν, μυρία
> εὐχόμενος ἀγαθά· λαμβάνων μου κατεφίλει
> τὰς χεῖρας.

[1] X, i, 69.

His peroration is equally terse. 'Conclusion. I gave you willingly one of my possessions. If it pleases you, keep it. If not, and you have changed your mind, give it back, inflicting no wrong and receiving none. But that you should have everything—part through my consent, part by force—is not right. I have finished.' Syriscus provides a perfect foil to this: his speech is florid, owes little to logic,[1] appeals openly to the emotions. He works up pathos about the child, bringing him forward in his arms as a mute pleader. 'He makes demand of you, Daos: these trinkets (he says) were hung upon him for his adornment, not to buy your meals.' It is a brilliant effect: good burlesque of the professional bar, yet perfectly sound emotional drama. Indeed Syriscus is in very truth "dramatic"—more so than anyone outside Sheridan's *Critic*: he appeals to the judge's theatrical experience. 'I am sure you have often been to the theatre (τεθέασαι τραγῳδούς, οἶδ' ὅτι): well, remember the story of Neleus and Pelias, how they were found by an aged goat-herd, dressed in skins like me, how by a wallet of tokens they found their true estate and the erstwhile goat-herd boys became kings. Now, if Daos had found *their* amulets and sold them for a few shillings. . . .' That is the acme of pathetic comedy: smiling yet earnest, charming yet utterly sophisticated.

We find only one other character so well drawn; for all that we know of Pamphile and Charisius [2] is two good emotional outbursts and the suggestive fact that Pamphile, for all her nobility, does not go so far as to tell Smicrines that she has born an illegitimate child.[3] But Habrotonon is a masterpiece. We have

[1] It does not occur to him to remark that Daos' whole argument implies that the baby is valuable, whereas he gave it away because it was a nuisance.

[2] Nevertheless his psychology is important to the action. Legrand (*Daos*, p. 407) excellently remarks: "Si Charisios était un brutal il aurait renvoyé Pamphilé et dévoilé au père la mésaventure de la malheureuse femme. S'il avait du sang-froid et s'il écoutait sa raison, il aurait pardonné de prime abord . . . une prétendue faute."

[3] "Else he would not be so arrogant in his attitude towards Charisius" (Capps, p. 39).

noted how self-seeking and thought for others are very naturally and engagingly combined in her device to discover the child's parents. She is a good-hearted girl: the baby delights her, and when she finds the mother she is full of sympathetic pleasure. If we had both this play and the *Shorn Lady* complete, it would be fascinating to compare her with Glycera. Even now the study is attractive. Both are kind, firm, and enterprising; but Glycera is a lady, whereas Habrotonon lacks delicacy: ἀγνὴ γάμων is her phrase to describe her relations with Charisius; she is just what the best of girls would be were she always attending Athenian wine-parties. A faintest faltering of that unequalled pen [1] would have made her either crude or " a perfect lady ".

Two passages are important both in themselves and also as showing Menander's ability to vivify a hackneyed theme. Near the close Smicrines, during his altercation with Onesimus, exclaims: ' Now by the gods. . . .' The slave pulls him up sternly. ' Smicrines! Do you imagine the gods have such abundant leisure that they allot evil and good to each person day by day? Let me explain. There are in the world approximately one thousand cities, each inhabited by thirty thousand people. Do the gods damn or save each of these individually? Impossible. That would mean a toilsome life indeed! " Then do not the gods take thought for us? " you may object. To each of us they assign, as commandant of the citadel, his character which dwells within and damns one man if he outrages it, but saves another. This character is the god in our life, the cause of each man's prosperity or ruin. Propitiate it by avoiding eccentric and misguided conduct so that you may prosper.' He applies this sermon to Smicrines' behaviour in attempting to take his daughter away by force, and ends superbly: ' Mind I don't catch you a second

[1] *Menander litterarum subtilitati sine aemulo genitus* (Pliny, *Nat. Hist.*, XXX, 27).

time acting so recklessly '.[1] Again, Charisius, bursting forth from his house in a passion of self-contempt and of adoration for his wife, astonishes us by a notably "modern" sentiment: he repudiates the so-called double law. Though Euripides often implies[2] this new moral equilibrium in discussing a woman's fate or conduct—indicating (that is) indirectly the double standard as the cause of her sorrow or sin—in no extant play does he raise the topic so explicitly as it is raised here. Charisius imagines God (τὸ δαιμόνιον) addressing him:[3]

> ἀκούσιον γυναικὸς ἀτύχημ' οὐ φέρεις,
> αὐτὸν δὲ δείξω σ' εἰς ὅμοι' ἐπταικότα.
> καὶ χρήσετ' αὐτή σοι τότ' ἠπίως. σὺ δὲ
> ταύτην ἀτιμάζεις. ἐπιδειχθήσει θ' ἅμα
> ἀτυχὴς γεγονὼς καὶ σκαιὸς ἀγνώμων τ' ἀνήρ.
> ὅμοιά γ' εἶπεν οἷς σὺ διενόου τότε
> πρὸς τὸν πατέρα.

'Thy wife's innocent mischance thou endurest not, but I will show that thou hast thyself stumbled into the same act. Then she shall use thee gently, but thou dishonourest her. Thou shalt be shown a wretch, stupid and heartless. Like thine own thoughts, verily, are the words she spoke to her father!'

We are now able to describe more at large Menander's quality under the three headings of style, dramaturgy and governing ideas or topics.

His style is one of the most perfect instruments to be found in any literature. A perfect instrument: that is, a style meant for a particular purpose and not for many: he wrote for the stage, and his excellence of style is a dramatic excellence. Certain purists cen-

---

[1] For the guardian genius cp. fr. incert. 550 Kock (pp. 167 *sq.*):

> ἅπαντι δαίμων ἀνδρὶ συμπαρίσταται
> εὐθὺς γενομένῳ, μυσταγωγὸς τοῦ βίου
> ἀγαθός.

A. Marpurgo (*Studi di Filologia Classica*, III, pp. 5-8) shows that the lecture as a whole is an absurd *pot-pourri* of Epicurus, Heraclitus, pseudo-Epicharmus and the Stoics.

[2] *E.g. Medea*, 606: τί δρῶσα; μῶν γαμοῦσα καὶ προδοῦσά σε; The active voice of γαμῶ is appropriate only to the man.

[3] vv. 493 *sqq.*

sured him viciously for incorrectness. " Menander's ὀψωνιασμός is abominable; he should have said ὀψώνιον."[1] " Αἰχμαλωτισθῆναι is so incorrect that not even Menander used it."[2] They would have had him employ good Attic words found in writers not later than Demosthenes, whereas like a sensible man he insisted on the speech of his own day. Vocabulary and idiom he uses precisely as does Plato[3] in his lighter dialogues, and precisely as every other writer of good conversation; he writes what is ostensibly the talk one hears while walking home from the theatre, but gives it point and finish. Yet it is also dramatic—brilliantly clear and thus tending to short sentences. With this simplicity is combined a limpid elegance, an unforced urbanity that defies translation and perhaps comparison. Terence has what measure of it the Latin language will permit; Congreve is more mannered, Goldsmith more commonplace; of all modern playwrights Schnitzler perhaps comes nearest, as one might have expected, the Viennese culture being a fascinating blend of the German and the French. Menander is rarely " brilliant "; except where the situation demands it, as in the pleading of Syriscus, he is never rhetorical. This explains why opinions may differ as to the precise degree of his excellence in style, even in the same reader's opinions from time to time. For it is a peculiarity of rhetoric that our estimate of it never varies. Henry the Fifth's harangue about St. Crispin's Day affects us always in exactly the same manner; not so the love-making beneath the stars of Verona. Lucan remains a steady blare of superhuman cleverness; Virgil changes like a landscape under sun, storm and twilight. Menander,

[1] Pollux, VI, 38.   [2] Phrynichus, *Epit.*, 418.
[3] The artistic principle is the same, but not (of course) the results. Wilamowitz makes the interesting remark (*Menander*, pp. 158 *sq.*) that between Plato and Menander the level of cultivated conversation has notably fallen : " the well-to-do Philistines of comedy and their sons have scarcely higher education and interests than their house-slaves". On the other hand, slaves in Menander are much " higher " than the Aristophanic.

for all that his range is narrower beyond comparison than Shakespeare's or Virgil's, shows this variable complexion too, because in him also humanity suffuses the very texture of the sentence.

There has been much ill-judged talk about his " poetry ". Menander is not a poet at all, except as the name is often conferred, by a natural looseness, on all dramatists using verse. He might as well have written in prose :[1] all the praises just given would have been equally in order. His verse, strictly as verse, possesses no merit whatever : it scans, that is all, sometimes easily, sometimes after effort : but how much rhythm is there in ὡς εὗρον, ὡς ἀνειλόμην· ὁ δὲ τότε μέν. . .? Other metres than the iambic are rare. In the *Samia* trochaics occur in the excited colloquy of the two fathers ; there was a lyrical scene in the *Possessed Woman* ; a few anapæsts survive from the *Woman of Leucas*. Poetry, then, in the strict sense must be denied to Menander ; but he has two other methods of intensifying literary effect. One is an occasional tinge of tragic diction where appropriate. That he was an enthusiast for Euripides is well-known ; and we find one direct quotation from his master. At the close of *Arbitration* Sophrone explains Pamphile's plight by a verse or two from the *Auge* :

ἡ φύσις ἐβούλεθ', ᾗ νόμων οὐδὲν μέλει·
γυνὴ δ' ἐπ' αὐτῷ τῷδ' ἔφυ.

'It was the will of Nature, which cares naught for law ; and a woman is born for this very purpose.' She threatens to recite the whole speech if Smicrines still does not understand. Syriscus in the arbitration scene quotes a precedent from the *Tyro* of Sophocles, and Demeas in the *Samia* gives " the tragedians " as his authority for Danae and the shower of gold. Menander's own diction rises at more solemn moments :[2] our best example is Charisius' soliloquy,

---

[1] Cp. Plutarch, *Quaest. Conviv.*, VII, 8, 3, 7 : ἥ τε γὰρ λέξις ἡδεῖα καὶ πεζή.

[2] Cp. Horace, *A.P.*, 93 : *interdum tamen et vocem comœdia tollit.*

where effect is gained by the simple device of avoiding resolved feet.

The other device is wit. From the "old" fragments one gathered that Menander was full of epigrams; this is hardly borne out by the recent discoveries,[1] and what general maxims we do find are mostly uttered by slaves, as in tragedy by the chorus-leader.[2] Downright jokes are not found, but there is plenty of quiet bizarrerie giving edge to perfectly relevant dialogue. In the *Samia*[3] Demeas, wishing to question his slave, begins: 'Listen, Parmenon: by the Twelve Gods, I have many reasons for my unwillingness to thrash you'. The spoiled young Moschion of the *Shorn Lady* recites a pompous speech that comes to a laughable anti-climax. 'In this present age many have sunk into misery, for throughout the Greek world (whatever be the cause) a flourishing crop exists thereof; but of all these, numerous as they are, I believe that no human being is so wretched as—I.'[4] The distraught Onesimus in *Arbitration* exclaims: 'Saviour Zeus, save me—if possible'.[5]

We have next to consider Menander's dramaturgy, his merits on the strictly dramatic side. Here our first impression may well be surprise at his submission to conditions that surely cramp his powers amazingly. First, why this omniscient prologue? Why introduce a deity who either reveals the progress and outcome of the action or at least tells us in narrative what should be revealed dramatically? The answer[6] falls into several parts. The prologue he inherited from Euripides; it is found in Aristophanes too, though less fully articulated; and at first social comedy (it appears)

[1] Cp. Sir F. G. Kenyon, *Quarterly Review*, 208, p. 341.
[2] Wilamowitz, *Menander*, p. 151.   [3] vv. 90 *sqq*.
[4] Περικειρομένη, vv. 282 *sqq*.   [5] v. 486.
[6] M. Croiset (*Revue des Deux Mondes*, 1909, p. 818) takes an utterly different view: "En donnant directement au public les explications nécessaires ... le poète s'affranchissait de certaines exigences gênantes qui l'auraient obligé à charger son drame d'entretiens peu animés. Il se débarrassait des difficultés qui auraient entravé son génie, et il lui assurait ainsi un jeu plus franc et plus vif."

could hardly be imagined without it. Again, ancient audiences were less interested than we in finding how all is to end and very engrossed in the method by which the end is produced;[1] they would not usually feel that a prologue had spoiled the drama by giving away the secret. Then, as to imparting such information dramatically, we may observe Menander working towards this method. Sometimes he sets his prologue later than the opening, as in the *Hero* and the *Shorn Lady*. This may seem a clumsy device,[2] but it secured attention by a bright dramatic first scene; a similar method is common in our novels. Had he lived long enough, he might have woven his exposition entirely into the genuine drama; even now we observe " an ingenious piecemeal surrender of contributory details "[3]—the *Rosmersholm* effect in embryo.

A second kind of narrowness is found in the topics —or topic. His invariable " story " concerns, not love at large, but love-escapades. Satyrus' *Life of Euripides* reinforces the impression made by our fragments: '... The quarrels that we remark in comedy between husband and wife, father and son, master and slave, or the climaxes brought about by rapes, supposititious children, recognitions by rings and necklaces; for these of course are the framework of New Comedy and were brought to perfection by Euripides.'[4] A strange manner of holding up the mirror to life![5] Such activities cannot be the staple

---

[1] Compare any extant tragedy, above all the *Œdipus Tyrannus*.
[2] Menander seems to have learnt it from Alexis, who employed it in his Κουρίς.
[3] Allinson, p. xvi. A later playwright (see p. 71 above) makes his prologuizing Dionysus ridicule the ordinary prologue-god.
[4] *Ox. Pap.*, IX, p. 49. Plutarch calls ἔρως the backbone of Menander's plays (ὁμαλῶς ἁπάντων ἓν συνεκτικόν ἐστιν, *ap.* Stob. 393), but praises him for his edifying treatment (*Symp.*, 712C). Croiset (*loc. cit.*, p. 824 f.) writes a brilliant comment on this feature. In Molière, "l'amour intervient généralement comme une cause de perturbation qui met l'homme en contradiction avec lui-même et par là fait ressortir plus fortement l'habitude morale qui le caractérise. . . ." In Menander, "le caractère se fait sous nos yeux et il se fait par l'amour."
[5] Quint., X, 70: *Ita omnem vitæ imaginem expressit.*

occupation of any society. Whatever we may have to say on Menander's method of filling in this outline, we cannot avoid astonishment that the outline satisfied him. Again the answer is complex. First, he must have been primarily more interested in treatment than in subject-matter,[1] herein resembling Shakespeare and differing utterly from Ibsen, whose combination of vital topic with superb workmanship makes him the greatest of all dramatists. Nor must the simple fact be forgotten that most playwrights wish their work to be produced: there is little sense in adopting an art-form that presupposes a large assembly and yet writing in a manner or on a subject that makes it certain there will be no assembly. Here lies whatever justification can be claimed for that oft-ridiculed couplet:

> The drama's laws the drama's patrons give:
> For they that live to please must please to live.

Menander was compelled to write on themes that would "please" and we are justified by his practice in assuming that no other than "love" had a prospect of success.

Thirdly, how small is the "world" whereof he treats! The *dramatis personæ* are few and stereotyped, their social conditions show little variety: the families belong to the undistinguished well-to-do or to the undistinguished poor. The social intercourse is notably casual. Every one at the slightest excuse goes off to live in the house of some one else; if that cannot be arranged, they run in and out of one another's houses or break holes in the walls like the ingenious Platæans in Thucydides. So constant is this practice that the street becomes more secluded than the hearth: if people have any private business to discuss they step out into the street, whereupon the neighbours edge up behind the porch to listen. All this social equality and unfettered coming and going will amuse us as crude technique until we observe that it is by no means

---

[1] What could be duller than the bald story of the *Priestess* set out above (pp. 325 *sq.*)?

confined to Menander.[1] We light here, in fact, upon a topic of the first importance for dramatic criticism.

Our customary use of the word " comedy " is absurdly wide and therefore misleading: the *Knights* and *Le Misanthrope* are both " comedies "; if we are to define comedy so as to include all such works we shall have to say that it is any drama of light tone, that (even if it treats of serious distress) at any rate excludes unrelieved agony. Such a definition is useless, and a great deal worse than useless, because it causes the innocent to compare work like Menander's with the Old Comedy. That is why discussion of critical labels is anything but waste of time, for blind acceptance of labels may ruin appreciation. Many plays are spoiled for us because we approach them in the wrong mood: it is disastrous to watch Euripides' *Helena* with a long face because Euripides is a tragedian, and *Arbitration* with a grin because Menander is a comedian. The *Helena* is a burlesque, the *Birds* is a farce; and many fail to enjoy them fully through taking Theonoe seriously and looking for a " message " in the streets of Cloudcuckootown. Most of fifth-century " comedy " is farce, not strictly comedy at all. The difference between these types is that in comedy people act in a fairly logical and natural way; in farce they, with their author, play the fool: comedy has poise, farce is lopsided. These facts are often ignored because of a widespread notion that farce must be bad, and we are too loyal to attribute farce to a great writer.[2] The fact is that, farce being unnatural, it is particularly hard to write it well. But it can be done: *Charley's Aunt* is good farce; the *Birds* is sublime farce. Between this and the writings of Menander, Molière, and

---

[1] In fact most of our evidence for this method comes from Roman Comedy which (for such externals) drew upon the whole New Comedy, not Menander alone.

[2] In the same way we are content to go on shaking our heads over certain elements in *Othello* because we refuse to see that it is not a tragedy but a melodrama.

Congreve, there is an almost [1] complete difference. That is why critics who happen to be more interested in comedy strictly so called than in comedy roughly so called—in farce, that is to say—occasionally astound us by their judgments; the French [2] have a great way of ignoring Shakespeare altogether when discussing comedy. We may put the distinction in other words—so as not to become the slaves of labels —and say that Aristophanes writes broad comedy, Molière and Menander the Comedy of Manners. This latter depicts more frequently types than individuals, and a situation that can without grave difficulty be supposed to occur every other week. It is " real " life made significant by deletion of irrelevance and alluring by skill in dialogue, deftness in construction. And here is the point at which we have been aiming throughout this paragraph: such qualities, realism, polish, deftness, necessitate precisely that circumscription which seemed a self-imposed clog upon Menander: it is a vital element in his art. This type of comedy needs people who fully understand one another's notions of life, who share the same accomplishments, the same degree of culture, even the same kind of language.[3] That is why the slaves are so near to their masters: one could not write a comedy of manners about Robinson Crusoe and Man Friday. Moreover, such work involves frequent confrontations or narrow escapes therefrom, so that they must all live close together, in the same house or contiguous houses. In brief, not only does the Comedy of Manners arise in a " world " that is small, sophisticated, equally sophisticated, and leisured; further, it is such a world,

---

[1] For they themselves now and then turn to farce, as in the "roast grandson" scene of the *Samia* and the sack-and-cudgel scene in *Les Fourberies de Scapin* (a passage censured by Boileau).

[2] Cp. Benoit, *La Comédie de Ménandre, e.g.* pp. 3 and 35; Croiset, *Hist. de la litt. grecque*, III, p. 631; Legrand throughout his magnificently copious *Daos*.

[3] On this, and the whole topic, see Meredith's sparkling and masterly *Essay on Comedy*.

and such a world only, that it depicts.[1] These conditions explain why our " Restoration " dramatists confine [2] themselves not merely to London, but to the fashionable world therein, with its attendant valets, seamstresses, and less reputable satellites; why even Molière is externally less varied than romantics like Rostand; why Crates was overshadowed by Cratinus in an Athens dominated by politics both domestic and imperial; why in the same city, as soon as politics became a remoter and less intelligible topic under Macedonian rule, Menander found excellent scope for this art by the simple device of ignoring both the great [3] and the lowly (save, indeed, the satellites aforesaid) and concentrating on the bourgeoisie; [4] why, in a field analogous to drama, Dickens wrote novels utterly unlike such comedy because he ranged so widely, whereas Meredith, an excellent Menandrian, dextrously carved for himself out of Victorian England a *milieu* containing only people of rank, fashion and culture—therefore leisured and sophisticated—who, with their dependants as always, gave him the ideal arena for his consummate wit and comedic genius.

So the tiny " world " of a Menandrian play is marked off, a circle containing some dozen people, each closely connected with the other eleven. Equally important, he is not connected with anyone outside the circle, unless indeed the plot demands that a child be born in his absence; if so, he is suddenly allotted absurdly vague business in Imbros or some other

---

[1] Wilamowitz seems mistaken, therefore, when he laments (*Menander*, p. 164) Menander's indifference to great events and achievements outside Athens, " which had become a little town ". Legrand (*Daos*, p. 651) develops the same lament with eloquence. So might one grieve that Jane Austen did not live in Paris.

[2] Not entirely: we find a fascinating hybrid in such plays as Farquhar's *The Beaux Stratagem*.

[3] It is often suggested that he and his school feared the Macedonian officials; as our own dramatists are said to fear the Tired Business Man. But the reason given above is in this respect better, that it accounts for a peculiarity shown by all social comedy.

[4] Cp. Aulus Gellius, II, 23: *illud Menandri de vita hominum media sumptum* (of a passage in the Πλόκιον).

island and duly packed off. But no one cares about Imbros.[1] Such places are mere starting-points whence the elderly uncle may arrive, bringing wealth or good news, just as he now arrives from Johannesburg or New Zealand. But the artificial congestion enables the artist to perform prodigies of skill, like Wilde's fan-scene that induces Lord Windermere and his wife to change completely, and in opposite directions, their opinions of Mrs. Erlynne; the marvellous dovetailing in the *Double-Dealer*, where Congreve achieves the ideal, *vera dicendo ut eos ambos fallam*[2]— ' to deceive them both by telling the truth '; the complications of Terence's *Self-Punishment* and the *Brothers*, where the fathers suppose the girl to be one youth's *inamorata* when she is really the other man's. The aim in such drama is not novelty of story, but novelty of treatment. The scheme stands, but different elements are emphasized and embellished in different plays. The exposed baby is found by a peasant: this can be dealt with in two lines, but in *Arbitration* it is wrought up into a long and splendid scene that gives its name to the whole. The hero comforts himself with a courtesan, but whereas in the *Shorn Lady* she has apparently no additional function, the whole action of *Arbitration* swings upon her. It is a standard feature that the amorous youth's real or supposed conquest should excite jealousy; but observe the difference between the passionate distress of Demeas and the naive misery of Polemon. The braggart always has a toady; in the *Flatterer* we see even from the scanty fragments that he outshone his principal. And in complication Menander, like his

---

[1] It has been said that for a Parisian the world is divided into three portions: Paris, the departments, and *là-bas*. This polished parochialism is equally marked in the descendants of Themistocles and Alcibiades. Imbros and Caria are *là-bas*, like "the Colonies" in a nineteenth-century novel or play: merely a dumping-ground for persons not wanted at the real centre. So John Worthing in Oscar Wilde says of his scapegrace brother: "He must choose between this world, the next world, and Australia".

[2] Terence, *Heaut.*, 711, which Congreve prefixed as a motto to his play.

successors, exhibits an eye-defeating virtuosity recalling those diagrams where at one moment the black squares stand out of a white background and, at the next, white squares on black. Habrotonon's device to trace mother by father, father by mother—to find two unknowns with only one equation to help her—is beautiful. Pamphile in the same comedy sacrifices her baby so as to keep her husband, but by that very plan she loses [1] him, yet later regains him because the device to keep him has failed. Polemon by quarrelling with Glycera binds her more closely to him: his ill-treatment brings about their marriage; and (most marvellous of all) the whole puzzle of that play solves itself. Some will have it that the presiding deity of New Comedy is Chance. This is a complete misunderstanding: Menander tells us, or allows his characters to tell us, that Chance governs life, but he will not admit her into the theatre. The neatness of his confrontations, the deftness wherewith events interlock, are not her work, but the outcome of that insistence upon a small homogeneous world which, once formed, compels his people to meet constantly.

But are there not certain misgivings that after a while chill our admiration: censure, perhaps, attaching to Menander alone, or to the whole Comedy of Manners?

Plutarch [2] relates that a friend of Menander once expressed surprise that though the Dionysiac festival was at hand the poet had not yet written his comedy. 'My play is written,' was his reply, 'for the plot is devised: I have only the lines to compose'. This of course implies that the plot (worked out in minute detail, to be sure) is independent of the actual words, which are only the matter filling in an outline. But in the perfectly-written play construction enters into

---

[1] This stage, it will be remembered, depends on the (probable) assumption that Habrotonon is for some considerable time recognized as the foundling's mother.
[2] *De Gloria Ath.*, 347e: πεποίηκα τὴν κωμῳδίαν, ᾠκονόμηται γὰρ ἡ διάθεσις· δεῖ δ' αὐτῇ τὰ στιχίδια ἐπᾷσαι.

details even minuter than those. Every word helps structure: pressure of the plot and its development tinges each crevice of the dialogue. It is not for nothing that the childless Electra calls Night ' thou nurse of golden stars '[1] or that Medea echoes a high-flown word of her husband's.[2] Can we believe that the *Œdipus Tyrannus* did not grow in and through its dialogue? Hervieu's work, especially *La Course du Flambeau*, derives much of its significance and intensity from this method. Ibsen has carried it to amazing perfection: one can hardly discover a passage in his superb later period that is not an example, the finest of all being the " casual " reference to little Thea Elvsted's hair, which gives such terrific power to the scene where the manuscript is burned. Plutarch's anecdote implies that Menander knew nothing of this. Wonderfully as his scenes interlock, they are not interfused: the dialogue serves its own purpose but does not echo and foretell by its mere turns of expression the dominant notes of scenes that precede or are to come. A strong example of this is seen in the *Samia*, where we find three passages, each splendid but out of tune with the others: anxious narrative, pathetic altercation, and farce. He composes a marvellous mechanism, not a fabric.

And is not all such comedy but a carving of cherry-stones, this superbly skilful manipulation of artifice in an unnaturally narrow area? Shall we not regard Menander as belonging to the race of Sardou and Pinero? Is he not a mere " man of the theatre," or, more accurately, a theatrical dramatist, by which is meant a dramatist whose " great moments " instil in the onlooker not a deeper appreciation of life but only admiration for the dexterity that has engendered them? No; because having perfected his vehicle he goes on to employ it for non-theatrical effects, precisely like Terence after *Phormio* and Ibsen after the *League of*

[1] Eur., *Electra*, v. 54.   [2] Eur., *Medea*, vv. 597, 1322.

Youth. Sardou and Pinero seek for "questions" and "problems" so as to ensure a thrilling scene of climax, what Sarcey called *la scène à faire ;* these others reverse the process, employing their dramatic powers to convey illumination about life and its distressing or ludicrous complexities. A playwright thus developing is menaced by a terrible danger. Will he become a propagandist pure and simple? That means ruin, for he will send his audience home arguing about "movements" and abuses, not glowing with a deeper vitality, a stronger relish for life itself.[1] Menander understood that art should not inculcate opinions but illumine the soul, bestowing not facts but spiritual appreciation. From him no one ever learned anything more definite than a knowledge of the human heart in all its quaint twists, its sudden meannesses, its unexpected nobility. In him is a splendid union of complete disillusionment and complete charity. The slave-characters so winningly drawn in *Arbitration*, those two delightful women, Habrotonon and Glycera, Charisius' outcry of self-discovery and protest, the separation of Demeas and his Samian concubine—all these penetrate far more deeply than the petty conditions of drawing-room comedy would suggest.

It may, indeed, be asked whether he does not transgress the bounds of comedy, far-flung as they are. Donatus in his commentary on Terence several times remarks: 'Here he diverges from Menander and does thus and thus lest his play should rise up into tragedy'. To suggest that it should not so rise is no vain pedantry. Too violent a change of tone may shake it to pieces, for nothing is more destructive of artistic effect than the crude juxtaposition of emotions that will not blend. Marlowe's *Dr. Faustus* sins horribly thus. The greatness of Shylock causes a splendid play to rock dangerously. Ford is a grave threat to the *Merry Wives :* his rage when alone should be care-

---

[1] The conflict between artist and propagandist in Mr. Galsworthy's plays is a drama in itself.

fully " over-acted ". The piteous anti-climax that follows Cæsar's noble address to the Sphinx is a *gaminerie* not only of Cleopatra, but of Shaw, and distresses the audience no less than it startles Cæsar. Now, in Menander, these dangers are, so far as we can now see, skilfully avoided. Why does he write, side by side, two accounts of Charisius' remorse ? First Onesimus reports what he has heard his master exclaiming within : next moment Charisius comes forth and says much the same to us. Clumsy ? Not so : we are prepared for what would otherwise be " too tragic " by Onesimus' report, which is mingled with the usual " comic " fears for his own safety. Similar tact marks the other emotional scenes : Polemon's agonized appeal to Patæcus is relieved by his artless insistence on showing Glycera's wardrobe to his reluctant hearer ; Demeas' torture of Chrysis and himself is relieved by her amazement at his perversity in breaking out now of all times.

Menander has realized that mere holding the mirror up to life soon grows tiresome and empty : he will be not an echo but a commentator. Yet he will not write treatises. Not only does he avoid advocacy of definite reforms or causes : it is difficult to maintain even that he puts forth any specific moral teaching. An obvious question arises : do his works set forth the doctrines of his illustrious school-fellow, Epicurus ? First, it is well known that Epicurus deplored the yoke cast upon men's hearts and minds by popular religion ; the outbursts of his disciple Lucretius on that theme are among the most renowned passages of Latin poetry. Now, Menander wrote at least four plays dealing more or less fully with this : the *Priestess* ('Ιέρεια), the *Superstitious Man* (Δεισιδαίμων), the *Charioteer* ('Ηνίοχος), the *Woman of Thessaly* (Θετταλή). The last dealt with witches who pull down the moon ; the *Charioteer* contained a biting remark[1] about strolling gods carried

---

[1] Fr. 202.

on a board from house to house by an old woman; the *Superstitious Man* ridicules the omen of a broken shoe-lace.¹ The *Priestess*, as we have seen, contained a grave censure of witch-doctor's " religion ". Secondly, the sermon of Onesimus, absurd jumble as it is, nevertheless puts forward an Epicurean doctrine, that the gods do not meddle with human affairs. Thirdly, certain fragments recommend the Epicurean impassivity (ἀταραξία), though they do not use that word or name the philosopher. Among them is that lofty passage ² about the quiet enjoyment of the august unchanging spectacle afforded by the material Universe. Fourthly, Menander often dilates upon the importance of affection or friendship; and Epicurus laid great emphasis on this. The proper conclusion to be drawn is plain. Menander, of course, knew the Epicurean doctrines, and the great passage about contemplation of the Universe is a notable borrowing. But there is no reason to consider him an actual convert, still less to suppose that he wishes to promulgate his friend's philosophy. Superstition is a theme that would easily offer itself, that could indeed hardly be avoided, in that age. Friendship or affection, unless we can show that Menander wrote plays to demonstrate its importance, provides no evidence at all; of course, no writer of social comedy can help saying much about it. We have at present no reason to suppose that Menander used the beautiful device of Terence, who bifurcates his plot and employs each half to solve the other. The upshot is that, though of course we cannot deny Epicurean influence, it is certainly not so strong that we can point to anything in Menander not fully intelligible without it. He is neither a propagandist nor a mere entertainer, but an urbane yet pungent commentator on the quaintness, pathos, and generosity of life itself as lived by unheroic yet deeply attractive men and women.

¹ Fr. 109. ² Fr. 481. See above, p. 321. Note ἀλύπως.

CHAPTER VIII

METRE AND RHYTHM IN GREEK COMEDY

§ 1. INTRODUCTION

POETRY is illuminating utterance consisting of words whose successive sounds are arranged according to a recurrent pattern. The soul of poetry is this illumination, its body this recurrent pattern of sounds; and it is with the body that we are now to deal. We must distinguish carefully between rhythm and metre. Rhythm is the recurrence just mentioned—the structure; metre is the gathering together of sounds into masses upon which rhythm shall do its work. Metre, so to put it, makes the bricks, while rhythm makes the arch.

Greek metre is based, not upon stress-accent,[1] but upon quantity—the length of time needed for the pronunciation of a syllable. In English the line

My bosom's lord sits lightly in his throne

is scanned as a series of five iambi; the iambus being a foot which consists of an unaccented, following by an accented, syllable. The word "bosom's" can stand where it does because the stress of the voice naturally falls upon the first syllable of "bosom"; to begin a line with "my controlled bosom" would clearly be wrong. The length of the syllables has no effect on the scansion. That "sits" needs as long a time for its utterance as the first syllable of "lightly" does not alter the fact that "sits light-" is an accentual

---

[1] A totally different thing from the written Greek accents `, ´, and ˆ, which refer to pitch, not stress.

iambus. Greek words, on the other hand, as metrical [1] material, are considered only from the quantitative point of view, not the accentual. The voice-stress in the word λόγους rests upon the first syllable, but the word is an iambus, a " short " followed by a " long " (marked respectively ⏑ and ‾).

When is a syllable long and when short ? *All* syllables are long—

(i) Which contain a necessarily long vowel (η or ω), *e.g.*, μῆν τῶν.

(ii) Which contain a diphthong or iota subscript, *e.g.*, οἶνος, αἰνοῦμεν, ῥᾳδίως, save that the first syllable of ποιῶ and τοιοῦτος (and their parts) is often short.

(iii) Which end with a double consonant (ζ, ξ, ψ), *e.g.*, ὄζος, ἔξω, ὄψον.

(iv) Which have the circumflex accent, *e.g.*, ὑμῖν, μῦς.

Most syllables are long the vowel of which is followed by two consonants. But there is some difficulty about this very frequent case. It can arise in three ways :—

(*a*) Both consonants may be in the same word as the vowel. Then the syllable is generally long, but the rules are complicated.[2] It may be noted specially that when the consonants are a mute followed by a liquid the syllable is usually short : *e.g.*, κᾰπνος, ἄγρος, ὀφρυς.

(*b*) One of the consonants may end its word and the other begin the next. Such syllables are *all* long. Thus, ὅσον στιλην, ανδρες σοφοι, although both these long syllables are " short by nature ".

(*c*) Both consonants may occur at the beginning of the second word. If the vowel is naturally short, the syllable is usually short, but if the second word begins with a double consonant or σ followed by another consonant, the syllable is always long. Thus ὁ ξενος, τί ζητεις, ταυτα σκοπουμεν.

---

[1] We shall see later that in *rhythm* stress-accent is important.
[2] See Prof. J. W. White, *The Verse of Greek Comedy*, pp. 364 *sq.*

A vowel, naturally short, when thus lengthened is said to be "lengthened by position".

The following types of syllable are *always* short :—

(i) Those containing a naturally short vowel (ε or ο) not lengthened by position, *e.g.*, ἕκων, ὅπως.

(ii) Final α of the third declension neuter singular (σῶμᾰ), third declension accusative singular (ἐλπιδᾰ, δρασαντᾰ), and all neuters plural (τᾰ, σωματᾰ, τοιαυτᾰ).

(iii) Final ι (*e.g.*, εστῐ, τῐ), save, of course, when it is part of a diphthong.

(iv) The accusative -ας of the third declension (ανδρᾰς, πονουντᾰς). But μουσᾱς (first declension). The quantity is that of the corresponding nominative.

Hiatus is rare. That is, a word ending in a vowel is not to be followed by a word beginning with a vowel, unless one vowel or the other disappears. Almost always it is the first vowel which is thus elided. In verse one would not write πάντα εἶπε, but πάντ' εἶπε : not ἔτι εἶναι, but ἔτ' εἶναι. When the first vowel is long and the second short, the latter is cut off by "prodelision," a much rarer occurrence. Thus τούτῳ ἀνεῖπε would become τούτῳ 'νεῖπε. Two long vowels, as in καλὴ ἡμέρα, are not used together at all. But the rule as to hiatus does not normally apply at the end of a verse; usually one can end a verse with an unelided vowel and begin the next with a vowel. If in any metrical scheme this liberty is not allowed, it is said that "synapheia [1] prevails". Hiatus, practically unknown in tragedy, is found here and there in the colloquial style of comedy : *e.g.*, περὶ Ἀλκιβιάδου (*Frogs*, 1422), τί ἐστι; (*Wasps*, 37). Occasionally two vowels are scanned as one by synizesis,[2] *e.g.*, μὴ οὐχί, which is a trochee (‾ ᴗ). Occasionally "weak hiatus" occurs : that is, a long vowel or a diphthong is shortened before a vowel.[3]

---

[1] Συνάφεια, "connexion," "continuity".   [2] Συνίζησις, "collapse".
[3] For an example see p. 167 (Plato). Cp. Prof. J. W. White, § 797.

§ 2. The Iambic Trimeter

This is the familiar line of ordinary dialogue: it consists of six feet, any one of which may be an iambus (⏑-). But a "pure" iambic line, one in which every foot is an iambus, as in *Plutus*, 1017:

$$\underset{μονος}{⏑\,-}\,|\,\underset{γαρ\ ηδ}{⏑\,-}|\underset{εθ}{-}\,\underset{ως}{⏑\,-}\,|\,\underset{εοικ}{⏑\,-}|\underset{εν}{⏑}\,\underset{εσθ}{-}|\underset{ιων}{⏑\,-}$$

is very rare. A speech written solely in such feet would be highly monotonous and far too rapid. Other feet are therefore allowed, under restrictions, to take the place of the iambus.

By far the commonest of these is the spondee, which consists of two long syllables (λόγχη, πάντων). This can occur in the first, third, or fifth places—one, two, or all three. Thus:

ἀλλ ὡς | τάχιστ|α τηνδ|ε την | Θεωρ|ιαν (*Peace*, 715).

ἐσθει | προς ημ|ας δευρ|ο πυρρ|ιχην | βλεπων (*Birds*, 1169).

ἐκ των | φρεατ|ων τους | καδους | ξυλλαμβ | ανειν (*Eccl.*, 1004).

Next, the lightness and variety is greatly increased by the use of "resolved" feet. Each long syllable being regarded as equal to two "shorts," it follows that the iambus can be resolved into ⏑⏑⏑, the spondee into -⏑⏑, ⏑⏑- (and ⏑⏑⏑⏑, but this last is not employed in iambics).

The anapæst (⏑⏑-) is the commonest of all the resolved feet, and may appear in any place save the sixth:

ἀλλ ει | δοκει | ρεγκωμ | εν εγκ|εκαλυμμ|ενοι (*Clouds*, 11).

The tribrach (⏑⏑⏑) can occur in any place, save the sixth:

παι παι | φερ εξ|ω δευρ|ο τον | γυλιον | εμοι (*Ach.*, 1097).

σφραγιδ|ας επιβ|αλλουσ|ιν ηδη και | μοχλους (*Thesm.*, 415).

METRE AND RHYTHM IN GREEK COMEDY

The dactyl (-⏑⏑) is allowed in those places to which the spondee is admitted, but somewhat rarely in the fifth. Thus:

ᾄδει | δε χρησμ|ους ο δε | γερων | σιβυλλ|ιᾳ (*Knights*, 61).
εχθρος ετ|ι προς | τουτοισ|ιν ανδρ|ι δημ|οτῃ (*Clouds*, 1219).
ου δειν|ον ουν|δητ εστ|ιν ημ|ας δεομ|ενους (*Birds*, 27).

Three important features, one metrical, two rhythmical, must be mentioned.

First, the last syllable of the line may be short: no doubt the pause at the end of the line was felt to help it out. Verses of this kind are innumerable, *e.g.*:

ησθην | δε βαι|α πανυ | δε βαι|α τεττ|αρα (*Ach.*, 2).

(This is followed by a vowel, α.) It matters little whether such final vowels are marked as long, or as short, or with the sign of doubtful quantity (⏑̄).

Next is the usage as to cæsura ("incision"). The rule in tragedy is that a word-ending must occur in the middle of the third or of the fourth foot. This usage is essential to rhythm. That co-extension of word and foot which is naturally frequent must at one point be emphatically excluded so that the whole line may be felt as a single rhythmical whole. Such "lines" as ταύτην ἄναξ λέγει καλὴν εἶναι πόλιν or Ὀδυσσέως φίλοι μαχούμενοι τάχα are utterly impossible: the first falls into six scraps, the second into two lumps, of equal length. But the cæsura may be dispensed with if the third foot ends with an elision, apparently because, if the word could be written in full, the fourth foot would be divided between two words. Whereas tragedy observes these rules closely, comedy allows a good many exceptions. Such lines as

εγω|δε θεισ|α || τους |στεφανους | περιδησ|ομαι (*Eccl.*, 122) are in this respect exactly like the tragic line. But exceptions are fairly common, e.g. :

ἵνα τοὐμ|ὸν ἱμ|άτιον | φορῶν | μεμνῆτ|ό μου (*Plutus*, 991).

δεδρακ|ας ειρ|ηνην | ποιησ|ας ως | προ του (*Peace*, 1199).

Thirdly, the " rule of the final cretic " [1] is ignored in comedy. The rule is that if the fifth foot contains a caesura, the foot must be an iambus. In tragedy there are hardly any breaches of this rule. In comedy they are numberless, e.g. :

σκεψασθε παιδες την αριστ|ην || εγχ|ελυν (*Ach.*, 889).

τῳ δητ αν αυτον προσαγαγοιμ|ην || δραμ|ατι (*Thesm.*, 849).

From this account it will be gathered that the iambic trimeter of comedy is (quite naturally) much rougher than the tragic and nearer to normal speech. It is often difficult to catch the rhythm at all owing to the absence of caesura and the frequency of resolved feet :

ουτως | υποκριν | ομενον |σοφως | ονειρ | ατα (*Wasps*, 53).

ο τοκος | ετ εν | πολει | τεκοιμ | ες την | κυνην (*Lys.*, 754).

§ 3. The Iambic Tetrameter

This consists of eight feet with catalexis [2] (that is, the last foot has not its full number of syllables, the remainder being filled by a pause in delivery) :

πλακουσ|ιν εστ|ιν εντ|υχειν | πλανωμ|ενοις | ερημ|οις (*Peace*, 1143).

But such a line, in which all the seven complete feet are iambi, is exceedingly rare. The spondee is very frequently admitted, in the first, third, and fifth, but never the seventh, foot :

οιμοι | ταλας | εχουσ|ι γαρ | πορπακ|ας ω | πονηρ|ε (*Knights*, 858).

ουκουν | ορᾳς | ορμωμ|ε νους | ημας | παλαι | προθυμ|ως (*Plutus*, 257).

[1] It is so called because the second half of the fifth foot *plus* the sixth will obviously have the metrical form – ⏑ –, which sequence of syllables, when it forms a single foot (as, of course, it does not in iambics), is called a cretic.   [2] From καταλήγω, "to stop short".

Tribrachs are much rarer :

$$\text{χωρωμ} \mid \text{εν αμα} \mid \text{τε τῳ} \mid \text{λυχνῳ} \mid \text{παντῃ} \mid \text{διασκ} \mid \text{οπωμ} \mid \text{εν}$$ (*Wasps*, 246).

Dactyls are scarcely ever found :

$$\text{συ δ ου} \mid \text{βαδιζ|εις ο δε} \mid \text{Χαρων} \mid \text{το συμβ|ολον} \mid \text{διδωσ|ιν}$$ (*Plutus*, 278).

Anapæsts are excluded.

No rule exists as to cæsura, but diæresis normally occurs : that is, the end of the fourth foot generally coincides with the end of a word, as in all the examples hitherto offered. But exceptions are fairly frequent :

$$\text{αλλ εστ|ι τουτ} \mid \text{ω Δημ|ε μηχ|ανημ} \mid \text{ιν ην} \mid \text{συ βουλ|ῃ}$$ (*Knights*, 851).

That tragedy should not employ this metre is perfectly natural. Its length combined with catalexis make it a splendid instrument of comic declamation, but it has no dignity. The same raciness marks its English equivalent :

> With Admirals the ocean teemed all round his wide dominions.
> (*The Gondoliers*.)

§ 4. THE TROCHAIC TETRAMETER

Under this head we shall deal with trochees (‾ ⌣) only as used in the non-lyrical passages of comedy. Originally all dialogue was written in this metre ; but in extant comedy it is mostly confined to recitative by the chorus. The metre is always the trochaic tetrameter catalectic (sometimes called the trochaic octonarius), that is, a line consisting of eight feet, mostly trochees, with catalexis.

Pure trochaic verses are occasionally to be found :

$$\text{ουκ ακ|ουσομ|εσθα} \mid \text{δητα} \mid \text{δεινα} \mid \text{ταρα} \mid \text{πεισομ|αι}_{\wedge}$$ (*Ach.*, 323).

The mark $_{\wedge}$ means that there is a pause equivalent in length to a short syllable. (It is often found in the scansion of lyrics, and there one also at times uses ⊤, ⌞, ⌞⌟ which mean pauses equivalent to two, three, and four short syllables respectively.) As in iambics, the last syllable may be short by nature:

ει δε | που πεσ|οιεν |ες τον | ωμον | εν μαχ|η τιν|ι ˌ (*Knights*, 571).

Such purely trochaic lines are rare. Spondees are used freely in the second, fourth, and sixth feet:

τουτ εκ|ει καλ|ον παρ | ημιν | εστιν | ην τις | τῳ πατρ|ι ˌ (*Birds*, 758).

εξελ|ων ημ|ων μεν|οινων | προς βι|αν τανθρ|ηνι|α ˌ (*Wasps*, 1080).

Tribrachs, too, are very common:

τον ιερ|ον χορ|ον δικ|αιον | εστι | χρηστα | τη πολ|ει ˌ (*Frogs*, 686).

της ε|ορτης | μη τυχ|οντες | κατα λογ|ον των | ημερ|ων ˌ (*Clouds*, 619).

This foot may occur in any of the seven places, but is extremely rare in the fourth and seventh:

αλλα | χουτος | ετερος | ουτοσ|ι μεν | εστι | Φιλοκλε|ους ˌ (*Birds*, 281).

Dactyls and anapæsts are very rare.

There is no rule as to cæsura, but, as in the iambic tetrameter, diæresis normally occurs at the end of the fourth foot.

It will be seen that the trochaic tetrameter catalectic is almost as regular in comedy as in tragedy. This magnificent metre is in fact one of the finest and best loved elements in all poetry. Aristotle [1] indeed imputes to it lack of dignity, if not of decency: we should rather call it popular. Throughout the history of western civilization its splendid leaping vigour has been employed wherever simple strong emotion was to be expressed. Archilochus, the earliest of personal poets, employs it in his virile songs of love and revelry:

> ὡς Διωνύσοι᾽ ἄνακτος καλὸν ἐξάρξαι μέλος
> οἶδα διθύραμβον, οἴνῳ ξυγκεραυνωθεὶς φρένας.

Epicharmus throws into this same form his vigorous popular philosophy:

> νᾶφε καὶ μέμνασ᾽ ἀπιστεῖν· ἄρθρα ταῦτα τᾶν φρένων.

---

[1] *Poet.*, IV, 14: τὸ μὲν γὰρ πρῶτον τετραμέτρῳ ἐχρῶντο διὰ τὸ σατυρικὴν καὶ ὀρχηστικωτέραν εἶναι τὴν ποίησιν, In *Rhet.*, III, i, 9, he calls it κορδακικώτερον.

Attic drama is full of it. Æschylus has set some of his most magnificent poetry in this measure:

> τῆλε πρὸς δυσμαῖς ἄνακτος Ἡλίου φθινασμάτων.

In Latin popular poetry it flourished inextinguishably in that exquisite Pagan lyric, the *Pervigilium Veneris*—

> totus est in armis idem quando nudus est Amor—

as in the noblest hymns of the Roman Church:

> qualiter Redemptor orbis immolatus vicerit.

Later popular verse favours it no less, as in the old Austrian national anthem:

> Über blühende Gefilde reicht sein Scepter weit und breit;
> Säuler seines Throns sind Milde, Biedersinn und Redlichkeit,
> Und von seinem Wappenschilde strahlet die Gerechtigkeit.

In English it moulds the best-known work of Longfellow (*The Psalm of Life*) and of Tennyson (*Locksley Hall*); it flourishes still in verse that one would call the complete antithesis of Æschylus, the comic song:

> In a cabin, in a canyon, excavating for a mine,
> Dwelt a miner, forty-niner, and his daughter Clementine.

§ 5. Anapæstic Systems

The dimeter (or tetrapody) is a verse of four feet:

$$\smile\smile- \mid \smile\smile- \mid \smile\smile- \mid \smile\smile-$$
ἐλελίζ | ομενης δ | ιεροις | μελεσιν (*Birds*, 213).

But lines consisting of anapæsts alone are very uncommon. Spondees and dactyls, but no other feet, are often substituted, at any place in the verse:

$$\smile\smile- - \mid - - \mid - \smile-$$
διακιν|ησας | φαιδροις | ωσιν (*Peace*, 156).
$$-\smile\smile-\smile\smile \mid -\smile\smile- \mid \smile\smile$$
καναπυθ|ωμεθα | τουσδε τιν|ες ποτε (*Birds*, 403).

Anapæstic dimeters are invariably closed by a catalectic verse:

$$- \mid \smile\smile- \mid \smile\smile- -$$
θεια | μακαρων | ολολυγη ⏑ (*Birds*, 222).

This is called a "parœmiac" (a term of uncertain derivation). In systems of considerable length such verses occur at intervals; Cratinus in his *Odysses* has a passage composed entirely in parœmiacs.

Unlike the dimeter, the tetrameter (eight feet) is unknown to tragedy, but in comedy it is extremely frequent, and is indeed called by Hephæstion τὸ Ἀριστοφάνειον, 'the Aristophanic line,' because of his skill in its use. The verse is always catalectic:

$$\smile\smile - \smile\smile - \smile\smile - \smile\smile - \smile\smile - \smile\smile - \smile\smile - \smile-$$
ο μεν ορτ|υγα δους | ο δε πορφ|υριων | ο δε χην | ο δε Περσ|ικον ορν|ιν $\stackrel{-}{\smile}$
(*Birds*, 707).

As usual, other feet are freely admitted: indeed the line just given is the only extant example of a purely anapæstic line. The spondee is frequent, being admitted to any of the first six[1] feet:

$$- - \smile\smile - \smile\smile - -- -- -- \smile\smile --$$
ον χρην | δια τας | προτερας | νικας | πινειν | εν τῳ | πρυτανει|ῳ $\stackrel{-}{\smile}$
(*Knights*, 535).

The only other foot allowed is the dactyl, which is rarer, and practically confined to the first and third feet: it is never found in the sixth or seventh:

$$-\smile\smile -- -\smile\smile -- \smile\smile - - -\smile\smile - -$$
αυτον επ|ηνει | προς το θε|ατρον | παραβας | εν τοις | αναπαιστ|οις $\stackrel{-}{\smile}$
(*Peace*, 735).

Diæresis is almost always to be found at the end of the fourth foot.

This metre, which exhibits better than any other the flexible vigour and the beautifully limpid though idiomatic Greek of Aristophanes, is often employed in those brilliant harangues that expound pompous theses, such as Socrates' lecture on the origin of thunder (*Clouds*); a series of this type regularly occurs in the parabasis. An excellent parallel is found in *Iolanthe*, *e.g.*:

> And you're giving a treat (penny ice and cold meat) to a
> party of friends and relations
> (They're a ravenous horde), and they all came on board at
> Sloane Square and South Kensington Stations.

[1] See p. 131 for a unique example (from Cratinus) of a spondee even in the seventh place.

§ 6. Lyrics

The metres and rhythms of Greek songs form a difficult and complicated study, as we do not know the music composed for them. Nevertheless, we find much help in the fact that they are normally arranged in stanzas which closely correspond in metre and rhythm. Any pair of these is called strophe and antistrophe.

Our best preparation is the habit of reading aloud, with correct quantities and natural emphasis, the non-lyrical parts of Aristophanes. Let us, so prepared, address ourselves to the following passage from the *Frogs* (534-541):

>   ταῦτα μὲν πρὸς ἀνδρός ἐστι
>   νοῦν ἔχοντος καὶ φρένας καὶ
>   πολλὰ περιπεπλευκότος,
>   μετακυλίνδειν αὑτὸν ἀεὶ
>   πρὸς τὸν εὖ πράττοντα τοῖχον
>   μᾶλλον ἢ γεγραμμένην
>   εἰκόν' ἑστάναι λαβόνθ' ἕν
>   σχῆμα· τὸ δὲ μεταστρέφεσθαι
>   πρὸς τὸ μαλθακώτερον
>   δεξιοῦ πρὸς ἀνδρός ἐστι
>   καὶ φύσει Θηραμένους.

```
-υ|-υ|-υ|-υ
-υ|->|-υ|->
-υ|υυυ|-υ|- ʌ
υυυ|->|-υ|->
-υ|->|-υ|-υ
-υ|-υ|-υ|- ʌ
-υ|-υ|-υ|-υ
-υ|υυυ|-υ|->
-υ|-υ|-υ|- ʌ
-υ|-υ|-υ|-υ
-υ|->|-υ|- ʌ
```

The passage is trochaic, three only of the feet being resolved. Seven feet are irrational: that is, a long syllable is substituted for a short. The result is often called a spondee, but there can be no doubt that (in trochaics) -›, while taking longer to pronounce than -υ, was yet shorter than --.

So much for the metre. As for the rhythm, our passage reveals structure effected by the use of catalexis at intervals. This marks the whole strophe into "periods" (περίοδος, "circuit") which are sometimes printed each as one huge "line". Why are they usually divided as above? Because as the strophe is built up out of periods, so is each period built up out of cola (κῶλον, "limb"). Each colon, then, of this lyric is a trochaic dimeter (tetrapody) and we may indicate the scheme of the whole thus:

$$\left\{\begin{matrix}4\\4\\4\end{matrix}\right. \quad \left\{\begin{matrix}4\\4\\4\end{matrix}\right. \quad \left\{\begin{matrix}4\\4\\4\end{matrix}\right. \quad \left\{\begin{matrix}4\\4\end{matrix}\right.$$

This is a very simple lyric. Similar examples are the antistrophe of course (*Frogs*, 542-8) and *Birds*, 1470-81 (= 1482-93). In the latter, however, as often, the end of a colon falls in the middle of a word:[1]

> πολλὰ δὴ καὶ καινὰ καὶ θαυμ-
> άστ' ἐπεπτόμεσθα καὶ . . .

Rather more difficult is the delightful song from the *Knights* (551 *sqq.*):

> ἵππι' ἄναξ Πόσειδον, ᾧ
> χαλκοκρότων ἵππων κτύπος
> καὶ χρεμετισμὸς ἀνδάνει
> καὶ κυανέμβολοι θοαὶ
>   μισθοφόροι τριήρεις,
> μειρακίων θ' ἅμιλλα λαμ-
> πρυνομένων ἐν ἅρμασιν
> καὶ βαρυδαιμονούντων,
> δεῦρ' ἔλθ' ἐς χορὸν ὦ χρυσοτρίαιν' ὦ
> δελφίνων μεδέων Σουνιάρατε,
> ὦ Γεραίστιε παῖ Κρόνου,
> Φορμίωνί τε φίλτατ' ἐκ
> τῶν ἄλλων τε θεῶν Ἀθην-
>   αίοις πρὸς τὸ παρεστός.

Like the former, this passage is trochaic, but we find rhythmical features hitherto unmentioned, which are of the first importance in lyric verse.

First, dactyls are admitted: the first colon is scanned:

> $-\,\smile\smile\,-\,\smile\,-\,\smile\,-$
> ιππι αν|αξ Ποσ|ειδον| ῳ ˄

(equivalent to four trochees), and the whole passage is plentifully sprinkled with dactyls. That is to say, trochaic

---

[1] See further p. 383.

lyric systems admit, not genuine dactyls, but " cyclic " dactyls. To the " long " of each foot and to the first " short " is given less than their usual length: the rhythm is accelerated, so that $-\smile$ is equivalent to $-$, and the whole cyclic dactyl, marked $-\smile\smile$, is equivalent to a trochee.[1] Whenever we see a number of apparent dactyls, we must examine the whole passage to find whether it is trochaic or not. Trochaic systems which contain cyclic dactyls are called " logaoedic ".[2]

Next, we encounter τονή (" stretching "). Lyric metres recognize syllables of greater length than $\smile\smile$. Most frequent is that marked L, equal to $\smile\smile\smile$. Lyric trochaic systems freely admit a single " long " syllable (L) as a complete foot, and the swing of the whole composition will generally show where such a foot is to be postulated. Thus the fifth colon above runs

$$- \smile\smile - \smile\mathsf{L} -$$
μισθοφορ|οι τρι|ηρ|εις ⋀.

If one asks " why not

$$- \smile\smile - \smile - >$$
μισθοφορ|οι τρι|ηρεις ? "

the answer is that the rest of the strophe falls into cola of four feet, not of three, and that therefore the assumption of τονή is better rhythm. So

$$\mathsf{L} -$$
βαρυδαιμον|ουντ|ων ⋀

The two longer cola are scanned

$$- > - \smile\smile \mathsf{L} - \smile \mathsf{L} -$$
δευρ ελθ | ες χορον | ω | χρυσοτρι|αιν | ω ⋀
$$- > - \smile\smile\mathsf{L} - \smile\smile \mathsf{L} \smile-$$
δελφιν|ων μεδε|ων | Σουνιαρ | ατ|ε ⋀

giving us six " trochees " in each colon.

Other lyrics show anacrusis. Many scholars refuse to believe in its existence; but whether it is a figment[3]

---

[1] Before condemning this statement as a mere evasion, the student should reflect that all such poetry is written for music, which would in performance make the rhythm "come right".

[2] Λογαοιδικός, "mingled of prose and verse".

[3] Ancient writers on metric know nothing of it: Gottfried Hermann introduced it a little more than a century ago.

or not, Greek lyrics are vastly easier to scan if it is postulated. It is an introduction (ἀνάκρουσις, "striking up"), standing outside the metrical structure, and plainly neglect of this will often throw our scansion out completely. Consider the following (*Peace*, 1127-30) :[1]

> ἥδομαί γ' ἥδομαι
> κράνους ἀπηλλαγμένος
> τυροῦ τε καὶ κρομμύων.
> οὐ γὰρ φιληδῶ μάχαις.

The scansion of the syllables is plain enough :

```
 - ᴗ - - ᴗ -
ᴗ - ᴗ - - ᴗ -
 - - ᴗ - - ᴗ -
 - - ᴗ - - ᴗ -
```

Without anacrusis one cannot arrange this intelligibly into feet unless one accepts the trochee as the equivalent of the iambus, which is impossible. But with anacrusis the scheme is easy :

```
        - ᴗ - | - ᴗ -
ᴗ | - ᴗ - | - ᴗ -
- |  - ᴗ - | - ᴗ -
- |  - ᴗ - | - ᴗ -
```

Whether the passage should be scanned as cretics (⁻ ᴗ ⁻) or as trochees (⁻ ᴗ ⌊) is another question.

Not only is the strophe usually analysable into periods: there are sometimes isolated cola: a period may be preceded by a prelude and followed by a postlude or epode; and such a member occurring between periods is called a mesode.

We have now become acquainted with three rhythmical masses: the colon, the period, the strophe. Are there others? What is a "verse" in lyrics? There is no such thing. One must of course distinguish between a line and a verse. Lines there must be: that is an affair of the scribe and the printer; verses are rhythmical units, and there is no rhythmical mass in Greek lyrics between the colon and the period.

We must now consider the most vital portion of

[1] Cola containing anacrusis are often printed so as to begin further to the left than others.

our subject. How are we to determine the cola ? The colon is the very soul of the rhythm. The period is generally too long for the ear (unaided by music) to receive it as one artistic impression. The foot is too short; moreover, the mere foot too often tends to play one false: irrational syllables and τονή are against us. But the colon is neither too long nor too short. The colon-division serves the same purpose as non-commissioned officers in a regiment, or the determination of water-sheds in geography: it gives a sense both of grouping and of control.

What precisely *is* a colon ? It is as much of a strophe as can be uttered without making a new start. It is the embodiment of rhythm: a series of feet bound into a rhythmical unity by the presence of one main ictus. Three questions, then, arise. (i) What is an ictus ? (ii) Which is the main ictus of a series ? (iii) Can we with certainty determine the beginning and end of a colon when we have identified the main ictus ?

(i) Ictus is stress-accent. The ictus of any single word is usually obvious: in πάντων, λυσαμένοις, and κατάπαστος, it falls upon the first, second, and third syllable respectively. Greek metre is based upon quantity, but Greek rhythm (like all other rhythm) is based upon ictus. A strophe can, and must, be scanned foot by foot on quantity alone; but when we go beyond the foot-division to exhibit the structure of the whole, we must refer to ictus and nothing but ictus—for structure is an affair of cola, and the colon is created by the main ictus.[1]

(ii) Among the many word-ictuses of a considerable passage, a few will be found which are heavier than the rest. These are simply the ictuses of the most important words. Each of these prominent ictuses gathers the neighbouring minor ictuses into a

[1] The doctrine of ictus here stated is that generally accepted. But a number of scholars deny any ictus to Greek poetry. See, for example, Prof. J. W. White (*The Verse of Greek Comedy*, § 28). If they are right, it is impossible for anyone bred on Germanic language and literature to understand Greek poetry at all on its formal side.

group round itself. We should begin then by fixing some example where the main ictus is unmistakable, and on this basis attempt, by the help of the correspondences which we expect, to determine other main ictuses. The strophe will thus gradually fall into cola.

(iii) Can we with certainty determine the extent of each colon? Unfortunately no simple rule can be given for the settlement of this vital point. A well-trained ear is the chief guide. Intelligent and careful reading aloud of an English prose-passage will show this. Take first a famous sentence of John Bright:

> The angel of Death is abroad in the land: you may almost hear the beating of his wings.

If we set a dash for each syllable and mark the ictuses by one or more dots according to their strength, we find this scheme:

$$\_\overset{\cdot}{\_}\_\_\overset{:}{\_}\_\_\overset{\cdot}{\_}\_\_\overset{\cdot}{\_}$$
$$\_\_\_\overset{\cdot}{\_}\_\overset{:}{\_}\_\overset{:}{\_}\_\_\_\overset{:}{\_}$$

So with longer passages, where, however, we shall find at times that our voice quite naturally makes a colon-ending in the midst of a grammatical sentence:

> Therefore let us also, seeing we are compassed about with so great a cloud of witnesses, lay aside every weight, and the sin which doth so easily beset us, and let us run with patience the race that is set before us (*Hebrews*, xii, 1, R.V.).

$$\overset{:}{\_}\_\_\overset{:}{\_}\_\_$$
$$\overset{\cdot}{\_}\_\_\_\overset{:}{\_}\_\_\overset{\cdot}{\_}$$
$$\_\_\overset{\cdot}{\_}\_\overset{:}{\_}\_\overset{:}{\_}\_\_$$
$$\overset{\cdot}{\_}\_\_\overset{:}{\_}\_\_\overset{:}{\_}$$
$$\_\_\overset{:}{\_}\_\_\_\overset{:}{\_}\_\_\_\overset{:}{\_}\_$$
$$\_\overset{\cdot}{\_}\_\overset{\cdot}{\_}\_\overset{:}{\_}\_$$
$$\_\overset{:}{\_}\_\_\overset{:}{\_}\_\overset{\cdot}{\_}\_$$

Let us now attempt so to catch the rhythm of a passage from Aristophanes (*Peace*, 774 *sqq.*) if set out as " prose ":

METRE AND RHYTHM IN GREEK COMEDY

Μοῦσα σὺ μὲν πολέμους ἀπωσαμένη μετ' ἐμοῦ τοῦ φίλου χόρευσον, κλείουσα θεῶν τε γάμους ἀνδρῶν τε δαῖτας καὶ θαλίας μακάρων · σοὶ γὰρ τάδ' ἐξ ἀρχῆς μέλει. ἢν δέ σε Κάρκινος ἐλθὼν ἀντιβολῇ μετὰ τῶν παίδων χορεῦσαι, μήθ' ὑπάκουε μήτ' ἔλθῃς συνέριθος αὐτοῖς, ἀλλὰ νόμιζε πάντας ὄρτυγας οἰκογενεῖς γυλιαύχενας ὀρχηστὰς ναννοφυεῖς σφυράδων ἀποκνίσματα μηχανοδίφας. καὶ γὰρ ἔφασχ' ὁ πατὴρ ὃ παρ' ἐλπίδας εἶχε τὸ δρᾶμα γαλῆν τῆς ἑσπέρας ἀπάγξαι. τοιάδε χρὴ Χαρίτων δαμώματα καλλικόμων τὸν σοφὸν ποιητὴν ὑμνεῖν, ὅταν ἠρινὰ μὲν φωνῇ χελιδὼν ἑζομένῃ κελαδῇ, χορὸν δὲ μὴ 'χῃ Μόρσιμος μηδὲ Μελάνθιος, οὗ δὴ πικροτάτην ὄπα γηρύσαντος ἤκουσ' ἡνίκα τῶν τραγῳδῶν τὸν χορὸν εἶχον ἀδελφός τε καὶ αὐτός, ἄμφω Γοργόνες ὀψοφάγοι βατιδοσκόποι Ἅρπυιαι, γραοσόβαι μιαροὶ τραγομάσχαλοι ἰχθυολῦμαι · ὧν καταχρεμψαμένη μέγα καὶ πλατὺ Μοῦσα θεὰ μετ' ἐμοῦ σύμπαιζε τὴν ἑορτήν.

If we first mark the quantities (ignoring, as we must at first, the possibility of ⌣) and go over the whole carefully, we soon find that it falls into two corresponding portions: Μοῦσα σὺ μέν ... ἀπάγξαι is the strophe, τοιάδε χρή ... ἑορτήν is the antistrophe. Next we look for rhythmical units. On the one hand, there is the great difficulty that, since we must have strophic equivalence, certain cola may take in words not belonging to the same sense-groups or grammatical clauses. On the other hand, we have enormous help in the fact that there are two great masses which correspond exactly. Next we read the first strophe aloud carefully to find the natural stress-arrangement, and so the cola. We shall soon find certain masses suggesting themselves:

τοῦ φίλου χόρευσον—σοὶ γὰρ τάδ' ἐξ ἀρχῆς μέλει—ἀλλὰ νόμιζε πάντας—ἀποκνίσματα μηχανοδίφας—ἑσπέρας ἀπάγξαι.

Let us then set out the strophe provisionally thus:

1. Μοῦσα σὺ μὲν πολέμους ἀπωσαμένη μετ' ἐμοῦ
2. τοῦ φίλου χόρευσον
3. κλείουσα θεῶν τε γάμους ἀνδρῶν τε δαῖτας καὶ θαλίας μακάρων
4. σοὶ γὰρ τάδ' ἐξ ἀρχῆς μέλει
5. ἢν δέ σε Κάρκινος ἐλθὼν ἀντιβολῇ μετὰ τῶν παίδων χορεῦσαι, μήθ' ὑπάκουε μήτ' ἔλθῃς συνέριθος αὐτοῖς
6. ἀλλὰ νόμιζε πάντας
7. ὄρτυγας οἰκογενεῖς γυλιαύχενας ὀρχηστὰς ναννοφυεῖς σφυράδων ἀποκνίσματα μηχανοδίφας
8. καὶ γὰρ ἔφασχ' ὁ πατὴρ ὃ παρ' ἐλπίδας εἶχε τὸ δρᾶμα γαλῆν τῆς
9. ἑσπέρας ἀπάγξαι

Is there any of these nine which is too long for a colon? The first probably, certainly the third, fifth, seventh, and eighth. The first falls into two correspondent parts : -ωσαμένη μετ' ἐμοῦ is the same as the earlier part, except for catalexis. In the third we detect two portions similar to those in the first, namely : κλείουσα θεῶν τε γάμους ἀνδρ- and καὶ θαλίας μακάρων with -ῶν τε δαῖτας in the middle. This collocation shows that we have to do both with real or apparent dactyls and with real or apparent trochees. These facts should help us in the fifth mass. Dactylic scansion suggests that we separate from the rest ἢν δέ σε Κάρκινος ἐλθών and -ης συνέριθος αὐτοῖς, which exactly equal one another.[1] As for the residue—ἀντιβολῇ μετὰ τῶν παίδων χορεῦσαι, μήθ' ὑπάκουε μήτ' ἐλθ- —the last four words exactly equal the second colon shown in the preceding sentence : ‿ ‿ ‒ ‿ ‒ L ‒ ⋏ and we soon observe that ἀντιβολῇ μετὰ τῶν παίδ- equals the first colon of that sentence. This fifth mass thus falls into four almost identical cola, with -ων χορεῦσαι in the middle, which is the same as -ῶν τε δαῖτας above.[2]

The seventh passage is plainly dactylic : indeed, for those familiar with Homer it reads like a bad attempt at two hexameters. But it is not for this reason that we divide after ὀρχηστάς : it is because there is great difficulty in hearing dactyls or spondees in the middle of the passage by any other means. The eighth mass is perfectly dactylic, with a final long syllable, but the whole is too lengthy for a colon. The reader's ear will probably tell him definitely that the end comes after ἐλπίδας. As for εἶχε τὸ δρᾶμα γαλῆν, dactylic scansion is best served by adding the next word, τῆς : ‒ ‿ ‿ ‒ ‿ ‿ ‒ ‒. Moreover ἑσπέρας ἀπάγξαι, not τῆς ἑσπ. ἀπ., is a familiar colon : ‒ ‿ | ‒ ‿ | L | ‒ ⋏ (an ithyphallic—see p. 389).

---

[1] Counting the trochaic -ιθος as equivalent to the dactylic Κάρκινος, on the assumption that the dactyls are cyclic.

[2] Shall we regard these two phrases, -ων χορεῦσαι and -ῶν τε δαῖτας, as too short to form separate cola, and the phrases that precede them as short enough to combine with them, thus making one colon of ἀντιβολῇ μετὰ τῶν παίδων χορεῦσαι and another of κλείουσα θεῶν τε γάμους ἀνδρῶν τε δαῖτας? This is a minor question, to be decided according as we wish either to emphasize the similarity of the four phrases indicated above in the fifth mass, or to avoid cola that are too brief to " fill the mouth ".

METRE AND RHYTHM IN GREEK COMEDY 383

The whole strophe is composed then of the following cola :

(i) Μοῦσα σὺ μὲν πολέμους ἀπ- (ii) -ωσαμένη μετ' ἐμοῦ (iii) τοῦ φίλου χόρευσον (iv) κλείουσα θεῶν τε γάμους ἀνδρ- (v) -ῶν τε δαῖτας (vi) καὶ θαλίας μακάρων (vii) σοὶ γὰρ τάδ' ἐξ ἀρχῆς μέλει (viii) ἢν δέ σε Κάρκινος ἐλθών (ix) ἀντιβολῇ μετὰ τῶν παίδ- (x) -ων χορεῦσαι (xi) μήθ' ὑπάκουε μήτ' ἔλθ- (xii) -ῃς συνέριθος αὐτοῖς (xiii) ἀλλὰ νόμιζε πάντας (xiv) ὄρτυγας οἰκογενεῖς γυλιαύχενας ὀρχηστάς (xv) ναννοφυεῖς σφυράδων ἀποκνίσματα μηχανοδίφας (xvi) καὶ γὰρ ἔφασχ' ὁ πατὴρ ὃ παρ' ἐλπίδας (xvii) εἶχε τὸ δρᾶμα γαλῆν τῆς (xviii) ἑσπέρας ἀπάγξαι

How are these eighteen cola to be set out ? This is a question of minor importance. If we do not object to lines ending in the middle of a word we may write them out as eighteen lines. Or we may continue a line till we reach a colon-ending that is also a word-ending. This we shall now do, but at times we shall carry the line past the point just mentioned, because if we stopped at that point there would occur in the antistrophe (which must be written out to correspond) a word-break at the end of a line. Thus, if the last line of the strophe contained only ἑσπέρας ἀπάγξαι, the last line of the antistrophe must begin at the middle of σύμπαιζε. Two of our lines are set more to the left to indicate anacrusis :

Μοῦσα σὺ μὲν πολέμους ἀπωσαμένη μετ' ἐμοῦ
τοῦ φίλου χόρευσον,
κλείουσα θεῶν τε γάμους ἀνδρῶν τε δαῖτας
καὶ θαλίας μακάρων ·
σοὶ γὰρ τάδ' ἐξ ἀρχῆς μέλει.
ἢν δέ σε Κάρκινος ἐλθὼν
ἀντιβολῇ μετὰ τῶν παίδων χορεῦσαι,
μήθ' ὑπάκουε μήτ' ἔλθῃς συνέριθος αὐτοῖς, ἀλλὰ νόμιζε πάντας
ὄρτυγας οἰκογενεῖς γυλιαύχενας ὀρχηστὰς
ναννοφυεῖς σφυράδων ἀποκνίσματα μηχανοδίφας.
καὶ γὰρ ἔφασχ' ὁ πατὴρ ὃ παρ' ἐλπίδας
εἶχε τὸ δρᾶμα γαλῆν τῆς ἑσπέρας ἀπάγξαι.

Certain detailed hints may be added :
(i) The tetrapody is the most frequent length, the pentapody the rarest. (That is why μήθ' ὑπάκουε μήτ' ἔλθ- above was scanned ⏑⏑ | -⏑ | L | -ᴧ rather than as a tripody : ⏑⏑ | -⏑ | ->.)
(ii) The end of a colon is often indicated in dactyls by a spondee, in trochees by a single long syllable (whether L or ‾ ᴧ).

(iii) In any one period there is a tendency to conformity in length. If 6 + 5 + 4 and 6 + 6 + 4 are *prima facie* equally possible, the latter is as a rule to be preferred. In spite of the difference in sum-total (6 + 6 + 4 = 16; 6 + 5 + 4 = 15), this point often arises, because of the possibility of τονή.

§ 7. A List of the Feet used in Lyrics

(a) Iambi. Iambic systems are frequent and various: *e.g. Ach.*, 948 ff. :

> ἀλλ' ὦ ξένων βέλτιστε συν-
> θέριζε καὶ τοῦτον λαβὼν
> πρόσβαλλ' ὅποι βούλει φέρων πρὸς πάντα συκοφάντην.

This is the rhythm of the English comic song :

> I'm Captain Jinks of the Horse Marines :
> I feed my horse on kidney beans.
> Of course it's far beyond the means of a Captain in the Army.

(b) Trochees. These are the most frequent feet in lyrics. Such systems express ordinary strong interest :

> καὶ τὰ τῇδε καὶ τὰ δεῦρο
> πάντ' ἀνασκόπει καλῶς (*Thesm.*, 666).

So in English :

> Then, upon one knee uprising,
> Hiawatha aimed an arrow.   (LONGFELLOW.)

Resolution into tribrachs, and the use of spondees (or irrational trochees), are frequent :

> ⏑ ⏑ ⏑ – >   – ⏑ – ⏑
> ὅτι μέν | οὖν ἦν | χρηστόν | ἦ τι (*Frogs*, 599).

Whenever more definite emotion is to be conveyed, either cyclic dactyls are introduced or a change is made to some other metre.

(c) Dactyls. These are found pure, or mingled with spondees or quasi-trochees (– ⏑). They are employed to convey a sense of majesty, as in the splendid entrance-song of the *Clouds* (275-313), or amid the dazzling finale of the *Birds* (*e.g.*, 1748-49) :

> ὦ μέγα χρύσεον ἀστερόπης φάος
> ὦ Διὸς ἄμβροτον ἔγχος.
> – ⏑ ⏑ | – ⏑ ⏑ | – ⏑ ⏑ | – ⏑ ⏑
> – ⏑ ⏑ | – ⏑ ⏑ | ⎵⎦ | – $\bar{\wedge}$

METRE AND RHYTHM IN GREEK COMEDY 385

Where $\mathrel{\sqcup\!\!\!\sqcup} = \smile\smile\smile\smile$, *i.e.*, (here) a dactyl. Ariel's lines in *The Tempest* (V, i):

> Merrily, merrily, shall I live now,
> Under the blossom that hangs on the bough,

are dactylic tetrapodies with catalexis.

(*d*) *Spondees.* It is not certain that these are used as a base, though as a variant in anapæstic and dactylic metre they are common. *Birds*, 1058-64, may be taken as spondees:

> ἤδη 'μοὶ τῷ παντόπτᾳ
> καὶ παντάρχᾳ θνητοὶ πάντες
> θύσουσ' εὐκταίαις εὐχαῖς.

But they may be quasi-anapæsts.

(*e*) *Cretics.* This foot ($-\smile-$) is frequent, being used to express strong excitement, whether gleeful or angry. It is therefore very often resolved as $-\smile\smile\smile$, called a pæon, *e.g.*, *Ach.*, 214-17:

> ἐκπέφευγ', οἴχεται φροῦδος· οἴμοι τάλας τῶν ἐτῶν τῶν ἐμῶν.
> οὐκ ἂν ἐπ' ἐμῆς γε νεότητος, ὅτ' ἐγὼ φέρων ἀνθράκων φορτίον
> $-\smile-|-\smile-|-\smile-|-\smile-|-\smile-|-\smile-$
> $-\smile\smile\smile|-\smile\smile\smile|-\smile\smile\smile|-\smile-|-\smile-|-\smile-$

Few cretics are found in English, though Tennyson's brief poem, *The Oak*, is written entirely in this metre, *e.g.*:

> All his leaves
> Fall'n at length,
> Look, he stands,
> Trunk and bough,
> Naked strength.

(*f*) *Bacchiacs.* The bacchius consists of $--\smile$, the system being invariably introduced by anacrusis.[1] It is rare:

> φάνηθ' ὦ τυράννους στυγοῦσ' ὥσπερ εἰκός (*Thesm.*, 1144).
> $\smile:--\smile|--\smile|--\smile|--\wedge$

> Ye storm-winds of Autumn!
> Who rush by, who shake
> The window, and ruffle
> The gleam-lighted lake. (M. ARNOLD.)

---

[1] Those who do not believe in anacrusis of course describe the bacchius as consisting of $\smile--$.

(g) *Ionics*: -- ⏑⏑. When anacrusis is found—the usual form—the foot is often called *Ionicus a minore* (*i.e.*, ⏑⏑--); otherwise it is called *Ionicus a maiore* :

χαρίτων πλεῖστον ἔχουσαν μέρος ἁγνάν, ἱεράν (*Frogs*, 335).
⏑⏑ : -- ⏑⏑ | -- ⏑⏑ | -- ⏑⏑ |⌊⌋ ⩘

A strange variant is -⏑-⏑ ; the variation is called "anaclasis" ("breaking-up"). Thus :

φλογὶ φέγγεται δὲ λείμων (*Frogs*, 343).
⏑⏑ : -⏑-⏑ | -- ⩘

Anaclasis is sometimes modified into ---⏑, but the corresponding verse regularly shows complete anaclasis. Thus

πολύκαρπον μὲν τινάσσων (*Frogs*, 328)
⏑⏑ : ---⏑ | -- ⩘

corresponds to

γόνυ πάλλεται γερόντων (*Frogs*, 345)
⏑⏑ : -⏑-⏑ | -- ⩘

in the antistrophe.

(h) *Choriambi* : -⏑⏑-. It depends upon our methods of scansion whether we find this foot often or very seldon in comedy.

(i) *Dochmiacs*. It is convenient to discuss these here, though the dochmius is not a foot, but a colon, of which the simplest form [1] is ⏑--⏑-, *e.g.*, κακορρημόνων.

τί ταῦτα στρέφει τεχνάζεις τε καὶ πορίζεις τριβάς ; (*Ach.*, 385).
⏑--⏑- | ⏑--⏑- | ⏑--⏑-

Resolution of one or more long syllables is very common. A frequent form is ⏑⏑⏑-⏑- :

πόλεμος αἴρεται, πόλεμος οὐ φατός (*Birds*, 1188).
⏑⏑⏑-⏑- | ⏑⏑⏑-⏑⏑-

There is much variety, owing to resolution and irrational long syllables. Thus :

μηδόμενος ποιεῖν ὅ τι καλῶς ἔχει (*Thesm.*, 676).
>⏑⏑-⏑- | ⏑⏑⏑-⏑-
λάβε δ' ἐμοῦ γ' ἕνεκα παρ' Ἱερωνύμου (*Ach.*, 386).
⏑⏑⏑-⏑⏑⏑ | ⏑⏑⏑-⏑-
ἀέρα[2] περινέφελον ὃν ἔρεβος ἐτέκετο (*Birds*, 1194).
-⏑⏑⏑⏑⏑⏑⏑⏑⏑⏑⏑-

[1] This important sequence may be conveniently memorized—if we substitute accent for quantity—by the sentence "Attack Rome at once".

[2] Scanned - ⏑ by synizesis.

The last line, of course, would by itself have no rhythm at all, being so completely broken to pieces, in order to express extreme agitation; but it gains rhythm from the clearer lines of the context, *e.g.* :

> πρὸς ἐμὲ καὶ θεούς, ἀλλὰ φύλαττε πᾶς.
> ◡◡–◡–|>◡◡–◡–

§ 8. Important Cola

Every colon has of course a name which is a description of its metre, *e.g.*, "trochaic tetrameter catalectic," describing the phrase –◡–◡––◡–◡––◡–◡––◡–. But certain cola of special form and frequent usage received brief additional titles. The following list will be useful:

ARCHILOCHIAN : –◡◡–◡◡––̄–––̄–◡–◡L◡–. This is a dactylic dimeter followed by an ithyphallic (see below):

> αὐτομάτη δὲ φέρει τιθύμαλλον καὶ σφάκον πρὸς αὐτῷ (Cratinus, 325).

It is of course a period of two cola, often described as dactylo-trochaic. Cp. Horace (*e.g.*, *Odes*, I, iv, 1):

> *solvitur acris hiems grata vice veris et Favoni.*

LESSER ASCLEPIAD : –––◡◡––◡◡–◡–. This non-catalectic form is familiar in Horace, *e.g.*, *Odes*, I, i, 1 : *Mæcenas atavis edite regibus*. In Aristophanes only the catalectic form occurs:

> ὥραν οὐκ ἀπολεῖς οὐδ' ἀπολήψει (*Eccl.*, 923).

GREATER ASCLEPIAD : –––◡◡––◡◡––◡◡–◡–.

> ὄρνιθες τίνες οἶδ' οὐδὲν ἔχοντες πτεροποίκιλοι; (*Birds*, 1410).

Cp. Horace, I, xi, 1 :

> *tu ne quæsieris, scire nefas, quem mihi, quem tibi . . .*

This is named also the "longer Sapphic" (Σαπφικὸν ἑνδεκασύλλαβον) from its use by that poetess :

> φοιτάσεις πέδ' ἀμαύρων νεκύων ἐκπεποταμένα.
> Large red lilies of love, sceptral and tall, lovely for eyes to see.
> (SWINBURNE.)

CHŒRILEUM : $-\cup\cup-\cup\cup---\cup\cup-\cup\cup-$. Two dactylic trimeters, the second catalectic :

ἄξια σῇ φρενὶ συμβουλευσαμένους μετὰ σοῦ (*Clouds*, 475).

Marius Victorinus (III, p. 2558) discusses this type, giving a Latin example :

nunc age Pierios versus dea Calliope.

COLON REIZIANUM is a modern name for the "acephalous"[1] Pherecratean, $\cup--\cup\cup L-$ *e.g.* :

τοῦ μηνὸς ἑκάστου (*Ach.*, 859).

CRATINEUM : $-\cup\cup-\cup-\cup--\cup-\cup--\cup-$. This is perhaps a pair of trochaic cola, the second catalectic :

εὗιε κισσοχαῖτ' ἄναξ χαῖρ', ἔφασκ' Ἐκφαντίδης.
πάντα φορητὰ πάντα τολμητὰ τῷδε τῷ χορῷ.

EUPOLIDEAN : $\cup-\cup--\cup-\cup\cup-\cup-\cup-\cup-\cup-$. This curious and ugly metre was in great favour with the comic poets, including Eupolis, after whom it was named. We have a long example of its use in the parabasis of the *Clouds* (518-62), *e.g.* :

ὁ σώφρων τε χὠ καταπύγων ἄριστ' ἠκουσάτην (529).
ἐξέθηκα, παῖς δ' ἑτέρα τις λαβοῦσ' ἀνείλετο (531).

The line appears to consist of two cola, of which the second is usually a catalectic trochaic dimeter. The second half of the first colon is invariably a choriambus :

$\cup- \quad -\cup \quad -\cup\cup- \quad -\cup--\cup-$
ὁ σώφρων τε | χὠ καταπυγ | ων αριστ ηκουσατην.

The first half has four syllables, each of which, except the third, may be short or long at the poet's will, though $\cup\cup$ is avoided. This random quantity is derived from the original Æolic verse in which all syllables might have any quantity. It is certainly impossible to get any feet out of the first four syllables of the colon.

GLYCONIC : $---\cup\cup-\cup-$. This lively and beautiful phrase is no doubt a logaœdic trochaic dimeter

---

[1] *I.e.* "headless"; an acephalous colon has lost its first syllable. It is hard to believe in the existence of such a freak.

(tetrapody): a retarded trochee, a cyclic dactyl, a trochee, a catalectic trochee:

ἥδιστον φάος ἡμέρας (*Knights*, 973).

Cp. Horace (III, xiii, 4): *cui frons turgida cornibus.* The second syllable may be short:

οὗτος οὐ δύναται μαθεῖν (*Knights*, 995).

ITHYPHALLIC: *e.g.*:

ἐν βροτοῖσιν ἕξεις (*Clouds*, 460).

This is a favourite close of the Aristophanic trochaic stanza. It is not a tripody but a dimeter—*i.e.*, scanned as four feet, thus: $-\cup|-\cup|\mathrel{L}|-\wedge$. Resolution is admitted:

νέκυσιν ἐπὶ πορείαν (*Thesm.*, 1055).

PARŒMIAC: $\overline{-}-|\overline{-}-|\cup\cup-|-\overline{\wedge}$. This is the regular close of an anapæstic system, *e.g.*:

τοῦ σεμνοτάτου δι' Ὀλύμπου (*Thesm.*, 1069).

PHALÆCEAN: $\cup-\cup--\cup\cup-\cup-\cup--$

πολλὰ δὴ διεκόμπασας σὺ κἀγώ (*Wasps*, 1248).

Occasionally both the first two syllables are short:

τανυσίπτερε ποικίλα χελιδοῖ (*Birds*, 1411).

This is the metre of the celebrated Harmodius-song in the first two lines of its stanza:

ἐν μύρτου κλαδὶ τὸ ξίφος φορήσω
ὥσπερ Ἁρμόδιος κ' Ἀριστογείτων.

Cp. Cratinus 321, Kock (p. 140 above). It is familiar also in Latin as the hendecasyllabic line of Catullus and Martial, *e.g.*, *quoi dono lepidum novum libellum?* (Cat., I, 1).

PHERECRATEAN: $-\cup--\cup\cup\mathrel{L}-$: ἢν Κλέων ἀπόληται (*Knights*, 976). This is a catalectic form of the glyconic. The metre is named after Pherecrates, from whom we have a fragment which gives a long syllable regularly in the second place:

ἄνδρες, πρόσσχετε τὸν νοῦν
ἐξευρήματι καινῷ,
συμπύκτοις ἀναπαίστοις.

Cp. Horace (III, xiii, 3), *cras donaberis hædo.*

Pherecrates himself calls these cola "collapsed anapæsts," meaning apparently that the third and fourth feet in each colon are abbreviated by τονή. The Pherecratean is often used to close a series of Glyconics.

PRIAPEAN : ‐ ⏑ ‐ ‐ ⏑ ⏑ ‐ ⏑ ‐ | ‐ ⏑ ‐ ⏑ ⏑ ‐ ⌊ ‐. This is a glyconic followed by a Pherecratean :

οὐδ' Αἰξωνίδ' ἐρυθρόχρων | ἐσθίειν ἔτι τρίγλην
οὐδὲ τρυγόνος, οὐδὲ δειν|οῦ φυὴν μελανούρου (Cratinus).

Catullus, *Carm.* XVII, is written in this metre :

O Colonia, quæ cupis ponte ludere longo.

The "first Priapean" (used in the fragment of Eupolis on p. 191) is a variation that makes the first foot of each colon a dactyl, and the second a trochee.

PROSODIAC : ‐ ‐ ⏑ ⏑ ‐ ⏑ ⏑ ‐. This, of course, can be scanned as anapæsts, but Professor White, who gives great importance to this colon, regards it (§ 630), on the authority of Hephæstion, as consisting of Ionic *a maiore* and choriamb. It is found, *e.g.*, in Cratinus, fr. 323, followed by a catalectic iambic dimeter :

χαῖρ' ὦ μέγ' ἀχρειογέλως ὅμιλε ταῖς ἐπίβδαις.

We have said little concerning the nature, structure, and correspondence of periods, subjects too doubtful and complicated for the present brief statement. We may perhaps work out the period on paper, but our ear often cannot appreciate the balance and contour of the whole as it can in English lyrics, where we have the immense assistance of a rhyme-scheme. But it is no sound deduction that the study of Greek lyric metre and rhythm is therefore useless. We cannot always hear the period—that is a question of music ; but we can always hear the colon—that is a question of language. To utter the cola correctly is easy after a little practice ; and it is these "sentences" which, by their own rhythmical nature and by the identities or contrasts existing between them, reinforce and more pungently articulate the sense of the words wherefrom they are moulded.

INDEXES

I. GREEK

ἄθυρμα, 130 n.
ἀκαταληψία, 70 n.
ἀμενηνὰ κάρηνα, 278, 278 n.
ἀμφιανακτίζειν, 137.
ἀπόλειψις, 338 n.
Ἀριστοφάνειον, 374.
ἀρκύωρος, 133.
αὐξανόμενος λόγος, 93 n., 94.
αὐτοκάβδαλοι, 72 n.

βάθρα, 151 n.
βουκολιασμός, 101 n.
βουλόμενος, 274 n.
βοῶπις, 126 n.
βρίκελοι, 140.

γέρανος, 106 n.
γέρων, 161 n.; γέρων ὤν, 310, 310 n.
γλυκὺς ἀγκών, 175 n.

δεικηλισταί, 72 n.
δίλογχος, 133.
δῖνος, 218 sq.

ἐγκεκαλυμμένος λόγος, 94 n.
ἐθελονταί, 5 n., 72 n.
ἐμαυτός, 176.
ἐν πέντε κριτῶν γούνασι κεῖται, 107 sq.
ἐπιδεύτερος, 151 n.
ἐπίνοιαι, 146.
ἐποικοδόμησις, 95.
ἐφιάλτης, 151.

θάλασσα, 148 n.
θεωρία, 231 n.

ἰαμβικὴ ἰδέα, 146 n.
ἴαμβοι, 7.
ἰδυῖοι, 278, 278 n.
ἱλαροτραγῳδία, 73 n.

κάπηλον φρόνημα, 69.
καπνίας, 17.
καταστολή, 80.

κερατίνης λόγος, 65, 65 n.
κεφεληγερέτα, 126 n.
κλῖμαξ, 94 sqq.
κόρυμβα, 278, 278 n.
κραμβότατον στόμα, 147.
Κρατίνειον, 140, 140 n.
κύβηβος, 133.
κύβιτος, 108.
κυνῶπις, 126 n.
κυσί τε καὶ κυνηγέταις, 175 n.
κῶλον, 376.
κῶμος, 111 n.
κωμῳδοτραγῳδία, 5, 37, 49.

Λέρνη θεατῶν, 139 n.
λόγος, 106.

μὴ κωμῳδεῖν ὀνομαστί, 26-29, 113 n. 125 n.
μιμηταί, 72 n.

ναὶ μὰ τὴν κράμβην, 86 n.
ναυτοδίκαι, 129 n.
νεφεληγερέτα, 126 n.
νόμος, 222.

ὀγκία, 108.
ὀρθίαξ, 101 n.
ὀστρακίνδα, 167 n.
οὐγκία, 108.
Οὖτις, 131.

παλαιστικός, 58 n.
παλαιστρικός, 58.
παλλακή, 338 n.
πανήγυρις, 52 sq., 320 n.
πάντα χωρεῖ καὶ οὐδὲν μένει, 86.
παράσιτοι, 280 sq.
παραχορήγημα, 233, 285 n.
παρουσία, 175.
παρρησία, 26, 205, 311.
περίοδος, 376.

Πριαμιλλύδριον, 102.
πρόβουλος, 245 *n*.
πρόλογοι, 13 *n*.
πρόσωπον, 123 *n*.

ῥογός, 100 *n*.
ῥωποπερπερήθρα, 65.

σκευοποιοί, 72 *n*.
σκηναί, 295 *n*.
σοφισταί, 72 *n*.
συνάφεια, 367 *n*.
συνίζησις, 367 *n*.
συρβηνεύς, 134.

σχῆμα κλιμακωτόν, 95 *n*.
σχινοκέφαλος, 127 *n*.

τάξαι, 168.
τέμενος, 202 *n*.
τετραδισταί, 328.
τονή, 377, 379.

φαλλοφόροι, 8, 72 *n*., 73 *n*.
φλύακες, 72 *n*., 74, 76, 108 *n*.
φλυακογραφία, 73 *n*.
φλύαξ, 73 *n*.
φρύγανα, 22.

χιτὼν εὐνητήρ, 69.
χωρίον, 187 *n*.

II. TOPICS

ACCENT, Athenian, 296.
Acephalous cola, 388, 388 n.
Acrostics, 84 n.
Actor, 9.
Æolic verse, 388.
Agon, 6 n., 252, 252 n., 275.
Albert Memorial, 311.
Alexandrian scholarship, 36, 108 n., 109, 119 n., 283.
— theatre, 40 n.
Alphabet, 97.
Amulets, 38.
Anachronism, 99.
Anaclasis, 386.
Anacrusis, 377 sq.
Anapæst, 368; anapæstic systems, 373 sq.
Antepirrhema, 239.
Antipnigos, 239 n.
Antistrophe, 375.
Antitheses in Epicharmus, 97.
Antode, 239.
Archilochian colon, 387.
Asclepiad, Greater, 387; Lesser, 387.
Asides, 60.
Athenian prose, 94.
Audience, culture of, 262.

BACCHIACS, 385.
Bastardy law, 125.
Beast-mummeries, 6, 7.
— -plays, 17.
Bifurcation of plot, 364.
Billingsgate, 208.
Bipartition or tripartition of Athenian comedy? 37 n.
Blackmailers, 21.
" Boxing-tune," 102.
Bucolic poetry, 101, 236.
" Building up," 95.
Burglar's " jemmy," 296 n.
Burlesque, 23; in Epicharmus, 87, 97-102; Cratinus, 118-25, 129-33; Eupolis, 189 sq.; Aristophanes, see under that heading; Plato Com., 175 n.; Strattis, 33; in Middle Comedy, 39; particularly Diphilus, 60; also Timocles, 50; dwindles in New Comedy, 62; in phlyakes, 73; particularly Rhinthon, 74 sq.; and Sopater, 75; Charition, 80.
Byzantine account of origin of Comedy, 5 sq., 8.

CABBAGE oath, 86 n.
Cæsura, 369.
Cairo papyrus, 318, 326.
Carrier-pigeons, 159.
Catalexis, 370, 371, 382.
Censorship, 25-9.
Chance, 67, 320, 360.
Character-play, 151 sq.
Character study in Middle Comedy, 59.
Chœrileum, 388.
Choriambus, 386, 390.
Chorus, 7, 9, 27, 249, 295 and Chaps. III-VI passim; none in Epicharmus, 9, 98; none in Odysses, 129 n.; developed from animal-masquerade, 7, 10, 16 sq.; this became comos, 10, 13; delivered parabasis, 11 sq.; and lampoons, 15; usually undifferentiated, 24; exceptions to this, 24, 187 n., 193 sq., 293; symmetry even when differentiated, 253, 281, 281 n.; subsidiary chorus (παραχορήγημα), 233, 257, 285 n.; became insignificant after Old Comedy, 11, 28, 29, 38, 39, 54, 54 n., 272; but still participated in action of Middle Comedy, 58; but not of New Comedy, 59; becomes once more a comos, 59; Menander's chorus, 321, 333, 342.
Church and stage, 77.
Cigars, 171 n.
Climax, 94 sqq.
Clown, 80, 113, 194.
Cockaigne theme, 19, 20 sq.
Coinage in Hades, 159.
Cola, 376, 379-384, 390.
" Collapsed anapæsts," 159.
" Colonies," 359 n.
Colossus of Rhodes, 75.
Comédie larmoyante, 248.

393

Comedy, defined, 1. See also Old, Middle, and New Comedy.
Commation, 239.
Commedia del arte, 113.
Communism, 265, 266, 268 sq.
Comos, 7, 10, 13, 59, 72, 250.
Compound words, 137, 138, 229, 266.
Contaminatio, 233.
Cooks and cookery, 42 sq., 62 sq., 65, 175, 344, 345 n.
Cordax, 153 sq.
Costume of comedy, 9 sq.
Cottabos, 172, 174.
Courtesans, 44 sq., 63 sqq.
Cratineum, 140, 140 n., 388.
Cretics, 385 ; " final cretic," 370.
" Crocodile," 219.
" Cupboard-love," 51.
Cyclic dactyls, 377, 384.

DACTYLS, 369, 384 sq.
Deicelistæ, 72.
Diæresis, 371.
Dialogue and plot, 360 sq.
Digamma, 108.
Dimeter, 373.
Dinos, 218 sq., 300, 305.
Dithyramb, 9, 139, 139 n.
Divine-birth *motif*, 22, 51.
Dochmiacs, 386.
Doric Greek of physicians, 72, 150.
" Double law," 350.
Drama, defined, 1.
Drunkenness, 116, 150.
Duel-drama, 105 sq.

ECCYCLEMA, 22, 256 sq.
Education, 216 sq., 277 sqq.
Eleatic School, 47 n., 86, 93.
Eleusinian mysteries, 100.
Elision, 367.
English Civil War and drama, 29.
Epicureanism, 65 sq., 363 sq.
Epigrams in Epicharmus, 96.
Epirrhema, 239.
Epirrhematic syzygy, 6 n.
" Episodes " in Old Comedy, 281, 281 n., 282, 282 n.
Epode, 378.
Erotic drama, 37, 173 sqq.
Eupolideans, 184 n., 195 n., 388.

FANTASY in Old Comedy, 19, 39.
Farce, defined, 1.
Fishmongers, 43 sq.
Florentine papyrus, 323.
Freedom of speech in Athens, 25 sq., 205.
Fun, defined, 304.

GENEVA fragment of Menander, 323.
Glutton's Eldorado, 19, 163.
Glyconic colon, 388 sq.
" Good old days," 20, 126, 139, 147, 155, 198 sq.
Gorgonzola, 273 n.
Gradatio, 95 n.
Græculus, 266.
Growth Proposition, 94, 94 n.

HADES, visits to, 75, 159, 162, 257 sqq., 289-92.
Heliæa, 129 n.
Heracliteanism, 93.
Hermes-outrage, 21 n., 153.
Hexameters, 382.
Hiatus, 367.
Hibeh Papyri, 91 n.
" Horned Argument," 65.
Humour, 109, 298 sq., 304 sq.
Hymns of the Roman Church 373.

IAMBICS, 368 sqq., 370 sq., 384.
Ictus, vi, 379 sq.
" Imitating Arcadians," 166, 176.
In uxoris loco, 338 n.
" Increasing Man Proposition," 94 n.
Indecency, 30, 30 n., 44, 147, 147 n. 249, 306 sqq., 339 n.
Innuendo in Cratinus, 119, 122.
Ionics, 386, 390.
Irony in Aristophanes, 216, 301.
Irrational feet, 375, 379.
Italian farce, 10, 72 n., 73-6.
Ithyphallic, 382, 389.
Ivory kipper, 150, 252.

JAZZ, 134.

LACONIAN goblets, 277.
Lampoon, 6, 7 sqq., 13, 23, 26, 143, 146 n., 241, 263.
Latin comedies and Greek originals, 39, 63, 70 n., 109, 113, 173, 315, 317, 319, 327 sq., 330, 336, 342 n., 362.
" Lex Antimacheia," 27.
Lex Plautia, 95 n.
Limits of comedy, 362 sq.
" Literature-comedy," 173 n.
Living guide-book, 36 ; utensils, 224.
Logaœdics, 377, 388.
Long syllables, 366 sq.
Lyrics, scansion of, 375-84.

MACEDONIAN, domination, influence of, 37, 39, 58 sq.
Magic wheel, 188.
Male and Female Mimes, 77 n., 78, 78 n.

II. TOPICS

"Man of the theatre," 361.
Marriage, 325.
Mascots, 296.
Masks, 39.
Megarian claim, see Old Comedy.
— farce, 11, 13, 15, 113 *n.*
— philosophy, 65.
Melodrama, 80, 356 *n.*
Mesode, 378.
Messengers' speeches in tragedy, 112.
Metre, 365-78, 384-7.
Middle Comedy, 37-58; transition from Old Comedy, 29-37; is there a genuine distinction between Middle and New Comedy? 37 *n.*, 58 *sq.*, 62; differences between Old and Middle, 38 *sqq.*; main topics, 41; influence of Euripides, 38, 50.
Mime, 4, 76-82, 84, 110, 112.
Minor Forms of Comedy, 72-82.
Monogram on shields, 199.
Morychides' decree, 129 *n.*
Mounting of plays, 29.
Music, degradation of, 164.
Mutes, 123.
Mythological Comedy. See Burlesque.

NARRATION instead of action, 99, 100 *sq.*
Nativity-plays, 22.
Navy-Board, 129, 280.
New Comedy, 58-71; is there a genuine distinction between New and Middle Comedy? 37 *n.*, 58 *sq.*, 62; new fragments, 71; influence of Euripides, 61, 66, 354; light thrown by Plautus and Terence, 317, 319, 356 *n.*; literary manner, 69 *sq.*
Nightshirt, 69.
Nomes, 137 *n.*
Non-choric drama, 9.
Number of actors in early comedy, 123.
Nuts thrown among spectators, 147 *n.*

OCTONARIUS, 371.
Ode, 239.
Old Comedy, its origin and elements, 5-13; Megarian "comedy" and its claim, 7, 10 *sq.*, 11, 13, 15, 83 *n.*, 113 *n.*; literary history in outline, 13-37; main topics, 18; transition to Middle Comedy, 29-37; Peloponnesian element, 10, 13; post-parabasic scenes, 7, 12 *sq.*, 23, 25-9.
Ostracism, 135.

PADDING of comic actor, 9, 73.
Paeonics, 385.
Pageants, 7.
Pantomime, 171 *n.*; English, 13.
Parabasis, 7, 11, 59, 129, 129 *n.*; its sections, 239; discontinued in the Middle period, 39, 59; part of its functions taken over by the prologue, 59. See also Aristophanes and Cratinus.
Parasites, 41, 62, 103 *sq.*, 190, 191.
Parodos, 229, 262.
Parœmiacs, 130 *n.*, 373 *sq.*, 389.
Pathos, in Cratinus, 137. See also Aristophanes.
Pauses in lyrics, 371.
Peloponnesian War, 27, 29, 30, 119, 122, 129, 160, 178, 194, 197, 204, 230, 244, 287.
Pentapody, 383.
"People in the Long Walls," 182, 183
Periods, 376, 390.
Phalæceans, 140, 389.
Phallic songs, 6, 8 *sq.*; phallic procession, 13; phallus, 8, 9, 10, 108 *n.*
Pherecrateans, 159, 388, 389 *sq.*
Philosophy, in Epicharmus, 84-93; in Old Comedy, 24 *sq.*, 32, 190 *sq.*, 199, 211-22, 269; in Middle Comedy, 46 *sqq.*; in New Comedy, 65 *sq.*
Phlyaces, 10, 23, 113.
Pitch-accent, 365 *n.*
Plagiarism in Middle Comedy, 50.
Pnigos, 239.
Political Comedy, 23, 25-9, 143.
Pony-postman, 169.
"Position," 367.
Post-parabasic scenes, 7, 12 *sq.*
Postlude, 378.
Poverty abolished, 163, 270, 276 *sq.*
Prelude, 378.
Priapeans, 163 *n.*, 390.
Pro uxore, 338 *n.*
Prodelision, 367.
Prologue, in Old Comedy, 13, 13 *n.*, 59; in New Comedy, 59, 70, 71; in Menander, 112, 353 *sq.*; his postponed prologues, 327, 339, 354.
Properare, 109 *n.*
Prose, in comedy, 257, 309; in mime, 77, 80.
Prosodiac, 390.
Prospectus-passage in Epicharmean Forgeries, 91, 91 *n.*
Psephism of Morychides, 26.
Puns, 23, 96, 256.
Pythagoreanism, 83 *n.*, 92, 93.

RAJAH'S ruby, 174 n.
Recognition, 38.
" Reformed " pronunciation of Greek, 121 n.
Regattas, 176 n.
Reizianum (colon), 388.
Research in Plato's School, 48.
Resolved feet, 368.
Restoration drama, 29.
Revolt of women, 159.
Rhetoric and poetry, 351 sq.
— in Epicharmus, 94-7.
Rhythm, 365, 366 n., 375-84.
Riddles, 46, 62.
Rising from dead, 172, 179.
Rollers used for boat in theatre, 130, 257 n.
Roman citizenship conferred on Pythagoras, 85.
— comedy, 356 n.; literature, 94; satirists, 74.

SALMON, 161 n.
Samian War, 29, 284.
Sapphic, Longer, 387.
Satyric drama, 111 n., 141.
Scapegoat, 184.
Scazon, 79.
Second Athenian Confederacy, 293.
" Second Comedy," 28.
Seduction-*motif*, 39, 41.
" Shop-keeping mind," 69.
Short syllables, 367.
Slaves, growing importance of, 228, 272.
Sorites, 94 n., 95 n.
Spartan farce, 72 sq.
Spondees, 368, 385.
St. Crispin's Day, 351.
Stoicism, 65, 71, 76, 350 n.
Stress-accent, 365, 366 n.

" Stretching," 373, 379.
Strophe, 375.
Subject-allies, 194, 283-7.
Swaggering Soldier, 105.
Synapheia, 367.
Synizesis, 367.

TAUROPOLIA, 343, 346, 347.
Tetrameter, 374.
Tetrapody, 373, 376, 383.
Thesmophoria, 250, 252.
Timepiece, portable, 70.
Tired Business Man, 358 n.
Tribrachs, 368.
Trick-chair in Epicharmus, 102, 102 n.
Trilogistic form in Epicharmus ? 99, 111 sq.
Tripartition or bipartition of Athenian Comedy ? 37 n.
Tripody, 383.
Trochees, 371 sqq., 384.

UNCIA, 108.
Utensils personified, 148, 149, 224, 228.

" VAMPIRE," 151.
Vase-paintings, 2, 6, 7, 9, 10, 73, 75, 108 n., 124.
" Ventriloquism," 223 n.
Verse-pause, 369.
Violation-*motif*, 38.
Virtus dormitiva, 218.
Vulgarity, 236.

WAITERS, 171 n.
Weak hiatus, 367.
." Whisper " on stage, 123.
Wit, 298 sq., 304 sqq., 353.

III. PERSONS, WORKS, AND PLACES

A. = Aristophanes; E., Epicharmus; M., Menander. Small capitals indicate Greek comic dramatists

Academus, 220.
Academy, 46 sqq.
Acarnanians, 198.
Acestor, 192.
Achæans, 32.
Achæus of Eretria, 200 n.
Acharnæ, 122, 203.
Acharnians, 229.
Acharnians (A.), 4, 8, 13, 27, 102, 105, 115, 115 n., 117 n., 122, 181 n., 196 n., 203-6, 208, 231, 254, 255, 264, 273 n., 282 sq., 283 n., 284, 286, 286 n., 289 n., 302 n., 303, 310 n.
Achilles, 164.
Acragas, 5.
Acropolis, 68, 148 n., 196, 245, 249.
Adæus, 55.
Adam, 44.
— J., 269 n.
Adelphœ (Terence), 6 n., 319.
Admetus (Aristomenes), 269.
Adonais, 235.
Adoniazusæ, 79.
Adonis, 138.
Adonis (Nicophon), 269.
Adrastus, 49.
Æacus, 161, 162.
— (*Frogs*), 258.
Ægina, 161, 178, 202.
Ægisthus, 50.
Ægospotami, 30, 178, 205, 268.
Ælian, 105, 178 sq.
Æneid, 100 n.
Æolosicon (A.), 42, 129 n., 202.
Æschinades, 237.
Æschines, 189.
Æschylus, 4, 100, 104 n., 110, 111, 111 n., 113, 141, 143, 160, 172 n., 173 n., 179, 236, 259, 297, 373.
Æsop, 172.
Ætnæan Women, 111 n.
Africa, 99.
Africanus, Sextus Julius, 82.
Agamemnon, 119, 164.

Agamemnon, 4.
Agathocles, 77 n.
Agathon, 50, 250, 252, 254, 255 sq.
Agis, 182 n.
Agora, 183.
Agoracritus (*Knights*), 207.
Air personified to deliver prologue, 70.
Ajax, 79, 127.
Ajax (Sophocles), 6 n.
Aladdin, 242, 318.
Alcæus (lyrist), 255, 278.
ALCÆUS, 36, 269.
Alceste (*Le Misanthrope*), 113.
Alcestis, 255 n.
Alcibiades, 28, 165 n., 167, 169, 178, 183 n., 184 n., 188, 189, 216, 217, 240, 259, 279, 359 n.
Alcimus, 87-91.
Alcmæon, 49.
Alcmæonidæ, 122.
Alcman, 198.
Alciphron, 314 n., 315, 315 n.
Alexander (Paris) (*Dionysalexandros*), 118, 122.
— Ætolus, 297 n.
— Aphrodisiensis, 86.
— of Thessaly, 51.
— the Great, 55, 59, 61, 75, 137, 314, 328.
Alexandria, 76, 233, 314.
ALEXIS, 38, 40-7, 49, 52, 54, 55, 56-8, 71 n., 72, 73, 113 n., 313, 318, 320 n., 354 n.
Alliance (Plato Com.), 166 n., 167.
Allinson (Loeb ed. of M.), 318 n., 334 n., 339 n., 354 n.
All's Well, 342.
Alope, 347.
Ambassadors (Leucon), 223.
Ameinias, 213.
AMEIPSIAS, 23-5, 115, 116 n., 151, 152, 154, 211, 213, 217, 238.
Amorgos, 194, 318.
Amphictyon, 21.
Amphictyonic Council, 20.
Amphictyons (Telecleides), 19, 20,

397

Amphipolis, 199.
AMPHIS, 43, 44, 45, 47, 51, 52.
Amphitruo, 173.
Amycus, 102.
Amycus, (E.), 102, 110.
Amynias, 197 *n*.
Anacreon, 255, 278.
Ananius, 86 *n*., 98, 98 *n*., 99, 100 *n*., 110.
Anaxagoras, 297.
ANAXANDRIDES, 37, 38, 40 *sq*., 47, 49, 55, 55, 61.
ANAXILAS, 44, 45, 54 *sq*.
Anaxilaus, 104.
Andria, 319.
Andromache, 33 *n*.
Andromeda, 140, 153.
Andromeda, 250 *n*., 251, 256, 262 *n*.
Andros, Girl of : see *Andria*.
Androtion, 198.
Anger (M.), 313.
Anonymus de Comœdia, 3, 19, 31, 32, 40, 53, 60, 60 *n*., 83 *n*., 84, 111 *n*., 141 *sq*., 141 *n*., 145 *sq*., 151 *n*., 154, 154 *n*., 165, 165 *n*., 166, 178.
Antenor, 85.
Antenor (pseudo-E.), 92.
Anthology, 106 *n*., 324.
Antiatticista, 92 *n*.
Antigone, 50 *n*.
Antigonus, 55.
Antilais, 45.
Antimachus, 27.
Antiope, 252.
ANTIPHANES, 37 *n*., 38, 40, 44, 47 *n*., 48, 50, 51, 53, 54 *n*., 55, 316 *n*., 318.
Antiphon, 176.
Antisthenes, 89.
Ant-Men (Pherecrates), 161 *sq*.
Anytus, 217.
Aphrodite, 22, 124.
— (*Dionysalexandros*), 118, 123 ; (*Phaon*), 175.
— Pandemos, 328.
Aphroditopolis, 318.
Apollo, 270.
APOLLODORUS of Carystus, 63, 67, 68 ; of Gela, 63, 67, 68 ; of Athens, 78, 91, 99, 109, 111 *n*.
Apology of Socrates, 215, 217.
Apparition (M.), 330 *sq*.
Apuleius, 37 *n*., 61.
Arabia, 163.
Arabian Nights' Entertainments, 163.
ARAROS, 51, 202.
Arbitration (M.), 318, 321, 339, 342-50, 352, 353, 356, 359, 362.
Arcadians, 166, 166 *n*.

Arcesilaus, 70.
Archestratus, 42.
Archilochi (Cratinus), 135 *sq*., 137.
Archilochus, 60, 108, 135, 136, 136 *n*., 141, 143, 231, 235, 372.
ARCHIPPUS, 23, 113 *n*.
Areopagus, 136.
Ares, 22.
Arginusæ, 257, 259.
Argives, 50, 231, 233.
Argos, 140, 160.
Ariel, 242, 385.
Aristarchus, 109.
Aristides (statesman), 170, 181, 183, 186, 187, 207 ; (rhetor), 125 *n*., 183.
Aristion, 155 *n*.
Aristippus, 47.
Aristocles, 269 *n*.
Aristocracy personified, 56.
ARISTOMENES, 269.
ARISTONYMUS, 22.
Aristophanes' Apology, 302 *n*.
ARISTOPHANES, v, vi, 6 *n*., 7, 11, 16, 18, 22, 23, 24, 27, 30, 31, 35, 37, 38, 40 *n*., 42, 50, 51, 104, 106, 113, 115 *sq*., 129 *n*., 130 *n*., 137, 140 *n*., 141, 141 *n*., 142, 147, 147 *n*., 150, 152, 153 *sq*., 154 *n*., 157, 159, 163, 165 *n*., 166 *n*., 169 *n*., 173, 176, 179, 184, 193, 199, 201, 202-312, 357, 375-8, 387, 389 ; called a foreigner, 200, 202 ; indicted by Cleon, 26, 282 *sq*. ; influenced by E. ? 113 *n*. ; produced by others, 24, 166, 202, 276, 282 ; re-wrote some plays, 212-6, 231-14, 271 ; "ventriloquism," 223 *n*. ; Byzantine selection, 259, 272 ; doubtful plays, 23, 202, 292 *sq*. ; ridiculed by Cratinus, 138 ; quarrelled with Eupolis, 190, 200, 210 *sq*. ; defence of himself and his art, 295 *sq*. ; broken by fall of Athens, 28, 30, 165, 265 *sq*., 271 *sqq*., 296 *sq*., 310 ; structure of his plays, 12, 243, 257, 302 *sqq*. ; mistakes therein, 249 *n*., 264, 275 *sq*., 299 *sq*. ; prologues, 59, 353 ; "episodes," 281 *sq*. ; parabases, 120 ; looseness of post-parabasic scenes, 12, 142, 142 *n*., 299 ; spectacular jokes, 238, 300 *sqq*. ; pathos, 205, 247, 248 ; seriousness, 242, 246 *sq*., 259 *n*., 274 ; irony, 216, 244, 301 ; bitterness in attack, 25, 210 ; outspokenness, 26, 311 ;

III. PERSONS, WORKS, AND PLACES 399

lampoons, 23; social comedy, 18; fantastic comedy, 18; political comedy, 18, 23; burlesque of tragedy, 18, 23, 204, 205, 230, 235, 251, 255 sq.; and perhaps of "Megarian" farce, 282; attacks on Cleon, 207, 210, 218; on Lamachus, 206; on Euripides 260 sq., 296, 297; on Socrates, 211 sqq., 217; on Plato the philosopher, 269; remarks on comic playwrights, 16 sq., 145 sqq., 154, 209, 236, 282, 291 sq., 295; on education, 216 sq., 219-22, 277 sqq.; on science 218 sq.; on economics, 228 sq., 265, 266, 268 sq., 270, 275, 294; on slavery, 296; lyrics, 206, 243 sq., 261 sqq., 267; style, 208, 221 sqq., 225 sq., 237, 308 sqq., 374; prosody, 108; no humorist, 298 sq.; limitations as a playwright, 299 sq.; "world-annihilation," 300 sqq.; wit, 305 sq.; indecency, 307 sq.; vitality, 310 sqq. See also *Acharnians*, etc.
Aristophanes of Byzantium, 316, 316 n.
Aristotle, 2, 3, 10, 17, 50 n., 110, 111, 298, 314, 316; confesses to ignorance as to first stages of Comedy, 5, 123; on phallic songs, 6, 9 sq.; on comos, 7; implies that Comedy arose from comos, 10; on Megarian claim, 11, 83 n.; development of plot, 5, 18, 110; on E., 9, 11, 16, 83 n., 86 n., 95 n., 97, 111 n.; Phormis, 5, 110 n.; Chionides, 15, 83 n.; Magnes, 16, 83 n.; Crates, 8, 18, 145, 146, 147; Anaxandrides, 40; Philemon, 40; indecency in Old and Later Comedy, 30, 44; on the trochaic tetrameter, 372.
Aristoxenus (of Selinus), 84, 110; (philosopher), 91 n.
Arnold, M., 385.
Arrian, 329 n.
Arsenius, 166 n.
Art of Terence, 317.
Artemis, 133.
Artemis (Ephippus), 51.
Asclepius, 175 n., 270.
Asopichus, 197.
Aspasia, 63, 122, 125, 126 sq., 129 n., 228.
Astyanax of Miletus, 328.
As You Like It, 51.
Atalanta (Strattis), 32.

Athena, 34, 57, 98, 118, 124, 209, 271, 294.
Athenæus, 3, 147, 149, 165, 198 n., 199 n., 233, 238, 241, 242, 246, 248, 249, 252 n., 259, 262, 268, 280 n., 284, 285 n., 295, 298.
ATHENIO, 62.
Athens, like Hades, 263; transformed into a country paradise? 288 n.; had fruits out of season, 294; her fall ruined Old Comedy, and brought in Middle Comedy, 37; it broke A., 265; and the Athenian spirit, 268 sq., 275; "Mecca of tourists," 35; Second Confederacy, 108, 293; Macedonian conquest brought in New Comedy, 59.
Attica, 46, 161, 162, 173, 176, 179, 182, 182 n., 197, 237, 280, 287, 289, 293.
Augustine, St., 221, 221 n.
Aulularia, 327.
Aulus Gellius, see Gellius.
Ausonius, 315.
Austen, Jane, 358 n.
Australia, 359 n.
Austrian National Anthem, 373.
Autolycus (Eupolis), 199.
AXIONICUS, 50.
Axiopistus, 90 n., 91, 91 n., 92, 106 n.

Babylon, 242.
Babylonians, 284, 285.
Babylonians (A.), 282-7, 302 n.
Bacchæ (Euripides), 310 n.; (Lysippus), 36.
Bacchis (Sopater), 75.
Bactria, 333.
Baedeker, 35 n.
Baiter-Orelli, 109 n.
Balzac, 305.
Banqueters (A.), 202, 276-87, 302 n.
Baptæ (Eupolis), 28, 178, 188 sqq.
Basileia (*Birds*), 240, 242, 243.
BATO, 62, 63, 65, 66, 67, 70.
Bdelycleon (*Wasps*), 223, 224, 226, 228, 229, 306.
Beasts (Crates), 147-50.
Beaumont, 322 sq.
Beaux Stratagem, 358 n.
Bebryces, 102.
Beethoven, 221.
Beggar's Opera, 59 n.
Bekker, 314 n.
Bellerophon, 230.
Bendis, 133.
Benoit (*La Comédie de Ménandre*), 319 n., 357 n.

Bergk, 24 n., 130 n., 136 n., 150 n., 167, 173 n., 269 n., 280, 280 n., 281 n., 282 n., 285 n., 287 n., 290, 290 n., 291 n.
Bernays, 94 n.
Bernhardy (*Gesch. d. gr. Litt.*), 109 n.
Bias (*Flatterer*), 327, 328.
Bieber (*Theaterwesen*), 75 n.
Birds (A.), 4, 23, 24, 28, 125 n., 152, 152 n., 155, 235, 238-44, 246, 253, 265, 267, 296 n., 301, 303, 304, 309, 310 n., 311, 384; (Crates ?), 146; (Magnes), 17.
Birt (*Antike Buchwesen*), 108 n.
Birth of Aphrodite (Nicophon, Polyzelus), 22.
—— —— *Ares?* (Polyzelus), 22.
—— —— *Athena* (Hermippus), 22, 51.
—— —— *Dionysus* (Polyzelus), 22.
—— —— *Muses* (Polyzelus), 22.
—— —— *Pan* (Araros), 51.
Blass (*Attische Beredsamkeit*), 94 n., 97 n.
Blepsidemus (*Plutus*), 270, 272, 273, 273 n.
Blepyrus (*Ecclesiazusæ*), 264, 265, 268.
Bluntschli (*Arms and the Man*), 69.
Boeckh, 197 n.
Bœotian (*Acharnians*), 204.
Boileau, 357 n.
Boston, 311.
Boswell, 315.
Botticelli, 221.
Bourgeois Gentilhomme, 250.
Boys (Theopompus), 30.
Brasidas, 230, 234.
Brigadiers (Eupolis), 197 *sq.*
Bright, John, 380.
Brobdingnag, 302.
Brothel-keeper (Eubulus), 44.
Browning, 302 n.
Buffoon (*Charition*), 80 *sq.*
Bulias, 79.
Busiris, 50, 99.
Busiris (E.), 4, 99 *sq.*, 112.
Byzantium, 77, 314.

Cæcilius of Calacte, 316 n.
Cæsar (*Cæsar and Cleopatra*), 363.
Caius, Dr. (*Merry Wives*), 73.
CALLIAS, 132 n.
Callias, 190, 199, 222.
Calligeneia (lost *Thesmophoriazusæ*), 252.
Callimedes, 114.
Callistratus (A.'s friend), 24, 202, 203, 238, 244, 276, 276 n., 282, 283; (statesman), 32.
Calvus, 95 n.

Calypso, 131 n.
Calypso (Anaxilas), 44.
Camirus, 202.
Canon (attrib. to E.), 91.
CANTHARUS, 166 n.
Capps, 59 n., 113 n., 154 n., 287 n., 314 n., 318 n., 338 n., 345 n.
Captivi (Plautus), 63.
Carcinus, 66, 224.
Caria, 333, 359 n.
Carion (*Plutus*), 270, 272.
Carystius of Pergamum, 41 n.
Casaubon, 171 n., 295 n.
Castor (*Hebe's Wedding*), 98.
Catullus, 389. 390.
Cecrops, 289,
Celarent, B., 106 n.
Celts, 55.
Centaurs, 126, 127.
Ceos, 150.
Cephalus, 133.
Cephisophon, 297.
Cerberus, 258.
Ceres (*Tempest*), 7.
Cervantes, 301.
Chærephon, 331.
Chærestratus (*Arbitration*), 344, 345.
Chæronea, 37.
Chairmen (Telecleides), 19.
Chamaeleon, 41.
Chaplin, Charles, 209.
Characters of Theophrastus, 313.
Charicles, 21.
Charioteer (M.), 363.
Charisius (*Arbitration*), 342-350, 352, 362, 363.
Charition (*Charition*), 80 *sq.*
Charition, 71 n., 80 *sq.*
Charixena, 129 n.
Charley's Aunt. 356.
Charmides, 237.
Charmides, 151.
Charon (*Frogs*), 130, 197, 257.
Chaste Man and Rake (*Banqueters*), 280.
Chaucer, 231, 254.
Chicago, 69 n., 171.
Chimæra, 45.
Chinese Emperor, 318.
CHIONIDES, 11, 15, 16, 83 n., 84, 143.
Chios, 197, 209.
—— (*Cities*), 193.
Chiron (*Chirons*), 126, 127.
Chiron (attrib. to E.), 91 n., 92, 92 n.; (Pherecrates ? Plato ? Nicomachus ?), 155 n., 164.
Chirons (Cratinus), 125-9
Chiron's Maxims, 126.
Choephoræ, 260.
Choricius of Gaza, 78.

III. PERSONS, WORKS, AND PLACES

Chremes, 49.
— (*Ecclesiazusæ*), 265.
Chremylus (*Plutus*), 270, 272-6.
Christ, W., 109 n., 313 n.
Chrysippus, 94.
Chrysis (*Samia*), 331-6, 363.
Chrysogonus, 91, 91 n.
Cicero, 189, 189 n., 293, 293 n.
Cilicia, 60 n.
Cimon, 127, 135, 195.
Cinesias, 28, 164, 239, 243, 245, 249, 290, 292, 303.
Cinnarus, 34.
Circe, 272.
Circe (Anaxilas), 44.
Citharistes (M.), 321 n.
Cities (Eupolis), 24, 36, 55, 187, 193-7.
Citium, 135.
" City of Pigs," 237.
City of Slaves, 140.
Clansmen (Leucon), 230.
Cleænetus, 324, 325.
Cleisthenes, 251.
Clement of Alexandria, 83 n., 160.
Cleobulina, 139.
Cleobulinæ (Cratinus), 46, 139.
Cleomachus, 138.
Cleon, 25, 26, 167 n., 169, 192, 194, 195, 198, 199, 202, 207-10, 218, 224, 230, 232, 234, 236, 258, 282-8.
Cleonymus, 231.
Cleopatra, 341, 363.
Cleophanes (Antiphanes), 47.
Cleophon, 259.
Cleophon (Plato Com.), 153, 167, 176, 257.
Cloudcuckootown, 267, 356.
Clouds (A.), 23, 25, 106, 115, 115 n., 116 n., 130 n., 137 n., 141 n., 153, 153 n., 173 n., 190, 193, 199, 199 n., 206, 210, 211-22, 259, 276 n., 277, 277 n., 278, 279, 281 n., 293, 293 n., 303, 303 n., 305, 309 n., 310 n., 384.
Cobet, 125 n., 171 n., 173 n.
Cocalus (A.), 38, 40 n., 202.
Colophon, 40.
Columella, 109.
Comarchides, 237.
Comedotragedy (Deinolochus), 5 ; (Alcæus), 37 ; (Anaxandrides,) 49.
Comedy (*Wine-Flask*), 116, 117.
— (Theophrastus' treatise), 313.
Commodus, 296 n.
Compton Mackenzie, 220.
Concert-Hall, 134.
Congreve, 351, 357, 359, 359 n.
Connos (Ameipsias), 23, 24, 115, 152 n., 211, 213.

Constantinople, 6.
Constitution of Athens (attrib. to Xenophon), 27.
Cookery (attrib. to E.), 92.
Cope, 95 n.
Corax, 94, 94 n., 96.
Cordelia (*King Lear*), 341.
Corianno (*Corianno*), 157.
Corianno (Pherecrates), 18, 157 sqq., 165.
Corinth, 10, 209, 324, 338.
Cos, 83.
Costumes (Plato Com.), 176.
Cotys, 55.
Cotytto, 188 sqq.
Count Robert of Paris, 265.
Course du Flambeau, 361.
Crapatali (Pherecrates), 159.
Crastos, 83.
Crateia (*Hated Lover*), 328 sqq.
CRATES, 8, 15, 18 sq. 30, 37 n., 66, 105, 143, 145-50, 154, 154 n., 165, 209, 231, 233, 236, 252, 358.
Crates (philosopher), 146 n.
— School of, 8, 145-77.
CRATINUS, v, 15, 17, 18, 22, 23, 28, 37 n., 46, 50, 74, 101, 114-44, 145, 146, 154 n., 175 n., 179, 181, 201, 203, 209, 211, 213, 235, 302, 358 ; died through Spartan invasion ? 114 n., 173 ; rebuts A.'s reproaches, 116 sq. ; chides A., 138, 211, 296 ; difference between him and Crates, 146 sq. ; structure of his plays, 12, 141 sqq. ; mythological comedy, 23, 50, 119, 124 sq., 129-133 ; originated Cockaigne theme, 19 ; " baldheaded " vituperation, 26, 141 ; mocked Pericles, 26, 122, 124, 134, sq.; and Socrates, 217 n. ; metre and rhythm, 129 sq., 140, 374, 374 n., 389, 390 ; literary manner, 138, 140 sq., 144.
Cressida, 33.
Crete, 43, 55.
Critias, 63.
Critic, 167, 348.
Croiset, 88 n., 111 n., 118 n., 123 n., 345 n., 353 n., 354 n., 357 n.
Crönert, 90 n., 91 n.
Cronos, 126, 139.
Cronos (Phrynichus), 154.
Crusades, 2.
Curé de Tours, 305 sq.
Cybebe, 133 n.
Cybele, 133 n.
Cyclopes (Callias), 132 n.
Cyclops, 272.
— (*Odysses*), 129-33.

Cyclops (E.), 101.
Cydathenæon, 202.
Cynics, 47 n.
Cynossema, 178.
Cypria, 124.
Cyprus, 159.
Cyrene, 47.
Cyril, 166 n.
Cythera, 159, 175 n.

Dædalus, 177.
Dame Partlet, 264.
Damnasyllis, 77 n.
DAMOXENUS, 63, 65.
Danae, 333, 352.
Dancers (E.), 108 n.
Daos (*Farmer*), 324 ; (*Hero*) 326 sq. ; (*Shorn Lady*), 340 ; (*Arbitration*), 342, 346, 347 sq.
Daughters of Danaus (A.), 295.
Dawn, 235.
Débats, 105.
Decelea, 182.
DEINOLOCHUS, 5, 37.
Deinomenidæ, 112 n.
Deipnosophistæ, 3 and *passim*.
Delphi, 50, 104.
Demeas (*Samia*), 331-6, 352, 353, 359, 362, 363.
Demes (Eupolis), v, 36, 179-88, 182 n., 184.
Demeter, 66, 189 sq., 259, 260.
Demetrius (of Phalerum), 46 n., 62, 68, 94, 313 ; (rhetor), 61 n., 96 n., 97 n. ; (of Troezen), 252.
Demiańczuk (*Supplementum Comicum*), 56 n., 71 n., 147 n.
Democracy personified, 56.
Demos (*Babylonians ?*) 284 ; (*Knights*), 206 sqq., 303.
Demosthenes (5th cent.) (*Knights*), 207, 228 ; (4th cent.), 38, 40, 55, 65, 95 n., 96, 96 n., 185, 266, 314, 351.
Demostratus, 199.
Denis (*La Comédie grecque*) 28 n., 109 n., 205 n.
Desdemona (*Othello*), 341.
Deserters (Pherecrates), 160 sq.
Deucalion (*Ant-men*), 161.
Diadochi, 55, 59.
Dicæarchus (pseudo-), 35 n.
Dicæopolis (*Acharnians*), 8 sq., 10, 203-6, 228, 229, 243, 268, 282, 283, 303.
Dickens, 238, 268, 307, 310, 358.
Didymus, 16, 143, 154.
Diels, 89, 91 n., 107 n.
Dindorf, 24 n., 181 n.
Dinos, 218 sq., 300, 305.

Diocleidas, 153.
Diocles, 175.
DIODORUS, 280 n.
— Siculus, 286 n.
Diogenes Laertius, 46 n., 65 n., 78 n., 83 n., 84, 85 n., 86 n., 87, 89, 90, 96, 136 n., 213, 214.
Diomos, 101.
Dionysalexandros (Cratinus), 12, 22 n., 23, 26, 118-24, 143.
DIONYSIUS, 42, 54 n.
Dionysius of Syracuse, the elder, 50, 77 n., 202 ; the younger, 89 n., 91.
— Thrax, Scholiast on, 3, 165 n.
Dionysus, 7, 8, 13, 75, 97, 140.
— (*Revellers* of Epicharmus, 102 ; (*Dionysalexandros*), 118, 124 ; (*Brigadiers*), 197 sq. ; (*Babylonians*), 285 sqq. ; (*Frogs*), 257 sqq., 262, 264, 267, 304 ; (*Gerytades?*) 291, 291 n. ; (Anon.), 354 n.
Dionysus Shipwrecked (A.? Archippus?), 23.
Diopeithes, 313.
Diotima, 48.
DIPHILUS, 60, 62, 62 n., 66, 66 n., 68, 69 n.
Dippers, see *Baptæ*.
Disraeli, 50.
Dobree, 154 n.
Dog's Dirge, 178.
Dog's Life, 209.
Doll's House, 6.
Don Quixote, 298, 301.
Donatus, 319, 362.
Donne, 305.
Dorian Greeks, 10.
Doris (*Shorn Lady*), 338, 340.
Double-Dealer, 359.
Dramatic Productions (Cratinus), 139 n.
Dryden, 29.

Earth and Sea (E.), 105.
Ecclesiazusæ (A.), 29, 30, 58, 264-9, 271, 272, 275, 304, 310 n.
Echo (*Thesmophoriazusæ*), 250 n., 256.
ECPHANTIDES, 17, 140.
Edgar (*King Lear*), 34 n.
Egypt, 91 n., 99, 135, 179, 202, 294, 318, 323.
Electra (Euripides' *Electra*), 361.
Electra (Euripides), 361 n.
El-Hibeh, 91 n.
Elmsley, 130 n.
Elpinice, 195.
Empedocles, 46 n., 92, 93.

III. PERSONS, WORKS, AND PLACES 403

Ennius, 85 *n.*, 109, 109 *n.*, 112.
Ephialtes, 179.
Ephialtes (Phrynichus), 151.
EPHIPPUS, 43, 47, 50, 51, 55.
Epicharmean Forgeries, 90 *sqq.*
EPICHARMUS, 3-5, 9, 11, 15, 16, 41, 50, 72, 77, 83-113, 141, 142, 145, 154 *n.*, 191, 227, 350 *n.*, 372; E. and Hiero, 92 *sq.*; relation to his predecessors, 3, 110; to Æschylus, 4, 111; to philosophers and philosophy, 84-93; to rhetoric, 94-7; earliest genuine playwright, 3, 83 *sqq.*; transformed narrative into action, 4 *sq.* 100 *sq.*; dramatic structure, 4, 99, 110 *sqq.*; his plays non-choric, 9; burlesque of legend, 23, 74, 97-102; comedy of manners, 102-5; invented stage-parasite, 3, 41 *n.*; duel-plays, 105 *sq.*; length of his plays, 108; shrewd maxims, 106 *sqq.*; the Epicharmean Forgeries, 90 *sqq.*; language, 108; metre, 108; style, 108, 112; Sicilian manner, 109 *sq.*; his reputation, 87, 108, 109; his influence on Crates and his School, 18, 66, 143, 144; on Plautus, 109, 113; on later comedy, 113.
EPICRATES, 45, 48, 54 *n.*
Epicurus, 65, 66, 313, 350 *n.*, 363 *sq.*
Epidaurus, 183, 316.
Epilycus, 146.
EPINICUS, 66.
Epstein, 311.
Eratosthenes (critic), 162, 189, 231, 233; (mythographer), 124, 124 *n.*
Eristics, 65.
Erlynne, Mrs. (*Lady Windermere's Fan*), 359.
Eros, 244.
Essay on Comedy, 357 *n.*
Eteocles (*Phœnissæ* of Euripides and of Strattis), 33.
Euæon, 268.
Eubulides, 65.
EUBULUS, 40, 41, 42, 44, 45, 46, 50, 53, 53 *sq.*
Eucleides, 65.
Euelpides, 155, 238 *sqq.*
EUETES, 15.
Eumæus, 89, 101.
Eumenides, 6 *n.*, 50, 111 *n.*
Euneidæ (Cratinus), 137, 181 *n.*
Eunuchus (Terence), 221 *n.*, 327, 327 *n.*, 330, 336.

EUPOLIS, 23, 24, 25, 36, 41 *n.*, 55, 74, 122 *n.*, 151 *n.*, 154 *n.*, 165 *n.*, 166 *n.*, 178-201, 230, 314 *n.*, 390; his dog, 178 *sq.*; Alcibiades and the *Baptæ*, 28, 178, 189 *sq.*; collaborated in *Knights*, 210 *sq.*; his *Flatterers* defeated A.'s *Peace*, 179, 190, 230; Cratinus twitted him with plagiarizing A., 211; quarrelled with A., 193, 200; gibed at by A. 153 *sq.*, 193; ridiculed Socrates, 190, 199, 217 *n.*; imaginative power, 179, 201; literary style, 191.
Euripides, vi, 21 *sq.*, 26, 32, 33, 34, 34 *n.*, 38, 50, 61, 66, 67 *n.*, 77 *n.*, 85 *n.*, 104 *n.*, 130 *n.*, 138, 138 *n.*, 152, 170, 170 *n.*, 171, 179, 182, 185, 204, 211, 213, 235, 248, 250, 251, 252, 253, 255, 256, 257, 258, 259, 260, 261, 288 *n.*, 289 *n.*, 290, 296, 297, 304, 309, 310 *n.*, 317 *n.*, 336, 347, 350, 352, 353, 354, 356.
Europa (*Europa*), 173.
Europa (Plato Com.), 173.
Eurybatus, 155.
Eusebius, 70 *n.*, 81 *n.*, 147, 316 *n.*
Eustathius, 44 *n.*, 95 *n.*, 160 *n.*
Euthymenes, 26, 27.
EUXENIDES, 15.

Fahræus (*De argumento atque consilio Daetalensium*), 281 *n.*
Falstaff, 31, 45, 113, 144, 159, 263, 298, 300, 336.
Farmer (M.), 323 *sqq.*
Farmers (A.), 234 *n.*, 287 *sqq.*
Farnell, 175 *n.*
Farquhar, 358 *n.*
Fates (Hermippus), 123.
Faust, 106.
Faustus, Dr., 362.
Fear personified to deliver prologue, 70.
Festivals (Plato Com.), 170 *sq.*
Fielding, 307.
Fielitz (*De Atticorum Comœdia bipartita*), 37 *n.*
" Fighting-Cock," 55.
Fisherman and Rustic (Sophron), 79.
Fishes (Archippus), 23.
Fisticuff (*Rustic*), 105.
Flatterer (M.), 327 *sq.*, 359.
Flatterers (Eupolis), 179, 190 *sqq.*, 230.
Flickinger, 119 *n.*, 121 *n.*
Florida, 37 *n.*, 61 *n.*
Flower-Girls (Eubulus), 53 *sq.*
Ford (*Merry Wives*), 336, 362.
Fourberies de Scapin, 357 *n.*

Fränkel, 56 n.
Fritzsche (*De Daetalensibus*), 287 n.
Frogs (Magnes), 17; (A.), 24 n., 28, 29, 34 n., 112, 130, 144 n., 153, 154 n., 160, 169 n., 176, 184 n., 197, 236 n., 246, 253, 257-64, 268 n., 271, 285, 290, 291 n., 304, 375 sq.
Frozen Sun (Aristonymus), 22.
Fugitive Wife (Apollodorus of Gela), 63.
Furies, 50.
Furies (Telecleides), 20.

Gadshill, 300.
Galen, 183 n., 278, 278 n.
Gall-Flies (Magnes), 17.
Galsworthy, 362 n.
Gamard, Mddle., 306.
Games (Crates), 146, 150.
Gamp, Mrs., 272 n.
Gargantua, 100.
Gargarus, 102.
Gauguin, 311.
Gauls, 55.
Gauls (Sopater), 75.
Gay, 59 n.
Geissler (*Chronologie der altattischen Komödie*), 19 n., 31 n., 32 n., 129 n., 165 n., 166 n., 169 n., 197 n., 198 n., 290 n.
Gellius, Aulus, 58, 61, 297 n., 313 n., 315, 358 n.
Gelon, 83, 105, 112 n., 181, 181 n.
Gerytades (A.), 289-90.
Geta, 225, 327, 329.
Gettysburg Speech, 308.
Gilbert, 138, 298, 301.
Gissing, 268.
Glaucinus, 27.
Glyce (*Corianno*), 157.
Glycera, 313, 313 n., 315.
— (*Shorn Lady*), 337-42, 349, 360, 362, 363.
Gnathæna, 60.
Gnatho (*Flatterer*), 328.
Gnesippus, 138 n.
Goblin (Crates), 146.
Goethe, 106, 300.
Golden Age, 198 sq.
Goldsmith, 308, 340, 351.
Gondoliers, 253, 276.
Good (Pherecrates? Strattis?), 155 n.
Gorgias, 94, 286.
— (*Farmer*), 324 sq.
Gorgias (Plato philos.), 222.
Gorgon, 139, 258.
Graces (lost *Thesmophoriazusæ*), 252, 253.
Gracie, 80.

Graux (*Textes grecs inédits*), 78 n.
Gray's Inn, 230.
Greece or Islands (Plato Com.), 167 sqq.
Greenwich Hospital, 148 n.
Gregory Nazianzenus, 78 n.
Grenfell and Hunt, 80 n., 91 n., 118, 118 n., 325 n.
Grote, 224.
Grysar (*De Doriensium Comœdia*), 111.
Gunning (*De Babyloniis Aristophanis*), 283 n., 284 n.

Habrotonon (*Shorn Lady*), 339; (*Arbitration*), 343-9, 360, 360 n., 362.
Hadrian, 37 n.
Hardy, 322.
Harman, 240.
Harmodius-Song, 389.
Harpalus, 55.
Harpers (Magnes), 17.
Harpocration, 162, 173, 194, 195 n.
Hated Lover (M.), 328 sqq.
Headlam, vi.
Heautontimorumenos (M.), 319 n., 321 n.; (Terence), 319 n., 338 n.
Hebe, 97 sq.
Hebe's Wedding (E.), 97 sqq., 100 n.
Hebrews, 226 n.
Hector, 33 n., 95 n., 176 n., 226.
Hector's Ransom, see *Phrygians*.
Hecuba, 34 n.
Hegelochus, 34.
Hegesistrata, 313.
Heine, 300, 300 n., 301, 311.
Heiress (M.), 321 n.
Helen, 125, 125 n.
— (*Odysseus the Deserter?*), 100, 119; (*Dionysalexandros*), 118-22; (*Nemesis*), 124 sq.; (*Helena* of Euripides), 251, 255; (*Thesmophoriazusæ*), 251, 255, 256, 305, 306.
Helena (*All's Well*), 342.
Helena, 251, 255, 256 n., 356.
Heliodorus, 3.
Hellenica, 259.
Helots (Eupolis?), 178 n., 198.
HENIOCHUS, 53-55.
Henry IV, 229, 229 n., 263, 263 n., 273.
Henry V (*Henry V*), 351.
Henry V, 55.
— *VI*, 257 n.
Hephæstion, 126, 129 n., 131 n., 140 n., 158, 374, 390.
Hephæstus, 43, 95 n., 296.
— (*Hephæstus*), 102 n.

III. PERSONS, WORKS, AND PLACES 405

Hephæstus (E.), 101 sq.
Hera (*Hebe's Wedding*), 98 n., 99; (*Revellers* of Epicharmus), 101; (*Dionysalexandros*), 118, 123; (*Chirons*), 126 sq., 126 n.
Heraclea, 41.
Heracles, 11, 125 n., 236, 236 n.
— (*Busiris*), 4, 41; (*Hebe's Wedding*), 97-102; (*Heracles and the Girdle*), 101; (*Heracles the Bridegroom*), 113 n.; (*Birds*), 240, 242; (*Frogs*), 257, 258, 263, 264; (*Zeus Reviled*), 173 sq.
Heracles (Alexis), 49 sq.; (Diphilus), 60; (Ephippus), 50; (Rhinthon), 74.
— the *Play-Producer* (Nicochares), 22.
HERACLIDES, 55.
Heraclitus, 86, 93, 95 n., 110, 350 n.
Herdsmen (Cratinus), 137 sq.
Hermann, G., 180 n., 194 n., 377.
Hermes (*Iliad*), 95 n.; (*Ichneutæ*), 22 n.; (*Dionysalexandros*), 119 n., 120; (*Nemesis*), 124; (*Peace*), 230 sqq., 236; (*Plutus*), 270; (in Phrynichus), 177; (in Plato Com.), 177.
Hermione (*Winter's Tale*), 45.
HERMIPPUS, 22, 51, 123, 124.
Hermit (Phrynichus), 24, 27, 39, 151, 238.
Hermogenes, 314 n.
Hermon (*Bacchæ* of Lysippus), 36.
Hero (M.), 318, 326 sq., 339, 354.
HERODAS, 79 sq., 104 n., 157.
Herodotus, 148 n.
Heroes (Crates), 146.
Hervieu, 361.
Herwerden, 131 n.
Hesiod, 107, 109, 126, 136 n., 164, 238.
Hesiods (Telecleides), 19, 22.
Hesychius, 17, 33, 128 n., 133, 137, 139 n., 189, 192, 279 n., 284 n.
Heydemann, 75 n.
Hiero, 4, 83, 92, 94 n., 104, 105, 109, 111 n., 112 n., 113.
Hierocles, 81.
— (*Peace*), 231.
Hippias, 275.
Hippobotus, 84.
Hippocrates, 298.
Hippolytus (Euripides), 6 n., 50 n.; (Sopater), 75.
Hipponax, 60, 75, 75 n., 108 n.
Hipponicus, 190.
Hirzel, 70 n.
Homer, 4, 22, 31 sq., 51, 95 n., 100, 101, 108 n., 126 n., 129, 130 n., 131, 132, 136 n., 142, 164, 226, 231, 235, 260, 261, 298, 306, 314, 322, 336.
Hoopoe (*Birds*), 238, 240, 243.
Hope (E.), 3, 102 sqq., 143.
Horace, 28, 28 n., 74 n., 101 n., 113, n., 144, 179 n., 278, 316, 352 n., 387, 389.
Houhymnmns, 302.
Hours, 22 n.
Housman, A. E., 337 n.
Hroswitha, 316.
Husbandry (lost *Peace*), 232, 234.
Hyginus, 124 n.
Hymn to Hermes, 22, 51.
Hyperbolus, 25, 118, 167, 192, 211, 213.
— (*Frogs*), 258; (*Hyperbolus*), 169, 170, 170 n.
Hyperbolus (Plato Com.), 167, 169 sq.

Iamblicus, 85.
Ibsen, 138, 355, 361.
Ibycus, 254.
Icaria, 14.
Ichneutæ, 22 n., 51.
Ida, Mt., 118, 120.
Idylls of Theocritus, 79.
Ignorance (*Shorn Lady*), 339, 340.
Iliad, 33, 95 n., 108 n., 122 n., 164, 176 n., 226.
Imbrians (M.), 325 n.
Imbros, 358, 359 n.
Imogen (*Cymbeline*), 341.
Indian Ocean, 80 sq.
Informer (*Birds*), 243.
Inopia (*Trinummus*), 330 n.
Iolanthe, 374.
Iolaus, 177.
Ion of Chios, 200 n., 235.
Ion (Euripides), 38.
Ionia, 197.
Iphicrates, 55.
Iphigenia at Aulis (Rhinthon), 74.
— in *Tauris*, 80.
Iris (*Birds*), 239, 242, 303, 307.
Isaeus, 280 n.
Isarchus, 213.
Isis, 80.
Islands (E.), 104; (A.? Archippus?), 23, 202, 292 sq.
Isocrates, 32.
Ithaca, 130.
Ixion in Heaven, 50.

Jacob, 226.
Jebb-Pearson, 198 n., 274 n.
Jerome, St., 81 n., 147 n.
Jerusalem, 242.

Jocasta, 49.
— (*Phœnissæ* of Euripides and of Strattis), 33 ; (*Crapatali*), 160.
Johannesburg, 359.
John Anderson, 247.
Jonson, 105, 154.
Joseph, 226.
Jowett, 209.
Joyce, 311.
Julius Cæsar, 6 n.
Juno (*Tempest*), 7.
Just and Unjust 'Arguments' (*Clouds*), 106, 149.
Justice (*Chiron*), 164.
Juvenal, 188.

Kaibel, 2 n., and *passim*.
Katisha (*Mikado*), 299 n.
Keil, 108 n., 180 n.
Kenyon, 353 n.
Kingsley, 161 n.
Kipling, 277 n.
Knight of the Burning Pestle, 117 n.
Knights (A.), 3, 7, 16, 19, 23, 25 n., 27, 114 n., 115, 115 n., 118, 137 n., 140 n., 141 n., 144, 146, 147, 176 n., 181 n., 190, 192, 192 n., 193, 200, 206-11, 228, 230, 230 n., 281 n., 303, 304, 310 n., 356.
Kock, 20 n., and *passim*.
Koko (*Mikado*), 118.
Körte, 6 n., and *passim*.
Kühn, 183 n., 278 n.

Labes (*Wasps*), 224.
Lacedæmon, 195, 199.
La Chaussée, 248.
Laches, 182 n., 224.
Laconia, 230.
Lacydes, 70 sq.
Laertes, 132.
Læspodias, 30.
Lagisca, 32.
Laius, 49.
Lamachus (*Acharnians*), 105, 204, 206, 303 ; (*Peace*), 231.
Lamb, Charles, 310.
Lamp-market, 118.
Lampoon, 35 n.
Landseer, 311.
Lar Familiaris (*Aulularia*), 327.
Latinus, 316 n.
Laughter-Lover, 81.
Laureion, 162.
Laws (Cratinus), 136.
League of Youth, 361 sq.
Lear, 34 n.
Leda, 121.
— (*Nemesis*), 124 sq.

Leeuwen, van, 207 n., 214, 223, 241 n., 269 n., 271 n., 273, n., 318 n., 328 n., 335 n., 345 n.
Lefèbvre, 179, 179 n., 318.
Legrand, 37 n., 59 n., 319 n., 348 m., 357 n., 358 n.
Leontini, 286.
Lesbians, 33.
Lesbos, 164, 174.
LEUCON, 223, 230.
Leuconea, 152.
Libanius, 329 n.
Life of Pythagoras, 85 n.
Lilliput, 302.
Lincoln, A., 308.
Lindus, 202.
Linus, 49 sq.
Little Iliad, 100 n.
Lobeck, 188 n.
Locksley Hall, 373.
Locri, 104.
London, 263.
Long Night (Plato Com.), 173.
Longfellow, 305, 311, 373, 384.
Lorenz, 83 n., 109 n., 113 n.
Lover of Euripides (Axionicus), 50 ; (Philippides), 66.
—— *Tragedy* (Alexis), 49.
Lucan, 351.
Lucian, 83 n., 136, 189 n., 314.
Lucilius, 74, 144.
Lucretius, 57 n., 65, 321, 363.
Lumpkin (*She Stoops to Conquer*), 340.
Luscius Lanuvinus, 330, 342.
Luxuria (*Trinummus*), 330 n.
Luxurious Man (Theopompus), 32.
Lycabettus, 214.
Lyceum, 47 n.
LYCIS, 24, 154.
Lydians (Magnes), 17.
Lydus, 74, 77 n.
Lynceus of Samos, 60 n., 316.
Lysander, 32, 37, 265.
Lysias, 268, 308.
Lysimachus, 61 sq.
LYSIPPUS, 35 sq.
Lysistrata (*Lysistrata*), 244 sqq., 248, 249.
Lysistrata (A.), 19, 167, 205, 244-50. 298, 303.
Lysistratus, 279.

Macbeth (*Macbeth*), 209.
Macbeth, 209.
Macedonians (Strattis), 34.
MACHON, 40 n.
Macrobius, 201 n.
Magas, 61, 68.

III. PERSONS, WORKS, AND PLACES 407

MAGNES, 7, 11, 15-17, 18, 83 *n*., 84, 143, 146 *n*., 154 *n*., 209.
Mahaffy, 109 *n*., 111 *n*.
Malade Imaginaire, 218, 250.
Male and Female Argument (E.), 96.
Man and Superman, 6 *n*., 253.
Man Friday, 357.
Manchester, 35 *n*.
Manes, 155 *n*., 237.
Manilius, 316.
Mantinea, 181 *n*., 182, 183.
Manual of Corax, 96.
Map, Walter, 105.
Marathon, 185, 225 *sq*., 244.
Marcus Aurelius, 82, 82 *n*., 289.
Mariage Forcé, 93.
Maricas (Eupolis), 192, 192 *n*., 193, 210, 211.
Marlowe, 362.
Marmor Parium, see Parian Marble.
Maro, 132.
Marphurius (*Le Mariage Forcé*), 93.
Marpurgo, 350 *n*.
Martial, 389.
Mary Ann, 155.
Mary Gloster, 277 *n*.
Maxims (attrib. to E.), 91.
— *of Menander and Philistion*, 82.
Mazon, 6 *n*.
Medea (Deinolochus), 5; (Euripides), 50 *n*., 130 *n*., 171, 185 *n*., 248 *n*., 350 *n*., 361, 361 *n*.; (Rhinthon), 74.
Megara (Hyblæa), 3, 4, 83, 110; (Nisæa), 11, 12, 230.
Megarian (*Acharnians*), 204.
Megarian Woman (E.), 104 *sq*.
Megarians, 233.
Meier, 185.
Meineke, 24 and *passim*.
Melanippides, 164.
Meletus, 217, 290, 292.
Men of Seriphos (Cratinus), 139 *sq*.
MENANDER, v, 37 *n*., 38, 40, 60, 67, 71, 103 *n*., 107, 113, 165 *n*., 313-64, 300, 309 *sq*.; M. and Philemon, 61, 314; and Philistion, 82; and Terence, 317, 317 *n*., 319, 319 *n*.; reputation, 314-17; new papyri, 318; plot-construction, 331 *n*., 335, 335 *n*., 339 *sq*., 345, 345 *n*., 347, 353-63; prologues, 4, 112; chorus, 58; characterization, 340 *sqq*., 347 *sqq*.; farce, 232 *sq*.; "thefts," 316 *n*.; iambic rhythm, 69 *n*.; metres, 352; style, 316 *n*., 350-3; love, 323, 326 *sq*., 328 *sqq*., 330, 332, 354 *sq*.; indecency, 329 *n*.; grotesque sermon, 349 *sq*.; serious sermon, 350; "only the lines," 360 *sq*.; no propagandist, 367 *sq*.; superstition, 363 *sq*.; Epicurus, 313, 314, 364; comedy of manners, 357-60.
Menander (Wilamowitz), 353 *n*., 358 *n*.
Menelaus (*Helena* and *Thesmophoriazusæ*), 251, 255 *sq*.
Merchant of Venice, 6 *n*.
Meredith, 254, 263 *n*., 357 *n*., 358.
Merry Wives of Windsor, 73, 336, 362.
Merrythought (*Knight of the Burning Pestle*), 117 *n*.
METAGENES, 19.
Methe (*Wine-Flask*), 117.
Meton, 152.
Metrobius (*Archilochi*), 135.
Miccotrogus (*Stichus*), 113 *n*.
Midas, 273.
Midsummer Night's Dream, 253, 281.
Millamant (*Way of the World*), 305.
Miltiades, 195, 207.
— (*Demes*), 181, 186, 187.
Milton, vi.
Miners (Pherecrates? Nicomachus?) 19, 155 *n*., 162.
Miranda (*Tempest*), 341.
Misanthrope, 356.
Miser (attrib. to Crates), 146.
Mnesilochus, 21 *sq*.
"Mnesilochus" (*Thesmophoriazusæ*), 250-7.
MNESIMACHUS, 53.
Mnesiptolemus (*Mnesiptolemus*), 66.
Mnesiptolemus (Epinicus), 66.
Molière, 93, 218, 253, 312, 316, 354 *n*., 356 *sqq*.
Montmartre, 311.
Moon-Goddess, 80.
Morsimus, 176.
Morychides, 26, 28 *sq*.
Moschion (*Samia*), 331-6; (*Shorn Lady*), 337-41, 353.
Moschus, 79.
Müller, K. O., 111 *n*., 113 *n*.
— L., 109 *n*.
Murray, 59 *n*., 229 *n*., 260 *n*., 261 *n*., 318 *n*., 320 *n*.
Muses, 106 *n*., 153; (lost *Thesmophoriazusæ*), 252, 253.
Muses (E.), 98; (Phrynichus), 151, 152, 176, 257.
Music (*Chiron* of Pherecrates), 164.
MYLLUS, 15.
Myronides (or Pyronides?), 180, 180 *n*., 185, 186, 188.
Myrrhine (*Lysistrata*), 245, 249, 303; (*Farmer*), 324, 325; (*Shorn Lady*), 337, 339, 339 *n*., 341.
Mytilene, 284.

Naeke, 166 n.
Naples, 78.
Nauck, 182 n., 252 n., 288 n., 297 n.
Neighbours (Crates), 105, 146, 150.
Neleus, 348.
Nemea (Theopompus), 31.
Nemesis, 124.
Nemesis (Cratinus), 124 sq.
Nephelococcygia, 239, 242.
New Zealand, 359.
Nicarchus (*Acharnians*), 102.
Nicephorus, 6 n.
Niceratus (*Samia*), 331-6.
Nicias, 21, 152, 167, 169, 197, 217.
— (*Demes*), 180-3, 186, 188 ; (*Maricas*), 192 ; (*Knights*), 207, 228; (*Farmers*), 287 n., 288.
NICOCHARES, 22, 269.
NICOLAUS, 62.
Nicole, 323.
NICOMACHUS, 162, 164.
Nicomachus Gerasenus, 164 n.
NICOPHON, 19, 22, 269.
NICOSTRATUS, 50 n., 202.
Nicostratus (general), 182 n.
Niobos (A. ? Archippus ?), 23, 202.
Noman, 130 n., 131, 227.
Non-Combatants (Eupolis), 198.
Norden, 97 n.
Nossis, 74.
Numenius, 70 n.

Oak, 385.
Odysses (Cratinus), 12, 23, 129-33, 142, 257 n., 374.
Odysseus, 32, 75, 97, 100, 101, 129-33, 164, 227, 306, 328.
Odysseus (Theopompus), 31 sq.
— the *Deserter* (E.), 100 sq., 108.
— *Shipwrecked* (E.), 3 sq., 101.
Odyssey, 100 n., 101, 129, 131 n., 168 n.
Œax, 251.
Œdipus, 49, 96.
Œdipus Tyrannus, 354 n., 361.
Œneis, 114, 191 n.
Old Joe, 155.
Old Mortality, 265.
— *Women* (Pherecrates), 159.
Olympia, 55 sq.
Olympus, 303.
One-Line Maxims (M.), 317, 320.
O'Neill, 4.
Onesimus (*Arbitration*), 342-7, 349, 353, 363, 364.
Opora (*Peace*), 231, 307.
Oppé, (*Greek New Comedy*), 71 n.
Oppeln-Bronikowski, von, 345 n.
Orators, the Greek, 336.
Orestautocleides (Timocles), 50.

Orestas (Rhinthon), 74.
Oresteia, 111, 112.
Orestes, 50.
Orestes (Euripides), 34, 50 n.; (Sopater), 75.
Origen, 82.
Orion, 282 n.
Othello (*Othello*), 329 n.
Othello, 356 n.
Ovid, 314 n., 315.
Oxyrhynchus, 78, 80, 118, 318.
Oxyrhynchus Papyri, 78 n., 80 n., 118 n., 325 n., 354 n.

Palamedes, 251, 255.
Pamphile (*Arbitrants*), 344 sqq., 348, 350, 360.
Pamphilus (Eubulus), 45 sq.
Pan, 51, 140.
Panathenæa, 199.
Pandionis, 202.
Paphlagonian (*Knights*), 192, 207.
Paphos, 75.
Papiri Greco-Egizii, 290 n.
Parian Marble, 14, 40, 83 n.
Paris (Priam's son) (*Dionysalexandros*), 118-22.
— (city), 358, 359.
Paris, 35.
Parmenides, 89, 305.
Parmenides, 89 n.
Parmeno, 321.
Parmenon (*Samia*), 331 sqq., 335, 335 n., 353.
Parnes Mt., 214.
Paros, 132.
Pascal (*Rivista di Filologia*), 84 n.
Pasiphae (Alcæus), 37, 269.
Patæcus, (*Shorn Lady*), 336-41, 363.
Pater, 310.
Patræ, 70.
Pauly-Wissowa, 6 n., and often.
Pausanias, 314 n.
Pausanias, see *Macedonians*.
Peace (A.), 101, 114 n., 123 n., 160, 160 n., 173 n., 179, 190, 197 n., 230-8, 241, 243, 249, 287, 287 n., 288, 290, 290 n., 298, 309 n., 310 n., 378, 380-3.
Pecksniff, 216.
Peele, 4.
Pegasus, 230.
Peisander (Plato Com.), 166, 176.
Peisistratus, 136.
Peleus, 49.
Pelias, 348.
Peloponnese, 113 n., 240.
Pelops (*Male and Female Argument*), 96, 106 n.

III. PERSONS, WORKS, AND PLACES 409

Pergamum, 233.
Pericles, 21, 22 n., 25, 26, 35 n., 63, 119, 121, 122, 123, 124, 125, 125 n., 126, 127 n., 134 sq., 143 n., 180, 180 n., 181, 181 n., 183 n., 184 n., 185, 186, 195, 218, 231; (the younger), 120 n.
Pericles (Plutarch), 21.
Perinthus, Girl of, (M.), 105.
Persa, 39.
Persæ, 111 n., 192 n.
Persephone, 198, 258, 264.
Perseus (Men of Seriphos), 139 sq.; (Andromeda and Thesmophoriazusæ), 256.
Persia, king of, 203 n.
Persian (Theopompus), 32.
Persians (Pherecrates ?), 155 n., 162 sqq., 165.
Persius, 315.
Pervigilium Veneris, 373.
Petale (Pherecrates), 159.
Phæacia, 101.
Phædo, 32 n., 217.
Phædrus (fabulist), 315.
Phædrus (Plato phil.), 47; (Alexis), 47 n.
Phalaris, 53.
Phales, 8 sq.
Phaon, 174 sq.
Phaon (Plato Com.), 174 sq.
Pheidias, 231.
— (Flatterer), 327, 328; (Apparition), 330.
Pheidippides (Clouds), 211 sq., 214 sq., 221 sq., 278.
Pheidon, 49.
PHERECRATES, 28, 135, 154-65, 268; follower of Crates, 19; comedy of manners, 18, 157 sq.; Plato and The Savages, 155; doubtful plays, 155, 162 sqq.; passion for music, 165; "collapsed anapæsts," 389 sq.
Philagrius, 81.
PHILEMON, 37 n., 60 sq., 65, 67, 69, 70, 82, 320 n.; acted in Anaxandrides' plays, 40; anecdotes of P. and Magas, 61, 68; and M., 61; contrasted with M., 61 n.; often defeated him, 314; fragment on Euripides, 61, 66; avoids indecency of language, 147 n.
Philetærus, 203.
Philinna (Farmer), 324.
Philinus, 14.
— (Cities), 196; (Samia), 338.
PHILIPPIDES, 60, 61 sq., 66, 66 n., 67 n., 68, 68 n.

PHILIPPUS, 202.
PHILISTION, 81 sq.
Phillimore, 236.
Philocleon (Wasps), 223-7, 299.
Philoctetas (E.), 101, 111 n.
Philonides, 24, 202, 211, 223, 257, 276, 276 n.
Philosopher (Philemon), 65.
Philoxenus, 175.
Phœbus with Admetus, 263 n.
PHŒNICIDES, 64 sq., 329.
Phœnissæ (Phrynichus trag.), 229; (Euripides), 33 n.; (Strattis), 33.
Phormio, 197 sq.
— (Brigadiers), 197 sq.
Phormio, 361.
PHORMIS, 5, 110 n., 145.
Photius, 17, 77 n., 102 n., 133, 137 n., 139, 162, 168, 199, 282 n., 284 n.
Phrygians, 297.
Phrygians (Æschylus), 297 n.; (Euripides ?), 22.
PHRYNICHUS, 19, 24, 27 150-4, 165, 211 n., 217, 238.
Phrynichus (tragedian), 229, 255, 257, 259.
— (grammarian), 58 n., 351 n.
Phrynis, 164.
Phrynondas, 155.
Phyle, 271.
Pickard-Cambridge, 6 n., 7 n., 11 n., 14 n., 83 n., 85 n., 90 n., 91 n., 94 n., 98 n., 99 n., 104 n., 106 n., 108 n., 109 n.
Pierides, 98 n.
Pieros, 98.
Pilgrims (E.), 104, 143.
Pimpleides, 98 n.
Pimpleis, 98.
Pindar, 22, 92, 98 n., 104 n., 107, 110, 128, 186, 198, 198 n., 274, 310.
Pinero, 138, 309, 361, 362.
Piræus, 175 n., 314.
Pisthetærus (Birds), 155, 238-44, 273, 303, 307.
Plangon (Hero), 326 sq.; (Samia), 333 sqq.
Platæa, 25.
PLATO, 28, 30, 38 n., 153, 164, 165-77, 257; follower of Crates, 19; "imitating Arcadians," 166; assigned by some to Middle Comedy, 30, 165; late linguistic features, 167, 168 n.; casual style, 167; ridiculed Euripides, 170 sq.; and A., 176; erotic plays, 173 sqq.

Plato (philosopher), 4, 32, 38, 47, sq., 53, 77, 78, 78 n., 85 n., 86, 87-91, 109, 110, 113, 113 n., 133 n., 138 n., 151, 155, 175 n. 184 n., 202, 202 n., 208, 215, 217, 219, 221, 222, 237, 269, 269 n., 296, 296 n., 305, 308, 309, 336, 351, 351 n.
Platonius, 3, 12, 26 n., 39, 129, 129 n., 130 n., 141, 142, 178 n., 179.
Plautus, 31, 39, 63, 70 n., 109, 110, 113, 173, 227, 273, 317, 319 n.
Pliny, 97 n., 314 n., 349 n.
Plocion (M.), 58.
Plunder (E.), 104, 143.
Plutarch, 21, 32, 53, 61, 68 n., 85, 92, 92 n., 93, 94, 125, 164, 169 n., 170, 180, 184, 192 n., 197 n., 284 n., 288 n., 315 sq., 352 n., 354 n., 360, 360 n., 361 ; pseudo-Plutarch, 92 n.
Pluto (*Frogs*), 258, 259, 263.
Plutus (A.), 18, 30, 36, 39, 112, 163, 163 n., 259, 269-76, 299, 299 n., 304, 310 n.
Pnyx, 117, 203, 264.
Poems of Epicharmus (Dionysius), 89 n.
Poetry (A. ? Archippus ?), 23, 202.
Poets, see Spartans.
Polemon (*Shorn Lady*), 329 n., 337-40, 359, 360, 363.
Polemos (*Peace*), 230, 232, 233, 234, 238.
Pollux, 46 n., 98, 100 n., 101 n., 102, 102 n., 159, 271, 280 n., 351 n.
Polonius (*Hamlet*), 305.
Polydeuces (*Amycus*), 102.
Polynices (*Phœnissæ* of Euripides and of Strattis), 33.
Polyphemus, 227.
— (*Odysses*), 130-3.
POLYZELUS, 22.
Poppelreuter, 7 n.
Porphyrius, 108 n.
Porridge (Sopater), 75.
Porson, 168 n.
Portia (*Merchant of Venice*), 341.
POSEIDIPPUS, 65 n.
Poseidon, 98, 168, 209, 274.
— (*Birds*), 240, 242, 304.
Possessed Woman (M.), 352.
Post, L. A., 319 n.
Poverty (*Persians?*) 163 ; (*Plutus*), 270, 274 sqq.
Prasiæ, 230.
Praxagora (*Ecclesiazusæ*), 264-8.
Premise, Major, 106 n.
Priam, 118 n.
— (*Phrygians* of Æschylus), 297.

Priapus (Xenarchus), 44.
Priestess (M.), 325 sq., 355 n., 363, 364.
Priscian, 58, 166 n.
Procrustes, 267.
Prodicus, 274.
Promatheus (E.), 111 n.
Prometheus (*Birds*), 239, 243.
Prometheus Unbound, 242.
Propertius, 315.
Propylæa, 207.
Prospaltii (Eupolis), 122 n.
Protagoras, 24.
— (*Flatterers*), 190 sq.
Protagoras (Plato phil.), 155 n.
Prusa, 81.
Prytanis ? (*Babylonians?*), 287.
Psalm of Life, 305, 373.
Psammetichus, 135.
Ptolemy I (Soter), 73, 314 ; II (Philadelphus), 55, 75, 79.
Pygmies, 101.
Pylos, 207, 210, 287 n., 288.
Pyronides, 185 n. See also Myronides.
Pythagoras, 84, 85, 86.
Pythagoreans, 47.
Pythias, 64.
Pythodorus, 154 n.

Quintilian, 74, 95 n., 179 n., 192, 314 n., 324, 347, 354 n.

Rabelais, 100, 307.
Ranke (*De Aristophanis vita*), 281 n., 286 n.
Reason, Masculine and Feminine (E.), 106, 106 n.
Rehearsal (A.), 223, 227.
Reich (*Der Mimus*), 81 n.
Republic (attrib. to E.), 91 ; (Plato phil.), 237 n., 269, 269 n.
Resident Aliens (Plato Com.), 176.
Revellers (Ameipsias), 24, 151, 152, 238 ; (E.), 101.
Rhadamanthys, 32.
Rhamnus, 124.
RHINTHON, 23, 73-6, 78.
Rhinthonica, 74.
Rhode (*Priestess*), 325.
Rhodes, 35, 40 75.
Richards, 200 n.
Riches (Cratinus), 19, 126 n., 139, 147.
Robert, 180 n.
Robinson Crusoe, 357.
Robinson Crusoe, 156 n.
Roetter (*De Daetalensium fabula*) 280 n.

III. PERSONS, WORKS, AND PLACES 411

Rogers, 214, 221, 224, 226, 237, 248 n.
Rohde, 84 n.
Romans, 85, 233.
Rosmersholm, 354.
Rostand, 358.
Rustic (E.), 105.
Rutherford, 120 n.

Sabazius, 293 sq.
Salaminia, 240.
Salamis, 127.
Salis, von, 113 n.
Samia (M.), 318, 331-6, 353, 357 n., 361.
Samians, 284, 284 n.
Samians (Crates), 146, 150.
Samos, 29, 83, 284 n.
Sampson Stockfish, 230.
Sancho Panza, 301.
Sannyrion, 290, 290 n., 291 n.
Sappho, 60, 387.
Sappho (Diphilus), 60, 66.
Sarcey, 362.
Sardis, 81.
Sardou, 361, 362.
Satyrus, 354.
Sausage-Seller (*Knights*), 207 sqq., 303.
Savages (Pherecrates), 155 sqq.
Schiedsgericht, 345 n.
Schmidt, vi.
Schnitzler, 351.
Scholiasta Ambrosianus, 346 n.
School of Crates, 145-77.
Schroeder (*Novae Comœdiae Fragmenta*), 71 n.
Scientist (Sopater), 75.
Sciron (E.), 113 n.
Scolion (Ameipsias), 25.
Scourge of Mankind (Strattis), 33.
Scylla, 45.
Seasons (A.), 293 sqq.
Secis, 155 n.
Seleucus, 55, 55 n., 66.
Sellius, 316.
Semele, 108.
Semos of Delos, 8, 73 n.
Seneca, 316.
Seriphos, Men of (Cratinus), 139 sq.
Servius, 174 sq., 175 n.
Sextus Empiricus, 168 n.
Shade-Seekers (Strattis), 34 sq.
Shakespeare, vi, 33, 263, 282, 300, 305, 307, 341, 351 sq., 355, 357.
Shaw, 69, 321, 363.
Shelley, 235, 242, 263.
She-Pythagorean (Alexis), 47.
Sheridan, 167, 317, 348.
She Stoops to Conquer, 340.

Shipwrecked Man (A. ? Archippus ?), 202.
Shorn Lady (M.), 318, 319, 336-42, 349, 353, 354, 359.
Shylock (*Merchant of Venice*), 362.
Sicily, 3, 70, 83, 84, 94, 104, 108, 113 n., 131, 142, 178, 189, 197, 224 n., 230, 246, 286.
Sicon, 42.
Sicyonians, 72 n.
Sidonius Apollinaris, 315.
Simonides of Amorgus, 318 ; of Ceos, 97 n., 198.
Sinon, 100 n.
Sinope, 60.
Sinister Street, 220.
Sir Clyomon and Sir Chlamydes, 4.
Sirens (E.), 101.
Skogan, 230.
Smicrines (*Arbitration*), 342-9, 352.
Smyrna, 60.
Socrates, 22, 24 sq., 63, 88, 133, 184 n., 190, 199, 206, 211-8, 374.
Soldiers (Telecleides), 20.
Solœ, 60 n.
Solon, 108, 127 sq., 128 n., 136, 136 n., 181, 182, 185, 187, 243, 274 n., 278.
Song of Solomon, 164.
SOPATER, 75 sq., 78.
Sophists, 47, 190 sq., 217.
Sophocles, 22 n., 50, 51, 67 n., 113 n., 137 sq., 152, 153, 179, 198, 198 n., 235, 274, 290, 290 n., 291 n.
Sophocles of Sunium, 46 n.
SOPHRON, 77 sqq., 85 n., 104 n., 106.
Sophrone (*Arbitration*), 344, 345, 346 352.
Sosias (*new Alexis frag*.), 56 sq. ; (*Wasps*), 223 ; (*Shorn Lady*), 337.
Sosibius, 72.
SOSICRATES, 69 n.
Sosipolis, 178.
Soteridas of Epidaurus, 316.
South Italy, 113.
Southern Gaul, 315.
Sparta, 72, 108, 118, 121, 124, 125, 168, 178, 203, 217, 230.
Spartans, 32, 72, 98, 173, 233, 246, 249.
Spartans (Nicochares), 269.
— *or Poets* (Plato Com.), 171 sqq.
Sphacteria, 182, 199 n.
Sphendone (Ameipsias), 25.
Sphinx (*Cæsar and Cleopatra*), 363.
Spinther (*Nemea*), 31.
Stasinus, 124.
Statius, 78, 109.
Sterne, 307.

Stesichorus, 198, 199.
Sthenelus, 173, 176, 292.
Stichus, 113 n.
Stiffs (Telecleides), 20.
Stiggins, 191.
Stilbides, 197.
Stobæus, 14.
Strabo, 60 n.
Stratocles, 68.
STRATTIS, 32-5.
Strepsiades (*Clouds*), 211 sq., 214 sqq., 218 sq., 222.
Strife (*Chirons*), 126 sq.
Struthias (*Flatterer*), 328.
Strymodorus (*Acharnians*), 247 n.; (*Lysistrata*), 247; (*Wasps*), 229.
Sudhaus (*Menandri reliquiae nuper repertae*), 318 n., 330 n., 337 n.
Suidas, 5, 32, 36, 40, 60 sq., 73, 77 n., 81 n., 83 n., 114 n., 146, 151 n., 154, 165 n., 166, 166 n., 178, 282 n., 284 n., 313, 313 n., 316 n.
Suitors of Bacchis (Sopater), 75.
Sun-God, 36, 168 n.
Sun-God with a Cold? (Aristonymus), 22.
Sunium, Cape, 176.
Superstitious Man (M.), 363, 364.
Supposititious Child (M.), 320 sq.
Susannah, 82.
SUSARION, 6, 11, 13 sq.
Susemihl, 92 n., 110 n.
Süvern, 240 n.
Swift, 26, 302.
Symposium (Plato), 47, 48, 151, 217, 302; (Xenophon), 7, 199.
Syra, 237.
Syracosius, 27 sq., 152, 196.
Syracuse, 3, 4, 5, 74, 78, 83, 85, 89 n., 105, 110, 112, 202.
Syriscus (*Arbitration*), 342, 343, 346, 347, 348, 351, 352.

Tantalus, 62.
Tarentum, 73, 74.
Tearsheet, Doll (*Henry IV*, Pt. II), 31.
TELECLEIDES, 19-22, 41, 162, 268.
Telephus, 205, 251, 255.
Telesias (Diphilus), 62.
Tempest, 7, 240, 385.
Tennyson, 104 n., 311, 373, 385.
Tenos, 193.
Teos, 255.
Terence, 67, 71, 200, 221, 315, 330, 336, 338, 342 n., 351, 359, 359 n., 361, 362; his work evidence for nature of lost Greek plays? 70 n., 317, 319; debt of his *Eunuchus* to *Flatterer*, 327 sq.; bifurcation of plot, 364.
Terpander, 137 n.
Teucer, 49.
Teucrus, 153.
Thais, 323.
Thales, 84.
Thalia, 29.
Thasos, 136, 136 n.
Thea Elvsted (*Hedda Gabler*), 361.
Thebans, 72 n.
Themistocles, 176 sq., 359 n.
Theocritus, 79, 80, 83 n., 102 n., 104 n., 109, 158, 238, 329 n.
Theodorus, 27, 154.
Theognis, 50, 312.
Theolyte (*Nemea*), 31.
Theonoe (*Helena*), 356.
THEOPHILUS, 50 n.
Theophilus, 6 n.
Theophrastus, 313.
THEOPOMPUS, 30 sqq.
Theoria (*Peace*), 231.
Theramenes, 185 n., 259, 261.
Thericles, 31.
Theseus (Diphilus), 60.
Thesmophoriazusæ (A.), 18, 23, 50 n., 142, 150, 250-7, 271, 282, 303 n., 304, 306.
Thesmophorus (Dionysius), 42.
Thirty Tyrants, 21 n.
Thompson, 175 n.
Thoreau, 310.
Thrace, 209, 230.
Thracian Women (Cratinus), 125 n., 127 n., 133 sqq., 143 n.
Thracians, 323.
Thrasippus, 17.
Thraso (*Eunuchus* of Terence), 328.
Thrasonides (*Hated Lover*), 329 sq.
Thrasybulus, 271.
Thrasymachus, 279.
Thucydides (historian), 25 n., 110 n., 122 n., 156 n., 176 n., 182 n., 184 n., 195 n., 199 n., 241, 289 n., 355; (statesman), 127.
Thurii, 40.
Timæus, 83 n.
TIMOCLES, 49, 50, 50 n., 55 n.
Timotheus, 164.
Tiresias (*Bacchæ* of Euripides), 310 n.
Tragicomedy (Deinolochus), 5; (Alcæus), 37; (Anaxandrides), 49.
Tranio, 228.
Transition-Writers, 30-37.
Treasure (attrib. to Crates), 146; (M.), 323.
Trevelyan, 264 n.
Trinummus, 63.
Tripodiscus, 14.

III. PERSONS, WORKS, AND PLACES 413

Tristia, 315 *n.*
Troad, 122.
Troilus, 33.
Troilus (Strattis), 33.
Trojans, 79, 100.
Trojans (E.), 102.
Trojan Women, 241.
Troy, 100, 121, 328.
Truth-Tellers (Telecleides), 19.
Trygæus (*Peace*), 230-6, 238, 267, 275, 303, 307.
Tucker, 144 *n.*
Tunison (*Dramatic Traditions of the Dark Ages*), 6 *n.*
Twain, Mark, 50.
Tyro, 352.
Tzetzes, 2, 13, 28, 123.

Unnatural Son (*Birds*), 243.

Vahlen, 109 *n.*
Valckenăr, 124 *n.*
Vanbrugh, 309.
Venice, 35.
Venus, 175, 318.
Verona, 351.
Verrall, 148 *n.*
Victories (Plato Com.), 176.
Victorinus, C. Marius, 108 *n.*, 388.
Victorious Athlete (E.), 108 *n.*
Villon, 254.
Virgil, 100 *n.*, 133 *n.*, 175 *n.*, 278, 314, 351 *sq.*
Virgin-Goddess, 68.
Visit to the Dead (Sopater), 75.
Vulgar Man? (Strattis), 33 *n.*

Waddell, 318 *n.*
Wallet (Antiphanes), 47 *n.*
Wasps (A.), 11, 18, 180 *n.*, 222-30, 235, 247, 249, 254, 282, 283 *n.*, 298, 303 *n.*, 310 *n.*
Water and Wine Contention, 105.
Water-Babies, 161 *n.*
Way of the World, 305.
Wealth, see Hope.
Wedding of Bacchis (Sopater), 75.
Welcker, 132.
Wellington, 197.
White, 366 *n.*, 367 *n.*, 379 *n.*, 390.
Wilamowitz-Moellendorff, 47, 56 *n.*, 57 *n.*, 58, 71 *n.*, 111 *n.*, 122 *n.*, 123 *n.*, 318 *n.*, 319 *n.*, 345 *n.*, 351 *n.*
Wild Beasts (Crates), 146.
Wilde, 359.
Wilhelm, 15, 16, 19, 20, 114 *n.*, 147 *n.*
Winchester apprentices, 161 *n.*

Windermere, Lord (*Lady Windermere's Fan*), 359.
Windsor, 45.
Wine Flask (Cratinus), 23, 114-18, 142, 211, 213.
Winter's Tale, 45.
Woman Gathering Mandrakes (Alexis), 72.
Woman of Leucas (M.), 352.
— — *Megara*, see *Megarian Woman*.
— — *Samos*, see *Samia*.
— — *Thessaly* (M.), 363.
Woman's Government (Alexis; Amphis), 44.
Women at the Festival of Adonis, 79.
— *Under Canvas* (A.), 295 *sq.*
— *Watching the Isthmian Games* (Sophron), 79.
— *Who Say They Will Drive Out the Goddess* (Sophron), 78 *sq.*
Woodland Muse, 239.
Wordsworth, vi, 106 *n.*
Worthing, John (*The Importance of Being Earnest*), 359 *n.*
Wycherley, 311.
Wyse, 281 *n.*
Wysk, 105 *n.*

Xanthias (*Wasps*), 223, 224, 227; (*Frogs*), 257, 258, 262 *sq.*, 264.
XENARCHUS, 43 *n.*, 44, 45, 50 *n.*
Xenarchus, 77 *n.*
Xenocrates, 46.
Xenophanes, 86 *sq.*, 90, 93.
Xenophon, 7, 107, 199, 217, 246, 259, 268; pseudo-Xenophon, 27.
Xerxes, 77 *n.*, 134.

Y.M.C.A., 311.
Yankee at the Court of King Arthur, 50.

Zeno, 65.
Zenobius, 107, 114, 185 *n.*
Zenodora, 202.
Zeus, 27, 39, 57, 58, 95 *n.*, 96, 98, 99, 102, 106 *n.*, 124, 125, 125 *n.*, 126, 126 *n.*, 157, 160, 161, 162, 163, 168, 218 *sq.*, 221, 230, 232, 239, 240, 242, 270, 273, 289, 333, 334 *n.*, 335 *n.*, 343, 353.
— (*Nemesis*), 124, 125; (*Thracian Women*), 134; (*Europa*), 173; (*Zeus Reviled*), 173; (lost *Peace*) 233, 234.
Zeus Reviled (Plato Com.), 173 *sq.*
Zieliński, 6 *n.*, 113 *n.*, 157, 173 *n.*, 234 *n.*, 253 *n.*

For Product Safety Concerns and Information please contact our EU representative GPSR@taylorandfrancis.com
Taylor & Francis Verlag GmbH, Kaufingerstraße 24, 80331 München, Germany

www.ingramcontent.com/pod-product-compliance
Lightning Source LLC
Chambersburg PA
CBHW071140300426
44113CB00009B/1036